THE ORGANIZATION AND RETRIEVAL OF ECONOMIC KNOWLEDGE

The Organization and Retrieval of Economic Knowledge

Proceedings of a Conference held by the International Economic Association at Kiel, West Germany

edited by
MARK PERLMAN

Routledge
Taylor & Francis Group
LONDON AND NEW YORK

First published 1977 by Westview Press, Inc.

Published 2019 by Routledge
52 Vanderbilt Avenue, New York, NY 10017
2 Park Square, Milton Park, Abingdon, Oxon OX14 4RN

Routledge is an imprint of the Taylor & Francis Group, an informa business

Library of Congress Cataloging in Publication Data
Main entry under title:

The Organization and retrieval of economic
knowledge.

Includes index.
1. Economics libraries—Congresses.
2. Economics—Information services—Congresses.
3. Information storage and retrieval systems—
Economics—Congresses. I. Perlman, Mark.
II. International Economic Association.
Z675.E25073 029′.9′33 76–30513

ISBN 13: 978-0-367-28201-1 (hbk)
ISBN 13: 978-0-367-29747-3 (pbk)

Contents

Acknowledgments of the International Economic Association

There are many to be thanked. First, and as always, are two principal sponsors, UNESCO and the Ford Foundation, whose grants make possible the continuing work of the Association.

The German Economic Association was given a most generous grant by the Volkswagen Foundation to underwrite most of the costs of this conference. In addition, the Pittsburgh National Bank (Pittsburgh, Pennsylvania, USA) gave a grant to the International Economic Association, which was, of course, the actual sponsor of the conference, to assist in meeting some of the conference expenses.

The Programme Committee, which, in the IEA tradition is an intellectually critical one, had four active members: Professor Mark Blaug (University of London), Professor Herbert Giersch (*Institut für Weltwirtschaft*, University of Kiel), Professor Jean Meyriat (University of Paris I), and Professor Mark Perlman (University of Pittsburgh), who, with Professor Giersch, served as co-chairman and has edited this volume. Professor Martin Bronfenbrenner was the rapporteur.

Professor Giersch was ably assisted by Mr Roland Vaubel and Mrs Heidrun–B. Aldegarmann of the *Institut für Weltwirtschaft*, University of Kiel.

The conference had eleven sessions. Each had a chairman. They were, respectively:

Session 1. Professor Giersch
2. Professor Perlman
3. Professor Jean Meyriat
4. Professor Carlos Diaz-Alejandro
5. Professor Wilfred Prest
6. Professor Harry G. Johnson
7. Professor Charles P. Kindleberger
8. Professor Edwin von Böventer
9. Professor Mark Blaug
10. Professor Ronald Coase
11. Professor Giersch

Dr Ruth B. Waxman has assisted Professor Perlman as copy-editor.

List of Participants

Professor Mark Blaug, University of London, London, UK
Professor Edwin von Böventer, University of Munich, Munich, FRG
Dr Yu A. Borko, Institute of Scientific Information, Moscow, USSR
Professor Martin Bronfenbrenner, Duke University, Durham, North Carolina, USA
Professor Ronald H. Coase, University of Chicago, Chicago, Illinois, USA
Professor Paul Chamley, University of Strasbourg, Strasbourg, France
Professor Carlos F. Diaz-Alejandro, Yale University, New Haven, Connecticut, USA
Miss Phyllis Deane, University of Cambridge, Cambridge, UK
Professor Otto Eckstein, Harvard University, Cambridge, Massachusetts, USA
Mr Glyn T. Evans, State University of New York, Albany, New York, USA
Mr John J. Fetterman, University of Pittsburgh, Pittsburgh, Pennsylvania, USA
Professor Herbert Giersch, Institut für Weltwirtschaft, Kiel, FRG
Dr Luiz Carlos Gomes, Istituto Brasileiro de Geografia e Estatistica, Rio de Janeiro, Brazil*
Professor Michael Gort, State University of New York at Buffalo, Buffalo, New York, USA
Dr Erwin Heidemann, Institut für Weltwirtschaft, Kiel, FRG
Mr Jack Hibbert, Central Statistical Office, London, UK
Professor Harry G. Johnson, University of Chicago, Chicago, Illinois, USA
Professor Isaac Kerstenetzky, Instituto Brasileiro de Geografia e Estatistica, Rio de Janeiro, Brazil*
Mr Frederick G. Kilgour, The Ohio College Library Center, Columbus, Ohio, USA
Professor Charles P. Kindleberger, Massachusetts Institute of Technology, Cambridge, Massachusetts, USA
Professor Jean Meyriat, International Committee for Social Science, and the University of Paris I, Paris, France
Professor James N. Morgan, University of Michigan, Ann Arbor,

Michigan, USA
Dr A. C. Olinto, Instituto Brasileiro de Geografia e Estatistica, Rio de Janeiro, Brazil*
Dr M. S. Palnicov, Institute of Scientific Information, Moscow, USSR
Mrs Naomi Perlman, *Journal of Economic Literature*, Pittsburgh, Pennsylvania, USA
Professor Mark Perlman, University of Pittsburgh, Pittsburgh, Pennsylvania, USA
Dr Anna J. Schwartz, National Bureau of Economic Research, New York, USA
Professor Emeritus Carl S. Shoup, Columbia University, New York, USA
Professor Joseph H. Spengler, Duke University, Durham, North Carolina, USA*
Mr George K. Thompson, International Labour Organization Library, Geneva, Switzerland*
Professor William G. Tyler, University of Florida, Gainesville, Florida, USA
Mr John Walton, Central Statistical Office, London, UK*
Professor Jack N. Wolfe, University of Edinburgh, UK
Dr Montague Yudelman, International Bank for Reconstruction and Development, Washington, DC, USA*

Discussants, Institut für Weltwirtschaft, Kiel, FRG

Dr Dieter Biehl
Dr Ulrich Hiemenz
Mr Ernst-Jurgen Horn
Dr Frieda Otto
Dr Klaus-Werner Schatz
Dr Frauke Siefkes
Mr Peter Trapp
Mr Frank Weiss

Observers

Mr Wilhelm Bartenbach, Public Affairs Information Service Inc., New York, USA
Dr M. V. Ercolani, Banca D'Italia, Rome, Italy
Dr H. Junkers, Stiftung Volkswagenwerk, Hannover, FRG
Mr A. Kazancigil, UNESCO, Paris, France
Professor Wilfred Prest, Australian National University, Canberra, Australia
Professor W. Scheper, Kiel University, Kiel, FRG

* Participants who did not attend the Conference.

Symposium Coordinator

Mr Roland Vaubel

Secretariat

Mrs Heidrun–B. Aldegarmann

Introduction

Mark Perlman

In a significant sense it was Charles Kindleberger's suggestion that I commission a paper for the *Journal of Economic Literature* on the card catalogue organizational system developed at the *Institut für Weltwirtschaft* Library in Kiel, FRG, which was the beginning of this Conference. I failed to find anyone willing to undertake the assignment but in the process I did visit Kiel twice. My reaction to the spectacular card catalogue was described in a brief Editor's Note in the *Journal of Economic Literature.*[1]

[1] *Loc. cit. XI* (1973), pp. 56–8.

'The *Institut* is over 50 years old; it was originally organized by Professor Bernhard Harms. During the Nazi period the library's director, Dr Wilhelm Gülich, managed to preserve the Library's integrity by procrastination. It was moved from Kiel to the old Cathedral in the City of Ratzeburg during World War II, which was just as well since the *Institut* site, opposite the submarine pens, was levelled.

Return of the library to Kiel was fortuitous; the British-Soviet demarcation line was a scant distance east of the Cathedral. The library was reestablished in Kiel in 1949 under the *Institut* directorship of Professor Fritz Baade and on the reconstructed original site rather recently. Professor Erich Schneider devoted his considerable personal drive to reestablishing the *Institut* and its library. His successor is Professor Herbert Giersch, and the present Librarian is Dr Erwin Heidemann. It is not the size of the library's holdings so much as its approach to cataloguing which sets the library apart and makes knowledge of its existence so important to scholars. Actually, it has well in excess of 1,000,000 volumes, but most of them (plus many others) are available to Americans in the Washington, DC complex of governmental department libraries. Moreover, as the *Institut* is largely sponsored by the Schleswig-Holstein State and the national government (plus some smaller contributions from other German sources), its collections as well as the ancillary services it provides are basically available only to those willing to use German or willing to hire translators.

Yet, the cataloguing system has so many unusual features that overcoming these very real limitations (to my mind at least) is not an excessive price.

There are several basic catalogues which give entry to this collection. First, in place of the conventional "author catalogue" (which lists only authors or editors of books), there is in reality a "people catalogue". It contains listings of authors, including authors of individual essays within books and journals, editors of books and journals, and writers of introductions and prefaces. Further, it is also a subject catalogue about people which contains access information to all material about these people. Thus, it is a combination of "an author and editor" catalogue with a "people-subject" catalogue".

The Kiel library also has a catalogue bank—the title catalogue—devoted to "annual reports, serials, newspapers, and on-going collections of works". Included under this

However, as I pursued the quest for 'Kindelberger's' article, it became apparent that there were several economists (Professor Fritz Machlup, then President of the International Economic Association, in particular) as well as many information specialists who were increasingly aware of something else, the 'library problem'. Professor Machlup even suggested that there might be an International Economic Association meeting on the topic. A decision was taken in August of 1973 to organize such a conference, when Professor Herbert Giersch and I agreed to undertake the task.

The 'library problem' relates to the increasing costs of acquiring, storing, and providing intelligent access to scholarly material. It is not a problem confined to economics libraries. However, as Giersch and I are economists, we decided to confine the Kiel Conference to economics material. Moreover, the International Economic Association stood spon-

---

catalogue of annual reports is a bank devoted to "corporate bodies" (the National Bureau of Economic Research might be such an example). These "corporate bodies" are associations (private or public corporations, institutions, foundations, learned societies, congresses, conferences, and international organizations). The cataloguers are particularly careful to maintain continuity in this series even though great time and effort are necessary to do so. As these organizations regularly mutate and develop new names and new identities, the extraordinary ingenuity of the library's staff in maintaining continuity is something which makes travel to Kiel a tremendous time- and money-saver. Another bank in this catalogue of "annual reports, etc." is the "official body catalogue" which contains information pertaining to publications of various national and local government units.

The other major cataloguing effort undertaken by the library staff is the subject catalogue developed according to its own system and arranged alphabetically under subject headings (with as many as three subdivisions). Here the two main divisions are by "subject reference" and by geographic (regional) unit. This is a very complete subject catalogue with a tremendous number of references for every item on the shelves. What is more, the library staff recognizes the user time and effort wasted in cross referencing; consequently, there is virtually no "see listing under the heading of—". Instead of using a cross-reference card, the staff has gone to the trouble of producing the bibiliographic reference itself.

The regional subject catalogue goes so far as to cover fairly small governmental units. For example, counties of the United States, to say nothing of the cities of at least 20,000 in population, are listed.

The *Institut für Weltwirtschaft* library is dominated by its economists, not by librarians. Consequently, the approach to information retrieval follows the thinking of professional economists. Of course, from time to time subjects have to be reidentified, but because it is economists who dominate this process (rather than librarians), the lag following the profession's "switch" or "reswitch" is small. For scholars interested in working at the library, I should add that there is a variety of good living accommodations nearby.

The *Institut's* approach to librarianship represents the acme of the traditional approach to economic literature retrieval. Its card catalogue has been produced in bound volumes by G. K. Hall and Company of Boston. There are 207 such volumes giving the card catalogues on printed pages as they existed in the period 1966–68 (when the work was originally done).

sor for our efforts, and it was clearly appropriate that we should so limit our efforts.

We established a Programme Committee. The results in some sense reflect the positive efforts (as well as the failings) of that Committee. Professor Giersch was able to get a sizeable appropriation from the Volkswagen Foundation to the German Economic Association to cover the lion's share of the costs of the conference. The Volkswagen Foundation, however, limits the number of attendees to conferences where it has underwritten the lion's share. Consequently, we had to limit the number of invitees, the number of papers, and consequently, the number of areas which we could cover.

Although Professor Vinogradov had seemingly agreed to cooperate (he accepted appointment to the original Programme Committee), he was apparently unable to enlist any support from the CMEA countries. Nonetheless, Professor Giersch was ultimately able to get the Soviet government to permit the attendance to two paper writers. Both were information retrieval specialists.

There are other aspects reflecting limitations. We are aware of a bias in the distribution (towards American participants) with reference to library science specialists. Responsibility for that bias is mine. I made serious efforts to find experienced scholars in this discipline in other countries, but the rate of return on these efforts was apparently overwhelmingly high mostly amongst my fellow citizens. I am consequently glad that we did have a number of English specialists; I am also pleased that we had Continental European specialists, as well. Unfortunately, because of budgetary limitations, we were unable to include people from the Pacific area, specifically Japan. This limitation is one which Professor Giersch and I particularly regret.

Initial attempts to organize the conference led us to request papers in essentially four areas:

I. The Technology of the Library Industry and Its Uses for Economic Research
II. The Economics of the Economics Library Industry and Its Implications
III. The Information Needs of Researchers and Their Implications for the Library Industry
IV. The Nature of Economics and Its Implications for the Organization of Economic Knowledge

When it came to organizing the conference, the Planning Committee sought to balance the many daily sessions. A total of 26 papers were presented in four and one-half working days. While there is some logic to presenting clusters of paper not only in the same day but in the same morning or the same afternoon, the participants' attention tends to grow thin.

Consequently, we tried to organize the programme most efficiently from the standpoint of encouraging useful discussion.

This last decision invariably had some impact on the readability of the volume. Those who wish to focus on one or another cluster of papers may discover that the cluster seems to have had one or two seemingly out of order; e.g. Dr Palnikov's paper appears later than might have logically been the case, and the Perlmans' paper appears earlier.

The method of presentation of papers should be explained. Authors did not formally read their papers; rather, each paper, prepared to be circulated beforehand, was summarized by a discussant who had been instructed to spend approximately 12 to 15 minutes describing the paper's content before going on to his (her) own comments. Generally, if written comments had been received from individuals not present at the conference, these comments, duplicated, were then summarized. At that point a general discussion ensued; summaries of these discussions follow in this volume the presentation of the actual paper. The discussion invariably ended with the paper's writer (except in the four instances when they were not present) answering criticisms.

After the conference, the paper writers were given an opportunity to revise their written papers, but they were cautioned not to change the content of the paper in order to make the discussant's assessment or the discussion seem irrelevant. The paper's authors and each designated discussant were given an opportunity to see Professor Bronfenbrenner's summary of the discussion. In a few instances they corrected (according to their memory) Bronfenbrenner's statement of what had transpired in the discussion.

The table indicates the order of the papers and who were the discussants (both those who were present and those who submitted written comments).

The first paper, by Professor Charles Kindleberger, discusses his experience with libraries, which he categorized four ways: the personal library, the specialized library, the teaching library of a college or university, and the research library. It is an informal piece, full of academic anecdotes as well as some insights which are almost universally useful.

The second paper, by Mr George Thompson of the International Labour Organization library, describes in considerable detail the computerization of that library's index system. It also suggests how this system is being adapted to a computer network.

The third paper, by Professor Otto Eckstein, describes the service or product sold by his commercial enterprise, a company providing terminal-accessible national economic information. His paper describes the company's computer system, the communications network as it developed, the software it employs, the data banks it has generated, and the application of the foregoing to the testing of econometric models. Eckstein's service as well as his paper reflected a use of quantitative data in one industrialized nation (USA).

The ensuing paper, by Professor Isaac Kerstenetzky and his colleagues at the Brazilian Institute of Economics and Geography in Rio de Janeiro, describes in rather tantalizing detail the programme the Institute developed for presentation and analysis of the Brazilian 1970 population and other censuses. The Kerstenetzky *et al.* paper evoked considerable heated discussion. Because Professor Kerstenetzky was unable to be at the conference, he was asked to reply to the discussion in a written statement; his reply appears at the end of the summary of the discussion.

The fifth paper was the first of six papers which together made up Part Two of the programme: The Economics of the Economics Library Industry and Its Implications. Professor Wolfe's paper reported on a survey of the attitudes of British users of technical information systems. The next paper, by Mr John Fetterman, dealt with the general problem of rising costs in the library industry and the aspects of the problem which are faced by large university libraries. Dr Heidemann of the *Institut für Weltwirtschaft* library presented the seventh paper (the third in Part Two); it dealt with the use of interlocking catalogues as one way of minimizing cost of acquisition and ultimately storage.

There followed two papers, each indicating attempts at organizing library network schemes. Mr Glyn Evans reported on the efforts made by the State University of New York, a multi-campus institution, in developing its library network. Mr Frederick Kilgour reported on the development of a large number of centralized library networks that focused ultimately on his experience with the Ohio College Library Center, which is a computerized on-line catalogue containing nearly four million location listings as of Spring 1975.

Naomi and Mark Perlman concluded the second part of the conference with a paper surveying articles from the *Journal of Economic Literature* 1970–74 data base in order to identify the division of research activity (as reflected in economics articles' titles) among the various subfields in economics. They also discussed the methodological popularity of empirical data, generally and by subfield.

There then followed fourteen papers, each devoted to a discussion of a subfield. The opening paper, by Jack Hibbert and John Walton of the Central Statistical Office, on developments in national accounts, speculated on prospective developments in the United Kingdom's national account system (particularly in relation to the United Nation's system). Professor James Morgan in reporting on the problems of drawing, using, and disposing of microdata samples, focused on the impact of changing computer technology and what these changes meant in terms of dispositional costs. The next paper, by Dr Anna Schwartz, dealt with a delineation of the hierarchy of libraries for the optimal use of research in the monetary subfield. Professor Carl Shoup presented a

Paper title	*Author*	*Discussants*
The Use of Libraries by Economists: A Personal View	Charles Kindleberger, USA	Jack N. Wolfe, Scotland
Computerized Approaches to the Literature of Economics: From ISIS to DEVSIS	*George Thompson, Switzerland*	Frederick Kilgour, USA
National Economic Information Systems for Developed Countries	Otto Eckstein, USA	Anna Schwartz, USA
The Organization of Quantitative Data in Brazil	*Luiz Carlos Gomes, A. C. Olinto and Isaac Kerstenetzky, Brazil*	*Lutz Hoffmann, FRG* Carlos F. Diaz-Alejandro, USA
The Effectiveness of Secondary Information Systems in Economics and Industry	Jack Wolfe, Scotland	James Morgan, USA John Fletcher, UK
The High Cost of Information and Some Approaches to Its Acquisition	John Fetterman, USA	*Werner Schuchow, FRG* Glyn Evans, USA
Interlocking Catalogues	Erwin Heidemann, Germany	Naomi Perlman, USA *Billie I. Salter, USA*
Organizing an Inter-Library Network: The State University of New York Approach	Glyn Evans, USA	John Fetterman, USA
Economics of Computerized Library Networks	Frederick Kilgour, USA	*Ralph Shoffner, USA* William Tyler, USA
The Changing Modes of Data in Economic Research	Naomi and Mark Perlman, USA	Phyllis Deane, UK
Developments in National Accounts	Jack Hibbert and *Jack Walton*, UK	Carl Shoup, USA
The Usefulness of Microdata and Some Strategies for Storing, Using, and Disposing of It	James Morgan, USA	Edwin von Böventer, FRG
Library Policies for Research in Monetary Economics	Anna Schwartz, USA	Martin Bronfenbrenner, USA

Development of Fiscal Economics During the Decade 1975–85	Carl Shoup, USA	*Alan Peacock, UK* Dieter Biehl, FRG
Information Needs in Regional Economics	Edwin von Böventer, Germany	Paul Chamley, France
Information Needs and Data Requirements for International Economic Research	William Tyler, USA	Jack Hibbert, UK
Data Needs in Development Economics	Carlos F. Diaz-Alejandro, USA	Ulrich Hiemenz, FRG
Information Needs for Agricultural Development, Policy and Planning	Montague Yudelman, USA	*Erik Thorbecke, USA* M. S. Palnicov, USSR
Competition versus Planned Specialization in the Development of Resources for Research in Industrial Organization	Michael Gort, USA	*F. A. Graham, UK* *Michael Lynch, USA* Ronald Coase, USA
Some Information about Technological Progress and Economic Growth	Yu. A. Borko, USSR	Klaus Werner Schatz, FRG
The Relevance of Recent Trends in Economic History to the Information Needs of Research Workers in the Field	Phyllis Deane, UK	Charles Kindleberger, USA
The Information Needs of Economic Researchers in the Field of Comparative Economic Systems	Paul Chamley, France	Yu. A. Borko, USSR
Data in the Planned Economy of the USSR	M. S. Palnicov, USSR	*T. Földi, Hungary* Frank Weiss, FRG
The History of Economic Thought and Analysis: Organization and Retrieval of Its Content	Joseph Spengler, USA	Mark Blaug, UK
Economics and Contiguous Disciplines	Ronald Coase, USA	Harry Johnson, USA
Methodologies of Economics	Harry Johnson, USA	Mark Perlman, USA

Persons listed in italics contributed but did not attend the Conference.

speculative view of the future of fiscal economics (he prefers the term public finance) and the kind of empirical and other materials which libraries should have available if productive research is to be done in that area in the next decade. Professor Edwin von Böventer dealt with the information needs for policy-oriented economic research in regional economics. He stressed that the lack of data has inhibited the development of operational theories. Professor William Tyler then considered future work in the international economic area. The discussion which followed quite naturally questioned Tyler's virtually total confidence in empiricism as *the* high probability pay-off method. One the whole, the exchange represents one of the liveliest sessions of the conference. Professor Carlos Diaz-Alejandro's paper discussed data needs in development economics, particularly macroeconomic aggregates. Diaz-Alejandro's major concern was that there was far too much theorizing with far too little data. He was particularly interested in analysing data on the two hundred largest corporations in each developing country.

Dr Montague Yudelman's paper on information needs for agricultural development was in some sense the most futuristic or speculative. He identified some new uses of satellite technology for developing agricultural economics series. Professor Michael Gort was rather skeptical about what librarians could contribute to the stockpiling of information for future research in the area of industrial organization.

Dr Yu Borko of the Institute of Scientific Information on Social Sciences in the Soviet Union then presented a paper on the state and the need for information about technological process. In one sense his paper is a subset of the paper on industrial organization; in another sense, however, it goes well beyond the typical market economy orientation towards industrial organization. His paper reported on the experience of the Institute of Scientific Information on Social Sciences in the Soviet Union generally, and on the different types of information retrieval systems used in the Institute, specifically. Miss Phyllis Deane's paper on the data and information needs for economic historians summarized recent trends. Specifically, she was interested in the traditional sources of information and data and the requirements of the 'new' economic historians (the cliometricians). Professor Paul Chamley's paper provided a matrix for organizing the subdiscipline of comparative economic systems. That matrix was then used to identify the bibliographic and data needs.

Dr M. Palnikov presented a paper reporting on data uses in the Soviet Union's planned economy. The work is also integrated with that done in other CMEA-countries. Finally, the last paper in the 'subfield areas' was by Professor Joseph Spengler. It was on the history of economic thought and its needs for bibliographic assistance. Spengler's conclusion was the most conservative of all of the papers given. Skeptical of the use of the computer, he concluded that future work in this field should be in terms of method largely similar to what has gone on previously.

The conference concluded with two rather sweeping but nonetheless intriguing papers. One by Professor Ronald Coase of the Law School of the University of Chicago attempted to identify the future delineation of the subject of economics from its 'contiguous disciplines'. He draws a useful distinction between the kinds of cognate relationship where the non-economist specialist has only to acquire the possession of the techniques or approaches offered by the economists and the situation where the cognate discipline is so intermeshed with the economic system as to make it impossible to discuss the cognate area without a thorough knowledge of economic institutional relationships. The final paper of the conference, by Professor Harry G. Johnson, was an assessment of current and future methods as well as current and future methodologies. Although the paper starts with a rather acerbic view of what has happened to the pleasures of work in libraries, it goes on to discuss the author's conviction that mathematical and quantitative methods have probably 'shot their bolt'. Thus, there is a suggestion that we may be at the end of an era (?), and that future work in economics may give greater attention to ethics and social welfare concerns rather than to quantitative series and use of statistical tests of significance. Moreover, rising publishing costs may yet rescue (or perhaps postpone) libraries from disaster.

At the end of the conference those present turned to formulating a statement of professional concern regarding the economics of economics libraries, access for economists to economic information, and the problems of informed decision-making regarding library collections. The following statement was adopted overwhelmingly:

> We (including economists and library information specialists from over eight nations and over fifteen academic subdisciplines), the participants of the International Economics Association Kiel Symposium on 'The Organization and Retrieval of Economic Knowledge', desire to draw the attention of both the economics and information retrieval professions to the following high priority needs:
>
> 1. *The immediate problem of developing a variety of accounting procedures for measuring library activities (research material provision, materials for teaching, creation of cultural archives, and the storage of quantitative data bases).* This area is ripe for dissertational research; it needs work on measuring cost effectiveness regarding both interdisciplinary and interlibrary operations.
>
>   Specifically, the economics of libraries has not been adequately studied, and research is necessary in such areas as:

- definition of 'unit of output' formula for cost effectiveness
- prediction method for item selection for use and retention
- the library as 'a public good'
- balance between economically effective and sociologically acceptable libraries
- the 'value' of the storage or archival function
- valid 'user expectations' *re* time and services.

2. *Experimental research on library size and utilization.* There is a need to develop information on (a) utilization, and on (b) unfilled needs, as functions of collection size. Work in this area may lead to the development of procedures for continuous monitoring and assessment of library collection policies. But to avoid making exclusive use of current circulation as a guide, better procedures for evaluation and selection are needed as indicators of what to destroy, what to store, and what to keep readily accessible. Researchers have an obligation, including but going beyond self-interest, to help with this difficult task.

3. *The problem of standardization of full identification of authors (full names, not substitution of initials for given names), wherever an article or book appears.* Subsequent bibliographic listings should use full author identification whenever it is economically possible to do so. There should also be full identification of book publishers—not just city of publication—as well as italization in references of the title of a volume or journal in which an article appears.

4. *Recognition of the existence of successful and cost-efficient on-line retrieval systems for bibliographic data (both monographic cataloguing and analytic indexing).* Such systems can be used to assist in organizing and retrieving published economic knowledge and in guiding access to sources of such knowledge. The critical problem areas are: copyright, access to data sets, and the development of systems that transcend national boundaries and individual network developments.

5. *Encouraging cooperation in abstracting and indexing services.* The creation of a comprehensive thesaurus for economics *following the pattern of* such macro-thesauri as the one developed by OECD leaves open the possibility for further refinement of highly specialized fields to create a number of microthesauri.

6. *Standard definitions for data collection.* International statistical agencies would be encouraged to standardize definitions and organize the publication of data in suitable forms. Such forms include not only printed books, but also magnetic tapes.

7. *Importance of union catalogues.* Current practices should be extended to promote access to, rather than possession of, such research material as is not frequently used.

8. *The importance of regional (national or multi-national) libraries.* For research puposes central libraries should become responsible for collection development in well-defined subject areas in economics. The goal is to minimize unnecessary duplication in acquisition and storage.

9. *Recent developments in machine readable data technology.* Library administrators should consider how to cope with the growing need for documenting fully, archiving, and retrieving these data.

10. *Freedom of information.* Great care must be exercised that computerization of data does not lead to restrictions on data access to foreign scholars.

11. *Sample data sets.* Because many kinds of data are accumulating in amounts too large to preserve, it is essential to work out schemes for conserving records of samples. Co-operation among researchers, sampling experts, and archivists is crucial.

Part One

The Technology of the Library Industry and Its Use for Economic Research

1 The Use of Libraries by Economists: A Personal View

Charles Kindleberger*
MASSACHUSETTS INSTITUTE OF TECHNOLOGY

The paper, by a 'consumer economist', discusses the use of libraries under four classifications: the personal library, the specialized library, the teaching library of a college or university, and the research library. In addition, it reflects briefly on the current problems of libraries ensuing from rising costs, increasing published materials, reduced budgets, etc. It gives the view of one who is not widely familiar with bibliographic aids, both literary and increasingly computerized, and concludes, perhaps erroneously, that such is the ambiguity in the words used by economists that it is unlikely that mechanical substitutes will be found for informal and personalized techniques, such as asking people who know a given field.

I. INTRODUCTION

This essay is personal. The writer is an economist and, to the same extent, an economic historian, with limited knowledge of the fine points of librarianship. Writing it has been, in fact, a voyage of discovery. In the past, I have worked extensively—i.e. for a period from two weeks to a number of months or years—in ten great or good libraries,[1] and for

* I acknowledge with gratitude the help of Edgar W. Davy, director of the Dewey Library at MIT, but, since our points of view differ in a number of respects, he is not to be regarded as believing everything I say. Many librarians and one or two economists commented on the first draft and corrected errors of varying significance, for which I am grateful.

[1] Among the great economics libraries are those of Harvard and Columbia Universities, including, at Harvard, both the Widener Library and the Baker and Kress of the Graduate School of Business Administration; the Bibliothek of the Institut für Weltwirtschaft at the University of Kiel in Germany and Edinburgh University Library. Among the good ones, I may list my own Dewey Library at the Massachusetts Institute of Technology (MIT); the United Nations (formerly League of Nations) Library at the Palais des Nations, Geneva; Nuffield College Library at Oxford; the Ministry of Finance library at 101 Rue de Rivoli, Paris; and the Library of the Bank of Italy in the Via Nazionale in Rome. Acquaintance with the collections of the University of Pennsylvania, the Federal Reserve Bank of New York, and the Board of Governors of the Federal Reserve System in Washington, the library of the Bank for International Settlements at Basle, was once intense but has eroded with the passage of time.

lesser periods, down to one hour, in perhaps ten more. Since undertaking this assignment, I have had a chance to visit or inspect another ten.[2] But, in forty years of teaching and research, it is appalling what I did not learn about libraries and, in particular, about library directories, books on subject collections, professional bibliographies and published catalogs.[3] I cannot claim to have repaired these long-term omissions. In addition to library visits, research for the paper included sending a questionnaire to a selected list of libraries. Returns were somewhat spotty and numerical material, in any case, is ambiguous because of imprecision over the limits of 'economics' on the one hand and what constitutes a book, volume, pamphlet, periodical, manuscript, item, etc., on the other.

As a personal effort, the paper does not deal with the economics of libraries, as for example in Baumol and Marcus [5], which applies regression analysis to statistics of academic libraries, or in Raffel and Shisko [34], which covers formally many of the issues touched upon in what follows.

The subject is organized under four headings: the personal library, the working library, the teaching library and the research library.[4] In each

[2] In these last two categories, in the United States: the Library of Congress, New York Public Library (Research Libraries) (NYPL), the Regenstein Library at the University of Chicago, the Firestone Library at Princeton and the Milton Eisenhower Library at Johns Hopkins University; in England, the British Library, the British Library of Political and Economic Science at L.S.E., the Middlesex and Goldsmiths Libraries of the University of London, and the Bodleian Library at Oxford; in France, the Bibliothèque Nationale, libraries of the Institut des Sciences Politiques, the University of Paris I (Sorbonne), the Institut Nationale de la Statistique et des Etudes Economiques (INSEE), and the Organization for Economic Cooperation and Development (OECD), all in Paris; plus the libraries of Hitotsubashi, Keio and Tokyo Universities in Japan.

[3] Cf., e.g. University of Warwick, *Guide to the Library*, p. 5: 'Social Sciences: Library materials in these subjects usually give the greatest problems to users, even relatively senior ones....' This line was probably written by John Fletcher, the Economics Librarian at the University of Warwick, who is the editor of *The Uses of Economic Literature* [20], and the author of 5 of its 24 articles, which I discovered only at the end of writing the first draft. This is a first-rate guide to the use of libraries by economists, together with bibliographical studies in particular branches of the subject. I disagree in part, however, with the emphasis of Michael Shafe, who writes, under 'Reference and Bibliographical Tools' (p. 31):

> The relationship between the librarian and the economist in a search of information is an important one. Too often the 'old boy network', mentioned in Graham Mackenzie's article in *Aslib Proceedings*, July 1969, on reader instruction, is the first source of information and the library is thought of only as a secondary source. That net is full of holes: ... members of the network ... can perpetuate errors and leave unknown areas still unexplored. Librarians can help to reduce the size of the holes in the net.... Time is money, and as specialists' browsing time dwindles, the librarian can help to increase the economists' productivity and effectiveness.

In my view, the word-of-mouth circuit can produce information which cannot be retrieved by bibliographical tools alone.

[4] This breakdown closely resembles that of the First Report of the General Board's Committee on Libraries of Cambridge University [17], which discusses undergraduates

section a number of problems facing the library user are explored. A penultimate section, preceding a concise conclusion, deals briefly with new problems facing all libraries, as seen by a user-economist. The paper is faintly analytical. Anecdotes abound but are relegated to footnotes.

Books are usually private goods; libraries, except for personal collections, are public goods. Books and periodicals are used to disseminate knowledge; old books, periodicals, manuscripts, and archives are needed to preserve old knowledge and to produce new. For the purpose of dissemination, books should be widely distributed; for preservation and the production of new knowledge, it is useful to accumulate books and papers in a single place, to provide reader-researcher convenience. Rare books, however, are also a private good for the owner, who is interested in their uniqueness. From this point of view, rare books should be widely shared in the interest of the equality of wealth. For use, they should be gathered in one place to provide shopping economies of agglomeration. The conflict between books as rare objects and as tools of research runs through the subject and, at times, results in some antagonism between librarians who occasionally seem to want to keep their collections untouched, like objects in a museum, and the scholar who wants to read. The collector wants originals; the scholar, as a rule, is content with facsimiles. Cheap and efficient reproduction is well on its way to resolve the conflict between them.

II. THE PERSONAL LIBRARY

Students of economics, along with those of other subjects, face the decision many times a year, of whether to buy a book or to wait for it to be provided by the library. It would have been a useful exercise in consumption theory—or, perhaps, the theory of production with intermediate goods—to study with multiple regression the size of the personal libraries of economists. Raffel and Shisko [34, p. 47n] observe that, in 1968, MIT faculty members each spent $130 annually on books (and students $110), but the variance is doubtless high both between and within departments. My casual empiricism suggests that, among economists, size of library is a function of subject of specialization, age, income or wealth, office wallspace available, nearness to the (say) university library, its efficiency, and personal characteristics, i.e. the extent of the economist collector's instinct, usually and retentiveness, but, perhaps, in a few cases, interest in speculation for profit.

Subject is critical. Mathematical statisticians go in for hardly any books at all—at most, a few periodicals. The burden of the pure theorist is light, unless he cultivates an interest in the history of thought. An

buying books—it is noted that they fail to spend their full local education authority maintenance grant of £35 for the purpose—and College (teaching), Departmental (working), and University (research) libraries.

economist with two specialties—say, trade and development—has more books than one interested only in trade or only in development. Within the development field, moreover, there is a question of the number of countries that the specialist tries to keep abreast of. The greatest burden is economic history and, I would guess, that of Western Europe.[5]

Age governs the integral, converting flow into stock. The relationship is not simple. Some scholars weed, some do not. The wife of a colleague—call her Mrs Murgatroyd—has enunciated the law of the ever-normal library (granary): 'Bring a book home tonight, you take one away tomorrow morning.' Mrs Murgatroyd cannot enforce her rule at the office, but, after time, wall and cabinet space tend to.[6] The burden of periodicals is particularly hard on the old. Copies of the *American Economic Review* for the 1930s and 1940s are eating their heads off in thousands of personal libraries, taking up space and earning their rent in only one or two cases. The constraint of wall space is self-evident. Modern architecture, with its large windows, has doubtless cut the demand for books. I know one scholar who built shelving out into the room away from the wall, as do libraries, but the practice is rare.

The coefficient in the regression of nearness to the university library is of great interest and importance.[7] Should the library be centralized for the convenience of the scholar who has come there and wants to explore other fields, or decentralized to bring certain books nearer to the teacher in his office?

Something depends, of course, on the speed of cataloguing and the

[5] In their formula for measuring the adequacy of academic library collections, Clapp and Jordan [16, p. 375], include 2000 books for each field in which a university offers graduate work at the master's level or equivalent, but note that, within this average, requirements differ by field: e.g. anthropology 2000, physics 1885, area studies 7000.

[6] There are two ways of weeding: by book and by subject. The latter has greater benefits for the recipient of the weeded objects. Some years ago I decided that I had done with economic development and gave to the library of a struggling college all my books on the subject. The weeding of working paper files calls for the impossible discipline of throwing out the conference papers when the published proceedings are received.

Weeding and duplication are even more serious problems for libraries, of course, but ones which we do not have time to explore below. Raffel and Shisko discuss weeding as a technique of saving on storage costs and anlyse a number of criteria: past circulation, age of book, and gross characteristics, such as those classified by the Dewey Decimal System in a library that has converted to the Library of Congress [34, pp. 15ff.] None seems to me acceptable. They conclude that the saving of storage costs is too small to validate the loss of reader benefit. The task of libraries in eliminating duplication is horrendous when articles are often produced numerous times as working papers, journal papers, in a collection, anthologies, etc. It would be invidious to name the economists who squeeze all possible mileage out of their work in this way and complicate the lives of librarians.

[7] My colleagues and I at MIT doubtless buy more books since the Dewey Library was transferred from the third floor of the Sloan Building to a new building, joined by an enclosed bridge to be sure, but down two floors. It is rumoured that a former star of the Johns Hopkins Department of Political Economy was moved to accept an offer from another university, in considerable part because of the transfer of the library from Gilman Hall outside his door to the new Milton Eisenhower Library building across a quadrangle.

putting into use of new books by the university's central, or department, library. Where the delay is long, purchase is necessary for recent books that are needed immediately. Considerable improvement seems to have been recorded lately in this area, as cataloguing in publication (CIP) and National Computer Bibliographical Networks and computerized ordering have reduced processing and cataloguing time by more than reduced budgets and book output have increased it by complicating the selection process. I am informed that the MIT library backlog has been sharply reduced from its peak of five to ten years ago.

One could devote time to the problems of the personal library. How should books be arranged: by subject?; alphabetically?; by height?; etc.[8] whether to keep reprints in cardboard boxes on shelves or in vertical file cabinets; the economics of marginal notes for information retrieval which reduce the second-hand value of the book in the usual case;[9] whether one should take typed notes on the books one owns, along with those on borrowed books, so that, when the time for retrieval is at hand, there is only one source to consult;[10] how to divide books between office and home, for those scholars who work part time at home. The footnotes skim a few of these topics. I restrict the text to what is called, in growth theory, the problem of terminal conditions: how to dispose of the per-

[8] I recall asking Alexander Gerschenkron to borrow a book and being surprised that he could move across the room to its exact location. Asked how he knew exactly where it was, he said that he had had a grant from a foundation to rearrange his books. I neglected, however, to ask him what system was installed.

[9] If one achieves immortality as an economist, it will, of course, prove to have been worthwhile to have made marginal notes, as they increase the value of the book. Josef Schumpeter's notes on his books were made on slips of yellow paper, which the Hitotsubashi Library, which acquired the bulk of his collection, extracted and filed separately. In examining the collection I sought to see his notes on Keynes' *General Theory*, but this book was not among those given to Hitotsubashi. Notes on Samuelson's *Foundations* were disappointing, merely two slips with some scrappy matrix notation.

[10] In a conference on the Organization and Retrieval of Economic Knowledge, some attention might perhaps be paid as to how to retain at the ready the knowledge which one has obtained from books. I find students, at least, in economic history, enormously interested in this simple methodological problem: are 3″ × 5″ card in file drawers, for example, better than 8½″ × 11″ loose-leaf notebooks, one to a subject? (I am a loose-leaf notebook man.) Should all notes be typed for easy visual retrieval? (I think so.) On note-taking in general, R. M. Hartwell had the discouraging experience of taking detailed notes on a book, losing them four or five years later, reading the book again and taking another set. On finding the first set and comparing the two, he found an overlap of no more than two-thirds. It is evident that, as interests change with time, the meaning of a book for the scholar changes.

Bibliographical card filing can be overdone: the office of a professor in the Harvard Law School has several hundred thousand 3″ × 5″ cards in trays on shelves, desk, tables, cabinet, chairs and floor. Many a scholar's office is similarly encumbered with a disarray of books piled high everywhere. I nominate for special distinction in this connection the office of Graham Martin at the University of Canterbury in Christ Church, New Zealand, a large room, knee deep in business archives, where it is necessary to move a stack of books, folders and papers before finding a place to sit.

sonal library. If the economist does not provide for its disposition, the surviving spouse or colleague must bear the burden.

A personal collection of books may be given away intact to a library that wants it, sold intact, sold piecemeal, given to book rummage sales, distributed more or less randomly to members of the family, colleagues, students, or left in an attic or cellar. In at least some cases, university libraries used to appraise a book collection for tax purposes, accept it as a gift, keep what it wanted and dispose of the rest through the dealer network. Such appraisals now must be undertaken professionally, as libraries recognize the perils of mixing in matters with tax consequences. One used to be able to recognize in the lists of second-hand dealers in New York when the library of a defunct Columbia professor reached the market. Notable collections, such as the two of Foxwell in the Goldsmiths' Library at the University of London, and the Kress Library at the Harvard Graduate School of Business Administration, the Seligman collection at Columbia, Hutzler at Johns Hopkins, and Hollander at the University of Illinois are given or bought and kept intact. Japanese universities have bought the libraries, or part of them, of Adam Smith,[11] Carl Menger, Karl Bücher, Werner Sombart, and Gustav Schelle. Hitotsubashi University was given the greater part of Josef Schumpeter's library by his widow. G. D. H. Cole's collection is the basis for the Nuffield College Library at Oxford; the National Bureau of Economic Research started with Wesley Clair Mitchell's books; Erich Schneider's private collection of theoretical economics, consisting of about 7000 volumes, was left to the Institut für Weltwirtschaft which he headed from 1961 to 1969; Keynes' books went to the King's College Library of the History of Economic Thought in Cambridge, England; the University Library in Uppsala was founded in 1620 with a gift, from King Gustavus Adolphus, of books and manuscripts from the nunneries and monasteries that were closed as a result of the Reformation, of some that were war booty, and of some from the royal collection, etc., etc.

Optimally, perhaps, given the need for spreading teaching materials on the one hand, and concentrating scarce resources on the other, rare books should be sold (or given) to the great research libraries, while ordinary books should be given (or sold) to the poorer colleges trying to rise in the scholarly world. For economists who have served in government, such papers as are left over from those days may well be given to archival sources, e.g. in the United States: the Hoover, Roosevelt,

[11] Adam Smith's library is, for the most part, in the possession of the Edinburgh University Library (308 volumes). The University of Tokyo owns 141 books, including a 1781 catalogue drawn up by Smith himself, bought at a London auction in July, 1920 [44]. The Hutzler collection of the Johns Hopkins library has a score of books belonging to Adam Smith, with his bookplate. Others are in the Kress collection, the University of Glasgow (the Livingston collection), Queen's College of Belfast and Kyoto University [8, 30]. This library is, thus, divided and spread over the world like pieces of the True Cross.

Truman, Kennedy, and Johnson libraries. The tax advantages in the United States of so doing are not what they used to be.

III. THE WORKING OR SPECIALIZED LIBRARY

The economist doing research on a particular problem will do well to consider applying to a library specialized in the field. This may be a great library with strength in the given field. It may, however, be one with 100,000 volumes or less, but narrowly concentrated. Many of these belong to research or operating agencies, either private or governmental. Since the library serves a particular purpose other than the needs of the general reader, there may be the necessity for the introduction of an outsider to establish professional *bona fides*.

The size of specialized libraries evidently depends upon their coverage in three dimensions: time, subject matter and countries. The International Labour Office (ILO), for example, has three times the number of volumes (340,000 to 126,000), twice the periodical subscriptions (5000 to 3000), and more than 10 times the number of microfilm reels (2000 to 140), of the Joint Bank-Fund Library of the International Bank of Reconstruction and Development (IBRD) and the International Monetary Fund (IMF), mainly, I suspect, because it has been going twice as long, having been set up after World War I instead of after World War II. Both have the incomparable advantage of official status, so that they automatically receive government publications. The collection of national governmental budgets of the Joint Bank-Fund Library, for example, is one of the best in the world. Both have world-wide coverage. The subject span of the ILO library in labour, education, training and management may, or may not, extend more widely than the IBRD-IMF interest in central banking, domestic banking, international monetary affairs and economic development. It is of interest, however, that both organizations have found it necessary to establish faster retrieval machinery for books, journal articles and governmental documents. The ILO has been abstracting since 1965 and has a computer file of 55,000 document abstracts, from which 2000 bibliographies are made each year. The system is known as Integrated Scientific Information System (ISIS) and is being developed in collaboration with Stockholm and Ottawa. The Joint Bank-Fund Library undertook its own periodical indexing for some 500 titles because other indexing and abstracting services are slow, limited in coverage, and weak in articles in collected works and proceedings. Another organization which produces its own abstracts and makes them available publicly is the French Institut National de la Statistique et des Etudes Economiques (INSEE). *Documentation Economique* is a quarterly review which has been published since 1934, though interrupted from November 1938 to January 1947, and most recently in a form in which the entries can be ripped out and filed on stiff cards. This covers abstracts. The *Bulletin de la Bibliothèque* is a weekly catalogue of accessions, without abstracts, which again can be used as file entries after cutting. INSEE was erected on the basis of the old *Statistique Générale de la France* and has 275,000 volumes, plus 2400 periodicals, with its primary strength evidently in statistics about France, but with attention as well to foreign country statistical sources and international documents. With governmental support, Hitotsubashi University in Tokyo maintains a Documentation Centre on Japanese Economic Statistics. The data go back to 1830, including archival material good enough to recognize the figures, and the book collection numbers 50,000.

Other libraries specializing in current economic statistics are those of the National Bureau of Economic Research (NBER) in the United States and the National Institute for Economic and Social Research (NIESR) in Britain. The former is putting more and more of its series on machine-readable tape. It notes that the early stages of this process generate considerable confusion among librarians, documentalists, information specialists and users, with a need for procedures for identification of content still to be developed. The basic collection consists of statistical yearbooks, studies in methodology and mathematical models for forecasting. The NIESR librarian observes that limitations on size and staff inhibit it from encouraging the use of the library by outsiders, and that space makes it selective in purchasing and rigorous in discarding working papers after five years, as well as underutilized material, including especially journals, pamphlets, and old statistical material.

Governmental department libraries are typically inadequately noted by the academic world. They are specialized—by subject and Agency, Commerce, Agriculture, Labour, Interior, Patent Office, Health, Education and Welfare, Tariff, Commission, Treasury, etc.—large, with wide international coverage from an exchange of reports with foreign governments, and not always well organized. Ash and Lorenz, *Subject Collections* [3], states that the Department of Commerce has 472,000 volumes. In its returned questionnaire, the Commerce Library noted in more detail that it had been collecting materials since 1903, that it held 60,000 catalogued books, 10,000 statistical publications for 100 foreign countries, and 36,000 items in the maritime section, not to mention 44,000 volumes in its law branch, which is strong on hearings, committee prints and other material from the United States Congress. The law library of the Supreme Court complements that of the library of Congress, which specializes in foreign law, legislative acts, and such compartmentalized fields as taxation. The Department of Agriculture Library is one of the strongest in the world, so much so that the Library of Congress does not collect in this field.

Among foreign, large specialized libraries, *Subject Collections in European Libraries* [37] mentions the Board of Trade Library in London with 200,000 'volumes', the library of the Chambre de Commerce et d'Industrie in Paris with 250,000 volumes, 3000 current periodicals and 150 microfilms, and the library of the Commercial University 'Luigi Bocconi', in Milan, with 143,000 volumes and 1200 current periodicals.

Another useful guide, *The World of Learning* [42], lists among the (smaller) specialized libraries in London of interest to economists: H.M. Customs and Excise Library, City Business Library, Institute of Electrical Engineers Library, Iron and Steel Institute, Institute of Metals, Joint Metallurgical Library and the Marx Memorial Library (of approximately 15,000 volumes and 25,000 pamphlets).

Smaller European libraries include those of the Organization for European Cooperation and Development (OECD), the European Economic Community (EEC), the Food and Agriculture Organization at Rome (FAO), the Bank for International Settlements (BIS) at Basel, etc. The OECD library is first rate, with a good supply of books, documents, and periodicals, room to spread out and a helpful staff. In 1965, *Subject Collections in European Libraries* [37], gave the EEC library as 25,000 volumes. I do not know the EEC or FAO libraries, but, judging by the fine research which has come out of American scholars spending sabbaticals in them, they provide what is needed. Perhaps one ingredient in specialized libraries in operating agencies is the presence of the operators. 'A peek is worth two finesses', and it frequently saves time to ask one who knows rather than to seek to learn entirely through the written word.

For some purposes, a small and unpretentious library is better than one with a greater outreach. For one who starts without great depth in a subject, enough is as good as a feast, and too brave a show of riches may merely inhibit.[12]

For particular purposes, libraries can be tremendously specialized. The Dag Hammerskjöld Library of the United Nations in New York is, understandably, very strong on government publications, but especially so in economic planning, where its collection is used by the Interdocumentation Company of Zug, Switzerland, to complete its microfiche edition of development plans of the countries of the world. Walter J. Levy, a private

[12] In the summer of 1960, I read French financial and economic history in the Ministry of Finance library in the cupola on top of the Louvre on the Rue de Rivoli side of the building. The library was primitive, perhaps 10,000 books in all, with no titles in any language other than French, and housed in three rooms, Salles I, II, and III. The catalogue referred the reader to room, tier and shelf number only, with the remaining requirement that the book be found by search among the 50 to 70 on each shelf. In looking for particular books, I uncovered other highly useful titles. At the end of three months of this serendipity, however, I was ready to move out into the rest of Paris' library treasures to tackle gaps in the Ministry's collection more purposefully. Similarly, in 1972, I read Italian economic history in the working library of the Bank of Italy in Rome. It was highly useful in getting a neophyte started efficiently. If I had started with the library of the Luigi Einaudi library in Turin, containing 120,000 volumes on Italian economics, history and politics, I should have been overwhelmed. The latter, it may be noted, receives 1500 periodicals from Europe and has several archival sources available.

economic consultant on oil, has 10,000 volumes on oil alone in his personal and business library, 150 periodicals, 59 Conserva shelves of clippings and financial information on 600 companies. Only one third of these 10,000 volumes fall within the Library of Congress classification of economics (LC HA to HJ), which suggests the difficulty of defining where 'economics' begins and ends.

In three sabbaticals in Europe and working with five libraries, I have been guided largely by information picked up osmotically and by word of mouth. Since the process led me to the European libraries mentioned in footnote 1, the system is efficient. One may, however, save time and effort and minimize the risk of a poor choice, by the use of materials of librarians and of research specialists. *Subject Collections* and *Subject Collections in Europe* have been noted above. UNESCO publishes a *Guide to National Information Centers* [38]. *World Guide to Libraries* [41], gives minimal information on numbers of books but includes an enormous range of libraries.

In the United States, the American Library Association publishes the *American Library Directory* [2]. Lewanksi is the author of *European Library Directory* [27].

One or two detailed and specialized guides have been prepared. Downs' *Resources of Canadian Academic and Research Libraries* [18], has a strong librarian interest. Welch has edited *Libraries and Archives in France, A Handbook* for the Council on European Studies [40], with detailed instructions on how to use the collections, down to the numbers of the buses to take to reach them. It lacks a reference to my Ministry of Finance library in the Louvre, but is superb. It also fails to mention the fact that the Bibliothèque Mazarine, the oldest public library in France, owns one of the four original gold-bound copies of Quesnay's *Tableau Economique*—a fact communicated to me by Professor P. N. Rosenstein-Rodan—but says practically everything else one would want to know. A particularly useful guide to economic history in France is contained in an appendix to *Essays in French Economic History* [13]. Professor Scott Eddie has been kind enough to furnish me with 'Post Arrival Information for American Fulbright Grantees to Austria' [47], which gives details on how to use the research facilities of Vienna, down to the discouraging information that it takes 24 hours for a book to be delivered after filling out an *Entlehnungsschein* or a *Bestellschein.*[13]

Having now seen the material available on how to choose and use a specialized or general library, I am not sure that I am willing altogether to part with the word-of-mouth information circuit.

[13] Professor Alexander Gerschenkron responded to this statement in the first draft by observing that this represents an enormous improvement over the early 1930s when it took two days to get a catalogue reference and another two days to get the book. Then, if no seat in the reading room were vacant, a further delay ensued.

If transport costs were zero, there could be a big research project to tell where to study a given problem from a comparison of the comparative strengths of collections. For railroad history: the Pliny Fisk collection of the Firestone Library in Princeton, the H. V. and H. W. Poor Collection in the New York Public Library (NYPL), or the Bureau of Railway Economics Library in Washington, DC. For Physiocrats: the British Museum and the Goldsmiths' Library of the University of London, recommended by Hoselitz [23], the Kress Collection at Harvard, the Seligman Collection at Columbia, the Eleutherián Mills Historical Library in Wilmington, which contains, along with its 98,000 volumes of United States economic and industrial history, the library and manuscripts of DuPont de Nemours (1000 volumes), or the Gustav Schelle collection (1269 items) at the University of Otaru in Hokkaido, Japan [21]? Or all of them? But transport costs are not zero, not is the opportunity cost of the scholar's time, though it may appear so to outsiders. Where transaction costs are high, the golden rule is to exhaust the general resources close at hand, and to move to specialized libraries thereafter in some order, dictated partly by holdings and partly by the costs of overcoming distance, until diminishing returns approach the reserve price unless, of course, as in a sabbatical, the objective function includes in it an argument of considerable weight for leaving home. But Albert Hirschman tells me that if one wants to study, e.g. Argentina, one can do much outside, for example, at the Pan American Library in Washington, the University of Texas at Austin, or the University of Miami, but that there is no escape from the need to go to Buenos Aires.

IV. THE TEACHING LIBRARY

No ancient pure teaching library exists. Yesterday's teaching material is today's research material. And even libraries started *de novo* have a dual goal, to provide teaching materials for students and research materials both for students when they write papers and for faculty in its research. The distinction between teaching and research functions has been emphasized by the separation of undergraduate and graduate course materials from research collections in the Lamont Library at Harvard, and new undergraduate libraries at Stanford, Michigan, and other American and British universities. The Cross Campus Library at Yale is an 'intensive-use' library for undergraduates and graduates alike to relieve the pressure on the Sterling Library. The Cambridge General Board's Committee on Libraries notes that the research community in Cambridge, England consists of some 1500 members of the senior teaching and research staff, 1750 resident research students and visiting scholars, and nonresident members of the University using the Universities library sources, who may number up to 1500 in any year.

Undergraduates, with a different, though overlapping, need for books, add up to some 8500 [14, p. 1195].[14]

Great public libraries, moreover, have a difficult time separating out the high school or college graduate student, who is cranking out a term paper, from the serious scholar, and the New York Public Library went so far as to establish a new Midtown Branch library, above the old Arnold Constable store and across 5th Avenue from the famous stone lions, to care for the students who used to overwhelm the main building in the Christmas and Easter vacations.

Book/student ratios differ sharply for what we may loosely call students and scholars. For students who use texts and a few books for supplementary reading for courses, not to mention standard monographic literature, periodicals and reference and statistical material, it may run 75 to 1. For scholars, the ratio should start at 200 and has no upper limit. In the British Library in Great Russell Street, there are say 7,500,000 books and 600 seats in the reading room, a ratio of 125,000. For teaching libraries in normal times, the problem is overuse. For research libraries, after winnowing out students working for courses and the large body of the public seeking to verify a 'fact' or pin down an elusive reference, the problem may be underutilization—a large social expenditure for small immediate social gain.[15]

As a college or university library ages, its expansion of teaching

[14] A crude rule of thumb is that a teaching library should consist of a minimum of 100,000 volumes, with 75 volumes per student overall, and 200 volumes per graduate student. The Association of College and Research Libraries of the American Library Association established a standard, in 1959, of 50,000 carefully chosen books for 600 students (at the four-year college standard), with steady growth at the rate of 10,000 books for each additional 200 students, up to a level of 300,000 books, at which point the rate of increase could decline. A more refined standard of Clapp and Jordan (op. cit.). starts with a basic undergraduate library of 35,000 titles (42,000 volumes) 250 periodicals (with 3750 bound volumes over 15 years) and 5000 volumes of documents, and adds to it for each faculty member, student and field of concentration at the bachelor's, master's and doctor's degree level. The 2000 titles (2400 volumes) per field at the master's level or equivalent has been mentioned in footnote 5. For each Ph.D. field 15,000 titles (18,000 volumes), 100 periodicals (1500 bound volumes) and 5000 volumes of documents are suggested.

It is of some interest that when the formula is applied to a group of large American universities, the University of Illinois is 35 per cent above the Clapp-Jordan norm, Michigan 32 per cent above, and UCLA 22 per cent above, whereas one unnamed university with 1,675,000 volumes is 35 per cent deficient, and another, with 268,000 volumes, is 55 per cent deficient. In Canada, only the University of Toronto and two small colleges, met the Clapp-Jordan criteria.

[15] See Carpenter [15]: 'The Great Collections in the History of Economic Thought', paper presented to the Midwest Economics Association, April 1974: 'Kress and Goldsmiths' are both underused in terms of the curators' wishes. We would welcome more demands on us.' But, contrast Black [7, pp 702–3], who characterizes the Goldsmiths' Library as 'well housed, equipped and staffed; well sited, well supported, and well used'. When I visited that Library on a Saturday afternoon in January 1974, it had but one reader.

materials slows down and levels off, while that of research materials continues to grow. The first appetite may, in fact, become sated; the second never. Some additional monographs are preferable to others, but, apart from the congestion problem, an increase in holdings through purchases and through accumulation of periodicals and transient texts is always positive, as it adds to the opportunities for research. Unhappily, many books in college libraries are never consulted or borrowed.[16]

The problem of the teaching library is best illustrated by the issues faced by the new library in the new university. The amount that it could spend for back materials is virtually unlimited. Retrospective statistical yearbooks and abstracts for the major countries are mandatory, but what about old primary materials: the British Parliamentary papers offered in some 80 sets, by subject, by the Irish University Press, at a total cost of more than $60,000, for example, with 95 volumes on slavery available at $6889; 44 volumes on industrial relations at $3842;[17] or 80 volumes on the United States at $3250; British government statistics, 1809–1965, on microfilm ($9185), or statistical yearbooks for Germany, France and Italy from about 1880 on microfilm, available from Chadwyck-Healey, Ltd; 35 books on the evolution of capitalism available from the Arno Press (subsidiary of the *New York Times*) for $584 or 27 volumes of Temporary National Economic Committee (TNEC) reports for $800, 33 volumes of Tennessee Valley Authority reports for $415; 105 books on American labour for $1,409·50; 32 books on British labour struggles between 1727–1850 for $400; 51 books on Big Business for $932; 10 volumes of Annual Reports of the National Labour Relations Board, 1936–65, for $335; 53 books on Technology and Society for $1075. The Goldsmiths'/Kress Library of Economic Literature is to be reproduced in three segments in microfilm. Segment 1, reproducing all books up through 1800, has a price of $42,000 for approximately 30,000 titles or about 1500 reels. One can replace old serials or periodicals from reprints from the Johnson Reprint Corporation or Xerox and H. W. Wilson. The *American Economic Review* from 1919 to 1944 at $910 from the Johnson Reprint Corporation and the *Economic Journal* ($383·50 for 1891 to 1958 and $6·20 a year thereafter) and the *Economist* ($2462·40 for 1863 to 1964) from Xerox and Wilson.

[16] Of ten books pulled at random out of the shelves of a small library of a black college, not in Georgia, only one had been borrowed and all looked in mint condition.

[17] I understand that this venture has not been an enormous success, and that sales of complete sets of Parliamentary Papers have taken place in the following orders of magnitude: 20 sets to the United States, 10 to Japan, 2 to Australia, 1 to the Union of South Africa and none to Europe. Since Parliamentary Papers are a mine of information about the economic history of Europe as seen from Britain, this lack of purchases says something about (1) European interest in economic history; (2) European knowledge of historical sources; (3) European library budgets, or some combination of the three.

The reproduction of economics classics started with Augustus M. Kelley in New York in a small way, each book taken apart and filmed page by page by Mr. Kelley. Copyrights were in the public domain or bought outright for a small sum. Bit by bit, as technical progress in reproduction spread and new colleges were increasingly formed in the 1950s and '60s, the industry grew. Kelley's 1969 catalogue offered 2000 titles. The latest issue of *Reprints* put out by Kelley, not dated but probably 1973, deals with items published since 1969 and contains some 800 to 850 titles of reprinted works in economics, political science and economic, political and social history.

In starting up a new university, the University Grants Committee in Britain gives the library an extra budget for five years. The Carnegie Corporation has continued the interest of its founder in libraries with start-up grants in the case of at least one Scottish university, Stirling. But the problem faced by the new collection emphasizes the advantage in an ancient origin.

There may be external economies to a location in a city with other universities. The libraries may be combined, as in the Joint University Library in Nashville, which is operated by Vanderbilt University, Scarritt College and Peabody College, and was started in 1936. Inter-library loans should, perhaps, be accomplished more expeditiously when libraries are located close to one another, although major libraries which have many demands on them may tend to discourage business by slow service, and national systems of inter-library lending have lately come into being, as discussed in the next section.[18] At the same time, rumour that a certain book bears on the answer to a question about to be asked on an examination may lead to that book being stolen out of every library in Paris which does not keep its books under lock and key. Theft is a serious problem in teaching libraries in every country today, as competition for academic achievement mounts and the rewards are higher. The other technique of monopolizing a book under competitive conditions when stacks are open is to misshelve it. Most university libraries

[18] Students of international economics may be interested in pursuing the analogy between the European Payments Union and interlibrary lending. Any system which will work well with bilateral balancing will break down if some countries (university libraries) are persistent debtors and others persistent creditors. (The same point could be made about the tuition exchange plan for free tuition among faculty children, which collapsed as undergraduate colleges, and especially those for women, found themselves called upon to provide more places than their faculty members needed outside.) Dewey Library finds it more expeditious to undertake interlibrary loans at a distance so as not to add to its persistent deficit at the Library of Congress or Widener. On the other hand, the Yale Sterling Library's gross imports are highest from the Library of Congress and from Widener, to which it can furnish effective reciprocity. The creation of a National Centre for Research Libraries with its own resources is comparable to infusing the European Payments Union with capital of its own.

must now spend time and money in searching the shelves for 'lost' books which are accidentally or deliberately misshelved.[19]

In economics, the teaching library is very much aided by the periodical *Economic Selections: an International Bibliography* [19]. This periodical, sold on a subscription basis, is divided into Series I, a record of new books in economics appearing quarterly, and Series II, a Basic List in a specialized field such as economic theory, international economics, or public finance. Both lists are broken down into categories A through E. A refers to a junior college, or a first-rate high school, or a college with a combined department of social sciences, which spends up to $500 a year on economic books; B is a good college library emphasizing collegiate teaching rather than graduate study, budgeting between $500 and $900 a year. Category C refers to a university which wants a well rounded collection for teaching purposes, and spends $900 to $1500 a year, while category D is a university library emphasizing graduate research as well as graduate teaching, with a budget of $1500 to $2500.[20] A fifth category, E, comprises 'alternative selections'. The classes are, of course, cumulative. Items listed are described or characterized concisely.

A problem of some interest is presented by the question of foreign materials and materials in foreign languages. *Economics Selections* is called 'International' and the subject matter is. In one randomly chosen Series I issue (that for March 1970), there were roughly 135 selections dealing with foreign or international subjects, as contrasted with United States or theoretical, out of a total of 404, and in the Series II issue on Public Finance (dated December 1966) there were 68 foreign items out of 295, a somewhat lower proportion because the basic list of classic items is more heavily weighted with theoretical and synthetic treatments. But the Selection I issue had only 28 items in foreign languages, and Selection II none. Students bodies are more and more international in composition, but teaching libraries are entirely, and research libraries mostly, confined to works in the native language. Even more casual empiricism indicates

[19] At Yale, 15 per cent of all new books purchased for the Cross Campus Library between January and May 1973 were replacements for missing volumes [437, p. 8]. The same report notes further (p. 11) that a reorganization of the main Sterling book stack and extensive inventorying of the French literature collection reduced the number of books unaccounted for to 1·3 per cent and is thought to have contributed to a reduction of 22 per cent, from 10,130 to 7951, of search requests from readers using the central stack.

[20] An indication of the inflation of the last twenty years in books is provided by the 1954 corresponding categories: A up to $250; B $250 to $500; C $500 to $1000; D $1000 to $2500. A librarian at the university level comments that the figures are not helpful; his library spends $11,000 a year on books in economics alone, plus another $25,000 a year for serials and journals. To keep within the first sum requires rigorous selection, since it covers something less than 75 per cent of the English-language output of economics books.

that the position is identical in periodicals. There is a variety of English, Canadian and international journals, largely in English, in most American libraries, but few foreign ones. The position would be the same, with French substituted for English, in France. In other countries, the proportion of non-native books and journals would be far larger, since international scientific discourse today is conducted largely in English.

One of the more interesting ventures for a new library is that of the University of Warwick, established in 1964, which has only 25,000 volumes in economics but has specialized in two ventures: one, a statistics collection of 10,000 titles and 2000 current serials filed according to the Board of Trade Statistics Classification Scheme, with numbers for countries and letters for the subject of the statistics; and the other a collection of Working Papers from 360 series worldwide, with 10,000 in hand and weekly increments of 50 or 60.[21] This is the 'largest collection of unpublished working papers in the UK (possibly the world?)', as the University answer to the questionnaire states, and with it the Library publishes a quarterly Bibliography of Economics Working Papers [39], provides an allied microfiche service to subscribers, and has a loan service for working papers in the United Kingdom and Europe. Here is a library rapidly converting itself into a major one for research.

V. RESEARCH LIBRARIES

The great research libraries in economics are, with one or two exceptions, the great research libraries in general. In the United States, there come to mind the Library of Congress, NYPL, the Harvard University Library, Sterling at Yale, for width, and the Kress Collection of the Baker Library of the Graduate School of Business Administration at Harvard, plus the Seligman Collection at Columbia University for depth. In Britain there are three, four or perhaps as many as six: the British Library, the Bodleian at Oxford, the Cambridge University Library and, perhaps, the Edinburgh University Library, the British Library of Political and

[21] A number of other institutions have organized themselves to list working papers, so that readers of the list may write away to receive them. Among them is the Office of the Assistant Secretary for International Affairs (OASIA) of the Treasury Department, which operates an International Clearing House for International Economics intending to send out lists quarterly. At times, I have taken the view that there is too much material in too many periodicals, and that I would not read any article, no matter how beguiling the title, until I had seen or heard it mentioned twice, a test which no computer-aided bibliography is likely to apply. For thesis writers, however, and scholars working in a popular field, it may be vital to scan the literature in press as well as that in print. (Since writing the above, I must eat my words. The Social Sciences Citation Index, published by the Institution for Scientific Information in Philadelphia, does provide a computer count of the number of times various articles and papers are cited. It may not, however, distinguish between citations by scholars whose judgment I trust and those by others. It is particularly important to eliminate references by economists to their own work.)

Economic Science, and the Goldsmith's Library of the University of London. In France, the Bibliothèque Nationale in Paris. In Germany, the Bibliothek of the Institut für Weltwirtschaft at Kiel. In Japan, the library of Hitotsubashi University at Kunitachi outside Tokyo.

A library is great because of width and/or depth. As indicated above, it helps to be an ancient collector. Economies of scale abound. Large collections attract gifts of books and money, plus subventions from the government. Governmental collections thrive on the exchange of governmental documents with other governmental libraries. Where more than one library in a country is designated as a repository for copyright material, the larger collections are chosen.[22]

The Library of Congress and the British Library, alone of the national libraries, have strong collections of foreign materials. Governmental materials are received in exchanges. Much is bought. In the United States, PL 480 counterpart funds have been used to buy books in eight countries: Ceylon, India, Indonesia, Israel, Nepal, Pakistan, the United Arab Republic, Yugoslavia and, for a time, Poland. The programme, which was started in 1962, provides materials for 350 libraries, not all of which find it useful. One librarian noted that the programme was a 'horror', having shipped over material indiscriminately, including comic books and instructions on boiling water, and filling up two valuable rooms with material which the library lacked time and staff to winnow. In addition, the Library of Congress, with its National Programme for Acquisitions and Cataloguing, first authorized under the Higher Education Act, receives an annual appropriation for current materials, plus a small sum to repair gaps, and maintains offices all over the world in which it purchases and catalogues material, the cataloguing being available to other libraries using the LC catalogue classification.

The Library of Congress was established in 1800, when the government left the cultivated city of Philadelphia to establish itself in an entirely new location. Among the original 152 titles in 740 volumes with which it started were Adam Smith's *Wealth of Nations* and Postlethwayt's *Dictionary of Trade and Commerce.* As of June 30, 1973, it had 72,500,000

[22] Such a choice in the early 19th century had costs as well as benefits, and two libraries, at least, of the ten originally designated in the United Kingdom, gave up the privilege. The University of Glasgow, in 1830, yielded it for an annuity from the government of £600; the Edinburgh University Library sold its privilege to the local city library. Designation as a copyright depository does not guarantee complete coverage. Some works are not copyright. Some copyright works were not deposited. And some libraries, from time to time, sold off books received in this way in order to acquire cash to convert into other assets, which is why, early in the process, the British Copyright Office would harass the depository libraries to check up on their holdings.

The Library of Congress is the only copyright depository in the United States. The process began in 1846, but was interrupted by the Civil War. Part of the early collection was lost in an 1851 fire when the Library was in the Capitol. One copy of each book was received until 1870; thereafter, two.

'pieces', consisting mainly of 16,500,000 volumes and pamphlets, 31,000,000 manuscripts (pieces), 8,500,000 photographic negatives, prints and slides, 3,500,000 maps, etc. [17, 1973, p. 103]. The LC classification 'H' covering economics and sociology, consists of 1,537,000 volumes [17, 1973, p. 110], with more than 1,200,000 volumes in classes HA to HJ covering economics, representing at least 450,000 titles. There is no possibility of estimating how many of the 100,000 periodicals are in economics. Its strength lies in American economic history, communism, socialism and anarchism, the legislative proceedings and public records of the United States and foreign governments, and statistical compilations from all official and unofficial sources.

In works close to economics, such as science and technology, the Library is very strong, based on collections of the Smithsonian Institution, which transferred to the Library 40,000 items in 1866 and 566,554 volumes, pamphlets, charts in 1930 [17, 1973, p. 110]. A scholar on its staff states that its collection in American history is virtually complete, although doubt has been cast whether it may not lack one or two regimental histories of the Civil War.

The New York Public Library (NYPL) is an amalgam of two institutions, the branch libraries, 82 in number, which lend books to the New York public, and the Research Libraries, formed in 1911 from the Astor, Lenox and Tilden foundations. The Economic and Public Affairs Division was organized in 1914. It has an estimated 630,000 volumes in economics, plus 1200 current periodicals and several hundred thousand microforms. Its librarian believes that the library has 75 per cent or more of what has been published of research value on the United States and each of its regions, 75 per cent of the research materials on economics published in England, France and Germany; 60 to 70 per cent of output for the rest of Europe published in the Roman alphabet, and for Eastern Europe and the remainder of the world using non-Roman alphabets, about 50 per cent of what has been published.

Much less information on economic collections is available for other great libraries not specialized in economics. The British Library has 10–12 million total volumes in all, with 7 or 8 million in the British Library Building in Great Russell Street where Gibbon, Hume, Shaw, Marx, Lenin and the Webbs worked; 1 or 2 million more in storage at Woolwich Arsenal, available with a 1 to 2-day lag; a substantial collection of technical material, including scientific literature and patents, in two buildings of the Scientific Reference Library in London; and the Lending Division of 1,750,000 volumes at Boston Spa in Yorkshire, but is unable to estimate how much is in economics. Harvard has 8,900,000 volumes overall, and 60,000 periodicals. Its economics shelf list in Widener runs to 65,000 entries, and is published in two volumes. Baker has 478,000 items, including 65,000 manuscripts, 45,000 corporate records, and the Kress library of 25,000 items. Littauer (a departmental collection) and the Law Library also hold much of interest to economists. For the *aficionado* it should be noted that Harvard has the best collection in the world on bimetallism. The Bibliothèque Nationale, 'one of the great libraries of the world', has a book collection in excess of 7 million volumes and a distinguished manuscript collection of 150,000 pieces. It is better on the Middle East than is the Library of Congress, very limited on other non-French European and North American matters, and the extent of its economic collection is unknown. Yale, the second largest university collection in the United States after Harvard, with 6,200,000 volumes,[23] estimates that its economics collection amounts to about 300,000 volumes and 6300 serials. The Beinecke Rare Book and Manuscript Library has a notable collection of British and Irish economic and political tracts, the Wagner collection with more than 10,000 volumes;[24] the Cowles Foundation for Research in Economics Library, emphasizing mathematical and statistical works, runs to 5400 volumes and 158 serials; the Economic Growth Center has a Library focused on statistics, economics and planning in 100 developing countries, with 30,000 volumes and 3800 serials. Supporting these are social science, statistical and area collections in the Sterling Memorial Library, plus the intensive-use collection at the Cross Campus Library. The overall collection in the Bodleian in Oxford is measured linearly, rather than counted, running to 98,600 metres of shelf space equal to 3,210,530 volumes, not including manuscripts [32, p. 2]. The economics proportion of this is unknown, but economics in Oxford is represented in Nuffield College library with an estimated 50,000 items, especially strong in British trade unionism; in the Rhodes House Library on Commonwealth and United States history, including economic history; the Institute of Economics and Statistics; the Institute of Queen Elizabeth House in developing countries, the Institute of Agricultural Economics, and St. Anthony College. Cambridge University Library has 1,900,000 books and 600,000 volumes of periodicals

[23] See [1]. After Harvard and Yale, the largest general academic libraries in North America are Illinois (5,200,000 volumes), Columbia (4,500,000), Michigan (4,400,000), California at Berkeley (4,300,000), Toronto (4,100,000), Cornell (4,000,000), Stanford (3,900,000) and Indiana (3,500,000). The Universities of Texas and of Toronto lead Harvard and Yale in volumes added in 1972–73. British Columbia, Syracuse and Missouri lead in microform holdings. Berkeley with 98,000 (to Harvard's 48,000 [*sic*] in 7th place) is the leader in current periodicals, etc.

[24] Frank W. Fetter tells me that the Wagner collection was assembled by a mining engineer with an amateur's interest in economics books and pamphlets, who, between 1900 and 1915, bought for his collection, not in the normal markets but wherever he happened to be working. He was interested less in complete collections than in provincial material, and collected books and pamphlets in Manchester, Leeds, etc., and acquired material not available in Kress or Goldsmiths'. Professor Fetter notes that Edgar S. Furniss used the collection for his book on the *English Village Labourer*, but, apart from him, the only use that has been made of the collection of which he is aware is by Jacob Viner and Fetter. A Yale informant finds this statement libellous and wrong.

and serials, for a total of 2,500,000; supporting it is the Marshall Library with 65,000 volumes and the Department of Applied Economics with 5000, both in economics [14, pp. 1236, 1238, 1249].

Among the great libraries of the world there should no doubt be included the Lenin Library in Moscow and the public library in Leningrad. In 1940, the Librarian of Congress stated that his collection was as numerous as those of the British Library, the Bibliothèque Nationale and, possibly, the Leningrad Public Library [17, 1954, p. 3].[25] In 1956, the Library in Leningrad, the Saltykov Schedrin (the public library?), had 12 million printed units, but the Lenin Library of the U.S.S.R. in Moscow had 19 million books and periodicals [36, pp. 409–10].[26] Unhappily, the writer has to leave both institutions out of account, beyond this mention.

Expansive collections concentrated in economics (and allied social sciences) are located in the British Library of Economic and Political Science at the London School of Economics and Political Science, the Institut für Weltwirtschaft at the University of Kiel in Germany, and Hitotsubashi University. The British Library of Economic and Political Science has 600,000 bound volumes, and 2 million items in all, divided among the social sciences and the law but with the main concentration in economics and political science. The Bibliothek of the Institut für Weltwirtschaft, founded in 1914 to commemorate the 25th anniversary of the Kaiser's accession to the Imperial throne, and miraculously surviving World War II, contains 1,185,000 volumes on world economics, 770,000 on Europe, of which 274,000 are on Germany, 89,000 on Great Britain and 56,000 on France; 45,000 items on Asia; 32,000 on Africa; and 243,000 on the Americas, of which 168,000 are on the United States [24, pp. 10–13]. It is supported by the German government as the chosen instrument in the field. The Library of the Seminar of Economic Science at the University of Tübingen, in the founding of which Friederich List took part, consists of 80,000 volumes and 800 economics, statistics and historical periodicals. K. E. Born believes it to be the best library in Germany for historical research [10, pp. 61, 79, 87, 109, 177–87]. Knut Borchardt, of the University of Munich, has expressed an understandable scepticism about this claim and informs me that if one combines the libraries of the University and the Landesamt, the bibliographical resources of Munich overwhelm those of Tübingen. The great Hamburg Commerce Library was destroyed in World War II.

Hitotsubashi University is specialized in economics, commerce, law and social science, so that its library is heavily weighted in economics. In 1972, it consisted of 640,000 volumes, half in Japanese and Chinese and half in foreign books. 'As a library devoted to social sciences, it is un-

[25] Information kindly communicated by Professor E. L. Domar.

[26] The totals given are understated since they represent cumulative acquisitions between 1925–26 and 1973. By 1926, the collection had reached 100,000 volumes [31, p. 75].

rivalled in Japan, bearing comparison with almost any university in the world.' It is, moreover, as presently to be noted, specialized in rare books [22, p. 91].

After breadth, depth. There are four great libraries in the development of economic thought, the Goldsmiths' at the University of London, Kress in Baker, the Seligman collection at Columbia, and the Menger and Franklin collections at Hitotsubashi. The first two were collected by Herbert S. Foxwell, who used to fill his house with rare books and sell off the collection as he needed room and funds. Two housefuls went to the Goldsmiths guild, which ultimately gave them to the University of London. A third was bought by Claude W. Kress for the Harvard Business School.[27] The Columbia collection, assembled by Professor E. R. A. Seligman, is reported to have emerged from a bargain between brothers, with one leaving the other free to take over the banking business in exchange for an agreement to buy his books in academic life. The Hitotsubashi collection started with the Menger collection, bought for $30,000 in the 1920s, grew with the Schumpeter collection left to the University by Mrs. Schumpeter, and has most recently been enriched by the purchase of the collection of Burt Franklin, a New York bookseller and publisher, for a vast sum contributed by a Japanese trading company. The Menger collection consists of 19,000 items, much in German, but with strength in English and French, and somewhat less in Italian items.[28] The Franklin collection consists of more than 20,000 items, including many rare pamphlets. It has only just been received in Tokyo and will not be catalogued for several years. The Kress Library, which focuses on economic literature prior to 1850, has an annual budget of $6000 to $15,000 for acquisitions, and acquires approximately 400 titles a year, largely foreign, in an effort to raise the foreign proportion of its library, now 40 per cent of the total collection of 25,000 items. Goldsmiths' Library collects only in English, and the Seligman collection is not being added to [15].

For many of the major libraries it is not necessary to describe the collection in economics, since catalogues have been published in book form and are available for inspection without a journey, e.g. The Library of Congress, the British Library, and the Bibliothèque Nationale all have published catalogues, parts of the NYPL—of interest to economists

[27] In a book from Baker, there was pencilled inside the front cover: 'This book was compiled by - - - from his notes on historical lectures at the School of Economics, including even some of the little jokes with which I tried to keep the class awake. The lectures were delivered from 7–8 P.M. Not a word of acknowledgement, of course.' Kenneth Carpenter, Curator of the Kress Library, readily identified the handwriting as that of Foxwell.

[28] Other European collections in Japan, not previously mentioned, are the library of Werner Sombart at the Municipal University of Osaka [35], consisting of 10,000 items, and the collection of Karl Bücher, the German Economic historian, of 11,466 volumes, acquired by the University of Kyoto in 1920 for $4000 [12].

mainly—the 40 volume Catalogue of Government Publications, the Baker Library at the Harvard Business School, the Hoover Institution on War, Peace, and Revolution, the Institut für Weltwirtschaft, and many more. The G. K. Hall Catalogue mentions card catalogues published in book form for a long list of specialized collections, including those on Middle East economics, World War history, African government documents, agricultural economics, colonial history, and industrial relations. Locating these catalogues may require consulting the Library of Congress National Union Catalogue (NUC), which attempts to list all books catalogued in approximately 800 libraries in North America and reported to the Library of Congress, including its own collection. I am informed that NUC is not always complete, and note that one edition of NUC covers only three of the seven catalogues of the Institut für Weltwirtschaft's described admiringly by Perlman [33], the *Behördenkatalog* (Catalog of Administrative Authorities published in 10 volumes at $825); the *Körperschaftenkatalog* (Catalog of Corporations published in 13 volumes at $1100); and the *Regionenkatalog* (Regional Catalog published in 53 volumes at $5775), but not the other four, Person, Subject, Title and Periodical, amounting in all to 142 volumes costing $14,840. It was not originally clear to me whether even the Library of Congress had the four volumes not listed. The other three are held by the Library of Congress and by six, five and four libraries each, with only Harvard, Yale and the University of Minnesota being common to all three lists. (A later edition of NUC listed six of the seven, all but the *Sachkatalog*.) The useful Dictionary Catalog of the Giannini Foundation of Agricultural Economics Library of the University of California at Berkeley, in 12 volumes, priced at $985, seems to have been acquired only by the Library of Congress and Indiana University at Bloomington. The Harvard Shelflist in Economics is perhaps more widely spread, along with the catalogues of collections of rare books, but a shelflist is less encompassing than a subject catalogue, because it records each book only once, and not several times under different subjects.[29] The Harvard Shelflist, however, does include lists by author and by date of publication.

To a hardbitten bibliophile, the collection is all, but to most economists service counts, too. We want amenities. The Dartmouth library is good, but perhaps not great in terms of collection, with perhaps 100,000 volumes in economics, including bound periodicals, out of the 1 million books in the college's system. Located in a vacation area, with an excellent staff, who are not overworked in the summer and are eager to please, it has been chosen as a location for writing books by Milton Friedman, J. Kenneth Galbraith, Gunnar Myrdal, and Simon Kuznets, and as a pole for retirement by Frank W. Fetter and the late Bray Ham-

[29] In a given year, the Bibliothek of the Institut für Weltwirtschaft will acquire 50,000 works (in 1972) and make 240,000 entries in its various catalogues [24, p. 30].

mond. My personal predilection is for open stacks, rooms for typing, photocopying facilities handy, and a little help with problems.

Open stacks, with ample desk space bespeak a new building, such as the handsome Basil Spence-designed library of Edinburgh University, with the magnificent facility of widely spaced shelves housing Parliamentary Papers, and large desks nearby to spread them on.[30] The University of Toronto librarian, answering the questionnaire, stresses that, in the new building, economists have been well taken care of in terms of space. If one must choose between open stacks and space, however, I think I choose open stacks, though most librarians like them closed,[31] and one can make mistakes with open ones.[32] But the preference for open stacks is based on speed of access, and the serendipity from browsing—an important ingredient in research—that is mentioned in footnote 12.

Typing and desk space is usually too little, and what there is, is usually overwhelmed by insiders. At the Library of Congress there are three categories of facilities for scholars: reserved shelves on which to keep books, study desks on the decks and in the stacks, and some typing

[30] In the 1920s and 1930s, among the undergraduates at the University of Pennsylvania, it was believed that the reason the University Library resembled the Philadelphia, Baltimore and Ohio railroad station was because it was the same building. According to the legend, the City planned to extend Locust Street through the campus, and was prevented only by insistence that the University had begun the construction of a Library. Asking to see evidence, they were shown the hastily modified plans for the railroad station on which the University's architects had last worked.

[31] Sir Roy Harrod tells of visiting Harvard University at a time when he was a member of a committee considering open stacks for the Bodleian Library. He asked Paul Buck, the Harvard Librarian of the time, about Widener's experience with open stacks and, on learning of large losses through theft, recommended against them. In a subsequent visit, he learned that, in the meantime, almost all the three or four thousand books reported stolen had been recovered in the possession of a single kleptomaniac. Today, Cambridge University boasts of being the largest open-stack library in Britain.

[32] When I wanted to consult Boudet, *Le Monde des Affaires* [11], it was not on the shelf nor was it charged out at Harvard, Princeton, or Chicago. A visit to Columbia University brought forth a helpful reference librarian who consulted the National Union Catalogue, and noted that it was available at NYPL. There, with closed stacks, my slip was brought back to my seat with an 'idiot card' attached to it, saying 'Take the card catalog tray to the Librarian and ask about the book again.' I did so and learned that the small + in the upper corner meant that it was oversized and filed separately. It should be said in my defense that the Widener catalogue card did not have an F for folio size nor was the catalogue entry so marked in Regenstein. Incidentally, if I had been knowledgeable enough to consult the National Union Catalog myself before setting out in search of the book, I should not have looked for it at Harvard, Princeton or Columbia libraries, all of which have it but are not listed in NUC. It is of some modest unscientific interest that Boudet, which I have converted into a shibboleth for libraries, is found in the British Museum, but not in LSE, the University of London, Edinburgh, Aberdeen, The Palais des Nations Library at Geneva or the Royal Library in Copenhagen. It is listed in NUC as held by NYPL, the Universities of Chicago, Michigan, Oregon and Virginia, Duke, Rutgers, Ohio State, Stanford, the Union Library of Pennsylvania in Philadelphia, and Air University at Air Force Base, Montgomery Ala., but not by Yale and Illinois and, as noted, not by Harvard, Princeton or Columbia.

rooms. The last are always in use by government officials. The NYPL has a typing room with 8 desks, where books can be held out; the Wertheim study, given by Barbara Tuchman in memory of her father, has every convenience, including facilities for keeping 30 books for a month, but it is restricted to scholars with contracts to publish the work produced. The Library of the Palais des Nations in Geneva had a substantial typing room in 1954, plus an office in which my research team of 4 could keep books, type and operate calculating machines. I doubt that many libraries can offer that service today.

VI. NEW PROBLEMS AND TECHNIQUES IN LIBRARY ORGANIZATION

The knowledge explosion has been widely commented on. In economics, as in science in general, monographs, periodicals, students, Ph.D.s and the like seem to be growing at a rate of about 5 per cent a year, resulting in a doubling every 15 years [28].[33] Recent trends may be unsustainable as the knowledge industry changes from rapid growth to a sideways trend, and the deceleration causes problems for publishers, universities, libraries, etc., that are adjusted to expansion.

One particular aspect of the growth of recent years, in my judgment, has been the tendency of publishers to take advantage of the pressure on libraries to stay abreast of growing knowledge and to buy all books and periodicals. Some publishers have made a profit by bringing out books of dubious significance as contributions to learning, pricing them at monopoly prices and selling small editions, largely to libraries. The function of screening additions to the stock of knowledge is, thus, turned over from the publisher to the librarian. Harvard University does not, as a rule, place standing orders for books, and employs 6 bibliographers, specialized by broad region or discipline, to order selectively. Cutting down on library budgets and orders, along with the slowdown in the rate of growth of universities, is likely to produce bankruptcies in publishing which will modestly alleviate the problem.

A further technique is specialization by libraries. At the teaching level, libraries cannot specialize until universities specialize in the courses they present, but specialization in research is well under way in the United

[33] For an artistic impression of the problem, see Borges [9]. Sr. Borges was for many years the director of the National Library of Argentina. The reference was brought to my attention by Professor Carlos F. Diaz-Alejandro. Historical perspective may be obtained from Jacob:

'It is a very general and well founded complaint, both among authors, booksellers and others, that too many books are published. The constructed nature of German society, and the want of a point which could be considered the force of literature, occasions this excess of writing. Every man who thinks he has anything to communicate, runs to the press with eagerness, and is sure to find some admirers in some circles. . . .' [25, p. 308].

States. The Joint Universities Library at Nashville, Tennessee, involves a complete merger of the library function among a number of contiguous universities. Less formal sharing takes place between Duke University and the University of North Carolina, some miles apart. There is a consortium of Western universities and colleges, founded in 1968, and built around the Hoover Institution Library at Stanford, with pre-eminent resources in the western two-thirds of the United States. Nation-wide facilities have been developed in the Centre for Research Libraries in the United States, and the National Lending Library in Britain. The Centre for Research Libraries has some 60 members and 50 associate members to which it furnishes specialized materials requested by a teletype network—largely back issues of foreign newspapers. The National Lending Library in Britain, a governmental body, has a collection of its own, and also organizes inter-library lending among other libraries within Britain and between Britain and foreign countries.

The Farmington Plan of the Association of Research Libraries provided for specialization in the collection of foreign materials among 60 research libraries. This appears, after thirty years of operation, to have fulfilled its purposes, and a looser arrangement for exchange of information on the acquisition of foreign materials has been substituted for it. A Farmington plan for Canada was rejected. In Britain, a Standing Conference on Library Materials on Africa (Scolma) assigns to different universities the task of collecting materials on specified African regions.

Most recently, new groups are forming. In Canada, the Ontario Council of University Librarians plans closer co-operation among Brock, Guelph, McMaster, Toronto, Western and York Universities. In the United States, a Research Libraries Group has been formed, consisting originally of the libraries of Columbia, Harvard and Yale Universities, plus the New York Public Library, but later to be opened to other members, to explore the joint use of computer facilities and to share in the development of collections. It is, of course, strenuously opposed by publishers and author organizations.

At the same time, it is tragic that some libraries are being pulled apart. I am given to understand that the separation of the French from the Flemish portion of the University of Louvain will result in dividing the library in half, not by language, but arbitrarily, by title—the odd numbered ones to one university, even to the other. The thought evokes the judgment of Solomon.

Schemes for co-operation or integration are a response to the necessity for cutting library budgets on the one hand, and the opportunities presented by falling costs of communication, photocopying and machine information handling on the other. In the ultimate, as I understood it, the thought of Project Intrex at MIT was that there was need for no more than one copy of a book in the world which could be found, examined, and, if thought useful, photocopied from anywhere in the United States or the world by remote-controlled televiewing and photocopying. The question, of course, is whether the costs of electronic handling of information are declining fast enough to enable libraries to maintain or improve service in the face of exploding materials, and still cut budgets.[34] It may be necessary to spend vast sums of money for hardware to save money, but it is not obvious that the technique will work. One small indication in the pessimistic direction is that the Project Intrex experiment, now completed, has not been extended in new directions.

Space remains a problem for all libraries. New buildings are under construction in many locations; the Library of Congress, Harvard University, International Labour Office, INSEE, the Hoover Institution, etc., or have just been completed—the University of Toronto. Collections of rare books are underutilized, as noted, and so are some libraries that are located off the beaten track, such as that of the Institut für Weltwirtschaft. For others, space is critical. One technique is to transfer older books to depositories at a distance, reducing service to the occasional scholar who needs them but easing congestion. Especially popular libraries have to limit use by rationing or by the price system. The Library of Congress is open, apart from governmental officials, and especially the Congressional Reference Service, only to those whose research is likely to result in a published work. The British Library requires demonstration that the works sought are not available elsewhere. The Bibliothèque Nationale restricts foreigners through the cultural attachés of embassies who must vouch for visitors; the routine of the United States embassy in Paris is to refuse recommendation to undergraduates and to those below a certain age, except where a compelling case is made.

MIT, Harvard, Yale and Princeton use the price system to control outsiders. For full library privileges at MIT, industrial users are charged $500 a year, individuals $100, and alumni $50, a neat example of discriminatory pricing based on elasticities of demand. Scholars not on the university's rolls at Harvard are given a month's use of the library each year gratis, but pay thereafter. The fee is $125 a quarter, $175 for six months, and $300 a year. Alumni may use the library for $75 a year. Yale charges $40 a month ($10 a month or $100 a year to alumni), for full borrowing and stack-access privileges. Faculty from beyond a 100-mile range are accorded a three-month 'visiting scholar' status without charge, and special materials and special facilities are open to special categories of student and scholar, with any adult non-student free to use books in the library without access to stacks and with no period of grace.

[34] The financial plight of the New York Public Library is especially serious, since it has benefited from several one-time grants and transitional subventions but is still running a substantial deficit annually and has drawn down its endowment from $90 millions to $70 millions.

Between 1971–72 and 1972–73, the number of readers paying Yale for the privilege rose from 295 to 363, and the fees from $10,000 to $14,000, or two-tenths of one per cent of the library budget. The Princeton charge is $40 a year. This is held low because of the state aid received by the library in certain fields and the need to provide service to the public in return. It is not believed that market competition is so perfect that the prices of these several universities reflect marginal utilities.

The questionnaire request for general remarks about the problems of organizing and retrieving economic knowledge brought forth a limited response but one largely emphasizing the need for more, better, and especially, more current indexing of articles in periodicals, pamphlets, symposia, Festschriften, and foreign governmental statistical materials. This effort has begun with machine techniques in the sciences, where verbal ambiguity is less than in economics. The initial attempt in business and management has not been a great success: the indexing of a limited number of periodicals for a limited number of years. But statistical material will shortly be available in machine readable form, up-to-date. One librarian is convinced that library networks using the new machinery are the wave of the future. Another notes that the time is not far off when Computer Output Microform, telefacsimile, etc., will provide the user with what he wants when he wants it—adding, however, that this is only relatively speaking, as she has been listening to these discussions for a good many years.

The writer is incompetent to discuss the issue of the new technology, which will be dealt with by others at the conference. He would, however, raise a question whether it will ever be possible to dispense with the technique of search by asking someone knowledgeable in the field. The retrieval of statistics by machines is readily done, although the librarian of the NBER notes that the field is in some disarray. At the other extreme, however, machine translation of foreign languages has been proven a failure. Too much ambiguity resides in words with different meanings in different contexts.[35] I am concerned that the user seeking a bibliography on a given subject would get too much[36] and that even a

[35] A historian at the Library of Congress who was using its MARC system of machine readable records which use a 10-digit system and one key word in context (KWIC) to check the monthly flow of black studies, turned up 125 to 150 cards in each of three months but these included a number of titles relating to Black Hills, the Black Forest, black holes and the like. I have tried to contemplate how a reading machine using KWIC would respond to Landes' *Unbound Prometheus* [26]. With fuller subject references, it would, of course, show up on lists dealing with the industrial revolution, technological progress and European economic history. Project Intrex used an 'augmented' catalogue entry for information retrieval in a narrow field—materials science—with a conventionalized vocabulary. The average document in its file ran to six pages. The expense of producing these catalogue entries is, of course, formidable.

[36] The late Norbert Wiener once stated that it was true that a million chimpanzees typing at random for a million years would produce the works of Shakespeare and the

bibliography which catalogued a book under four or five subjects would miss out on some important uses to which it could be put.[37]

More bibliographical aids are doubtless needed. Articles in *Festschriften* and symposia are, in most cases, *spurlos versenkt*. I have no idea how scholars learn where various manuscript collections are located without NUCMUC, the National Union Manuscript Catalogue now in preparation by the Library of Congress, except by the word-of-mouth circuit.[38] Timeliness is important for the reasons mentioned in footnote 21 (p. 30). But I detect a professional division between librarians on the one hand, who believe that a librarian should be able to find a reference for use in answering all questions, and a user relying on more organic methods: ask a few colleagues and friends, get a few references, and the sources used in those will lead you out into the field. Formal bibliographies are suggestive, and often serve as reminders of works noted and temporarily forgotten, but it is unthinkable to me to start on research by compiling a bibliography which one then would proceed to read systematically. The 90-page bibliography in Volume VI of the Cambridge Economic History of Europe gives me intellectual indigestion. Bibliographies abound: Besterman's *A World Bibliography of Bibliographies* [6], has 36 columns (18 pages) of bibliographies in economics, including such specialized ones as that by a German governmental agency on the Marshall plan and another on French 16th century economic documents. The bibliography prepared in advance of the research will very little resemble the list of references contributing usefully to the project after completion.

An economist looking at libraries cannot help but be struck by the slow pace in achieving economies of scale in classification and cataloguing. The gain to the user would be trivial. If he reads a book in

---

Holy Bible, but the problem would be to find them in an accumulation of paper larger than the earth. I am told that the ILO computer retrieval system produces, on the average, 59 abstracts per inquiry.

[37] In work on technical education in France, I tried to find out about the education of businessmen in France, working both from Centenary volumes of the Ecole Polytechnique and of the Ecole Centrale des Arts et Manufactures to industry, and from the businessmen to their education. In the latter connection, since the *Dictionnaire de Biographie Française* goes only to E, I found great difficulty until I asked Professor Maurice Lévy-Leboyer who suggested Boudet's *Le Monde des Affaires*, mentioned in footnote 31, which proved enormously helpful. I do not see how it would have been possible to locate this work through a bibliographic search, whether or not aided by Machine Readable Records. Professor M. M. Postan, in commenting on the issue, adds: 'Even if the computer can give you the name of a book, can it tell you whether it is a good book?'

[38] I see no way of knowing, for example, that the John Hopkins Library would hold correspondence of Scott Nearing from 1912–22; of Josef Schumpeter from 1913–24; of E. R. A. Seligman from 1893–1918; or of Francis A. Walker from 1870–96. Nor do I see how scholars like Richard Kuisel and Charles Maier would know that papers of Louis Loucheur, who worked in the French government on industrial and reparations questions, would be at the Hoover Institution library, as they evidently do, from their writings.

one place, he is not likely to read it elsewhere, and the cost of looking it up in another card catalogue is small. The gain to libraries where so much work goes into cataloguing, however, would be large. There are the Library of Congress and the Dewey Decimal systems, with a Bliss system, which preceded them, used by the University of London and the several University Colleges in Africa patterned after it, with libraries of 100,000 books. The British Library, Harvard and Princeton have their own classifications. Some libraries, like those at MIT and Yale University, are engaged in the long drawn-out process of shifting from Dewey to the Library of Congress at the margin. As MIT shifts from Dewey to LC, moreover, the Edinburgh Library shifts from its idiosyncratic system to the Dewey Decimal.

Like 33, 45 and 78-rpm records which can all be played on the same phonograph, fitted with an adaptor, the Library of Congress seeks in its cataloguing to provide LC and Dewey Decimal classifications for new books as they are produced in the United States and bought abroad. An International Standard Book Number is assigned for acquisition purposes, and the LC, Dewey Decimal and ISBN numbers are listed in the Marc project for Machine Readable Classification. Libraries like the Dewey at MIT shifted over to LC for current acquisitions in 1964, but made no attempt to reclassify the existing collection. In economic history, and the history of thought, where obsolescence is slow, this means the necessity to keep two classifications side by side. For smaller libraries, with accumulation, the new standard system, now LC, tomorrow perhaps an international one, gradually overwhelms the old. But, for ancient libraries, the cost of reconverting ancient treasures to modern systems is too great. They are, thus, unable to take full advantage of standardization and the economies that it affords.

VII. CONCLUSION

Time was when the great library had the task of buying it all. Except for national libraries dealing with national literature, that was received for copyright purposes, that day is over. Large libraries, like small ones must choose. The specialized library has an easier time, since comparability needed to make intelligent choice is more readily achieved within specific fields than across them. Inter-discipline comparisons, like those of utility between persons, are hard, if not impossible.

To this user of library services, it is shocking to realize that he has been getting along with only a limited understanding of the rich bibliographic resources available in libraries. In part, he has been aided by professional librarians who provided results without revealing how the machinery worked. In part, however, there may be diminishing returns to organized knowledge retrieval, and merit in sequential scanning and search, starting with a few sources and spreading out, relying on word-of-mouth communication and serendipity. Bibliographies, guides to literature, etc., have a short half-life, except in the rare-book field. The economist and the librarian are each sceptical of the other. The resulting tension (not antagonism) is doubtless fruitful.

A librarian makes the cogent point that reliance on the old-boy network is difficult for new boys. I suppose that the reply would be that that is why there is some use left for the instructor, particularly the one who is prepared to exploit his friends and acquaintances.

REFERENCES

[1] 'Academic Library Statistics, 1972–73, A Compilation of Statistics from the Eighty-one University Members of the Association of Research Libraries' (Washington, D.C., 1973).

[2] American Library Association, *American Library Directory, 1972–73*, 28th edition (New York: R. R. Bowker and Co., 1972).

[3] Ash, Lee and Lorenz, Dennis, *Subject Collections*, 3rd edition (New York: R. R. Bowker and Co., 1967).

[4] Austrian-American Educational Commission, 'Post-Arrival Information for American Fulbright Grantees to Austria' (1972).

[5] Baumol, William J. and Marcus, Matityahu, *Economics of Academic Libraries* (Washington, DC: American Council on Education, 1973).

[6] Besterman, Theodore, *A World Bibliography of Bibliographies*, 4th edition, (Lausanne: Societas Bibliographies, 1965).

[7] Black, Collison, review of 'Catalogue of the Goldsmith's Library of Economic Literature', *Economic Journal*, 81, No. 323 (September 1971), pp. 702–3.

[8] Bonar, James, *A Catalogue of the Library of Adam Smith* (London: Macmillan, 1894, rev. edition 1932).

[9] Borges, Jorges Luis, 'The Library of Babel', *Ficciones* (New York: Grove Press, 1962), pp. 79–88.

[10] Born, Karl E., *Geschichte der Wirtschaftwissenschaften an der Universität Tübingen* (Tübingen: J. C. B. Mohr (Paul Siebeck), 1967).

[11] Boudet, Jacques, *Le Monde des Affaires* (Paris: Société d'Edition de Dictionnaires et Encyclopédies, 1952).

[12] *Katalog der Karl Bücher, Bibliothek in der Wissenschaftlichen Fakultät der Universität Kyoto* (Kyoto, 1970).

[13] Cameron, Rondo, ed., *Essays in French Economic History*, Homewood, Ill., Richard D. Irwin, for the American Economic Association and the Economic History Association, 1970.

[14] Cambridge University, General Board's Committee on Libraries, 'First Report', *Cambridge University Reporter*, XCIX, No. 4653 (28 March 1969).

[15] Carpenter, Kenneth E., 'The Great Collections in the History of Economic Thought', paper presented to the Midwest Economics Association (April, 1974).

[16] Clapp, Verner W. and Jordan, Robert T., 'Quantitative Criteria for Adequacy of Academic Library Collections', *College and Research Libraries*, XXV, No. 5 (September, 1965).

[17] Congress, Librarian of, *Annual Report* (Washington DC: Library of Congress, various years).

[18] Downs, Robert B., *Resources of Canadian Academic and Research Libraries* (Ottawa: Associations of Universities and Colleges of Canada, 1967).

[19] *Economic Selections: An International Bibliography* (Baltimore, Md.: Johns Hopkins University, 1954–62; New York: Gordon & Breach, 1965–70; New York: Augustus M. Kelley, Inc., 1971–). [This publication, which has appeared under

several names, was originated at the Department of Political Economy of the Johns Hopkins University and was moved to the Department of Economics of University of Pittsburgh in 1963. Ed.]

[20] Fletcher, John, *The Uses of Economic Literature* (Hamden, Conn.: Archon Books, 1971).

[21] Hambayashi, Masuo, *Catalogue de la bibliothèque du Professeur Gustav Schelle* (Tokyo: Libraririe Keiso Shobo, 1962).

[22] Hitotsubashi University, *Bulletin of Information, 1972–73* (Kunitachi, Tokyo, 1973).

[23] Hoselitz, Bert F., *A Reader's Guide to the Social Sciences* (New York: Free Press, rev. edition, 1970), p. 245.

[24] Institut für Weltwirtschaft, Bibliothek, 'Statistiche Ubersichten für den Zeitraum 1971–73' (Kiel, 1974).

[25] Jacob, William, *A View of the Agriculture, Manufactures, Statistics and Society in the State of Germany and Parts of Holland and France* (London: John Murray, 1820).

[26] Landes, David S., *Unbound Prometheus* (Cambridge, Cambridge University Press, 1969).

[27] Lewanski, Richard C., *European Library Directory, A Geographical and Bibliographical Guide* (Firenze: L. S. Olschki, 1968).

[28] Lovell, Michael C., 'The Production of Economic Literature: An Interpretation', *Journal of Economic Literature*, XI, No. 1 (March 1971), pp. 27–54.

[29] *Katalog der Carl Menger-Bibliothek in der Handels-Universität* (Tokyo: Bibliothek der Handels-Universität I, 1926; II, 1955.

[30] Mizuta, Hirosji, *Adam Smith's Library: Supplement to Bonar's Catalogue* (Cambridge: Cambridge University Press, for the Royal Economic Society, 1967).

[31] Otto, Frieda, 'Die Bibliothek des Instituts für Weltwirtschaft', in *Institut für Weltwirtschaft an der Universität Kiel, 1914–64*, (Kiel, 1964).

[32] Oxford University, 'Annual Report of the Curator of the Bodleian Library for 1971–72', Supplement No. 6 to the *University Gazette* CIII, (June 1973).

[33] Perlman, Mark, 'The Editor's Comment', *Journal of Economic Literature*, XI, No. 1 (March, 1973), pp. 56–58.

[34] Raffel, Jeffry A. and Shisko, Robert, *Systematic Analysis of University Libraries, An Application of Cost-Benefit Analysis to MIT Libraries* (Cambridge, Mass.: MIT Press, 1969).

[35] *Katalog der Werner Sombart* (Osaka: Bibliothek in der Stadtischen Universität, 1967).

[36] Soviet Union, *The Large Soviet Encyclopedia*, Special Edition of Volume 50.

[37] *Subject Collections in European Libraries* (New York, R. R. Bowker and Co., 1965).

[38] UNESCO, *Guide to National Information Centers*, 3rd edition, revised and enlarged (Paris, 1970).

[39] Warwick, University of, *Bibliography of Economics Working Papers*, quarterly.

[40] Welch, Erwin K., 'Libraries and Archives in France, A Handbook', Pittsburgh: Council on European Studies: 1973).

[41] *World Guide to Libraries* (New York: R. R. Bowker and Co., and Munich: Verlag Dokumentation, 1970).

[42] *The World of Learning*, 24th ed. (London: Europa Publications, Ltd., 1973).

[43] Yale University, 'Report of the University Librarian, 1972–73', *Bulletin of Yale University*, Series 70, No. 2 (15 January, 1974).

[44] Yanaihara, Tada, *Catalogue of Adam Smith's Library* (Tokyo: Iwanami Shoten, 1951).

Summary of the Discussion

After introductory remarks by *Professor Giersch* as Chairman of the Conference, *Professor Wolfe* presented the Kindleberger paper as an exercise in meta-bibliography, admirably adapted to the keynote position in the *Proceedings* volume, and likely to become a standard source. Rather than outlining the entire paper, *Professor Wolfe* chose to emphasize its analytics. Professor Kindleberger has treated the decision problems of libraries under four main heads: private libraries, specialist libraries, teaching libraries, and research libraries. For the first two categories, at least, the most important decision problem is the allocation of *space*; it is even more important than the allocation of its budget. (Similar ideas could be found in Professor Becker's studies of the allocation of time, in inventory [queueing] theory, and in the economics of transport.) There was less analytical content in Kindleberger's treatment of the specialist library; many such exist in various branches of Economics, but not all are in places of ready access. For teaching libraries, *Professor Wolfe* mentioned the work of Professor Perlman at Johns Hopkins, and later at Pittsburgh, in preparing *Economics Selections* for their use. Another problem, theft and mis-shelving, might also be important for research; in general, the line between teaching and research libraries is foggy, in that yesterday's research is today's textbook—and sometimes vice versa. A peculiar problem of the teaching library, at the same time, is student demand for multiple copies of textbooks and readings. *Professor Wolfe* suggested that his own university rule (Edinburgh) of no more than two copies of any one volume, might help here. As for research libraries in the true sense, Professor Kindleberger estimates that there are only three or four in the entire world, and they attract scholars from all countries. (We know little of who they are or why they come.) *Professor Wolfe* doubted that university libraries should attempt to duplicate many of their facilities, but noted that Professor Kindleberger was more liberal.

Some problems common to many classes of libraries are: the weeding out of obsolescence—evading 'Parkinson's Law' that numbers of books always expand to fill space, the inadequacy of the expenditure budget, the use of technical aids such as computers and duplicating equipment; the pooling of resources between libraries, and the resulting transport costs.

Perhaps, following the Kindleberger paper, discussion might settle on such problems as amounts of money to be spent, optimal library sizes, optimal patterns and degrees of inter-library co-operation, the technical sub-structure of libraries, and the types of information media needed by economists generally. (The paper suggests that libraries may include *too much* along the lines of computers, bibliographies, and abstracts, since many researchers rely mainly on colleagues and friends for bibliographical information—the so-called 'old-boy' network—and want more space for research and typing within the library and fewer unused books.)

Going beyond the Kindleberger paper itself, *Professor Wolfe* pointed out that the library budget is only a small part (perhaps 10 per cent) of the information budget of the typical university, which is itself only a small part of the research budget. At Edinburgh, the library budget is about 2 per cent of the university budget, and Edinburgh has ambitions to support a research library. (*Professor Wolfe* believes that the percentage may be lower in the United States, but the absolute sizes of library budgets are higher, and also that libraries in the United States tend to come closer to teaching libraries than do the British ones.) Professor Wolfe's final point was that Economics was an outlier in its relative non-use of non-library bibliographical materials patterned after *Chemical Abstracts, Psychological Abstracts*, etc., which are major works in their respective fields.

Beginning the discussion from the floor, *Professor Morgan* expressed the opinion that universities do a poor job of costing libraries (as well as other facilities). Universities would be appalled, *Professor Morgan* believes, to learn the true cost of their libraries, especially their capital costs. Cost-benefit analysis is underdeveloped in this field; how do we measure the input and output of a library? We also need to know more about the political science and sociology of libraries: Who makes the basic decisions (political problem)? How do we learn the use of libraries and rules of behaviour in them (social-psychological problem)? But this would be material for another paper.

Professor Eckstein directed attention to recent changes in both economic research and library management. For example, more mathematical and statistical research methods are being used, with less emphasis on traditional literary bibliography. At the same time, students are demanding greater control of universities, including libraries. On the first point, libraries are adapting quite well—more journals, fewer books, more statistical records but (as yet) inadequate computerization. Libraries are, in some sense, losing out to computer research stations. On the second point of student satisfaction, libraries do a poor job, especially at the undergraduate level, and students are disengaging themselves from the library. For example, at his own university (Harvard), students are required to buy all of their basic reading materials even in basic graduate courses, since the library cannot keep enough copies.

Mr. Fetterman made the point that size is a poor measure or proxy for the value of a library, especially a university library. (This point is not realized by universities in the United States, which rate libraries by number of volumes.) *Availability* of materials is important; this is usually a question of access, not of possession. From the University of Pittsburgh, the librarian can communicate with Chicago as quickly as with a crosstown library in Pittsburgh. It would save money if numerous libraries could use the same volumes.

Professor Shoup suggested, following on the last point, that research libraries should include duplicating facilities in lieu of reading and writing space. He had found himself unable to use his own university library (Columbia) because of this lack; on the other hand, the less-celebrated Dalhousie University library was ideal, with large numbers of copiers. The library of the future, *Professor Shoup* felt, will no longer be a place to read.

Professor M. Perlman disagreed. Libraries are to him both intermediate and final products. Professor Kindleberger's paper had stressed the library as a final product, a temporary living space. His critics had treated the library only as an intermediate good. *Professor Perlman* himself agrees with Professor Kindleberger.

Professor Meyriat pointed out that economists differ among themselves. One economist wants to read great books; another wants only data and documents. Libraries would like to know more precisely who wants what; there are real communication problems between users and suppliers. Data banks, document libraries, and bibliographical services are somewhat separate in France, but French specialists are trying to build up 'switching mechanisms' between them.

Professor Morgan insisted that economists need approximately 10 minutes to look at a document to judge its relevance to their work. They cannot trust bibliographies or reference services exclusively.

Professor Kindleberger opened his response to this discussion by agreeing with Professor Morgan in what he (Kindleberger) interpreted as basically a dispute between open stacks and closed ones (or inter-library loans). To some extent, therefore, he disagreed with the comments of Professors Eckstein and Meyriat, and also with those of Mr. Fetterman. In his view, a scholar needs much more than statistical data. He, therefore, agrees also with Professor Perlman that libraries are *more* than intermediate products. He is of two minds on Professor Shoup's comment. It is important to skim, and duplicators will not skim for you. At his own institution (MIT) there is even a problem of disposal of excess xerox copies. He agrees with Mr. Fetterman that many libraries are too big, their book numbers 'padded' with unused titles. The problem of student use he sees as a function of university, rather than of library, size. He sees a major library as a public good—a memory, or an insurance policy against the loss of knowledge. On these terms, the Library of Congress in Washington is clearly worthwhile.

Professor Kindleberger closed on a confessional note. He admitted that he was old-fashioned, and rather hoped that computers may go the way of machine translation, which had been ineffective. He also admitted placing trust in the 'old boy' network as a supplement to, if not a substitute for, formal bibliography.

2 Computerised Approaches to the Literature of Economics: from ISIS to DEVSIS

George K. Thompson
INTERNATIONAL LABOUR ORGANIZATION LIBRARY, GENEVA

Of the hundreds of computer-readable bibliographic data bases in existence in the world today, indexing and abstracting services in the social sciences have only recently started making use of computers. This paper examines those services and systems directly relevant to economists. High cost of indexing and abstracting and lack of coordination among secondary services are two factors which hamper the growth of improved or new services. International sharing of resources (data banks and indexes) by means of computer networks appears to be the only reasonable approach to take—even in the short run.

There are hundreds of computer-readable bibliographic data bases in existence in the world today.[1,2] While the natural sciences pioneered in the use of computers as an aid in the production of secondary services, a number of computer-assisted indexing and abstracting services in the social sciences have recently started up as well. The development of these services has been paralleled by the launching of several international information networks which link institutions that are willing to co-operate in the effort of preparing input and sharing information resources.[3] The purpose of this paper is to examine the present situation with respect to those services and systems which are of direct relevance to the literature of economics.

I. WHY USE COMPUTERS?

Three main factors determine whether indexing and abstracting services use computers or not, and a fourth factor lurks on the horizon. There is

[1] Gechman, Marvin C. 'Machine-readable Bibliographic Data Bases,' *Annual Review of Information Science and Technology*, 7 (1972), pp. 323–378.

[2] Schneider, John H. *et al.*, *Survey of Commercially Available Computer-readable Bibliographic Data Bases* (Washington: American Society for Information Science, 1973).

[3] Tocatlian, Jacques 'International Information Systems' (to be published in *Advances in Librarianship*).

the need to hold down processing and production costs, a desire to accelerate the production cycle so that information about new documents can be made available to users more quickly, and pressure to provide other services, such as a retrospective searching capability. Having gone to all of the trouble of computerizing, secondary services can then think in terms of linking together into international networks, with a further improvement in their cost-effectiveness to be hoped for, to say nothing of an augmented chance for survival!

COSTS

In a forecasting study prepared for the OECD, Anderla points out:[4]

> On the one hand, the mass of information is growing steadily and rapidly and the costs of manual/mechanical handling are increasing even more rapidly owing to rising wages and the absence of any appreciable productivity gains. On the other hand, the efficiency of electronic technology is growing exponentially and even faster, causing an almost parallel decrease in operating costs.
>
> The massive substitution of automated information processing for manual/mechanical processes will begin independently of official intervention as soon as unit costs of the two technologies will have reached parity towards 1979–80. Before then few spontaneous, unsubsidized automated systems will be set up, but after this date systems will become more numerous and widespread.

Much has been written over the years about the so-called 'information explosion', but there is little hard data about the explosion of rising costs which is beleaguering managers of libraries, information centres and bibliographic services. American economic journals have gone up in price by 84 per cent in the last five years,[5] and it is likely that subscription rates for non-American journals may have increased even more sharply.

Within the ILO, which is certainly typical of European-based agencies of the United Nations family, the cost of a professional indexer or abstracter increased by 53 per cent over the past six years (in constant 1970 dollars), or by 70 per cent, based on mid-1974 dollars. The average cost to the organization, of a professional staff member in 1976–77, has been reckoned at well over $40,000 per annum, based on the exchange rate prevailing for the dollar in February 1975.

[4] Anderla, Georges *Information in 1985; A Forecasting Study of Information Needs and Resources* (Paris: Organisation for Economic Co-operation and Development, 1973.)

[5] Brown, Norman B. 'Price Indexes for 1974', *Library Journal* (July 1974), pp. 1775–1779.

Faced with such staggering cost increases, management must think in terms of fresh approaches to the problem. Index or abstract less? Try to improve productivity? Cut back on the quality of indexing? Unless one can be content with the very shallow indexing that computers can perform automatically on titles, of the so-called KWIC (Keyword-in-Context) type,[6,7] one has to accept that there are inevitable indexing and abstracting costs associated with the production of a good quality secondary service, and seek other ways of keeping costs down, as, for example, by networking.

For secondary services which produce a printed index bulletin or journal of abstracts, yet another cost has to be taken into account: printing. In 1974, a decision was taken by the ILO to switch to computer photocomposition of its *CIS Abstracts* in the field of occupational safety and health, when it was found that the cost of manual typesetting of this monthly journal was almost identical with the cost of computer photocomposition of the same text. Computerization did not decrease the production costs of individual issues, but it meant that annual indexes could thenceforth be prepared automatically; moreover, the existence of a machine-readable data base offered a retrieval capability not previously possible.[8]

TIME-LAG IN PUBLICATION

Another very good reason to make use of computers is to speed up the production cycle of secondary services. As individual index entries or abstracts are prepared they can be put into machine-readable form and proof-read on a daily basis. When the time comes to prepare the 'copy' for printing, the computer merges the entries, sorts them into proper sequence, and prepares the author, subject, or other indexes as required. While not eliminating the intellectual effort of indexing each item in the first place, it does do away with the time-consuming, tedious task of preparing such indexes manually, and it also makes it possible to prepare cumulations very quickly. Examples of such computer-produced services include the British National Bibliography, which is issued weekly, with triannual and annual cumulations, and the *Social Sciences Citation Index*, issued triannually with annual cumulations.

[6] Jahoda, Gerald *Information Storage and Retrieval Systems for Individual Researchers* (New York: Wiley-Interscience, 1970).

[7] Maloney, Ruth Kay 'Title Versus Title/Abstract Text Searching in SDI Systems' *Journal of the American Society for Information Science* (Nov.–Dec. 1974), pp. 370–373.

[8] Torkington, Roy B. *Computer Typesetting vs. Manual Typesetting—Cost Estimates Based on CIS Costs* (Geneva: ILO, 1974). (ISIS Technical Note G-13).

NEW SERVICES

As these secondary services already exist on magnetic tape for production purposes, copies of the tapes can be made available for purchase. The *BNB* tapes, for example, would be useful mainly for large libraries having access to computing facilities, and their use should theoretically enable subscribing libraries to cut down on their own cataloguing costs of new British imprints.

Another more cost-effective approach is to record all bibliographic information about books on a central computer, and to connect to it by telephone lines, with visual display computer terminals in dozens or hundreds of libraries.[9,10,11] Each library can have instantaneous access to whatever data it requires at very low cost indeed, and individual libraries contribute new records to the central file when they acquire particular items not already in the system. An outstanding example of such an operating on-line cataloguing system is the Ohio College Library Center in Columbus, which serves not only libraries in the state of Ohio, but in certain adjacent states and Canadian provinces as well. The OCLC experience has been so successful that a number of other regional centres have come into existence, and together these regional centres recently created (Nov. 1974) a Council for Computerized Library Networks.

The computer can also make possible new services to users that would either be impossible, or exorbitantly expensive to produce by using manual methods.[12] In the new ILO Library, opened in February 1975, readers who manifest an interest are encouraged to do their own bibliographic browsing through the file of some 60,000 abstracts which is presently available for on-line searching. Several visual display computer terminals are located at various points in the reading room for this purpose.

Over the past decade 13,280 printed searches were produced on the computer at the ILO (2978 in 1974 alone). In addition, selective dissemination of information (SDI) services are provided. A profile of the individual user's interest is constructed, and this is matched at given intervals, say once a month or once a quarter, against the file of new abstracts recorded in the system. When there is a 'hit', the computer prints out a notification which is sent to the user. The ILO library staff who provide this service are somewhat skeptical, however, about its widespread

[9] Olson, Edwin E. *et al.* 'Library and Information Networks', *Annual Review of Information Science and Technology*, 7 (1972), pp. 279–321.

[10] Hookway, H. T. 'The Resources of the British Library', *Aslib Proceedings* (Jan. 1975), pp. 2–7.

[11] *Canadian Library Systems and Networks; Their Planning and Development* (Ottawa: Canadian Library Association, 1974).

[12] Lawrence, Barbara, *et al.* 'Making On-line Searching Available in an Industrial Research Environment', *Journal of the American Society for Information Science* (Nov.–Dec. 1974), pp. 364–369.

usefulness. It would appear that most researchers' interest profiles shift after they have been exposed to a retrieval system and have consulted some of the abstracts or the documents to which they refer. Moreover, their interests usually change as they proceed more deeply into their projects. For this reason, most of ILO's 'regular' SDI customers are those individuals, or research teams, who constantly need to be alerted to all new publications in a very specific field. A case which comes to mind is the following profile: statistical results and/or methodology of household or family budget surveys. After ten years of operation, only 80 SDI profiles are currently processed at the ILO.

Another new service of interest to economists that has been made possible through the use of computers is the citation index. The Institute for Scientific Information in Philadelphia publishes the *Social Sciences Citation Index* every four months. Every new article appearing in leading journals is recorded, together with every reference cited by the author of the article. In this way it is possible to X-Ray the activities going on in a specific subject area and, also to get some idea of the influence that certain scientific writings are having in adjacent areas.

II. EXISTING COMPUTER-ASSISTED SERVICES HANDLING ECONOMIC LITERATURE

It is beyond the scope of this present paper to attempt to evaluate the usefulness of existing indexing and abstracting services. Instead, an effort will be made to describe those services of relevance to the field of economics which make use of computers, because it seems reasonable to assume that the computer will become an increasingly important tool in information handling. The five services described in this section all use computers in quite different ways. As I have pointed out in an earlier paper, there is perhaps no single 'best way'.[13] To say the least, the computer allows one to use a great deal of imagination in approaching the problem of information handling.

An attempt has been made to see how well the journal literature is covered by four of the services (the fifth only deals with books). A recent issue of the *Journal of Economic Literature* contains a listing of 219 economics journals.[14] While this listing is far from complete (no journals from the Soviet Union or the Middle East are mentioned, for example), it was used for checking purposes because the new edition of UNESCO's

[13] Thompson, Georges K. 'Abstracting Services in Education and the Social Sciences; A Study of Document Analysis Techniques Useful for the Development of a Computer-based Decentralized Information Network', *EUDISED Technical Studies 1971* (Strasbourg: Council of Europe, 1971), pp. 43–83.

[14] 'Subscription Data—Journal Listings' *Journal of Economic Literature* (Sept. 1974), pp. 1012–1024.

'World List of Social Science Periodicals' was still being printed when this paper was written.

Each of the 219 titles was checked against the lists of journals scanned, indexed or abstracted by the four services. *Social Sciences Citation Index* handles 116 of them, or 53 per cent, *Economic Titles* 69, or 32 per cent, *International Labour Documentation* 137, or 63 per cent; and *Agrindex* 21, or 10 per cent. Each service, of course, 'handles' the periodicals in an entirely different way. If Soviet and Middle Eastern journals were added, the coverage of the *Social Sciences Citation Index* would fall below 50 per cent and that of *International Labour Documentation* would increase. The full listing with the coverage of each service is available on request from the author of this paper.

Characteristics of the five services are given in summary form in the table on p. 55, and in narrative form below:

SOCIAL SCIENCES CITATION INDEX

All articles published in some 1200 journals and a selection of articles from some 1300 more are regularly recorded in the *Social Sciences Citation Index* published by the Institute for Scientific Information in Philadelphia. Although this index contains a pseudo-subject index made by permuting keywords in the titles of articles, its main interest resides in the fact that index entries are generated for all references cited in each journal article (making an index of absolutely colossal proportions).

Each issue contains three main sections, the citation index, the source index and the permuted word title index. The citation index is arranged alphabetically by cited author and then by cited year of publication. Under each cited item, which may be a monograph, a government publication, a journal article, etc., appear the source articles which cite the work. The source index provides a complete author index to the current literature and a full description of each citing item. It should be underlined that only journal articles are recorded in the source index. The title index is a permuted index using each non-trivial word in a title. In the case of non-English language titles, the permutation is performed on the English translation of the title.

In addition to the printed index, which, because of its price, is unlikely to be purchased by individual researchers, the ISI offers an 'Automatic Subject Citation Alert' selective dissemination service which produces weekly computer printouts of new articles by matching subject profiles against words in the titles of items recorded in the system, truncated words, cited references or authors, corporated addresses, names of journals thought to be highly relevant to the subject of the profile, and so on.

Because of the looseness of vocabulary some amusing results can occur when the same term has quite different meanings in other disciplines, and one attempts to search on words alone. 'Migration' means one thing

COMPUTER ASSISTED SERVICES HANDLING ECONOMIC LITERATURE

Titles	*Publication period*	*Frequency*	*Subject scope*	*Coverage*	*Economic entries per year (estimates)*	*SDI or retrospective searching services*	*Availability of original documents*	*Annual subscription price*	*Classified order of entries*
Social Sciences Citation Index	1970–	Every four months; cumulates annually	Social sciences	Journal articles only	70,000	Both	$3 for articles up to 10 pages; $1 per 10 pages after first 10	$1250.–	By author
British National Bibiolography	1950–	Weekly; cumulates every 4 months and annually	All fields of knowledge	British books only	3,800	—	—	£74.50 incl. annual volume	Dewey Decimal Classification
Economic Titles	1974–	Semi-monthly with subject index which cumulates annually	Economics	Mainly journal articles, some books, government publications, reports, directories	16,000	Manual SDI at present; computerized SDI + retro-searching in 1976	Photocopies of journal articles guilders 0,45 per page	750 guilders	Universal Decimal Classification adapted to users' needs
International Labour Documentation	1965–	Semi-monthly; cumulates every two years	Relevant to programme of work of ILO	Books, journal articles, government publications, documents of international organizations	4,000	Both	ILO publications only	$17.– (semi-monthly issues only)	—
Agrindex	1975–	Monthly	Agriculture in general; incl. agr. economics, rural dev., dist. and marketing, etc.	Journal articles, monographs, technical reports	Several thousand	—	—	$25.–	Own Classification

to an economist, another to a biologist, yet another to a geologist, and so on. Weekly printouts on the subject prepared for the ILO have brought to light such items as:

'Cellular basis of movement of migrating grex of slime-mold dictyostelium-discoideum'

'Migration-inhibitory factor in gold hypersensitivity'

'Relation of oil migration to secondary clay cementation'

and

'Radar study of autumn migration of wood pigeons Columba-Palumbus in Southern Scandinavia'

These non-'economic' titles appeared because the computer was searching all new items entered in all of the ISI data bases. In all fairness, it should be pointed out that in each of several profiles run weekly for the ILO there have been occasional relevant titles which have appeared in non-social science journals. Normally, these would have been overlooked. Since no intellectual indexing has been done at all, one should be grateful for finding a few pertinent items each week, particularly when one considers the vocabulary problem and the fact that authors often do not convey accurately enough the thrust of their articles in their titles.

A full explanation of the technique of citation indexing, and a guide to the specific services available with respect to the *Social Sciences Citation Index* has been published by the Institute for Scientific Information.[15] In addition, a slide/cassette tutorial explaining how to use the indexes can be obtained, as can wall-charts.

One is tempted to say that the existence of this service may transform the old 'Publish or perish' adage to 'Perish unless your publications are cited!'.

BRITISH NATIONAL BIBLIOGRAPHY

The *BNB* is a weekly list of new British books prepared by the Bibliographic Services Division of the British Library. Entries are arranged according to the Dewey Decimal Classification, and a weekly author index is provided. Cumulations are published every four months, containing a subject index as well.

Each book is indexed by a system known as PRECIS (Preserved Context Indexing System). PRECIS is able to preserve the correct meaning of a set of index entries by means of an operation called concept analysis. Descriptors are assigned in such an order that one term establishes the wider context in which the next term had been considered by the author.

[15] *Social Sciences Citation Index, 1973 Annual Guide and Journals List* (Philadelphia: Institute for Scientific Information, 1974).

Then 'manipulation codes' are prefixed to each descriptor so that the computer can recognize how it is to treat it in relation to other terms when it prepares the subject index for printing.

The following subject entries were generated by this system for the book, *Inner Dualism: An Outcome of the Center-Periphery Relationship During Modernization Processes in Uganda*, by Baruch Kimmerling:

Economic Development. Rural regions. Uganda. Policies of government, ca.1950–ca.1970. Effects—Case studies
Policies. Government. Uganda. On economic development of rural regions, ca.1950–ca.1970 Effects—Case studies
Rural regions. Uganda. Economic development. Policies of government, ca.1950–ca.1970. Effects—Case studies
Uganda. Rural regions. Economic development. Policies of government, ca.1950–ca.1970. Effects—Case studies

At the end of each year an annual bound cumulation is published. National bibliographies of other countries as well are, of course, often prepared by computer-assisted systems. The *BNB* has been described here because it is a rather exemplary case of a national bibliography which can be easily understood and used by researchers and students as well as by librarians.

ECONOMIC TITLES

Economic Titles is a semi-monthly journal of indicative abstracts prepared by the Library and Documentation Center, Economic Information Service of the Ministry of Economic Affairs of the Netherlands. It began publication in 1974 and is also available on magnetic tape (9 track, 800 BPI) from the publishers, Martinas Nijhoff, in The Hague.

Some 16,000 entries are published each year. These are made up of a selection of articles from some 2500 journals in the economic field (economic science, applied economics, management and organization), as well as books, research reports, government publications, important annual reports and directories. The main emphasis of the collection is on journals published in the English, French, German and Dutch languages. The source of these journals is as follows:

Europe	1750
Americas	470
International org.	230
Africa	150
Australia + Oceania	55

Some 100 journals in the field of economic science are processed from cover-to-cover, with the exception of articles in the field of pure mathematical economics, studies of a very specific local character and short notes.

Entries are arranged in classified order according to the Universal Decimal Classification, and the brief abstracts accompanying each entry are written in one of the following languages: English, French, German or Dutch.

One to three descriptors (in English only) are used to index each entry and to prepare the subject index which appears in each issue; this index cumulates annually. The descriptors are in a one-to-one correspondence with UDC numbers which are also recorded on the magnetic tapes. In many instances, the tapes also contain a number of descriptors in addition to those printed in *Economic Titles*, and about 15 per cent more abstracts. Beginning in 1976, the Economic Information Service will offer computerised SDI and retrospective searching facilities including free-text searching on the abstracts by means of the software package STAIRS.

INTERNATIONAL LABOUR DOCUMENTATION

For the past ten years the Central Library and Documentation Branch of the International Labour Office in Geneva has prepared a semi-monthly bulletin of indicative abstracts entitled *International Labour Documentation*. Subject descriptors selected from the 'ILO Thesaurus' (to be published in September 1975) are embedded into the text of the abstract itself. These descriptors are flagged so that the computer can easily pick them out. All descriptors appearing in the first sentence or phrase of each abstract appear in the subject index prepared by computer, together with the title of the document.

All abstracts are written in English. The thesaurus, however, is trilingual (English, French, Spanish), and computer programmes are being prepared which will permit abstracts written in any of the three languages to be merged into a single file and to permit on-line searching in any one of the same languages. Magnetic tapes of the file of 60,000 abstracts can be made available (9 track, 800 or 1600 BPI).

The computer programs used to prepare *International Labour Documentation* are part of a set of general purpose library management, printing and retrieval programs developed by the ILO, and known as ISIS.[16, 17] A technical paper also exists which describes how 'manage-

[16] Schieber, William D. *ISIS (Integrated Scientific Information System); A General Description of an Approach to Computerised Bibliographical Control* (Geneva: ILO, 1972).

[17] Schieber, William D. *Technical Manual on ISIS; A Generalised Information Storage and Retrieval System Designed at the International Labour Office* (Stockholm: Statskontoret, 1972).

ment information' derived from the operation of the ISIS system can be used.[18]

AGRINDEX

Agrindex, published by the FAO, is the product of the newly established International Information System for the Agricultural Sciences and Technology (AGRIS), discussed later in this paper. The first issue, containing 2557 entries, was published in January 1975. For this reason it is not possible to estimate yet how much material on the literature of economics will be recorded each year. It is anticipated that, when AGRIS is fully operational, in two or three years time, *Agrindex* will report on some 200,000 items per year. It is likely, therefore, that several thousand items on such topics as agricultural economics, rural development, distribution and marketing will be picked up each year.

The entries are presented in classified order, using a plan worked out for the AGRIS system, and may be subdivided by commodities, according to a classification schedule printed in each issue. *Agrindex* also contains a personal author index, a corporate entry index, a report and patent number index, and a commodities index. The maximum number of subject access points for any document is two.

III. NETWORKING: A KEY TO FURTHER IMPROVEMENT IN ACCESS TO THE LITERATURE OF ECONOMICS

In recent years, a number of mission-oriented co-operative ventures have been started which attempt to provide an international mechanism for controlling literature that is useful for a certain mission, as opposed to literature that is necessarily relevant to a single discipline. The first of these was INIS, the International Nuclear Information System which functions under the aegis of the International Atomic Energy Agency in Vienna. The second was AGRIS, the International Information System for the Agricultural Sciences and Technology, which is not only patterned after the INIS model, but which makes use of the computer facilities of the IAEA for the production of its *Agrindex*.

The INIS model consists of three basic elements: decentralized identification and recording of information about literature produced in a country or region; centralized merging of this information under the aegis of an international organization; the production of various kinds of output amenable either to further computer processing or to use by in-

[18] Piazzalonga, Doris *A Collection of Basic Data on Library and Information Retrieval Services of the International Labour Office, Based on an Analysis of Several Machine-readable Files* (Geneva: ILO, 1973). (LD/NOTES/61).

dividuals working without access to automated retrieval facilities. Each national or regional input centre is responsible for collecting information only from its local territory. This gives local control over the decisions about what to include and what to leave out and provides an equitable formula for distributing input costs. Flexibility in the mode of input is accepted; central processing costs are shared according to a formula agreed upon by member states of the organization who accept this responsibility; and output products are geared to all levels of users. Such a model has the further advantage of encouraging the development of national and regional information infrastructures.[19]

Two proposed new international information systems are presently being studied, one in the field of population (IDEMIS—International Demographic Information System) and another in the field of economic and social development (DEVSIS—Development Sciences Information System).[20] One of the problems facing the designers of IDEMIS and DEVSIS (other than the problem of how the two systems would interface with each other) is the question of the institutional infrastructure required to make the systems function. In most countries, atomic energy is highly centralized, and agriculture somewhat less so, but a great variety of different government departments and other institutions concern themselves with population questions and economic and social development. Both IDEMIS and DEVSIS represent, to a considerable extent, a shift out of the so-called 'hard' sciences into the social sciences, where the terminology is less precise and problems of classification and indexing are more complex.

Both initiatives bear watching, as co-operative networking seems the logical way to improve information resources. Moreover, from the outset, a variety of different types of institution are engaged in their design, not only government agencies, but, also, international governmental and non-governmental organizations, national research bodies and university research institutes.

[19] Wild, Kate and Woolston, John E. *Social and Economic Development: How DEVIS Would Link into the Emerging Network of International Information Systems* (Ottawa: International Development Research Centre, 1975).

[20] Tocatlian, *op. cit.*

Comment by N. Roberts (University of Sheffield)

Economists have not been well served by the 'tools' for literature control and exploitation that are provided by traditional bibliographical methods. It must be admitted, however, that economists, as a group, have shown few signs of concern over known bibliographical deficiencies despite being beset by one of the fastest growing bodies of specialist literature [1]. Nonetheless, despite this apparent unconcern and a documented reluctance to rely upon bibliographical aids [2], Thompson's paper brings the news to economists that improvements in the bibliographical situation are to be expected as the literature of economics and of related fields becomes more widely subject to the forms of control and manipulation made possible by the introduction of computer-assisted and computerized bibliographical systems. Present trends would seem to support this interpretation. There are strong grounds for recognizing that bibliographical progress is to be associated, in the future, with the increasingly intensive application of computers to bibliographical problems. What cannot be predicted with any accuracy, of course, is the speed and degree to which these developments may be expected to influence the literature and the literature-using habits of economists.

The computer may be employed (as Thompson points out) simply to assist in the production of what amount to versions of the traditional, printed forms of bibliographical aids (e.g. national bibliographies, indexes, etc.) and, on occasion, types of bibliographical publications not previously feasible (e.g. the *Social Science Citation Index*). Although the contribution of the computer in these areas has been significant in maintaining the scale and currency of the international bibliographical effort during a period of wildly escalating costs, its most promising bibliographical potential has yet to be realized on a large scale. This potential is based upon the facility which computer systems offer for 'on-line' working. Translated into bibliographical terms, this means the ability to consult and search immense literature and data bases rapidly and easily according to individual needs, and manipulating masses of bibliographical data in ways not previously possible. Provided that the literature of economics and related fields is 'captured' and organized usefully by the various computerized services, economists (and other researchers) will have at their command an unprecedented ability to exploit an ever-growing literature. For many economists this is likely to be a vision of the future; for many researchers in the 'harder' sciences such a service is already a routine facility.

Most operational 'on-line' systems manipulate elements of bibliographical references, i.e. authors, titles, dates, publishers, subject descriptions of various kinds, etc. that are attached to documents as retrieving labels, or tags. For many research economists, however, discovering 'about' documents may be a matter of secondary importance; access to quantitative data may well be a more frequent, urgent and fundamental need. The difficulties of using statistical sources and, at another level, simply discovering what statistical data exist to be used have been much discussed, but with only marginal improvements to the researcher. The ultimate solution may well be an all-encompassing system of computerized data-banks; in the meantime, less-ambitious, but exceedingly useful, projects have been undertaken to improve access to published statistical data. Two British examples may be used to illustrate the trend. The computerized macroeconomic data service for the British Parliament (MEDHOC

Project) demonstrates how simply and neatly statistical data may be obtained from a specialized data base [3]. The STIR (Statistics Indexing and Retrieval) Project is intended to improve the accessibility of statistics published in the major time series by the computer-assisted preparation of indexes to table level [4].

As might be expected, the costs of an 'on-line' service are fairly high. The promise of cost reduction is implicit in expected technical developments [5] and in a forecasted substantial expansion in 'on-line' working—

> The demand for 'on-line' access for scientific and technical information in Europe is expected to increase dramatically, as is indicated by the forecast number of users, 1976—60,000, 1980—960,000, 1985—2,350,000 [6].

In the last resort, however, the economic exploitation of computerized systems must be based upon the wholehearted acceptance of co-operation, co-ordination and standardization at international, national, regional and subject levels. Economy alone is a powerful incentive for the acceptance of these ideas which are basic to the concept of networks and networking (i.e. a complex of computer services connected in such a way as to facilitate the searching, or interrogation, of a number of geographically dispersed literature, or data, bases from any one of a number of separate service points).

The foregoing considerations are usually regarded as the province of the information specialist, but the developments and projections of which they treat have important implications for economists as a body of researchers. Economists may need reminding that the Council of Ministers of the European Community, in 1971, passed a resolution with a view to co-ordinating the actions of Member States regarding scientific and technical information and documentation (this formulation includes economic data and information). Member States were asked, *inter alia*, to assist in 'the creation and rational development of systems for scientific and technical information and documentation so that a European network (EURONET) could be established' and were advised that 'it is planned to commence the first operations of EURONET by mid-1976 with a limited number of services and to expand the network and the services it offers from there' [7]. In addition, the efforts of EURONET, within Europe, are roughly paralled by those of UNISIST (a world science information system which will embrace the social sciences) at the international level.

Inevitably, these activities involve the bureaucracies of national governments and international agencies at a number of levels, all seemingly far removed from the immediate and pressing preoccupations of the research economist. However, the message of recent and expected developments is clear enough. If economics as a subject is to receive its due share of the modern forms of bibliographical effort, and if individual economists are to benefit from the new forms of bibliographical assistance rendered by the computer, then economists must expect to devote considerably more time to what may be broadly termed bibliographical issues. The development of relevant forms of computer services with appropriate literature and data bases, the most effective forms of literature and data organization, the problems of terminological standardization, the influence of language barriers on the transmission of 'information', the realistic costing of the bibliographical effort in research programmes—these, and many other, problems call for the attention of professional economists. It has been said before but it bears repeating—the information business is too important to be left to information specialists.

REFERENCES

[1] Holt, C. C. and Schrank, W. E. Growth of the professional literature in economics and other fields, and some implications. *American Documentation*, 19 (1) Jan., 1968.

[2] Line, M. B. *and others. Information requirements of researchers in the social sciences.* Bath University Library, 1971. (Investigation into Information Requirements of the Social Sciences, Research Report no. 1).

[3] Poole, J. B. and Van Dongen, J. A. A computerized macro-economic data service for Parliament: the MEDHOC Project. *Program*, 9 (1), Jan. 1975.

[4] Hamilton, G. E. and Smart, K. I. *U.K. statistics: sources, use and indexing requirements. 1st Report on the STIR Project.* Loughborough University of Technology, Library Report no. LUT/LIB/R7, 1973.

[5] Anderla, G. *Information in 1985*. OECD, 1973.

[6] P. A. International Management Consultants Ltd. *Forecasts of users of on-line retrieval services for scientific and technical information in Europe 1976–1985.* I.M.C., 1974.

[7] Davies, G. W. P. *Information networks in the European Community.* Paper presented at a conference on 'The future of Information Science: patterns and policies' held at the University of Lancaster, 10–11 April, 1975.

Summary of the Discussion

Mr Kilgour introduced Mr Thompson's paper with the question: why do libraries use computers? Mr Thompson's answers were: (1) to save money, (2) to accelerate availability of data, (3) to provide computer-oriented services for users, and (4) to provide co-operative networking for libraries. American economic journals have increased 84 per cent in cost in the last five years. *Mr Kilgour* noted that technical journals tend to gobble up what had traditionally been new book money. The acceleration of availability, the paper goes on, extends to computerized *bibliography* and *search procedures*. For these purposes, a computer may be more 'personal' than a library in indicating which volumes contain which ranges of materials, when a book is shelved in only one place.

Computer-assisted services of this type deal with journals only. The *Social Sciences Citations Index* covers approximately 55 per cent of specialized journals. The International Labour Office (ILO) and Food and Agriculture Organization (EAO) have data bases of 200,000 abstracts keyed to computers, and a similar service exists in the Netherlands.

On networking there is much hope in the future. Agencies like INIS and AGRIS are popular in Europe. These services integrate work in separate countries, as *Chemical Abstracts* does in chemistry. ILO is moving in the same direction with its DEVSIS service, which is, however, just getting started.

Commenting on the paper, *Mr Kilgour* pointed out that material could be made available in both hand-copy and magnetic-tape form. As between alternative computerized services, batch-processing methods are difficult and make inter-action with users impossible. On-line systems may be cheaper, as well as providing more inter-action. A key problem is: can services be inter-faced in an on-line system as between several computers. Computers may eventually be able to machine-translate between different computer systems, but such developments are only beginning. In conclusion, *Mr Kilgour* considered Mr Thompson's paper a good account of the current 'state of the art', but it over-estimated, perhaps, the developments already made and under-estimated the improvements needed.

Mrs Siefkes, in the opening interpellation, pointed out that on-line facilities are not yet as developed in Europe as in the United States. She hopes, however, that American methods can be transferred. On the newer services, she expressed much the same doubts as did Mr Kilgour in his conclusions. She added that cost-cutting was largely the result of networking. If there is no networking, there will be little or no cost saving; there may even be diseconomy.

Professor M. Perlman then digested for the conference the written comment submitted by Professor Roberts. Professor Roberts rates traditional economic bibliographies as poor, and as only rarely used by economists. Improvements are expected, but will economists respond? Not right away, Professor Roberts believes, unlike the record in the natural sciences. The initial response will be confined largely to statistical data. We may develop a universal data bank, but the data will probably not be comparable across national boundaries nor across varying terminologies. An all-European network is planned for 1976 in a number of scientific disciplines—but not in Economics.

Professor Wolfe doubted the wisdom of extrapolating the recent-past growth trend in the use of computerized library services. The 'Political Economy of information retrieval' is that everyone is waiting for someone else to pay for the necessary research and development before the results become practical. *Professor Wolfe's* own guess is that the United States will eventually pay for most of it, being the homeland of major computer companies and under pressure from organized information specialists as well. In Economics, there seems quite generally to be less research and development than in the natural sciences, because it seems less important to avoid 're-inventing the wheel', and because it has been less important for the economist to shift rapidly from one speciality to another.

Professor Giersch wondered if the savings expected from computerization represented lower costs for the same output or the spreading of the same (or higher) costs over a greater quantity of output. Professor Johnson claimed that many of the larger econometric models already in use for forecasting purposes over-strained the existing data bases.

Professor Eckstein felt that the impact of the computer on economic information had been virtually nil so far except for data banking. He criticized economists' standards of scholarship for not requiring the sort of literature search which is taken for granted in mathematics or chemistry. The libraries are obvious middle-men in this connection, but are not at all being fully used. This is because neither students nor faculty are required to prove that they have searched the existing literature.

Professor Kindleberger repeated the point that the use of computerized facilities is expensive. In the natural sciences it is funded, but not in Economics. Why is it not funded in Economics? Because it has not yet been proved sufficiently useful.

Comparing the situation in Economics and in Psychology, *Professor Morgan* maintained that the psychologists made better and more extensive literature searches than did the economists, but were less inclined to read their own technical journals. What economists really want most, *Professor Morgan* continued, are working papers which cannot yet be filed intelligently and expeditiously in key-word indexes.

Mrs N. Perlman returned to the subject of costs. She believed the cost of preparing abstracts in the ILO systems to be extremely high, relative to their limited use. She also believed that standard printing (including computer printing) might be cheaper. The high-cost problem in duplication, she argued from experience, is proof-reading, which must be done with any system.

In Mr Thompson's absence, *Dr Bartenbach* responded to the comments individually. (To Professor Morgan) Mr Thompson believes that 60 per cent of the ILO sources are 'grey' (working-paper) literature of the sort that Professor Morgan mentioned, and that DEVSIS is trying to collect more 'grey' materials. (To Mrs N. Perlman) Indexing is expensive, but the number of indexings is subject to reduction. In Economic Development, some articles are abstracted many times—perhaps the same abstract is used many times. As a cost-reduction move, many authors are willing to do their own abstracting. (To Professor Eckstein) Lockheed's on-line system now has over 900 users in the United States alone. (To Professor Roberts) Indexes are available but not widely used, perhaps because indexing systems (key-words) are imperfectly compatible. (To Mrs Siefkes) The Lockheed Dialogue System is available in Europe. The Public Affairs Information Service publishes two indexes, one in English, the other in 5 foreign languages. The second is computerized, and may also be used on line. (To Mr Kilgour) Several on-line systems are by now available, but most users do not know about them and/or cannot afford their high prices. Also, DEVSIS has sent out questionnaires to a number of journals about their indexing policies. Many of them use indexes on a selective or a complete basis.

Two postscripts to the discussion were provided by *Mr Kilgour* and *Professor Wolfe. Mr Kilgour's* point was that taping is, indeed, cheaper than printing, and involves better control over unnecessary duplication. Also, 'grey' literature is being studied, and since the timing of computer retrieval is so short, the cost per unit is not high and many are willing to pay. Finally, on international networks, problems can be avoided if the user will 'do it himself' by consulting information services in several countries. *Professor Wolfe* agreed that time could be speeded up and cost reduced by computerized retrieval, but there is no evidence (from his own OECD experience) as to how these costs would be met.

3 National Economic Information Systems for Developed Economies

Otto Eckstein
HARVARD UNIVERSITY

A National Economic Information System (NEIS) is defined as having five elements: (1) computer systems; (2) a communications network; (3) software; (4) databanks; and (5) econometric models. The characteristics of each element are discussed, and the contributions of such systems to the various types of centres of economic analysis are indicated. It is concluded that time-sharing computer technology does have particular benefits for economic analysis.

The computer is the principal technological advance of our era. It is changing productive processes in every industry. The information revolution has made it possible to store and analyse data in quantities greater by many orders of magnitude. Every field of inquiry is provided with new opportunities, and economics is among the fields with the greatest protential benefit.

During the last seven years, my work has been devoted to the application of computers in the development of national economic information systems (NEIS). In this paper, I survey the role of information in economic analysis, the needs of different organizations, the logical components of a national economic information system, and the various methods by which such systems can best be organized for the different types of institutions.

THE ROLE OF INFORMATION IN ECONOMIC ANALYSIS

The traditional function of economic analysis is to analyse the historical record in search of systematic regularities. Alternative hypotheses describing various aspects of the economic process are defined and tested by statistical means, using the historical record as a sample. This record may consist of time series records of various economic statistics or cross section data sets for an historical point in time. If several hypotheses are combined, an economic model may be identified which seeks to represent the economic structure of the period under analysis.

Economic analysis is also used to forecast developments in the economy and to explore alternative possible future patterns. Forecasts are essential ingredients of business short-term production and marketing decisions, as well as of longer term planning. Governments need to develop forecasts as a basis for devising policies.

Economic analysis is also used to assess public policy alternatives. Formal or informal models have always been used to help define desirable budget and monetary policies. Microeconomic policy proposals are assessed by cost-benefit analyses which apply the logic of welfare economics in a quantitative framework.

THE LOCATION OF ECONOMIC ANALYSIS

Economic analysis is conducted in five different types of settings: first, the universities still possess the largest concentration of research economists and, so, the largest part of hypothesis testing and model building is conducted within university economics departments and business schools. Typically, the universities do not engage in forecasting or in policy analysis. The universities are principally concerned with historical hypothesis testing. This determines much of the nature of their needs for economic information. Libraries have been the principal repositories of data for the universities in their collections of government statistics. Scholars use research assistants to 'gather' the data. Analyses are run on university computer centres, using card or tape inputs for each analytical task.

A second major location of economic analysis is the research centre or institute, which may or may not be attached to a university. Its activities consist principally of historically oriented hypothesis testing, but, at least in some instances, it may also engage in current economic analysis and in forecasting. Research is likely to be more mission-oriented, and time schedules somewhat more rigid. Some institutes have made an effort to develop their own data collections, software packages and computing facilities.

Government agencies are a third major location of economic analysis. Some of the agencies are principally developers of the basic economic statistics; others perform analyses of public expenditure programmes, of the macroeconomy to aid fiscal and monetary policy formation, or of world conditions for international economic policy.

A fourth centre of economic analysis is private industry and finance. Here, the need is primarily to understand the workings of specific micromarkets, production functions, factor markets and product markets and, secondarily, to relate these microelements to macroeconomic conditions. Economic analysis is a background for capital budgeting, employment decisions, inventory and production planning, financial planning, and market research. This is the sector in which the growth of economic analysis is currently highest. One can look forward to the day when the largest concentration of individuals performing economic analysis will be in these day-to-day applications which will aid the actual operation of the economy.

A fifth location of economic analysis is the household sector. Here, reliance is principally on price information obtained from markets, word-of-mouth information about job opportunities and government programmes and, perhaps, published information about the quality of consumer products. The individual household obtains virtually all of its information on a decentralized basis, except for some data about the macroeconomy obtained through the mass media.

THE NATIONAL ECONOMIC INFORMATION SYSTEM (NEIS)

The computer technology has made possible the development of national economic information systems (NEIS). Such systems contain five sets of elements. I shall use the Data Resources System, for which I have responsibility, as an illustration.

The NEIS has been a response to the requirements of government agencies and private industry, where need relates more to forecasting, model building and policy analysis than to historical hypothesis testing. In a subsequent section, I shall discuss the relation of national economic information systems to the needs of universities and research centres.

(1) COMPUTER SYSTEMS

The NEIS is installed on general purpose computer systems. The machines must be able to handle many simultaneous users in a time sharing mode. They must be particularly efficient in managing large flows of data, since the users will be accessing large databases and performing analyses with them. The machines must also have a considerable numerical processing capacity, although they need not be the typical large, scientific use configuration because the complexity of calculations is not near the upper end of the range of computer applications. The systems should be large because the programs for statistical analysis and model simulation are large applications by time sharing technology standards.

The Data Resources system is run principally on a four-processor Burroughs 7700 computer, a very large machine dedicated to the NEIS purpose. The computer's operating system, or Master Control Program, is adapted to run as many as 150 users of the application programs. Data storage devices, containing six million bytes, are principally disk packs, a relatively recently developed high access speed, high density device. No use is made of card storage, and very little of tape storage. As the design of storage devices continues to bring down costs, it becomes possible to store on-line data with low frequency use.

(2) COMMUNICATIONS NETWORK

The Data Resources NEIS can be accessed through local telephone calls from the metropolitan areas in the United States and Canada, and from selected cities on other continents. The network consists of error-correcting minicomputer concentrators that send data twice to check against transmission error. The network uses the lines of the national telephone system, on either a leased or dial-up basis. In some European countries, where the postal service has the telephone monopoly, government policies have delayed the development of cost-effective data networks. Necessity will soon overcome the bureaucratic obstacles.

(3) SOFTWARE

The NEIS has to contain the software that lets the analyst do his work. It should not require programmer skills, but should let the analyst or an assistant operate directly on the system through the use of high-level computer languages. There are five essential types of programs.

(*a*) *Data entry and retrieval:* Every computer system now provides some data entry software. For economic databanks, which are principally time series or cross section data, it is possible to develop programs that greatly increase the efficiency of data entry, and which build in automatic internal checks to help assure accuracy.

(*b*) *Data analysis programs:* These may include seasonal adjustment, turning-point analysis, search and scanning, plotting and general data transformations. Such programs should handle repetitive tasks efficiently so that the analyst can set up routines that will perform the work without repeated intervention.

(*c*) *Statistical estimation packages:* In order to derive the basic relationships and test the hypotheses, a statistical program package has to be included which performs various forms of simple and complex regressions such as non-linear least-squares, distributed lag methods, other kinds of time series analysis such as Box-Jenkins and spectral analysis, model estimation such as two- and three-stage least-squares, mixed cross section and time series regressions, and the unending series of new techniques that econometric methodology is turning up.

The statistical package also has to be able to handle cross section data and to perform survey analysis. This includes the arrangement of survey data according to various characteristics, calculation of percentiles and other types of frequency distributions, analysis of variance and covariance, principal components analysis and other such routines.

(*d*) *Optimizing programs:* If the NEIS is to be usable for policy analysis by public and private organizations, it must contain optimizing techniques such as linear, integer, quadratic and other non-linear programming, capital budgeting decision algorithms, and techniques which include random elements to allow Monte Carloing of the analyses.

(*e*) *Modelling programs:* To install, solve, and use econometric models. Models must be defined by combining equations obtained statistically or algebraically. Equations must be ordered for efficiency. Different solution algorithms, including Gauss-Seidel and Newton-Raphson, have to be available. The program has to be able to use the output of one model as the exogenous inputs of a satellite model. This is a fundamental feature of an NEIS because much of the practical use revolves around this function.

(4) DATA BANKS

An NEIS will contain the principal time series data that are useful for analysis and that are produced by a nation's statistical system. These data must be entered on a computer as soon as they become available for immediate use. In the case of the Data Resources NEIS for the United States, 26,000 weekly, monthly, quarterly, and annual time series are banked, typically within an hour of the release time specified by the government. Because initial release of data is still in hard-copy form, a staff is required to obtain the data and enter them on the computer.

For other countries, including the principal European countries, Japan and Canada, we have developed a more limited, continually updated set of databanks. These are essential because of the interdependence of the major economies.

A national economic information system also contains secondary databases in machine-readable form. These may be large blocks of government data, such as the full industrial detail of the employment, wage and hour statistics of our Bureau of Labor Statistics, the full flow of funds data prepared by our Federal Reserve System, or proprietary bases for financial data of individual companies or industry variables. These data may be used less frequently or with less urgency. The lack of standardization of machine-readable data is a nuisance, but not a serious obstacle.

The Data Resources NEIS contains no data for identifiable individuals, in order to leave the system free of the legal, political and social problems of invading the privacy of individuals through computerized databanks.

(5) DATA BANK CHARACTERISTICS

Databanks should be accurate, timely, comprehensive in concepts and history, logical in structure, and properly documented.

(*a*) *Accuracy* can be achieved, in part, through checks built into the data entry programs. Aggregates can be checked against their components, full intervals against subintervals, real and price data against nominal data, etc. But such checks will be, at best, incomplete. Databanking is a technical craft with professional standards of its own. The work must be conducted in a calm environment, free of interruptions and under close supervision. Where internal checks are impossible there has to be duplicate entry to permit a full accuracy control. Even the computer and peripheral equipment and communications network have to be error-proof.

(*b*) *Timeliness and Updating:* The process of producing data is quite time-consuming, and in most countries the release of the principal economic statistics is much too slow. Because the data-producing agencies have little sensitivity to the needs of their users, the statistical description of economic developments is frequently several months behind calendar time. This is a serious problem for the management of the modern economy and most governments have spent too little effort in bringing the operations of the statistical source agencies into reasonable balance vis-à-vis the needs of users.

The national economic information system is able to reduce the subsequent loss of time to virtually zero. Data are banked immediately upon release, and can then be accessed anywhere from the network. Databanking techniques have been pushed to the point where even the full revision of the National Income Accounts each year can be entered on the computer system in relatively few hours.

The NEIS also has to contain the latest vintage of data. The government source agencies revise their statistics regularly. The NEIS has to replace obsolete data just as soon as the revised series becomes available. This is a problem for the scholar because it means that the particular statistical tests he is performing may yield different results depending upon the vintage of the data which he has employed. In our work, we use the rule that one should always use the latest vintage of data. We do not attempt to preserve the older data, although for purposes of analysing the accuracy of statistics and for verifying scientific results of earlier scholars, it might be desirable to retain a record of older vintage series.

(*c*) *Comprehensive:* An NEIS databank should contain all of the more important time series of the nation's statistical system. Presumably, the size of the databanks that can be justified economically depends upon the number of users and the value of their use. Beyond a certain easily defined set of data, it is most efficient to make the databanks grow in response to user requests. In this way, the databanks are sure to bear some relationship to the needs of users.

Most short-term economic analysis nowadays confines itself to the use of data since World War II. Thus, the typical time series stored in the databanks begins in 1947, or in the early 1950s. The basic annual National Income Account data are stored for the period beginning in 1929, the starting date of the official government accounts. Other kinds of pre-war data are given a different treatment. They are still found in a variety of books and government publications, and are banked only as they are needed for specific projects.

(*d*) *Hierarchical Mnemonic Structure:* Our databanks contain over one million time series. This creates a problem analogous to library classification. How can such time series be identified in a logical way so that it is possible to retrieve them? Data Resources adopted the mnemonic structure first developed at the Brookings Institution. This is the most widely used system. It is hierarchical in concept, and follows the normal usage of economists. For example, the mnemonic for consumption is 'C', for consumer durables, 'CD', for consumer durables-automobiles, 'CDA', for consumer durables-new automobiles, 'CDAN', for consumer durables-new foreign automobiles, 'CDANF', for consumer durables-new foreign automobiles in constant prices, 'CDANF58'. The mnemonics may also include identification by country, by region, by company, by industry, etc.

(*e*) *Documentation:* To be usable, the databank must include documentation. As part of the record stored for each series, we include five lines of textual description. This includes the name of the series, the source, when it was last updated, whether it is seasonally adjusted, the period for which the series is available, and other such information. When a user accesses a series, he has the choice of whether just to obtain the figures or whether also to get the accompanying description.

(6) ECONOMETRIC MODELS

An NEIS contains a collection of econometric models for forecasting, alternative analyses and policy assessment. The Data Resources system, for example, contains a 1200-equation short-term model of the US economy which includes explicit modelling of the traditional circular flow of income and expenditure, the flow of funds of households and businesses, a wage-price sector which develops the national price indexes by a stage of processing approach, a detailed international trade sector which decomposes exports and imports by type, an input-output sector which converts final demands into 80 individual industry production indexes, investment equations for industries which, in turn, are used to estimate capacity and utilization rates, and numerous other detailed features. The system also contains long-range models for the economy, including the Hudson-Jorgenson growth model, an econometric representation of neoclassical growth theory. It also contains detailed industry models which serve as a bridge between macro-estimates and the variables needed by specific industries. Economic filter equations and models are also stored in order to identify the information content of survey results and of other leading indicator statistics.

MEETING THE NEEDS OF VARIOUS TYPES OF INSTITUTIONS

The National Economic Information System has been designed for the future-oriented analyses performed by government agencies, private industry, and forecasting centres. For them, it is a necessity. The state-of-the-art requires that data be updated quickly and analysed by modern methods, and this is really possible only by the use of the centralized databanks of an NEIS. Typically, users will wish to relate these forecasts and analyses to variables of a microeconomic nature of special importance to them, and this is most readily accomplished by combining their own data with the central databanks. They need advanced analytical software and the modelling capabilities.

In the United States today, most serious forecasting is conducted by using national economic information systems, and longer-term planning is moving in that direction. The time-sharing computer technology allows a rational decentralization of economic analysis. The information that will be used as a common resource by many economic units is banked and stored centrally where it can be accessed through the communications network. The work of building national econometric models is also conducted on a centralized basis, and it is a large-scale undertaking of which very few organizations are capable. The highly specialized software development is also conducted at the centre.

On the other hand, it is impossible for a central organization either to build models or to apply serious human understanding to the workings of specific markets or other microvariables that are of great importance to particular organizations. For example, a Ministry of Finance will have a finer understanding of the ins and outs of revenue collection than will a central staff of econometricians. An automobile company will bring much knowledge and proprietary data to the analysis of its own sales and costs. A retail chain will know its own strengths and weaknesses in various regions and product lines, and will obtain feedback from its own markets. Time-sharing technology allows these organizations to blend the national data, models and forecasts with their microdata and understanding to allow economic analysis to be performed within the organization best equipped to do so by combining central and local information structures. The goal of a fully effective NEIS is to produce an optimal organization of economic information and analysis in a market economy.

HISTORICALLY-ORIENTED HYPOTHESIS TESTING

For the university or research centre not principally occupied with forecasting, the NEIS may be a useful component for its quantitative work, but it is only a partial answer. While the NEIS achieves some economies of scale by the sheer size of its computers and the commonality of data storage, it does require the use of a communications network. Also, the time-sharing mode requires more computer resources than does the same task run in the batch method. Further, some kinds of research, particularly the analyses of very large cross section data sets, are of a job size that is impractical in the time sharing technology, both because of the volume of data that would have to be transmitted over long distances, and the computer requirements for the specific task.

Time is also less critical in the university or research centre. The value of student time is, presumably, lower than of professional workers. Their initial learning experience can be in a more primitive computer environment where mistakes are less costly, where an overnight wait for results is less critical, and where data preparation may be inefficient but educational.

On the other hand, there are some elements of university research that benefit from the NEIS and some for which it is essential. In the past, the data used for statistical analyses in academic research have not been accurate. Few published results can be reproduced precisely because errors were allowed to creep into the data and the data used were obsolete. All too often, we accept theses or manuscripts that test hypotheses that are several years old. Would the results stand up later? That is a question to which we have had to close our minds as professors and journal editors, knowing that the researcher could not reopen the study without further loss of his career time. Now the excuses are gone. There is no reason to ignore the recent data now that they are so easily available.

There are other advantages to the academic use of NEIS. Smaller scale time series analyses are low in cost and do benefit from the instant updating of the data and the sophistication of the available statistical techniques. The educational importance of training students in the use of national economic information systems is also rising.

In the near future, the practical approach for universities and research centres is to obtain tapes of data sets from the national economic information systems. For most research purposes, a quarterly updating of the data is probably adequate. Such tapes would contain the series most commonly used in academic research. Data Resources is collaborating with the National Bureau of Economic Research in developing such a service.

CONCLUDING COMMENT

The use of quantitative data in economic analysis has been well established for 50 years. While there is a continuing development of estimation techniques, the fundamental methods were developed in the late 1940s and early 1950s. The computer has made it possible to apply the techniques much more easily and, therefore, has led to an explosion of quantitative economic analysis. The national economic information system has been developed to meet the needs of analysts concerned with future-oriented work in government agencies, private and financial institutions and forecasting centres. For the more traditional, historical hypothesis testing, the in-house computers of university and research centres continue to be an economical method. However, at this time, the treatment of data in these centres remains far behind the current state-of-the-art, and they must find ways to offer accurate, comprehensive, documented and updated data sets for the researchers.

Summary of the Discussion

Mrs Schwartz, introducing Professor Eckstein's paper, divided it into four topics: (1) the role of information in economic analysis; (2) different organizations involved in processing and/or using this information; (3) elements of a national information system; and (4) methods of tailoring information systems to the needs of users.

(1) Under this head Professor Eckstein included the search for patterns and regularities in the historical record, the testing of hypotheses and models, the forecasting of future developments under alternative policies (both micro and macroeconomic) and, finally, the evaluation of these alternative policies.

(2) The principal users of quantitative economic data include: (*a*) universities with staff members involved in historical analysis and testing; (*b*) independent research centres and institutes, which may be included in historical hypothesis testing or in forecasting, or may possibly be 'mission-oriented' in favour of a particular approach or model; (*c*) public agencies; (*d*) private industry, currently the fastest-growing of these subdivisions, and, finally (*e*) households, whose involvement is still minimal.

(3) Here Professor Eckstein uses his own enterprise (Data Resources Inc., or DRI) as an example. DRI works in the areas of forecasting, model-building, and policy-consulting. It also operates time-sharing systems which give to its subscribers access to its databank. (This would be more difficult under a few of the Government-operated telephone systems of Europe.) Its system contains software in matters of computer language, entry and retrieval, analysis programs, 'packaged' regressions, optimizing algorithms, and modelling the users' own programs.

(4) DRI's databank includes over one million series, including many for countries outside the United States, and a substantial degree of disaggregation.

(5) DRI's tailoring procedures centre around the availability of alternative econometric models, some with as many as 1200 equations. Most of these are short-run, but there are longer-term models in the armoury as well.

Professor Giersch inquired whether, in studying business oscillations, Professor Eckstein attached much weight to expectational factors. *Professor Morgan* pointed out that expectational data is of various types and levels. Its nature has changed greatly in the last 25 years, and much of the University of Michigan survey research data is being rearchived in consequence. Professor Morgan does not know what, if any, expectations data are used by the DRI.

Professor Giersch then raised the question of the need for the larger and more elaborate econometric model. He wondered why Mrs Schwartz had not questioned the need for large and detailed models of the DRI type. Smaller models, he suggested, might do just as well. Professor Giersch also wondered whether the DRI would survive competition with other firms, and raised the possibility of such service becoming a public good.

Professor Johnson noted the crisis—the run on the pound sterling—faced by the British in June of 1975. What, he wondered, could a firm like DRI have supplied to Prime Minister Wilson's Government in a form that it could use quickly over the crucial weekend, and, simultaneously, in a form that the British people could understand and trust? The economy is not timeless, in the sense that a model which worked at time t will work equally well at time $t + 1$—contrary to the assumptions of many American econometricians. We might already be possessed of more computer technology than we have brains enough to use, and Mrs Schwartz might have gone further than she did in pointing out the need for brains along with mechanical simulation. Professor Johnson also felt that macroeconomic models were applicable, if at all, to large, rich countries, and that they might be made *international* public goods.

Mr Hibbert insisted that economists should keep on trying to influence short-term policy, and not retreat into ivory towers. But he wonders whether the *most recent* estimate, embodying the latest data, should always be used as the basis for recommendations, as Professor Eckstein says. Many compilers disagree; some revisions of data introduce biases of various kinds; some of our data may not even be worthy of the title 'economic knowledge'. With regard to property rights in data, everything used by agencies like DRI is in the public domain, and the agency has merely increased their availability.

Replying to Mr Hibbert, *Professor Johnson* said that Britain has had 25 years of short-term forecasting. The National Institute of Economic Research in London is an excellent statistical agency, but as a policy consultant it has a bias in favour of incomes policies as universal remedies, a bias which statistical expertise has not helped it to overcome.

Professor von Böventer wondered how much of our data were really economically relevant. He would like to see a cost-benefit analysis of data collection and, likewise, a policy of substitution between types of data in spending a statistical budget. (These points would come up again, Professor von Böventer said, in connection with a later paper.)

Professor Wolfe tended to agree with Professor Johnson. Naive models are often just as accurate as more elaborate ones. When Professor Eckstein is adding microdimensions to macromodels—the major explanation for their size—he may be adding degrees of uncertainty, lowering degrees of statistical freedom, and compounding errors.

In his reply, *Professor Eckstein* discarded as irrelevant the questions involving the use of econometric models in policy formation as not being the subject of his particular paper or of the conference. On forecasting, of course, no one is perfect, whether or not he uses formal models. *Professor Eckstein* believes that the econometric models are now about 40 per cent better than either naive models or crude monetarism. Over the period 1974–75, in the United States, DRI's record was nothing to boast about, but would have been better (as would the performance of the economy in the United States) if the Administration had not attempted 'fine tuning'. His choice of a 50-year period to encompass the econometric revolution was justified by the quantum jump after the 1920s, particularly in the use of regression analysis.

Passing to the issues at the Conference, *Professor Eckstein* expressed his views on the choice of material to be stored centrally, as in databanks. These should be only data used by many people, not merely for occasional scientific work by one particular person. As for households, they do not now use the data available for them, but they may in the future. On the international front, data are available and are used. The eventual logic of the DRI methodology is international. DRI stays away from 'private' databanks about individual families or firms, to ensure privacy. But (in reply to an interpolated question from Professor M.

Perlman) computerized output is private property even though its basic data are not. It is a problem for a firm like DRI to stay ahead of imitators. In competing with them, DRI takes a 'workable competition' approach toward both private and public competitors. They are a spur, hastening progress in the field of economic information systems.

On literature search, the problem is that the technology is not yet ready. Existing slow-speed terminals do not permit sufficiently rapid literary reproduction. Some experiments are under way, such as the *New York Times* text bank.

Expectations are in the DRI models, at least in proxy form. In *Professor Eckstein*'s view, the issue of 'technology *versus* brains', that was raised by Professor Johnson, is a non-issue. The real issue is to induce first-class economists *not* to leave the data in the databanks while they engage in abstract theorizing. More technology is available than is being used. There is no other way than the econometric for economics or economists to come up with answers to quantitative questions. This is especially true, *Professor Eckstein* now believes, in connection with microeconomic problems like the energy crisis. But as regards 'vintages' of data, he agreed reluctantly that old editions may sometimes be better than revisions, though this runs counter to the theory by which governments operate their statistical programs.

Professor Morgan added a postscript on the subject of telephone service to consumers from a central agency like DRI. In his view, this service is available (on prices and qualities of particular commodities) as an aspect of the consumer movement, but political forces prevent its being used in conjunction with a public utility (the telephone company). Provision of such information may ultimately be possible on a completely private basis.

4 The Organization of Quantitative Data in Brazil

Luis Carlos, A. C. Olinto and Isaac Kerstenetzky

INSTITUTO BRASILEIRO DE GEOGRAFIA E ESTATISTICA, RIO DE JANEIRO

The efforts made in Brazil for the production of quantitative data for economic and social research are described as a case study on developing countries. A description of the current computer-based organization that is given to data collected in censuses and surveys is presented, together with the packages being developed for access to the organized information.

I. *INTRODUCTION*

Two major sources of quantitative data that contribute to our knowledge on the macroeconomic level can be identified: one comes from statistical surveys of socioeconomic information, and the other comes from administrative records of the government such as on the budget, foreign trade and social security, to mention a few important ones. In Brazil, as in other countries, these two sources are, to a great extent, independent. The administrative records of macroeconomic interest are mostly under the Ministry of Labour, the Ministry of Finance and the Ministry of Social Security; the statistical surveys of socioeconomic information are conducted by the Secretary of Planning of the Presidency of the Republic through the Brazilian Institute of Geography and Statistics, which we refer to, from now on, as IBGE.[1] In this paper we consider only the organization and retrieval of quantitative data generated by the statistical surveys conducted by IBGE.

IBGE came into existence in 1938 by the merging of the National Institute for Statistics (Instituto Nacional de Estatistica) and the National Council for Geography (Conselho Nacional de Geografia). Statistics was understood mainly as the gathering of descriptive information about the geographical space and it had little to do with the economic and social planning of the country as we understand it today. This descriptive understanding of the geographical space certainly was much needed at that time (and it is still needed today) due to the continental dimension of the

[1] IBGE—Instituto Brasileiro de Geografia e Estatistica.

country. The main activities of IBGE were reflected in the publication of descriptive maps and the many cross-tabulations of collected data which were broken down at the level of political units of the country.

Quantitative economic planning in Brazil is a relatively recent activity at the government level. In 1964, at the peak of a very high inflation, a political change took place that brought into power a strong central government and, with the new government, the necessity to plan the economy with quantitative data. At that time the government organized the Ministry of Planning and, soon afterwards (1965), a Research Institute for Applied Economics was created in this Ministry for the purpose, among others, of informing the government about alternatives for economic strategies. Soon a great demand was felt for economic information to be fed into the different analyses being made. IBGE, with its broad experience in collecting information on a nationwide scale, was transferred, in 1967, from the orbit of the Ministry of Interior to the Ministry of Planning with the design of producing the needed information. This required a basic reorganization of IBGE and the opportunity for that came with the general census of the country to be carried out in 1970. It is with the efforts made after 1970 in IBGE, related to the organization and retrieval of quantitative data, that we will be concerned in the next sections of this report.

In section II we give a description of the basic concepts related to the organization of the data. In section III we give the dimensions of the data collected, and in section IV we connect the information content with the need for simulating the Brazilian economy.

II. *GENERAL CONSIDERATIONS*

There are two ways of looking into a document, one from its contents and the other from its structure. It is from the latter standpoint that we will be looking into the documents used for collecting information through IBGE's surveys. The framework for analysing the structure of the documents for the purpose of acquiring the data is based on the concepts of segments, registers, and fields, and, for retrieving the information, on the concepts of primary and structural variables. In this section we will discuss these concepts in order to fix the context within which we will use them to describe our organization of quantitative social and economic data and to evaluate the extension and complexity of the information collected in the surveys.

Let us take as an example the document used in the 1970 population and housing census in Brazil. For what we will say below it is sufficient to know that inquiries were made about attributes of the housing unit and characteristics of households in the housing unit (if more than one), and observations were collected on social attributes of the persons belonging to the households. Thus, this document has three hierarchically disposed segments, as exhibited in Figure 4.1.

The identification of hierarchical segments is easily understood if we recall that one of their basic properties is to extend the attributes of the higher to the lower levels of the hierarchy. Therefore, disposing the segments as shown in Figure 4.1, we are saying that the attributes of the housing unit apply to all of its households and, also, to all of the persons belonging to the households of that housing unit.

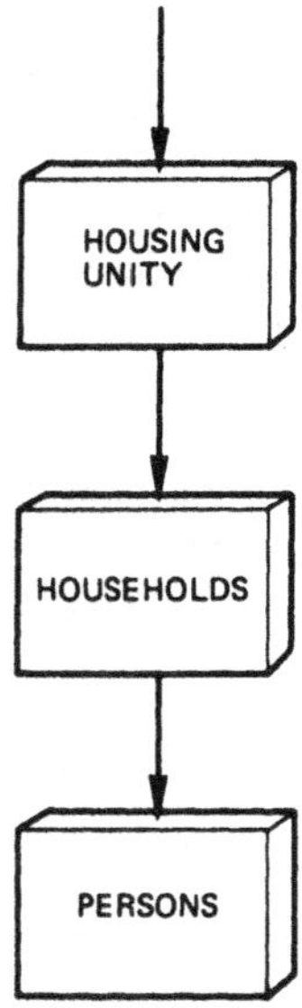

Fig. 4.1

This property, by itself, is not enough for a full characterization of a segment and we also need the property that a segment is a collection of homogeneous records. To illustrate what we mean by a homogeneous record, let us consider the segment 'person'. The above mentioned survey asked a fixed number of questions about persons, whose observed answers constitute the record of each person, each question corresponding to a field in the record where its answer is registered. The homogeneity of the records on persons results from the fact that *every* record contains exactly the same number of fields in a previously specified order, each field corresponding unequivocally to a question. Otherwise, the number of records in a segment is variable, changing from one document to another according to the number of persons in the households.

Figure 4.2 illustrates the resulting structure of a filled-out document whose segmented structure corresponds to that of Figure 4.1. The structure indicates the existence of two households in the housing unit, one with three and the other with five persons. Due to the variability of the number of households in housing units and persons in households, the actual structure of individual documents may vary enormously, though the segmented structure is the same. This invariant property of the segmented structure is what enables us to choose it as the natural framework to organize the observed data, i.e. the elementary pieces of information collected in the surveys.

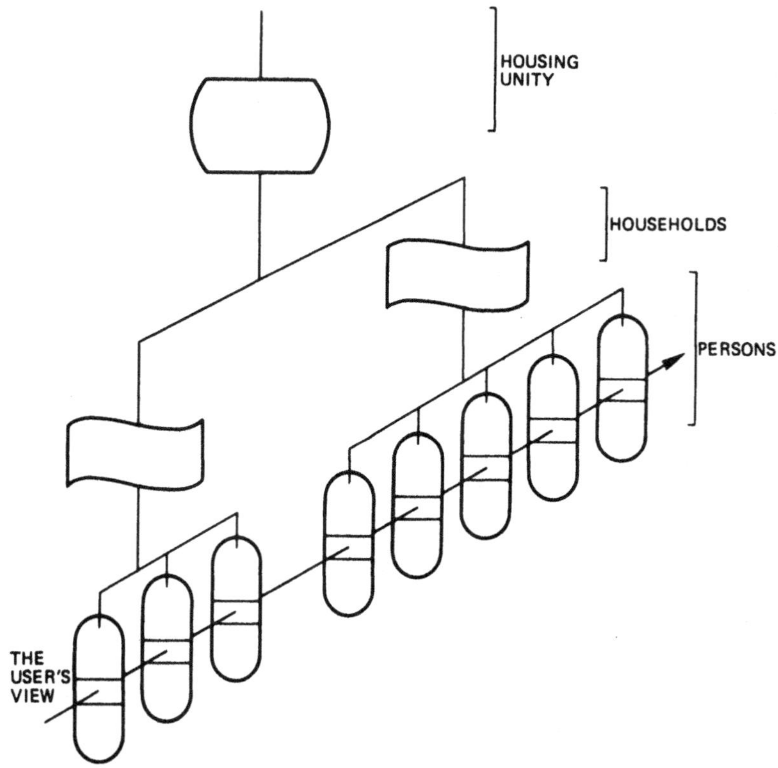

Fig. 4.2

From the user's point of view, for every investigated question there is a corresponding random variable which is its object of study. We may say that the user of the data looks into the collection of documents from a cross-sectional angle as it is illustrated in Figure 4.2 and, due to the randomness of the data, his instruments for 'reading' the information are statistical in character. It would be hopeless to try to describe the increasing number of such statistical instruments. What makes a unified approach to data analysis possible is that, whatever those instruments are, they all operate from a single point of departure which may be thought of as a rectangular array where the columns represent the variables and the rows correspond to the individual observations. In other words, the (i, j) cell of the array contains the i-th value observed for the j-th variable. This array has a simple geometrical interpretation. We may imagine each row as defining a vector in a space of dimension equal to the number of variables being considered, with the whole array corresponding to a cloud of points in this space. The problem of grasping the information contained in this array is the same as the problem of recognizing patterns in the clouds of points. The statistical instruments put forward in this domain are tentative techniques of pattern recognition. The complexity of this general problem in data analysis is easily perceived once we remember that there is no 'natural' metric in the space of observations and, furthermore, the values of some of the variables do not represent any numerical ordering but only an arbitrary coding of different answers to the same question.

From what is said above we observe that the user deals with a single set of homogeneous records. On the other hand, the collecting document, with its possibly segmented structure, is, generally, a non-homogeneous collection of records. Consequently, we must describe the transformations for going from the collecting set of documents to the user's array. Let us anticipate that these transformations result from the fact that, in general, we cannot go from the array to the segmented structure of the document. In particular, the information content of the array is invariant with respect to permutations of its rows, while the hierarchical interconnections among the registers of different segments make such a symmetry property meaningless with respect to the set of registers representing the collection of documents.

In defining the transformation, the first step taken by the user is the specification of his unit of observation. Considering the example given in relation to Figure 4.1, the user may choose the household unit, the housing unit of the person as his unit of observation. The choice of unit of observation is, to a great extent, connected to the level of the segment. Let us suppose that he has chosen the household unit. Next, he may decide which variables to include in his array. He may choose the variables from the segment level corresponding to the chosen unit of observation, which can be directly transferred to his array without any further transformation. He may choose variables from a higher level of segmentation which, when transferred to the array, take a constant value on all of the observation units, connected to a single higher unit, due to the property that the attributes of the higher level of the segment apply to all lower levels. This, again, causes no difficulty in specifying the transformation from the segmented structure to the user's array. For lower segment variables there is no simple transformation for using them in higher units of observation, for the individual attributes of persons bear no unique relation to attributes of the household as a unit.

For the characterization of the transformation, we have introduced the concept of the structural variable of a segment as being an operator in the variables of the immediately inferior segment. Examples of such operators could be the household income as the sum of the incomes of the persons belonging to the household, the occupation of the head of the household, the number of children in the household below ten years of age, etc. Even without going into the details of which operators can be implemented in an actual retrieval facility, we may appreciate that the creation of structural variables is the mechanism through which the user explores the segmented structure of the documents by statistical analysis.

Segmented structures of survey documents can be much more elaborate than the one shown in Figure 4.1. In Figure 4.3 we show the

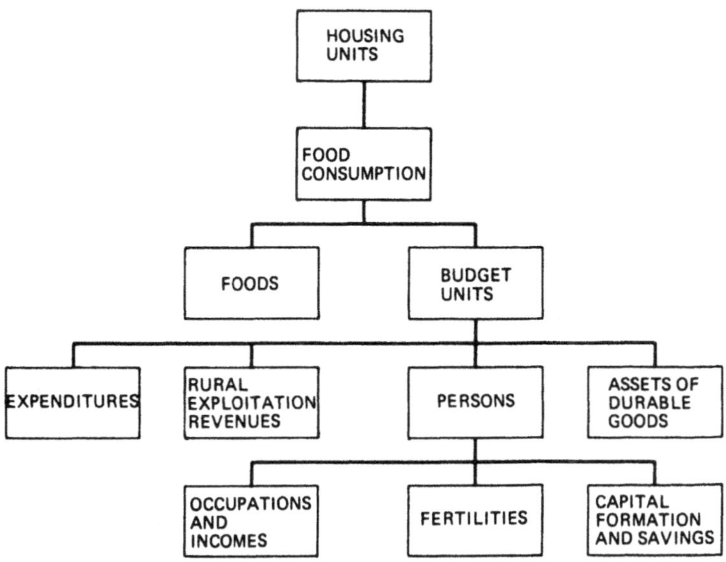

Fig. 4.3

structure of the survey which is currently being carried out on food consumption and family budget. We may observe five levels of eleven segments.[2] This is, at the moment, the most complex structure that we have encountered in IBGE, and we note the appearance of parallel segments like 'foods' and 'budget units'. If the segmented structure has been correctly analysed there will be no need to build arrays with the

[2] Figure 4.3 shows a simplified version of the segmentation of this document. The actual structure contains 33 segments and 6 levels of hierarchy.

simultaneous use of variables from different parallel segments, for the record in the parallel segments refers to total non-homogeneous pieces of information, such as 'foods' and 'budget units' in the example of Figure 4.3.

Structural variables complete the mechanism by which the flux of information moves through the segmented structure of the document. It is, therefore, by the use of structural variables that the user fully explores the collected information. From what we have said, the number of possible structural variables can be very large even in a simple structure as shown in Figure 4.1. Let us call primary variables those which are directly associated with the questions made in the survey. With this distinction between structural and primary variables, we may say that a good measure of the depth of the survey is its number of primary variables. Analogously, we say that the number of segments and the number of levels which are in the segmented structure measure, to a certain extent, the complexity of the survey, while the size of the sample measures its extension.

III. *THE ORGANIZATION OF DATA*

We will now describe the actual organization of quantitative data at IBGE.

IBGE adopts a nested division of the country for the specification of the spatial co-ordinates of its statistical data, which coincides, wherever possible, with the political boundaries inside Brazil. There are five levels of division, ranging from large regions to small ones and called, respectively federal units, microregions, municipalities, districts and sectors. Up to the district level the spatial division is common to both economic and populational data. A sector for populational data corresponds in the urban area to approximately a city block, while for economic data it represents a larger area. In rural areas the sectoral unit is common to both economic and populational data. To give a feeling of how fine the mesh for spatial division is, we observe that the whole country is divided into 27 federal units, 361 microregions, approximately 4000 counties and 8000 districts. The number of sectors can be as high as 300 per district.

We may consider these five levels of regional subdivision as constituting a hierarchically segmented structure in which the structure of the documents is imbedded, with these higher segments corresponding to the spatial organization of the data. Sample surveys have their design based on the municipalities' division of the country and, therefore, they do not usually contain the district and sector variables. These latter normally occur only in census data. Initially, there was an effort to organize all data in an integrated data base. This has proven to be too cumbersome and of little value. We have, therefore, discontinued this effort. We now organize the data in separate volumes, one for each survey of census, with the exception of those periodic economic surveys that are applied to a fixed panel and which will be organized in volumes integrating the time co-ordinate. In all cases the full document structure is preserved in the filing of the data.

Before the data are inserted in the data base, they pass through a screening process for the detection of transcription errors. The screening thoroughly checks errors that can lead to (i) invalid segmentation of the document, (ii) invalid field values and (iii) logical inconsistencies among fields of records. The use of techniques for the detection of statistical outlyers has been excluded, so far, from the screening process, as have imputation methods for the elimination of missing values. After the collected data have been satisfactorily passed through the screening and the surveys concluded, the resulting volume goes through a process of automatic recoding to compress its size, and a decoding module is automatically created to make the compressing strategy of the data transparent to the user of information. These compressing techniques have contributed up to a factor of ten in the reduction of the physical size of the file, when applied to economic data originating from the census. This large reduction in size can be understood as due mainly to the fact that a single detailed document was applied to the whole universe of economic establishments, resulting in a large incidence of missing data due to the high frequency of small establishments where the document was not applicable in its full details.

We shall now describe the efforts made to access the data. We divided the access process into two phases. First, the user defines his array with all of the necessary primary and structural variables, together with the specification of his unit of observation. We call this the theme definition phase and it permits the system to retrieve the user's theme for analysis from what we have collected. The second phase consists of the actual analysis where the user applies to the theme the many statistical instruments that are at his disposal. The characterization of these two phases came about by observing that there was a large difference in the number of requests for each one. Usually, the data analysis module accessed on theme many times before a second theme was requested. For the generation of themes, a set of primitives was developed that permits a PL-1 program to access logically the segmented structure of documents, thus easing the task of creating structural variables at the user's request.

As far as the data analysis module is concerned, one would think that a good statistical package would fulfil these objectives. Unfortunately, it did not. After some frustrating experiences with well-known packages, IBGE decided to develop its own data analysis module. Some of the features of this module are (i) a full control of the precision of the algorithms being used, (ii) flexibility for including future needs of new instruments of analysis at IBGE's request and (iii) a programming language that is close to Portuguese in order to ease the understanding, on the user's part, of the analysis requested from the computer.

The development of this package was a major venture, as the development of a high level computer language had never before been carried out in Brazil. Due to the risks involved, the first version that was developed was somewhat restricted in scope and lacked the flexibility for the inclusion of new instruments. The data analysis package currently being developed will correct limitations of the first version and will include two new features for analysis: Tukey's exploratory analysis[3] and Benzecri's correspondence analysis.[4]

Not all of the demands for information are made in the form of requests for the analysis data by the research units of IBGE, and many are formulated directly in terms of cross-tabulations. For the fast recovery of information in the form of cross-tabulations we are developing a package[5] which generates these cross-tabulations, without the need for producing the intermediate array.

We now come to the description of the actual data being stored. Demographic data are collected during the housing and population censuses that are carried out every ten years, and by the annual surveys in other years. The first set of stored data was collected during the 1970 housing and population census. The document used in this census is very similar to that recommended by the United Nations.[6] There was a single sample designed for the census, covering approximately a quarter of the population, which corresponds to about five million housing units. The annual household sample surveys used to cover only data on manpower. Since 1972, however, these surveys have included new areas of study. Thus, in 1972, the household sample survey covered approximately 150,000 housing units and included questions on income distribution, consumer durables, internal migration and fertility. The 1973 survey continued to cover migration and fertility (excluding income distribution) and added a supplement with questions related to social mobilities. The 1974 survey was completely redesigned for the study of food consumption and family budgets. Table 4.1 gives a summary of these surveys and censuses showing the size of the sample, the number of primary variables generated by the surveys and their structures, i.e. the number of segments and the number of levels. One observes that the 1974 survey considerably exceeds the others in the complexity of its documents,[7] thus opening new ares of research in IBGE.

[3] J. W. Tukey, *Exploratory Data Analysis*, vol. 1, limited preliminary edition. (Reading, Mass.: Addison Wesley Publishing Co.)

[4] J. P. Benzecri, *Analyse des correspondances.* (Paris; Dunod, 1973), vol. II.

[5] At the moment, this function is being fulfilled by an adapted version of CENTS, a package developed by the U.S. Bureau of Census.

[6] *Handbook of Household Surveys*, (New York: Statistical Office of the United Nations, 1964).

[7] See footnote 2, p. 85.

As to economic data, every five years IBGE takes the economic census covering separately the three basic economic sectors. In 1970 the census covered the whole universe, which contained nearly six million rural establishments in the primary sector and close to 1·3 millions establishments in the secondary and tertiary sectors of the economy. We refer to Table 4.1 for further details on each separate census.

Besides the censuses, surveys on a monthly and yearly basis have been conducted. However, due to lack of standardization of the collected information and, also, due to bias in the samples chosen, we have not tried to include the information in the date base, and we will not discuss them any further. Let us only mention that the results of the 1970 census are leading to a full revision of all economic surveys. With the results of the economic census fully available after September of this year (1975), we expect a whole year to be spent in revising these surveys. Similarly, the

TABLE 4.1

Surveys and Censuses	*Segments*	*Levels*	*Primary Variables*	*Documents*
Census				
Housing and population	3	3	52	5×10^6
Industrial	4	2	187	$1{\cdot}6 \times 10^{5*}$
Commercial	2	1	213	$7{\cdot}5 \times 10^{5*}$
Services	1	1	215	$2{\cdot}5 \times 10^{5*}$
Agricultural	1	1	120	$6{\cdot}2 \times 10^{6*}$
Household sample survey				
1971	3	3	36	$3{\cdot}5 \times 10^4$
1972	3	3	128	9×10^4
1973	3	3	109	9×10^4
1974	33	6	188	$6{\cdot}2 \times 10^4$

This table gives an indication of the complexity, depth and extension of some surveys made by IBGE. The first column gives the name of the census of survey; the second and third columns give the number of segments and number of levels, respectively, corresponding to the structure of the documents, taken as indicators of their complexity; the fourth column gives the number of primary variables, indicator of the depth of the survey and finally, and the fifth column gives the number of documents collected or, equivalently, the size of the sample. Those with asterisks correspond to the size of the universe.

wholesale and consumer price indexes will be developed once the results of the food consumption and family budget survey and the new input-output table are available.

IV. *THE USE OF INFORMATION*

We now come to the point where something should be said about the use of information. To describe the collected information in any detail would make this paper longer than it was originally planned. Therefore, we will mention only the major goal for which the information was collected, that is, for use in policy design.

Figure 4.4, in a schematic way, exhibits a typical demonstration model

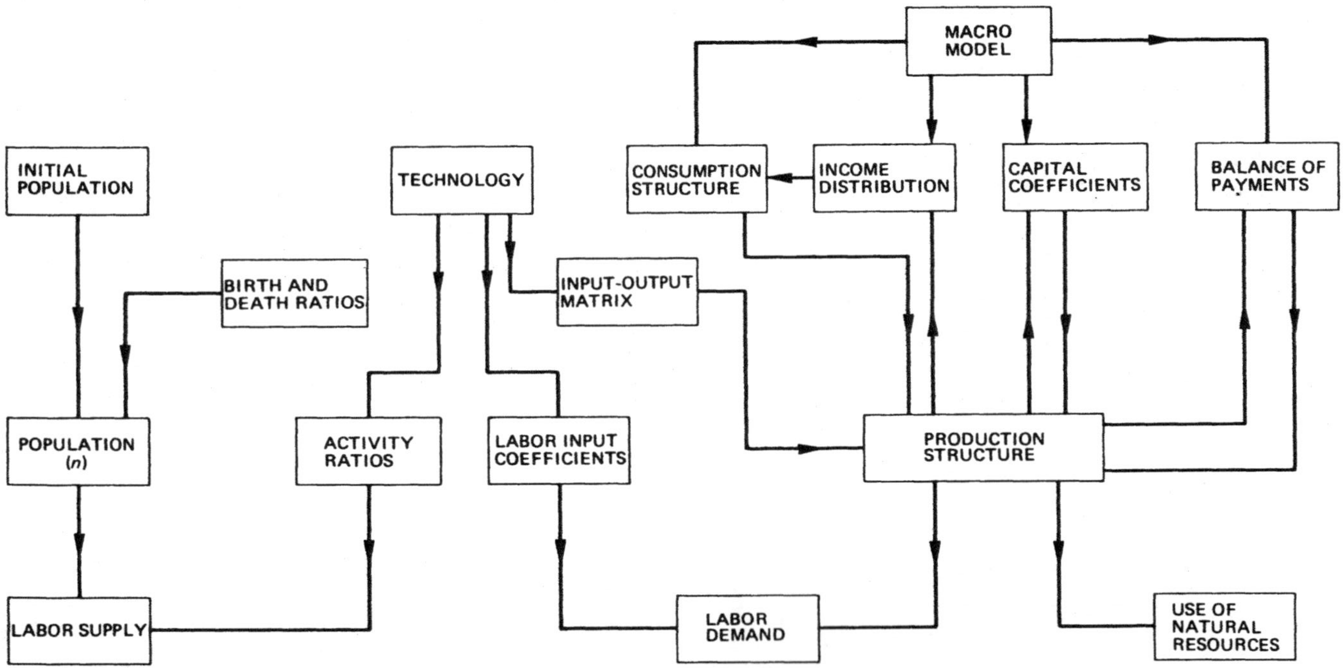
MACRO MODEL
INITIAL POPULATION
TECHNOLOGY
CONSUMPTION STRUCTURE
INCOME DISTRIBUTION
CAPITAL COEFFICIENTS
BALANCE OF PAYMENTS
BIRTH AND DEATH RATIOS
INPUT-OUTPUT MATRIX
POPULATION (n)
ACTIVITY RATIOS
LABOR INPUT COEFFICIENTS
PRODUCTION STRUCTURE
LABOR SUPPLY
LABOR DEMAND
USE OF NATURAL RESOURCES

Fig. 4.4

for the simulation of the Brazilian economy. The model has two major subsystems: (i) the demographic, represented by the blocks on the left and (ii) the economic, by those on the right of the figure.

The scheme for the demographic model is rather simple. Starting from an initial population, say in 1970, and an estimate of fertility and mortality ratios, the population at the period *n* can be predicted. By knowing the activity ratios of the population projected for the future, the supply of labour is determined. What is important to realize is that, with the data from the housing and population census of 1970 and the yearly simple surveys on households, the parameters of the simulation can be estimated, not only on a national scale, but, to a certain extent, on a regional scale, which makes the demographic system more realistic. Similarly, the feedback of the economic variables to the parameters of the demographic model (not shown in Figure 4.4) can be studied.

In the economic subsystem we see, in Figure 4.4 that the demand for labour is specified by the labour input coefficients and the production structure of the economy. The production levels are determined in the usual way, by the final demand and the input-output matrix.

The following submodules interact separately by feedback to the production structure: (i) the consumption structure with the income distribution, (ii) the capital coefficients, and (iii) the balance payments. A macro-model specifies the tolerable levels of consumption, capital formation and balance of payments. The total level of consumption, together with the income distribution, determines, through the consumption structure, the final demand and, therefore, the production. On the other hand, any change in the production structure affects the income distribution and, eventually, the final demand, thus exhibiting the feedback mechanism of this loop. In addition, it shows that the loop involving the consumption structure, income distribution and production structure imposes a consistent solution of the problem. Similarly, the structure of production has to be consistent with tolerable levels of capital formation and balance of payments. One of the results of the simulation is the estimate of the order of magnitude of future needs for natural resources.

It is important to note that the data organized since 1970 have made possible the elaboration of an input-output matrix of the economy with more than one hundred sectors that can eventually be regionalized. This same set of data is also being used for the study of annual labour input coefficients and capital coefficients. The annual household sample surveys are being used for income distribution studies and the determination of the consumption structure. The import and export vectors in the input-output matrix give the interactive mechanism of the foreign trade with the national economy. Due to the programmed five-year interval between economic censuses, these coefficients can be revised on the same time interval which we think short enough to justify a fully linear approach to the simulation model.

We have said that the data collected so far are enough to generate the parameters of a simulation model of the Brazilian economy. This does not mean that the only goal for collecting the data was to generate the necessary parameters of the economy. We are perfectly aware that the quality of our data justifies a more detailed and sophisticated approach at the social and economic level. For example, studies are being conducted by IBGE on social indicators to monitor the welfare impact of economic policies. Other examples are the study conducted with the collaboration of FAO on food consumption of the Brazilian population and a joint project with the ILO world employment project.

Comment by Lutz Hoffmann (University of Regensburg)

The paper by Gomes, Olinto and Kerstenetzky is of a rather technical nature. In some way it may be considered as an introductory manual for potential users of the Brazilian census and survey data stored in a newly developed databank at the Instituto Brasileiro de Geografia e Estatística (IBGE). The first part describes the system of data ordering, which follows a hierarchy of segments. From the user's point of view, these segments may be thought of as different levels of aggregation which permit the user to assess the data at the level of his choice. In analysing income distribution, for instance, he may choose household incomes or, at the next lower segment, personal incomes or, at an even lower segment, personal incomes of a certain age group.

In the second part, the authors specify the hierarchy of regional segments, the regional levels at which census and survey data are collected, and, in rather general terms, the actual data being stored. They further report about data screening and compressing procedures as well as about problems encountered in applying statistical programs for data evaluation. As stated in the third part, the basic purpose of the databank is the construction of simulation and planning models for the Brazilian economy. A short description of the model presently in use is given.

When reading the paper one gets the impression that the IBGE has succeeded in realizing the pipe dream of planning technocrats all over the world. As a planning officer you do not have to run around between statistics departments, ministries, private sector organizations, etc., to obtain your data, to make the data consistent with each other and, finally, to raise doubts and eventually ask for revision of the data. You simply sit down, develop a model, ask the operator to apply the prescribed statistical tools and that's it.

I can imagine that an economist who has been working with a critical mind in a planning agency of a developing country will feel uneasy about this kind of technology transfer from advanced countries. A fairly sophisticated databank, as described, has its justification where first, statistical clerks are scarce; second, the data are supplied in a final form—i.e. revisions are usually not necessary or, if so, only of marginal magnitude—and third, the analytical capacity exists for a systematic evaluation of the stored data. Though my own practical experience is more with Asian countries, my reading about Brazil has not convinced me that these three conditions are given there.

A common argument against manual operation with data states that the extraction and transcription of data by hand produce many inaccuracies and are too time-consuming. This conclusion may be true; but to eliminate those errors is simply a matter of installing sufficient checking procedures, and the time needed depends on the number of clerks employed. One may also note that in Brazil a census becomes available only after five years! Besides this, it is quite likely that in most developing countries such inaccuracies are negligible as compared to the estimation errors. If private investment or total savings are estimated twenty per cent too low or too high—a quite realistic error margin—it really does not matter whether here or there a single number is mistaken.

Once a wrong estimate has been transferred to the databank it has a tendency to remain there, though, in principle, it could, of course, be revised. This is because errors cannot be as easily detected in the anonymity of a databank, or because revisions are postponed since they involve time-consuming rearrangements of tapes or disks.

If the analytical capacity is lacking, the databank may be a tremendous waste of money (and skill). To produce simulation models for the Brazilian economy and to analyse a specific problem here and there, one definitely does not have to store several entire years of census information and surveys. One only can hope that the IBGE is able to attract sufficient analytical capacity from Brazilian sources and that its databank is not just another toy for jet-set economists from the North.

It is difficult to comment on the technical aspects mentioned in this paper, as it would require more detailed information. However, the following questions may be raised for further discussion. The construction of a hierarchy of segments could make the system unduly rigid. It probably limits the possible choices of cross-tabulations and aggregations. As the authors themselves state on pp. 84–5: 'For lower segment variables there is no simple transformation for using them in higher units of observation. . . . ' The question then is, what criteria determine the selection of a specific hierarchy. There is no 'natural' hierarchy, as a glance at Figure 4.3 immediately reveals. More important than the construction of a specific hierarchy is, therefore, the development of a perfectly flexible data code which enables the user to build-up any hierarchy (i.e. to choose any aggregation level) which is suitable for his purpose.

With regard to the data actually being stored, the question may be raised whether the changes in coverage of the annual surveys (e.g. the household sample surveys) do not severely limit their analytical usefulness. It is obvious that only fairly constant coverage enables the analysis of changes over time. A smaller sample with constant (or continuously increasing) coverage may be more helpful than a larger one with irregularly changing coverage. The models where simulation and planning have to rely on estimates of certain structural parameters for one year only tend to be systematically biased. A case in question is the labour and capital input coefficients mentioned in the paper. Both are anything but constant over time. The fact that explicitly or implicitly, other planning models assume the constancy of these coefficients is not at all reassuring.

Finally, I may raise some doubts as to whether it was a wise decision to develop a programming language 'close to Portuguese'. This could well turn out to be an inefficient kind of import substitution, as it will impede the future adoption of new programming techniques developed overseas.

Summary of the Discussion

Professor Diaz-Alejandro presented this paper as dealing more explicitly with the organization of quantitative data in Brazil. It can hardly be considered a case study for the 'Third World' as a whole, since Brazil is a special and relatively advanced country.

Brazil makes extensive use of administrative and census data. (The Brazilian census is under the planning department.) The paper is a good potential guide for users, with its discussion of the hierarchy of the data—how they are aggregated and disaggregated. The organization is largely on a geographical basis, since regional problems are important in Brazil. They are screened for transcription error and reduced in size for storage, at some cost, in accessibility, since stored 'modules' are not immediately usable. The data cover housing, industry, commerce, and households. The over-all stress is on a planning model for Brazil, highly disaggregated by regions and with an input-output table for inter-industry relationships. The Brazilians also attempt to analyse the nutrition, welfare, and distributional aspects of alternative policies.

If this report can be taken at face value, Brazil has provided a statistical miracle to match its economic one, and the information industry is the 'steel industry of the 1970s'. However, *Professor Diaz-Alejandro* viewed the paper with some distrust. How can errors be corrected, once they get into the system? The transition costs of shifting methods of recording data are high. Perhaps the Brazilian planning agency, should instead accelerate publication. Brazilian students, particularly students abroad, complain that Brazilian data are not available outside of the Brazilian Government. As for the planning model itself, *Professor Diaz-Alejandro* wondered whether it was more than a toy, and doubted whether it would really be used. And, if it were used, he wondered whether it would raise or lower the Brazilian growth rate. As for the non-growth applications (to welfare, etc.,) these seemed merely afterthoughts. In conclusion, *Professor Diaz-Alejandro* characterized the report as a 'premature transfer of advanced technology'.

A written comment submitted by *Dr Hoffmann* was likewise negative. He doubted that IBGE had, indeed, realized the dream of planners the world over. The elaborate model, with inaccurate data, seemed poorly adapted to a country like Brazil. Checking seemed insufficient to *Dr Hoffmann* and he pointed out that estimation errors were often more dangerous than transcription ones, while databanks of erroneous materials may waste both time and money. He raised the same doubt that had surfaced in connection with the previous paper, whether the agency collecting the data (IBGE, in this case), had the brains to handle them efficiently. Its hierarchy was too rigid, as was the hierarchy of the data. Outsiders had inadequate access to raw data, and could not check effectively upon handling of the complex sampling and transformation of IBGE's problems. He feared that bias of a self-justifying sort might be introduced within the Brazilian Government. Finally, he saw no merit in an IBGE suggestion to develop a new computer language 'closer to Portuguese' than those currently in use.

Professor Tyler rose to the defence of the Brazilian system. There may, indeed, be misallocation, but long strides have been made as the result of IBGE's efforts. Previous planning attempts have broken down in Brazil because of inadequate data outside of the national income accounts—which are now themselves being revised as a result of IBGE's work. Some of the census data are available in $1\frac{1}{2}$ years; economic data is later. *Professor Tyler* also referred briefly to a problem relating to income-distribution statistics, where census data became available to a visiting foreign scholar before publication in Brazil. As a result of the ensuing controversy, IBGE now pays more attention both to income-distribution problems and to earlier publication of data.

The discussion turned to problems of checking and correcting data. *Professor Morgan* said that checking and correction was possible on a machine-readable basis. *Professor Eckstein* referred to a study by Professor Stigler, indicating that regressions in published articles were often wrong, so that it is a mistake to use only printed results. It is, indeed, possible to check such results, but spill-overs have not occurred into general research practice even in the United States.

Mr Kilgour made the point that, for centuries, libraries have not met all the needs of users, and neither have museums. We can hardly expect better results from databanks. A special problem arises because librarians cannot yet operate computer rooms.

Professor Chamley inquired whether public policy makers do, in fact, respond to econometric models. *Professor Eckstein* assured him that they did.

Professor M. Perlman expressed additional scepticism about Brazilian data as based on inadequate field research, and feared that many LDC's were creating large and immovable bureaucracies blocking outsiders' access to data. He referred, then, to the Brazilian census of 1960, which had been overly ambitious and had broken down, and inquired whether new methods had been adopted to avoid repetition of this fiasco. *Professor Tyler* assured him that such had been the case, and, in particular, more and better use was being made of economists. But, *Professor Diaz-Alejandro* wondered, was access to outsiders being improved? In connection with the income-distribution study, had it been necessary for foreign scholars to obtain data surreptitously? *Professor Tyler* replied that the study would have been done anyway by Brazilians, and that IBGE would eventually have given access to the data. Up to now, however, access is limited to government agencies and government-approved projects.

Discussion of the access problem become more general. *Professor Wolfe* mentioned that, in Britain, one government office may not be given access to the data of another, the usual excuse being that revision is still under way. *Professor Eckstein* said that, in the United States, an organized Federal Statistics Users Group avoids this problem, at least to the extent of avoiding suspension of any publications. *Professor Morgan* mentioned a frequent LDC rule barring removal of data from a country unless a complete set is left behind. Under these circumstances, it is very helpful to make data computer-readable to begin with.

Mr Hibbert made two points, one British and one Brazilian. Replying to Professor Wolfe, he believed that the main obstacle to British inter-agency data transfers has been confidentiality, rather than revision. On Brazil, he expressed satisfaction with the great strides made during the decade 1960–70, but felt that it had been assumed (rather than demonstrated) that the data were sufficiently accurate to justify all of the uses to which they were being put.

Professor Blaug suggested that the 'computerology' and 'accessibility' problems might be related on a cost-benefit basis, meaning that it would be beneficial, on balance, for organizations like IBGE to put fewer resources into computer-science *minutiae* and more into the acceleration of publication.

Professor Kindleberger believed that the critics were being too harsh on Brazil, particularly as regards income-distribution data. After all, in the United States data are also highly questionable on this point, especially in the black community. (*Professor M. Perlman* wondered how much accuracy was really necessary.)

The discussion returned to the confidentiality problem in inter-agency data transfers. *Professor Wolfe* felt, in disagreement with Mr Hibbert, that the problem was minor in Britain, and repeated that statistical agencies were prone to wait too long to 'polish' unreliable data before releasing them. *Professor Morgan* argued from his experience that qualms about confidentiality could usually be broken down if one took sufficient time, but that the time was not usually worth taking.

Professor Johnson feared that the first generation of trained Brazilian economists might be largely wasted in the sorts of activities reported in this paper. He felt that much talent had been wasted elsewhere during the 1950s in compiling detailed, inaccurate, and unusable input-output tables, despite objections from himself and from other economists, and he anticipated a repetition of the arguments of that period.

None of the three Brazilian authors was able to attend the conference, and no other participant felt competent to reply to the critics on their behalf. The session ended, therefore, with *Professor M. Perlman* proposing to ask IBGE for cost data on its methods, and with *Professor Giersch* proposing to give IBGE an abstract of the discussion of this paper.

Comment by the authors on the Summary of the Discussion

We regret not having attended the meeting; the more so after having known the considerable discussion excited by our paper. We are somewhat perplexed at the comments raised during the discussion as they were not centred on the content of the paper but on general politically biased issues, resulting from an incomplete knowledge of what has happened at IBGE during the last five years. We are, therefore, taking this opportunity to add a few comments of our own in the hope of clarifying some of the points raised.

As far as the 1960 census is concerned, it must be pointed out that the economic censuses were concluded and published in time. What broke down was the demographic census, which had only a subsample and 20 per cent of the collected data published in final form. This experience led to the reorganization of IBGE. It is not surprising, therefore, that the 1970 demographic census had an advanced tabulation based on a 1·3 per cent sample published as early as six months after collecting the information. By early 1973 all the data were published and available to the public. The 1972 household sample survey focussing on income distribution was also published and has been available to the public since 1973.

The two procecesses, one for getting the census returns for publication and the other for organizing the census data, are co-operative in nature and not competitive, as suggested by Prof. Blaug. Actually, the computer-based organization of the data comes as a by-product of the census returns. Too frequently the by-products, are not organized and much of the gathered but not published data are wasted. This was the pattern used by IBGE before the last census. It was the main purpose of our paper to show, among the many alternatives open for the organization of the data, the one now adopted by IBGE. We must further add that the IBGE's data organization and retrieval is not 'miraculous' beyond the fact that any use of the computer in processing socio-economic data organization is miraculous.

IBGE does not charge the costs for development of software on the cost for retrieval of special tabulations. Therefore, the efforts made by IBGE (and described in our paper) to improve the retrieval facilities has contributed to lowering the actual cost of the information for requests outside the government. These requests, since 1972, amounted to about 40 per cent of the total number of requests received and we can safely conlude that IBGE's data is not for the exclusive use of the Brazilian government. In several cases involving Brazilian students abroad who needed data for developing theses and did not have financial support, IBGE has provided the data requested free of charge.

Regarding Professor Tyler's reference to the availability of census data to a visiting foreign scholar before publication in Brazil, this simply did not happen. Scholars, both national and foreign, had access to the data at the time of publication.

Nowhere in the paper did we say that the demonstration model described was *the* planning model of the Brazilian economy, and we are afraid that a few participants jumped to the erroneous conclusion that the model represented is *the* planning model of Brazil. Such is certainly not the case.

Mr Hibbert correctly pointed out that we have not demonstrated the accuracy of the data. We believe that by using the data in a logical scheme as suggested by the model described in the paper, purposefully over disaggregated, we can correctly detect inaccuracies and inadequacies of the data. Such an activity is very valuable for an agency like IBGE, which is vigorously pursuing a policy of improving its data in a country which in the past has not paid much attention to quantitative socio-economic information.

Part Two

The Economics of the Economics Library Industry and Its Implications

5 The Effectiveness of Secondary Information Systems in Economics and Industry

Jack N. Wolfe
UNIVERSITY OF EDINBURGH

The article reports briefly on a survey of the attitudes of users of technical information systems—mainly scientific research workers in British industries—concerning their benefits from such systems. It reports a parallel study of a survey among economists in Scottish universities as well. In both cases, advanced information techniques are rated rather poorly as compared with more orthodox techniques. Some tentative inferences for policy are drawn from those results which encapsulate some 15 man-years of work. It is concluded that personal contact and follow up of references are of great importance in economics.

INTRODUCTION

The growth of economic research has meant that a great deal of time and attention must be paid by all of those attempting to keep up with the whole field by simply scanning and reading the literature on the subject. The increase in literature has apparently varied from seven per cent to ten per cent per annum, which means a doubling of output in from seven to ten years. One of the effects of this expansion of output is that economists are forced more and more into specialization. This is, as Adam Smith observed, a necessary precondition for an improvement in technique, but it does lead to considerable difficulties in ensuring that technical advances in one are spilt over into other areas with appropriate rapidity. Until now, the economics profession has been surprisingly lax in the development of media for increasing its rate of assimilation of the products of its own profession. It is only in the last decade or so that any substantial effort has been made to produce an abstract journal in economics; I believe that such a journal is, in fact, available only for English language literature of a 'scientific' or, more properly, theoretical character. Classified lists of publications by subject matter have, of course, been available for a long time with respect to books, and more recently with respect to periodical literature. In this context one would mention particularly the American Economic Association *Index of*

Economic Journals, and the volumes produced by UNESCO. The rate of expansion of output is so great, however, that it cannot be very long before more active steps are taken to develop further techniques for making the search of economic literature easier. As an indication of what I have in mind I think it would be reasonable to forecast that, on the present basis of coverage, the present four issues per year of the *Journal of Economic Literature* would, within fifteen years, have to become a monthly volume of the same size. If coverage were to be extended to governmental and less 'scientific' material, the state of affairs might well mean that a volume of the present size would have to be published fortnightly in order to provide the same coverage as at present.

On top of this general spread of current publications we must bear in mind the spread of economics farther and farther throughout the world and into a wide variety of languages. It can hardly be expected that the dominance of English is likely to continue indefinitely in the changing world situation, and calls must soon come for equivalent abstract journals to be available in several other leading languages. In addition, the enormous volume of statistical material currently being made available throughout the world presents a rather specialized problem with which I should not like to deal in this paper.

Perhaps the best way of approaching this whole problem is to consider what has been done in other branches of science and technology. In most other branches the process of abstracting literature has been carried much farther, and so has the development of other forms of secondary information processing. It is not completely easy to see why the process has gone so much farther in other areas than economics. Two possibilities must, however, be mentioned. The first is the somewhat tendentious nature of a good deal of economic literature, which makes its scanning and knowledge of questionable value in the minds of the government and business officials who ultimately have to pay for any processing. The second point is that scientific and technical material is of interest to a wide range of private and public bodies who are themselves spending very large sums on research activity. In the case of economics, a great proportion of research activity is restricted to the universities and to government agencies. The former have been rather slow in demanding information processing procedures, even in the scientific field, and the latter are relatively few in number and, as many close observers will confirm, somewhat provincial in temper and disinclined to give credence to out-house material.

In spite of these dampening influences it is difficult not to believe that the increasing activity of economic researchers within government will not ultimately result in an effective demand for secondary information sources of the sort which have developed in other scientific branches. In this spirit, the present paper reports on a study of the effectiveness of the use of various secondary information media in scientific and technical fields in the United Kingdom. This study was commissioned by the Department of Education and Science in the United Kingdom, in co-operation with the OECD. It was motivated partly by the desire to consider the extent to which the more orthodox methods of secondary information analysis needed to be supplemented or replaced by more technically advanced ones.

The development of nonprimary information services must be seen in the context of the expansion of R & D (research and development) activity over the past three or four decades. A great boost to this activity has been given by the wartime expansion and continued postwar plateau of defense expenditure and, especially, the great bursts of effort involved in nuclear and aerospace development. This R & D activity has, indeed, found an echo in purely commercial sectors, but it is clear that it is still highly sensitive to fluctuations in defence procurement activity. The development of nonprimary information services is, to a considerable degree, an adjunct of this R & D activity, although it would be wrong not to see this development as a potentially self-sustaining one whose value renders highly unlikely a regression to older information forms.

We intend to study how efficiently nonprimary information services are produced, and to what degree consumers' wants are satisfied. We shall distinguish between several types and elements of information service in the following way. Those nonprimary information services provided within the firm or establishment (e.g. information offices or special libraries) will be called technical information services. Those nonprimary services provided by specialist information agencies outside the firm or establishment will be called secondary information service. The total nonprimary information activity encompassed in these two ways will be spoken of as the total secondary information service. It will be observed that a technical information service may make use of the activity of a secondary information service, but, normally, not vice versa.

The use of quantitative cost benefit analysis need not be confined to governmental or foundation-supported projects. It is not sufficiently appreciated that many of the activities within the private firm are only indirectly subject to the discipline of prices or markets. A great deal of the staff and support work of the modern corporation has this character. Moreover, a service unit within the firm may be profitable when considered as a whole, but many of its detailed activities may be of little use. For example, the detailed conduct of information work within the firm is usually left to the discretion of information experts, and little effort seems to be made to ensure that the material provided by the information service renders value for money in every instance. Some informal techniques may be utilized to ensure that the information system is not grossly wasteful, but a full analysis of the system would, in fact, require something very much like a cost-benefit study. The practice in some companies of making the information agency dependent for funds upon allocations from operating departments does not, in itself, ensure the most efficient detailed operation of the information agency, unless each item of information service is priced separately.

There are, unfortunately, little readily available data covering the field in which we are interested. One of our objectives in the study, therefore, is the generation of relevant data. Our scope is necessarily confined to certain areas of activity. A number of British industries were selected for special study: chemicals, aircraft, and electrical engineering were selected for their high R & D content, textiles because of its traditionally low R & D effort, and agriculture because it is not a manufacturing industry in the same sense as the others but does have a certain amount of research and development. The basic population of users from which we estimate the effectiveness of secondary information is the total R & D personnel in each of these industries. This entailed the random selection of a number of firms in each industry up to a prescribed maximum and the random selection of a set number of R & D personnel within each firm that carried out research and development. The application of statistical techniques in this rather complex sampling and estimation situation constitutes one of the important aspects of the study.

For present purposes it is sufficient to note that the sheer volume of the papers published in each field, throughout the world, renders it impossible for the typical scientist or technologist to meet his current-awareness need, i.e. to keep abreast of new papers by scanning all of the primary publications (periodicals, reports series, etc.) in which they appear. Moreover, he cannot ensure that he has obtained details of all of the work already done on a subject by searching a limited number of primary publications. (This latter requirement is frequently termed his information-retrieval need.)

To assist in coping with these problems there have been two main developments. First, information services have been established within the organizations employing scientists and technologists to look after their information needs, namely, to notify them of items of interest, to collect and organize the primary information so that it is available when they need it, and, if required, to search the mass of literature on their behalf. Such information services have increased rapidly with the development of the science-based industries. They are now common, at various levels of sophistication, in all government research establishments and technical departments, in research associations (where information services are one of the main services provided to members), and in most industrial and commercial organizations of any importance.

The second development has been that of services seeking to organize the information within a particular discipline or subject field, sometimes on a worldwide basis. Normally, all of the primary publications produced throughout the world within a subject field, or a proportion of them as decided by the publisher, will be scanned and their details listed in a periodic publication. Such publications are designated secondary and their contents as secondary information, since they contain references to, or representations of, primary items of information and do not reproduce the items themselves. Although these secondary information services have been produced for many years (e.g. *Science Abstracts* has been produced by the Institution of Electrical Engineers since 1898), their role has expanded with the massive increase in primary information. They have become one of the main tools of the technical information services individual organizations.

In considering the role of secondary information services, one must bear in mind the total environment in which they operate. Although there are a very large number of such services operating throughout the world, their influence on the individual scientist or engineer may be less than that of his local technical information service (through whom he normally will receive the products of the secondary service). Although in some organizations the scientist or engineer may receive the secondary publications on circulation from the library or information service for current-awareness scanning, in many organizations the relevant abstracts or titles from these publications are added to the information bulletin issued regularly by the local information service. Similarly, although some users conduct their own searches of the literature and, thus, make use of the abstracts journals and other tools, others have the search carried out on their behalf by the information staff (i.e. as a local enquiry-answering service) and, therefore, have less contact with the secondary information services used in the search.

The products of the total secondary information service may be conveniently divided into four main classes: abstracts journals, titles listings, SDI (selective dissemination of information) services, and enquiry-answering services. Abstracts journals provide listings with the following features: the title of the document, the author or authors, the bibliographic reference, and an abstract (that is, a brief objective condensation or summary of the document). The items in the abstracts journal are normally arranged by subject or by periodical title and series. Author, subject, and other indexes may be provided either in each issue of the journal or in periodic cumulations. An abstracts journal may thus be used for current awareness by scanning the individual issues, or for retrospective searching by means of its indexes and its classified arrangement. Titles listings normally are produced for current-awareness purposes and are seldom indexed. Apart from abstracts, they normally contain the same elements as the items in abstracts journals.

SDI, or selective dissemination of information, is a system, either manual or computer-based, by which those publications that are likely to be of interest are selected for an individual from the mass of publications produced. In the manual system this is done by information workers who scan the incoming literature and are aware of the information requirements of those individuals who are to be served. In a computer-based system the requirements of each individual are 'indexed' to form a profile: these profiles are then compared with the indexing of the documents entering the system and, where the match is sufficient, details of the documents are sent to the individual possessing the matching profile. If the individual returns an assessment of the relevance to his interests of the notifications sent to him, his profile may be modified to reflect his requirements more accurately. A variation on this SDI service tailored to the requirements of an individual is the standard-profile SDI service in which a profile is established to cover a stated subject, aspect, or facet, and any number of subscribers may receive the output.

Enquiry-answering services are also commonly referred to as information retrieval or retrospective searching services. In these the published (and often the semipublished) literature is searched in response to a specific enquiry in order to obtain documents that deal with the subject of the enquiry of a piece of information that provides the answer to the enquiry. In the latter instance, the answer may be augmented or entirely provided by a specialist in the subject from his own knowledge; such a service is frequently provided by research associations. However, the provision of a list of references is probably the more usual method of enquiry answering by information services and libraries. The references are normally obtained by searches of either the catalogues and indexes compiled by the local information service or of abstracts, journals, titles lists, and bibliographies produced by the secondary information services.

This discussion has centred mainly around published information such as periodical articles, conference proceedings, and patents and semi-published material such as theses, dissertations, and technical and research reports. Similarly, it has been confined to the formal or institutional information network represented by libraries, information centres, and secondary information services. In addition to this formal network, there is an extremely important informal system for the transmission of information. This is conducted mainly on a personal basis, either with colleagues in the organizations or with those working in the same field, through correspondence or at conferences and meetings. A large proportion of the information transmitted in this informal way is either oral or in manuscript or consists of unpublished reports, copies of papers that are to be published subsequently, etc.

In addition to this informal system there is a specialized system dealing with trade or manufacturer's literature, that is, advertisements, handbooks, catalogues, specifications of equipment, components, and materials available. This has its own specialist secondary information services but it is mainly transmitted by periodicals (including free controlled-circulation publications) and by direct mailing by the manufacturers.

It may be useful to provide an indication of the quantitative importance of the nonprimary information field. Our studies indicate that total expenditure of secondary information services in the United Kingdom may be about £5 million per annum.[1] Expenditure for the total secondary information services in all of the OECD countries may have been about £400 million in 1970.

The introduction of mechanized and computerized systems of secondary information appears likely to raise the costs of secondary information services in the fields affected to some multiple of their present level. On the other hand, these increases in expenditure may have as an offset the reduction of expenditure in the much more extensive field of technical information services within government and industrial firms. And they may also result in savings through the closing down of a number of national secondary information services. This question of the true social costs of the substitution of advanced computerized information systems for more conventional systems is of practical importance. The present study, however, does not focus upon this issue, although some of its results do throw some light indirectly upon the question.

We now come to the question of the international provision of secondary information services. This is perhaps the fastest-growing and certainly the most dramatic section of the market, coupled as it is with complex cataloguing and retrieval systems. The forces making for the internationalization of secondary information services are essentially the same as the putative forces making for monopoly in the secondary information service of a single industry or profession in a single country. Briefly, these forces are the savings available from performing secondary information activities on the same body of material for the same body of customers in a single agency. In the case of international co-operation, decreasing costs appear especially important because of the heavy initial costs of programming and storing information in computers.

But the introduction of large fixed-cost elements in production will not be worthwhile unless the extent of the market covered is increased. Thus, the introduction of computerized secondary information systems leads to pressure for a wider and international market and to pressure for the elimination of competitive national agencies. These developments in the secondary information field offer obvious advantages for the computer-producing industries and the computer-producing contries. The advantages may be somewhat less marked elsewhere. The internationalization of secondary information services opens up problems of fee setting and cost sharing. It is not easy to generalize about the basis of fees and cost sharing in international secondary information services. To some degree, this will remain the outcome of international bargaining. One possible system, however, involves the cost contribution of any particular country

[1] £1 = $2·50 at time of writing.

being confined to a commitment to process information generated in that country. Such a system involves a charge on production of primary information. Insofar as production and the use of primary scientific information is perfectly correlated, this seems fair. But it is arguable that the basic costs of the international facility should be borne by the largest information user, with only incremental costs being borne by other countries. There is, in fact, probably no simple system of fees and costs that will be thought 'fair' by everyone concerned. The scope for bargaining is certainly considerable, but the net effect is internationalization of information services, together with a considerable transfer of resources from the United States to other countries, at least in the first instance.

From the practical point of view it may be that the most important economic issues in the secondary information field in the next decade will be the extent to which European countries should contribute to the accelerated development of international systems, even at the expense of increased secondary information budgets or of the running down of their own national secondary information agencies. The subject is a complex one and the present study can throw only incidental light upon it. But one important element in the problem is the extent to which the characteristics of the services provided by international agencies conform to those most desired by national R & D workers. Some useful light is thrown on that subject in the present study. There is limited value in providing secondary information services of great technical capacity if the particular characteristics of the services they offer are not much appreciated by those who use them and if the services which they displace offer characteristics that are more strikingly appreciated.

We must now turn to a consideration of the main theoretical and methodological assumptions underlying the present study. It is a commonplace of quantitative work in economics that economic data can seldom be accepted at face value. Statistical data in economics require a theoretical interpretation. This is the foundation stone of the econometric method. It applies with as much force to the present study as to the traditional problem of the estimation of supply and demand curves.

The study was based upon the assumption of the existence of a stochastic production function of research output. One of the arguments of this function is the volume of information reaching the research-conducting scientists. Thus, we assume the existence of a research production function having the form

$$R = f(S,I)$$
$$S = E + N$$

where R = research output
S = scientific input
I = secondary information input

N = information activity among scientific personnel
E = scientific research activity of such personnel

We assume that an increase in I will increase R if S is constant—i.e. $\partial R/\partial I > 0$,—by reducing N-activities and increasing E-activities among scientists. We do not deal with the possibility that an increase in I will reduce the efficiency of E-activities by causing a diversion of E-effort into wasteful reading activities. We assume that scientists will optimize their reading activities and will not read more than is necessary, regardless of the secondary information flow. If this assumption were violated so that an increase in the secondary information available to scientists caused them to divert their efforts into unproductive lines of study, then the conclusions of our work would have to be modified. Put symbolically, this assumption may be expressed thus:

$$R = f(S,I)$$
$$S = E + N$$
$$E = g(Q,T)$$
$$Q = Q(I)$$

Here T is the number of hours of scientific effort devoted to scientific work and Q is the 'quality' of these hours. We assume that $Q = Q(I)$, and that $dQ/dI > 0$. Further, our main calculations are based on the assumptions that

$$N = N(I)$$
$$E = E(I)$$

and that

$$\frac{dN}{dI} < 0$$

$$\frac{dE}{dI} > 0$$

Briefly, this says that the amount of information work performed by scientists depends upon the secondary information services available and that an increase in secondary information services available will reduce the amount of information-type activities performed by scientists. Furthermore, these relationships indicate that the volume of scientific research activity increases with the volume of secondary information supplied to the research personnel.

There are certain psychological assumptions upon which our calculations also depend. We assume, in particular, that the amount of research output depends in a proportional fashion upon the number of hours of research effort undertaken by each scientific worker. There is no evidence offered for this proposition and if some other relationship—say, a logarithmic one—prevailed, our numerical results would be affected.

The testing of this assumption is, however, rather beyond the scope of economic study and lies in the field of psychology.

A further notable characteristic of this study is its acceptance of the information user's satisfaction as the proper basis of benefit evaluation. Again, there is the acceptance of the existing salary structure as a measure of the research worker's research productivity. These assumptions naturally affect the quantitative results of this study. If, for example, it should be desired to test the implications of the proposition that younger research workers are underpaid in terms of their productivity, while older workers are overpaid, an adjustment in terms of a 'shadow wage' based on age is possible within the terms of this study.

One characteristic of this study that will be specially noted by economists is that cost-effectiveness measures are calculated on the basis of total provision rather than on the basis of incremental provision. This is made necessary by the fact that the provision of particular sorts of secondary information does not have any clearly defined quantitative measure. It is not possible to think in terms of varying the quantity of abstracts available. The situation must be considered in terms of full provision or of no provision. The method principally adopted is most easily conceived of as answering questions about the desirability of continuing a particular service.

Our procedure in this study is to value each particular information service separately and to arrive at total values to the firm and to the economy by amalgamating these individual values. This procedure depends upon the assumption that relations of substitutability and complementarity between services are not very great and that the degree of commercial competition between establishments engaging in research and development is not excessive. Our method could be modified to relax those assumptions if this were thought necessary. Such an alteration would reduce somewhat the values attached to information services as a whole.

A further aspect of the study is that, wherever possible, alternative measures of cost-effectiveness are derived on the basis of alternative assumptions. One of the merits of this approach is that it is possible to examine the sensitivity of results to the choice of assumptions made, and this is done wherever possible.

In the past, economists have been relectant to rely upon surveys of consumers' expressed preferences. They have mainly inclined to the view that only choice revealed in the market could offer evidence about consumers' underlying preferences. This self-denying ordinance has not prevented economists from developing exceedingly useful theoretical structures of demand analysis. Nevertheless, it has resulted in the neglect of a rich source of data which, in fact, has been exploited largely by psychologists and marketing specialists. An essential feature of the study is its attempt to utilize questionnaire techniques to evaluate the benefits of certain economic activities. Some economists will reject this 'attitudinal' approach out of hand; others will accept the validity of the approach as dependent upon the predictive success of the method. The study does not, however, lend itself to predictive test, and the reader must be referred to the extensive marketing literature for analysis of the problems involved and the success of the general approach.

Our study provides an opportunity for examining the extent to which simple and readily available measures, like those derived from questioning information officers, will provide good proxies for measures derived from more complex, time consuming and expensive procedures.

It would be tedious and unnecessary for me to provide here a detailed indication of the results of the study which we performed. The study is based on the reactions of scientific and technological research workers in a number of British industries. These workers were classified in a variety of ways in accordance with professional background, degree of research commitment, years of experience, and so on. Perhaps the most striking results are that, within the sample chosen, rather limited enthusiasm was expressed for more advanced forms of information retrieval and dissemination systems. On the other hand, this is only one of a wide variety of results achieved which include, for example, estimates of 'best practice' volume of secondary information activity in different industries and in relation to research activity.

CONCLUSION

The study undertaken of secondary information systems has proved to be far from conclusive with respect to some of the main issues involved. In particular, it does not appear to be conclusive on the question of whether it would be advantageous to add further expenditure to existing secondary information expenditure, in order to bring into use more technically advanced computer based information retrieval systems. It does, however, indicate, not conclusively, but with a considerable persuasive power, that the reduction of orthodox secondary information procedures in order to provide funds for financing more technically advanced information retrieval and dissemination systems are not likely to be advantageous. This conclusion is tentative for three particular reasons:

1. because only average effectiveness values can be obtained by the methods employed;
2. because it is not clear to what extent the so-called 'gate-keepers'—well informed individuals—are themselves utilizers of highly advanced secondary information systems; and
3. because the members of the sample studied may be thought to have had too limited an exposure to more advanced technical forms really

to represent a fair test of the ultimate usefulness of such forms once their acceptance has become general and new habit patterns of work have been developed.

These conclusions relate entirely to the field of technical information as demanded and desired by applied scientist working in industrial research laboratories. They offer little definite guidance for pure scientists in universities. And they offer no guidance at all with respect to the information needs of economists either in government departments or in universities.

Nevertheless, one might speculate by analogy from these results as to the implications for the priorities for information development in economics. One might suppose, for example, that the first priority might be to develop to the fullest extent possible current awareness of, and, information retrieval systems like, the *Index of Economic Journals* of the American Economic Association. Secondly, priority might then be given to expanding the coverage and depth of abstracting journals like the *Journal of Economic Literature.* Thirdly, high priority might be given to increasing the rate of speed of publication of both of these forms of secondary information. Fourthly, it would appear that only after all of these services have been developed to a satisfactory degree might priority be given to the development of mechanized information retrieval systems and information dissemination systems. Fifthly, the scope for the development of internationally orientated and computer-based systems would appear, at present, to be relatively small. Finally, more emphasis might be placed upon the fact that information flow occurs most rapidly and with greatest effect through personal contact and personal visits, rather than through reading, and this suggests that both national and international visits of people engaged in different institutions and in different types of economic work are highly advantageous and far from being a wasteful form of activity.

In order to check on some of these hypothetical extensions of these results into economics, I have undertaken a limited mail survey of approximately sixty economists in Scottish universities, intended to elicit their estimate of the importance to them of a variety of secondary information materials and techniques. The sample suffers from the usual bias of mail questionnaires. It is, further, of limited interest, because the characteristics of staff in Scottish university departments of economics may not correspond exactly with those elsewhere. A summary of the responses to the questionnarie follows.

The questionnaire on which this survey was based will be provided to those who write directly to the author. The principal conclusions are as follows:

1. Percentage of respondents 28
   (within thirteen days of sending out questionnaire)

2. Age group of respondents by percentage

under 32	54
32—45	38
over 45	8

3. Percentage of respondents answering Section C.3 in a positive spirit . . . 58
   (interpreted as indicating an interest in SDI and computerized services; negative response is usually general)
4. Percentage of respondents having had experience of SDI 8
5. Percentage of respondents having had experience of computer retrieval 0
6. Percentage of respondents listing *A*.1 (following up references as very important)

Teaching	50
Research	79

7. Percentage of respondents listing *A*.2 (suggestions made by professional colleagues) as very important

Teaching	12
Research	25

8. Percentage of respondents listing *B*.1 and *B*.4 (abstracts and indexes) as having high priority

Teaching—*B*.1	50
Research—*B*.1	50
Teaching—*B*.4	21
Research—*B*.4	25

   (Call this group *X*.)
9. Age of Group *X*

under 32	64
32—45	36
over 45	0

10. Percentage of Group *X* regarding following up of references as very important

Teaching	44
Research	66

The conclusions which it seems reasonable to draw, at least tentatively, from these results are as follows:

1. The low response rate to this questionnaire may indicate a relatively low importance attached to information media (28 per cent).
2. This is confirmed by the relatively large group giving no definite answers to Section *C*.3 listing improvements desirable in information procedures (42 per cent).
3. The relatively low weight given to discussion with colleagues contrasts somewhat with evidence from other scientific professions.

4. The relatively high proportion of those respondents relying mainly on follow-up through footnotes (*A*.1) indicates a relatively high proportion of respondents following older information procedures.
5. It would be interesting to compare these answers with those obtained from a sample of university staff in the social sciences, in the physical sciences, or in economics in other countries. A further stratification by highest degree obtained might be interesting. An interesting contrast might be obtained by comparing these results with those obtained from a sample of workers in research departments of universities, government or business.
6. It is noticeable that only limited enthusiasm appears to be felt for the provision of SDI or computer retrieval systems.
7. It seems possible to conclude that the greatest return to expenditure on information might come from increasing awareness among university staff of the advantages to be obtained from modern information techniques, rather than by extending the availability of such techniques.
8. The results of this survey did not differ markedly from those of a similar survey of the thirty-odd participants at the present conference of the International Economic Association.

Comment by John Fletcher (University of Warwick)

Professor Wolfe attempts to draw conclusions about the adequacy and future development of secondary information services in economics by analogy with the equivalent services in science and technology used by R & D personnel in British industry.

Only in the final section does Professor Wolfe draw implications for economics from his research project: that *Index of Economic Articles* and *Journal of Economic Literature* should be expanded, speeded up, and made more international in scope, and that perhaps their production should be mechanized. It seems unlikely that these services would be used more if they were of the size suggested by Professor Wolfe and the cost of such expansion would be very great.

More hopeful, surely, is an expansion of the coverage and use of 'current contents' services such as *Contents of Recent Economics Journals* (published by Her Majesty's Stationery Office for the Library of the British Department of Industry). Useful as abstracts are, most researchers would surely prefer a speedy index to a tardy abstracting service, and the Dutch Economische Voorlichtingsdienst has shown us the way with its *Economic Titles*. This fortnightly service indexes articles in six to ten weeks after their publication in the journals, is international in coverage, indexes by subject (though, alas, not by author), and uses a computer to help with the enormous task.

The existing secondary information services are used by less than ten per cent of economists, who rely much more on word of mouth, mimeographed discussion papers, and on following up references in journal articles and books for their information. These are inefficient and costly methods of research, but only by improving the speed and coverage of published services shall we woo researchers from their traditional lines of information gathering.

Professor Wolfe has written an interesting paper, but the two projects carried out at Bath University, INFROSS (Investigation into Information Requirements of the Social Sciences) and DISISS (Design of Information Systems in the Social Sciences) have produced large amounts of detailed data on this subject, and there is now scope for a much more penetrating analysis of the use and efficiency of secondary sources in economics.

Summary of the Discussion (University of Warwick)

Professor Morgan introduced Professor Wolfe's paper, and pointed out a regrettable lag in the processing of secondary economic data. The material was often controversial; public agencies are slow in publishing it; users have not demanded speed; cost-benefit studies of data acceleration have not been made. The situation, furthermore, is worse in Economics than in many other disciplines. This is because economic research is so largely concentrated in slow-moving institutions like universities. In other disciplines, working technicians keep up better with developments in their specialties, there is more money available for processing, and abstracting services are more available. International co-operation may be necessary if the situation is to be improved, and the United States may well be called upon for much of the 'seed money'.

If secondary information were more effective and available, Professor Wolfe believes, one might set up a 'virtuous circle' or 'double-whammy' model of its results. Researchers, spending less time to accumulate data, could spend more time doing actual research. This would produce more results available to others as secondary data, giving these others more time to do research and producing more data, and so proceed.

Professor Wolfe had prepared and circulated a questionnaire dealing with improving retrieval from secondary sources. (Copies were circulated at the conference.) The response rate among economists had been low, as compared to responses from technicians in other fields; some of their replies had been uninterested in the problem and unenthusiastic about possible improvements. Professor Morgan pointed out that there is seldom any great demand for an improvement before the improvement has been made available, and that reduced funding of the present (inferior) system will not in itself produce a better alternative. Also, the Wolfe questionnaire may be criticized as 'too hypothetical', and the sample may not have been scientifically selected.

In more general comments, *Professor Morgan* preferred to blame the lag in data processing ultimately on the deductive and analytical tradition of Economics itself. (Political Science, for example, has changed drastically, 'leap-frogging' Economics. It used to be less empirical than Economics, and is now more so.) He wondered whether information generally goes from universities to government and industry or the vice versa. (The university community may be lagging behind without realizing the fact.)

With regard to the Wolfe questionnaire, Professor Morgan wanted more detail as to the sample and its selection. He wondered how people respond to questions about a demand which is latent, if not absent. As an alternative, he thought that researchers might have been asked more explicitly what it is that they want. (Perhaps they want primarily greater ease in following up each others' footnotes. If so, they can be helped primarily by substantive experts, not by information specialists, whose advantage lies in the storage of data.)

Professor M. Perlman made the initial interpellation, pointing out that people's views change with their problems. Professor Morgan, he thought, expressed the viewpoint of the publisher of research and of the public policy specialist. He, himself, believes that many and more serious problems result from poor secondary source material. Citation analysis is inadequate in economists' work, and better secondary retrieval systems would reduce the 're-invention of the wheel' in Economics. The purpose of this conference is to make different groups see each other's problems.

In reply, *Professor Morgan* doubted that 'following the footnote trail' was a helpful research procedure in most cases. In fact, it seems to work better in other fields than in Economics. In any case, *evaluation* is necessary, and this must be provided by people who know the field, rather than by information specialists.

The next interpellation, from *Professor Blaug*, dealt with the Wolfe questionnaire. It seemed to him strange that economists show so little interest in computerized retrieval. His own International Labour Office experience would have suggested otherwise. Perhaps the problem is lack of experience. That is to say, more experience would increase enthusiasm for modern methods of secondary retrieval.

Mrs Schwartz suggested that retrieval often involves going through a number of serial volumes, so that no computerization is needed. To this *Professor M. Perlman* replied that when it is important to learn what *critics* as well as authors have said, one must go beyond the serial volumes to material available from secondary retrieval. In his special field of survey research, *Professor Morgan* said, computerized cross-referencing is especially difficult because the individual surveys are so variegated. *Dr Bartenbach* mentioned that bibliographical indexes, even without abstracts, represent an alternative secondary retrieval instrument. Summarizing this series of interpellations, *Professor Morgan* suggested that ordinary market research is needed to find out why researchers have been so hesitant to use advanced retrieval methods of all kinds.

Mr Fetterman doubted that the problem was much different in Economics than in other fields, giving Chemistry as his example. Relatively few people want to know or learn, most are stuck in the mud and satisfied with existing knowledge. Their reluctance to learn new subject matter extends, naturally, to the new methods of information retrieval. This is one of the oldest problems in the entire information industry. Most chemists, for example, don't even look at what the information specialists give them.

Mr Kilgour felt that footnoting and the footnote trail are obsolete. At his university (Ohio State) the Michigan type of service is available. It has helped to double circulation at the Ohio State library, and produced better rapport between faculty members and librarians like himself. (At certain other American universities, including Harvard, there is widespread faculty *discontent* with library facilities which on paper, appear better than those of Ohio State.)

Professor M. Perlman then digested and commented upon a written response to the Wolfe paper from Mr Fletcher. Mr Fletcher felt that the Wolfe paper had too little direct relevance to economics, and doubted that expansion of the *Journal of Economic Literature* (JEL) bibliographical services would be worth its cost. He preferred indexing to abstracting services, and cited HM Stationery Office as providing good indexing services in Britain. He had a dim view of both the footnote trail and the old-boy network, and suggested that the Wolfe questionnaire might be supplemented by similar work done at another British university (Bath). To the criticism of JEL, *Professor M. Perlman* replied that its time lag was being reduced by computer techniques, and that much of it was due to authors rather than to the journal itself.

Returning to the Wolfe questionnaire, *Professor Meyriat* wondered whether there were any marked differences between the answers of technologists and economists, and inquired as to the reasons for them. *Professor Wolfe* replied that technologists seemed more interested in his problem. All answered his questionnaire. All had used retrieval services and abstracting services. Personal contacts were also very important. Economists, on the other hand, placed greater reliance on indexes. Personal contacts were less important than among the technologists, while the footnote trail seemed almost entirely an economic phenomenon.

Professor Wolfe began his response by agreeing with Professor Blaug's distinction between visible and latent demand for improved secondary retrieval. Natural scientists, with experience in computerized systems, feel that more experience will help even them; economists, with little or no experience, are more skeptical. His questionnaire study was unpopular, perhaps because it seemed to suggest the possibility of replacing 'informational specialists' by computers during a slack period in the academic market-place. (There may even have been an attempt to influence the conclusions of the questionnaire by 'stuffing the ballot box'.) Turning next to Professor Morgan's concern with what people may really want, Professor Wolfe replied that they did not usually know, but 'voting with their feet' eventually counts, as the people most in demand move to places most supportive of their research. *Professor Wolfe* then turned to another question, the sources of funds for data-retrieval research. For this purpose universities use part of their surpluses on public contracts, and hope to reduce 'wasteful duplication' of their efforts—part of which is actually useful competition. (In the USSR, Professor Wolfe believes, information work is more highly advanced than in the West, and a new 'explosion' may come either from there or from some UN agency.) He felt that some of the discussion was not based firmly on experience, but inquired of Mr Kilgour the costs of the impressive Ohio State experiment. ('It is cheap', replied *Mr Kilgour.*) *Professor Wolfe* went on to comment that the great bulk of academic work (including that of many recipients of his questionnaire) is not research or even research-oriented, but that there is pressure on the information-retrieval front from the research minority. Perhaps one of the most desirable features of improved retrieval will be increased interest in research.

At the close of the formal discussion, there arose a dialogue on the old-boy network. *Professor Morgan* felt that this network might be adequate for established senior professors, but that the younger men with fewer contacts were discriminated against. *Professor Johnson* replied that such a network is an *exchange* of information. One should not expect to receive much until one has something to offer.

6 The High Cost of Information and Some Approaches to Its Acquisition

J. Fetterman
UNIVERSITY OF PITTSBURGH

The cost of information, especially in its imprinted form, has been rising at an exponential rate for more than twenty-five years. This cost increase is coupled with a similar increase in the amount of material being produced and the number of users requesting it.

Several approaches to these problems are suggested. One is resource sharing, where access to material is considered to be more important than possession. Another is the development of acquisition programmes based on usage and providing remote storage facilities where the material is under bibliographic control and available through efficient delivery systems.

OVERVIEW

There are two critical variables in the library environment. The first is the amount of material—past, present and future—for which the library must be responsible. These variables are multidimensional insofar as the format of the material ranges from imprinted to microform to computer-processible. Another significant dimension lies in the variable needs of users which are sometimes not understood and, at other times, totally unpredictable. The second critical variable is that of cost. Typically, cost is a function of materials, labour, demand, and volume. Both critical variables have been increasing at an exponential rate for at least twenty-five years.

These library issues ought to be addressed at several levels. First of all, individual libraries must examine their own procedures associated with acquisitions, processing, storage, and the delivery of services. A Cartesean methodical doubt can effectively be applied to all of these processes. Secondly, libraries ought to consider resource sharing as a way of providing more goods and services to satisfy user needs than their individual budgets can support.

The space for any of these materials is often as expensive as the materials themselves. Critical methodologies ought to be employed to determine the cost-effective use of this space. Storage facilities, whether used individually or collectively, can provide feasible alternatives to overcrowded central facilities. Both storage and delivery systems are available to alleviate the problems caused by exponentially expanding amounts of material which must be stored in virtually unexpandable space.

The key to cost-effective library operations is to have programme oriented systems which can identify what the user really needs and the time frame for its delivery. These issues of acquisition, processing, storage, and delivery of services will be addressed in terms of a whole system which has fixed resources, but variable demands, and whose goal is the best possible performance for the most reasonable cost.

THE NATURE OF THE PROBLEM

Keyes Metcalf has been, for several decades, one of the outstanding leaders in the library field in America and he considers library growth as the cause of nearly all of the libraries' financial problems. This pattern of growth became typical since the turn of the century. Numerous studies have indicated that university libraries have been growing at an exponential rate, with their collections doubling, on the average, every sixteen years. In large university libraries the average doubling interval has been 9·5 years.

A study by Oliver Dunn plots library growth factors from 1951 through 1969 and projects the growth curves to 1980. He reports:

> The average composite of the 58 University libraries included in this study indicates that the number of volumes held doubles every seventeen years; the number of volumes added to the collections each year has doubled every 9–12 years; and library operating expenses double every seven years. The report concludes: In short, the records of growth since 1951, including the most recent years, and the unfaltering growth may not soon decelerate.[1]

If your library happens to be primarily in the business of collecting in science and technology, the problems of growth are of even greater proportions. The growth in the number of scientific journals has been charted by D. J. deSola Price in his book, *Science Since Babylon.*[2] He shows that there were about ten scientific journals being produced in the late 1600s. By the beginning of the 1800s this number had increased to about 100. By the beginning of the 1900s this number had increased to about 10,000. His evaluation of the *World List of Scientific Periodicals*

[1] Dunn, Oliver. *The Past and Likely future of 58 Research Libraries 1951–1980: 'A Statistical Study of Growth and Change'*, 6th Issue (Lafayette, Indiana: Purdue University Library, 1970).

[2] Price, D. J. deSola. *Science Since Babylon* (New Haven: Yale University Press, 1961).

is that we are well on our way to the 100,000 mark. The data he presents show a remarkably constant doubling time of fifteen years, now maintained for nearly three centuries.

This extraordinary growth rate in publishing does not necessarily correlate with a growth rate in usage. A study of the use of currently published serials done at the John Crerar Library in Chicago found that 65 per cent of the journals it currently receives are used less often than once a year. Another study of inter-library loan use at the National Library of Medicine found that 88 per cent of its serial titles were used less often than once a year. According to a recent study done by the Center for Research Libraries, there is evidence that 25 per cent, and probably more, of the journals received are used no oftener than once in every 25 to 100 years in any one library. Put another way, 100 per cent of the use during the twelve month period was satisfied by only 4347 titles out of the approximately 37,000 in the NLM collection.

THE COST OF MUCH OF IT

Up to this point I have been trying to give some data-based substance to the assumptions or insights that you may have had about the information explosion. I have already suggested that there has not been a corresponding growth in the use rate and I will spend more time on that aspect later. For the present, I would like to spend some time discussing the rising cost of all of this material, most of which is not being used much.

To confirm your intuitions about what has happened to your information dollar, aggregate statistics for the United States indicate that, in 1964, 15,000,000 volumes were added to academic library collections. By 1968, this number had risen to 25,000,000 and has remained there as a constant through 1974. During this same time frame, the expenditures for books and other library materials rose from $90,000,000 in 1964 to $188,000,000 in 1968. Then, from 1968 to 1974, this figure rose to $283,000,000 at the same time as the number of volumes added per year remained constant.

A similar kind of trend can also be seen at the other end of the spectrum if one looks at average prices per volume and the index of growth. At the time of writing, the figures for 1974 were not yet available, but the trend is clear and not likely to be reversed. I refer the reader to the following table:

	1967		*1971*		*1972*		*1973*	
	Av. Price	*Index*	*Av. Price*	*Index*	*Av. Price*	*Index*	*Av. Price*	*Index*
Hardcover books	$8·43	100·00	$13·25	157·18	$12·99	154·00	$12·20	145·00
Periodicals	8·02	100·00	11·66	145·39	13·23	164·96	16·20	202·00
Serial Services	66·98	100·00	90·05	134·44	95·38	142·40	103·45	154·45

SOURCE: *Publishers Weekly*, February 4, 1974, p. 57.

The indicative factors to take note of are the index figures given after 1973. It is unrealistic to suppose that anyone's budget has increased by anything like 45 per cent, 102 per cent, and 54 per cent respectively. As in every other sector of the economy, the inflationary factor is running far ahead of budget increases.

Many of you have a special interest in periodicals. Bowker's Annual provides some additional statistics on their increasing costs. The following data are taken from the 1974 edition:

Year	*Number*	*Average Price*	*Index*
U.S. Periodicals (97 titles dropped; 191 added)			
1967–1969	6,944	$8·66	100·0
1970	2,372	10·41	120·2
1971	2,415	11·66	134·6
1972	2,537	13·23	152·8
1973	2,861	16·20	187·1
1974	2,955	17·71	204·5

It is important to note than the greatest increase, 35 per cent, took place in 1973 and that the rate of increase seems to have lessened.

The response of some libraries to this extreme rise in periodical costs has been the severe one of cancelling subscriptions to many periodicals. For example, the Center for Research Libraries in Chicago reports that of the fifty major libraries in its membership, two thirds have already cancelled an average of 300 titles. Some members have had to cancel as many as 2000 titles.[3] The damage done to a collection by this kind of cancellation policy is extremely difficult and expensive to repair. The difficulty lies in finding the backruns of these periodicals at a later date, and the later acquisition puts an additional strain on a budget that is hard-pressed to keep up with current acquisitions.

CO-OPERATIVE PROJECTS

One alternative to cancelling periodical subscriptions is to enter into a co-operative acquisition programme whereby the expensive and the less-used items are acquired by a regional library. The group would have to agree, of course, as to which items were to be acquired by the regional library and the participating institutions would have to have adequate assurances that the runs would be continued. This operation can function like a star network in which a central institution acquires the goods and then distributes them to the participating institutions.

An alternative to this configuration would be a distributive network in

[3] *Background and Proposal for a National Lending Library for Journals* (Chicago: Center for Research Libraries, 1972), p. 2.

which each institution agreed to share an approximately even portion of the acquisition responsibility and then have completely reciprocal borrowing privileges.

The co-operative acquisition of serials is one of the more productive ways to maximize the function of your information expenditure. It has the great advantage of producing a noticeable reduction in costs and increasing the amount of goods available. Furthermore, these benefits can take place with a minimum of disruption to normal library service. The principle embodied here is an important one, I believe, for implementing cost-beneficial resource sharing operations. The goal is to change some very expensive and not-so-beneficial acquisition practices. One of the better ways to accomplish that is to begin with changes which involve low risks and high rewards. To acquire more and yet spend less is just such a reward system in operation. It has the corrolary effect of inducing librarians to look at many other operations with the hope of duplicating this cost-beneficial innovation.

These co-operative concepts mentioned here function really as entrance points into a broad spectrum of co-operative activities. They suggest co-operative programme planning in which these acquisitions might be used. They suggest co-operative processing in which there would be enough volume to justify the use of automation and achieve economies of scale. They suggest delivery systems that would move the goods from one location to another within reasonable time frames and at cost-beneficial prices.

There are two points I would like to emphasize at this time. The first is the inter-connected characteristics of all of these resource sharing activities. As soon as one begins to function in a co-operative mode in any of the four basic areas of acquisitions, processing, storage, or delivery of service, appropriate activities in each of the other three areas must be considered if the project is to be cost-beneficial.

The cost-beneficial factor is the second point I wish to emphasize. In the long run, the benefits should be such that much more in goods and services is achieved in the co-operative mode than in the self-sufficiency mode. In the self sufficiency mode one plus one may equal two; but in the co-operative mode, one plus one should equal four. In short, there would be a noticeable synergistic function in the co-operative mode which will produce the desired cost-beneficial effect.

THE COST OF NON-USE

The rise in costs is more dramatic in periodicals than in books, but the non-use rate in books is more measurable at the present time. The examination of this non-use factor in books can give us some valuable insights into more cost-beneficial library operations.

A book is like a bridge, and I don't mean this in a metaphorical sense.

I mean it in the sense of a collective good decreasing in cost per unit use once the initial investment has been made. The decreasing average cost is a function of use as conditioned by the initial investment. If, for some reason, use does not occur at all, the cost remains at its initial level. In the library world we have many bridges which have never been used. The amount of non-use in any given academic collection is in the order of 40 per cent. For the sake of understanding the cost of this non-use factor in libraries, let us assume that we are talking about a collection of moderate proportions, that is, in the order of 600,000 volumes. On the basis of studies done at the University of Pittsburgh and elsewhere it is reasonable to say that at least 40 per cent of these 600,000 items have never been used. If we assume an average purchasing cost of $15·00 per volume and an average processing cost of $15·00 we then have a total cost of $7,200,000·00 for books which have never been used, or the price of a small bridge which will never be crossed. Mancur Olson, a professor of Economics at the University of Maryland, makes a good point by saying that 'in the aggregate the production and dissemination of scientific and humanistic knowledge is usually characterized by sharply decreasing costs'.[4] This is true if, and only if, there is use of the material. Otherwise, these books become some of the most expensive artifacts which our society is producing.

People frequently respond to this cost-analysis approach by saying that an academic library has a serious obligation to perform an archival function and that there is no cost-value which can be attached to knowledge. I would agree with both of these premises, but add that neither provides a sufficient reason for operating the expensive form of acquisition and storage systems for books which we now maintain.

A COUNTER PROPOSAL

Use should dominate. I would suggest that if material is needed it should be acquired with as many multiple copies as are necessary to satisfy the actual demand of users. This high use collection will probably be a relatively small portion of the total collection and ought to be housed in the most convenient place possible in relation to the user. Maximum ease of access ought to be the guiding principle not only in terms of location, but also in terms of library hours and procedures. As the use rate diminishes, fewer copies should be acquired and they should be located at points proportionately remote from the user. The logical extension of this concept is that several colleges or universities could profitably join in a local common storage facility which would function as a regional

[4] Olson, Mancur. 'Information as a Public Good', *Economics of Information Dissemination, A Symposium*, ed. Robert Taylor (Syracuse, NY: Syracuse University, 1973), p. 11.

resource centre. In the case of material with extremely low use, a larger grouping could be utilized, serving a substantial region in any given country. At this level of use it may even be more cost-beneficial to transport users to the materials than to provide these materials throughout the system and have them wait for an occasional rare use.

The concept which is being proposed here can be pictured as a series of concentric circles with the user in the centre. The inner circle has the greatest density of books with the greatest ease of access and the outer circle has the least density of books with appropriately complex methodologies of access.

THE USER

This kind of layered system is entirely feasible now even with the application of low to moderate level technology. The bibliographic searching can be carried out both manually and by TWX or, in some cases, via computer. As large bibliographic centres develop, such as the Ohio College Library Center (OCLC), more and more bibliographic data will be online and the searching throughout a large system can be done most efficiently.

If the user is part of a larger computerized system he can find out very quickly if the material exists in the system, where it is and approximately how long it will take to reach him. The slight delay in time which may be associated with delivery in a large system such as this does not seem to be a critical factor in reality. There is a myth, widely circulated and atrociously popular, which says that all users must have instant satisfaction or terrible things will happen to both the user and the librarian. In point of fact, immediate satisfaction is rarely required even in the natural and experimental sciences or in the medical profession. Most mail systems can have material in a user's hands in a few days and that is soon enough.

It is critical to remember that the trade-off for the brief delay in delivery is access to a larger system than any user could realistically hope to have available to him at the local level. The 'system' is not being proposed here as any kind of panacea, but, rather, as a larger environment in which many more possibilities for attaining goods and services are made available to the library administrator and user. With the funds available to him severely limited, the library administrator can attempt to acquire some miniscule portion of the information available in any given field or can invest that same money in user studies and consortia membership. User studies would go a long way towards giving some kind of profile to these groups and to identifying what they actually need, instead of what others think they need or ought to have. I suspect that, as more and more information system managers carry out such studies, they will find that they have wasted more money on unused materials than they are asking for as increments in their budget. To refer to the previous metaphor, library administrators have built more bridges than need to be crossed.

THE INFORMATION EXPLOSION

A few minutes ago I suggested that any given library can purchase only a minuscule portion of the available imprinted material. Allow me to sensitize you with a few statistics. Thus:

1. There have been 30 million titles published since Gutenberg. How many libraries have anything more than 5 per cent of these? I guess some have less than $\frac{1}{2}$ per cent.
2. There are about 100 thousand journals published currently. How many libraries subscribe to more than 10–15 per cent? Some subscribe to less than $\frac{1}{2}$ per cent.
3. About 500 thousand books were published in 1974. How many libraries will buy more than 10–15 per cent? Some will buy less than $\frac{1}{2}$ per cent.[5]

Given these vast amounts of information, it is an illusion to think that any local institution, even one of the largest size, can acquire any significant portion of this material. The critical factor to keep in mind is that owning is not the most important consideration; access is. The most cost-effective way of gaining access to this material is to belong to a system in which a modest investment is made, say in the order of $15,000, to gain access to millions of dollars' worth of material. This is precisely what we have done in our region by joining the Center for Research Libraries in Chicago.

DELIVERY SYSTEMS

I have proposed the concept of an information system pictured as a series of concentric circles with the user in the middle and the greatest density of books closest to him and the less used books more remotely located. An information system like this implies the existence of a delivery system to distribute the goods. Such systems for information networks can be constructed with the same concerns about optimization as exist in all of the branches of Operations Research. It is possible only to suggest areas of investigation at this point, but such OR techniques as Transportation Models, Markov Analyses and Queuing Theories can all be profitably applied to the information delivery system question.

A brief example may be in order here. In our region of Pennsylvania we have a truck delivery system which services all of the academic

[5] Kent, Allen. *Resource Sharing in Libraries* (New York: Marcel Dekker, Inc., 1974).

libraries and the major public ones. Pennsylvania is 450 km from east to west and 253 km from north to south. These trucks go to each of the libraries requesting a stop on a twice weekly basis and carry unlimited loads of virtually anything and everything that one library has to send to another. The start-up financing has been provided by substantial grants from the Federal Government, with a modest enrolment fee on the part of the participating institution. For example, the most recent enrolment fee was $400·00 for two years of service. At the end of two years, this fee would go up to about $800·00 for the same time frame. The managers of the system think that the system can be self-supporting at the $800·00 level if enough members can be induced to join at a lower rate and experience the benefits of the system. I think that the system is extremely worthwhile, especially as more libraries in the State are joining the OCLC system. Of equal importance is the principle of the Federal Government providing funds for the heavy start-up costs. There are many operations like this in the information processing world which could not have begun were it not for a large portion of Federal seed money at the beginning—but that is the subject of another paper.

OCLC

I would like to use OCLC as an example of a networking operation in the context which has been established here. A single system such as this, set up in a large number and variety of libraries can do many other things besides cataloguing. I wish to emphasize two functions in terms of the system I have been talking about. The first is that it provides a way of learning which other libraries on the system hold a particular title. Librarians should query the system *before* they make a decision to buy a particular title. This buy or no-buy decision will be made in consideration of a number of complex factors such as user needs, location of the item within the system, available delivery mechanisms, inter-library loan policies, etc. The point that I wish to emphasize is that libraries could save a great deal of money if they would use a network in this way.

THE STORAGE NODE

The final component of the information system that I have in mind would be a storage library. There are many systems available for the compact storage of books. Ralph Ellsworth, in his classical monograph on storage libraries, lists twelve.[6] They differ widely in their cost and space requirements per volume stored. The ranges are from $·49 to $1·42 per volume stored and from 15 to 147 volumes per square foot of space. The

[6] Ellsworth, R. E. *The Economics of Book Storage in College and University Libraries* (Metuchen, NJ: The Scarecrow Press, Inc., 1969).

traditional reasons for considering a storage facility are generally (1) to save money; (2) to solve a space crisis; and (3) to improve access to the books in the book-stacks. The issue of saving money through remote storage has to be examined very carefully because there are substantial costs associated with acquiring more space and staff, changing records and providing for an efficient delivery system, etc. It seems to be a practical impossibility for a single library, regardless of its size, to afford a storage library of its own. To achieve any real economies, a great deal of attention must be given to value analysis in considering what is gained and what is lost. Ellsworth warns that the institution must be aware that 'it might be creating conditions that could, in the long run, increase costs that might be much larger than are the short-term savings it might make by adopting a storage program'.[7]

CONCLUSION

Information is as critical a resource to man as food and water, light, and heat. Man needs information to survive. The challenge facing us is to manage our production and distribution mechanisms well enough so that men will have as much of it as they need, provided to them at the most reasonable cost. I think that the search for solutions must lead us, not merely to seek more money, but, also, to examine critically the reasons why we acquire information and the ways in which we process, store, and deliver it. We may very well be spending too much and getting too little.

[7] Ellsworth, R. E., *op. cit.* p. 15.

Comment by Werner Schuchow

(Studiengruppe für Systemforschung, Heidelberg)

In his conclusion, John Fetterman states that information (and he means, in particular, scientific and technical information) is as critical a resource to man as food and water, light and heat, and that we should, therefore, seek production and distribution mechanisms for this most important 'substance' which enables us, within the limits of the available financial means, to obtain as much of it as we need. From this conclusion, restricted to the consideration of (science) libraries, it is only a small step to considering the economics of the entire process of producing and transferring scientific and technical information from a similar angle.

The process of transferring scientific and technical information from the producers to the users takes place in many different ways:

directly, without permanently fixing the information on any particular medium (letter paper, books, periodicals, microfilms, tape recordings, magnetic tapes, etc.) and without various different types of transformations and intermediate storage. Examples: personal conversations, conferences, seminars, lectures and symposia.

indirectly, with more or less permanent fixation of the information to be transmitted on data media and transmission through different channels and stages of processing and condensation. Examples: publishing houses for scientific literature, libraries, science archives, bibliographic documentation systems, scientific databanks, information analysis centres.

The phenomenon described by John Fetterman is not restricted to libraries alone. Exponentially growing quantities of scientific information, accompanied by (as a result of inflation) still more steeply rising acquisition, processing and storage costs on the one hand, and, on the other hand, ever more specific and differentiated user needs, result in extremely uneven use of the accumulated store of information. These are tendencies evident throughout the entire system of indirect information transfer. Hence, in searching for ways out of the situation described by Fetterman, one should regard this system as a whole.

The indirect transfer of scientific and technical information involves a step-by-step process, meaning that the individual parts of the process are attuned to one another in their mode of operation. Publishers of scientific literature, for example, concern themselves with the publication of research results in technical periodicals which are arranged and stored in libraries and made available to interested persons upon request. Bibliographic documentation systems, in turn, analyse the individual periodical articles from the point of view of content, and supply references in response to specific information needs. The user can then follow these references and obtain the required literature via, for example, a library. Databanks permit access to isolated scientific and technical data gleaned from, e.g. articles in technical periodicals. Information analysis centres critically evaluate material from, among other sources, technical periodicals, and make comparisons from various points of view. Special reference services (referral centres, clearing-houses) provide information, for example, on the current state, and the latest results, of research in specific areas, and refer those interested in specific material to institutions or persons who can supply the requested information.

If one wishes to analyse the economics of the entire system of indirect information transfers, one must not fail to consider the interdependent relations between the individual parts of this system. The government of the Federal Republic of Germany sees this object in its 'Program zur Förderung von Information und Dokumentation' (Programme for the Promotion of Information and Documentation), which it made public this year [1]. For the period 1974–77, the government plans to appropriate 440 million marks for long range restructuring of scientific and technical information transfer in the FRG in co-operation with the Bundesländer (federal states) and private enterprise. The emphasis of the programme lies on the integration of bibliographical, data and project documentation, centralized technical libraries, science archives and scientific translation services for larger subject fields and disciplines (among others, for the field of economics).

Economically organizing the entire indirect transfer system for scientific and technical information involves, moreover, an effort to organize its subsystems. John Fetterman's contribution, concentrating on the area of science libraries, represents an effort in this direction. In the following analysis, computerized bibliographical documentation systems will be used as an example to demonstrate that more or less the same set of problems applies to the other subsystems.

The factor which Fetterman represents as critical for libraries, namely, the exponential growth rate of scientific and technical literature, is of at least equally critical importance for documentation systems. Owing to the enormous increase in new literature within the last years, 'manual operations' are now no longer adequate for storing the annual increment of titles, abstracts and descriptors or for searching through accrued data bases. The penetration and continued advance of computer technology into the field of documentation is based on these developments. Already in the year 1972, for example, a few large international documentation systems were faced with the following numbers of new scientific and technical literature entries (number of titles) to be processed and stored:

ISI	Institute for Scientific Information (USA)	400,000
CAS	Chemical Abstracts Service (USA)	377,800
MEDLARS	Medical Literature Analysis and Retrieval System (USA)	232,000
BIOSIS	Biosciences Information Service (USA)	240,000
INSPEC	Information Service for Physics, Electrotechnology, Computers and Control (UK)	152,000
	National Agricultural Library (USA)	120,000
	Engineering Index, Inc. (USA)	85,000
INIS	International Nuclear Information System (IAEO)	21,000
SDS	ESRO's Space Documentation Service	150,000
	American Geological Institute (USA)	60,000

If, furthermore, one is aware that, in mechanized documentation systems, the cost per title merely of the activities of selection, cataloguing, indexing, abstracting, thesaurus maintenance, data preparation and computer input processing (i.e. without acquisition) was of the order of 40 DMs [2, 3] at that time (1972), it becomes clear what an avalanche of expenses was set in motion by the development of retrievable data bases for the various disciplines and subject fields. Since personnel expenses account for approximately 75 per cent of these input costs, the quantity component (growth of the volume of literature) is greatly augmented by a price component (sharp rise in the cost of labour in some countries).

Here one should add that, from system to system, this value for the input costs per title is naturally subject to great fluctuations according to the respective structure and size of the observed systems, subject fields, type and exhaustivity of the indexing and classification procedures, etc. [2, 3]. Roughly approximated, this value already lies at about 60 DMs for mechanized documentation systems in western nations today. For documentation in the field of chemistry, this value would more or less double, though in some nations with lower costs of labour (e.g. Great Britain), it would be lower. Within one nation, this value would vary for individual systems dealing with identical or neighbouring fields according to the extent of co-operation in indexing and abstracting documents and in building up retrievable data bases. There is a prevailing tendency to lower the input costs per title through co-operative division of labour in indexing information sources and building up co-operative data bases on the national and international levels. A current example of this trend is the plan for a network to transmit scientific and technical data within the European Community (EURONET).

Analogous to Fetterman's deductions and solution proposals for the problems of science libraries, what conclusion can now be drawn from the constantly rising input costs in computerized documentation systems? Here, just as for science libraries, the steadily rising storage growth rate is accompanied by an at-most halting, if indeed any, increase in the demand for this stored material on the part of the user. In most computerized documentation systems today, the relation between input and output costs varies, according to concrete circumstances, anywhere between 8:2 and 6:4 [2, 3]. This relationship can actually be regarded as symptomatic of the 'degree of maturity' which a system has attained. For documentation systems which have already been in operation for some length of time and which have built up a clientele, the relation of the output costs to the input costs is favourable. (In some cases, the output costs are already higher in absolute value than the input costs.)

Since the purpose of documentation systems is to satisfy the information needs of certain groups of users, and not to restrict themselves to building up the most comprehensive storage facilities possible, critics observing the predominating relation between input and output were incited to coin the expression 'input graveyards'.

However, compared with that of libraries, the situation of documentation systems provides somewhat less grounds for pessimism regarding the future development of this problem. This divergence has the following reasons:

1. Today, most computerized documentation systems still find themselves in the planning, development and implementation phases, at the initiation of operation or in a stage of reorganization. These, by definition, demand a high per cent of input costs—more or less as an investment towards a more effective supply of services in the future.
2. In the future, the significance of documentation systems (compared to that of libraries) will grow for the rapidly developing areas of science, technology, economics, management and planning. One reason for this is that the organizational structure of libraries hardly adapts them for satisfying specific information needs (e.g. for information related to the latest results of research

in a specialized field of space research) with sufficient rapidity and pertinence.

3. Consequently, in the future, there will be an increase in demand for the manifold services offered by documentation systems (searching, upon special request, for particular subject material or material under a specific subject heading; continually keeping certain users abreast of the latest literature, compiled on the basis of closely defined user need profiles; generally offering running reports on the latest realizations and developments in certain areas of science and technology, etc.). Documentation systems will thus be in a position to produce their services at a lower unit cost than presently possible, since the ratio of input costs per service unit will fall tendentially (as, in fact, will all fixed costs), while the volume of services increases.

The increased output of documentation systems will also lead, however, to an increase in demand for the services of science libraries. The users will turn to libraries to find the complete texts of the citations and abstracts to which they have been referred. Here, once more, is proof of the necessity for completely integrating the organization of the entire indirect transfer system for scientific and technical information.

4. Finally, growing national and international co-operation of documentation systems (perhaps culminating at some point in networks operated on-line) will lead to a reduction of the input costs per title—i.e. to more economical construction of data bases—and to an increase in the use, i.e. to more economical use, of existing data bases across national boundaries.

REFERENCES

[1] Bundesministerium für Forschung und Technologie (ed.). *Programm der Bundesregierung zur Förderung der Information und Dokumentation* (Bonn: 1975), [will be published this summer].

[2] Organization for Economic Co-operation and Development, (ed.), *The Costs of Mechanized Information Systems* (Paris, 1974).

[3] Drees, G., 'Die Kosten von wissenschaftlich-technischen Informations- und Dokumentationssystemen (Brussel: Kommission der Europäischen Gemeinschaften, 1974). Dok. III/520/74 D (work paper, initial version; will shortly be officially published).

Summary of the Discussion

Both Mr Fetterman and *Mr Evans*, who introduced his paper, agreed in what they called a minority view among librarians. This view is that libraries should re-examine their individual needs and share their joint resources. Also, they should become user-oriented or, in the case of university libraries, curriculum-oriented. The key variable prompting eventual change may well be space, with (unit) cost in second place. Co-operating libraries may form either star-shaped patterns around a dominant central library or a circular association among approximate equals. The dead-weight cost of unused capacity may force libraries to re-define their roles in terms of services to people rather than as repositories of books. User expectation is that libraries should bring books to people rather than *vice versa*. This expectation may not be completely viable, but it is not illogical in terms of saving time.

Under these circumstances, *access* to books is more important to a library than actual *ownership*. The solutions to a library's space and financial problems will lie in some form of better distribution of books among libraries, an on-line network of libraries for resource-sharing (the Ohio plan, represented at this conference by Mr Kilgour), and specialized storage responsibilities.

Mr Fetterman's paper does not go quite far enough to satisfy *Mr Evans*. One omission is the problem of serial subscription, i.e. the integrity of a particular series. Once the series is cut and a subscription cancelled, it may not be worth a library's while to resume that subscription. Also, the difficulties (rivalry aspects) of co-operative acquisition policies are not stressed sufficiently. It should be emphasized that librarians are not apt to disemploy other librarians, and that co-operation in one field (with Library A dominent) may lead to further co-operation in others (in which Library B will dominate).

Mr Evans went on to consider the complaints of earlier speakers about their home university libraries. They had considered libraries from three angles: cost, which implied some evaluation of benefit as well; sociology, involving the expectations of both users and librarians; and politics, the question being who makes the decisions. *Mr Evans* wanted to stress the political point that the base decisions about libraries are not usually made by librarians, who are not masters of their own fates. If libraries are to be rescued, it will be by an alliance between librarians and academicians. The librarians believe that they know what needs doing, but not how to do it or how to make their cases. Economics and economists could help here.

Professor Kindleberger opened the general discussion with a question on possible conflicts between efficiency and sociological considerations as determinants of optimum library size. The optimum size from the economic point of view may be larger than optimal from the sociological one, which stresses friendly relations between librarians and library users. *Mr Evans* admitted that libraries tend to ignore sociological considerations and are, therefore, too large. The Harvard library continues to be used as a model, although it, too, is in trouble with its clientèle. *Mr Kilgour*, however, saw the problem as involving the propensity of large libraries to use rules and procedures more appropriate to smaller ones. He mentioned the 'Farmington plan' for inter-library co-operation in acquisitions, which, he felt, worked only when the material involved was not really wanted by any of the co-operating libraries.

While *Professor Wolfe* expressed himself as impressed particularly with the Ohio experiment, he felt that co-operation might be even more fruitful over shorter distances and would like to see an Ohio plan over a smaller area. He also thought that the price mechanism should be used, with people required to pay for improvement of 'their own' individual libraries.

Professor Shoup expanded on the difficulty he had found in using the Columbia library. One point was its distance from his office. Another was his personal idiosyncrasy—he is a book-*marker*. He felt that libraries are primarily for younger faculty members and students, but that older faculty members should place major reliance on their private collections.

A comment by *Dr Shuchow* was introduced into the record by *Professor M. Perlman*, who suggested that it might merit separate publication. Two important points in the Shuchow comment were that the library had declined as a centre for reading and scholarly activity, and had become a general service institution for the general public.

Professor Blaug commented on the politics of libraries, with special reference to the London School of Economics (LSE). Librarians are low in the LSE pecking order, and most economists are unconcerned with retrieval. As a result, the library is in bad shape, with a high disappearance rate, while it is run by a 'library committee' of senior scholars who do not themselves use it. Its collapse is explainable on essentially the terms presented to the conference by Professor Wolfe—disassociation between interest and control.

Mrs N. Perlman spoke as a discouraged user of libraries. In her editorial capacity, she must constantly write to authors to check their own footnotes and quotations, rather than consulting the University of Pittsburgh library. Use is just too difficult. *Professor Bronfenbrenner* suggested that users typically have somewhat better luck at somewhat inferior libraries, since the particular materials they want are often there but not in great demand. *Professor Morgan* argued that decay, once it begins, tends to be a cumulative process. This applies to specialized, departmental, general, and personal libraries. Once it slips, a library seldom recovers—like an urban transportation system.

Professor Giersch pointed out that shifts of user interest must be considered, and that libraries find it difficult to adapt to them. Among the shifts he had in mind were for articles as against books, for policy as against history, and for discussion papers and survey articles as against standard texts.

Professor Chamley pointed out an undesirable consequence of scholars relying primarily on their private libraries. This reduces their mobility because such libraries are so expensive to move even across town to new offices.

Professor Wolfe wondered whether Professor Blaug's account of LSE conditions was typical of Britain. At Edinburgh, the library committee of senior scholars largely ratifies the decisions of nominally-subordinate librarians. Only one or two people in each department do the ordering, so that the collection is lop-sided; the librarians buy only the more obvious items. Also, staff reading rooms have been replaced, in the interest of 'democracy', by large comfortless general reading rooms where students congregate to keep warm in winter.

Mr Evans said that library budgets had been victims of economy drives. At his university system (State University of New York, or SUNY) there had been drastic cuts in three of the main campuses.

Stronger arguments are needed by the librarians against similar slashes in the future, and it is in providing such arguments that economists should be helpful.

Professor Prest raised the endemic campus issue on general versus departmental libraries on the individual campus. Much pressure has been exerted to centralize libraries on Australian compuses, to save money and satisfy librarians. Faculty members, however, could exercise a greater degree of control over decentralized departmental facilities.

Summing up the discussion, *Mr Fetterman's* first point was that, in the past, librarianship had been more of an art than a science, but that this state of affairs must change as a result of the 'information revolution'. Librarians were finding it difficult to adjust to the new world. Librarians should also realize better than they have, that they cannot acquire or retain complete control over libraries. There is insufficient money and space; the *desideratum* should shift from possession to access.

In this new world, *Mr Fetterman* believes that the proper model for the library is hierarchical. The ordinary library would hold items most in demand; it would be closest to users, easiest of access, richer in duplicate copies. The central library would have storage systems, delivery systems and bibliographic control (cataloguing). He personally approves of the Ohio system, which, in his view, is under-utilized; perhaps old-fashioned librarians are afraid of it.

The non-use problem is very real—unused material must be weeded out and relegated to storage. At *Mr Fetterman's* home library (Pittsburgh) $9 million worth of inventory has been unused in seven years, but the delivery system must be improved so that 'storage' does not mean 'loss'. These are key problems.

Co-operative acquisition by libraries is the logical next step, but it is complex because of rivalries and problems of cost division. Perhaps some sort of algorithms will eventuate from the experience of the next few years.

7 Interlocking Catalogues

Erwin Heidemann
INSTITUT FÜR WELTWIRTSCHAFT

To meet the need for economic information, national and international co-ordination and co-operation are necessary. Within the whole spectrum of library and documentation activities, only the conditions for interlocking catalogues, with a view to networking and interaction, are described in this paper. The existing cataloguing rules and classification scheme for alphabetical and subject cataloguing are discussed, in general, and from the aspect of effective international co-operation and cataloguing. The author mentions the present international activities and plans, including NATIS, in the library and information field. He discusses the advantages and disadvantages of alternative prospects for interlocking cataloguing in economics.

I. THE EXTENT OF PRODUCTION OF ECONOMIC LITERATURE

The present organization of the world-wide system of libraries does not guarantee a complete supply either of literature or of information in all branches of knowledge. This also applies to economics. First of all, I shall make some general remarks on the possibilities and the conditions of co-operation between libraries and then I shall make proposals on how to improve the current systems of information in economics by an international division of labour.

The aim of a catalogue system is to show the holdings of the respective library. No library in the world stocks all the publications, i.e. books, journals, annual reports and newspapers, which economists need. Only a limited number of libraries hold non-conventional literature, i.e. literature published outside of publishing houses. In order to assess the present information deficit of all library catalogues, it would be useful to have an idea of the extent of the production of relevant economic literature.

There are no reliable statistics concerning the production of economic literature in the world. The UNESCO statistics included—in an older classification—a section on economics and social sciences, but it was not made clear whether or not non-conventional literature was taken into consideration. Nevertheless, it is this kind of literature which is of special importance to economists. The reports of firms and organizations and the statistics of international corporations and authorities like the IMF, EEC and OECD, of states, countries or municipalities, are absolutely essential instruments and just as important as non-conventional literature.

In the two largest economic libraries in the Federal Republic of Germany such reports amount to 60 per cent of all new acquisitions. As we have no reliable figures I shall try to estimate the annual extent of new publications which are of interest to economists.

My estimations are based on the UNESCO statistics[1] and on my knowledge of the acquisitions of a large economics library. For monographs, i.e. books and pamphlets, the figure is about 110,000 every year. For works not separately published the figure is still higher. About 130,000–150,000 articles in journals and other periodicals, congress reports etc. are published annually. At present, the total number of new publications including articles on economic subjects amounts to 250,000 per annum.

Of course, it is impossible to be accurate when trying to estimate the extent of economic literature. The border between economics and other subjects is not always clear. The overlapping literature is considerable when we think of such subjects as politics, mathematics, law, sociology or geography, just to mention the most important ones. The interdependence of all branches of knowledge very often requires multidisciplinary research and results in respective publications.

There is another aspect that makes a clear calculation difficult. The catalogues of a large library disclose the process of 'marketing' of the literary production of some authors. You will often find the same essay as a working paper and later on as an article in one or more journals. And it is not surprising to find the same title as a translation or, completely unaltered, in a collection of readings.

II. DEFINITION AND FIXING OF THE AIM

The national, as well as the international, co-operation of libraries and documentation centres could form a comprehensive information system in the future. We shall call such a system interlocking cataloguing. In such a catalogue you would find not only the call number of books etc. but, also, further information on the topic in question. The aim of interlocking cataloguing is to provide a world-wide information system for economic science which would enable every user to get the publication required—book, journal or collection of statistics—or information about economic literature within a short time. In this system the function of the libraries would be the physical storage of the publications. The libraries would acquire the material required, record the necessary data in their catalogues and offer them to the user. The function of documentation centres, on the other hand, would be to inform the user about all

[1] UNESCO *Statistical Yearbook 1972*, pp. 713 ff.

publications after having analyzed and catalogued them. Co-operation between both kinds of institutions is necessary if the retrieval process is to function smoothly.

III. CONDITIONS FOR INTERLOCKING CATALOGUING

(*a*) AUTHOR AND TITLE CATALOGUES

Cataloguing is done in order to allow a search for publications according to bibliographical or subject criteria. The interlocking of bibliographical data on a basis of national and international co-operation would require an adjustment of the working-rules of this process. The formal elements of cataloguing are set down in rules to enable the identical registration of the titles. The larger the stocks of a library, the more complicated the cataloguing rules would have to be. Cataloguing means not only the registration of standard literature, but, also, of reports, etc. with a limited circulation. The latter very often lack a front cover.

Standardization is a necessary condition for the exchange of cataloguing data. What has been achieved up to now? In the past, many people tried to unify the rules of cataloguing, but they had little success. For historical reasons, the libraries in different countries went in different directions. Some European libraries made use of the cataloguing rules of the American Library Association for developing their own rules. In 1967 the Anglo-American Cataloguing Rules (AACR) were re-codified, but were too late to be of use for the new university libraries. In the end, however, new technologies were introduced and people again became interested in standardization.

The International Conference on Cataloguing Principles in 1961, in Paris, gave a strong impulse to the library associations to make new efforts in the direction of standardization. Ten years later, the International Standard Bibliographic Description for Monographs ISBD(M) was accepted by the national libraries and the bibliographic centres. This was a decisive step towards a system of interlocking catalogues. 'Three objectives were considered in establishing a standard form of bibliographic record, to make records from different sources interchangeable, to facilitate their interpretation across language barriers and to facilitate the conversion of records into machine-readable data.'[2]

By means of data processing, formats were produced for the exchange of bibliographic data. Electronic data processing and the establishment of a concordance allow machine transformation, so that different catalogued bibliographical records can be used in a common system.

First of all, we have to mention the MARC-II format which came from the United States. In some European countries deviating versions of

[2] Anderson, Dorothy 'International Standard Bibliographic Description for Monographs Checklists', *UNESCO Bulletin for Libraries*, vol. 28 (1974), No. 1, pp. 34–39.

this system were developed. These national versions proved to be very different from the original system, so that there was still no compatibility. When this became clear, retrogressive efforts were made in order to make possible an international interchange. 'INTERMARC' is one example. This format is still at the development stage.

Based on the MARC format, the documentation centres are trying to develop their own exchange format. MADOC is internationally promoted by the Fédération Internationale de Documentation (FID).

For the natural sciences, special bibliographic formats for input and exchange have been developed and have become internationally accepted.

Due to the sluggishness of library organization, specialists have worked out their own solutions for their respective branches. May I illustrate this by referring to the International Nuclear Information System (INIS), which has been operated by the International Atomic Energy Agency in Vienna since 1972. At the moment our library is testing whether this system can be expanded for the social sciences in order to manage both library cataloguing and retrieval problems. These efforts to achieve an international standardization of formal cataloguing have gradually brought about an assimilation of the different principles.[3] Nevertheless, we are not yet able to recommend to one country that it adopt the rules of another.

At first glance, the proposal that all libraries adopt the Anglo-American Cataloguing Rules may be tempting. But these rules, which were re-codified in 1967, now need to be revised again for internal reasons within the Anglo-American sector.[4] The rules must be adapted to the principles laid down in the ISBD. In addition, it will be somewhat difficult, for all non-English speaking countries, as all kinds of names must be in English and not in the original language. But only the original formulation can be used in an internationally uniform way. The AACR does not always require uniform headings. Identical names and titles are not infrequently represented by several headings. In the United States this problem, which hampers data processing, is solved partially by printing catalogue cards with all necessary references. Nevertheless, this would interfere with the European habit of sorting data by machine.

In the Federal Republic of Germany, all additional suggestions for national and international co-operation are based on the new rules for

[3] Verona, Eva *Statement of Principles: Adopted at the International Conference on Cataloguing Principles*, Paris, October 1961. Annotated ed. with commentary and examples by Eva Verona assisted by others. Definitive ed. International Federation of Library Associations (Committee on Cataloguing) (London, 1971).

[4] Kaltwasser, Franz Georg 'Die Regeln für die alphabetische Katalogisierung (RAK)'. Bericht, vorgetragen auf der Schlussitzung des 64. Deutschen Bibliothekartages, p. 153; in: *Organisation und Technik in Bibliotheken,* (Frankfurt 1975). *Zeitschrift für Bibliothekswesen und Bibliographie,* Sonderheft 21.

alphabetical cataloguing ('Regeln für die alphabetische Katalogisierung' = RAK).

We have, however, already encountered considerable difficulties in obtaining recognition for the RAK in our country, so that there will be little chance of their being internationally accepted as a basis for alphabetical cataloguing. The librarians in the FRG would be pleased, of course, if this happened. But as the extent of literary production in the German language is comparatively small and the costs of reorganization of all libraries would be high, we will have to drop this idea for the time being.

Perhaps there are some prospects for an agreement in the long run. 'Up to now we have not been successful in attaining a total international standardization. First of all there are no rules which would make that possible without difficulties, as all of us to a certain extent are fixed to our own traditions. This may be a task for the twenty-first century and requires an international agreement.[5]

(*b*) SUBJECT CATALOGUING

For the subject analysis of publications which is necessary for the arrangement of titles in bibliographies and catalogues, there are, in principle, two possibilities: subject headings or classification. Both solutions have advantages and disadvantages. In the catalogues of the libraries for economic science in Western Europe the subject heading principle dominates. Cataloguing elements are subject headings and/or keywords and regional terms. The users of this system need not be familiarized with them; the data required is in alphabetic order. Disadvantages are created by language problems: terms denoting a similar subject may be separated by the alphabetical order. Definitions might be lacking and synonyms might not be excluded. Foreigners not acquainted with the specific language will have their problems with this system. For interlocking catalogues this kind of subject cataloguing would be suitable if we could use only one language.

Of all the classification systems, the Universal Decimal Classification is the most well-known. Economics are part of this system. There are no language problems here as, according to an international agreement, all terms are expressed by numbers. There are, however, some disadvantages in this system because, for most research workers, it is not sufficiently differentiated and new terms cannot be included quickly enough because of lacking flexibility. The mechanism of international agreement takes much time, and the main objection is that this classification reflects a hierarchy which is somewhat controversial.

There are various other classification schemes used by national libraries and bibliographic centres, which are widely adopted in their

[5] Kaltwasser, *op. cit.*

respective countries. Users and librarians pick out of the lists of new publications those they are interested in. For economic reasons or because of lack of their own specialists, university libraries very often take over the schemes dominating in their countries. The libraries which subscribe to the tape or card services of the Library of Congress (LoC), are acquainted with the classification of the LoC. As this classification is at the same time, of great importance for the shelving of the stocks of the libraries concerned, you can imagine the limits of this system.

The information requirements of researchers cannot be satisfied by classification schemes, because their categories are too broad and not precise enough for special fields of study.

Let me now mention those specific schedules that are used for economics in the internationally known bibliographies. The titles are selected and arranged according to subject by economists and, thus, research workers are able to inform themselves about new publications in their special branch. As a matter of fact, all bibliographies only will contain a part of all the new economic literature and, accordingly, the classification will systematize only this part. In spite of this, these bibliographies are very useful for interlocking cataloguing as there are points of application for international co-operation.

The *Journal of Economic Literature* is the economics periodical with the widest distribution in this field. Its classification system includes newer developments in economic science. In this journal, published by the American Economic Association (AEA), foreign titles are taken into consideration, so the idea of international co-operation in the bibliographic field has already found some form of expression. It is very possible that the editors have arranged this symposium in order to broaden the connections and to improve the bibliographic situation on an international basis. Another bibliography of the AEA is the 'Index of Economic Articles in Journals and Collective Volumes'. When the classification of this bibliography was introduced it was the most up-to-date in its field, so many institutes adopted it.

For one bibliography, the *International Bibliography of Social Sciences*: *International Bibliography of Economics*, the collection of titles and editing is already organized on an international basis. This bibliography, which is published yearly, contains 8000 titles per annum, and is edited by the International Committee for Social Science Information and Documentation in Paris. The classification schedule is given in English and French. Economists from different countries and continents are working on this system together.

A further bibliography with systematic classification in two languages is the *Bibliographie der Wirtschaftswissenschaften* (*Bibliography of Economics*) edited by the Kiel Library. Here we have a collection of 10,000 titles selected annually from a total of 50,000 catalogued titles.

The most important bibliographies in economic science, arranged by subject headings, are published by the Public Affairs Information Service which works in close co-operation with the Research Division of the New York Public Library. Their comprehensive *Bulletin* is restricted to publications in the English language. Since 1968 this service has been widened. In the *Foreign Language Index* the journals of some European countries are analyzed. Here we have a good combination of an effective library, on the one hand, and an information service in economics on the other. One of their two bibliographies is already produced by means of electronic data processing. Thus, we have some idea of the possibilities for co-operation with other similarly organized institutes.

A good basis for interlocking catalogues would be a unified system for subject cataloguing which is internationally approved and accepted. But, even if we had such a system, we should have to be aware of the fact that it will be nearly impossible to get completely objective analyses. And even if we worked out detailed instructions, the selection of criteria to characterize a publication would be a personal one.

Each library participating in an interlocking system will thus have to make some decisions. A library must either completely take over the subject cataloguing done by other institutes, or it must revise it for its own purposes. The alternative would be subject cataloguing itself, without the advantages of a division of labour.

A good and useful method of processing subject data in a computerized information system for retrieval processes is the application of thesauruses. A thesaurus combines both forms of analysis, the systematic and the alphabetical. For libraries and documentation centres collecting publications on economics, the *Macro-Thesaurus* of the OECD has become the basis of their own subject arrangements, either by adoption or by adjustment to their respective purposes. In the German Democratic Republic the *Thesaurus Ökonomie* has been developed, but we do not know to what extent this system has been adopted. It is universally based and very suitable for the subject analysis of literature in the socialist countries.

The following conditions are necessary for effective international co-operation in cataloguing:

an agreement on the principles of bibliographical description,
an agreement on the form of subject cataloguing and/or classification, and
the application of modern technical equipment.

Only by means of modern, data processing technology will it be possible to record the extensive literary production quickly enough. Centralized cataloguing as practised up to now has shown us how important the time factor is. In particular, economists need their information within a short time, whether they are working in university institutes, in public administration or in industrial enterprises. Only large libraries can stock extensive collections. And such libraries work, necessarily, with a certain sluggishness when they catalogue in the conventional way. Here we have one explanation why—apart from some local attempts—there has been, up to now, no central cataloguing and no interlocking activities in economics. Nevertheless, we should endeavour to bring about a world-wide information system in economics which should be:

as comprehensive as possible (principle of completeness),
as actual as possible (principle of actuality),
as inexpensive as possible (principle of economy-of-effort).

IV. PROPOSALS FOR INTERLOCKING CATALOGUING

(*a*) EXISTING INTERNATIONAL ACTIVITIES AND PLANS

There are already some networks working successfully, co-operating either on a regional or a subject basis. Some of them have already been described at this conference.

Economists are mainly interested in subject-oriented information systems and their improvement, and not so much in general library and documentation systems. Since economic literature is part of literary production as a whole, economics would also benefit from a well-functioning library organization.

In September, 1974, in Paris, UNESCO, in co-operation with the international archivists', librarians', and documentalists' associations, organized an 'International Conference on the Planning of National Documentation, Library and Archives Infrastructures'.[6] The goals which were formulated at this conference comprise all of the important requirements of a co-operative information system. For economics, no special recommendations have yet been made. The references to existing world-wide interconnected systems, e.g. to INIS (atomic energy) or AGRIS (agriculture), are, however, just as valid for economics. Only for a section of economics has preliminary work begun. As can easily be imagined, the developing countries represent the weakest link in the information chain. Information specialists from several continents met in June, 1974, in Ottawa at the suggestion of the International Development Research Centre (IDRC) and in co-operation with the OECD and the UNESCO. They dealt with proposals for the establishment of an international information system for the development sciences.[7] The suggestions which were worked out at this conference take into con-

[6] Intergovernmental Conference on the Planning of National Documentation, Library and Archives Infrastructures, Paris, 23–27 September 1974. *UNESCO Bulletin for Libraries*, vol. 29 (1975), No. 1, pp. 2–15.

[7] Brandreth, M. Summary Record of the Meeting on the Feasibility of an International Information System for the Development Sciences (DEVSIS), (Ottawa, 1974). (DEVSIS W. P. 8 Rev. 1).

sideration the particular circumstances and information requirements of the developing countries. A directorate committee was appointed to work out a plan as well as a feasibility study. No results are known as yet. The principles of the assignment to the directorate committee of DEVSIS are, to a great extent, identical with the demands of the Paris conference in September, 1974.

(*b*) NATIS

In each country, a 'National Information System' (NATIS) is to be established, where all library and documentation activities would be merged and co-ordinated. The corresponding demand of the conference was:

> Objective 7—Planning the organizational structure of NATIS
>
> 'the functions of all documentation, library and archives services should be co-ordinated through a central body (or bodies) to form the national information system (NATIS), so as to ensure the optimum use of available resources and the maximum contribution to the cultural, social and economic development of each nation.'[8]

The fundamental principles were described in the following way:

> 'Effective co-operation between all these networks and services should be promoted, particularly for the production of the national bibliography, and in the following fields: co-operative acquisition of materials, centralized processing, use of reprographic, audio-visual and other equipment, and translation and preservation facilities. Planning the development of NATIS is therefore a complex operation; prerequisites are acceptance at governmental level of its vital role, analysis of the existing physical and human resources and of user needs. The targets for this planning are: (a) elaboration of development plans for each of the institutional networks composing the system; (b) co-ordination of the network plans so as to achieve a comprehensive plan for the development of NATIS; (c) incorporation of the comprehensive plan and its components in the national over-all and sectoral development plans; (d) harmonization of the NATIS development plan, particularly in specialized fields, with international aims for world-wide information systems.'[9]

In Objective 12—Universal Bibliographic Control (UBC)—the way to the realization of the long-term programme is shown. It is premature to hope for early results from these international plans. To begin with, international centres must be founded which have to carry out the introduction of all of the necessary standardization in their own countries.

[8] Intergovernmental Conference, p. 7.
[9] Intergovernmental Conference, p. 8.

Librarians are convinced that rationalization and international division of labour could help to solve the pressing problems. Still, very little is being done. To carry out such plans will be more difficult in a federal state, where the competence for library and information tasks is decentralized, than in a centrally organized state, where the political representatives are convinced that such steps have to be taken. Only when all states are provided with the necessary infrastructure and institutions, can international adjustment and co-operation begin. Substantial and political difficulties will be mastered, eventually. Even now, in some countries, effective co-operation has been brought about, which shows us what can be done. In Great Britain, several independent institutions have been merged to constitute the 'British Library' which offers improved services. In the United States, the Office of Science Information Service of the National Science Foundation has presented seventeen specific research and development targets.[10] In 1974, the National Commission on Libraries and Information Science published 'A National Programme for Library and Information Service'. The Congress of the United States is expected to take up the problem in the course of this year and to grant the means required for national co-operation. The USSR and other socialist countries have been organizing co-ordinated national information systems for some time. In the FRG a national plan for the promotion of information and documentation is being developed. Economics is one of sixteen subjects for which an information centre is to be founded.

V. ADVANTAGES AND DISADVANTAGES OF THE ALTERNATIVE PROPOSALS FOR INTERLOCKING CATALOGUING

Interlocking cataloguing can, in principle, be realized in different ways, i.e.

by a world-wide hierarchical system,
by world-wide co-operation of national centres,
by a subject-oriented hierarchical system,
by co-operation on subject basis of competent institutions.

(*a*) WORLD-WIDE HIERARCHICAL SYSTEM

One large institution would have to take over all of the tasks of acquisition, cataloguing and user services and share the results with the other participants. This would mean that one institution would have to acquire and process all publications of every country in every language on every

[10] NSF Floats New Approach to IR Support. Information, Retrieval and Library Automation. Mt. Airy. Vol. 10 (1974), No. 5, p. 1–3.

subject. Few will support this solution, because the disadvantages obviously outweigh the advantages. The advantage would be to have one location for all publications. But this task would have to be carried out by a gigantic, hardly operable organization. Experiences with large libraries have been rather discouraging. It takes much longer to process a book in a large library than in a medium-sized or small one. Acquisition offices must be set up in every country and provided with the necessary authority to collect all publications. Even now, copyright laws do not suffice to secure the acquisition of all publications by the national libraries. How much more difficult would it be to buy all publications in order to send them to the centre.

For cataloguing, as much personnel would be needed as all the national libraries need together. Specialists would be needed for languages and subjects. It might be possible to solve the organizational problems of such a huge library, but, obviously, processing would be more complicated than in smaller working units. Accordingly, cataloguing would take up more time.

The following advantages of the hierarchical system can be listed:

Books would be processed according to consistent rules. These rules would be determined by the processing institution itself. No agreements with others would have to be sought.

For all participants of the system, cataloguing would not cost anything. They would only have to take over cataloguing data in a form which suits them. Costs would arise merely for the transport of data from the centre to the participant. In any case, these costs would be lower than the costs for individual cataloguing.

Each participant could depend on a comprehensive pool of bibliographical information which would allow him to select what is of importance to him. He could base his acquisition decisions on the most comprehensive information. The acquired works could be used right away, because no time is needed for cataloguing.

The following disadvantages must not be forgotten:

It cannot be guaranteed that all publications will be acquired.

Acquisition is very expensive.

Additional transportation to the centre is necessary, which means delay.

Large working units require more time for processing.

(*b*) WORLD-WIDE CO-OPERATION OF NATIONAL CENTRES

The introduction of NATIS and UBC could substantially further co-operative interlocking. First, a national centre in every country has to be established. Its task would be to acquire all the publications of that country by means of copyright laws, and to process and catalogue them according to uniform rules. In every country, each publication would be catalogued only once. The national centre would provide everybody in that country with all required data. Since international norms for cataloguing have been created, the international exchange of cataloguing data is possible. This exchange of data would be at the disposal of all national centres.

National institutions are better able to control the publications of their own countries. They can acquire them quickly and, usually, at low cost. Since the capacity of these libraries would be limited to the national literature, the working units would not be too large. Each national or international participant of this co-operative system could select titles according to his wishes and, after acquisition, request the pertinent cataloguing data.

It is a disadvantage that only publications of the respective country would be readily available. To extend this system to a world-wide basis, the national centres would need equipment for information transfer. They would have to take over and process the cataloguing data of other countries, in order to make them accessible to users in their particular country. If the rules and norms were not completely homogeneous, cataloguing data would have to be transformed in order to integrate them into the national system. This means additional expense.

The advantages of the co-operative system are:

Acquisitions in the particular country are rather likely to be complete.
Actuality can be kept in collecting and cataloguing.
Cataloguing will be done only in the publishing country.
There are no language barriers in the country.
Transportation costs for use in the country are low.

The disadvantages are:

In order to establish an exchange of data, an agreement about cataloguing principles must have been reached. This concerns the bibliographical description as well as subject cataloguing and/or classification. It would not be easy to reach such an agreement.

The costs of transportation and transformation of the output of other institutions would be high.

There would be difficulties in using data and books across national border lines.

(*c*) SUBJECT-ORIENTED HIERARCHICAL SYSTEM

The proposals for interlocking cataloguing which have been described up to now do not pertain to a special subject, they are concerned with the entire literary production of all of the countries of the world. But interlocking cataloguing systems for a special subject, e.g. for economics, are also conceivable. The task of acquiring the entire material relevant to economics, of cataloguing it and storing it for use, could be assigned to one large library for economics. This library would have to possess all of the existing material in all languages. The advantage of such a library would be that specialists could select the works significant for economics from the great mass of literature. The extent of the literary production in economics amounts to no more than could be handled by a large library. This central special library would have to have an acquisition agent in every country for the transmission of bibliographical data to the centre and for the acquisition of publications according to directions from the centre.

The above-mentioned disadvantages of the universal hierarchical system also apply to this proposal. Costs for acquisition and transportation will be high; so will the loss of time. In this central special library all publications on economics would be available, catalogued according to consistent rules. Cataloguing data would be accessible to all interested libraries, institutes or other organizations. The data could be supplied as catalogue cards, on tape, or in any other suitable form, so that these libraries could use them to catalogue their own book stock or decide about new acquisitions.

In particular, there would be the following advantages:

All economic publications would be available in one place.

Cataloguing and/or classification would be done according to uniform principles.

Each publication would be processed not only according to library principles, but, also, according to principles relevant to the subject and to research demands.

In this hierarchical system all publications would be catalogued only once. Each participant could select from the pool and, thus, utilize the advantages of centralized processing.

Co-operation with other documentation centres would be simplified.

The central library should also possess a comprehensive documentation centre.

The first three objections to a central universal library also hold true for the central special library. It would be even more difficult to attain completeness. A large amount of non-conventional literature is more or less confidential and not easily sent out of the country, as experience shows. Using literature which is available only in the central library, necessarily implies delay. The indispensable speed in the transmission of information could be attained only by very expensive technical equipment (television satellites?).

(*d*) CO-OPERATION ON SUBJECT BASIS OF COMPETENT INSTITUTIONS

Compared with the perfect systems which have been described up to now, co-operation in the area of economics between existing large libraries, bibliographical institutions and documentation centres seems to be a more realistic concept. Each library collects only a small part of the publications of the whole world. To a great extent, each collects and catalogues identical titles. All institutions use their own cataloguing rules and classification system. There is as yet no co-ordination. In comparison with the information requirements, the progress so far is quite unsatisfactory. The information supply could be substantially improved, without any additional expense, merely by co-ordination. To this end, partners must agree to use the same cataloguing rules, so that they can utilize each other's cataloguing data. Data collection could be restricted to the titles published in the respective countries in correspondence with the NATIS proposals. Since the information systems for development sciences (DEVSIS) is not yet in existence, those countries with a highly developed information infrastructure should be commissioned to supply data to those countries which do not yet possess efficient libraries and documentation centres. Disadvantages, as far as completeness, speed, and transportation costs are concerned, have been mentioned earlier. They will weigh less, if useful information can be obtained this way.

A division of labour would be possible in different regions. The records of United States publications, for instance, could be collected quite comprehensively by co-operation between the New York Public Library with the *Journal of Economic Literature* and the Public Affairs Information Service. When this information is supplemented by the records of government publications of the Superintendent of Documents, the United States Government Printing Office, and the accordingly classified titles of the LOC, a comprehensive information pool for economics would be achieved. These catalogue data could be distributed to every interested institution in the form of catalogue cards, a printed bibliography or on tape.

In Europe, the British Library of Political and Economic Science at the London School of Economics could collect and process all British and Commonwealth (or Sterling bloc) publications. The Bibliothek des Instituts für Weltwirtschaft could do the same for German-speaking as well as for other European countries. The above-mentioned documentary activities could also be supplemented by each other, so that information would be much more complete than has hitherto been possible. This concerns (I propose) the following bibliographies:

Economic Titles, edited by the Library and Documentation Center of the Economic Information Service, Ministry of Economic Affairs, The Hague, the bibliographies which are edited by the International Committee for Social Science Information Documentation in Paris, and

the *Bibliographie der Wirtschaftswissenschaften*, edited by the Bibliothek des Instituts für Weltwirtschaft.

But co-ordination is not only a matter of common sense. Commercial interests are also involved. Private publishers editing bibliographies must be taken into account.

Some institutions already use electronic data processing equipment for cataloguing and/or operating special information systems. This could be of essential importance to the planned system.

The thing to be done now is to convince the responsible statesmen and librarians that they themselves will profit considerably by the results of international co-operation and division of labour, without being faced with exorbitant additional expenses. Who will dare to take the first step and begin?

Comments by Billie I. Salter (Yale University)

Dr Erwin Heidemann's paper presents the broad range of problems that exist and must be faced in considering the options for the establishment of systems to provide universal control of the literature in general, and the economics literature in particular. Not the least of these is the profusion of competing schemes now being employed and developed to catalogue and classify the full range of library materials.

It is doubtful that the international co-ordination of library and documentation activities for the development sciences alone, or for the economics literature as a whole, would be well served by developing new specialized networks between libraries. I question whether this is a feasible solution to the problem of controlling this literature.

Co-ordinating activities in the industrialized countries, where very strong academic, government and research institutions support important libraries in the fields concerned, presents its own problems. Quite apart from these is the complicated problem of maintaining access to the publications of governments and research institutions located in the developing countries where national bibliographies and other such tools often do not yet exist. We all have had experience in trying to trace key sources based on references passed along by word of mouth with the frequent result that the researcher must travel to the country concerned. (And, I suspect, these trips are sometimes followed by a reluctance on the part of the researcher to share these elusive sources with the library on his return!)

While supportive of the goals of co-ordination in principle, it is true that economics libraries, like research collections in many other disciplines, have also been reluctant to burden themselves with time-consuming co-ordination commitments to shakily-organized or poorly-financed consortia, especially when this means that they must relinquish autonomy or compromise local or national standards, and special retrieval needs, in order to co-operate. Financial constraints restrict them to service goals formulated in response to immediate and long-term expectations from their own communities of users for the on-site acquisition of materials, as well as the local documentation of those received. Little time or money has been left to devote to the study of organizational alternatives in the absence of other directives from parent bodies.

There is also the question of assigning priorities in selecting out a discipline or group of subjects for special treatment from within a large research collection. The political scientists might be the first to say, in the United States, that they at least have gone far enough to compile a thesaurus designed '. . . to be one of the underpinings [*sic*] of an information system for political science'.[1]

Improved access to the literature, coupled with a real financial benefit, does tempt libraries already burdened by shrinking budgets, rising prices and the growth of the literature. A striking example of this in the United States is the recently-organized Research Libraries Group formed by the libraries of Columbia, Harvard and Yale Universities and the research libraries of the New York Public Library which '. . . are developing a programme designed to rationalize collection building, reciprocal reader access, bibliographic control, information

[1] Beck, Carl, Dym, Eleanor D. and McKechnie, J. Thomas, *Political Science Thesaurus* (Washington, D.C.: American Political Science Association, 1975), p. 2.

delivery and computer applications for participating libraries and their clientele. Whereas the initial effort involves four libraries with all of their diversity and complications, it has always been the desire of the initiators of this consortium to open its membership to other like libraries when the project is firmly launched'.[2] Its Bibliographic Center will '. . . maintain extensive runs of national and specialized bibliographies, library catalogues, and similar tools to aid in locating publications desired by readers in participating libraries'.[3] The combining of the strengths of the catalogues to these great libraries will be a giant first step toward co-ordinating access to the literature. Papers on other networks and co-operative systems are being presented at this symposium.

The International Federation of Library Associations established its International Office for Universal Bibliographic Control in July of 1974 and it is already making progress in acting as a liaison about standards, publishing recommendations, and promoting the use of standards.[4] It holds that 'the pattern for the future is the creation of national bibliographic organizations with comprehensive computer-based systems for controlling internal operations, producing national bibliographic records, and transmitting and receiving bibliographic information in national, regional and international networks'.[5]

Consortia are being developed nationally or regionally throughout the world, but they cannot become interactive on an international basis unless compromises occur in establishing shared standards for descriptive and subject entry. Compatibility is the basic foundation for effective communication through computer applications. Differences in handling geographic and personal names, along with other problems of form, can be resolved. Interaction can be even more of a realistic goal among the large libraries if computerized systems can accommodate special satellite collections within their superstructures by accepting differing levels of subject analysis and distinguishing between them.

Let us start out by not burdening interdisciplinary superstructures with demands for new levels of subject analysis, but not neglect to build into national and regional schemes the possibility of detailed subject analysis. When we do not even have control of the first level of retrieval via broad subject, how can we proceed to complicate this first and fundamental effort? Is comprehensive coverage desirable enough to justify the cost?

An extension of personalized service can attractively supplement the basic 'interlocking catalogue'. This combination is discussed by the Librarian of the National Central Library, London, Maurice B. Line, in his paper, 'Information Requirements in the Social Sciences'[6] in which he states 'The preference for informal services on the part of many users; the immense personal variations between users, even within disciplines and environments, and the consequent need for flexibility; the difficulties of using formal services (unawareness, ter-

[2] Rogers, Rutherford D. *Report of the University Librarian, 1973–1974*. Bulletin of Yale University, series 71, no. 1 (New Haven, Conn. 1975), p. 5.

[3] *Ibid.*, p. 6.

[4] Anderson, Dorothy *Universal Bibliographic Control—a Long Term Policy, a Plan for Action* (Pullach bei München: Verlag Dokumentation, 1974), pp. 47–48.

[5] *Ibid.*, p. 83.

[6] 'Conference on Access to Knowledge and Information in the Social Sciences and Humanities, New York, 1972.' *Proceedings* . . . (Flushing, N.Y.: Queens College Press, 1974), pp. 146–158.

minology, etc.); the probable greater complexity of future formal services, especially if they are computer-based; and the sheer amount of time required for information hunting all seem to point in one direction: the deliberate development of informal personal services, exploiting on the user's behalf the formal services which can then be developed to any level of complexity."[7] Very complex factors—human, financial and technical—must be considered.

The co-ordination of interactive catalogues, personalized services, and standard bibliographic sources (subject indexes, special bibliographies, citation indexes and others) will improve service to economists. Such combinations could develop very satisfactorily, even if libraries go no further than the first broad level of subject analysis in defining a base for retrieval.

The more librarians learn about the needs and desires of users through personal contact, user studies and symposia of this kind, the better able they will be to evolve effective and balanced services. We must do more to foster financial and moral support of the primary goals of universal bibliographic control from the users of libraries as well as from the private and public agencies to which libraries are affiliated.

[7] *Ibid.*, p. 155.

Summary of the Discussion

Mrs N. Perlman presented Dr Heidemann's paper on the inter-relationships between different library and other subject-matter classification schemes in cataloguing technical economic materials. The explosion of literature now amounts to 250,000 titles per year, of which 60 per cent are not in 'standard' works. International co-operation is necessary for this volume of information to be retrievable. The ultimate aim is a comprehensive classification and sub-classification system keyed to all languages with all categories translatable. Meanwhile, citations need to be standardized, and this has not been achieved. (The natural sciences apparently do better in this regard). The citation system may be alphabetical or numerical. In any case, detailed thesauri are required to permit the non-specialist librarian to decide which term (in one system) corresponds to which term (in another system). There already are international systems in existence, including those used by the Institut für Weltwirtschaft library at Kiel, by UNESCO, by PAIS, and by JEL for the various sub-disciplines of economics. Dr Heidemann would like to see the acceptance of a single system, with computerized equipment permitting its use by libraries retaining other systems. This ideal system might be an international one worked out by an international body. It might involve the co-operation of national centres and the publication of an international thesaurus keying national classifications to each other. The national agencies might alternatively be, *ad hoc* subject-oriented groups of specialists, or representatives of the major libraries in the various countries. In any case, what is needed is a set of common, or at least consistent, cataloguing rules.

While *Mrs Perlman* approved Dr Heidemann's desire to make libraries more efficient, she confessed some uncertainty as to the optimal degree of co-operation, in view of the high economic and social costs of instituting such a system and changing it once adopted. She interpreted the sense of the conference as likewise sceptical.

As an example of the difficulties involved, even with a relatively simple straight-forward issue, *Mrs Perlman* cited the suggestion by Professor Machlup for 'author-title' standardization. Professor Machlup would like to see all catalogue cards and all journal and book references include the full first name of authors, plus the publisher's name, the place, and year of publication. In the case of articles, Professor Machlup would like to see the title of the article in quotation marks and the full title of the book or journal in italics, as in the conventional US system. This suggestion, particularly with respect to the full first name, has met with some opposition, because, as compared with less complete systems, it increases cataloguing and printing costs far beyond expectations. JEL experience with an attempt to verify full names indicates that it is sufficiently costly to involve a trade-off of a larger databank for accuracy. On a more important level, namely subject indexing, co-ordination presents serious, although not insupperable problems: inconsistences between 'key words' and numerical bases; the problems involved in technical vocabularies and between languages; and the biases in different classification methods.

Dr Otto, in the first interpellation from the floor, summarized her previous written comment. Co-operation in cataloguing has been under way in Germany, and author-title standardization has been largely accomplished. Subject classification is, unfortunately, lagging. The Kiel group has tried to spread its own system, which has been difficult for other libraries to use. On the Machlup proposals, Dr Otto added that good international practice calls for the full first names of senior authors only, and that the desirability of full citation of publisher, date and place of publication are all recognized.

Mr Evans' view was that authors should provide such information themselves; librarians and editors have too much other work to do. He is himself working on committees which worry about standard forms for classifying journals, because no standardization exists at the production end. He also mentioned a proposal that journals not be listed separately, but working papers and articles fed into central agencies for classification and transmission.

Professor Blaug, commenting on the Machlup proposal, said that many difficulties would be avoided if authors read the University of Chicago *Manual of Style*. The listing of first names, however, should be up to the author; why bother librarians? *Mrs N. Perlman*, however, responded that each editor may have his own style which may differ from the Chicago one. Furthermore, *Professor Coase* commented, the standard citation style in the law differs from that in economics; it works well in the *Journal of Law and Economics* which he edits.

Professor M. Perlman referred to citation as a special and ultra-complex issue. While full names add to cost, full identification of authors is necessary and may be difficult in name-change cases. In the United States the copyright office has imposed its own rules. He thought that Dr Heidemann's most interesting point had been the suggestion that standardization be extended to subject-matter classification, and mentioned a written comment by Miss Salter opposing any 'freezing' of subject categories. But he, himself, doubted that a standard system would have to be forced. If a system had wide acceptability, people would be aware of it and use it voluntarily.

Dr Otto said that if central authorities take over cataloguing within individual countries, unification may proceed naturally. *Mrs Schwartz* pointed out that authors are often over-ruled by editors on such matters.

Professor Meyriat agreed with several previous speakers on the desirability of co-operation. In his view, UNESCO and other international agencies have provided a basis for standardization, and have laid the groundwork for international agreement on a compromise basis. As for standard subject cataloguing, this will, of course, be difficult, but thesauri, such as are used by ILO, will be useful. No economic thesaurus is yet available, but one is under way; the preparation process needs more co-operation from economists. Publication is planned in English and French; a German edition is also possible.

Dr Heidemann agreed with Professor Meyriat on his thesaurus proposal for key words in economic terminology.

Professor Wolfe was more pessimistic. Economists, he said, have no clear views on these subjects. The main trouble is with pamphlets and working papers, where standardization is particularly lacking. He did not think that conference, as such, should take a stand in favour of even the Machlup proposals.

Mr Kilgour felt that computers dominate bibliographers, and that no great progress could be expected, short of a machine-readable format for bibliographical references. He mentioned the UNISIS manual as a first step in this direction, but as unsatisfactory and obsolete.

There followed some discussion as to the effect of bibliographical reform and inter-library co-operation on the number of publications. *Dr Weise* inquired whether better bibbliography could reduce duplication. *Mrs Schwartz* felt it might particularly reduce the number of books found necessary. *Professor Giersch* said that the loss would not be great, because we would have working and discussion papers instead. *Professor Kindleberger*, on the other hand, worried about quality. Books and journal articles, he felt, passed a more rigorous market test than did discussion papers, commissioned papers, working papers, and *Festschrift* contributions. The effect on quality was, he thought, obvious, and the need was for academic contraception.

Mr Fetterman raised the issue of the effect on the publishing industry, which was not represented at the conference. He felt that inter-library co-operation, in particular, was already having its effects in the form of smaller runs of even good books, which were going out of print unusually rapidly.

Mr Kilgour quoted Mr Benjamin, President of the McGraw-Hill publishing company, as believing that the scientific monograph as a form of publication may be obsolete as early as 1980, to be replaced by the 'twigging' of technical-journal articles. Although not an economist, Mr Kilgour expected something similar to happen in economics.

Professor Giersch worried about language problems, linguistic inconsistencies, and the treatment of new words in standardized bibliography. *Dr Bartenbach* replied that computer technology was easing such transitions as that between 'Negro', 'coloured', and 'black', but *Mr Evans* said that the case was more difficult when a word is split up in consequence of scholarly advances.

Dr Heidemann felt himself in general agreement with most of the discussion of his paper, and felt that the conference should issue some sort of policy statement in aid of international co-operation in economic bibliography. He went on to express surprise that the figures on the number of publications do not terrify people. No place on earth keeps more than one-fifth of the new output; at the same time, there is a great deal of duplication, and the same material appears in two or more publications. (*Professor M. Perlman* interposed the comment that the Library of Congress in Washington has a larger proportion, but not in readily accessible form. *Professor Morgan* added that a great deal of material is forgotten or overlooked because of turnover within academic departments.)

Dr Heidemann added a comment on the Machlup suggestions, which he felt more useful for large catalogues than for smaller ones. (*Dr Otto* noted the tendency of catalogues to expand with time.) In *Dr Heidemann's* view, also, electronic data processing would reduce the importance of Professor Machlup's problem, and render his proposals somewhat obsolescent.

8 Organizing an Inter-Library Network: The State University of New York Approach

Glyn T. Evans
STATE UNIVERSITY OF NEW YORK

The State University of New York is a multicampus university which, in response to the fiscal and operational problems which are facing higher education, is developing a library network. Proposals to increase the cost efficiency and cost effectiveness of the libraries are made, and some of the unknown elements, including library output measurement, collection size formulae, and the balance of emphasis between the collection or archival and user service functions are discussed.

Brief statements of project description and progress are made and a prognosis is offered.

I INTRODUCTION

This paper reports on the work which has been done, is being done, or is proposed, to transform the libraries of the State University of New York into a library network. The paper describes the University, the environment in which it is operating, and the problems which its libraries face. The theoretical basis for the work is outlined and the difficulties which are encountered are reported. Finally, progress on each project is reported and a prognosis is offered.

II STATE UNIVERSITY OF NEW YORK

The State University of New York is a public funded University in New York State. It is the largest University in the world, with 350,000 student enrolment. The University is a centrally co-ordinated network of 64 campuses distributed within the 40,000 square miles of the State. It is comprised of four University Centres, offering programmes to Ph.D. level, four Medical Schools, thirteen four-year Colleges of Arts and Science, offering programmes to the Master's level, six two-year Agriculture and Technical Colleges, a number of specialized colleges (Maritime, Ceramics, Agriculture, etc.) and twenty-seven two-year Community Colleges specialized in vocational and technical education.

The University does not provide public higher education in Metropolitan New York, where public higher education is the responsibility of City University. There is a very strong tradition of private academic education in the State.

Administratively, the University is directly responsible to the State Legislature. Its policies are defined by a publicly-appointed Board of Trustees. Each campus is autonomous within the planning and administrative guidelines established by the University. The Central Administration is a very small group, charged with co-ordinating the activities of the campuses. My office reports to both the Vice Chancellor for Academic Programmes and the Assistant Vice Chancellor for Computer Systems Development.

This paper does not specifically highlight the disciplinary problem of economics. Rather, the paper discusses the problems of developing and implementing a general framework for library network development in which specific disciplinary problems are recognized but are handled within a total system of service.

III PROBLEMS

The University and its libraries face several classes of problem:

(*a*) FISCAL

The general problem of inflation in prices is further compounded by a diminishing tax base in New York State. This is coupled to one of the highest tax rates in the United States and a legislature which is reluctant to raise taxes to even higher levels.

The total State University budget is close to $630 million and in Fiscal Year 1975–76 the increases in the budget did not cover price increases. The total library budget is approximately $28 million, of which some $8 million is spent on acquisitions. In 1975–76, for the first time, the acquisitions budgets at three of the University Centre campuses were cut in the number of dollars allocated. A total of $636,000 was taken from the budgets based on the application of a collection size formula, and, at all the others, increases in dollars did not cover price increases. The University operates on a 'base plus' budgeting system, rather than having to rejustify every dollar each year, and, therefore, such cuts are highly unusual.

Another aspect of the fiscal problem, that of the general increase in the unit costs of services, is now, following the excellent studies by Baumol and Marcus[1] (see Figure 8.1). These facts, when placed in the general

[1] Baumol, William J. and Marcus Matityahu. *Economics of Academic Libraries* (Washington, DC: American Council on Education, 1973).

fiscal context, place the libraries in a perilous budgetary position. It is, for the immediate future, unrealistic to expect budgetary relief. We can not buy our way out of trouble and, therefore, the libraries must, as a matter of extreme urgency, increase both the cost efficiency and cost effectiveness of their programmes.

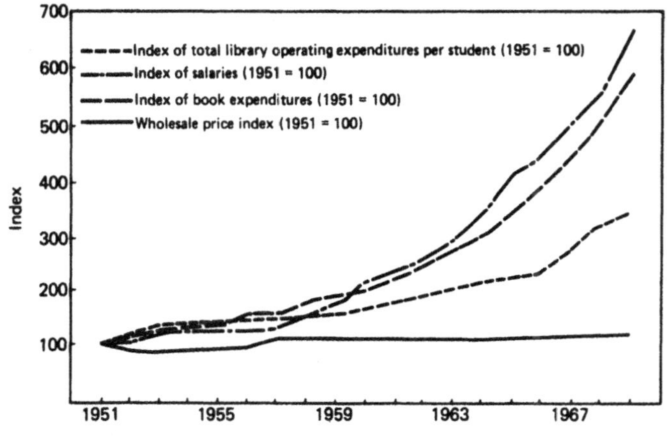

Source: Table 2.2

Fig. 8.1. Unit Costs in Fifty-eight University Research Libraries in Comparison with Wholesale Price Index, 1951–69 (from Baumol and Marcus, p. 46).

(*b*) GROWTH OF THE UNIVERSITY

The University is very young, only 26 years old, although it includes a number of older campuses. It entered a period of massive growth in the very late 1950s, although four of its campuses are still classed as 'emerging' or growing campuses in which massive construction is still taking place. The result is that most of the physical plant is new and the library space on each campus is adequate for the next few years.

The basis for this growth, however, has been enrolment projections. The Student Full Time Equivalent is the basic building block for budgeting, in which this number for each campus generates the income. Thus, the period of growth was based on the expectations of continuing annual increased enrolments. In 1972, however, it became apparent that this growth curve would not continue. Present projections expect that the enrolment (and, under present budgeting practice, the income) will continue to grow until the late 1970s, will plateau until about 1984, and then will decline.

This pattern will have a severe fiscal impact on the University. It also makes it extremely unlikely that much building construction will take place, although the need for library space will increase as the libraries continue to grow, even though there may be less need for classroom or dormitory space.

The University is responding to the expected curtailment in growth, at least in the traditional 18–25-year-old student group, by developing 'life-long learning' programmes to serve the changing informational and educational needs of the citizens of the State. This diversity, however, with many off-campus, part-time students, will demand from the libraries a greater flexibility of service procedures such as can be obtained only from a cohesive network rather than from a group of independent units.

(*c*) GROWTH OF LITERATURE

The growth of literature in all fields is always cited as a cause of library difficulty, as, indeed, it is. The study by George Anderla[2] is perhaps the most recent, wide ranging study of this growth.

It is perhaps uncertain that this growth will continue in the changing fiscal environment. What is of greater concern, however, is whether or not the pattern of publishing will change, and, if it does, whether the libraries can recognize and respond to the change in a responsible and timely manner. Since many of the libraries are operationally on the wrong foot and are continuing to operate in older modes of service, they may not be able to react as necessary.

Whether or not the growth of literature continues at its present pace, the libraries still have to contend with the results of past growth, even though the inexorable rules of natural selection are working on the literature output of the last few years.

(*d*) OTHER PROBLEMS

A number of other concerns affect the library problem and these should be mentioned briefly at this point. They are:

(*a*) General administrative concerns which arise from being a State agency, such as the requirement for book dealer and other service contracts.

(*b*) Library personnel problems, including the changed expectations of librarians, morale problems caused by the failure fully to implement faculty status, equal pay grievances, etc.

(*c*) Resistance to, and educational unpreparedness for, change, on the part of librarians, faculty, administrators and budget officials.

(*d*) Unrealistic faculty expectations, based on years of unlimited funds in a period of rapid growth.

[2] Anderla, George, *Information in 1985; a Forecasting Study of Information Needs and Resources*, Organization for Economic Co-operation and Development (1973).

(*e*) The problems of transmitting a sense of urgency to decision makers.
(*f*) The social expectations of library users and, perhaps particularly, administrators, based on memories of past practices and easier, quieter times.
(*g*) The structure of the University with its strong tradition of local autonomy and, hence, some resistance to central service planning and implementation.
(*h*) Inter-agency and inter-group rivalry.
(*i*) The difficulty of measuring the output value of higher education in general, and of libraries in particular, leading to problems in convincing budget officials that they need to support investment in innovation and change.
(*j*) The absence of sound management data, even to general uncertainty as to the definition of basic terms of measurement, such as volume, serial, etc., and no accepted procedures for measuring the outputs of libraries, such as reference services.
(*k*) The decline in the prestige of higher education.
(*l*) The lack of basic management formulae, for example, the failure to develop a soundly based, rational library collection size formula or personnel performance formula.

Most of the problems cited above are completely outside the ability of libraries to solve, and yet they have profound impact on the search for a solution to the library problems. The library solutions have to be found within this environment at a time when the library problem is only one part of the total concerns of higher education.

IV APPROACHES TO SOLUTIONS

It is possible to group the library problems into three areas, cost-efficiency, cost-effectiveness and cost-benefit; and to attack each with different and appropriate methodologies.

For the purposes of this paper, I propose acceptance of the following usage of the above terms.[3]

Cost-efficiency is devoted to the relationship between input and output costs of a library operation; thus, the smaller the gap between the two, the more cost-efficient the operation.

Cost-effectiveness is concerned with the resources required to achieve a specific output and the effective use of those resources.

[3] Humphry, David, *Costs and Effectiveness of Instructional Development.* Paper presented at the annual conference of the American Association for Higher Education, unpublished (March 1974).

——, *Instructional Development: the Problems of Costs and Effectiveness*, ERIC ED 092 045 (October 1974).

Cost-benefit is used to define the broad 'societal' benefits of the programme.

In a specific library environment, the following examples of the usage of the terms may assist in clarification. If it is possible, through a change in technique, to reduce the cost of cataloguing a book, then the cost-efficiency of that operation has been improved. A reduction of a cost of $1·00 per title in a library cataloguing 10,000 titles a year, would realize an annual saving of $10,000. If, however, of the 10,000 titles catalogued, only 2000 are ever used, and 8000 have been bought and catalogued never to be used, the resource investment is very high for a limited return and the programme is not cost-effective. Since libraries are generally regarded as an academic support service, it is difficult to isolate the general societal cost-benefit of a library programme; rather, its cost-benefit is a factor in the total programmatic analysis. And, yet, the library does play a major role in that analysis. For example, the development of a major research collection to support a Ph.D. programme in history can take a concentrated acquisition effort over a number of years and an acquisitions expenditure of some millions of dollars, plus processing, housing, and personnel costs. The decision to mount such a Ph.D. programme must take full account of the cost involved.

The importance of this analysis is the recognition which it forces that no one technique will ever provide the total solution to library problems. There is, in other words, a limit to what the computer, or an on-line network, can do. It can, and does, greatly improve the cost efficiency of libraries but does little to improve the cost-effectiveness of collections. Conversely, careful attention to collection-efficiency is equally self-limiting if the potential benefits and existence of on-line networks is ignored.

The work being undertaken in the State University of New York is designed to establish the best library system by developing a network in which cost-effectiveness and cost-efficiency have the most harmonious relationship, and combine to support the 'societal' cost-benefit of the University's programmes.

The line between cost-effectiveness and cost-efficiency is by no means rigidly defined and, in fact, continual osmosis between the two elements is a natural phenomenon. By far the most fruitful result of this osmosis is the development of management data as a by-product of attempts to improve cost-efficient (i.e. computer-based) programmes. These data are invaluable in improving the cost-effectiveness of library collections as it is realized how library collections are used—or not used.

In fact, this osmosis is leading to a synthesis of revolutionary-versus-classical librarianship. The *revolutionary mode* of the computer is being used to preserve the concepts of classical librarianship, by improving the cost-efficiency of *traditional concepts*, for example, the library operation of cataloguing. On the other hand, *revolutionary concepts* regarding the cost-effectiveness of library collections are being stimulated by the analysis of management data from the automation of the *traditional mode* of library circulation.

V COST-EFFICIENCY

The attempts to improve the cost-efficiency of State University Libraries centre almost exclusively on the introduction of on-line computer technology into the libraries.

In 1973, the present author offered a paper on the 10th Clinic on Library Applications of Data Processing held at the Graduate School of Library Science, Urbana, Illinois, entitled 'Bibliographic Data Centers for New York State'.[4] This paper described the framework in which network development was foreseen within the State University. It is not necessary to repeat that paper here, but the basic theory underlying such development is important. Essentially, a bibliographic data centre (or centres), whose functions are the delivery of bibliographic data via an on-line network to libraries, was proposed. Such centres would not handle physical library materials but would be, essentially, computer centres.

Further, three linked layers, or concentric rings, of data are proposed, the first consisting of volatile, inventory-type files of circulation, serials control, or inprocess records, alterable by member libraries; the second of standard bibliographic data for serials, monographs, etc., immune from local tampering; and third, a surrounding circle of abstract and index data, inviolate from local interference, but, nonetheless, providing vital information retrieval and subject services. (See Figure 8.2.)

It should also be noted that there is a fourth or outer layer of files which is comprised of relatively unformated raw data, such as census data, economic data, and data from the physical sciences, such as meteorological data. It is an open question whether these data should be provided as a service from a bibliographic data centre or not, but it is important to recognize that these data exist.

State University is developing its computing network services within the above framework. Work is being done on discrete segments of the system, while, for the time being, the attempt to link these segments is postponed. It should be noted that it is not necessary for all of the pieces to be developed from the ground up by the University. In fact, one of the advantages of on-line networks is that a library, or a library network, can take its services where it finds them, thus avoiding expensive research and development and hardware investments costs.

[4] Evans, Glyn T., 'Bibliographic Data Centers for New York State', *Proceedings of the 1973 Clinic on Library Applications of Data Processing*, ed. F. W. Lancaster (Champaign: University of Illinois, 1973), pp. 150–64.

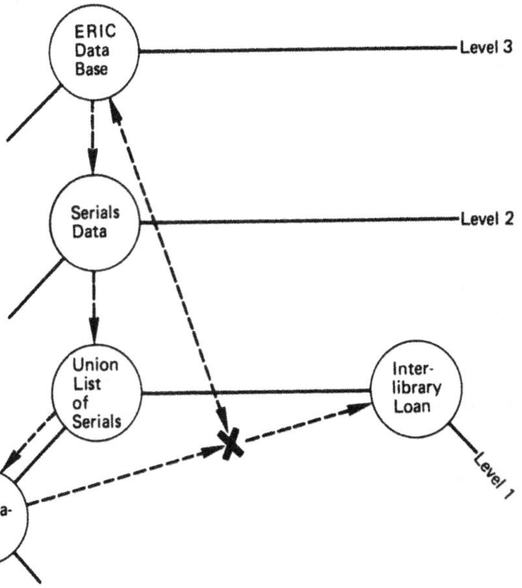

Fig. 8.2. (From Evans, p. 156.)

(*a*) CATALOGUING

We expect to have 104 terminals serving 90 libraries, including non-SUNY libraries, by the end of this year.

Particular attention has to be paid to the training of the librarians and clerical staff who will use the system. Many who come to the system for the first time are nervous and apprehensive, and many fear change. Thus, the training has not only to be rigorous, but it has to be sympathetic and non-threatening to the individual. In addition to the mechanics of using terminals, and learning the changes in cataloguing practice that use of the system entails, librarians are also trained in the techniques of introducing terminals into the work flow to ensure the best utilization of the system, and are advised of the physical requirements of terminal installation. A total of four days of individual training is given to each library staff. In addition, training manuals and implementation memoranda are essential to provide adequate documentary support for the system and its usage.

This careful attention to detail has shown excellent results. The terminals have been accepted rapidly and easily by the libraries and are now a familiar piece of library equipment. There is no evidence of unconscious sabotage of the system caused through fear or ignorance and a technological revolution has been achieved within the libraries.

Reports are now beginning to come into my office from libraries using the system indicating that it is, indeed, demonstrating an improvement in cost-efficiency. For example, one library reports a 38 per cent reduction in the cost of cataloguing a title, and another has reallocated to other positions 12 clerical staff members whose total salaries exceed $90,000 per year.

(*b*) SERIALS CONTROL

Serials inventory control is an extremely difficult and expensive part of academic library operation because so many variables can intercede between the publisher issuing a new part of a serial and the library putting it on the shelf. Further, the size of the task is overwhelming. State University checks in over 900,000 discrete issues per year although, of course, this is the total of all campuses, not of one centralized receiving point.

The libraries can readily add serials control to the same terminal installation.

In order to help the libraries use the Serials Control system, State University is providing a once-for-all conversion of serials records into the system from one central point. A small staff is participating in the nationwide CONSER national serials data base development which is using the OCLC system. Other libraries in CONSER are the Library of Congress, the National Agriculture Library, the National Library of Medicine, and the National Library of Canada. This joint effort is expected to produce a data base of some quarter of a million records within three years. This project is an outstanding example of the use of technology to produce a cost-efficient technique of providing an essential library service.

(*c*) ACQUISITIONS

OCLC is developing an acquisition system which is planned for readiness in mid-1976, and it is our current expectation that the libraries will use that system also.

(*d*) CIRCULATION

The University has been interested for some time in developing a University-wide circulation system. As a first step, the University acquired the programmes for the Ohio State University on-line system[5] and installed them on the Central Office computer to service the Albany campus. This replication was successful and the system has been operating for over 18 months. It has been subject to continuous evaluation during this time with a view to its expansion through the University.

[5] Atkinson, Hugh, 'Ohio State On-line Circulation System', *Ibid.* (1972), pp. 22–8.

The major disadvantage to the system expansion is the need to do a massive conversion of all manual shelf list records into machine readable form. This conversion would, in fact, give the system its strength, particularly since the use of OCLC archival tapes provides ongoing support to the converted file, so that the problem lies in the unlikelihood of getting adequate fiscal support in the immediate future, no matter how desirable the project.

One other recent development has changed the picture, and that is the fairly recent development of off-the-shelf minicomputer systems which may provide a viable alternative. Finally, few libraries have severe service problems at the 'point-of-sale'. All libraries, however, have difficulty in maintaining the files and providing adequate circulation support services. Most crucial of all is the almost total lack of adequate management data about collection usage on either a campus or a university-wide basis, yet, as will be seen in the discussion of the improvement of cost-effectiveness, it may be worth the cost of installation of the circulation system just to get the management data.

It is clear, therefore, that, at present, the whole circulation system proposals are in a state of flux.

(*e*) INFORMATION RETRIEVAL

State University developed one of the earliest on-line information retrieval systems when, in 1969, it inaugurated its Biomedical Communications Network.[6] This system began with the Medlars Medical data base, but, in 1973, it expanded its services by adding Psychological Abstracts and the Eric Educational Research data bases. Thirty-three libraries, including many outside of New York, now use the system. Users can 'log-on' to any data base of their choice, using the same terminal, and perform Boolean searches on the data. The use of the system is gradually increasing, 4438 searches having been performed in January, 1975 and 4623 in March, 1975.

As the variety of data bases grows and more disciplines can be served through the same terminal, the system is becoming demonstrably more cost-efficient. Machine searching is more complex, more precise and much faster than comparable manual search, and, as the cost of the paper-printed abstracts increases, shared use of the same machine readable data base by many institutions is becoming cheaper than each library buying its printed copy.

To summarize this section of the paper, I would say that the library network is improving the cost-efficiency of its operations by the introduction of on-line computer technology. The network is buying services (cataloguing, serials control, and acquisitions), replicating services

[6] Pizer, Irwin H., 'On-line Technology in a Library Network', *Ibid.*, pp. 54–68.

developed elsewhere (circulation) and developing its own where necessary (information retrieval). It does not seek to invest in expensive wheel reinvention and, yet, does invest in Research and Development as necessary where a service is needed but is not available from any other source. Finally, the University is providing leadership and services to other libraries in the State of New York, thus fulfilling its social obligations as a public institution.

VI COST-EFFECTIVENESS

It is not too difficult to establish measures for demonstrating an increase, or decrease, in the cost-efficiency of an operation, since inputs and outputs are known. Further, it is possible to define an increase in efficiency as a precise management target by a planned change in technique.

Cost-effectiveness is, however, much more diffuse and uncertain, and, yet, before discussing its improvement, one needs some idea of what one seeks to improve and a technique to measure the success or failure of the efforts.

It is proposed, therefore, that library cost-effectiveness be defined very simply as:

$$\frac{\text{library costs}}{\text{library usage}} = \$n \textit{ or } \text{unit cost of library service.*}$$

This can be expanded as follows:

$$\frac{|\text{COSTS}|}{|\text{USAGE}|} \quad \frac{\text{Selection + acquisition + cataloguing + housing + reference + locating + circulation + personnel}}{\text{Item usage (i.e. inhouse reading + reference + lending)}}$$

$$= \$n \textit{ or } \text{unit cost of library service.}$$

Each library can redefine its goals by isolating, for emphasis, the output components of the formula.

It is readily seen that, by decreasing the costs above the line and increasing the usage below the line, the unit cost will lower and the cost effectiveness will increase.

This apparently simple formula is, in fact, however, extremely difficult to administer, for three reasons. First, the gross terms need very precise

* It became apparent during the discussion that, at present, it is extremely difficult to define a 'unit of output' for a library.

definition. Second, while it is relatively easy to establish costs above the line, with the dollar as the normative factor, there is, as yet, no similar normative factor which establishes an equal relationship between references, storage, lending or inhouse reading, unless one says (and this could well be true) that all uses, or 'units of output' are equal in that either reading a whole book or having one reference question answered can be seen as 'one user-need satisfied'. It should be noted, however, that the type of use or output will vary from library to library, by both library objective and disciplinary speciality or will be performed at different degrees in the same library. Third, at present, the management data to support this formula is generally not available in individual libraries. In a group of autonomous libraries in a network such as State University there is also gross inconsistency in data gathered and reported by different campuses to one central source.

Two additional observations are necessary. First, the relationship between cost-efficiency and cost-effectiveness is well demonstrated in the formula since, clearly, the impact of the introduction of technology to reduce costs above the line favourably influences the cost effectiveness of the library. Second, each library unit cost will be different, depending on the purpose of the library. At opposite extremes, a major research library that is building collections for posterity will have a higher unit cost than will a small lending collection in a public library, local service branch. And, yet, each research library or public library branch should have costs which, given due regard for local conditions such as salaries, share the same range of costs.

It is the latter of the two observations which is guiding the planning to improve the cost-effectiveness of the State University Library network. When the purposes of the different types of libraries and their users' needs are examined it is clear that some blurring of objective has taken place. Redefinition of the objectives of each library will guide all efforts to plan the network.

It is important, at this point, to recall the way in which the library network grew. The libraries developed as independent entities on autonomous campuses, responding to violent growth needs as local campuses established a wide range of programmes in response to rising enrolment expectations, with adequate funds to support such growth. Such electronic computing as was appreciated was expected to be local batch computing; it was not until the late 1960s that on-line technology became a viable option for library networks. But, by that time, the pattern was set, and more than 95 per cent of the investment in the library system had been made. The problem lies in redefining the objectives of the libraries to respond to current and expected conditions.

(*a*) OBJECTIVE SETTING

The essential choice which faces college and University libraries is whether to place a priority on storage versus use. There is a real danger that the large research collections, whose goals are completeness, are becoming increasingly unusable, particularly by an undergraduate community. Conversely, there is an equal risk that the college libraries, primarily focusing on undergraduate services, will try to become university research collections. Evan Farber points this out when he regrets 'the attempt to pattern college library services after University library services (since) their needs and clientele are entirely different'.[7]

The fact is that in current conditions a library has to choose between excellence in service or excellence in collections. Seldom, except in well defined disciplinary areas, can a library aspire to both. It would seem that the most appropriate mode of development is to encourage the continuation and maintenance of strong research collections that are already in existence, and transform other collections into volatile use-oriented collections.

(*b*) DECISION OPTIONS

Within the terms of the cost-effectiveness formula, the choices are as follows:

For collection completeness:
- a selection policy of wide-ranging scope, including all countries and languages;
- heavy expenditure in acquisitions and cataloguing;
- large, expensive library building;
- difficulty in locating material;
- minimal circulation;
- heavy personnel cost, over the line.

Under the line, probably heavier inhouse and reference use, but little emphasis on circulation.

For collection use:
- rigorous selection policy based on expected use, with little variety and much duplication;
- comparatively reduced expenditure on acquisition, and some portion of collection planned to be obtained from an external source on request;
- reduced cataloguing expenditure;

[7] Farber, Evan, 'College Librarians and the University-Library Syndrome', in *The Academic Library: Essays in Honour of Guy R. Lyle* (Metuchen, NJ: Scarecrow Press, 1974).

smaller physical libraries;
easy location of material;
heavy emphasis on circulation;
probably lowered personnel budget, over the line.

Under the line, very heavy collection usage figures.

(*c*) INVENTORY LAW

A number of workers, in different libraries, and, at different times, have studied the use of library material.[8] Time and again, the 'inventory law' associated with supermarkets, spare parts stores, etc., has been demonstrated. This law indicates that some 20 per cent of the collection (of books or groceries) satisfies 80 per cent of the requests made of the collection, and that the remaining 80 per cent satisfy a part of the other demands, the rest of the demands being unsatisfied by the collection. This data is emerging from the analysis of large automated files of circulation records.

Similarly, analyses of the fifteen years of files held at the Institute of Scientific Information demonstrate supportive data. These files are the basis of Science Citation Index and Social Science Citation Index. The files report the relationship between journals by linking the citations found in each journal. Each discipline is found to have first, a core of heavily used journals which constantly cite each other, and, then, steadily, but rigorously receding, outer concentric rings of diminishing citation relationship.[9] This finding confirms observations made by Bradford, in 1953,[10] which suggested that the journal sources of citations in disciplinary areas are related to each other in the series 1, N, N^2, N^3 ... Weinstock, of the Institute of Scientific Information,[11] suggests that 80 per cent of the reference questions in science over the last 10 years could be answered with 200 journals. Further, it is now becoming possible to identify these journals.

A recent paper by Worthen,[12] has examined the applications of Bradford's Law to the publishers of monographs and concludes that 'Bradford's Law of distribution can also be applied to the monograph-publisher relationship for a subject literature'.

[8] Trueswell, R. W., *Growing Libraries: Who Needs Them? A Statistical Theory of the No-growth Collection*. Paper presented at the ACM Conference on Space, Growth and Performance Problems of Academic Libraries, Chicago, April 1975 (to be published).

[9] Garfield, Eugene, 'Citation Analysis as a Tool in Journal Evaluation', *Science*, 178 (1972), pp. 471–9.

[10] Bradford, S. C., *Documentation*, 2nd ed. (London: Lockwood, 1953).

[11] Weinstock, Melvin, *Economics of Information Dissemination: A Symposium* (Syracuse: Syracuse University School of Information Science, 1973), p. 67.

[12] Warthen, Dennis B., 'The Application of Bradford's Law to Monographs', *Journal of Documentation*, 31, no. 1 (March 1975), pp. 19–25.

This and other evidence is beginning to indicate very clearly that, for much of our teaching purpose, small libraries are better than large ones and, more, that we can begin to identify very precisely the materials which we should buy for both small and large libraries. Perhaps the most interesting proposal in this regard is that for a 'Dynamic Library' made by Salton, of Cornell University.[13] There the library would maintain a steady size but would be a volatile, heavily-used collection of materials based on measured usage and expected usage predicted both from past patterns and the recognition of the laws of natural selection working on past publications.[14]

Buckland and Hindle[15] have further proposed a formula, based on past use and performance and on the cost effectiveness of buying rather than not buying a particular item, which would offer a prediction of future use to be used at the time when a selection decision about any book is being made.

Library selection procedures will almost certainly have to be altered to account for this mounting evidence.

(*d*) MANAGEMENT FORMULAE

There is a total lack of adequate library management formulae, whether for collection size, personnel performance, and even space allocation, although much excellent work has been done on the last topic. Furthermore, many of the formulae which do exist are based on the measurement of past or current practice, with a heavy overlay of subjective value judgments regarding that which is 'good'. Unfortunately, budget officers, from sheer desperation, fall on, and use, formulae no matter how valid.

It is important to concentrate on formulae for library collection size. The earliest work on this was done by Clapp and Jordan,[16] who proposed a formula for minimal adequacy for college and university collections based on their measurement of libraries which were in existence. The formula is based on a basic number for a collection plus so many extra volumes per type of student, etc. This formula has come to be accepted, even though Clapp and Jordan were at great pains to describe the ten-

[13] Salton, Gerald, 'Proposal for a Dynamic Library', *Information, part 2*, vol. 2, no. 2 (1973), pp. 1–27.

[14] Line, Maurice B. and Sandison, A., 'Obsolescence and Changes in the Use of Literature with Time', *Journal of Documentation*, XXX, no. 3 (September 1974), pp. 283–350.

[15] Buckland, Michael and Hindle, Anthony, *Acquisitions, Growth and Performance Control Through Systems Analysis*. Paper presented at the ACM Conference on Space, Growth and Performance Problems of Academic Libraries, Chicago, April 1975 (to be published).

[16] Clapp, Verner W. and Jordan, Robert J., 'Quantitative Criteria for Adequacy of Academic Library Collections', *College and Research Libraries*, XXVI (September 1965), pp. 371–80.

tative nature of their work and urged that much more research be done on the topic before a formula be developed. Almost no research has been done since that date and the only action has been to raise the numbers in the formula, giving an even larger collection. To make matters worse, the Association of College and Research Libraries has endorsed the formula, or one of its later higher derivatives, in its 'Standard for College Libraries'.[17] Even worse, budget officers are now threatening to use the formula to curtail library growth without any regard for the effectiveness of the library that may result.

In State University, we have been examining the question of 'factors which underlie library collection formulae' and have completed the first phase of our work. The proposed formula is based on the discipline, its own characteristics, and the objective of the institution regarding the practice of that discipline. In outline, the factors are:

Group 1
- A. Discipline
  - Mass of material published in a discipline
  - Publication rate
  - Volatility
- B. Collection Purpose
  - Teaching
  - Research
  - Basic library use

Group 2: Operation Factors
- A. User population size
- B. Extant collection (quality and quantity)
- C. Dispersal of holdings
- D. External environment:
  - Planned co-operative acquisition programmes
  - Availability of other resources
  - Availablity of technological support
- E. Physical format of material
- F. Loss and physical deterioration
- G. Inflation
- H. Programmes
  - Level (undergraduate, graduate, post doctoral)
  - Number
  - Variety
  - Structure (multi- and inter-disciplinary).

It is expected that these factors can now be evaluated, weighted and linked into a collection formula into which any library can define its

[17] 'Draft: Standards for College Libraries 1975 revision', *College and Research Libraries News*, XXXV, 11 (December 1974), pp. 284–6, 299–305.

objectives, evaluate its present collection and the availability of other support services, and then define its collection needs in specific dollar terms.

(*e*) PROGRAMME SUPPORT

One aim is to increase the relationship between curricula and collections on a University-wide basis. There is evidence that some campuses have developed, or wish to develop, programmes where library support is lacking, while, on other campuses, library collections are being built long after the programmatic need has been satisfied. The attempt to rectify these situations will further increase the cost-effectiveness of the libraries.

(*f*) CENTRAL SUPPORT

The libraries, as has been stated, have been growing autonomously with little relationship among them, although, of course, there is the normal interlibrary loan traffic by mail and, in some cases, by local delivery service.

One possible mode of providing service in an effective way is to develop a central store which will house the lesser used materials and then deliver them to the libraries on demand. This is a well-established procedure, the most outstanding example of which is the National Lending Library Unit of the British Library. It is necessary to consider user requirements, the delay in service, and modes of transport, as well as the relative costs of developing such a store, as opposed to allowing each library to continue in its present mode.

One very valuable and increasingly viable option is the possibility of transmission of pages of text by cable TV or telefacsimile from store to library. The technology in both of these fields is advancing, particularly with the advent of freeze-frame TV, and the costs are decreasing.

As we plan for the future we need increasingly to take account of the changing technology and examine 'travel/communications substitutability'. A recent paper by Day reviews developments in this field and makes some fascinating suggestions.[18] It is clear, however, that the development of such a service would have to take place *before* changes are made in library operation; that is, it would be necessary to demonstrate excellent service from an external central source before instituting local changes.

(*g*) INCREASED USE

One very simple and cheap way of increasing the use of the collections is to allow very easy access to the campus libraries by students, faculty and

[18] Day, Lawrence, 'An Assessment of Travel/Communications Substitutability', *Futures*, V, 6 (December 1973), pp. 559–72.

staff from other campuses. In February, 1974, the university initiated a policy which encourages this service by allowing any member of the University community to use any library on presentation of a valid University ID card. Books may be borrowed and returned to the lending library either from one's own campus, or from any other within the system.

In the first year of operation, some 4500 users, primarily students, borrowed 13,500 items in this way. The traffic between pairs of libraries, and the use of collection by discipline, has been analysed.

Briefly to summarize this section, it is possible to define library objectives in terms of collection size or collection use and plan based on the objective selected. Using the elements in the cost-effectiveness formula, and acquiring evidence of use and relative importance of materials selected, it is then possible to build, using a new 'collection size' formula, dynamic service oriented collections (perhaps supported by on-line computing, cable TV or telefacsimile services offered by a central back up service point), with careful integration of curricula and collections.

The result would be expected to be a cost-effective library service in which maximum utilization is made of library resources, on the one hand, and resources are tailored to achieve maximum use on the other.

VII PROGNOSIS

In this paper, the problems facing the libraries of State University have been addressed in the context of the conditions under which higher educational institutions in the United States are presently operating.

It is apparent that libraries cannot survive if they continue to operate in an outmoded manner in an era of financial stringency. Network development offers a hope for the future. Technology can be, and is being, harnessed to increase the efficiency of library operations. In a wider sense, it is possible to improve the cost effectiveness of libraries by a careful redefinition of objectives based on an understanding of emerging patterns of collection usage and current developments in library management formulae and technique. If severe financial strains induce libraries to improve themselves, whether out of necessity of in defence, the experience, though difficult, will be worthwhile.

Work on these lines is either underway or being planned for the libraries of State University. This work relies on external services which are provided by other agencies, either within New York State, such as the interlibrary loan network, from other states, e.g. OCLC, or nationally. Where services are not readily available, the University may develop its own.

This revolution in approach requires a major educational effort directed, in different ways, at librarians, administrators and budget officials. Research, development and implementation funds are needed.

Results are now being obtained which demonstrate savings from projects which have been successfully initiated. One is optimistic that similar success will be attained in future projects.

It is the hope of the project that changes in techniques and approaches to library service will allow reallocation of funds within the libraries so that they become a more cost-effective component of the educational process.

The really critical issue is whether funds to support further development will be made available at a time of extreme financial stringency. The decision to allocate funds will demand courage, foresight and imagination.

One's greatest fear is that funds will be cut irrationally because of expediency, resulting in a severe down-turn of both efficiency and effectiveness, rather than through a planned development in library services techniques.

Summary of the Discussion

Mr Fetterman began his introduction of Mr Evans' paper with an account of the State University of New York (SUNY), a relatively new institution and unfamiliar to non-American participants. SUNY, where Mr Evans is employed, is the largest university in the world, with approximately 80,000 faculty members and 375,000 students. It is responsible to the State legislature of New York, and each of its numerous campuses has a relatively high degree of autonomy.

SUNY's main problems were characterized as 'fiscal' and 'growth'. The fiscal problem is that support is tax based, in competition with other government functions, and it is no longer possible, as it had been in the first days of the SUNY experiment, to 'buy one's way out of trouble'. This leads directly to SUNY's growth problem or, rather, to SUNY's deceleration problem after the rapid expansion of the 1960s. The new libraries on the various campuses are now trying to 'catch up' in the face of both the 'information explosion' and the decline in the growth rate of student population. These problems are outside of the ability of libraries to solve, and the library's problems cannot be examined in isolation.

Mr Evan's paper explores cost-efficiency, cost-effectiveness, and cost-benefit approaches, which are distinguished more fully in the text than *Mr Fetterman* felt necessary to reproduce orally. (In developing these ideas, Mr Evans, not himself an economist, hopes for the assistance of economists.)

In the aid of cost-efficiency, SUNY has introduced on-line computer technology (not fully explained) to provide 'concentric circles' of data for library administration. SUNY has also become a participant in The Ohio College Library Center (OCLC, or the Ohio plan) for cataloguing and serials control, but not for acquisitions. In Mr Evan's view, SUNY's participation in the Ohio plan should be greater than it is, but the plan has been explained inadequately to an older generation of librarians with fears for job security. On its own (outside of the Ohio plan), SUNY has installed a circulation monitoring system, also computer-based, to show what is used and by whom. On the subject of cost-effectiveness (which attempts to measure cost per unit of user-need satisfaction), the SUNY system assumes, as a first approximation, that all needs are of equal value. There appears to be a trade-off between the excellence of a library's collection (itself a service to one group of users) and the excellence of its service (to its users in general) with a given budget. Mr Evans pleaded for some better basis for optimizing this trade-off than what the library profession has itself supplied. In the short run, SUNY has instituted a system whereby students and faculty members on any campus may use library facilities at all other campuses as well. For the longer term, Mr Evans saw inter-library networking as a main hope.

In his own comments, *Mr Fetterman* emphasized the more foreboding aspects of the Evans paper. Investments in automation and in networking are both large, not small. Even with good management, they will take years to pay for themselves. They are certainly not panaceas, in Mr Fetterman's opinion —especially if library management is not of the best.

Professor Giersch opened discussion from the floor with two questions: (1) Can any academic library be self-supporting? (2) Are there any management consulting firms specializing in library problems? *Professor Blaug* mentioned a historical library in London which is self-supporting. No conference participant knew of a library-management consulting firm.

Professor M. Perlman went on to raise more questions. He wished for more information as to the aims of institutions which support libraries. At his own university (Pittsburgh), the library and the computer centre rival the Medical School as sources of the deficit, and he did not know how this could be justified. He wondered how much of the Evans paper would be relevant outside of the SUNY system, and, also, how much of SUNY's problem may be due to its late establishment and rapid initial growth. *Professor Perlman* hoped that Mr Kilgour's account of the Ohio plan might be more generally helpful. *Dr Otto* asked whether SUNY was, indeed, a specialized research collection. The figures she had seen suggested otherwise, and she repeated Professor M. Perlman's doubts as to the relevance of the SUNY experience for older institutions.

Professor Kindleberger expressed the view that, since 20 per cent of the average library gave 80 per cent of the services, part of the solution of the problems of such a library might be a reduction in size. On the other hand, he questioned all cost-effectiveness calculations which assumed that one 'bit' of service or satisfaction was equal to any other. His own diagnosis was that SUNY might be duplicating Harvard's mistake of neglecting its teaching-library functions.

Mr Hibbert was dubious about the distinction between cost-efficiency and cost-effectiveness. What is the output of a library, he asked—the range of services *offered*, or the range *used*? (The first, he believed, makes better theoretical-economic sense.) It is also wrong, he thought, to equate all user-need units to each other. What is needed is a set of 'shadow prices'. Also, in discussing user satisfaction, he felt that some consideration might be given to the *level* of this satisfaction, even though this were outside the library's control. He hoped for a weighting system for library services, but doubted its practicality. (*Mr Fetterman*, in reply, suggested that the sociological concept of 'social audit' might have something to offer.)

Mr Evans replied that economists' expertise was needed by librarians, and that he would be satisfied if his paper excited the economists' interest. He mentioned also that the data in that paper was probably already obsolete, as New York State had dipped into the SUNY budget to assist New York City in its financial crisis. He also believed that SUNY would make better use of OCLC advantages after the completion of its shakedown period.

Referring more specifically to Professor M. Perlman, *Mr Evans* thought that the SUNY problems to be of general interest. Other institutions, too, had a multiplicity of libraries and difficulty in co-ordinating acquisitions. Many institutions had multiple campuses and had the problem of deciding what should be done on which campus and on what level. SUNY may just be facing these problems *sooner* and *on a larger scale* than other institutions. Replying, then, to Dr Otto, *Mr Evans* agreed that SUNY was basically a teaching institution, with pockets of specialized research (for example, at Cornell in industrial relations). But there was a great deal of inter-campus rivalry; in particular, many of the present undergraduate-teaching institutions had research ambitions for the future, while there was pressure for reducing the number of doctoral programmes (for example, the four in history, some of which are lagging precisely because of inadequate library facilities).

Basic decisions must be made as to the weighting of various aspects of SUNY activity. Formulas are weak—more precise than accurate or relevant. But, without this kind of support, the library is 'going naked into the conference chamber'. *Mr Evans* concluded by repeating his hope that OCLC might be part of his solution, and that economists might furnish additional parts.

After Mr Evans had completed his summary, *Professor Giersch* remarked that it had become quite common for specialists in many fields to appeal to economists (and management scientists) to go behind conventional book-keeping to determine appropriate measures for inputs and outputs. *Professor Kindleberger* agreed, citing the specific example of hospitals. *Dr Otto* repeated her doubts about the applicability of American experience to European problems, since the representative European research library must do more of its own cataloguing, computer-based facilities were less developed, and making costs were, necessarily, higher.

9 Economics of Computerized Library Networks

Frederick G. Kilgour
OHIO COLLEGE LIBRARY CENTER

Except for the introduction of the photocopying machine, there have been no significant developments in library operations for nearly a century. Libraries are highly labour-intensive organizations, with salaries and wages constituting between 50 to 60 per cent of their expenditures. Because of a lack of increase in productivity of library staffs, the per-unit rate of rise of costs in academic libraries in the United States averaged six per cent per year in the two decades following 1950, whereas, during the same period, the wholesale price index rose about one per cent per year.

With the recent development of computerized library networks having a large on-line, central catalogue servicing all libraries, there has been a significant introduction of economies of scale. Productivity of library staffs is being dramatically increased. Moreover, computerized networks make it possible for libraries to have new objectives while reducing the rate of rise of per-unit costs. These objectives include making the resources of a region or nation rapidly available to library users, supplying users with information when and where they need it, and enabling libraries to give personalized service. Further development in the computerization of library processes and of patrons' use of libraries will invoke a continuing, increasing productivity that will make libraries and the use of them economically viable in the future.

Libraries have contributed little to economy-wide productivity, for they are extraordinarily labour intensive. Librarians have struggled for decades to achieve efficiencies and actually have invoked some limited economy of scale by sharing cataloguing, the most costly of library activities, but they have gained little in productivity. For example, it is doubtful that a library cataloguer of today is significantly more productive than was a cataloguer of a century ago.

The advent of a high-speed data-processing machine, the electronic digital computer, has presented librarians with an opportunity to apply sophisticated technology to library operations. In addition, the marriage of modern telecommunications and the computer to form a library network has widely extended the availability of a machine which has the potential for dramatically improving library staff productivity.

This paper will first examine the historical background of the development of library operations in the mid-nineteenth century and compare these developments with the evolution of the so-called American System of Manufacture, a phrase employed by economic historians to describe mass production using interchangeable parts, that has made enormous contributions to economic growth; it will then show how, through the use of computerized library networks, libraries can increase productivity by invoking principles of the American System.

HISTORICAL BACKGROUND

Prior to the nineteenth century, librarians collected, catalogued, and conserved books. Libraries were little used, and most of them were entirely unavailable for use. It was during the nineteenth century that the free public library came into being, with its emphasis on library book use by the community and on self-education. In the latter part of the century, academic libraries were also increasingly available for faculty and students. Until then, some academic libraries in the United States had been open for only an hour or two each week.

It was also during the nineteenth century that librarians made important advances in the techniques of library operations. In 1843, Charles Coffin Jewett, then at Brown University, introduced the structured, alphabetical subject-heading list, thereby enabling library users more readily to obtain information rather than just a specific book. Five years later, William Frederick Poole, at Yale University, introduced the periodical index wherein articles in periodicals were catalogued, thus making available to library users information contained primarily in articles.

Prior to the middle of the nineteenth century, libraries printed their catalogues in book form in multiple copies, although some French librarians had been promoting card catalogues since the Revolution. Book catalogues are expensive to print and can never be up-to-date. With the rise, during the last century, of the importance of information, and particularly of recent information, librarians introduced the card catalogue, at once less costly than the book catalogue and more easily kept up-to-date. The major disadvantage of the card catalogue is that there is but one for each library; a user must go to the library to consult it.

In 1873, Melville Dewey, then an undergraduate at Amherst College, developed a narrow subject classification scheme, now in its eighteenth version and widely used in libraries for the arrangement of books on shelves. Prior to Dewey's invention, classification schemes were extremely broad, with books arranged within each subject by author, or by date of imprint or, possibly, by chronological accession. Books under broad subject heads did not facilitate retrieval of information by subject, but Dewey's narrow classification scheme, with many subject classes arranged hierarchically, made it possible for a user to find information on a given subject by going directly to the bookshelves.

Dewey also made the last important library innovation in the nineteenth century when, in 1884, he assigned two staff members of the Columbia University Library, where he was librarian, to work full time in assisting users in finding materials that they needed. Dewey recognized that subject indexing, periodical indexing, up-to-date catalogues, and narrow subject classification were not, in themselves, adequate to enable a user to locate information. Hence, he invoked the full-time reference librarian to assist users.

The five major innovations just described are the basic procedures of modern librarianship. In the nineteenth century, library staff performed these tasks; many professional librarians are still performing them today without mechanical assistance other than such low technological tools as the typewriter.

There have, however, been advances. For example, librarians standardized the size of catalogue cards at 75 by 125 millimetres, making it possible to interchange cards and, thereby, cataloguing information among libraries. Some libraries, such as the Library of Congress in the United States, and commercial concerns sell catalogue cards, making it unnecessary for libraries to duplicate the costly effort required to catalogue a book. The provision of catalogue cards made possible limited scale economies in cataloguing, but violated various labour-saving principles such as flow-production logic. Librarianship is still extremely labour intensive.

W. J. Baumol and M. Marcus have recently published the first major economic analysis of libraries,[1] finding that per-student costs in academic libraries rose over 6 per cent per year during the two decades following 1950, by comparison with a 1 per cent per year rise in the wholesale price index. They point out similar per-unit percentage cost increases in elementary education, public and private universities, and hospitals, and ascribe this commonality to a slow rate of labour-saving innovation. It is abundantly clear that if libraries are to decelerate their rate of rise of per-unit costs to an increase comparable to that in the economy as a whole they must invoke labour-saving technology.

THE AMERICAN SYSTEM AND PRODUCTIVITY

American mechanics were still making important contributions to the American System of manufacture in the mid-nineteenth century when

[1] Baumol, W. J. and Marcus, Matityahu. *Economics of Academic Libraries* (Washington, D.C.: American Council on Education, 1973).

American librarians were initiating the evolution of new library operations. The development of labour-saving machines and principles had no effect on librarianship, however, because of the unavailability of machines that could be adapted to library operations. Librarians were aware of the benefits of mechanization and made abortive efforts to introduce machines to libraries. For example, Charles Coffin Jewett, who had introduced the structured, alphabetical subject-heading index in 1843, attempted a decade later, to introduce scale economies in cataloguing with a stereotyped catalogue. As already mentioned, most catalogues in the United States at mid-century were printed in book-form, and Jewett proposed to use clay stereotyped plates containing cataloguing information. His plan was to keep the collection of plates continuously up to date as libraries catalogued additions to their collections. When a library wished to print a new edition of its catalogue, those plates containing entries for books in the library would be selected and used to print the catalogue. Jewett's ambitious project failed because his inexpensive clay plates shrank and warped, making their adjustment on a press impossible. Even if clay plates had worked, it is likely that his system would have failed because of weaknesses in other areas of design.

As is well known, the early evolution of the American System took place largely in firearms and clock manufacture. The principal characteristics of the system that enabled it to contribute to economic growth were the interchangeability of parts, specialized machinery, and assembly-line production flow.[2] Although mechanics had introduced interchangeable parts manufacture into the clock industry to achieve scale economies, the United States Government armouries that invented interchangeable parts manufacture for firearms had done so, not for the benefit of economies of scale, but, rather, for a more efficient firearms system whereby a firearm with a broken part could be rapidly repaired in the field. It was only with the development of a commercial firearms industry that the benefits of economy of scale were recognized as being inherent in interchangeable parts manufacture.

To produce interchangeable parts, special-purpose machine tools are required, such as milling and die-forging machines, to reproduce parts exactly. It is impossible for manual processes to attain the precision required for interchangeability.

The third component of the American System is a production flow wherein all processes are integrated into one system. Flow production need not take the form of a continuous flowbelt assembly line, but it is usually contained within one building.

These three characteristics of the American System make possible scale economies resulting from low unit production costs at high volumes

[2] Uselding, Paul. 'Elisha K. Root, Forging, and the "American System" ', *Technology and Culture*, 15 (Oct. 1974), pp. 543–568.

of output. The labour-saving principles of the American System that can be important now for librarianship are (1) maximum mechanical work and control, (2) maximum use of non-human sources of power, (3) high volumes of output, (4) high operating speeds, (5) mechanical continuity in operations, and (6) automatic error detection.

Another characteristic of the American System that will undoubtedly have an impact on librarianship is the system's ability to make new products. The Colt revolver is an example of such a product, for although Colt was the inventor of it, his mechanic, Elisha Root, made possible the manufacture of the inexpensive Colt revolver by developing a series of specialized machines.[3]

Despite efforts to apply special purpose machinery (as distinct from such machines as the typewriter) to library operations, libraries have been almost totally unable to enjoy the benefits of the labour-saving principles enunciated above. Rather, libraries have continued, up to the present time, to be highly labour-intensive and are unfortunately characterized by high unit-production costs no matter how high the volumes of output.

COMPUTERIZED NETWORKS

As already mentioned, computerized library networks consist largely of a computer or computers wedded to a telecommunications net. Together, they form an operation not unlike the production flow in one location that characterized the American System. Of the two components, it is the computer that is the more important because of its tremendous power to achieve interchangeability, to perform as a special purpose machine, and to effect integrated production flow.

Prior to the introduction of the computer, libraries achieved some degree of interchangeability of bibliographic information by standardizing catalogue card size and providing cataloguing codes designed to standardize bibliographic information on the cards. In computerized library operations, the equivalent of the standard card size is a standardized machine-readable format containing essentially the bibliographic information found on catalogue cards. Catalogue cards, however, require uniform physical size to be interchangeable, whereas the physical characteristics of the machine-readable record do not need to be physically uniform to achieve interchangeability. Here, the network designer can exert the power of the computer by programming it to convert machine-readable records in the data base of one network to the format required for manipulation in a second network. This power of the computer to achieve interchangeability of 'parts' without requiring physical uniformity has yet to be fully realized by library networks.

[3] *Ibid.*

The computer also has the extraordinary power of operation as a special purpose machine. Electronic digital computers are often thought of as 'general purpose' machines, and so they may be from the viewpoint of a manufacturer or a computer-centre director. From the user's point of view, however, a computer is a special purpose machine which he instructs to carry out his particular purpose. So it is with a computer in a library network, an observation that is more clear when the computer is dedicated full time to the operation of the network.

A computer can also be thought of as a continuous flow system or assembly line with stations. A library network computer is programmed to process bibliographic information and, at various stages, the computer displays the results of the processing at remote terminals where human intervention and interaction with the computer occur. After appropriate manipulation, the terminal operator instructs the computer to proceed further with its processing.

To the extent that a computer system employs only one entry of information in its memory in processing for multiple libraries, the system achieves economies of scale.

A computerized library network embodies the half-dozen labour-saving principles enunciated above that the classical, labour-intensive library cannot enjoy. First, the design of a computerized network should provide for maximum mechanical processing and control with minimal human participation. The system should not, however, control human participation, as is the case, for example, in the manual feeding of an automatic printing press; rather, the human must exert overall control.

Second, the system should make maximum use of non-human sources of power, a requirement easy of attainment when employing electronic machinery. Computers produce physical products such as catalogue cards, and, in the handling of these products, the system designer must employ non-electronic special purpose machines.

The third and fourth labour-saving principles are large-scale production and high operating speeds, and here the computer excels. The computer's incredible swiftness of operation yields extremely high volumes of output. In the case of the Ohio College Library Center (OCLC) at Columbus, Ohio, participating libraries on the network were able to catalogue over ten thousand books in a single day when there was but one computer in operation. For these ten thousand and more books, the computer often produced more than eighty thousand individually formated catalogue cards in final form, ready for filing in specific catalogues in participating libraries. This daily production is twice the annual production of the largest of special libraries.

The fifth principle of mechanical continuity and elimination of manual operations is another principle that can be invested in a computerized network. Finally, a computer can be programmed to effect extensive automatic error detection.

Just as the American System has made possible the manufacture of new products, so does the computerized library network. An example of a new product is the on-line library catalogue, which is a wholly new device. The printed book-form catalogue made its appearance in the seventeenth century and largely disappeared in the latter part of the nineteenth when the card catalogue replaced it. An on-line library catalogue is neither an on-line printed book catalogue nor an on-line card catalogue. The on-line catalogue is a late twentieth-century catalogue and actually consists of huge numbers of small catalogues. In the case of the Ohio College Library Center's on-line catalogue, there are well over a million small catalogues that constitute the catalogue system, and the size of these small catalogues varies from one to thirty-two entries. The maximum size can vary, of course, according to system design, but at the present time no user of the OCLC on-line catalogue must search through a listing of more than thirty-two entries.

The fact that a catalogue, by design, may never contain more than thirty-two entries suggests that elaborate cataloguing codes, consisting of hundreds of pages, and designed to make it possible for a cataloguer to produce a unique description of a unique book, so that the description can be entered into a precise location in a catalogue for future reference, will no longer be necessary. It appears that, once a library has its entire catalogue on-line, it may very well be possible, with minimal human intervention, to construct a catalogue merely by transcribing the text from a title page or from the head of a periodical article. Such a technical development would, of course, greatly enhance economies of scale.

OPERATING NETWORKS

There are at least three computerized library networks in operation. The LIBRIS network in Sweden and the Ontario Universities Computerized Library System in Canada each has about a dozen participating libraries. The Ohio College Library Center in the United States is the largest of the three, having in the Spring of 1975, over four hundred participating libraries. As already mentioned, these libraries often catalogue more than ten thousand books a day on the system, for which the Center produces seventy to eighty thousand catalogue cards.

The principal objectives of the Ohio College Library Center are to increase the availability of resources in network libraries to users at individual libraries, while at the same time reducing the rate of rise of per-unit costs. This paper deals only with the second objective. As for the first objective, the OCLC on-line catalogue is a union catalogue that contained nearly four million location listings in Spring, 1975.

The OCLC system design calls for six subsystems: (1) on-line union catalogue and shared cataloguing; (2) serials control; (3) technical processing; (4) interlibrary loan request communication; (5) user access by subject, title words, date, and language; and (6) remote catalogue access and circulation control. The on-line union catalogue and shared cataloguing system have been operational since the late summer of 1971. The serials control system has been partially in operation since the summer of 1974, and it is scheduled to be completely operational by the end of 1975. Programming has begun on the technical processing system that will largely involve acquisition of materials and the information retrieval system.

There is but one cataloguing record per title in the system, except for unwanted duplicates; a participating library, cataloguing a book represented by a record in the system, employs the existing record and does not have to redo the cataloguing. About three-quarters of the cataloguing done by the four-hundred-odd libraries uses records already in existence, and it is the number of times that each record is used that determines the economy of scale. Many participating libraries have demonstrated that use of the system not only reduces the rate of rise of per-unit costs, but also effects net savings.

R. D. Rogers and D. C. Weber have observed that, in large university libraries, manual cataloguing production is approximately 1000 titles per year per full-time staff member, but if cataloguing copy from another library is used, 'cataloguing should take from 20 per cent to 50 per cent as much time'.[4] If cataloguing takes 50 per cent as much time, then each full-time person would work at the rate of 2000 titles per year or slightly more than 1 title per hour. A recent study[5] of the OCLC system revealed that, in 19 participating libraries, the estimated mean rate of cataloguing at a CRT terminal on the OCLC network was 14 per hour when a cataloguing record was already in the system—the equivalent of 'cataloguing copy from another library'. If it is assumed that, in addition to the terminal operator, a full-time equivalent of one more person is required physically to process the book and to file cards in the catalogue, the rate of this type of cataloguing productivity on the OCLC system is 7 titles per person per hour—a seven-fold increase. Since the five large university libraries (those spending more than $500,000 a year for materials) in the study find 66 per cent of their cataloguing already in the system (a percentage probably higher than would be located by manual procedures) there is at least an overall 4·6 times increase in cataloguing productivity for those large libraries on the OCLC computerized network.

With the future introduction of further scale economies and

[4] Rogers, R. D. and Weber, D. C. *University Library Administration* (New York: H. W. Wilson Co., 1971). p. 176.

[5] Hewitt, Joe A. *The Academic Library and On-line Cataloguing: a Study of the Charter Members of the Ohio College Library Center* (Columbus, Ohio: The Ohio State University Libraries (In press)).

mechanization, it can be expected that a computerized library network will greatly increase productivity of staff.

SUMMARY

Classical libraries are highly labour intensive and, as Baumol and Marcus have shown, their rate of increase of per-unit costs has been six times that of the wholesale price index. Computerized library networks are introducing to librarianship a new system that increases staff productivity, thereby decelerating the rate of cost rise. It now appears certain that libraries, at long last, will join that vast majority of the economic community contributing to economic growth.

Comment by Ralph M. Shoffner (Ringgold Corporation)

The purpose of this comment is to provide counterpoints to some of the points raised in the main paper in order to identify extensions or qualifications that should be made of these points. In general, I am in agreement with Mr Kilgour's theme that information technology, particularly that associated with the electronic digital computer, presents the libraries of the world with the opportunity for, and perhaps the requirement for, rapid innovation.

LIBRARIES DON'T PRODUCE STUDENTS

The macro-economic data used by Baumol and Marcus[1] does not provide a measure of library's output. The measure which they used, library cost per student, is simply the total library cost divided by the number of students (full time equivalent) in the population served. Nothing is indicated about the number of units of service provided. If we ratio total expenditure for convenience foods to total population and find its value is increasing, we know only that people are spending more—not how much output and prices are changing.

An increase of library budgets with the intention of increasing the level of library cost per student. And we know that one of the intentions of the post-Sputnik decade was to increase library output. Unfortunately, we do not have the national data on library output with which to determine the extent to which output did change.

One can make the definition of library output as complex as, say, that of a petroleum refinery. However, there are some simple counts that would give some idea of the level of performance of academic libraries. Total usage is the most obvious. It could be counted and segmented by: place of use—in library/out of library; type of material—monograph, journal, microform, . . . ; cause of use—assigned/independent; source of material—local/inter-library loan; and, type of user—faculty, graduate student, under-graduate . . . . Such segmentation would be useful as changes occur in our national policy of support for academic institutions.

Some useful secondary counts are the number of reference questions answered, the number of references provided, the number of different users served, the amount of telephone traffic and the amount of floor traffic.

A LIBRARY IS A DISTRIBUTOR

Although the wholesale price index is a handy one to use, it gives a misleading impression of the performance of libraries (even assuming a constant level of output) relative to comparable enterprises. Libraries are not manufacturers or producers; they are distributors.

Libraries are no more technologically retarded, or labour-intensive, than other distributing enterprises, e.g., groceries, automobile dealers and clothing stores. Indeed, if a library had to buy a book each time it provided one to a borrower, as these other distributors must, then the public library would be as labour intensive

[1] Baumol, William J. and Marcus Matityahu, *Economics of Academic Libraries* (Washington, D.C.: American Council on Education, 1973).

as a grocery store, and an academic library less so than a clothing store.[2] Since most production technology has been irrelevant to the major activities of distribution enterprises, it is not surprising that, as Mr Kilgour points out, production technology has been little used in libraries.

On the other hand, information technology is highly relevant to the critical problems of distribution. These include: location of the library (store); size; layout; access, physical and intellectual (exposure and advertising of the merchandise); and selection (inventory) policy and control. As a result, we can expect many uses of information technology to be developed for libraries.

LIBRARIES ARE BUYING MORE THAN CARD SETS FROM OCLC

At present, the average library is paying OCLC on the order of $2 per card set delivered. By contrast, this library could purchase card sets containing the same information from commercial firms for less than half the cost. There are at least four firms in the United States that are currently offering computer-produced catalogue card sets containing Library of Congress source cataloguing: Baker and Taylor, Blackwell North America, Bro-Dart, and Josten's. At least two of these offer the ability to modify the information contained and to provide cataloguing for material not covered by the Library of Congress. The price for a minimum card set (two author cards, one title card, subject and added author cards as needed) begins at about $0·30.

Assuming that OCLC customer libraries are aware of the alternatives and that they are making rational purchasing decisions, then they are buying more than card sets. There are two aspects of the service provided which is likely to be desired by the libraries: the immediate ability, via the video display terminal, to review and modify the contents of the catalogue record on file that will be used to produce the card set to be sent out; and the building and maintenance of an on-line union catalogue of the holdings of the participating libraries, with costs covered by the card set pricing.

As the cataloguing records in the on-line files grow older, they will be used less for the production of card sets. Thus, current revenues to cover the cost of holding the records will be reduced. There are different pricing strategies which can be used to cover these holding costs: the original price of the card set could

[2] National Center for Educational Statistics, *Statistics of Public Libraries Serving Areas With at Least 25,000 Inhabitants, 1968*: (Washington, D.C.: US Government Printing Office, HE 5.215: 15068-68, May, 1970).

Oregon State System of Higher Education, *Biennial Report of the Interinstitutional Library Council, 1972–1974* (Ashland, Oregon, October 1974).

Public, 1968	*Total*	*Margin*	*Materials*	*Staff*	*Capital*	*Other*
Actual	100%	0	14	48	12	13
Adjusted 'sale'	100%	10	77	9	2	2
OSSHE, 1972–4						
Actual	100%	0	31	64	*	5
Adjusted 'sale'	100%	10	67	21	*	2

* Not available. Inclusion would reduce the other percentages.

be calculated to cover the holding costs for the indefinite future; the current price of card sets can be set to recover total current holding costs; or, separate pricing, which is independent of card set supply, could be established for other services relating to these records or simply for holding these records.

Pricing other services is the most direct approach. However, it may suffer from customer resistance since it is placing a price on an activity which appeared to be 'free' in the manual analogue. Yet, unless the purpose of the pricing relates to the maintenance of these records on-line, there will be cost and capacity pressures to remove these 'unused' records from the system.

OCLC IS AN ALTERNATIVE ORGANIZATION

Previously, I have hypothesized that the rate of library automation cannot be significantly increased unless there is a change of approach:[3]

1. The economic advantages of using computers are unclear.
   (*a*) Both development costs and operating costs (including staffing and maintenance) are uncertain.
   (*b*) If money is saved through the use of computers, it may not benefit the library, since its budget is set by a controlling institution.
2. Monetary commitment to innovate is large, compared to the individual library budget.
3. The systems and procedures developed by one library have been difficult to understand and adapt to the uses of another library. Staff who are competent in information technology, and who are normally in short supply, are required to install and maintain such systems.

An organization such as OCLC absorbs the uncertainty of the development cost, reduces the relative size of the monetary commitment, and provides the staff competence necessary for the technological transfer.

These advantages could be provided by any other development organization. However, OCLC offers a different organizational approach. As a not-for-profit corporation whose board of trustees are customers, OCLC is between the consolidated library system on the one hand and the private corporation on the other. It offers the reality of a large number of library customers and concomitant usage than a consolidated library system could hope to achieve. It allows the possibility (though in some cases, not the political reality) that the individual library may withdraw as a customer. It allows access to public risk capital with an established customer base to benefit from successful development.

Interestingly, OCLC also provides the prospect that the library customers may funnel 'saving' from computer use into continued technological development. That is, the price of services provided could be set to provide excess revenues for development work. Since they may not be able to divert the money to other library uses, libraries are likely to be willing to pay without regard to present library costs or the prices quoted by for-profit competitors, so long as they are in favour of the work done.

[3] Shoffner, Ralph M. 'The Economics of National Automation of Libraries', *Library Trends*, 18:4, (April, 1970), p. 448–63.

WE NEED PRODUCT INNOVATION

Providing faster access to the same catalogue content via on-line computer systems is better than slower access by manual methods, but it will take us only so far. To make major progress, it is critical to improve the nature of the intellectual access provided. We will need to continue to provide access by author and title. We will need to maintain our authorities and catalogue codes, because to organize and maintain access to millions of pieces of recorded language requires that thousands of people understand the cataloguing structure and use it in a consistent manner. While the use of KWIC (or KWOC) key word indexing of titles has been demonstrated to be of use, there is no prospect that it will replace catalogue codes because consistency would demand that tens of thousands of authors understand the ground rules for representing the content of their books in their titles.

What is needed is more subject cataloguing and more cataloguing codes concerned with the representation of subject content. At present, there are, on the average, less than two subject headings assigned to a book. Though the theoretical foundations are not especially firm, this level of indexing has been shown to be inadequate from a quantitative point of view.[4] As a practical matter, few would argue.

To increase the access to books will require the development of an improved subject cataloguing procedure. At present, the authority is the Library of Congress list of some 100,000 subject headings. These headings are listed, but they are not defined or delimited in relation to each other. Here would seem a good place to start, since deeper indexing of books will require a larger and more redundant indexing structure. Improving our current access structure is a large job and it will probably take decades to accomplish as an operational reality. We should get started with it.

[4] Resnikoff, Howard L. and Dolby, James L. *Access* (Los Altos, California: R & D Consultants Company, May, 1971).

Summary of the Discussion

Professor Tyler introduced Mr Kilgour's paper. In the 19th century, libraries were largely repositories with limited clienteles. After the spread of free public libraries in the latter part of the century, such features as card indexes, card catalogues, classification systems, and separate reference libraries developed. But these advances, largely concentrated in the 20th century, have left libraries labour intensive and increasingly inefficient. (A study by Baumol and Marcus is often cited, showing operating cost per student as rising 45 per cent in a period of near-constant wholesale prices.)

It has become obvious to Mr Kilgour that libraries should shift to the labour-saving technology, the so-called 'American System', involving such features of modern industrialization as assembly lines, integration, interchangeable components, and automation. In addition to saving labour, these improvements can provide better control and increase the economies of large scale. On the other hand, such technology is impractical for the individual library. The answer, according to Mr Kilgour is computerized networking.

The computerized network with which Mr Kilgour is himself associated is the Ohio College Library Center (OCLC), whose services extend well beyond the State of Ohio. *Professor Tyler* feels that the description of OCLC is the most interesting part of the Kilgour paper. The basic service of OCLC has been to share cataloguing costs for its member libraries, blunting the rate of rise in library costs and postponing the need for computerization of other activities.

Professor Tyler's own comments concentrated upon Mr Kilgour's omissions. He would have liked more description of OCLC services. He wondered whether more traditional libraries could not share machine-readable data on their own and, if so, how it might be done. He wondered also about the cost of library computerization for libraries of various sizes and types, and how these costs should be priced. He professed himself unclear about the definition of the OCLC's output, a public good with derived demand and, therefore, like research and education generally, difficult to evaluate. Like other critics, *Professor Tyler* found cost per student a misleading measure of efficiency, particularly because it was affected so sharply by changes in the number of students. Why not consider costs per book, *Professor Tyler* asked, or, perhaps, per employee? If costs are rising for other reasons than higher labour costs, *Professor Tyler* also wondered whether OCLC would reduce them. He was not sure what benchmark or standard Mr Kilgour had used in calling the library industry labour intensive, and felt that, librarians still being relatively cheap, labour intensive methods might still be more economical than capital intensive computer networking. *Professor Tyler's* own hope was to get to a system of machine-readable databanks as quickly as possible and by any method which will prove practical, rather than waiting for largescale networking.

A comment by Mr Shoffner was summarized by *Professor M. Perlman.* Mr Shoffner objected to Mr Kilgour's measure of output, and, also, to his analogies between a library and a seller of labour-intensive services on the private market. As for OCLC, private firms compete with it in supplying card sets to libraries; to justify the claims made for OCLC, it must offer more than card sets. In general, more comparison should have been made between OCLC and its alternatives.

Also, more innovation is required in cataloguing by subjects, i.e. in the classification of library holdings.

Dr Heidemann made the first oral comment. He inquired whether the savings on cataloguing costs under OCLC might not be balanced by higher capital costs? He wished to know more about overall savings to participating libraries. Also, he desired more information about possible internationalization of the OCLC system. Is access limited by language, or by type of use? Is it intended to take over other systems? Is it necessary for participants to maintain card catalogues?

Mr Evans defended Mr Kilgour's use of cost per student as a unit. It is used as a basis for public budgetary allotments; good or bad, librarians must pay attention to it, although some try to break away.

Professor Shoup doubted that a library was a true public good. For a true public good, no demander can be excluded by pre-selection, and service is joint over consumers. Libraries, it seemed to him, are more like large theatres with unused capacities, so that their economic decisions should take account of marginal, as well as average, costs. *Professor M. Perlman* asked whether, on the Shoup definition, a highway which excluded motorcycles would still be a public good. Professor Kindleberger identified the public-good aspect of the library as the preservation of information for the future, as in the case of a museum.

To *Professor Blaug*, the key question in distinguishing public from private goods was whether exclusion of demands or demanders was practicable either by pricing or by some other form of rationing. The library is a multi-product enterprise; some of its outputs may be public goods and others may not. Any overall estimate of library efficiency requires subjective weighting of units of output when prices are unavailable. This is a problem of subjective valuation, and librarians operate on the basis of implicit preference functions which Professor Blaug wishes could be made explicit and explained to the public and to legislators. *Professor Wolfe* characterized what Professor Blaug had in mind as PPBS analysis (planning-programming-budgeting system), which, he agreed, was extremely difficult.

Professor M. Perlman recalled a PPBS study of the division of time in the University of Pittsburgh hospitals, which was terminated by the hospitals because it gave what doctors considered 'wrong' answers, namely, that research cost more in terms of patient care than doctors believed it did. *Professor Blaug*, however, said that time constraints might be fitted into a PPBS study with other objectives being of major concern. He mentioned studies at the University of Durham in England as having contributed to the solution of Professor Perlman's problem.

Replying to these comments, *Mr Kilgour* reminded his audience that OCLC dates only from 1967 and that on-line services began only in 1971. It is the largest network of its kind in the United States with 726 terminals serving 430 institutions from coast to coast and with European connections as well. Its objectives are to make resources available and to reduce the rise in costs. Shared cataloguing is rising, in any event, and he believes OCLC to be cheaper than alternative systems.

When costs are saved in cataloguing, changes in library objectives become possible, and this is an important point for the future. Mr Kilgour agreed with most of the criticism of cost per student as a basic unit, but called it part of the conventional wisdom. OCLC plans to improve interfacing to provide access to data bases outside of its own system; other secondary services by libraries have been successful for nearly 150 years. He has not reached any firm decision as to whether the conventional card catalogue now in existence can ever be dispensed with, but is convinced that future catalogues will be on-line. And, as a final note, *Mr Kilgour* assured his critics that his cost estimates included capital costs. OCLC's current financial problem, he went on, is largely one of short-term cash flow, not long-term capital at all.

10 The Changing Modes of Data in Recent Research

Naomi Perlman*
UNIVERSITY OF PITTSBURGH
ASSOCIATE EDITOR, *JOURNAL OF ECONOMIC LITERATURE*

Mark Perlman*
UNIVERSITY OF PITTSBURGH
MANAGING EDITOR, *JOURNAL OF ECONOMIC LITERATURE*

Using two overlapping samples of articles from the JEL 1970–74 *data base, the authors analyse the distribution of economics articles among the subfields, the changes in the distribution 1970–74, and the importance of empirical data generally and by subfield. There is also a casual examination of the quality of empirical data used.*

INTRODUCTION

This article is an effort at evaluating the nature of the current output of economics articles. We focus on a small number of points which, in turn, affect a large amount of professional effort. Our principal task is to indicate the distribution of articles over subfields of economics and the degree to which empiricism dominates economists' research.

The line of thought starts by identifying the material bases for our own investigation. We have used two universes, both being sets of journals, 1970–74. We then describe the classification system that the American Economic Association has developed, and we analyse briefly some implications inherent in the way that system has grown.

The major part of our findings is in the second section of this paper. There we report on the distribution of research effort (as shown in a number of articles) by subject category. Next, we turn to the incidence of empirical effort by detailed subject category. We end by drawing some tentative conclusions (essentially inferences) about some problems that we see emerging in empirical research in economics.

* Two administrators at the University of Pittsburgh have been of inestimable assistance in our work on this paper. Professor Jerome Rosenberg (Dean of the Faculty of Arts and Sciences) allocated funds for data processing at the University's Computer Centre, and Mr Philip Sidel, Technical Director of the Social Science Computer Research Institute, gave us considerable personal assistance in the necessary data programming.

I. THE COMPOSITION OF THE DATA BASE

A. THE DATA BASE

The *Journal of Economic Literature* classifies the economics articles found in about 220 journals for immediate use in the quarterly journal and for subsequent use in an annual index. As we use student and professorial talent in the University of Pittsburgh Economics Department to do this classifying and checking, and as these individuals are not always fluent in non-English languages, our data base consists almost exclusively of articles in English. We do include articles where English summaries appear in some of the 220 journals, but the general rule is that our data base pertains primarily to articles in the English language.

We began our effort in September of 1968. At that time, material was processed on typed pages. In 1971 we moved to the use of a computer. While we have put the 1969 material on tape, that tape is not presently available for use. At the present time (February, 1975), we have a computerized data base for material for the period 1970 to mid-1974. Because of the inevitable lags in processing the data, less than half of the 1974 entries are available at the time of writing.

This paper presents results from two overlapping selections of journals drawn from the overall journal collection. The first group, List A (see Appendix I), contains material from 47 journals that we believe represent the 'hard core' general journals whose objective is to cover the entire economics discipline. The larger group, List B (see Appendix I), adds to List A material from an additional 67 journals (making a total of 114 journals). The additional ones consist of specialized journals where the intent is to provide depth or intensive investigation of particular subfields (e.g. monetary, labour, or agricultural economics). Of course, most of our conclusions are largely shaped by what we included in the two lists. Although our List B covers only about half of the journals, it represents about 70 per cent of the articles that the *Journal of Economic Literature* classifies; the distribution within the two groups is, of course, weighted by our decision to include one specialized or exclude another specialized journal. However, after one has perused the list of journals (and inevitably discovered a few that should have been included or a few that should have been excluded) the likelihood is that most people would have made a selection roughly similar to ours.

A more serious problem, of course, deals with the assumption that all articles are essentially homogeneous in importance and length. We know that they are not, particularly since we include notes, comments, and communications as well as articles. However, we have treated them as though they are; in fact, we treat articles on a binary basis rather than weighting them by length, by some measure of footnote citation consequence, or by some other similarly elaborate technique.

B. THE JOURNAL OF ECONOMIC LITERATURE CLASSIFICATION SYSTEM

There are several classification systems for materials in economics. Most of them were designed for the classification of books. In the 1960s, the classification of articles was begun by the American Economic Association, with a broad grouping of 18 categories used in the *Journal of Economic Abstracts* and a 700 category breakdown, developed at Yale University (in part for the Association) by Professors John Perry Miller and Richard Ruggles, used in the *Index of Economic Articles*. In 1968, the American Economic Association appointed a classification committee who developed a new system to replace these other systems and to co-ordinate it with the American National Scientific Register.

In the last few years, classification systems have been developed for computerized systems such as the International Labour Organization's system and the UNESCO related International Committee for Documentation in the Social Sciences. The ILO and the International Committee are considerably more detailed than is the *Journal of Economic Literature* plan.

The present American Economic Association's classification system consists of a 1-digit, 10-pigeon hole system, which is further divided into a 2-digit, 36-pigeon hole system; then into a 3-digit, 100-pigeon hole system; and, finally, into a 4-digit, 300-pigeon hole system. The whole system may be found in Appendix II.

Analysis in this paper makes alternative use of the 2-digit, the 3-digit, and the 4-digit classification systems. Since these systems are related (e.g. the 3-digit system is a disaggregation of the 2-digit contents, and the 4-digit system is a further disaggregation of the 3-digit material in the same general class), we have, in the body of the article, simply referred to the most aggregated form which demonstrates the point that we are trying to make.

Classification systems, like facts, do not really speak for themselves. Articles are classified with certain specific criteria in mind. The *Journal of Economic Literature* classification system has major elements that control the analytical results. To start, all economics material is divided into ten very broad groups—the last is so widesweeping as to be almost a residual. These groups are then divided and subdivided into increasingly narrow units. By contrast with the Yale University *Index of Economic Journals* system, the subfields include theory articles as well as empirical articles.

The system was perceived, secondly, as operating for published format, rather than for popular access to a centralized computer data bank. Third, the system was designed for research analysis rather than for teaching purposes. For example, although growth theory is usually taught in macro-theory courses, our instructions were to treat it as a separate category.

In the actual task of classification, three policies emerge:

(*a*) Limit the number of categories and cross classifications.
(*b*) Apply the criterion 'If you were a research person interested in a particular topic heading, would you be interested in having this article drawn to your attention?—that is, should it be listed in this classification?'
(*c*) Favour empirical content (i.e. subject matter) over analytical method. This decision implies that someone interested in cost-benefit methods used in analysing returns to education would not automatically be led to cost-benefit methods used in transportation economics. He would be led, however, to other methods used in the analysis of the education area.

The consequences of the foregoing policies are limited numbers of categories and cross classifications. The intent is to have classified in one, two, or three categories, all articles that might interest a researcher pursuing a particular topic. At the same time, the number of items in a classification was to be sufficiently limited to enable a user to distinguish among items. We have also been concerned with the number of items in a category, in a negative as well as a positive sense. That is, in the development of the 4-digit system, if the number of articles in the 3-digit classification was relatively sparse, we did not introduce subdivisions in the 4th digit. In other cases, where the number of entries appeared to us too large or where clear cut distinctions were apparent in the field, we did break the categories. Thus, the Scylla of excessive classification (too many locations) has been avoided and, at the same time, we have avoided the Charybdis of too few classifications. One of the criticisms of the previous system used by the American Economic Association (that is, prior to the present one) was that it tended to lump too much in the 'theory' group. Consequently, we have classified articles in the theory group only if they deal exclusively with theory, narrowly perceived, or if the content appears to be such as would interest people concerned only with purely theoretical discussions. This decision has resulted in reducing somewhat the size of the general theory category and transferring a great many essentially theoretical articles elsewhere.

We have also tried to be internally consistent, although, at the same time, we have recognized that the classification system takes account of changing perceptions of concepts and of the discipline, itself. We have continued to use a particular category for one type of article until it becomes apparent that a new category would be clearly useful.

II. ANALYSIS OF DATA BASE

A. DISTRIBUTION BY SUBJECT CATEGORY

Theory as distinct from other categories. Certain elements stand out in any analysis of the indexed material. Table 1 indicates the 2-digit breakdown of the classification of articles. In both Lists A and B, 'theory' is the largest single category. In List A, consisting of the core group of journals, the general economic theory category (group 02) included, during 1970–74, between 27 and 33 per cent of the total articles; in other words, almost one-third of the articles carried a general theory classification. Yet there are several other categories, particularly on the 3- and 4-digit levels, which are clearly theory, rather than empirical, entities. These are:

111	Economic growth theory and models
1342	Inflation theories; studies illustrating inflation theories
3112	Monetary theory; empirical studies
3135	Portfolio selection: theories and studies
3212	Fiscal theory; empirical studies illustrating fiscal theory
411	International trade theory
4312	General balance of payments and adjustment mechanisms; theory
4410	Theory of international investment and capital flows
821	Theory of labour markets and leisure
9411	Theory of regional economics.

Adding these ten categories, List A suggests that at least 45–50 per cent of all articles are theoretical. In List B, 15–17 per cent are of the 02 category and 24–28 per cent should be considered theoretical according to the augmented perception.

The relative size of our categories. What follows relates primarily to List B and is intended to provide in-depth or intensive investigation of particular subfields as well as of the so-called core areas of modern economics. It is important to note that we are aware that this List B represents only a bare half of the titles of journals that the *Journal of Economic Literature* classifies; however, the number of entries covered in List B represents approximately 68–80 per cent of the total number of entries that our classifiers processed.

The theory group, as mentioned immediately above, is by far the largest group of articles. The next largest subject area is the 1-digit labour division (consisting of five 2-digit groups); it is 16–20 per cent, and although it contains some theoretical material (class 821), it is overwhelmingly empirical. The third largest is the industrial organization, technological change, and industry studies division (again a 1-digit division made up of four 2-digit groups); it contains about 14–15 per cent of the total number of articles. Monetary economics is the fourth largest entity with 11–14 per cent. Much to our surprise, business administration, including business finance, marketing, and accounting, is the fifth largest cluster with 10–14 per cent of the citations. The sixth largest is inter-

TABLE 10.1 DISTRIBUTION OF 2-DIGIT CLASSIFICATION (LISTS A AND B, 1970–74)

Per cent of entries

	List A					*List B*				
	1970	*1971*	*1972*	*1973*	*(Partial) 1974*	*1970*	*1971*	*1972*	*1973*	*(Partial) 1974*
01 General economics	2·84	2·81	3·48	2·64	3·56	2·29	2·60	2·76	2·15	3·31
02 General economic theory	27·85	28·85	30·73	26·77	32·57	16·00	15·48	17·16	15·19	16·87
03 History of thought; methodology	3·03	4·43	5·16	4·19	4·27	2·51	3·01	3·30	2·56	3·24
04 Economic history	1·68	2·81	1·74	1·95	1·85	4·31	4·99	4·07	3·99	4·35
05 Economic systems	2·97	2·89	3·65	2·13	2·13	2·17	1·64	1·91	1·43	1·23
11 Economic growth; development; planning theory and policy	9·99	9·57	7·80	7·70	5·83	6·60	6·16	5·04	4·79	4·02
12 Economic development studies	6·83	5·35	4·21	5·40	3·13	7·23	4·56	4·02	4·74	3·18
13 Economic fluctuations; forecasting; stabilization; inflation	5·67	7·95	8·69	8·73	9·39	4·20	6·16	5·56	6·65	7·40
21 Econometric, statistical and mathematical methods, models	4·71	3·31	4·37	4·14	3·84	5·91	5·17	6·68	6·85	5·71
22 Economic and social statistics	4·77	2·96	3·31	3·68	3·98	4·14	3·53	3·45	3·90	4·87
31 Domestic monetary and financial theory and institutions	11·93	10·06	10·71	11·14	10·81	11·09	12·53	11·67	12·53	14·47
32 Fiscal theory and policy; public finance	8·51	9·50	9·03	7·70	8·82	9·00	8·50	8·87	8·73	7·07
41 International trade theory	6·64	5·21	4·77	5·00	3·70	3·34	3·10	2·68	2·64	1·82
42 Trade relations; commercial policy; international economic integration	4·96	4·64	5·05	4·19	2·99	3·74	3·48	3·48	3·29	2·21

43 Balance of payments; international finance	5·22	4·71	3·87	6·15	2·99	3·11	3·42	3·43	3·85	2·14
44 International investment and foreign aid	4·00	3·10	2·47	3·22	2·84	3·14	2·42	2·31	2·83	2·79
50 Administration, business finance; marketing; accounting	—	—	—	—	—	—	—	—	·02	—
51 Administration	1·61	1·27	1·40	1·32	2·56	4·54	3·01	2·58	3·99	4·67
52 Business finance and investment	3·42	3·17	2·08	2·76	2·56	4·37	4·00	3·20	3·77	4·61
53 Marketing	·45	·28	·22	·69	1·56	2·80	1·72	2·01	1·98	1·69
54 Accounting	·06	·14	·06	—	·28	2·40	1·96	2·23	1·60	2·53
61 Industrial organization and public policy	6·33	6·33	5·78	4·88	9·10	5·63	6·66	5·12	5·49	6·68
62 Economics of technological change	1·83	1·83	1·96	1·84	·57	1·80	1·55	2·06	1·38	1·82
63 Industry studies	5·67	5·21	5·10	6·84	6·97	5·94	5·32	5·61	6·90	6·49
64 Economic capacity	·58	·21	·34	·11	·43	·29	·15	·20	·07	·26
71 Agriculture	2·13	2·18	1·46	1·84	·85	7·03	7·13	6·31	5·66	5·26
72 Natural resources	1·35	2·32	3·42	2·93	3·27	2·66	3·97	4·40	3·27	3·50
73 Economic geography	·06	·07	·11	—	—	·46	·44	·35	·27	·39
80 Manpower; labour; population	·06	—	—	—	—	·03	—	—	—	—
81 Manpower training and allocation; labour force and supply	1·55	2·32	1·12	1·67	1·56	2·83	3·62	2·26	2·76	3·11
82 Labour markets; public policy	8·19	7·32	8·75	10·40	4·13	9·37	8·76	8·57	9·68	9·73
83 Trade unions; collective bargaining; labour management relations	1·03	·49	1·18	1·03	2·70	2·54	2·45	2·31	2·13	2·73
84 Demographic economics	·90	·91	1·35	2·47	4·13	1·09	1·11	1·32	2·23	2·27
85 Human capital	1·55	1·55	1·74	1·95	2·70	1·34	1·40	1·51	1·65	1·75
91 Welfare programmes	6·00	4·93	4·43	5·97	6·12	5·51	5·34	5·02	6·75	7·40
92 Consumer economics	2·77	2·39	2·97	2·87	1·99	2·60	2·45	2·68	2·56	2·53
93 Urban economics	2·39	3·10	2·02	2·93	2·56	3·26	3·80	3·38	4·52	2·73
94 Regional economics	2·84	2·60	2·64	3·22	3·27	3·80	3·86	3·40	4·77	4·15

national economics, with 9–13 per cent of the citations. The seventh largest is fiscal economics, with only 7–9 per cent of the citations.

Some observations on particular classes. We examined the 3-digit classes; Table 2 presents a 3-digit breakdown for those 2-digit classes where we felt a further breakdown was useful.

Microeconomic analysis. Half of all the general economic theory articles are in microeconomic analysis. On the basis of data not included with this article, but which is available from us in mimeographed form, the theory of household-comsumer demand (cell 0222) seems to be of falling interest during the five years that we surveyed. Interest in the theory of production (cell 0223) peaked in 1971 and has been falling since; apparently, interest in microanalytic production functions has also waned. Finally, interest in price and market theory of the firm and industry in noncompetitive relations (cell 0226) also peaked in 1971 and has since declined.

Welfare theory. Starting with 1971 (that is, after 1970), interest in welfare theory seems to have been rather stable.

History of economic thought. Interest in economic thought grew between 1970 and 1972 and seems to have remained fairly stable since then. Perhaps it reflects the impact of the Nobel Award in Economics, first given in 1969. In any event, although the classification is not a large one, the number of articles is substantial, particularly in view of the decline in courses in the field. This may be explained, in part, by Keynesian economics having become history of thought.

Economic growth; development; planning theory and policy. As a whole, interest in this category has diminished sharply in the five years that we have been classifying articles. Both growth theory and models (class 111), the biggest category comprising about one-half of the total group, and economic development theory and models (class 112) are the subgroups causing the decline. One sub-category in this group, economic planning (class 113), seems not to have suffered from a diminution in interest as the others have.

Economic development studies. This group has lost relative ground. Most of the decline has been in the area of less industrialized country studies.

Economic fluctuations; forecasting, stabilization; and inflation. This group, as one might expect, has experienced an increase in interest. There has been a marked rise in activity in general outlook and stabilization theories and policies (class 133). Another subgroup, inflation (class 134), is up even more.

Monetary economics. This is a particularly popular field in the core group of journals and the larger list (List B). Within it, policy, theory, and institutions (class 311) is particularly significant, containing about 75 per cent of all of the monetary economics articles. Monetary theory (cell 3112) is a very important cell in the whole monetary field. Interest in this area may have been stimulated by the combination of theory and empirical work perceived by Professor Milton Friedman. There are those who emulate his views, while many others are stimulated by them to disagree with him; all, however, seem to be influenced by his partly theoretical, partly empirical methods. Financial markets, including portfolio selection (class 313), has had a marked increase in interest. Credit (class 315) never seems to have 'gotten off the ground'. We speculate that, although this topic is of considerable interest to practitioners both in business and government, it apparently has not been of similar concern to those scholars who write articles in the field.

Fiscal economics. Although this group is only the seventh largest in economics, interest in it has remained relatively stable. About half of the articles are in fiscal theory and policy (class 321). Within that class, fiscal theory (cell 3212) peaked in 1971 and has now suffered a somewhat diminished interest. National government expenditure studies (cell 3221) also peaked in 1971. Finally, state and local government financing (class 324), including particularly revenue sharing, has always been of unexpectedly small academic interest; interest in it peaked in 1971.

International economics. Somewhat to our surprise, this subject category, perceived since Ricardo's time as the 'guts' of economic analysis, was only the sixth largest category. Articles on this topic have diminished in both Lists A and B, although the 1974 figure may be unrepresentative for all of the articles for that year. International trade theory (group 41), in particular, has suffered a very large decline; decline in this area is even greater in the so-called core journals (List A) than it is in List B. It may be that there will be a lagged revival of interest in the future—lagged only in the sense that it takes about two years for a new set of problems to emerge as a new group of articles.

Business administration; finance; marketing; and accounting. The relatively important quantitative role of studies in this area, usually perceived by academic economists as somewhat peripheral to the conventional or traditional focus of their interests, was (as we noted) a particular surprise to us.

Industrial organization; technological change; and industry studies. This cluster of articles was the third largest. We found relative size puzzling. We saw no clear trends regarding its relative importance or its composition. Apparently, economics of transportation, a very small class, seems to have peaked in 1971. On the other hand, industry studies, themselves, have grown in number—with service industries, initially a very small category, swelling in size.

Agricultural economics. Overall, there has been a marked decline in interest in agricultural economics.

Natural resources; conservation; and pollution. This has never been a large category. Conservation and pollution peaked in 1972. Natural resources, as a group, is of growing importance. Again, there is probably a lag between the impact of the OPEC monopoly pricing, first evident in 1973, and the emergence of a large number of articles.

Labour economics. This is, as we noted above, the second largest division of articles. Part of its relative strength stems, doubtless, from a recent emphasis on theoretical and empirical analysis of labour markets (group 82), which constitutes about half of all the articles within the general labour area. Further analysis of group 82 reveals that the bulk of the articles are divided between theory of labour markets and leisure (class 821) and labour market studies, wages, and employment (class 824). Interest in labour theory has increased very sharply in this period. Demographic economics and the economics of human capital (groups 84 and 85, respectively) are not large, but are rapidly increasing in size. Interest in trade unionism and collective bargaining (group 83) seems to be unchanged over the period of our investigation.

Welfare programmes. Interest in this area has gone up since 1970.

Regional economics. Interest in this area may have gone up, although it is probably too early to discern any real trend.

B. THE QUESTION OF LINKAGES

We have developed a programme for checking linkages between classes on the 3-digit level. The purpose of investigating pairs between classes is to determine whether we have sailed too close to the Scylla of too many classifications or to the Charybdis of too few classifications. On the whole, there are relatively few surprises.

We are aware that certain cells are intimately related; that is, a large percentage of certain articles classified in one cell is very likely to carry a cross-classification in another. Roughly 45 per cent of the articles carried no cross-classifications. In the main, the cross-classifications were scattered across the groups. This situation particularly pertains where microanalytic theory (class 022) has ties to applied areas such as organization and decision theory (class 511) or managerial economics (class 512). We were interested that there are fewer pairs between microanalytic theory and the applied fields than there are between macroanalytic theory and certain applied fields. One reason why this situation obtains is, undoubtedly, that much of what is now accepted as macroeconomic theory was perceived, until relatively recently, as 'business cycle theory', monetary theory, or fiscal economics (to name but a few of the many alternatives).

We have noted a strong relationship between macroeconomic analysis (class 023) and monetary theory, the consumption function (class 921—consumer economics), growth theory (class 111), and microanalytic theory (class 023) as well. Similarly, we have noted strong ties between welfare theory (class 024) and fiscal economics (class 321) and environmental studies (class 722).

Not unexpectedly, growth theory (class 111) pairs very frequently with macroeconomic analysis (class 023) and studies pertaining to technological change (class 621).

Country studies pertaining to less developed economies have a much heavier cross-pairing with work in the international economic area (the classes in the 400's series) than do developed countries. Country studies pertaining to less developed countries also have a large number of cross-pairings with labour market analysis (class 820).

We discovered that monetary theory and policy (class 311) has many pairings with macroeconomic analysis (class 023)—as we noted above, but there is also considerable cross-pairing with fiscal analysis (class 321) and, above all, with financial markets, including portfolio theory (class 520).

The group of articles on financial markets and portfolio theory (class 313) had considerable (about 40 per cent) pairing with the monetary economics areas (classes in the 310 series), as did those in financial markets and portfolio theory with business investment and finance. What surprised us somewhat, however, was the large number of articles on financial markets and portfolio theory that carried cross-referencing to general microanalytic theory (class 022).

Not unexpectedly, fiscal theory and policy (class 321) carried many pairings with welfare theory (class 024), with taxation (class 323), and with outlook and stabilization studies (class 123).

We found, interestingly, a rather pronounced pattern of studies on taxation (class 323) which overlapped studies on business finance (class 522) and on labour markets (class 824).

The international economics group (class 400) is probably over-subdivided. We are too close to the Scylla side. In any event, we noted a considerable amount of pairing between entities within the class 400 group.

One could proceed with this analysis indefinitely, but because of the shortage of space we will simply point out that the class 900 contains the heterogeneous mixture, and we discovered, consequently, virtually no cross-classification between applied welfare economics (class 911) and regional economics (class 940) and consumer economics (class 920).

Suffice it to remark that the experience of six years of classification probably should serve as a basis for a new look (perhaps by a select com-

TABLE 10.2 DISTRIBUTION OF 3-DIGIT CLASSIFICATION FOR SELECTED 2-DIGIT CLASSES

Per cent of entries

		List A					*List B*				
		1970	*1971*	*1972*	*1973*	*(Partial) 1974*	*1970*	*1971*	*1972*	*1973*	*(Partial) 1974*
02	General Economic Theory										
020	General Economic Theory	·32	—	·79	·29	1·42	·14	·12	·37	·19	·65
021	General Equilibrium Theory	2·39	2·11	2·41	1·72	2·42	1·40	1·26	1·47	·97	1·10
022	Microeconomic Theory	13·67	12·60	13·74	13·56	14·22	7·94	6·86	7·55	6·99	7·33
023	Macroeconomic Theory	7·29	7·04	7·68	6·09	7·54	3·71	3·65	4·22	3·46	3·76
024	Welfare Theory	5·74	7·81	7·68	5·80	7·54	3·29	4·18	4·22	3·77	4·22
025	Social Choice	1·87	2·53	1·96	2·18	3·13	1·14	1·23	1·07	1·28	1·49
11	Economic Growth; Development; Planning Theory and Policy										
110	Economic Growth; Development; Planning Theory and Policy	—	·07	—	—	—	—	·03	—	—	—
111	Economic Growth Theory and Models	5·29	3·87	3·93	4·08	2·84	2·89	2·19	1·99	2·20	1·36
112	Economic Development Models and Theories	3·03	3·17	1·79	2·13	1·71	2·00	2·10	1·47	1·38	1·69
113	Economic Planning Theory and Policy	1·48	2·18	1·79	1·32	1·85	1·37	1·61	1·22	·94	1·10
114	Economics of War, Defence, and Disarmament	·64	·70	1·23	·34	—	·66	·53	·82	·36	·13
12	Economic Development Studies										
120	Economic Development Studies	—	·07	·11	—	—	·09	·03	·05	—	—
121	Economic Studies of Less Industrialized Countries	3·87	2·89	2·52	2·81	1·42	4·80	3·04	2·83	2·98	2·08
122	Economic Studies of More Industrialized Countries	1·35	1·06	·95	1·32	1·28	·97	·73	·70	·80	·65
123	Comparative Economic Studies Involving Both More and Less Industrialized Countries; International Statistical Comparisons	2·06	1·41	·84	1·44	·43	1·63	·79	·55	1·09	·45

13	Economic Fluctuations, Forecasting, Stabilization, and Inflation										
131	Economic Fluctuations	1·87	1·34	·62	1·44	1·42	1·03	·96	·42	·73	·78
132	Economic Forecasting and Forecasting Models	1·35	1·62	1·57	1·95	1·28	1·06	1·49	1·34	1·67	1·36
133	General Outlook and Stabilization Theories and Policies	1·42	3·80	3·87	3·62	4·27	1·43	2·66	2·46	2·86	3·63
134	Inflation and Deflation	1·29	2·39	3·20	2·87	3·13	1·00	1·75	1·66	2·35	2·08
31	Domestic Monetary and Financial Theory and Institutions										
311	Domestic Monetary and Financial Theory and Institutions	8·64	7·39	7·85	7·75	6·12	6·09	6·45	6·18	5·93	5·58
312	Commercial Banking	·84	1·34	·73	1·15	·85	1·37	2·51	1·89	2·03	2·47
313	Financial Markets	2·71	2·18	2·64	2·53	3·70	3·63	4·09	4·20	4·72	6·10
314	Financial Intermediaries	·13	·21	·28	·52	·28	·40	·67	·55	·58	·97
315	Credit to Business, Consumer, etc. (including mortgages)	·52	·14	·17	·86	·43	·57	·50	·89	·92	1·30
32	Fiscal Theory and Policy; Public Finance										
321	Fiscal Theory and Policy	4·58	5·49	5·27	4·02	5·97	3·11	3·50	3·38	3·31	3·18
322	National Government Expenditures and Budgeting	·84	1·41	·95	·86	·57	·83	1·29	1·27	·94	·71
323	National Taxation and Subsidies	2·90	2·53	2·75	1·78	2·28	3·51	2·37	3·46	3·46	2·53
324	State and Local Government Finance	1·29	1·48	1·23	1·78	1·28	2·09	1·84	1·96	1·94	1·30
325	Intergovernmental Financial Relationships	·13	·28	·28	·57	·28	·51	·99	·42	·46	·32
43	Balance of Payments; International Finance										
430	Balance of Payments; International Finance	·06	·07	—	·06	—	·03	·06	·02	·02	—
431	Balance of Payments; Mechanisms of Adjustment; Exchange Rates	4·19	3·59	3·03	5·05	2·70	2·40	2·60	2·38	3·12	1·75
432	International Monetary Arrangements	1·48	1·41	1·18	1·67	·57	·91	1·11	1·44	1·23	·52

Table 10.2 (*Continued*)

		Per cent of entries									
		List A					List B				
		1970	*1971*	*1972*	*1973*	(*Partial*) *1974*	*1970*	*1971*	*1972*	*1973*	(*Partial*) *1974*
61	Industrial Organization and Public Policy										
610	Industrial Organization and Public Policy	—	—	—	—	—	·03	·03	—	·02	—
611	Industrial Organization and Market Structure	2·58	2·18	3·14	2·64	5·12	2·26	2·45	2·14	2·24	3·37
612	Public Policy Towards Monopoly and Competition	1·03	1·27	1·07	·80	1·99	1·29	1·84	1·39	1·14	1·62
613	Public Utilities and Government Regulation of Other Industries in the Private Sector	1·81	1·20	·90	·40	2·42	1·49	1·17	·77	1·04	1·95
614	Public Enterprises	·32	·42	·39	·23	·14	·20	·32	·22	·22	·06
615	Economics of Transportation	1·68	1·83	·90	1·03	·85	1·11	1·72	·99	1·14	·71
63	Industry Studies										
630	Industry Studies	·32	·63	·45	·92	1·14	·17	·32	·30	·65	·91
631	Industry Studies: Manufacturing	2·90	2·53	2·86	4·14	3·41	2·57	2·72	2·66	3·68	2·86
632	Industry Studies: Extractive Industries	·52	·42	·45	·46	·85	·91	·50	·45	·60	·84
633	Industry Studies: Distributive Trades	·32	·28	·11	·17	—	·57	·44	·52	·58	·26
634	Industry Studies: Construction	·64	·42	·17	·06	—	·54	·47	·60	·17	·13
635	Industry Studies: Services and Related Industries	·97	1·13	1·18	1·09	1·71	1·17	1·02	1·19	1·26	1·69
72	Natural Resources										
721	Natural Resources	·52	·42	·73	·92	1·42	1·71	1·49	1·51	1·62	1·88
722	Conservation and Pollution	·77	1·83	2·80	2·24	2·13	·94	2·57	3·03	1·84	2·08

82	Labour Markets; Public Policy										
821	Theory of Labour Markets and Leisure	2·32	2·81	3·76	5·11	4·27	1·23	1·87	2·14	2·88	2·21
822	Public Policy; Role of Government	·52	·63	1·35	·92	·57	1·37	1·14	1·44	1·35	1·43
823	Labour Mobility; National and International Migration	1·68	1·13	1·07	·98	·57	1·54	1·14	·99	1·06	·78
824	Labour Market Studies, Wages, Employment	4·38	3·59	3·87	4·94	3·41	5·14	4·70	4·37	4·96	5·32
825	Labour Productivity	·39	·42	·39	·52	·28	·60	·64	·57	·58	·65
826	Labour Markets: Demographic Characteristics	·45	·07	·39	·34	·43	·94	·53	·52	·44	·65
91	Welfare Programmes										
911	General Welfare Programmes	·39	·42	·28	·29	·71	·43	·50	·40	·73	1·17
912	Economics of Education (consumption side)	1·35	·63	·56	1·61	1·00	1·31	·85	·89	1·86	1·69
913	Economics of Health	1·81	1·27	1·12	1·21	1·00	1·20	1·11	·94	1·35	1·69
914	Economics of Poverty	1·23	·84	·56	·57	1·28	1·17	·85	·70	·77	·78
915	Social Security	·13	·07	·17	·06	·14	·29	·15	·27	·60	·19
916	Economics of Crime	·32	·21	·34	·69	·43	·20	·15	·25	·44	·39
917	Economics of Discrimination	1·42	1·90	1·63	1·90	2·28	1·51	2·31	2·06	1·52	2·08

mittee of the American Economic Association) at the classification system. Our reaction is that, although there were few surprises provided by the pairing system of analysis, such a system of analysis does suggest one way of steering a wise course between the two aforementioned rocks.

C. EMPIRICAL DATA

When we classified articles for use in our system, we did not include indicators of the presence, the date, or the quality of (episodic versus systematic) data in the article. Such information is, of course, useful, but it did not occur to us at the time when we first computerized the data base that this information was worth the additional cost of gathering it. Consequently, the best that we can do to indicate what proportion of the articles used empirical data is to employ proxy information.

Fortunately, we had a reasonably good proxy. Our classifications included the possible presence of up to five geographic descriptors. Whenever a geographic descriptor was assigned to an article, there was a strong presumption that that article had descriptive (episodic or quantitative) data because the geographic descriptor is intended to flag an article for any research investigator who is interested in a topic about a particular geographic area. There are certain adjustments that we made to correct for elements inherent in the classification system. In many comparative country studies where the number of countries exceeded five, we listed the article in comparative country studies (class 123) and did not use a geographic descriptor. Thus, when we came to studying our data base, we summed all of the articles that carried geographic descriptors and added all of the articles in class 123 (described above), made some allowance for duplication, added virtually all of the economic history articles (most of them carried geographic descriptors, anyway) and came up with the results that we are about to discuss. We should add, however, that we excluded several cells within the business administration division because the data in these divisions were often based on microanalytic studies pertaining to firms rather than to particular countries.

Overall, about 50 per cent of the articles had empirical content. As shown in Appendix III, the adjusted percentages ranged from 44–56 per cent; the unadjusted percentages from 39–52 per cent. Over time—that is, since 1970—the proportion seems to show neither an upward nor a downward trend.

The actual proportions of articles with geographic descriptors by 3-digit classes can be found in Appendix III. Most classes were characterized by geographic descriptor percentages well over the average. In particular, categories containing historical studies, the country studies, certain of the statistical data, some of the monetary and fiscal fields, and most of the international, industrial, labour, and welfare topics had a large proportion of geographic descriptors. Why, then, is the overall percentage so low?

As we noted before, a very large proportion of the total number of articles were essentially theoretical. Theoretical articles have a relatively low usage rate of empirical data. Consequently, the high incidence of theoretical articles and their low use of data explain why the total use of data applied to only about half of the number of articles.

There are exceptions to the previous generalization. Articles in macroeconomic theory (class 023) contained data about 25 per cent of the time. Similarly, articles in domestic monetary and financial theory (class 311) often carried descriptive material because they were concerned with policy as well as with theory. Finally, the theory of labour markets and leisure (class 821) had a high incidence of empirical material in its articles; whether this is the result of the labour field having been historically an empirical field and only recently perceived as a *a priori* political field, or whether the impact of behavioural studies (implicit in any study of this area) results in the use of empirical data is anyone's guess. Other theory classes had low percentages.

Besides the theoretical group, others with low empirical content were the statistical, econometric, and mathematical models (group 21), decision and organization theory (classes 511 and 512). Less expected were the relatively low percentages in the following classes: development theory and models, planning, inflation, and some of the monetary, international economics, and agricultural groups. Initial expectation was that the bulk of the articles would be tied, in some way, to empiricism in terms of either systematic statistical data or episodic descriptions. Several factors contributed to our view. One was a prevalent conviction (at least voiced) that hypotheses must be analysed in terms of data. Were such the case, it seemed logical to us that there would have been even greater reliance on data than we found. Another element that might reasonably have contributed to our initial expectation was that there seemed to be an increasing proportion of economists interested in the solution of policy dilemmas. We had thought that the tendency to discuss policy in truly abstract terms had been almost thoroughly offset by a preference for 'knowing the facts'.

After looking at our general results, we concluded that our initial expectations were erroneous because many hypotheses are tested by use of simulation (involving the use of non-specific data) or many policy alternatives are discussed on the basis of hypothetical costs and hypothetical benefits. As an indication of this point we observed that articles on natural resources (class 121) and conservation and pollution (class 722) had less than half of the articles containing empirical material.

There are three questions that may be raised about empirical data that are used in economics articles and books. Are data used? How good are the data for the purpose of the article—recency, relevancy, consistency? How are the data manipulated and for what purposes?

We have already identified the extent to which we found data used. In so doing, we have taken care to indicate the influence of the construction of our data base on our conclusions and to indicate that our classification system was set up for research rather than for teaching purposes.

In our effort to explore the other two questions, at least tentatively, we accessed our data base and went back to the original articles. We looked at articles for the United States in 3 cells for 1970 and 1973: income distribution (cell 2213), population (cell 8410), and economics of discrimination (cell 9170). We had selected these topics in part because they are areas in which policy decisions are being made, and it seemed to us that articles on these topics would probably be concerned with providing an empirical basis. There were fewer articles than we had anticipated, particularly in the income distribution and population areas. Consequently, such findings as we have are impressionistic and are fleshed out by impressions of books as well as articles.

There is an inevitable lag in the data used of at least a couple of years—inevitable in the sense of data publication delay, time required for analysis, and publication delay of the journal in which the article appears. In many articles, given this delay, the data used are up-to-date.

Some articles or books used data which were 4–6 years old as relevant to current issues without any proviso as to their recency. An example may be found in an OECD study published in late 1974 on population trends and forecasts in OECD countries. Although noting that most countries conducted censuses in 1970–71, the OECD requested its information prior to the availability of results. Thus, the figures for 1970–74 were estimated, and the forecasts for the period up to the year 2000 were not based on recent censuses. For the United States, for example, although population projections had been revised downward three times by 1972, only the first of these revisions were included. In a 1973 article, which carries as part of its title 'Some New Evidence', the conclusions were based on data (unpublished) from a 1967 Current Population Survey.

A fair proportion of the articles was primarily concerned with developing a model or a theory. The authors used data to support the model or theory, but were apparently unconcerned that these data were not the most recent. For example, several of the papers given at the National Bureau of Economic Research conference on fertility, in 1972 (printed in the *Journal of Political Economy* in 1973) used 1960 data. Certainly within the confines of the articles the data were appropriate; whether the theories would be upheld by later data remains unresolved.

Finally, in some instances, in the income distribution and discrimination areas, there are examples of models differing in variables or in form applied to much the same data, which yield different, but not necessarily definitive results.

In sum, we found that only about 50 per cent of the articles have empirical content. Statistical data cited are inevitably somewhat dated.

Although many articles use current data, others, for which currency is equally relevant, do not. A sizeable proportion of the articles are concerned more with the structure of a model or the important elements in a theory than with the recency of the data used for demonstration. Finally, conclusions from data may, in the final result, require examination of the statistical manipulation as well as of the data.

An explanation of these findings is suggested by studies that analyse citation usage and journal ratings. For example, Hawkins, Ritter, and Walter conclude in their article that

> . . . the more 'theoretical' or 'general' a journal, the greater its assessed prestige or status tends to be; the more 'applied or specialized' its focus, the lower its apparent reputation. A 'theoretical' or 'quantitative' paper published in a general journal (regardless of its quality) is likely to be perceived by one's colleagues as inherently superior to an 'applied' or 'institutional' paper in a more specialized journal (no matter how well done or how useful).[1]

[1] Hawkins, Robert G., Ritter, Lawrence S. and Walter, Ingo. 'What Economists Think of Their Journals', *Journal of Political Economy*, 81 (4), (July/August 1973), p. 1024.

Appendix I
Journals included in both A and B

(List A journals carry an asterisk)

Accounting Review
Agricultural Economics Research
Agricultural Finance Review
* *American Economic Review*
* *American Economist*
* *American Journal of Agricultural Economics*
American Journal of Economics and Sociology
Annals of Economic and Social Measurement
Antitrust Bulletin
* *Applied Economics*
Australian Economic History Review
* *Australian Economic Papers*
Australian Journal of Agricultural Economics
* *Banca Nazionale del Lavoro*
Bell Journal of Economics and Management Science
* *Brookings Papers on Economic Activity*
Bulletin of Economic Research
* *Bulletin of Economics and Statistics*
Bulletin for International Fiscal Documentation
Business History Review
California Management Review
Canadian Journal of Agricultural Economics
* *Canadian Journal of Economics*
Econometrica
* *Economia Internazionale*
Economic Development and Cultural Change
Economic Geography
Economic History Review
* *Economic Inquiry*
* *Economic Journal*
* *Economic Record*
* *Economica (NS)*
Economics of Planning
Engineering Economist
* *European Economic Review*
Exploration in Economic History
Federal Reserve Bank of St. Louis Review
Federal Reserve Bulletin
Finance and Development
Food Research Institute Studies
* *German Economic Review*
Growth and Change
Harvard Business Review
* *Hitotsubashi Journal of Economics*
Illinois Agricultural Economics
* *Indian Economic Journal*
Industrial and Labour Relations Review
Industrial Relations
* *International Economic Review*
International Labour Review
International Monetary Fund Staff Papers
Journal of American Statistical Association
Journal of Bank Research
Journal of Business
Journal of Common Market Studies
Journal of Developing Areas
Journal of Development Studies
Journal of Econometrics
Journal of Economic Education
Journal of Economic History
* *Journal of Economic Issues*
* *Journal of Economic Literature*
* *Journal of Economic Theory*
Journal of Finance
Journal of Financial and Quantitative Analysis
Journal of Human Resources
Journal of Industrial Economics
Journal of International Economics
Journal of Law and Economics
Journal of Marketing Research
Journal of Money, Credit, and Banking
* *Journal of Political Economy*
Journal of Regional Science
Journal of Royal Statistical Society
* *Kyklos*
Land Economics
* *Law and Contemporary Problems*
* *Lloyds Bank Review*
Management Accounting
* *Manchester School*
Monthly Labour Review
National Tax Journal
Natural Resources Journal

* *Nebraska Journal of Economics and Business*
* *Osaka Economic Papers*
Oxford Bulletin of Economics and Statistics
Oxford Economic Papers
Philippine Economic Journal
* *Public Choice*
Public Finance
Public Finance Quarterly
Public Policy
* *Quarterly Journal of Economics*
* *Quarterly Review of Economics and Business*
* *Review of Economic Studies*
* *Review of Economics and Statistics*
Review of Income and Wealth
* *Review of Radical Political Economics*
Review of Regional Studies
* *Review of Social Economy*
* *Schweitzerische Zeitschrift für Volkswirtschaft und Statistik*
Science and Society
* *Scottish Journal of Political Economy*
Social Security Bulletin
* *South African Journal of Economics*
* *Southern Economic Journal*
* *Survey of Currrent Business*
* *Swedish Journal of Economics*
* *Tijdschrift voor Economie*
Urban Studies
Water Resources Research
* *Weltwirtschaftliches Archiv*
World Development
* *Zeitschrift für Nationalökonomie*

Appendix II
Journal of Economic Literature Classification System

- 0 General Economics; Theory; History; Systems
  - 01 General Economics
    - 011 General Economics
      - 0110 General
      - 0111 Teaching of Economics
      - 0112 Role of Economics; Role of Economists
      - 0113 Relation of Economics to Other Disciplines
      - 0114 Relation of Economics to Social Values
      - 0115 Methods Used by Economists
  - 02 General Economic Theory
      - 0200 General Economic Theory
    - 021 General Equilibrium Theory
      - 0210 General Equilibrium Theory
    - 022 Microeconomic Theory
      - 0220 General
      - 0222 Theory of the Household (consumer demand)
      - 0223 Theory of Production
      - 0224 Theory of Distribution (factor) and Distributive Shares
      - 0225 Prices and Markets Theory of Firm and Industry in Competition; Single Market Equilibrium
      - 0226 Prices and Markets Theory of Firm and Industry in Noncompetitive Relations
    - 023 Macroeconomic Theory
      - 0230 General
      - 0231 Developments in General Macroeconomic Theory 1930–45
      - 0232 Theory of Aggregate Demand; Consumption
      - 0233 Theory of Aggregate Demand: Investment
      - 0234 Theory of Aggregate Supply
      - 0235 Theory of Aggregate Distribution
    - 024 Welfare Theory
      - 0240 General
      - 0242 Allocative Efficiency Including Theory of Cost/Benefit
      - 0243 Redistributive Aspects
      - 0244 Externalities
    - 025 Social Choice
      - 0250 Social Choice
  - 03 History of Thought: Methodology
    - 031 History of Economic Thought
      - 0310 General
      - 0311 Ancient, Medieval
      - 0312 Pre-Classical Except Mercantilist
      - 0313 Mercantilist
      - 0314 Classical
      - 0315 Austrian, Marshallian, Neoclassical
      - 0316 General Equilibrium until 1945
      - 0317 Socialist until 1945
      - 0318 Historical and Institutional
    - 032 History of Economic Thought (continued)
      - 0321 Other Schools Since 1800
      - 0322 Individuals
      - 0329 Other Special Topics
    - 036 Economic Methodology
      - 0360 Economic Methodology
  - 04 Economic History
    - 041 Economic History: General
      - 0410 General
      - 0411 Development of the Discipline
      - 0412 Comparative Intercountry or Intertemporal Economic History
    - 042 Economic History: North America (excluding Mexico)
      - 0420 General
      - 0421 History of Product Prices and Markets
      - 0422 History of Factor Prices

and Markets
0423 History of Public Economic Policy (all levels)
043 Economic History: Ancient and Medieval (until 1453)
0430 General
0431 History of Product Prices and Markets
0432 History of Factor Prices and Markets
0433 History of Public Economic Policy (all levels)
044 Economic History: Europe
0440 General
0441 History of Product Prices and Markets
0442 History of Factor Prices and Markets
0443 History of Public Economic Policy (all levels)
045 Economic History: Asia
0450 General
0451 History of Product Prices and Markets
0452 History of Factor Prices and Markets
0453 History of Public Economic Policy (all levels)
046 Economic History: Africa
0460 General
0461 History of Product Prices and Markets
0462 History of Factor Prices and Markets
0463 History of Public Economic Policy (all levels)
047 Economic History: Latin America and Caribbean
0470 General
0471 History of Product Prices and Markets
0472 History of Factor Prices and Markets
0473 History of Public Economic Policy (all levels)
048 Economic History: Oceania
0480 General
0481 History of Product Prices and Markets
0482 History of Factor Prices and Markets
0483 History of Public Economic Policy (all levels)
05 Economic Systems
051 Capitalist Economic Systems
0510 Market Economies; Includes Cooperatives in Predominantly Market Economies
052 Socialist and Communist Economic Systems
0520 Socialist and Communist Economic Systems
053 Comparative Economic Systems
0530 Comparative Economic Systems
1 Economic Growth; Development; Planning; Fluctuations
11 Economic Growth; Development; Planning Theory and Policy
111 Economic Growth Theory and Models
1110 Growth Theories
1112 One and Two Sector Growth Models and Related Topics
1113 Multisector Growth Models and Related Topics
1114 Monetary Growth: Models
112 Economic Development Models and Theories
1120 Economic Development Models and Theories
113 Economic Planning Theory and Policy
1130 Economic Planning Theory and Policy
1132 Economic Planning Theory
1136 Economic Planning Policy
114 Economics of War, Defence, and Disarmament
1140 Economics of War and Defense
12 Economic Development Studies
121 Economic Studies of Less Industrialized Countries
1210 General
1211 Comparative Country Studies
1213 European Countries
1214 Asian Countries
1215 African Countries
1216 Latin America and Caribbean Countries
1217 Oceanic Countries

122 Economic Studies of More Industrialized Countries
1220 General
1221 Comparative Country Studies
1223 European Countries
1224 Asian Countries
1225 African Countries
1226 Latin American and Caribbean Countries
1227 Oceanic Countries
1228 North American Countries
123 Comparative Economic Studies Involving Both More and Less Industrialized Countries; International Statistical Comparisons
1230 Comparative Economic Studies Involving More and Less Industrialized Countries; International Statistical Comparisons
13 Economic Fluctuations; Forecasting; Stabilization; and Inflation
131 Economic Fluctuations
1310 General
1313 Fluctuation: Studies
132 Economic Forecasting; and Forecasting Models
1320 General
1322 General Forecasts for a Country
1323 Specific Forecasts for a Sector
1324 Forecasting Models; Theory and Methodology
133 General Outlook and Stabilization Theories and Policies
1330 General Outlook
1331 Stabilization Theories and Policies
1332 Wage and Price Controls
134 Inflation and Deflation
1340 General
1342 Inflation Theories; Studies Illustrating Inflation Theories
2 Quantitative Economic Methods and Data
21 Econometric, Statistical, and Mathematical Methods and Models
211 Econometric and Statistical Methods and Models
2110 General
2112 Inferential Problems in Simultaneous Equation Systems
2113 Distributed Lags and Serially Correlated Disturbance Terms; Miscellaneous Single Equation Inferential Problems
2114 Multivariate Analysis, Information Theory, and Other Special Inferential Problems; Queuing Theory; Markov Chains
2115 Bayesian Statistics and Statistical Decision Theory
2116 Time Series and Spectral Analysis
2117 Survey Methods; Sampling Methods
2118 Theory of Index Numbers and Aggregation
212 Construction, Analysis, and Use of Econometric Models
2120 Construction, Analysis, and Use of Econometric Models
213 Mathematical Methods and Models
2130 General
2132 Optimization Techniques
2133 Existence and Stability Conditions of Equilibrium
2134 Computational Techniques
2135 Construction, Analysis and Use of Mathematical Programming Models
2140 Computer Programs
22 Economic and Social Statistics
221 National Income Accounting
2210 National Income Accounting Theory and Procedures
2212 National Income Accounts
2213 Income Distribution
222 Input-Output
2220 Input-Output (including regional)
223 Financial Accounts

2230 Financial Accounts; Financial Statistics
224 National Wealth and Balance Sheets
2240 National Wealth and

225 Social Indicators and Social Accounts
2250 Social Indicators and Social Accounts
226 Productivity and Growth Indicators
2260 Productivity and Growth Indicators
227 Prices
2270 Prices
228 Regional Statistics
2280 Regional Statistics
229 Micro-data
2290 Micro-data
3 Domestic Monetary and Fiscal Theory and Institutions
31 Domestic Monetary and Financial Theory and Institutions
311 Domestic Monetary and Financial Theory and Institutions
3110 Monetary Theory and Policy
3112 Monetary Theory; Empirical Studies
3116 Monetary Policy (including all central banking topics)
312 Commercial Banking
3120 Commercial Banking
313 Financial Markets
3130 General
3132 Financial Markets Studies and Regulation
3135 Portfolio Selection: Theories and Studies
314 Financial Intermediaries
3140 Financial Intermediaries
315 Credit to Business, Consumer, etc. (including mortgages)
3150 General
3151 Consumer Finance
3152 Mortgage Market
3153 Business Credit
32 Fiscal Theory and Policy; Public Finance
321 Fiscal Theory and Policy
3210 Fiscal Theory and Policy
3212 Fiscal Theory; Empirical Studies Illustrating Fiscal Theory
3216 Fiscal Policy; Studies
322 National Government Expenditures and Budgeting
3221 National Government Expenditures
3226 National Government Budgeting
3228 National Government Debt Management
323 National Taxation and Subsidies
3230 National Taxation and Subsidies
324 State and Local Government Finance
3240 General
3241 State and Local Government Expenditures and Budgeting
3242 State and Local Government Taxation, Subsidies and Revenue
3243 State and Local Government Borrowing
325 Intergovernmental Financial Relationships
3250 Intergovernmental Financial Relationships
4 International Economics
41 International Trade Theory
411 International Trade Theory
4110 General
4112 Theory of International Trade: Prices, Comparative Advantage, etc.
4113 Theory of Protection
4114 Theory of International Trade and Economic Development
42 Trade Relations; Commercial Policy; International Economic Integration
421 Trade Relations
4210 Trade Relations
422 Commercial Policy
4220 Commercial Policy and Trade Regulations; Empirical Studies
423 Economic Integration
4230 General
4232 Theory of Economic Integration
4233 Economic Integration: Policy and Empirical

Studies

43 Balance of Payments; International Finance

431 Balance of Payments; Mechanisms of Adjustment; Exchange Rates

4310 General

4312 Balance of Payments and Adjustment Mechanisms: Theory

4313 Balance of Payments and Adjustment Mechanisms: Studies

4314 Exchange Rates and Markets

432 International Monetary Arrangements

4320 International Monetary Arrangements

44 International Investment and Foreign Aid

441 International Investment and Capital Markets

4410 Theory of International Investment and Capital Flows

4412 International Investment and Capital Flows: Studies

442 International Business

4420 International Business; Management and Policies; Economic Imperialism and Host Country Policies

443 International Aid

4430 International Aid

5 Administration; Business Finance; Marketing; Accounting

51 Administration

511 Organization and Decision Theory

5110 Organization and Decision Theory

512 Managerial Economics

5120 Managerial Economics

513 Business and Public Administration

5130 Business and Public Administration

514 Goals and Objectives of Firms

5140 Goals and Objectives of Firms

52 Business Finance and Investment

5200 Business Finance and Investment

521 Business Finance

5210 Business Finance

522 Business Investment

5220 Business Investment

53 Marketing

531 Marketing and Advertising

5310 Marketing and Advertising

54 Accounting

541 Accounting

5410 Accounting

6 Industrial Organization; Technological Change; Industry Studies

61 Industrial Organization and Public Policy

611 Industrial Organization and Market Structure

6110 Industrial Organization and Market Structure

612 Public Policy Towards Monopoly and Competition

6120 Public Policy Towards Monopoly and Competition

613 Public Utilities and Government Regulation of Other Industries in the Private Sector

6130 Public Utilities and Government Regulation of Other Industries in the Private Sector

614 Public Enterprises

6140 Public Enterprises

615 Economics of Transportation

6150 Economics of Transportation

62 Economics of Technological

621 Technological Change; Innovation; Research and Development

6210 General

6211 Technological Change and Innovation

6212 Research and Development

63 Industry Studies

6300 Industry Studies: General

631 Industry Studies: Manufacturing

6310 General

6312 Metals (iron, steel, and other)

6313 Machinery (tools, electri-

cal equipment, and appliances)
6314 Transportation and Communication Equipment
6315 Chemicals, Drugs, Plastics, Ceramics, Glass, and Rubber
6316 Textiles, Leather, and Clothing
6317 Forest Products, Building Materials, and Paper
6318 Food Processing (excluding agribusiness), Tobacco, and Beverages
632 Industry Studies: Extractive Industries
6320 General
6322 Mining (metal, coal, and other nonmetallic minerals)
6323 Oil, Gas, and Other Fuels
633 Industry Studies: Distributive Trades
6330 General
6332 Wholesale Trade
6333 Retail Trade
634 Industry Studies: Construction
6340 Construction
635 Industry Studies: Services and Related Industries
6350 General
6352 Electrical, Communication, and Information Services
6353 Personal Services
6354 Business and Legal Services
6355 Repair Services
6356 Insurance
6357 Real Estate
6358 Entertainment, Recreation, Tourism
64 Economic Capacity
641 Economic Capacity
6410 Economic Capacity
7 Agriculture; Natural Resources
71 Agriculture
7100 Agriculture
711 Agricultural Supply and Demand Analysis
7110 Agricultural Supply and Demand Analysis
712 Agricultural Situation and Outlook
7120 Agricultural Situation and Outlook
713 Agricultural Policy, Domestic and International
7130 Agricultural Policy, Domestic and International
714 Agricultural Finance
7140 Agricultural Finance
715 Agricultural Marketing and Agribusiness
7150 Agricultural Marketing; Cooperatives
7151 Agribusiness
716 Farm Management
7160 Farm Management; Allocative Efficiency
717 Land Reform and Land Use
7170 General
7171 Land Ownership and Tenure; Land Reform
7172 Land Development; Land Use; Irrigation Policy
718 Rural Economics
7180 Rural Economics
72 Natural Resources
721 Natural Resources
7210 General (for agricultural irrigation aspects see 7172)
7211 Recreational Aspects of Natural Resources
722 Conservation and Pollution
7220 Conservation and Pollution
73 Economic Geography
731 Economic Geography
7310 Economic Geography
8 Manpower; Labour; Population
81 Manpower Training and Allocation; Labour Force and Supply
811 Manpower Training and Development
8110 Manpower Training and Development
812 Occupation
8120 Occupation
813 Labour Force
8130 General
8131 Agriculture
8132 Manufacturing
8133 Service
8134 Professional

8135 Government Employees
8136 Construction
82 Labour Markets; Public Policy
821 Theory of Labour Markets and Leisure
8210 Theory of Labour Markets and Leisure: Empirical Studies Illustrating Theories
822 Public Policy; Role of Government
8220 General
8221 Wages and Hours
8222 Workmen's Compensation
8223 Factory Act and Safety Legislation
8224 Unemployment Insurance
8225 Employment Services
8226 Employment in Public Sector
823 Labour Mobility; National and International Migration
8230 Labour Mobility; National and International Migration
824 Labour Market Studies, Wages, Employment
8240 General
8241 Specific Labour Market Studies
8242 Wage and Fringe Benefit Studies
8243 Employment Studies; Unemployment and Vacancies
825 Labour Productivity
8250 Labor Productivity
826 Labour Markets: Demographic Characteristics
8260 Labour Markets: Demographic Characteristics
83 Trade Unions; Collective Bargaining; Labour Management Relations
831 Trade Unions
8310 Trade Unions
832 Collective Bargaining
8320 General
8321 Collective Bargaining in the Private Sector
8322 Collective Bargaining in the Public Sector
833 Labour Management Relations
8330 General
8331 Labour Management Relations in Private Sector
8332 Labour Management Relations in Public Sector
84 Demographic Economics
841 Demographic Economics
8410 Demographic Economics
85 Human Capital
851 Human Capital
8510 Human Capital
9 Welfare Programmes; Consumer Economics; Urban and Regional Economics
91 Welfare Programmes
911 General Welfare Programmes
9110 General Welfare Programmes
912 Economics of Education (consumption side)
9120 Economics of Education (consumption side)
913 Economics of Health
9130 Economics of Health
914 Economics of Poverty
9140 Economics of Poverty
915 Social Security
9150 Social Security (public superannuation and survivors' benefits)
916 Economics of Crime
9160 Economics of Crime
917 Economics of Discrimination
9170 Economics of Discrimination
92 Consumer Economics
921 Consumer Economics; Levels and Standards of Living
9210 General
9211 Living Standards Studies and Composition of Over-all Expenditures
9212 Expenditure Patterns and Consumption of Expenditure on Specific Items
9213 Consumer Protection
93 Urban Economics
931 Urban Economics and Public Policy
9310 Urban Economics and Public Policy
932 Housing Economics
9320 Housing Economics (including nonurban housing)

933 Urban Transportation Economics
9330 Urban Transportation Economics
94 Regional Economics
941 Regional Economics
9410 General
9411 Theory of Regional Economics
9412 Regional Economic Studies
9413 Regional Economic Models and Forecasts

Appendix III
Percentage of Articles carrying a Geographic Descriptor Code List B, 1970, 1972, 1973, 1974[1]

3-Digit Classification		*1970*	*1972*	*1973*	*1974*
011	General Economics	26	23	27	35
021	General Equilibrium Theory	6	0	0	0
022	Microeconomic Theory	10	5	8	8
023	Macroeconomic Theory	23	26	27	17
024	Welfare Theory	10	4	12	12
025	Social Choice	10	14	21	13
031	History of Economic Thought	17	6	6	14
032	History of Economic Thought (cont.)	6	10	5	0
036	Economic Methodology	—	0	8	0
041	Economic History: General	25	47	6	33
042	Economic History: North America (excluding Mexico)	100	100	100	100
043	Economic History: Ancient and Medieval (until 1453)	100	100	100	100
044	Economic History: Europe	100	100	100	100
045	Economic History: Asia	100	100	100	100
046	Economic History: Africa	100	100	100	—
047	Economic History: Latin America and Caribbean	100	100	100	—
048	Economic History: Oceania	100	100	100	—
051	Capitalist Economic Systems	61	37	27	83
052	Socialist and Communist Economic Systems	78	65	58	71
053	Comparative Economic Systems	27	14	10	—
111	Economic Growth Theory and Models	6	6	13	10
112	Economic Development Models and Theories	24	12	21	35
113	Economic Planning Theory and Policy	54	29	56	53
114	Economics of War, Defence, and Disarmament	52	64	80	50
121	Economic Studies of Less Industrialized Countries	74	58	64	78
122	Economic Studies of More Industrialized Countries	82	71	82	100
123	Comparative Economic Studies	100	100	100	100
131	Economic Fluctuations; Forecasting; Stabilization; Inflation	61	47	73	83
132	Economic Forecasting and Forecasting Models	65	69	65	52
133	General Outlook and Stabilization Theories and Policies	58	67	64	71
134	Inflation and Deflation	54	43	55	56

[1] 1971 tape is being corrected. Much of the material was put on tape before the Geographical Descriptor Code was added.

3-Digit Classification		*1970*	*1972*	*1973*	*1974*
211	Econometric and Statistical Methods and Models	12	10	10	6
212	Construction, Analysis, and Use of Econometric Models	7	16	29	15
213	Mathematical Methods and Models	6	4	3	13
214	Computer Programs	—	25	0	—
220	Economic and Social Statistics	48	100	100	—
221	National Income Accounting	65	62	67	69
222	Input-Output	46	43	27	38
223	Financial Accounts	75	50	75	75
224	National Wealth and Balance Sheets	60	67	67	100
225	Social Indicators and Social Acounts	85	22	57	—
226	Productivity and Growth Indicators	61	39	65	100
227	Prices	64	67	75	78
228	Regional Statistics	0	76	67	100
229	Micro-data	—	100	80	81
311	Domestic Monetary and Financial Theory and Institutions	39	42	57	57
312	Commercial Banking	63	58	69	82
313	Financial Markets	28	38	52	57
314	Financial Intermediaries	50	55	58	67
315	Credit to Business, Consumer, etc. (incl. mortgages)	75	39	82	95
321	Fiscal Theory and Policy	31	26	39	35
322	National Government Expenditures and Budgeting	72	59	62	64
323	National Taxation and Subsidies	55	56	71	67
324	State and Local Government Finance	79	58	84	75
325	Intergovernmental Financial Relations	94	65	68	80
411	International Trade Theory	18	13	14	25
421	Trade Relations	56	60	60	76
422	Commercial Policy	47	56	63	77
423	Economic Integration	83	67	74	71
430	Balance of Payments; International Finance	100	0	0	—
431	Balance of Payments; Mechanisms of Adjustment; Exchange Rates	52	28	26	51
432	International Monetary Arrangements	16	14	18	0
441	International Investment and Capital Markets	47	47	46	75
442	International Business	52	45	51	46
443	International Aid	42	22	12	38
511	Organization and Decision Theory	19	6	14	11
512	Managerial Economics	19	4	15	6
513	Business and Public Administration	27	19	33	28
514	Goals and Objectives of Firms	64	10	15	11
520	Business Finance and Investment	0	67	0	—
521	Business Finance	18	16	30	29
522	Business Investment	33	32	39	19
611	Industrial Organization and Market Structure	54	44	65	63
612	Public Policy Towards Monopoly and Competition	80	71	85	68

3-Digit Classification		*1970*	*1972*	*1973*	*1974*
613	Public Utilities and Government Regulation of Other Industries in the Private Sector	67	52	51	63
614	Public Enterprises	33	52	44	100
615	Economics of Transportation	64	58	72	82
621	Technological Change; Innovation; Research and Development	41	39	51	43
630	Industry Studies: General	100	100	100	100
631	Industry Studies: Manufacturing	100	100	100	100
632	Industry Studies: Extractive Industries	100	100	100	100
633	Industry Studies: Distributive Trades	100	100	100	100
634	Industry Studies: Construction	100	100	100	100
635	Industry Studies: Services and Related Industries	100	100	100	100
641	Economic Capacity	78	100	100	25
710	Agriculture	75	42	77	80
711	Agricultural Supply and Demand Analysis	57	63	74	76
712	Agricultural Situation and Outlook	72	56	80	100
713	Agricultural Policy, Domestic and International	75	63	67	79
714	Agricultural Finance	40	41	86	100
715	Agricultural Marketing and Agribusiness	67	73	90	75
716	Farm Management	41	51	52	80
717	Land Reform and Land Use	73	47	60	78
718	Rural Economics	0	70	87	93
721	Natural Resources	45	41	43	34
722	Conservation and Pollution	52	25	25	49
731	Economic Geography	63	50	45	67
811	Manpower Training and Development	74	76	74	100
812	Occupation	73	73	66	92
813	Labour Force	60	79	88	93
821	Theory of Labour Markets and Leisure	37	38	50	56
822	Public Policy; Role of Government	88	66	86	86
823	Labour Mobility; National and International Migration	63	58	75	83
824	Labour Market Studies, Wages, Employment	76	66	87	91
825	Labour Productivity	81	83	79	90
826	Labour Markets: Demographic Characteristics	94	67	89	100
831	Trade Unions	81	81	52	87
832	Collective Bargaining	94	75	81	95
833	Labour Management Relations	83	76	86	75
841	Demographic Economics	61	34	66	57
851	Human Capital	55	64	72	63
911	General Welfare Programmes	67	69	90	100
912	Economics of Education (consumption side)	80	50	79	78
913	Economics of Health	69	66	80	67

3-Digit Classification	*1970*	*1972*	*1973*	*1974*
914 Economics of Poverty	83	50	84	100
915 Social Security	50	45	96	100
916 Economics of Crime	57	60	39	67
917 Economics of Discrimination	81	63	71	75
921 Consumer Economics; Levels and Standards of Living	49	43	58	67
931 Urban Economics and Public Policy	66	52	52	86
932 Housing Economics	80	63	66	33
933 Urban Transportation Economics	38	71	45	0
941 Regional Economics	57	61	64	64

Summary of the Discussion

The objective of the Perlmans' paper was a double one, according to *Miss Deane*'s introduction. They have attempted to apply the *JEL* classification system to papers in a wide range of other journals and, simultaneously, to investigate the question: To what extent does empiricism dominate the economics profession?

Their sample of journals covers the period 1970–73 plus part of 1974. 47 general (and relatively prestigious) journals comprise their A List; this list plus 67 specialized journals comprises their B List. Taken together, these 114 journals cover 83 per cent of *JEL* entries.

In the first general 2-digit field, 'General Economic Theory', from 27 to 33 per cent of the core group (List A) citations are found, and if one also adds theoretical sub-fields from other 2-digit fields, 50 per cent of the core group articles were theoretical. About half of the more prestigious journals were primarily theoretical, as against one-fourth of the remainder. Some bias may be introduced by classifying as empirical all cases where empirical content is implied by geographical descriptors and similar devices; even with this bias, only about 50 per cent of the articles had empirical content. Furthermore, sampling estimates of the quality of empirical data led the Perlmans to conclude that its purpose was primarily illustrative rather than substantive. *Miss Deane* found too brief for easy comprehension the Perlmans' description of their linkage programme between 3-digit sub-classes, i.e. their examination of articles which combined two or more such sub-classes.

The period was, of course, too short to permit trend analysis, but the Perlmans noted a strong upward movement in Demographic Economics among the fields of interest studied, and a corresponding decline in Economic Development, which, *Miss Deane* suspected, might be due to a drying-up of foundation grants. *Miss Deane* wondered whether a peak in History of Economic Thought (noted by the Perlmans in 1972) was more than the spin-off from a conference or two. In general, she also saw time-lag problems throughout the Perlman data; when, she wondered, was the actual research done?

Miss Deane was surprised at certain of the Perlmans' results. The preponderance of theory surprised her, and likewise (within the theoretical group) that of micro- over macro-economics. Did the Perlmans distinguish adequately, she inquired, between full-scale articles and mere 'notes and communications'? She also surmised that the data on empirical content assembled by the Perlmans might not represent the division of research effort, in that empirical work is more likely to avoid the article form, but to move directly to the book, monograph, or other report. Perhaps the Perlmans have told us mainly what sorts of material lend themselves to article publication. In summary, *Miss Deane* was still awaiting further evidence about the usefulness of the *JEL* classification system as such.

Dr Otto presented a digest of a comment. She had found the Perlmans' study more useful than preceding studies, and a desirable addition to the volume of such studies. Libraries could use their evidence in framing acquisition policies; they might even try to keep ahead of the trends. (The current conference might also have similar effects.) The Perlmans' work required electronic data processing, but the Kiel library could use the *JEL* classification to analyse its own withdrawals. It would hardly be possible to transfer the Kiel system of cataloguing by subject to the *JEL* system of classification without something like a concordance.

Within economic theory, however, *Dr Otto* continued, there are two main bodies, 'capitalist' and 'socialist'. This distinction is true for many other aspects of economics, and should be handled by the classification system. Also, more and more theoretical articles include major empirical support; this may be particularly true of *regional* materials.

The validity of the Perlmans' analysis is one problem, said *Professor Blaug.* The usefulness of the *JEL* classification to the Kiel library for studying its withdrawals is quite another, and the two should not be confused. He also inquired how one classifies Soviet materials: purely geographically? necessarily Marxist? And where do Soviet materials in mathematical economics or dynamic programming fit in? A 'super-task', *Professor Blaug* thought, was involved in valid classification.

Professor Kindleberger called the group's attention to the 'sociology of knowledge' aspects of the Perlmans' study. Do the changes observed by the Perlmans represent basic trends or merely 'fashion and fancy?' Consider his own field (international economics). The decline that the Perlmans observed there may or may not represent an 'inward turning' of economists' interests. They also may, or may not, represent a shift from pure trade theory to International Finance (balance of payments) problems.

Professor Johnson also raised some points about the shift in content of articles published. A great deal depends, he felt on referees' and editors' judgments about what was worth publishing, and on foundations' judgments about what research was worth supporting. *Professor Blaug* doubted that from the short period anything conclusive could be observed. The rises that the Perlmans had noted in price theory and in monetary economics did not surprise him, but he had doubts about the apparent rise of interest shown by their figures on doctrinal history and economic methodology. But, said *Professor Johnson* in reply, one should consider the (possibly temporary) stimuli to production in these fields. Look at the appearance of the Keynes papers, the revival of Marxian and radical economics, and the methodology sessions at the American Economic Association (AEA) conventions. (Also, added *Professor Bronfenbrenner*, a new journal in the field, *History of Political Economy.*) Agricultural economics, continued *Professor Johnson*, seems to have a life of its own, independent of others' interest in agricultural problems. Finally, *Professor Johnson* thought, considerations of diminishing marginal utility might well bring some of the temporary bulges to early ends.

Mr Evans asked whether this conference could be expected to generate articles in economic journals, and *Professor Morgan* asked the Perlmans, where, in the *JEL* classification, such articles might go. (*Mrs N. Perlman* answered that a decision would have to be made between the 01 and 02 classifications.) *Mrs Schwartz* inquired why the *JEL* classification is imperfectly consistent with that used by the *Index of Economic Articles.* (*Professor M. Perlman* replied that the *Index* is shifting to the *JEL* system.)

Dr Biehl noted that the bulge observed by the Perlmans in monetary economics is now appearing in job applications. He believed that there were longer swings in economists' interests. (Another example, said *Professor Perlman*, might be the theory of yesterday reappearing as today's history of thought.)

Miss Deane returned to the issue of referees' and editors' prejudices. She believed that most good work eventually gets published, but agreed that the Perlmans' A List might be affected by the prejudices of a relatively few people.

Mrs N. Perlman, responding for her husband and herself, began with a history of their efforts in this field. The AEA undertook to establish a consistent classification system for books and journal articles. A classification committee developed a compatible 2- and 3-digit system and the Perlmans then developed a compatible 4-digit level of classification for the annual indexes; these replaced the non-compatible classification system used in the volumes covering the period 1886–1968. *Mrs Perlman*, noting that every classification system has its own flavour, observed that the *JEL* criteria in classification were designed for economic research workers, rather than for teachers who ask 'In what course do I cover this topic?'. Cross-referencing was used to ensure that articles would be drawn to the attention of any researcher interested in the topic.

Mrs Perlman said that with reference to the analyses of linkages, it identified subject areas which tended to be related; for the moment, the usefulness may be limited to internal improvement of the classification system. She agreed that the time period covered by the data was too short for definitive conclusions about trends, but thought that some of the indicated trends were valid. For example, the increased interest in history of thought is genuine; explanatory factors include a renewed interest in Marx, Keynes having become history of thought, and the establishment of a journal devoted to the topic.

As for *Miss Deane*'s conjecture that books and articles differed in their reliance upon the empirical method, *Mrs Perlman* said that her experience in annotating some 1200 books per year did not bear out a conclusion that books and monographs actually contain a larger portion of empirical content than do journal articles. Although the geographic descriptors are not perfect proxies for the evidence of empirical content, their use clearly yields significant results. They are not, however, identical with statistical data, since they refer to descriptive and qualitative data as well. The quality of the statistical data, as indicated by the casual sampling of policy related articles, raised some questions: the data were often out-moded, were used primarily for illustrating a model, and the use of the same data apparently yielded differing conclusions in different articles. Except for the inclusion of sub-categories in the general theory area she did not agree with Dr Otto's suggestion that separate 'socialist' classifications are necessary. Much Soviet material is now cross-classified under both 'Theory' and 'Economic Systems' headings. Finally, Mrs Perlman agreed, some of the short-term trends represent mere fads; some, cycles of various lengths, and some growing trends. It was difficult if not impossible to state *ex ante* which was which.

Part Three

Information Needs of Researchers and their Implications for the Library Industry

11 Developments in National Accounts

Jack Hibbert and John Walton
CENTRAL STATISTICAL OFFICE, LONDON

The main developments in national accounts over the next decade are examined under the four main headings of (1) developments of United Kingdom national accounts in relation to the United Nations system, together with its complementary systems and sub-systems; (2) national accounts in support of conjunctural analysis; (3) inflation and the measurements of quantum changes; and (4) possible extensions of the national accounts and the storage and dissemination of national accounts data.

INTRODUCTION

This paper describes our view of the main developments likely in national accounts statistics over the next decade. We have examined the needs of those using national accounts statistics both in the context of our own United Kingdom experience and, so far as we were able, in the international context.

National statistical agencies are faced with the problem of determining the optimum disposition of professional and other resources between competing claims. Not only must choices be made between competing claims for the collection of new data, but between more collection and more analysis or the improvement of existing data sources. Users may press for more information, more reliable data, more timely figures, changes in classification or presentation—the list sometimes seems endless—and the official statistician must respond to these demands in a constructive and responsible manner. He must bear in mind what is, in fact, possible, given the basic information systems from which he can collect the information. He must also consider the costs which he is imposing on those providing data in relation to the benefits arising from the information becoming available. With these considerations in mind and, in addition, describing all the main areas in which we know faster development is considered to be desirable, we have indicated where we see development as most likely to be achieved. The views expressed here are our own and it may be that our scale of priorities will differ from that of other practitioners; we are not attempting to present here an official

United Kingdom Government Statistical Service view. Despite our reservations about the feasibility of developing national accounts in certain directions, however, we are generally sanguine about what can be achieved, and look forward to considerable progress during the next decade.

The paper comprises six sections, the first four of which deal with possible developments in national accounts estimates. Within each of these sections, separate but related topics are considered. There is, inevitably, some duplication where the same issues arise in different contexts, but we trust that this will prove helpful rather than tedious. In the first sections of the paper the need for information and sources and methods of estimation is mentioned, and in the final sections some consideration is given to the storage and dissemination of national accounts estimates. The list of topics covered is as follows:

1. Developments of United Kingdom national accounts in relation to the UN system, together with its complementary systems and sub-systems.
   (*a*) Input-output estimates
   (*b*) Development of accounts for sub-sectors within the system
   (*c*) Real and financial wealth of economic sectors
   (*d*) Disaggregation by characteristics of individuals or households
   (*e*) International comparisons of real product
   (*f*) Geographical analysis
2. National accounts in support of conjunctural analysis and forecasting
   (*a*) Quarterly data
   (*b*) Time series analysis
   (*c*) Consistency of the data base
   (*d*) Revisions to the data base—computerized systems
   (*e*) The monetary dimensions of short-term forecasting models
   (*f*) Redistribution of income through public finance
3. Inflation and the measurement of quantum changes
   (*a*) Conceptual problems
   (*b*) Unique products
   (*c*) Non-market services
   (*d*) Factor incomes at current prices
   (*e*) Value added at constant prices
4. Possible extensions of the national accounts boundaries
   (*a*) The treatment of regrettable necessities
   (*b*) Industrial pollution
   (*c*) Non-market services
   (*d*) The boundary between consumption and capital accumulation
5. Need for supplementary information by users of national accounts
6. Storage and dissemination of national accounts data

II. DEVELOPMENT OF UNITED KINGDOM NATIONAL ACCOUNTS IN RELATION TO THE UN SYSTEM, TOGETHER WITH ITS COMPLEMENTARY SYSTEMS AND SUB-SYSTEMS

INTRODUCTION

The present UN system of national accounts (SNA) was adopted by the fifteenth session of the UN Statistical Commission for the use of national statistical authorities and for the reporting of internationally comparable national accounts data. It provides a comprehensive framework within which to record estimates of the flows and stocks of the economy [12]. This section of our paper examines those parts of this framework to which particular attention is likely to be directed in the next few years by UK national accounting statisticians.

INPUT-OUTPUT ESTIMATES

In many countries a set of detailed input–output tables[1] form the cornerstone of the national accounts estimates. By contrast, work on input-output tables in the United Kingdom in the past, has largely taken the estimates for the main national accounts aggregates as given, and has been regarded as supplementary to, rather than forming the basis for, the main accounts. The optimal approach to all of these related tasks of statistical compilation is, of course, a matter of judgment in the light of the reliability of each set of data available, and in this respect the situation may differ significantly from country to country. We now feel, however, that in the United Kingdom we may not have given sufficient attention to input-output estimates of value added as a means of checking the quality and plausibility of estimates derived from other sources (e.g. tax administration data on incomes). Similarly, we have tended to rely solely upon data for capital expenditure by investing units without supplementing it with a commodity flow approach to estimating capital formation. We are changing the emphasis of our work in order that the approaches not so far fully utilized should play a more important role in helping to identify inconsistencies and discrepancies in the estimates.

One difficulty encountered when attempting to use the input-output approach as a basis for estimating the recent past is the shortage of detailed data needed for this purpose. The collection and analysis of this information will typically require several years to complete, and for many uses to which the national accounts estimates are put this is not sufficiently timely. There is a further point of difficulty in that certain detailed information, in particular that relating to each industry's purchases, can be ob-

[1] I.e. a commodity or industrial analysis of the goods and services flowing into (inputs) and out of (outputs) each industry or productive process in the economy.

tained only with the agreement and goodwill of the firms providing such information. There is an understandable reluctance amongst firms to go to the trouble and expense of arranging for this to be done more frequently than is absolutely necessary, and in the United Kingdom such purchases inquiries have been held only about every five years. In those circumstances, it has been necessary to develop techniques for the updating of 'bechmark' input-output tables and in the future we are likely to see an increasing effort devoted to this kind of work.

To users of national accounts estimates it may be that much of this work will pass unnoticed because the format and detail of the published data may not be very different. As compilers *and* users of the national accounts, however, we attach very great importance to that part of our work which is aimed at improving the reliability of our estimates. There may often exist a difficult choice to be made between devoting additional resources to the extension of national accounts or other areas of statistics and concentrating upon the improvement of existing series. We refer below to numerous areas where we see probable development and extension of national accounts, but overall we see the next decade as a period in which, in the United Kingdom, at least, as much attention, if not more, will be given to improving the quality of our existing national accounts estimates as to extending them.

DEVELOPMENT OF ACCOUNTS FOR SUB-SECTORS WITHIN THE SYSTEM

In the United Kingdom national accounts, the construction of current and capital accounts for the main institutional sectors (persons, companies, central and local government, public corporations and overseas) was, from the outset, regarded as essential. The development of financial accounts (though now well-established) came rather later in the day and led to the creation of sub-sectors for industrial and commercial companies, banks and other financial institutions. More recently, the need for the sub-division of the personal sector has become apparent in a number of different contexts.

Within the personal sector we can, in principle, distinguish households, individuals living outside of households (mostly in institutions), unincorporated businesses, non-profit-making bodies serving households, and life assurance and superannuation funds. For most purposes, there is little reason for wishing to distinguish between the first two groups, and in practice it is usually impossible to separate all of the business and household transactions of the proprietors of unincorporated businesses. So far, therefore, work in the United Kingdom has been restricted to the construction of estimates for (1) non-profit-making bodies serving households, (2) life assurance and superannuation funds, and (3) the rest of the personal sector (mainly households).

The main objectives of this sub-division are not difficult to appreciate. In studying the income, expenditure and saving behaviour of the personal sector, the disaggregation may enable more reliable relationships between the various aggregates to be established. Personal sector consumption, for example, is mainly by households and might be expected to be better explained in terms of household income, exclusive of transfers to superannuation funds and non-profit-making bodies serving households but inclusive of transfers from these sub-sectors (e.g. pensions). We also see this development leading to the possibility of further disaggregation of the household sector itself, not, perhaps, in terms of a full set of accounts, but in terms of the income and expenditure behaviour of different household types. For this pupose, household types might be defined in terms of the population characteristics or the income characteristics of the household, or even a combination of the two. Such an approach is very ambitious, however, and may prove to be impracticable because of the constraints imposed by the data limitations. It may be that work of this kind will have to take the form of simulations rather than the construction of estimates based on data collected from households. Sections 1d. and 2f. of our paper also refer to possible developments of this kind.

A separate requirement for estimates of household income, as distinct from total personal sector income, arises from the need to have control totals for estimates on the distribution of personal incomes. The data on distribution of incomes that are at present available for the United Kingdom are somewhat limited in scope and, with the increasing need for estimates of income and wealth distribution, we are now devoting more resources to this area of our statistics.

Improvement of estimates for the company sector will include better estimates of the flows of interest, etc, between industrial and commercial companies and financial companies, and a fuller identification of lending and borrowing, particularly in the form of trade credit. The link between estimates of income, outlay, transactions in financial assets, and balance sheets giving estimates of the level of assets and liabilities will assume greater importance (see the next section). More attention will also need to be paid to the 'interface' between operating or production accounts showing the operating surplus accruing to units analysed according to industries and income and outlay accounts showing the transactions of units under common ownership.

REAL AND FINANCIAL WEALTH OF ECONOMIC SECTORS

The system of national accounts as we know it now records economic *transactions* in the form of production accounts (analysed by industries), which are then brought together (for the main sectors of the economy) as income, and outlay and capital accumulation accounts. In these sector accounts, the Keynesian identity that, for the whole economy, saving (or unconsumed income) equals investment is made up by including the net balance of dealings in the (financial) claims of one sector or another. The system has been regarded as being completed by accounts showing the financial transactions of the various sectors (or flows of funds), which are analysed by sub-divisions of the corporate sector to show the accounts for the various types of financial intermediaries. A number of countries now prepare regular estimates of the flow of funds, but their usefulness is limited both practically and conceptually: practically, because there are often huge, unidentified residuals between the balance of a sector's estimated receipts and expenditure on current and capital account (the implied net acquisition of financial assets) and the balance of its identified purchases and sales of financial assets; and, conceptually, because decisions on current and capital spending, and on financial investment are not only affected by borrowing and lending in the sense of *transactions* in financial assets, but, also, by the *holdings* of financial assets.

To complete the picture, therfore, there is a need for balance sheet types of estimates which will show in aggregate, for each sector, the level of assets held, distinguishing between 'real' assets and financial claims, and of financial liabilities (i.e. the claims of other sectors). Estimates for the United Kingdom relating to the mid-1960s were put together by Revell [5] and Roe [6], and, recently, the UN Statistical Commission approved a document [16] setting out guidelines for the conceptual framework of such a system of estimates. This framework has the following main characteristics:

(i) For each sector which is distinguished there is a balance sheet (balanced, like all balance sheets, by an estimate of the net worth of the sector)
(ii) For each period, the opening and closing balance sheet is integrated into the rest of the system of national accounts through the financial transactions (capital finance) account and a 'reconciliation' account showing changes in the valuation of assets and liabilities and adjustments such as the natural growth or depletion of certain real assets (e.g. timber and sub-soil deposits), reclassifications of institutions from one sector to another, and the disappearance of equities when a company is taken over and becomes a subsidiary.
(iii) The basis of valuation is market values (rather than book values) where an effective market exists; otherwise the basis is a proxy (such as written down replacement cost for plant and machinery) for market values.
(iv) The boundary is drawn at the same point as in the SNA, e.g. consumer and military durables are not capitalized, though there is provision for supplementary estimates evaluating the existing stock of these goods.

(v) If the separate sector accounts are consolidated (rather than being combined) a statement emerges for the nation as a whole, showing the value of its stock of real assets plus its net claims on the rest of the world. For other analytical purposes, it is desirable to go some way towards analysing the financial claims of each sector on a 'to whom, from whom' basis, i.e. to analyse financial assets according to the sector issuing the claim as its liability.

The development of such estimates in a comprehensive form and their regular maintenance, will place a substantial burden on national statistical offices, even for those countries already compiling flow of funds estimates. In the United Kingdom, even with the advantage of the pioneering work already mentioned, the completion of the programme is at least five years off. The potential uses of such estimates seem considerable; they are outlined in paragraphs 2.1 to 2.17 of the UN's guidelines [16]. However, certain sub-systems can be developed independently, viz, estimates of the value of fixed assets and buildings, which can be developed from the existing estimates of capital accumulation by the so-called 'perpetual inventory' method, and estimates of holdings of the most liquid of financial assets (money or near-money), which are available from balance sheets produced by banks and other credit institutions. With other claims, however, the problems of estimation loom large, particularly when the asset is highly transferrable (viz, bearer bonds, time certificates of deposit) so that the debtor institution cannot report its liabilities by sector. Amongst real assets, the main problems are in the valuation of land, or of plantations and natural resources, while unquoted securities provide problems on the financial side. There are also difficulties in the classification of institutions, particularly holding companies. Sector balance sheets are a relatively new statistical field, and there is little experience on which to draw, so it may take some time to find satisfactory solutions to these problems.

The main relevance of comprehensive balance sheet-type estimates to conjunctural forecasting models would revolve around the question of how, and to what degree, spending decisions, particularly on durables, stocks and fixed assets, are influenced by the level of assets held by an economic agent, the liquidity 'profile' of such assets, the range and efficiency of facilities offered by financial intermediaries, etc. The theoretical background is mainly in terms of the 'portfolio adjustment' type model of behaviour, developed by Tobin [7] and others. In the next ten years it should become possible to begin using models of this kind to the extent that the national accounts estimates are progressively expanded to include balance sheet-type estimates, first for financial institutions and then for the non-financial sectors of the economy. But the preparation of comprehensive balance sheet estimates will be costly, and progress towards that completion must be conditioned by the need of the national accounts statistician to order the priorities of his work on this and on other (but perhaps less costly) developments.

In one area—the distribution of the wealth of the nation in the hands of the ultimate beneficiaries of that wealth, viz, the household sector—the need for better data is all too obvious, not merely for the light that it might throw on decisions whether to spend or to re-invest income, and on other aspects of behaviour affecting output in aggregate, but for the study of the structure of society and welfare. It is often held, other things (including the rate of growth of aggregate wealth) being equal, that a relatively equal distribution of personal wealth will contribute more to economic welfare than will a relatively unequal distribution of the same wealth. To what extent, in the progression towards equality, can 'other things' be expected to remain equal? At what point do diseconomies such as dispersion of cultural heritage, shortage of supply of investable funds, become material? In the United Kingdom, questions of this kind are to be studied by a Standing Royal Commission. One thing is clear, however, the study of all of this will be impossible unless the data on the distribution of personal wealth can be improved. This is likely to be a major 'growth area' in the national accounts in the next decade. Unfortunately, however, the data problems are very great, and progress will not be easy. It will help, for a start, to have estimates of the total of wealth held by households, as described above. For the study of its distribution, there are at present three known methods; the estate duty multiplier method (where the dead, whose assets are known, are taken as a sample of the living), though this relates to individuals rather than households; the method of estimating the value of assets from the amount of (investment) income received from them, this being often known by fiscal administrations; and sample surveys of households. The latter lead to intractable problems if required as a principal source of comprehensive estimates (people do not know the detailed make-up of their wealth even if they are willing to reveal it), but will be useful for determining the structure of assets held by the middle and lower income groups. A fourth approach, covering only the upper end of the wealth distribution, is available when a wealth tax exists. In the opinion of the authors, progress will come from a mixture of all four approaches, and the development of each so as to interlock with the others. Orders of magnitude for the proportion of total wealth owned by the most wealthy 1 per cent and 5 per cent of the population of the United Kingdom, together with an account of some of the problems in basing estimates on the estate duty multiplier method, are contained in an appendix to the recent 'Green Paper' on a Wealth Tax [18].

DISAGGREGATION BY CHARACTERISTICS OF INDIVIDUALS OR HOUSEHOLDS

The SNA's income and outlay accounts evidently give only very summary information in respect to the household sector, and there is both need and scope for the disaggregation of either income or outlay in various dimensions—the distribution of income, the commodity composition of consumption—or for comprehensive estimates relating income to consumption and saving as analysed by size of income, by socio-economy category, by size of household, etc. There is no need to outline here the shape of such a complementary system; it has been done by the UN [15]. Of more interest are the uses of such data and, most important, the problems in the way of contructing estimates which can be related to the aggregates in the national accounts as a whole. What we have at the moment (in the complementary system) is a well-ordered and detailed account of what might be called the conventional symbols of a map of the terrain; but the actual observations are either completely lacking or are a confused jumble of seemingly unrelated numbers, with huge gaps.

The UN system delineates the uses of such information under two main headings: the welfare of the population, and global economic questions. The relevance of income distribution data to welfare is obvious enough. Questions of welfare and perceptions of welfare may also be relevant to the effective management of the economy, e.g. in the aim of attaining steady growth and limiting inflation. The regulation of demand in a conjunctural sense through public finance also depends on much better data than are generally available of household income and outlay disaggregated by size of income, etc. For instance, not only does the estimation of tax yields depend on such data, but so does the assessment of the response of consumption to changes in the level of indirect taxes. The relationship between income and consumption can be better understood with the help of cross-section data rather than aggregate time series alone. There is also a need for a number of social and economic purposes for comprehensive studies of the redistribution of income through public finance (direct and indirect taxes, subsidies and grants). For an example of the most recently published United Kingdom work of this kind see [10].

The problems in constructing such estimates are partly definitional but mainly practical. The unit of observation (household, family, tax unit, individual) affects the analysis, and so does the definition of 'income' (despite Mr Micawber's adage, notoriously an amorphous concept). Data on income may be obtained from employees, as a by-product of fiscal administration, by direct enquiry to households through sample surveys, or from data obtained from other sectors (e.g. investment income). The statistician's problem is that no single source is likely to be capable of development into a comprehensive set of estimates, so that he has to relate one to the other. In general, if data from the fiscal administration cover a large part of the field and are used as a main source for the aggregate measure of the factor income generated by the national product, the task of compiling distribution data which are as comprehensive as the aggregate is less forbidding, but, even so, there will be many gaps to fill in and problems in obtaining analysis by socio-economic characteristics or by using a wider unit of observation, such as the household.

INTERNATIONAL COMPARISONS OF REAL PRODUCT

The usefulness of international comparisons of the main national accounts aggregates may be severely limited when estimates are converted to a common basis of valuation by means of official exchange rates. Following earlier work for OECD in the 1950s by Gilbert and Kravis, in 1968 the United Nations began work on an international comparison project, a report on the first stage of which was published this year [13]. The purpose of the project is to establish a system for the international comparison of real product and purchasing power.

Work of this kind is likely to be further developed during the coming years and it is important that the potential uses of its results as well as of their limitations, be properly understood. The results are useful in analysing the processes of economic growth and development, enabling valid cross-sectional comparisons to be made between different stages of economic development and facilitating the assessment of the success of development efforts. Particular areas of interest are savings ratios, the composition of output, growth rates and the role of government. The results are also useful for such purposes as a basis on which to allocate aid to developing countries or to share the costs of international projects between participating countries.

Amongst the qualifications to be attached to these results are the sampling and other estimation errors which inevitably arise in the completion of such an extensive and complex statistical exercise. But perhaps more important is the need to understand that the purchasing power parities which are calculated are not intended to approximate to equilibrium rates of exchange, which depend upon many factors in addition to the relative purchasing power of currencies over the goods and services which constitute the gross domestic product. Also, comparisons of real income between different countries involve a number of implicit assumptions which certainly do not hold in any strict sense. The price structure existing in the countries being compared, for example, may differ to an extent sufficient to render the significance of the results open to question, since a rigorous set of conditions for such a comparison would require that the price structure be identical.

Despite these limitations, we regard the results of this work as being extremely valuable and expect to see the participation of national statistical agencies in its further development.

GEOGRAPHICAL ANALYSIS

Until fairly recently there had been little official interest shown in the United Kingdom in compiling regional accounts, except for some work on separate estimates for Northern Ireland, Scotland and Wales. With the entry of the United Kingdom into the European Economic Community, however, it became necessary to compile official regional estimates in connection with the formulation of a Community regional policy. The first results of this work were published in November, 1973 [9], and further work will be necessary to develop these estimates over the next few years.

III NATIONAL ACCOUNTS IN SUPPORT OF CONJUNCTURAL ANALYSIS AND FORECASTING

QUARTERLY DATA

The development of quarterly national accounts, as distinct from key short-term economic indicators, has varied in degree from one country to another. Some countries, such as Canada and the United States, have compiled and published a comprehensive set of quarterly national accounts for many years, whilst others, usually because the necessary professional statistical resources were not available, have relied upon annual national accounts and a set of selected short-term indicators. The importance of the contribution to be made by quarterly national accounts is, no doubt, debatable. Even if the relevant economic transactions could be measured accurately, problems of interpretation would still remain, so that even in principle the usefulness of the quarterly accounts clearly depends upon the economic significance to be attached to quarterly movements in the aggregates measured. In practice, the question of whether monthly or quarterly measurement is, in fact, possible also assumes some importance. If businesses do not prepare quarterly accounts of their transactions in the detail required, it will usually not be possible for statistical agencies to collect the necessary data from which to construct quarterly national accounts. There are also special problems arising from the appropriate treatment of agriculture where the normal production cycle is longer than a calendar quarter and the industry's 'work-in-progress' takes a rather different form from that encountered elsewhere.

The main strengths of a quarterly system of national accounts lie in their comprehensiveness and internal consistency. The annual accounts attempt to portray the essential structure of the economy and, even though the available quarterly data may be incomplete, it will usually be possible to infer from it a good deal about the remainder of the accounts. The data underlying the short-term economic indicators such as an index of industrial production, data on external trade, retail sales, wholesale and retail prices, etc, all play their part in the construction of quarterly national accounts, but what finally emerges is, in a sense, greater than the sum of its components because it has been fitted to the economic framework defined by the accounts.

The degree of detail in which quarterly national accounts should be constructed is a matter to be decided in the light of the considerations already mentioned—usefulness, accuracy, economic significance—but a further consideration of equal importance is that of timeliness. Generally, those responsible for short-term economic management are concerned with the present and immediate future rather than with the events of a rapidly receding past. Given this need for an up-to-date assessment of the present, it might be thought that quarterly national accounts could most usefully take the form of a continuous forecast of the present in the light of the latest estimates relating to the immediate past. As far as we are aware, however, no official statistical agency regularly publishes information in this form. One reason for this may be the extent to which official statisticians are subjected to criticism when their estimates are repeatedly revised; clearly, any system of continuous assessment of the present and recent past would be particularly subject to revision.

The present signs are that quarterly national accounts are likely to be more widely developed during the coming decade. There is a growing interest in their development, both nationally and internationally. The OECD, for example, an organization with particular interest in monitoring developments in national economies, is anxious to set up a system of standard national accounts reporting on a quarterly basis to supplement the existing annual system. Discussion at international meetings confirms that, where national quarterly accounts are not already constructed, countries are putting resources into this work. In those countries where such estimates are already well established they appear to be regarded as an essential tool of economic policy and the aim of improving their reliability and usefulness as deserving high priority.

TIME SERIES ANALYSIS

Attention was drawn in the preceding section to the possibility that improvements in reliability may be of limited value where interpretation is difficult. By interpretation we mean an assessment of the significance of the events observed for the actions of government, business and other interested parties. It is not sufficient to know with virtual certainty that consumer spending rose or fell by x per cent in a recent period, since without some understanding of the reasons underlying this change it may be impossible to judge what action, if any, it is appropriate to take. (It may well be that, even where there is agreement about the reasons for the observed change, views will differ as to the appropriate action, but this is a separate issue.)

One aid to interpretation which is now well established is, of course, the process of seasonal adjustment. Many different methods have been devised of estimating the systematic seasonal variation of a series of observations about its trend, and it seems, at least to us, that we are unlikely to see any further substantial advances in this field. One point over which it seems possible that some controversy will centre, however, is whether there is benefit to be gained by choosing some optimal method for application to all series. This view seems to be held quite strongly by some who are mainly concerned with achieving comparability between different series, in particular where comparisons are to be made between different countries. But if it is accepted that seasonal adjustment is, essentially, an aid to interpretation, rather than a transformation of the series into an alternative form, we would argue that its successful application depends as much upon a detailed understanding of the characteristics of the series in question as upon the choice of an appropriate method. This is mainly because of the need to identify special factors influencing the series before attempting to measure the regular seasonal variation, and our experience suggests that this first stage can be achieved better by the individual statistician than by mathematical methods. A further technical point is that one can expect, on theoretical grounds, that some series will be better fitted by one type of model rather than by another, and it seems counterproductive to ignore this point in the pursuit of 'consistency'.

Perhaps worthy of more attention than seasonal variation in the behaviour of the economy is its cyclical behaviour. With the availability of short-term data covering an increasing number of economic cycles, the potential for fruitful work in this field seems to exist. Certainly, the timing of counter-cyclical action by governments has been, rightly or wrongly, the subject of much criticism, and one might expect resources to be devoted to the anaysis of past cycles in order that future action of this kind be more effective. Businesses, also, can be expected to continue to devote resources towards a more accurate assessment of the likely turning points in the behaviour of the economy.

CONSISTENCY OF THE DATA BASE

In constructing the national accounts for the United Kingdom we have always recognized the importance of compiling estimates for all of the time periods on a consistent set of definitions. Much of the work of economists and of other users of the national accounts depends upon our following this principle. As would be expected, however, one encounters many difficulties; these arise in at least two different ways.

First, in the light of experience there may be general agreement that changes in the systems of classification and methods of compilation are desirable. In this way, the present UN system of national accounts (SNA) was formulated during the 1960s and agreement was reached that this should replace the former system, at least as a basis for reporting national accounts data to the international organizations. There is no doubt that, in due course, these changes will be demonstrated to have been worthwhile. For the present, however, we are faced with a situation in which few countries are now able to provide more than a minimum of consistently defined time series for the past 20–25 years. Indeed, the publications of the international organizations currently contain a variety of series which, for any given year, may be on the basis of the former or the present SNA, depending upon the country in question. The transition to the new system is proving to be a troublesome and lengthy process, whilst the compilation of estimates for past years on the new basis is difficult or even impossible. In the future, views about the desirability of changes to the system for international reporting may be influenced by the experience of changing from the former to the present SNA and greater wight may be given to the need for stability.

A second problem in achieving consistent time series arises from the institutional changes which occur in the economy. The growth of the company sector as the result of businesses changing their legal status to that of an incorporated enterprise, for example, can be regarded, in one sense, as a 'legitimate' reason for the growth in company profits and, thus, properly recorded in the national accounts as such. But the nationalization or denationalization of enterprises, and other substantive changes occurring at particular points of time, can make comparisons of the estimates for the institutional sectors in the accounts of limited value. These problems are unlikely to assume any less importance in the future.

Problems of consistency of a rather different kind arise in the compilation of estimates at constant prices (and the associated implied price indices). For both international reporting and national use it has been customary to choose a base year for the calculation of constant price estimates which has generally been retained for some time, perhaps five-years but sometimes considerably longer. When a change in the base year is made, it usually means that the constant price national accounts aggregates are recalculated for some periods, yielding a new set of estimated volume changes in gross domestic product, etc. (because the individual volume changes in the components are now combined according to a different set of relative prices). The differences between the old and new estimates would usually be relatively small, their extent normally depending upon how 'out of date' the base year had become. If one considers a series of 20 years' data, the question then arises as to what constitutes a 'consistent' set of constant price estimates for the whole of this period.

The position taken for the United Kingdom national accounts has been to say that calculation of the volume changes, in the aggregate, over such an extended period, at the relative prices of a single year, would be less useful than the retention of the estimates calculated at the relative prices of a year closer to the period in question. Thus, although the present base year for constant price estimates in the United Kingdom national accounts is 1970, the volume changes between the years 1948 to 1954 are based on the relative prices of 1954, those between 1954 and 1958 on 1958 relative prices, and those between 1958 and 1963 on 1963 relative prices. This may be a reasonable approach for the periods mentioned, but we have recently moved into a period where relative prices have changed very dramatically, and there are legitimate doubts as to whether retention of the relative prices of 1970 for constant price calculations until 1978 (when revised calculations based on the relative prices of 1975 would be introduced) will adequately meet the needs of users.

Research is under way into the probable sensitivity of the constant price estimates to a sharp change in the relative price of certain products. There is, in fact, a strong theoretical case for changing the base of the constant price estimates every year and, indeed, some countries already publish and use estimates on this basis, in addition to those described above. The difficulties encountered are primarily of two kinds. First, there is the need for more detailed data than will normally be available from existing annual inquiries. But, second, there are practical difficulties for the user, since the constant price estimates are no longer additive (i.e. except in the case where only two years are being compared it is necessary to work in terms of index numbers rather than of constant price aggregates which can be manipulated in the same way as current price data).

In view of recent world economic developments, it does seem probable that we shall see more frequent rebasing of constant price series, even though the resulting estimates may be less easy for users to handle and will require additional data for their compilation. The time series calculated in this way would no longer be in the form of base weighted Laspeyres or current weighted Paasche indices, but in that of a chained index, probably chained Laspeyres volume and, thus, chained Paasche implied price indices. It could well be argued in terms of consistency over time that such estimates would be preferable to those generally compiled at present, since each year-to-year change would be defined in a consistent manner.

REVISIONS TO THE DATA BASE—COMPUTERIZED SYSTEMS

If all of the data for national accounts were collected in a single inquiry, then once they were completed and processed, the estimates would be published and, seemingly, no revision would be necessary. Even if such a procedure were feasible, one suspects that publication of the results would be possible only long after the event and that they would be of little relevance to current policy needs. In practice, the national accounts are compiled from a multiplicity of data sources, some of which may have to be utilised with considerable ingenuity in order to provide a basis for estimating the aggregate in which the national accounts statistician is interested. This is particularly true of preliminary or provisional estimates made on the basis of incomplete information. In this situation, one may well find that information bearing upon the national accounts estimates becomes available on many different occasions during the year. A decision has to be taken how frequently to revise the estimates in these circumstances.

The need to make frequent revisions may involve the compiler in additional costs and the user may find frequent revisions tedious, but, at the same time, the user presumably wishes to be made aware of any significant changes to the estimates as more reliable information becomes available. We try, therefore, to strike a balance between avoiding frequent revision to the estimates and making available additional information where it significantly affects the estimates.

The increasing availability of sophisticated computerized systems for data handling, transmission and presentation provides an opportunity for dealing with these problems in a more systematic and efficient way. Those concerned with conjunctural analysis and forecasting are particularly interested in estimates for the present and recent past and, thus, perhaps more than most, will wish to have available a continous updated picture of the economy which takes account of all relevant information. Although, in the United Kingdom, we have not yet organized our procedures in this way, the prospect does now exist of an operational system which would automatically update all of the national accounts estimates as new information became available. Precisely now this would work in practice is not yet clear because it depends, to a significant degree, upon how far the updating procedures can be automatic or dependent on the judgment of the national accounts statistician. What the computerized system potentially makes possible is a method of rapidly taking account of many separate pieces of additional information as each of them becomes available. We expect to be developing our own national accounts work along these lines, as well as seeing more extensive use of computer facilities for the checking and testing of date reliability at a disaggregated level.

THE MONETARY DIMENSIONS OF SHORT-TERM FORECASTING MODELS

Typically, short-term forecasting models have been concerned with the counter-cyclical regulation of aggregate demand for the resources being supplied by the production of an economy or by imports. The quantitative expression of this demand—in the most summary form it is the final domestic expenditure of the economy plus foreign expenditure on the economy's exports (which, less imports, equals the value added in domestic production of goods and services)—is, therefore, in terms of data, expressed at constant prices. Some of the behavioural relationships (e.g. those concerned with imported or domestically produced investment goods) have been expressed wholly or mainly in terms of data at constant prices; little weight has been given to the question of the income or borrowing facilities available to sustain the demand. The prediction of consumers' expenditure, however, has typically taken account both of disposable income (after taxes) and of borrowing facilities; also, in order that the effect of taxes in redistributing income can be taken into account, it has always been necessary, for this element of demand, to work, in terms of forecasts at current prices as well as at constant prices. Also, the balance between imports and exports is influenced by relative costs, changes in the terms of trade and in exchange rates, so that data at current prices are required for forecasts of overseas trade in goods and services. In recent years, the question of the likely rate of inflation in different circumstances, viz., at different levels of *ex-ante* demand, has become more and more important. For all of these purposes it has become necessary to try to forecast the income, expenditure, lending and borrowing accounts of all of the main institutional sectors. In the past in the United Kingdom the process has been in two *successive* stages. The first is a forecast of the income and expenditure account, including expenditure on real capital assets (fixed assets and stocks) leading to the so-called 'financial surplus or deficit'—the excess (if a surplus) of saving over expenditure on real assets, which is available for net lending in the form of financial claims. The second, and separate process, has been to attempt to forecast the flow of funds (financial transactions), giving for each sector the balance of its lending and borrowing in response to a predetermined forecast of its financial surplus or deficit. This procedure is obviously unsatisfactory, since there will be a feed-back from the lending or borrowing to expenditure. Hitherto, the financial flow forecasts have been used only judgmentally to assess the plausibility of the given expenditure forecasts, for there is, as yet, no integrated system of an econometric kind to indicate how financial conditions do influence spending decisions. No mention has been made, so far, of rates of interest, which, classically, bring the demand for funds into line with the available supply; nor about the inter-relations between the banking system and the borrowing requirement of the public sector of the economy, with their effects on the availability of credit (or what is largely its counterpart, the growth of the 'money' stock) and on rates of interest.

The integration of a complete financial sector into the short-term forecasting model of the economy of the United Kingdom is still incomplete. So far, research has concentrated on models of bank behaviour, since this is the key sector, and comprehensive balance sheet and flow-of-funds data are already available. Progress will be inhibited, to some extent, by lack of suitable data (viz., estimates of the levels and composition of assets held by all of the institutional sectors mentioned above). It will also be affected by the rather large statistical discrepancies in the sector accounts. Though the balance of the consolidated current and capital accounts should be the same as the balance of identified borrowing and lending, it is not. The extension of the data base to cover balance sheet-type estimates as well as the improvement in the accuracy of the sector accounts and the flow of funds data should contribute to the effectiveness of this use, as will the build-up of longer-time series of (preferably) quarterly data. In the United Kingdom, however, the available time series already cover 17 years of quarterly income and expenditure data, and 12 years of quarterly flow of funds data.

REDISTRIBUTION OF INCOME THROUGH PUBLIC FINANCE

The section on a complementary system disaggregating income and expenditure data by the characteristics of individuals or households, has already touched on one use for such data—the analysis of the effects on the economy of the redistribution of income through the agency of public finance. In the United Kingdom, studies of this have been regularly published for some time [10]. They have been wholly based, however, on a regular sample survey of family incomes and expenditure, the results of which are affected by non-response and response bias (under-reporting of certain types of expenditure and under-reporting of incomes). There is a need, therefore, for estimates of this kind which are recorded consistently with the corresponding aggregates in the national accounts, which, as mentioned above, raise major practical problems which will not be mastered quickly or easily.

The uses of such data are of great potential value. One area is the study of the effect of aggregate demand of changes in rates of taxation, direct or indirect, or of changes in their degree of progressivity or regressivity. Information on income/expenditure relationships for differing types of households—e.g. age, number of children—would enable more reliably based measures to be formulated on social security benefits. Information on the commodity composition of consumption, analysed according to the income and other characteristics of households, may well add precision to predictions of the response of changes in the demand for particular commodities to changes in income or in borrowing facilities. The redistributive effect of taxation can be viewed systematically only through information which relates factor income, through direct taxes and cash benefits from the State, to disposable income, to saving, and, through indirect taxes and benefits in kind, to consumption. The redistributive effect can thus be quantified in terms of measures of inequality before and after the process of redistribution through taxes and benefits; changes in each over time can be assessed. A further, as yet largely unexplored, dimension will be to extend the range of benefits in kind covered by the analysis (viz., non-market services, such as health and education, and even services provided by public goods, such as roads and other infrastructure) in terms of the benefits to the recipients. One interesting feature of this kind of analysis is that the distinction between the income and expenditure sector of the accounts seems blurred. Some benefits (e.g. subsidies) are treated effectively as negative expenditure, others as income, some as reductions to direct taxes (viz., child allowances) while still others are treated as income (viz., family allowances in cash).

IV. INFLATION AND THE MEASUREMENT OF QUANTUM CHANGES

CONCEPTUAL PROBLEMS

A system of national accounts may be thought of as being primarily concerned with recording, according to a given methodology, transactions between different industries or sectors in the economy. These transactions may take one of several different forms—the exchange of real assets (goods and services) and financial assets, or transfers from one institutional unit to another (e.g. the payment of taxes). The flows of goods and services in the accounts are of particular interest to some users, and for the analysis of these flows it will often be preferable to work in quantity rather than value terms. Estimates at constant prices are constructed for this purpose.

Although estimates at constant prices are often presented in the same national accounts framework as those at current prices, the implication which this form of presentation carries—that the estimates are subject to the same accounting constraints as those at current prices—is questionable. Estimates at constant prices are, in all fundamental repects, quantity index numbers and are subject to all of the limitations and problems of the construction of index numbers. Reference has already been made in Section III to the question of how often the base period for constant price estimates should be changed. It was suggested that, given the recent, large changes in relative prices, more frequent rebasing than hitherto might prove to be necessary, and that a case could also be argued for annual changes on theoretical grounds. The reasons for arguing along these lines are briefly as follows.

A major area of difficulty in constructing either price or quantity indices is the treatment of quality changes and what, in a sense, may be regarded as essentially the same thing—new and disappearing products. Unless we have some way of equating the old and new quality or variety of product, there is no way in which two periods, each containing one product but not the other, can be compared. In practice, this problem may be tackled in a number of ways, but it would be fair to say that they are rarely, if ever, very satisfactory and we have to recognize that the resulting estimates may be deficient in not adequately taking account of quality changes which have occurred. Given this situation, however, it is evident, first of all, that the longer the period of comparison the more likely it will be that the results are subject to such deficiencies. But, furthermore, it suggests that in calculating aggregate quantity or price changes by means of index numbers, the use of the relative prices or quantities of a recent period as weights for the calculations will be far preferable to the use of data relating to a more remote period.

If quantity changes were always calculated initially for adjacent years only, using the relative prices of one of these years, and comparisons between non-adjacent years obtained by chaining together these initial calculations, then the problems arising from quality change would be minimized.

It has sometimes been argued that, by proceeding in this way (use of a chained index), the comparisons obtained between non-adjacent periods were, in some sense, less valid than those obtained by directly comparing the two periods in question in terms of the relative prices (or quantities) of one of the two periods concerned. In some circumstances, this would be true because the chaining procedure can lead to perverse results which would be unacceptable. Where, for example, the cyclical behaviour of different parts of the economy varied very substantially, the use of a chained index might prove to be a less reliable method of comparing two periods at the same point of the cycle than would a direct comparison. But, where structural changes in the economy are of greater significance than changes within the economic cycle, the use of chained indices would seem to be preferable. As we have already observed, it does seem likely that we shall see an increasing use of chained price and quantity indices in the future.

UNIQUE PRODUCTS

A related, but somewhat different, problem to that of dealing with new and disappearing products arises when output may sometimes take the form of a tailormade product which cannot readily be compared in quantity terms with other forms of output. Much civil engineering and construction work is of this kind; some plant, machinery, shipbuilding, etc. may also take this form. Here there are two possible solutions open to the statistician. One approach is to attempt to disaggregate the products into component parts of a kind which can be compared with the components of similar products produced in other periods. An alternative approach is to revalue, at constant 'prices', the expenditure on these products with an index of input cost which incorporates an assumption about changes in productivity (actual changes in productivity cannot be measured if we have no way of quantifying the volume of output). So far, in practice, the second approach has usually been adopted, but, in view of its obvious disadvantages, we hope to see the development of more soundly based methods. The construction of standardized indices of tender prices is a first step in this direction.

NON-MARKET SERVICES

The precise definition of the goods or services whose changes in price or quantity are to be measured may play a crucial role in determining the results obtained. This is particularly true of services where the nature of the service purchased may differ according to the point of view taken. For example, should the treatment provided by a dentist be regarded as (*a*) simply a means of eliminating pain or avoiding it in the future, (*b*) the extraction or filling of a tooth, or (*c*) the composite set of goods and services used to provide the treatment (i.e. the time of the dentist and his staff, the use of their equipment and the materials needed)? If the dentist is to be regarded as a producer, then either (*a*) or (*b*) should be taken as output, since (*c*) is simply an aggregate of the inputs of the producing unit (*a*) is not acceptable as a measure of output, since it is dependent upon factors outside of the scope of the national accounts. We are left with (*b*) which is fine, provided that, with the service so identified, there exists a price with which we can value the quantities produced for aggregation with other goods and services.

The main problems encountered when attempting to construct quantity measures of changes in non-market services (i.e. services provided by private or public institutions not making a direct charge related to the services provided) are the identification of the services to be measured and the appropriate set of relative prices at which the different services are to be valued. No country yet seems to have made any real impression on these problems, the practice usually adopted being that of measuring the quantity of inputs into these services and making an assumption about changes in productivity ranging from that of no change to that of taking the movements estimated for the rest or a part of the economy.

For certain non-market services it seems most unlikely that any atempt to measure output as anything other than the sum of inputs would be possible. The output of a nation's military defence services, for example, might conceivably be quantified in some way but it is difficult to see how. In such circumstances, national accountants should perhaps recognize that the boundary of production, in this instance, lies between the public authority purchasing the goods and services necessary for military defence and the market economy, not between the public authority and the individuals on whose behalf that defence capability is being maintained. If that were recognized, one would not be faced with the possible paradox that the 'output' of military defence services might increase sharply during periods of active hostility and fall when the objective (peace) was achieved.

Other non-market services, such as education and health services, may be measurable in quantity of output terms. A set of provided services which were capable of measurement might well be defined, but, as yet, there is no general agreement about the precise form which these services might take. In our view, it would be wrong to attempt to measure the ultimate objectives of these services (i.e. a better educated and healthier population). Rather, we should try to measure changes in the quantities of different tuition and treatment provided. Where these various forms of 'output' have, themselves, changed over time, we should, of course, be faced with yet another example of the new and disappearing 'products' discussed above.

Any developments along these lines would be difficult to achieve and a necessary condition for them would seem to be the adoption of such measurement systems within the administrative organization of the services in question. It would be quite unrealistic to think in terms of the necessary data being assembled purely for national accounting purposes. Such a set of developments in the national accounts would be feasible only if, as part of the running of such public services, it were considered useful to have quantity measures of output in the terms suggested. Much depends, therefore, upon whether those concerned with the administration of these services would find such measures of value.

FACTOR INCOMES AT CURRENT PRICES

A long-standing technique in the construction of the national accounts has been to exclude stock appreciation (inventory valuation adjustment) from the measurement of the factor incomes generated by production. This is because the value added in the process of production (by the factors labour and capital) is best measured as the surplus of outputs over the concurrent cost of non-factor inputs. The use of materials is measured, therefore, at the replacement cost of the materials, and the book value of the change in the opening and closing levels of stock during any accounting period is split between the physical change, valued at current prices, and the rest of the increase in value (between purchase and the point of use in the productive process, or the stock valuation date), which is known in the United Kingdom national accounts as stock appreciation. Since, however, profits as measured commercially are generally based on a valuation of stock at historic cost (typically on the 'first in, first out' principle), separate calculations have had to be made of 'stock appreciation', which is then deducted from profits, on the factor income side of the accounts, to show (effectively) what profits would be if materials used were charged at replacement cost rather than at actual (historic) cost.

Similarly, in the national accounts it is arguable that depreciation (the provision for the consumption of fixed capital) should also be based on the replacement cost principle. If this is so, the net national product, after deducting provision for capital consumption, is shown after full provision of the replacement of the stock of fixed capital assets. This is the approach recommended in SNA and it has been adopted in the United Kingdom, the estimates of capital consumption not being based at all on commercial depreciation figures, but on a model of the stock of fixed assets valued at replacement cost, which is constructed from past figures of investment revalued to current replacement cost, using the so-called 'perpetual inventory' technique. (The link with commercial figures of profits is at the level of profit *before* provision is made for depreciation.)

These features of the existing system of evaluation for the purpose of the national accounts are highly relevant to the question now being considered of the adjustment of company accounts to allow for inflation—the question of 'inflation accounting'. In the United Kingdom this is being considered by a Committee on Inflation Accounting which is reporting in the summer of 1975. Broadly speaking, there are two schools of thought on 'inflation accounting'; one is the 'replacement cost' school and the other the 'current purchasing power' school. The former envisages the construction of balance sheets in which fixed assets are valued at replacement cost (estimating the replacement cost, so far as possible, as the cost specific to each asset), and the profit is based on charges for asset replacement at current cost; other assets may or may not be valued at market value (as opposed to book value). The latter starts from the existing system of provision for asset replacement at historic cost, but then adjusts the historic cost figures for the acquisition of assets and the subsequent depreciation provision according to a general index of changes in the value of money—the concept being to measure corporate earnings in terms of what would be necessary to maintain the purchasing power of the shareholders' original stake in the business. (Assets, other than fixed assets, and liabilities other than the shareholders are, therefore, also revalued.) It is evident that the former system is very close to that now used in the national accounts, so that, if it were adopted, the figures in the national accounts (as extended to balance sheet estimates) and those in commercial accounts would become very similar over the next decade, and with substantial advantages for many analytical purposes. In an article on inflation accounting published last August [1], a colleague expressed the view that inflation accounting should be viewed in two stages: in the first, the construction of a balance sheet evaluating the written down position of wasting assets at current cost, and other assets at current market value, and, in the second, the revaluation to the prices of a common base of the whole sequence of balance sheets, perhaps using a general price index.

VALUE ADDED AT CONSTANT PRICES

An industry's contribution to the gross domestic product is its 'net output' or 'value added'; in other words, the value of its gross output less the cost of its intermediate inputs, i.e. goods and services which it purchases from other industries, or imports, for use in production. Thus, its net output when value at factor cost equals the sum of the factor incomes—income from employment and gross trading profits—earned in the industry after deducting stock appreciation. In principle, value added at current factor cost can be measured either as the difference between gross output and intermediate inputs (taking into account net indirect taxes), or as the sum of factor incomes.

Similarly, an industry's contribution to the gross domestic product at constant prices—its 'real product' or 'real output'—is its value added measured at constant prices. Conceptually, this can be calculated as the difference between its gross output and intermediate inputs, each measured at constant prices. This method is known as double deflation. It is not possible to measure value added at constant prices as the sum of deflated incomes, since profit incomes are a residual with no corresponding quantity unit and, hence, no price per unit.

In practice, it is often not possible to apply the method of double deflation because sufficient information (particularly adequate information about prices) is not available for estimating both gross output and intermediate inputs at constant prices. Indeed, for the United Kingdom, the method has so far not been used at all for the published estimates, except in the case of the agriculture industry. As an alternative, movements in a single indicator—usually gross output at constant prices—are used to project from the value added by the industry in the base year, on the assumption that changes in the ratio of gross output at constant prices to net output at constant prices are likely to be small. Even if estimates of both gross output and intermediate inputs do, in fact, exist, single indicator methods are often to be preferred because of the sensitivity of double deflated estimates to errors in price deflators.

Given the availability of *accurate* data on both gross outputs and intermediate inputs at constant prices, it is clear that the method of double deflation will give an accurate measure of value added at constant prices, while single indicator estimates will fail to do so, except in the special case where the ratio of net output to gross output at constant prices does not change. In practice, however, the basic estimates of inputs and outputs are inevitably subject to error; and the relative error in their difference, and, thus, in the double deflated measure of value added, may well be greater than in either the input or the output series. Depending on the size of the error variances, on the divergence between the (true) movements of inputs and outputs at constant prices, and on the ratio of net output to gross output in the base year, it is possible for a single indicator method to give more accurate estimates of value added at constant prices than are obtainable by the double deflation technique. In practice, most of these parameters are usually unknown; but a single indicator estimate based on gross output is probably preferable, unless there is evidence of significant divergence between the movements of inputs and outputs. For a full theoretical discussion see [4].

In the past, there has been no possibility of compiling regular, double deflated estimates of net output at constant prices for the United Kingdom (except for the agriculture industry) because information on intermediate inputs was available only at infrequent intervals. (In recent years it was collected only for 1963 and 1968, when full censuses of production were held.) However, with the regular annual collection of total purchases of materials by manufacturing industries, input-output tables are now being compiled for every year from 1970 onwards, using updating techniques for years when detailed input data is not collected, and these will provide estimates of intermediate inputs. Although updated tables tend to perpetuate the technological relations of the base year, it is hoped that these annual tables will provide for each industry a basis for assessing the divergence of movements in inputs and outputs at constant prices, and whether double deflated estimates of value added at constant prices should be preferred to the single indicator estimates currently used for the output-based estimates of changes in gross domestic product at constant prices. This work, however, is in its early stages and improvements in basic data sources may be necessary before sufficiently reliable estimates can be made.

The input-output tables will be available only annually and with some delay, as compared with the single indicators. Thus, even for those industries for which they are preferred, double deflated estimates of value added at constant prices could be used only for adjusting, retrospectively, estimates of industrial output and of gross domestic product based on single indicators of output which had been compiled and published much earlier. There is no prospect of using double deflation for the latest quarterly estimates.

V. POSSIBLE EXTENSIONS OF THE NATIONAL ACCOUNTS BOUNDARIES

From time to time, national accounts aggregates of output or income come under criticism because of their inadequacy as measures of welfare or standards of living. These criticisms draw attention both to inclusions and exclusions which are considered to be inappropriate. The former generally comprise what may be termed the 'regrettable necessities' (for example, expenditure on military defence) and the latter the non-marketed output of various kinds (such as that of housewives). These topics are receiving increasing attention internationally [17] and in Japan the results of some official work on measuring changes in economic welfare have been published [3]. In other countries, published results so far seem to be limited to work by statisticians outside of government agencies. This section of our paper puts forward a view of how work in this field seems likely to develop.

THE TREATMENT OF REGRETTABLE NECESSITIES

It is argued by some that where the use of increased resources is not accompanied by an increase in welfare (for example, the use of a larger police force which succeeds only in restricting the level of crime to that of some earlier period when fewer resources were used for this purpose) this should not be regarded as an increase in the volume of output. Our view is that one must recognize that there are limitations to the scope of national accounts and that the measurement of changes in welfare, in the sense implied by those who would exclude the regrettable necessities from output, is necessarily outside of their scope. Changes in external circumstances may, of course, materially affect the quality of life but the consequences of attempting to take account of such changes when measuring national output seem too far-reaching to contemplate as part of a national accounting framework. It would not be sufficient simply to exclude from output the services of the police and others engaged in 'non-productive' activities, since the logic of a welfare approach would lead inexorably to the need to measure the extent to which changes in the level of crime affected the quality of life (i.e. if it is argued that additional resources devoted to crime prevention do not constitute output unless the level of crime falls, then, any change in the level of crime presumably represents a change in 'output'). Statistical systems concerned with the levels and distribution of welfare are, in fact, receiving attention elsewhere by social and demographic statisticians [14]. This seems to us a much more promising approach than that of attempting to extend the national accounts framework to encompass this added dimension.

INDUSTRIAL POLLUTION

It is important to draw a distinction between the effects of changing circumstances external to the economic system and the results of using particular production processes in that system. If the environment is increasingly polluted by the emission of waste products arising from particular methods of production, it is the concern of the national accountant that resources devoted to combating this pollution should be properly reflected in the accounts. It is argued in [17] that the costs of controlling industrial pollution should be treated as intermediate expenditure (i.e. not contributing to changes in volume of final output). Although this would seem to be correct in principle, it gives rise to problems of measurement, since some of the costs of combating industrial pollution are usually borne by government and financed from taxation. Where the principle that 'the polluter pays' is followed, it would seem feasible to treat the costs of combating industrial pollution as intermediate expenditure, since the taxes levied on pollutors could be regarded as the purchase of a service from government. At present, however, it seems that expenditure by government on pollution control is generally treated as final expenditure, and is, thus, regarded as contributing to final output. This is true of the United Kingdom and would also seem to be the case in the United States, where the collection and publication of expenditure statistics relating to pollution abatement and control has been significantly developed in the last two or three years [2]. A rationalization of the treatment of the costs of controlling industrial pollution would seem to depend very largely upon the extent to which comprehensive provisions for the control of pollution are introduced by governments, and how far these follow the principle that 'the polluter pays'.

NON-MARKET SERVICES

Where goods and services are bought and sold through the market, they automatically fall within the production boundary drawn for the national accounts. Most countries also include, within the production boundary, in addition to the non-market services provided by general government and private non-profit-making bodies, certain other services not provided by the market, an important example of which is the service provided by owner-occupiers of private dwellings to themselves as consumers of housing services. We do not, however, take account of the services provided to themselves by private owners of motor cars or household durables; nor do we regard the labour services provided by housewives and others as falling within the production boundary. What is it which determines where we choose to draw the line?

Those responsible for compiling national accounts have generally been reluctant to extend the boundary of production beyond the area of market transactions. This is probably because the basis on which such non-market transactions could be imputed usually appeared, at best, rather unreliable and, at worst, quite arbitrary. However, the problems of valuation encountered when attempting to include imputed transactions in the national accounts can often be solved in a reasonably satisfactory way (as for the imputed rents of owner-occupied dwellings). A more serious problem is that one is still faced with the question of where the production boundary is to be drawn since, having included the services of housewives for example, do we then regard those services as being consumed or as intermediate inputs combined with other intermediate inputs in a further stage of production? Is final consumption one further stage down the production chain—the meal served to the family—or do we need to look even further, treating some part, at least, of the family's food intake as an intermediate input necessary to maintain it in 'good working order'? (Professor Stone's UN paper [17] aptly refers to this as owner-occupied slaves.) National accounts statisticians are more concerned with the task of compiling useful, timely and reliable data than in pursuing such esoteric arguments. Since our principal users (the economic policy arms of government) do not regard the exclusion of housewives and other household services from production as a serious deficiency in the national accounts, we do not see the extension of the accounts in this direction as deserving of any special priority.

There are some other aspects of non-market services, however, to which considerable attention has been directed by national accounts statisticians over the years, though so far not with any noticeably useful results. The appropriate concepts for the services provided free, or for a nominal charge, by general government or private non-profit-making bodies serving households seem to have been subject to considerable uncertainty. In the former UN system of national accounts (SNA) these institutions were regarded, not as producers, but as final consumers. In the present system they are regarded both as producers and consumers, consumption of the services they provide being on behalf of the community as a whole. But, although one can agree that, in principle, the production boundary might be drawn between such institutions and those to whom they provide their services (present SNA), rather than between the market economy and those institutions (former SNA), the practical effect of this change has been minimal. This is because the value of the 'output' of these institutions is still regarded as equal to the value of the sum of their inputs. Thus, the formal extension of the production boundary has no effect on the value of production, provided that the scope of the 'inputs' under the new system is the same as that of the items consumed under the old system. The implications of different definitions of the production boundary for changes in the *volume* of non-market services (as distinct from changes in their value) was touched upon in Section IV, above.

THE BOUNDARY BETWEEN CONSUMPTION AND CAPITAL ACCUMULATION

In the national accounts, we currently restrict what is regarded as capital formation to reproducible assets such as buildings, plant, machinery, vehicles and producers' stocks of goods and work-in-progress. The suggestions for extension include research and development expenditure and investment in human capital. Also, in the context of economic balance sheets, it is thought that natural resources in the form of mineral ores or fossil fuels should be taken into account, and that provision should be made for supplementary estimates of the stock of consumer and military durables not regarded as capital formation of the main accounts. Although these areas of activity may be relevant to the consideration of certain economic problems, we do not see them as leading to any major changes in the form of mainstream national accounts development work.

VI. THE NEED FOR SUPPLEMENTARY INFORMATION BY USERS OF NATIONAL ACCOUNTS

We have laid some emphasis in earlier sections of this paper upon our view that improvements in the quality of national accounts estimates are at least as important as their extension or further elaboration. However, the estimates will never be perfect and it is likely that there will always be differences in the reliability of component series. The availability of a description of the relative reliability of the mail series seem to us important, therefore, if the user is to derive maximum benefit from the published figures.

For the United Kingdom national accounts, such a description of the methodology is given in *Sources and Methods* [8] and this is regularly updated in the notes to the annual national income and expenditure Blue Book (as in the latest edition [11]). Recent changes or developments are also noted in the publication *Statistical News*. It is our impression that, with few exceptions, the data sources and methods of estimation underlying other countries' national accounts estimates are not so readily available from published sources. This seems to us regrettable, since a valid interpretation of the estimates may well depend upon a proper appreciation of their reliability. Although we have no specific plans for extending the range of this background material in respect of the United Kingdom national accounts (it will, of course, continue to be updated), we would, nevertheless, very much welcome the growth of such practices in other countries.

VII. THE STORAGE AND DISSEMINATION OF NATIONAL ACCOUNTS DATA

In addition to requiring varying sets of data, particular users may put a premium upon rapid turnround time. Those concerned with monitoring short-term movements in the economy, for example, will wish to have the latest available figures readily to hand. By contrast, an academic researcher may be more concerned that long time series of consistently defined data be made available, access to estimates for the most recent period being of marginal value only in the context of a particular research project.

The needs of the former group are best met by a reliable databank service of the kind described in the paper by Eckstein. Where such a service is not available, users will look to the regular statistical publications of national agencies as the media through which the information should be made available. This may be supplemented (as in the United Kingdom) by other means of making data available prior to its appearance on the printed page, such as through the issue of press notices or cyclostyled sheets. The researcher who wishes to make use of more detailed data covering a longer period will, presumably, not regard rapid turnround time as so important. For these needs, the important factors would seem to be access to clearly and consistently defined data on as detailed and extensive a scale as possible. Here the international agencies clearly play a crucial role, since the criterion of consistency of definition is one to which they attach great importance for the national accounts data which they collect and publish. But, in addition, where it is available, the researcher should also have access to the kind of supporting material in the previous section.

All of these considerations suggest to us that the order of priorities to be followed in determining the service to be provided by academic libraries should be broadly on these lines. There should be quick access to the latest national accounts aggregates in whatever form they are first issued by the national statistical agency concerned. Libraries should give first priority to the figures relating to their own country, but, where possible, could extend their coverage to include the figures for other countries likely to be of interest to their own economists. We would suggest that the material on which this service was based should be disposed of, however, whenever it has been superseded by a further set of estimates. There should also be access to long runs of consistently defined national accounts series which are most readily found in the special publications of the United Nations Organization for Economic Co-operation and Development and the Statistical Office of the European Communities.[1] It is noteworthy that the summary publications of the last-named organization includes estimates for the main national accounts series relating to the United States and Japan, as well as estimates for member countries.

One obvious need is to ensure that very long time series derived from publications issued at different times are consistently defined. The international organizations are well aware of this and it seems likely that, wherever possible, they will publish long runs for the main national accounts aggregates. In any event, their latest issues usually contain a run of data covering about ten years, which may be sufficient for much

[1] The national accounts definitions followed by these three international organizations can be regarded, for most practical purposes, as identical; differences arise mainly in the form of presentation adopted.

research work. Finally, we would mention again the value of supporting material describing the sources and methods underlying national accounts estimates. Librarians may need to devote special effort to obtain this kind of information but, once made, this effort seems to us likely to be a worthwhile investment. The researcher is most unlikely to be able to obtain a similar service from a computerized databank.

REFERENCES

[1] Cowley, A. H., 'Accounting for Inflation', *Economic Trends* (August 1974).

[2] Cremeans, J. E. and Segal, F. W., 'National Expenditures for Pollution Abatement and Control, 1972', *Survey of Current Business* (February 1975).

[3] Economic Council of Japan, 'Measuring Net National Welfare of Japan', Report of Net National Welfare Measurement Committee. (1974).

[4] Hill, T. P., *The Measurement of Real Products* (OECD, 1971).

[5] Revell, J., et al., *The Wealth of the Nation—the National Balance Sheet of the United Kingdom 1957–1961.*

[6] Roe, A. R., *The Financial Interdependence of the Economy, 1957–1966* (Cambridge: Dept. of Applied Economics, 1971).

[7] Tobin, J. and Brainard, W. C., 'Pitfalls in Financial Model Buildings', *American Economic Review*, Papers and Proceedings (May 1968).

[8] United Kingdom Statistical Office, *National Accounts Statistics: Sources and Methods* (London: Her Majesty's Stationery Office, 1968).

[9] United Kingdom Central Statistical Office, *Economic Trends, November 1973: Preliminary Estimates of Regional GDP.*

[10] United Kingdom Central Statistical Office, *Economic Trends, December 1974: The Incidence of Taxes and Social Security Benefits in 1973.*

[11] United Kingdom Central Statistical Office, *National Finance and Expenditure, 1964–1974*, (London: Her Majesty's Stationery Office, 1975).

[12] United Nations, *A System of National Accounts* (New York: United Nations, 1968).

[13] United Nations, *A System of International Comparisons of Gross Product and Purchasing Power*, (New York: United Nations, 1975).

[14] United Nations, *Towards A System of Social and Demographic Statistics* (New York: United Nations, 1975).

[15] United Nations Statistical Commission, Seventeenth Session, *A Draft System of Statistics of the Distribution of Income, Consumption and Accumulator* (New York: United Nations, 1972).

[16] United Nations Statistical Commission, Eighteenth Session, *Report of the Secretary-General on Draft International Guidelines on the National and Sector Balance Sheet and Reconciliation Accounts of the SNA* (New York: United Nations, 1974).

[17] United Nations Statistical Commission, Eighteenth Session, *Supplementing the National Accounts for Purposes of Welfare Measurements* (New York: United Nations, 1974).

[18] *Wealth Tax, Cmnd 5704* (London: Her Majesty's Stationery Office, August 1974), Appendix 2.

Summary of the Discussion

After noting that this paper was technically more advanced than most of the others presented at this conference, *Professor Shoup* discussed it under four main heads:

1. Restatement of the British system of national accounts and comparison with the system recommended by the UN. Professor Shoup preferred to save most of his queries for more controversial issues, but noted the wider use of input-output analysis to improve the accuracy of estimates by checking sales against purchases. He inquired whether value-added taxation (VAT) was also an aid in improving accuracy, as income taxation had been in earlier periods. While agreeing that the quality and timeliness of national accounts are being improved in Britain and elsewhere, *Professor Shoup* wondered about the uses of the new data, particularly in mitigating economic fluctuations. He made one substantive suggestion, namely, the clearer separation of households from the unincorporated enterprises which they often conduct.

2. Use of the accounts in support of economic forecasting. The paper frequently stresses this use, as well as distributional issues (by income size, income type, family type, region, etc.) Such other uses as measurement of growth and international comparisons are apparently played down in the accounts, in view of the limited funds available. Professor Shoup felt that the continual revisions, which the British practice, have both good and bad points, and doubted the justification of any 'welfare' interpretation of either total or per capita income. This is because spending decisions are affected by stocks (both inventories and financial assets) as well as flows, and by the sectoring (distribution) of the flows. *Professor Shoup* hoped for annual reports from a standing Royal Commission currently studying income distribution and redistribution in Britain, and commented that wealth distribution data remain poor. *Professor Shoup* did not believe that the effects of the public finance system on income distribution can be determined except at the margin, and thought that too much reliance was being placed on national income figures in the allocation and sharing of international costs between, e.g. UN members.

While agreeing that, in principle, national income accounts can be used in forecasting, *Professor Shoup* placed greater reliance on 'leading indicators' of the American type, particularly the securities markets. Pehaps the national income data might be more helpful if firms were required to report more frequently (perhaps even daily!) and were subsidized for that purpose. Such a change would catch rapid shifts, such as the making and cancelling of multiple orders. (*Mr Hibbert* agreed only that 'the present' could be estimated more readily with more immediate reporting.)

3. Adjusting for inflation and measurement of quantum changes. The paper proposes more widespread reliance on chained indexes and a more complete integration of the financial sector. *Professor Shoup* would prefer, instead, more household data as an aid in stabilization policy. As inflation has increased in intensity and continuity, a shift to replacement cost depreciation is surely needed. Some special problems of adjustment relate to unique items, to quantifying services, and to including non-market transactions. *Professor Shoup* was more ambitious than the paper as to both the latter points. He would prefer to measure, even if subjectively, the number of units of, e.g. crime reduction and the cost per unit, rather than simply to include the input cost of crime reduction in the accounts as representing its output in terms of crime reduced. He would also like to see housewives' services included in national income accounts. And, as for firms, *Professor Shoup* felt that data on inter-firm purchases were weak, and repeated his hope that VAT would help the situation.

4. Extending the boundaries of the accounts. Consider consumption, said *Professor Shoup*. How much of it is real, and how much consists of 'regrettable necessities' like adjustments to cold winters, expenditures for police protection and national defence? Even at the cost of increased subjectivity, let us try to measure output rather than continuing the present admixture of input items. On the other hand, *Professor Shoup* felt it was a mistake to attempt the measurement of 'quality of life' or 'net national welfare' as such. He expressed himself as generally unfavourable to the 'welfare approach' in national income accounting. He had often been asked why, if the principal users of the accounts are unconcerned with housewives' services, for example, the national income statistician should consider them. His reply to such criticism has been that, to some extent, users should be told what to want, on the principle of 'merit wants' in public finance.

Opening the discussion from the floor, *Professor M. Perlman* regretted the absence in the paper of any assistance to librarians. Can much be said, beyond that libraries should have data from leading countries?

Miss Deane wondered who the major demanders of data were—policy makers, researchers, businessmen, teachers? She also felt that it should be made easier for users to interpret the results, and inquired about developments such as the up-dating of obsolete British publications and indicating margins of error.

Professor Morgan argued that competing groups of users exacerbate the documentation problem. Forecasters want speed, businessmen detail, and researchers attention to basic problems. Perhaps much small-sample, small-area data should be omitted. *Professor Morgan* also regretted that the whole topic of 'social indicators' was being left so largely to sociologists and psychologists. He suspected that 'how early teenagers leave home' might have more economic consequences than many details of non-money income. On the accounts themselves, *Professor Morgan* thought that time as well as money inputs might be measured, as leisure was in other connections, and would like more information about the estimation and imputation methods used throughout the accounts.

Mr Fetterman inquired about the levels and availability of information. Librarians and information scientists would like to know what material needs to go where, and how soon. *Professor Morgan* replied that the answer varies with the users, and that the question could not be answered in general.

Professor Bronfenbrenner said that plausible adjustments, e.g. for inflation, can be made on one side of the double-entry national income accounts, but wondered whether the balancing entries on the other side might not be arbitrary and hard to justify? *Mr Hibbert* denied that this was a serious problem; *Professor Morgan* added that, when it is, the adjustments should be delayed. A preliminary single-entry statement could suffice for puposes of immediate availability.

Professor Kindleberger worried about specious accuracy in arbitrary solutions to valuation problems. He felt this to be a particularly serious matter where wealth and other stocks were concerned.

Mr Evans mentioned the library as an example of a service whose input (cost) is conventionally equated with its output. He said that the problem is more serious for libraries than for such other service institutions as retail stores.

Mr Hibbert replied to these comments, beginning with an acknowledgement that the paper needed to be expanded in order to deal more directly with the problems of librarians as suggested by Professor Perlman (see sections V and VI of the published paper). He next dealt with Professor Shoup's desire to see the boundaries of the national accounts extended. The accounts do not, and never will, answer all of the questions directed at them and one might well argue that they included too much guesswork already. Further extension of the boundaries beyond the market sector would be unlikely to help the user; more promising was the development of special studies in problem areas of public policy interest.

On Professor Shoup's question about the possible use of the VAT system, this had been viewed as a rich potential source of statistical material, but in the United Kingdom those responsible for administering the tax had evidently set their face against the inclusion, in the system, of any features purely for statistical purposes. This meant that the system's potential would not be realised to any significant degree. In Mr Hibbert's opinion the timeliness-accuracy trade-off on quarterly accounts is nearly optimal. Estimates for the household transactions of unincorporated businesses could be compiled but would merely be a reflection of the conventions adopted and probably not worth publishing.

On net economic welfare comparisons there was generally little impetus for such work in the United Kingdom at present, though attention had been drawn recently to the important short-term changes in real income (as compared with real output) arising from changes in the terms of trade. There was, however, great interest in welfare comparisons between different sections of the population, and the Royal Commission will be reporting regularly.

On forecasting, Mr Hibbert saw possible dangers in combining the role of compiler and forecaster in the same office.

The measurement of short-term quantum changes at a time of rapid inflation and little growth in real terms was inevitably subject to an unusually wide margin of error. The attention of users had been drawn to this feature of the estimates for recent periods. On guidance and supporting services to users generally, the material is published in the United Kingdom but perhaps not sufficiently publicised. The standard work of reference for the United Kingdom national accounts (published in 1968) is updated every year in the notes to the annual national accounts volume, for example, but evidently this fact had gone unnoticed by some users.

On Professor Kindleberger's point about the difficulties of valuing wealth, Mr Hibbert said that it seemed preferable for official statisticians to attempt this task, indicating clearly the problems and underlying assumptions, rather than to leave it to others who might fail to recognize all of the pitfalls.

In summary, plans for *fundamental* change to national accounts concepts were not the main pre-occupation in the United Kingdom at the present time. Detailed checks on consistency and accuracy are currently of greater concern. Different users may have different needs, some of which may be competing. The official statistician does his best to strike a satisfactory compromise.

12 The Usefulness of Microdata and some Strategies for the Storing, Using, and Disposing of it

James N. Morgan
UNIVERSITY OF MICHIGAN

The storage and retrieval of microdata involve serious problems because of the complex documentation required. The changing computer technology and the complex data-manipulation are statistical procedures. At best, secondary use will remain expensive, and its funding a problem. Reductions in cost of access require investments in anticipation of later use which may be self-justifying (by increasing that use) but cannot be funded by those future users. A stepwise procedure for access will probably involve securing and reading the initial published analysis, then securing volumes of printed documentation (code books are not enough) and ultimately securing a data file. Now there is a problem of knowing who else has worked, or is working, on the same data.

I. *INTRODUCTION*

In this world of exploding archives we are clearly in need of some guidelines to deal with the storing or disposal of data. Even with the reductions made possible by modern technology there are bound to be storage costs, and trade-offs between these costs and ease of access will have to be considered. With the passage of time, material stored under one method becomes increasingly difficult to retrieve under more modern technology and keeping all information easily retrievable is likely to be prohibitively expensive.

If storage is costly, and keeping archives in the best storage involves repeated costs for updating, we need some criteria for deciding what to keep most easily accessible, what to keep in various states of accessibility, and what to store or even to destroy.

A basic principle, of course, is that things which can be easily recreated from other information need not be saved. One does not need tables of square roots if they can be computed as they are needed. Secondary analysis of data, particularly sets of tables running everything by everything, are less crucial for storage and retrieval than are basic data.

One of the best things about common statistical procedures is that, at least in theory, anyone using the same data set and the the same model should be able to come up with the same results.

Hence, basic data are more important than much of the analyses published on them. This is doubly true if the data are high-quality measures of something likely to change, where the understanding of the change is important. Both in the selection and archiving of data, attention to comparability across space and time is important.

Data from systematic official records or probability samples are more likely to provide clean comparisons than are non-sample data, or data from small sub-populations. An exception is, of course, a sample of a sub-population that is easily identifiable, persists over time, and is likely to undergo changes.

Probability samples of well-defined populations are more useful than are poorly-defined sub-populations or quota samples. The major advantages of a probability sample are that the sampling variances are known, or can be estimated, and that any definable subgroup in such a sample is a representative probability sample of that subgroup.

It should not be necessary to add that we mean a completely carried-out probability sample, not one that, at the last stages, has allowed the uncontrolled selection of dwellings or respondents. The potential biases from such departures are well documented.

Good interviewing or data collection methods are more likely to be reproducible than are bad ones. Even when personal interviews are involved, a fixed-question open-answer system, content-analysed under controls, is far more useful for replication and estimating trends. One can always re-code the original protocols or a sample of them, to be sure that the same answer is being interpreted the same way. What seems like the precision of check boxes in questionnaires hides unknown and uncheckable variety in the interpretation of the question by respondent and/or interviewer.

Looking at the storage and retrieval of information as one more example of cost-benefit analysis focuses our attention on the systematic inclusion of all of the costs and benefits. Let us start with the benefits.

II. *BENEFITS*

The value of information is, of course, difficult to quantify. More important yet, its total social value increases the more it is used, and the exclusivity principle does not apply. That is, I can give you information and still have it myself. Utility curves add vertically rather than horizontally. We must, therefore, project how much use might be made of any given set of data, and for what purposes. It seems likely that any rich set of microdata will be useful for some re-analysis as new theories develop to be tested and as new statistical procedures become workable. But the sets most likely to be used by many people over many years are those which provide benchmark data for intertemporal comparisons. At a point in time not much of real interest changes. Differences in income and prices are confounded with other things and the dynamics of adaptation are difficult to uncover.

The passage of time and the great changes that take place, provide a series of natural experiments, confounded of course, and not optimally designed, but at least some crucial explanatory variables change. There have been vast changes in prices, in relative prices, in real incomes, in racial and sex differences in earnings, and in labour force participation. There have been dramatic changes in the prices of various financial and other assets, and in the impact of unemployment on different occupations.

All of these, and other changes have affected peoples' condition, behaviour and belief, their plans and strategies. We can, of course, attempt to rely on people's memory, at least as to changing facts, but repeated survey data from probability samples allow much richer analysis, even if the repeated measurements are not of identical individuals.

III. *COSTS*

When we come to costs we must be sure to include them all, and their measurement is more important than it is with many other things because we have no market mechanism where customers decide whether the price warrants their purchase. Some policymaker must decide, first, whether the total benefits are greater than the total costs, and, then, how the costs are to be financed, i.e. whether there should be some user charges.

Storage of data has a number of costs, some of them one time, some intermittent, and some associated with each use. There are investment costs in preparing data and documentation for archives, and some strategy decisions. For instance, a larger investment in documentation and storage costs may make each later use less expensive. Such an investment pays off only if easy access to the data encourages sufficient use to amortize the extra costs.

The initial preparation of proper documentation is difficult and costly because it must be done by a busy researcher trying to finish a project, and because he must be able to put down many things absurdly obvious to him. It is difficult to foresee how essential it will be for someone to know the information in a different time or place.

Another cost, also involving strategy, is that of updating files and maintaining them in a form optimal for the current generation of computers. The speed with which computer *procedures* (as distinct from *technology*) change is what matters, and that has been substantial. Even at my own university there are currently two different ways of storing numbers, one of which uses 9s to indicate missing data, the other minus zeros. One keeps twelve letters of alphabetic description of each variable, the other twenty four. One can complain and urge some uniform and consistent system for labelling data files, storing them and describing them, but so long as the present heterogeneity exists, and changing heterogeneity at that, we shall have to think of the costs of keeping up with it.

Both the archivist and the future users have to invest in the acquisition of knowledge and skills, and this is part of the total cost. It is the capital investments in learning about each new change that are the most costly, and the most likely to be ignored. The enthusiastic developers of new and better systems for both storage and computing persistently underestimate the costs of retraining people and of transmitting the new information or methods. I have watched for more than a quarter of a century, as generation after generation of students and new researchers struggled to acquire a body of expertise that was often obsolete within a few years. I have seen good researchers get out of the analysis of microdata in frustration over the problems of keeping up with the sheer mechanics of their use. I have seen many discussions of new computer systems, with promises of *automatic* translations from the old system, most of which proved to be illusory.

There is, of course, some transfer of learning. But the proliferation of courses on how to use the computer, and of mechanisms for consultation and help, are clearly far short of providing sufficient access to data for those who need it. Much of the learning takes place informally, at great cost to the gracious and willing people who teach others what they have just learned through difficult experience. If one wanted an estimate of one small fraction of this cost, one might start with the number of aborted computer runs, plus those which ran but had to be rerun because of errors, and ask what they cost in terms of researcher time, computer time, delay, and discouragement. Indeed, the discouragement factor may be the most important social cost of all. We have traded great efficiency in data manipulation for those who are in the know, for a massive barrier to access for all the rest of the scientific community. The comparative advantage of the great university relative to the small college, and of the large firm relative to the small one, in getting and using information, is thus increased.

Hence, one might ask for the development of some relatively simple, even if inefficient, and stable (unchanging over long periods)—but well documented—system for storage and access. Only thus will access to data be close to the kind of open, democratically available resource that books in libraries have been for centuries.

Another cost to the user, even more difficult to deal with systematically, is the cost of searching for the existence of data sets to meet specified needs. Even if each data set were well documented, easily transferable in some uniform way, the user must discover that it exists, and be able to tell whether it is potentially adaptable to his needs. Since data sets are not usually uniquely associated with one publication, the process is difficult. Again, we have rationing by ignorance, with a comparative advantage to those who are in the circuits, e.g. the large professional universities.

One possible way to deal with this is to attempt to have one major publication associated with each major data set, its appendixes providing enough detail to help a reader decide whether to make the next step and ask for the full documentation. What tends to happen now is that the long distance telephone is used, partly out of laziness by people who hate to read, but partly because there is no assurance that all of the existing data are summarized, described, and their main findings spelled out in some publication that can be found by the usual library methods. Our own organization attempts to produce at least one major publication for each national survey that we do, but we do not always succeed.

An added difficulty arises in indexing microdata simply because they cover a broad range of topics. Cross-referencing, the librarian's usual answer, does not work well if a survey has collected data on several hundred variables, scores of which could be thought of as dependent variables to be explained, and most of which can be thought of as explanatory variables of some sort. One can imagine the indexing that would be required, for each data set, to allow them to answer such questions as:

> What studies tell us anything about racial differences? What do we know about quality of housing? What is inflation doing to people's mental health? How frequent are accidents with home appliances? Does life insurance compete with Social Security? Are people retiring earlier, and why? What do we know about living in the suburbs?

IV. *FLEXIBILITY*

If a major purpose of archiving microdata is to facilitate study of the natural experiments in history—the way changing events have affected the situation and behaviour of different subpopulations—then we need the data available in their most flexible form. No one can predict accurately which subgroups will need to be examined, and in connection with what other variables. Hence, it is not the published analyses of the data, nor the tables, that are crucial, but the basic data in all their richness. If the main report on a study that first collected and used the data provides a complete list of the data and the distributions of all of the variables or classifications, it may provide an introduction to the archive; otherwise, some documentation volume must. Particularly if the sample is special in some sense—not a probability sample or a whole population—then the actual distribution of the sample by income, age, education, family size, and the like, will be crucial in indicating its utility for assessing the effects of major trends.

If the interviewing is carefully done, with fixed-questions, and, where necessary, centrally controlled content analysis of open-ended answers, the possibility of comparable data collected later is greatly enhanced. Where we deal with attitudes, and expectations and reasons why, that comparability may require checking the current content-analysis (coding) of answers by re-coding a sample of the earlier protocols. Hence, there is an argument for storage and accessibility, somehow, of the basic questionnaires (with identification of names, but not of the earlier coded information removed). But they need not be stored in more than one place nor even in any expensive way that costs a lot now, hoping to reduce the later costs of re-coding. Microfilm, I might add, does not make re-coding easier.

V. *MANIPULATION*

When a library keeps books, people are assumed to know how to read. When it keeps complex microdata sets, their utilization requires not only that the scientist discover their existence, and have documentation of the data, but that some computer with adequate software be available and that the scientist know something about what to do and how to do it.

If it is sometimes difficult to transfer data from one computer to another, it is far more difficult to transfer computer programs. They tend to be written for maximal efficiency on a particular computer, not for maximum transportability. The problem is probably worse with 'data management' programs, rather than with statistical programs. Most users find it necessary to do some rearranging of the data, some creation of new or combined variables. It is not clear who is responsible for the development, documentation, and teaching of computer data-handling methods.

In addition, the statistical analysis of complex microdata files also requires a set of skills not automatically available, ranging from understanding the impact of clustered samples on statistical tests, to an appreciation of the need for separating the search for an optimal model (ransacking) from the test of one or two best models with an independent set of data. The statistical literature is replete with elaborate methods of dealing with: non-linear relations; intercorrelation among predictors; interaction effects; heterogeneous variances; autocorrelated errors; intercorrelated errors; categorical predictors; categorical dependent variables; errors in explanatory variables, or unobservable variables (measured with error by proxies); directed (causal?) relations, and structural models; searching for a model versus assessing the best one.

Little is said about how to deal with *combinations* of these problems, particularly with the kind of microdata now rapidly becoming available.

VI. *SYSTEMS AND FINANCING*

Assuming that we have some solution to the selection of the microdata to be saved, and their distribution among archiving methods ranging from heavy initial investment, well-documented, widely-distributed data to low overhead, high-retrieval-cost storage, there remains a problem of how the system should be funded, including the initial storage, the updating, and the distribution and dissemination.

The ultimate users cannot fund the investment in initial preparation and storage. Nor, given current funding systems, can the groups or agencies responsible for the initial collection and analysis always count on such funding. One could argue that any important data collection should have funding for its proper archiving. Systems to encourage and preserve funding for that purpose might be welcome.

The amount of added cost to be covered by users will depend on the quality and amount of the initial investment in archiving. For instance, one can simply store the master documentation and copy it (at 10¢ a page) as users need it; or one can print and store *copies* of it, at less than half that cost, provided enough of the copies are sold; or one can make it machine readable so that printing one more copy is relatively cheap and there is no investment in preparing and storing a lot of paper that may not be used. Clearly, some forecast of future use is required, but the amount of that use may itself depend on the user charges. One can be safe, and economize, and take little risk by simpler archiving that requires higher user charges later, or one can invest now in archiving that will allow very low (marginal) user charges.

From an economic efficiency point of view, since the more use the more social value, marginal cost pricing (or less) seems called for. Particularly if the benefits are themselves not market place benefits but social benefits from knowledge, better public policy, etc., user charges may well be disfunctional. Of course, the problem remains how the costs should be funded, and how they should be allocated between initial investment and variable, use-associated costs.

If is roughly correct to say that if anyone had enthusiastically invested in expensive archiving of the economic surveys of the last twenty-five years, the investment would hardly have been warranted by the use that has been made of those data. Perhaps the increased availability and lower marginal costs would have encouraged more use, but other barriers, lack of interest, lack of knowledge on how to use the data, and no earlier data for studying changes, may well have discouraged further analysis. Only recently has it become clear that we need to know more about the microbehaviour parameters of economic systems if we are to deal adequately with macrodynamics.

VII. *SUMMARY*

If there were to be funds available for improved archiving of microdata, their allocation would have to be based both on some assumptions about the future, and on some principles of equity and efficiency. First, priority should probably go to assuring that current data are being properly documented, and that the basic data stored in some reasonably uniform, easily accessible way. But large investments in many duplicate copies may not be called for, unless or until the rate of use seems to justify it. Second, at least one publication containing some findings and a description of every major data set should be encouraged and widely distributed, to ease the search process and provide the first access route. Beyond that, extensive assembling of lists, bibliographies, automated retrieval systems and the like, would seem far less useful than investment in retrieving data sets that are now practically inaccessible because of their inadequate documentation or the archaic nature of their storage. (It is extremely difficult even to *read* some old data sets with modern computers.)

Finally, along with investment in archiving should go an investment in training people to work with microdata. A whole new statistical outlook is required for those accustomed to aggregate time-series or small-scale experimental data. The explosion of both degrees of freedom and of measured variables for each unit allows tremendous flexibility in letting the data speak about what might be the best model. And the errors in measurement of explanatory variables, or the need to use proxies for the concepts of theory, lead to problems that had all but disappeared from the econometric literature until recently.[1]

The most important aspect of this new freedom is a crying necessity for the practical and conceptual separation of the process of ransacking data while searching for the best explanatory model, from the process of assessing the explanatory power of the best model, measuring its parameters, and testing crucial aspects of it. This requires separating data into independent subparts, something which can be done properly only by someone familiar with the details of the original sample. (A random half of a clustered sample is correlated with the other half, because members of clusters tend to get divided and fall into both halves.) The

[1] Goldberger, Arthur, 'Maximum-Likelihood Estimation of Regressions Containing Unobservable Independent Variables', *International Economic Review*, 13 (February 1972) pp. 1–15.

Zellner, Arnold, 'Estimation of Regression Relationships Containing Unobservable Independent Variables', *International Economic Review*, 11 (1970) pp. 441–54.

Leamer, Edward E., 'False Models and Post-Data Model Construction', *Journal of the American Statistical Association*, 69 (March, 1974), pp. 112–31.

Griliches, Zvi, 'Errors in Variables and Other Unobservables' *Econometrica*, Vol. 42 (November, 1974), pp. 971–98.

Goldberger Arthur, and Duncan, O. D., eds., *Structural Equation Models in the Social Sciences*, New York and London: Seminar Press, 1973).

Survey Research Center is now designating independent quarter samples in its data to facilitate this process.[2]

POSTSCRIPT

Comments lead me to the following additional observations.

There is a range of studies, from large scale ones done by enduring organizations using probability samples, to smaller studies by individuals who go on to other pursuits. Two decisions are required over much of this range: (a) whether the data should be archived and, (b) if so, where and by whom? We have implied that it is important to save data from well-conducted probability samples in areas where something is likely to change. It seems useful to propose controlled data archives for studies without a permanent source institution that has some expectation of immortality.[3] Funding of both kinds of archives remains a serious problem, even if we use the low-storage-cost high-accessibility-cost strategy.

As for facilitating the location of desired data, the attempt to designate one main published report for each data set seems crucial. And the establishment of the principle that the documentation and data should be available as soon as the first analysis report is published should become the accepted and expected standard of behaviour.

[2] Morgan, J. N., 'Using Survey Data from the University of Michigan's Survey Research Center', *American Economic Review*, May 1975.

[3] More than one such archive might be good, allowing for some specialization. As to substantive areas (economic, political, geographic), archives already exist at the universities of Michigan, Wisconsin, Illinois, and Florida, at Williams College, at the National Opionion Research Center (Chicago), and at the Bureau of Applied Social Research (Columbia).

Summary of the Discussion

Professor von Böventer introduced this paper with the comment that it contained material for numerous such papers. Among the subjects Professor Morgan had enriched were: the financing of the collection system, the benefits of storage and flexibility, the relative importance of data and analysis, the importance of comparability, replicability, and collection methods. *Professor von Böventer* would merely expand on a few of these topics.

There is, for example, a three-way trade-off among low storage costs, frequent up-dating of data, and maintaining ease of access to users. Optimization is a subjective matter, although quantitative proxies for, e.g. numbers of users and the probability of useful results may influence the decision. (Time preference may also be an influence.) Subjective elements cannot be eliminated, said *Professor von Böventer*; on the other hand, some of the problems may be formally reducible to standard ones in control theory.

Passing on to cost-benefit analysis, *Professor von Böventer* accepted the elementary criteria that benefits should exceed costs. But what prices should the users pay, to reduce the costs of the data supplier? Also, while dealing with costs, should the relevant estimates be of marginal or average costs per output unit? Another problem: while some costs are paid once for all, some are intermittent, and others recur at each use; low overhead costs may mean high retrieval costs, and vice versa.

One of the costs of acquiring knowledge and skills by archivists and computer technologists is the discouraging effect of constantly changing computer technology. Accordingly, *Professor von Böventer* favoured a simple, stable, well-documented system of storage and access, even at some loss in efficiency. Furthermore, one major explicatory publication should accompany each data set lent out to a user.

To provide flexibility for multiple users of data, basic data should be stored in all its richness; as for other materials. It is sometimes easier to give users actual data than to give them programs for getting it themselves. For this purpose the skills of statistical analysts may be important, so that it is also important that more be trained.

As for financing methods, *Professor von Böventer* favoured marginal cost pricing as most desirable, whenever possible. This choice might leave the statistical office with a deficit, which should be funded outside the market.

Professor von Böventer agreed with Professor Morgan's conclusion that more microdata is necessary for the macrodynamics of growth and fluctuations. But the many different levels on which Professor Morgan stresses this point makes both his (Morgan's) own writing and the commentator's task unusually difficult. To operate like a professional in this area one must be at once a statistician, an empirically-oriented theoretical economist, and an information specialist.

Turning to criticisms, *Professor von Böventer* claimed that Professor Morgan's report omitted a few important considerations. What sorts of data should be collected at all, and for whom? These questions, in turn, lead to all sorts of methodological problems, including, how does one entice people to *absorb* information. A related issue: Who determines what data should be collected and at what cost? Also, who should have access to them, and for what purposes? Such problems are 'solved' in practice by a trade-off or compromise among the interests of politicians, researchers, academicians (including non-economists, journalists, and the general public). Also, any successful compromise must bear in mind both the existence of trade-offs, and the possibility that data lead to theory as well as vice versa.

Perhaps Professor Morgan can say something useful about all these topics. He might also recall that funding comes more easily when one can show possible relevance to theories, particularly those of the particular politicians involved in the security market negotiations.

Professor M. Perlman presented a digest of written comments received from *Professor Ferber*. *Professor Ferber* felt that Professor Morgan's paper had placed too much stress on problems of storage and of funding. What should have been stressed for librarians and information scientists, in Professor Ferber's opinion, was, rather, the nature of the microdata, the reasons why many economists consider them important, and the ways in which they are used.

Professor Wolfe's impression was that many projects in microeconomics do not require much data or much funding. Short, small programs should come first. *Professor Johnson* commented that microdata is useful mainly as an antidote to the first impressions of the more stupid politicians and journalists who might more easily persuade the public in the absence of such data.

Professor Blaug was concerned that so much data may have already been scattered and otherwise lost, and cited the case of India. In Britain, on the other hand, the Social Science Research Council (SSRC) has been financing data banks for storage of both micro- and macrodata, which are routinely shipped there. He wondered whether similar institutions existed elsewhere. *Professor Tyler* said that in the United States there exist several data banks which cooperate with each other. For example, there is one at his own institution (Florida) which specializes in Latin American census data, but is not widely used. Apparently, Say's Law does not work in this case—supply does not create its own demand. Furthermore, *Professor Tyler* was certain that the whole problem was not price, because the University of Florida charges users only for the marginal costs of their requests.

Professor Morgan opened his response by asserting that many methodological problems in survey research have been theoretically, but not practically, solved. In general, political researches concentrate on making access to data cheap, and wait for demand to develop. Economic researchers, on the other hand, concentrate on improving the quality of the microdata as the major means of increasing its use. He was not sure how the two approaches could be combined optimally.

The basic problem, in *Professor Morgan's* view, was not what data are worth collecting in the first place, but what portion of the collected data may be worth saving and archiving. Data, hardware, and software are all involved; the practical question is, which should be moved to where the others are. His personal preference is for 'Model T' or 'VW' or 'exportable' programs, which can be moved to the users' institutions. Such programs secure access at some cost in efficiency. Some of his University of Michigan colleagues, however, favour highly efficient programs which can as yet be used at few computer centres outside of Ann Arbor. This specialization, in *Professor Morgan's* view, benefits the programmers and the users at major institutions at the expense of potential users of computers elsewhere.

In opposition to Professor Wolfe, *Professor Morgan* preferred to concentrate on large probability samples. Planning and collection are almost as difficult for small as for large sample surveys, and the larger probability samples are more readily replicable.

As for data banks in the United States, the Roper archive is simple to use, but is limited to public-opinion polls. The data at his own institution (Michigan) are too complex for the Roper bank, but some of them are retrievable from what *Professor Morgan* described as 'sub-backs'.

Professor Morgan closed his summary with suggestions for librarians, outlining what he called a 3-phase process. (1) If microdata are embodied in a report or similar publication, many librarians should store the report. (2) Few publications will include all documentation (appendices, etc.). When these exist separately, a few highly specialized libraries should have them. (3) For anything more, users must consult original data sets, often including questionnaires. Libraries will not be involved here.

After the completion of Professor Morgan's report, *Dr Bartenbach* complained that the shipment of data to the data bank at the City University of New York (CUNY) is often delayed until the data have been milked dry at the point where they were first collected. *Professor Morgan* responded that this was less true for Michigan data materials than, admittedly, it had been in the past. However, costs must be charged for the preparation of data for transmission to data banks, and it is still an unsolved problem of 'who pays for what'? in such fixed costs as, e.g. machine-readable code books.

13 Library Policies for Research in Monetary Economics

Anna J. Schwartz
NATIONAL BUREAU OF ECONOMIC RESEARCH, NEW YORK

A sketch of the questions dealt with in monetary economics is followed by a delineation of a hierarchy of libraries for the optimal use of library resources for research in the subfield. Different roles for four types of libraries are distinguished. In the future, materials that libraries will be expected to provide will include computer-based bibliographies, time-series data banks, and magnetic-tape cross-section data. Interlibrary exchanges will become essential. Indiscriminate duplication of titles will give way to shared responsibility among types of libraries for collecting research materials in monetary economics, and for providing access to a collective pool of research titles.

One of the purposes of this conference is to forecast what will be research developments during the coming decade in particular economic subfields, with the aim of assisting librarians to formulate appropriate acquisition and discard policies for the subfield. Two statements applicable to research in general may also be made with respect to the field of monetary economics in particular:

(1) Future developments of the principal topics of current or recent interest in monetary economics will generally build on results reached earlier, revising or modifying older conclusions. This is the usual case in scientific work.
(2) In addition, someone with a new insight is likely to come on the scene, transforming the specific issues that have occupied investigators and opening up new questions with only weak links to past research. Such breakthroughs are not predictable. Research surprise should be taken for granted.

The only forecast that it is, therefore, useful to make about the course of research in monetary economics in the decade ahead is the projection of present lines of inquiry. This I propose to do in section I of the paper. In addition, authors of papers dealing with economic subfields have been asked to speculate on the optimal role for different types of libraries with respect to materials related to those subfields. Section II discusses the organization of libraries; section III the kinds of materials that they will ideally provide. Section IV offers some conclusions.

I

Monetary economics generally covers developments in monetary theory dealing with the influence of the quantity of money on the economy and in the conduct of monetary policy-including the goals and instruments of policymakers, institutional arrangements employed in monetary decisions, as well as the effectiveness of policy. Particularly in the past quarter of the century, empirical work to test theories against the facts, much of it econometric, has increasingly characterized monetary economics. Even so, theory is still elaborated, generally in mathematical form, independently of possible subsequent efforts to verify the theory by empirical testing.

Monetary economics is concerned with the behaviour of the public—mainly firms and households—the commercial banks, and the monetary authorities—who, in many countries, are represented by the central bank and the federal Treasury Department. The public's behaviour with regard to holding money and the behaviour of the commercial banks and the monetary authorities with regard to issuing money are within the purview of the discipline. Corresponding to the liabilities which the banks incur when they issue money are the assets which they hold in the form of loans and investments. Consequently, the banks' behaviour in acquiring these assets is a subject for study. The government's fiscal policy—government expenditures and taxes—affects monetary authority behaviour and, also, financial markets, where households and firms are both borrowing and lending. Interaction by all of the actors specified determines short- and long-term interest rates. These are also subjects that monetary economics deals with. The quantity of money is linked not only to financial markets, but to the level of economic activity and, depending on the character of the country's exchange rate policy between the domestic money and the money of other countries, there are links between the quantity of money and the balance of payments. Obviously, the subfield has a broad range.

Before indicating some of the outstanding issues in recent research activity, let me say that there are battle lines in the field of monetary economics. On one side are arrayed neo-Keynesians and, on the other, monetarists. Their differences are both theoretical and empirical. Briefly, neo-Keynesians tend to favour large-scale econometric models of the economy; they assume that in order to know what changes aggregate expenditures or the price level, it is necessary to know what is happening in specific sectors; and they accept the proposition that fiscal policy is more potent than monetary policy. Monetarists, on the other hand, tend to believe that, in a complex world, achieving an understanding of single-equation relationships or of the interactions of small-scale econometric models of key variables is the best we can do, given our present imperfect knowledge of the detailed structure of the economy; that changes in aggregate expenditures and in the price level can be explained without knowledge of developments in specific sectors; and that the dominant impulse in altering the level of nominal economic activity is past monetary change.

It may be useful to librarians to know of this division in research strategy and theoretical framework of the two camps. Conceivably, this division may have a bearing on the character of the material that research workers of the different persuasions may require.

Without further ado, I shall describe, under three heads, the questions that recent research in monetary economics deals with: (1) questions concerning fundamentals; (2) questions concerning the link between monetary change and change in economic activity; (3) questions concerning the link between monetary change and financial markets.

(1) Some of the questions involving fundamentals are the following: Why does an economy shift from barter to money transactions? In theory, how should money be defined? What assets, held by whom, should be counted as money? Are there empirical data matching the theoretical specifications? What control do the monetary authorities exercise over the supply of money? What targets—such as bank reserves or market interest rates—should the monetary authorities aim at in deploying control over the supply of money? What are the effects of money substitutes—such as other financial assets—and of balance of international payments flows on central bank control of the money supply? Is all money wealth, whether issued by commercial banks or by monetary authorities, or is only the latter wealth? What is the relation of growth in money supply to economic growth? What is the optimum amount of money for an economy? Another group of questions involving fundamentals centres on the demand for money: What are the determinants of the quantity of money that holders desire? Do these differ for households and for firms? There is a variety of assets alternative to money-holding, including physical as well as financial assets with nominal yields. What is the effect on the demand for money of the yields on these alternatives? Is the demand for money determined by holders' wealth or by their current income?

Of all of the questions listed, the demand for money has probably had most of the work of the past 15 years devoted to it. There is some consensus as a result of this effort: the determinants can be specified and moneyholders apparently have fairly definite notions of the amount that they want to hold, in light of these determinants. If the amount supplied to holders is greater than the quantity of money they desire, they will attempt to reduce their holdings by increasing their spending, lending, and unilateral transfers. As a result, they will increase aggregate income.

If the amount supplied to holders is less than they desire, they will attempt to increase their holdings by reducing their spending, lending, and unilateral transfers. In the process they will decrease aggregate income.

(2) For monetarists it is the interaction between the quantity of money supplied with the quantity of money holders desire that results in changes in aggregate income. Keynesian theory, on the other hand, emphasizes the instability of business investment as being responsible for fluctuations in aggregate income, and hence, the need to employ government fiscal policy to offset the behaviour of the private sector. One area of research that received marked attention in the early 1960s was a test of the rival theories. Later, attention shifted to tests at the St. Louis Federal Reserve Bank of the relative strength and reliability of monetary and fiscal policy changes as policy instruments for affecting income change. Both sets of tests stimulated a controversial literature. An allied question was the length of the lag, if any, between a change in monetary (or fiscal) policy and the ensuing effect on incomes. Another set of questions that has since come to the fore relates to the division of nominal income change between price and output change. The studies under this head are usually offshoots of the Phillips curve analysis, relating the rate of wage inflation to the level of unemployment. The questions include the following: Are low unemployment rates attainable with a fixed rate of inflation? Can policies like wage-price guideposts make lower rates of unemployment attainable than would otherwise be the case? Is it possible to achieve a permanent reduction in unemployment with a fixed rate of inflation, or is a tradeoff possible only when inflation is unanticipated? How should anticipated price change be measured?

Accompanying this empirical literature, there has been a theoretical development referred to as the microfoundations of employment and inflation. This development seeks to explain why a slowing down of monetary expansion after rapid inflation is frequently associated with a decline in the rate of change of real output, even though price rise continues, and emphasizes information costs and relocation costs to explain unemployment of resources and simultaneous stickiness of prices. The theoretical development is still undergoing refinement.

Much empirical work on the determinants of the inflation rate has been neo-Keynesian in orientation, emphasizing links with a markup over minimized average cost. The monetary view of inflation attributes increases in unit labour costs, resulting from a faster rate of increase in wage payments, to faster growth of money and its effect on price anticipations. The monetary view has stressed the worldwide character of the current inflationary episode and explains it in terms of the acceleration in the world supply of money since 1965. Questions about the role of the balance of payments in transmitting inflation under pegged exchange rates, and the nature of the present monetary standard under floating exchange rates have also been given attention.

(3) Questions dealing with the link between monetary change and financial markets include the following: What are the effects on interest rates of increasing the quantity of money in the very short run, over the duration of a business cycle expansion, and over longer periods? Monetarists distinguish between nominal and real rates of interest—nominal rates less an allowance for price change. In this connection, there is a question of the length of the lag in the formation of price anticipations affecting interest rates. Are real rates of interest affected, and in what direction, by inflation? What variables determine the formation of anticipations? Are past rates of change in money, as well as past rates of change in prices, determinants of price anticipations?

Another set of questions focuses on the relation between long-term and short-term interest rates—known as the term structure of interest rates. The relation between changes in stock market returns and the change in the quantity of money has also been a subject of inquiry.

Studies of different financial institutions have dealt with their functioning and impact on the financial market.

One conclusion that is highlighted by the foregoing survey of the questions that have stimulated recent research activity is that the boundaries of monetary economics overflow the numbered heading assigned to monetary theory and institutions in the classification used in the *Journal of Economic Literature.* At least four numbered headings are relevant to the subfield and so are, on occasion, four additional numbered headings, as follows:

130 (Economic Fluctuations, Forecasting, Stabilization, and Inflation)
310 (Domestic Monetary and Financial Theory and Institutions)
320 (Domestic Fiscal Theory and Policy; Public Finance)
430 (Balance of Payments; International Finance).

The four additional numbered headings occasionally relevant are:

010 (General Economics) for textbooks, or a listing like Tobin's *The New Economics One Decade Older* (Princeton, 1974)
040 (Economic History)
610 (Industrial Organization and Public Policy) for studies of regulation of the banking industry
920 (Consumer Economics) for studies of effects of monetary change.

The question, then, is: how can a survey of past work help librarians? My answer is that such a survey is obviously useful for enlarging librarians' general fund of knowledge, but for the determination of specific acquisitions and discards, given the size of the budget, the advice of a monetary economist will be required.

In addition, as I started out by saying, it is certain that new lines of inquiry and new techniques of investigation that are unpredictable will emerge during the coming decade. Even if it were possible to suggest guidelines for librarians, based on a continuation of present needs, there is little help one can offer in anticipation of the changes in research emphasis, due to the breakthoughs that innovators will introduce.

II

I now turn to the second question. Given the character of present research in monetary economics, what is the ideal organization of libraries to further this activity? What kinds of materials should libraries ideally provide for research in monetary economics?

With the cost of books and periodical subscriptions skyrocketing, local self-sufficiency in providing library materials is no longer likely as a realistic option. Indiscriminate duplication of titles will give way to shared responsibility for collecting the materials for research in monetary economics. Co-operation among different types of libraries will be required to provide access to a collective pool of research titles.

Let me first distinguish the different roles that I conceive of for different types of libraries, with respect to materials related to monetary economics:

(1) a non-specialist training library attached to a graduate school of economics or business administration;
(2) a library specializing in particular areas of monetary economics, developed in conjunction with research centres or workshops associated with graduate schools or large commercial banks or nonprofit research centres;
(3) regional libraries with generalized strength in monetary economics, in a country as big as the United States, mainly, at the Board of Governors of the Federal Reserve System and at the regional Federal Reserve Banks, but, also, in libraries unaffiliated with the System;
(4) national libraries, like the Library of Congress or the New York Public Library in the United States, with comprehensive collections in monetary economics.

(1) A training library would have no particular depth in any area of monetary economics, but, ideally, should hold a generous sampling of current work in most areas. The aim of such a library would be to acquaint students with the range of issues that the subfield deals with and to whet their appetite to learn more. The material should be mainly of recent publication.

(2) A library specializing in monetary economics would have depth in several areas of monetary economics. Specialist collections should include not only current, but, also, historical materials related to those

areas, with particular reference to the United States alone or to some foreign country or group of countries. To give some concrete examples, studies of the effect of price anticipations on the level of interest rates have links to ideas expressed by Henry Thornton in 1811 and restated by Irving Fisher toward the end of the century. Studies of escalator clauses as a means of reducing the costs of inflation have a long history in many countries. A specialist collection serving scholars with an interest in such questions would presumably offer this kind of depth. The coverage of the holdings would vary with the research interests of the centre to which the library was attached.

(3) Regional libraries in the United States fall into two categories. One is the set of libraries attached to the Board of Governors of the Federal Reserve System in Washington, DC, and to the twelve Federal Reserve Banks throughout the country. The other is the set of unaffiliated libraries.

The Federal Reserve libraries, with largely duplicate collections, would provide generalized coverage of monetary developments since the establishment of the System in 1914, focusing on the central bank's activities here and abroad, but also including state banking operations in the region. The full record of Federal Reserve and Congressional publications and of government departments, such as the Treasury and Commerce, relevant to monetary economics would be available at these libraries. Federal Reserve unpublished documents of minutes of operations that are released on a schedule some years after the event would also be on deposit here. Research studies of the System's economists would be available at the regional libraries, which would also have substantial collections of non-government publications in monetary economics, exemplified by the bibliography on domestic aspects of monetary theory and policy published by the Board of Governors in 1965 [4]. Although no matching bibliography on international aspects has been published, such items would also be included in the regional collections.

Unaffiliated regional libraries in this scheme would provide collections representing financial institutions of the region, extending as far back as they exist in the history of the United States, as well as such unpublished papers of significant participants in local financial developments as the libraries may acquire.

(4) National libraries would be depositories, maintaining copies of all materials available in the specialist libraries and more. These libraries would acquire all of the listings in the *Journal of Economic Literature* under the numbered headings specified above related to monetary economics, and all federal and state government periodical publications, including those of Congressional committees dealing with monetary economics. For the United States, the coverage would date back to colonial times. An annotated bibliography of published and unpublished

work on money and banking, with such coverage, that was in preparation by Professor Herman Krooss of the New York University School of Business Administration, would have been an indispensable aid to librarians. His untimely death this spring leaves the completion of his undertaking uncertain. For other countries, the collection would presumably vary in richness and depth.

Having said this much about the desirable differences as I conceive them among the four types of libraries with respect to their holdings related to monetary economics, let me go on to discuss special aspects of library materials.

III

Great changes lie ahead in the kinds of materials that libraries will be expected to provide. I shall single out for comment: (1) computer-based bibliographies; (2) time-series data banks; (3) magnetic-tape cross-section data.

(1) Computer-based bibliographies. In monetary economics, as in other subfields, journal articles are the main outlet for research activity. One basic need for all research work that will surely be satisfied, sooner or later, is a regularly updated index of monetary economics, on line. An existing system is the London School of Economics bibliography of statistical literature, which permits retrieval by author's name, keywords identifying subject matter, and details of references to other papers [3]. It may be that users will fund such a system listing many papers not directly related to the question under investigation and, hence, wasteful; on the other hand, it is unlikely that references which users will find indispensable will be skipped. The optimal arrangement of giving access to the system would be through teletype terminals linked directly to the computer. Libraries at all levels would be encouraged to acquire time-sharing terminals to computer centres for use of the index. An index of unpublished working papers that are now proliferating is a further development that one can foresee.

(2) For a number of subdivisions of monetary economics, access to a time-series data bank is indispensable. Increasingly, training libraries will provide graduate students with time-sharing terminals to computer centres for this type of information. The data banks currently available cover post-World War II data only. Specialist or regional libraries may, in the future, develop historical data banks covering earlier periods.

(3) Cross-section data, becoming increasingly available on magnetic tape, will be useful for other subdivisions of monetary economics. This kind of material is expensive and requires some expertise in its use. The staff of the training library should be aware of the existence of this material and have enough familiarity with its sources to guide a research student to it. For practical reasons, however, the storage, maintenance,

and complete documentation of this material should be in the regional or specialist library.

In general, more and more materials will become available in microfilm or microfiche. These forms are most appropriate for regional or specialist libraries. Fascimile reproduction of materials may be the next development on the horizon.

If the system of specialist libraries takes hold, interlibrary exchanges will become essential for research that is not carried on at these centres. In addition, for the proper functioning of the system, a union catalogue of the holdings of the different libraries will be essential. Such a catalogue will help to locate listed sources for research work. A union catalogue will also be useful for librarians in arranging the redistribution of selected items among the collections, so that material not germane to the collection of the holder may be shifted to collections seeking such material. In this connection, it may prove helpful to design a clearing house to facilitate exchanges. A central office would be notified of items sought and items up for disposal and would be the intermediary for mutually beneficial exchanges.

I have said virtually nothing about the cost of these technologically feasible programmes. Start-up costs are high and the present troubled economic condition of most western economies may delay their implementation. The benefits of these programmes are such, however, that ultimately they will be adopted.

IV

Interest in monetary economics has intensified in recent years as new, theoretical insights have illuminated the key and pervasive role of money in modern economies. Theory has been accompanied by empirical work testing hypotheses and producing econometric evidence [2] on the relation of money to economic activity and to financial markets. There has been an enormous outpouring of articles and books on monetary economics and of professional journals devoted in whole or in part to monetary theory, policy, and institutions.

The very size of the stream of publications poses a question on which, in a period of tight budgets, librarians may feel driven to take a stand. A recent study [1] has documented that only a small fraction of articles published in economic theory, in 1945–68, ever achieves citation. What, then, is the justification for investment in the publishing, cataloguing, and shelving of journals of economics containing so much material that no one regards as of sufficient significance to cite either in praise or dispraise? I do not know whether the pattern of citation found for articles in economic theory would also characterize monetary economics, but the question surely merits investigation.

This paper has attempted to specify the optimal use of library resources for research in monetary economics. A hierarchy of libraries for the United States has been delineated. Training libraries would have limited, current collections, but would have access to data banks and to specialist or regional libraries for materials that may be in demand for occasional use. Specialist libraries would have depth in specific areas of monetary economics, attracting faculty with interest in these areas of specialization and students who want to work with them. These libraries would seek to streamline their collections by trading with other institutions those items that do not belong in their areas of specialization for items that do. Regional libraries attached to the Federal Reserve would be the main centres for research related to the System. Unaffiliated regional libraries would concentrate on historical collections of regional interest. National libraries would provide comprehensive coverage of materials available in specialist libraries.

In the decade ahead libraries will undergo great technological change as computer-based bibliographies, time-sharing terminals to computer data banks, and interlibrary exchanges are introduced and perfected.

REFERENCES

[1] Bordo, M. D. and Landau, D, 'The Pattern of Citations in Economic Theory 1945–68: An Exploration Towards a Quantitative History of Economic Thought' (unpublished paper, December 1974).

[2] Fisher, Gordon and Sheppard, David, 'Effects of Monetary Policy on the United States Economy, A Survey of Econometric Evidence', *OECD Economic Outlook, Occasional Studies* (December 1972).

[3] Jones, Susan, 'The London School of Economics Computer-Based Bibliography of Statistical Literature', *Journal of the Royal Statistical Society—Series A (General)*, 137, Part 2 (1974), pp. 219–26.

[4] *Monetary Theory and Policy: A Bibliography, Part 1: Domestic Aspects*. Board of Governors of the Federal Reserve System (November 1965).

Summary of the Discussion

Professor Bronfenbrenner introduced Mrs Schwartz's paper. Its first half, he said, attempted to explain to librarians (and non-economists generally) what contemporary monetary controversy was all about, on the explicit assumption by Mrs Schwartz that these controversies would continue to dominate the subject over the next generation or so. These three issues were (1) 'monetary fundamentals'—the appropriate definition of money, the relation of money and wealth, the motivations for holding money, etc., (2) the relationships between money and the economy, and (3) the relationships between money and other aspects of the financial system more particularly. *Professor Bronfenbrenner* felt that Mrs Schwartz's presentation of these issues, though carefully neutral in its content, sometimes betrayed her 'monetarist' predilections (which he shared) by understressing the 'anti-monetarist' relationships between the economy and the monetary system.

Mrs Schwartz supported, in general, a 'hierarchical' position relative to libraries and storage facilities for monetary data. The ordinary library, that is to say, needed rather little, so that centralization of a few major research centres within each country was probably optimal. *Professor Bronfenbrenner* thought that more account might have been taken of the close association between monetary economics, international economics, and public finance in assessing the ease or difficulty of building up collections in the monetary area. He also worried about possible costs if a centre of monetary research should shift to an area without 'core library facilities', and about 'separation of the facts from the figures' when data were archived without adequate coding of institutional peculiarities of the 'window-dressing' variety, which might make them mean something other than what they appeared to mean.

Dr Trapp made the first oral comment. He feared that wholesale adoption of Mrs Schwartz's programme might increase the cost of research over and beyond the continuation of the present lines of inquiry. He felt it risky, but not impossible, to forecast what some of these new lines might be. Mentioning a 1962 survey-article forecast by Professor Johnson,[1] *Dr Trapp* cited the relatively-undeveloped fields of the connection between money and growth and the determination of the money supply, and objected, on methodological grounds, to ignoring potential changes in research interests as 'unpredictable'. Although Mrs Schwartz had drawn a distinction between the relationships of money with the economy and with the financial system, *Dr Trapp* felt that the two sets of relationships were so closely connected that no distinction was legitimate. *Dr Trapp's* final point was that, while monetary authorities collect a great deal of data, most of what was disclosed promptly was self-justificatory in nature. There was a great deal of non-disclosure, and more delay in disclosure. *Dr Trapp* hoped for co-operation between researchers to remedy this situation.

Professor Kindleberger recalled the old-fashioned notion of the quality of money as distinguished from its quantity. In studying panics historically, one needs Gresham's Law and, perhaps, also, a kind of 'catastrophe' in which normal quantitative relationships are temporarily suspended or at least replaced by others.

[1] 'Monetary Theory and Policy', *Amer. Econ. Rev.*, *52* (1962), 335–89.

In support of Mrs Schwartz's contention that debate on 'standard' monetary issues would continue to dominate the field, *Professor Johnson* commented that debate on these same issues goes back over the centuries. He also thought that, while seasonal changes were easy to analyse, 'philosophy' is necessary for the analysis of longer-term changes such as those in research problems. He agreed that there might be something to 'Kindleberger on catastrophe', pointing out the difficulty of explaining the 1930s to people who had grown up in the post-1945 inflationary milieu. *Professor Johnson* then inquired what libraries might do, over and above storing the Great Books. They could avoid such errors as losing an excellent money stock series for the United Kingdom (in Dr Goodwin's dissertation),[2] and in storing mis-specified data which do more harm than good.

Professor Morgan felt that both Mrs Schwartz and Professor Bronfenbrenner had played down (if only by omission) the importance of behavioural research on monetary matters at the micro-level. The archiving of even small studies, *Professor Morgan* believed, would be useful and might cumulate into better macro-models than we now possess. *Professor Morgan* cited Professor Guy Orcutt as a leader among economists working along this line. (*Professor Johnson* noted that the defective Oxford surveys of the influence of interest rates on investment decisions had shunted Keynesian economies off on a wrong track.) *Professor Kindleberger* suggested that surveys imply that no one learns anything, and that it would be better to read biographies instead. Professor Morgan did not understand this interpretation of survey methods.

Mr Evans wondered which libraries could be expected to collect what, and where. He said that this question was not being answered by the conference, and that librarians needed guidance in connection with it. *Mr Kilgour* felt that, eventually, national libraries (the Library of Congress, the British Museum) would become the nation's libraries—libraries of first, as well as last, resort. *Mr Kilgour* also said, relative to micro-data collection, that libraries collect materials useful to significant numbers of people. If the banked data that Professor Morgan, for example, wanted kept, would eventually be useful to significant numbers of people, of course libraries should retain them. But if not, *Mr Kilgour* felt that the library should be free to reconsider its retention decision, as it does in areas other than Economics. *Professor Johnson* noted that monetary economics has become quantitative only recently, and that libraries were not sure how to react to what might, for all they know, prove to be only a fad.

Mrs Schwartz then responded to certain of the points raised. Changes in research interests have come about, of course, but they have resulted from the efforts of creative people, not from the decisions of any intellectual cartel on OPEC lines. Even if (as monetarists maintain) the private sector of the economy is basically stable, such changes cannot be forecast in advance. Her article should not be interpreted as seeking to *exclude* innovations—including points raised by Professor Bronfenbrenner and in the discussion from the floor. As regards libraries, her own position reflects having worked mainly in a small library at the National Bureau of Economic Research (NBER). She could offer

[2] Richard M. Goodwin, 'Studies in Money. England and Wales, 1917–38'. Unpublished Harvard University Ph.D. thesis, 1941. A summary, including a graph but no tables, appeared in Richard M. Goodwin, 'The Supply of Bank Money in England and Wales', *Oxford Econ. Papers*, *5* old series (1941), 1–29.

no organized suggestions as to who should collect what and how long. As far as she could tell, individual economists have been, and will continue to be, advised mainly by other economists on such matters—the 'old boy' network once again.

14 Development of Fiscal Economics during the Decade 1975–85

Carl S. Shoup
COLUMBIA UNIVERSITY

The largest share of fiscal economics (public finance) literature will continue to be occupied with taxation. Empirical studies of factors determining governmental expenditures will increase, but studies of levels of government services await an awakening of interest in inequalities of distribution among sub-groups. Transfer payment analyses, excepting subsidies, may increase. Part of public goods theory is moving into microeconomics (equilibrium conditions for goods non-excludable but joint over users), and most of externalities theory, into direct regulation. Inter-disciplinary efforts, which call for centralizing library facilities, will especially characterize public choice and fiscal stabilization literature. Journals, staff papers, services, and official reports will multiply more rapidly than will textbooks.

I

Fiscal economics is part of an inter-disciplinary body of studies that include, particularly, law, political science, and accounting. This paper will focus on the role of economists in each of the fiscal areas, with some comment on the extent to which the non-economists share the field. To the librarian, this cross-discipline characteristic must be a prime cause of concern. It probably renders more difficult the task of supplying scholars with what they need. As an illustration, a research worker engaged in studying income tax subsidies and their alternative, direct cash subsidies, may need to have at hand economic journals, law reviews, political science journals, and journals in accounting and management.

II

In sheer amount of activity, taxation will probably continue to dominate fiscal economics.

The income tax is everywhere growing more complex. One reason is an increasing tendency to use the income tax as a device to encourage this or that activity by granting tax preferences or reliefs. An increasing recognition of the haphazard manner in which these tax subsidies have been granted will probably lead, not to a replacement of them by outright cash subsidies, but to more systematic appraisals of their consequences. This means more work for the tax economist.[1]

Another cause of growing income tax complexity is the increasing role of multinational corporations and the corresponding importance, for income taxation, of 'transfer prices', that is, the prices at which one part of a business firm sells goods and services to another part of the same firm. When the two parts of the firm are in different countries, they are, in most instances, separately incorporated under the laws of the two countries. Taxing authorities have hitherto depended chiefly on lawyers and accountants, rather than on economists, to formulate rules for transfer prices that will be accepted. In the years ahead, however, this tendency may be reversed, as the economic aspects of transfer pricing become better understood. For example, internal struggles within the firm over the setting of transfer prices resemble the confrontations of bilateral monopolists in economic theory. Here, again, is a good example of the need for the research worker to have close at hand articles and books in several fields: economics, tax law, accounting, and business management.

Integration of the corporate income tax with the personal income tax has been the aim of a great deal of activity in income tax law in several countries over the past decade or so. This activity promises to continue, perhaps to accelerate. The goal is to avoid gross overtaxation of corporate earnings that are distributed in dividends to taxable individuals, out of profits that have already been subject to corporate tax, while not being too lenient with respect to that portion of the corporation's profits that is retained in the business and thus, for the time being, escapes the personal tax. Economists' tools have been useful in comparing different techniques of partial integration within one country, and should prove even more useful in untangling the issues involved when the shareholders live in one country and the corporation operates in another. In that case, integration involves two different income tax systems as well as two levels of income recipient (corporation and individual shareholder). Once more, however, the economist must work in close co-operation with the tax lawyer and the tax accountant, who will be aware, as the economist commonly is not, of the disturbances that will spread throughout the complex web of the income tax system when a substantial change is made at any one point.

Quite another cause of complexity is the gradual alteration of the income tax by something between an income tax proper and a tax on consumer expenditures, that is, an income tax that exempts saved income. This change is taking place, not by careful design, but in fits and starts,

[1] Omitted here from the paper as presented at the conference are three sentences that essentially duplicated the cash-subsidy remarks in Section V below, except for the inclusion of a more optimistic conjecture as to future research in this area than is given in that section.

and is thus creating complexities and inconsistencies, to be uncovered by tax lawyers and appraised by economists, or vice versa. In any event, the economic consequences of this partial transformation deserve far more economic analysis than they have received so far.

A good deal of saved personal income has been exempted in the United States, or, at least, taxation has been deferred for a potentially long period, by a succession of special provisions concerning, for example, employers' contributions to pension funds, interest accumulated for the insured's account by a life insurance company, and savings by the self-employed that are invested in a specified manner. Much investment spending by business firms has been virtually exempted in the United Kingdom by allowing full depreciation, in the year of acquisition, for manufacturing plant and equipment. Various other methods of reducing or deferring income tax by spending on investment goods are to be found in most income tax laws, e.g. investment credits, accelerated depreciation, and excess depreciation. These measures are a subset of the 'tax incentives' or 'tax subsidies' noted above. They promise to grow in importance, withouth being transformed into cash subsidies, if only because the savers and the spenders on investment goods who do not fit into the existing provisions will be demanding the same tax benefits.

Alongside these specific problems of income tax policy there will remain the unresolved empirical issues of broader scope, a notable example being the question of whether the corporation income tax is shifted, and, if so, to what degree and in what direction. Equally important, and unknown, are the effects of income tax rate changes on the amount of risk-taking, supply of labour, and flow of capital. How much further such problems will be pursued seems not quite clear at the moment, in view of the inherent difficulties that face econometric studies in these areas. On the other hand, theoretical analyses of particular provisions or proposals—say, a tax on business firms granting wage increases— can be useful in suggesting the directions in which the effects will move, at least if the analysis is carried out within a carefully detailed model. There will surely be an increasing amount of this type of study of aspects of income taxation, appearing chiefly in journal articles.

III

Leaving the income tax, we may note the recent spread of the value-added tax in developed countries and the probability that developing countries, most of them without any general sales tax at all, will at least be exploring the possibility of using this fiscal instrument, so powerful in the developed countries. Here the advice of the tax economist may be sought on a large scale, especially in deciding what regime to apply to each major sector of the economy, the farm sector for example.

Still other taxes could be cited to make the point that 'tax engineering' will continue to absorb more of fiscal economists' time, and probably more of libraries' resources, than any other single sector of fiscal economics in the years ahead.

IV

Study of the other two chief ways of raising government revenue —money creation, and the borrowing of existing money—could well expand appreciably. But the expansion may occur more under the aegis of monetary economics, as in studies of inflation, and of effects of open market operations on the stock of money and on interest rates. Yet there are many interesting questions that could be pursued by the public finance scholar, e.g. changes in ownership of the public debt, and new techniques of public borrowing from the private sector. The United States Treasury's publication, the *Treasury Bulletin*, contains each month some 60 pages of data on the Federal debt, most of it as relatively unmined by the fiscal economist as has been its counterpart in the tax field, the annual *Statistics of Income*. The mere existence of data, however, has evidently not been the determining factor in the allocation of public finance research resources. Public debts seem not to raise questions of the immediacy and urgency that are so numerous in the tax area.

V

As to government expenditures, the research here promises to be, as it has been in the past, more oriented to questions raised by scholars than to demands for information by policy makers, who seem rather slow in picking up some important social and economic issues that have been developed in the public finance literature of the past ten or twenty years: for example, the unequal distribution of a government service among area sub-groups or ethnic or income sub-groups.

One exception to this statement is transfer payments of the welfare type. Politicians are struggling to reform current welfare systems, and are seeking advice on the relative merits of the negative income tax, the flat-rate taxable demogrant, and other alternatives. Here the fiscal economist will need to work closely with social workers, sociologists, and tax administrators, if only to avoid a too simple transference of positive income tax procedures to negative income taxation. Continuing study of the social security system, especially with respect to old-age benefits and the methods of financing, will have to be keyed to studies of the rapidly expanding private-pension sector.

Government subsidies to encourage output of specified private-sector goods and services are to be distinguished from welfare payments. Subsidies are so numerous and so large that it seems odd that no English-language economist has devoted a book to this subject (two such books appeared in Germany in recent years). The United States Congressional Joint Economic Committee sponsored a study of subsidies that appeared in some dozen volumes of staff studies, hearings, and compendium papers in 1972–73. At present, however, there seems little prospect of further extensive output in this field, except as parts of studies devoted to housing, transportation, and other particular industries. Libraries will cover this branch of public finance through the acquisition of books and journals in the several industrial fields.

An increasing number of huge private-sector business firms have been bailed out in the past few years by the governments of several industrialized economies, as much to prevent sudden and massive unemployment as to encourage the use of these firms' products. The drift toward nationalization that is implied in some of these instances should stimulate literature on state enterprises.

A striking development in the study of government expenditures has been the large number of articles in which correlation and regression analysis has been used to estimate the relative influence of various social and economic forces on those expenditures. The results have been especially interesting in a multi-level government setting, involving various types of inter-governmental grants for particular services, say education. More of this seems to lie ahead, given the ease with which computers can now be employed for finding the coefficients. There may even be some question as to whether this ease of computation may not be producing some studies of little permanent value, or with possibly misleading conclusions. In any event, this type of research seems destined to continue to expand, especially since it can be, and has been, used in other sectors of fiscal economics: for example, in attempting to explain variations among countries in the ratio of the government sector to the total economy.

It seems doubtful that the existing public finance journals can, or should, absorb the increase in this type of study. Perhaps there is room for a fiscal economics journal that would specialize in these econometric or statistical studies.

Empirical studies of levels of particular government services seem urgent from a social point of view, but expansion appears unlikely here in the immediate future, partly because of relative lack of interest on the part of policy makers, and partly because the units of measurement of services have been only crudely defined, if at all. Data are not only scanty because of lack of interest, but are, in some instances, deliberately kept secret by the government unit involved: many police departments will not release—if indeed they gather—information on the varying levels of crime among precincts. Perhaps for this area of fiscal economics the next decade will be one of foundation building with emphasis on further achievements by students of programme and performance budgeting in formulating concepts for units of output, especially for fire protection, education, and medical care.

To be sure, cost-benefit analysis has already produced a copious literature and there is more to come, but many of these studies have been of ventures that yield physical units of marketable goods, hence not involved in the problems of concept and measurement just referred to. The appropriate social rate of discount to use in these studies does reflect some peculiarly 'public' finance problems, and can be expected to generate further journal articles.

VI

In some countries, inter-governmental fiscal relations within a single national will be a steadily expanding field of research, much of which will appear in documentary form, from government departments, quasi-governmental organizations, or special commissions. Librarians of the United States, Canada, Australia, and Germany, in particular, will need to cope with what may seem at times a flood of material, much of which, however, will be used only sporadically by their clients, and may soon become outdated, although they often contain novel concepts and concrete suggestions that could be valuable in many other contexts.

The economic theory of intergovernmental relations is still in a confused enough state to invite more articles in all sorts of journals, even the most abstract, where real of apparent conflicts between distributive goals and Pareto-efficient equilibria are a common theme.

Some of the pressure for further output in this area is coming from the growing discipline of urban economics, which involves, of course, much more than fiscal economics, but is heavily dependent on it. Sociological and political science studies of the urban scene will prove indispensable to the urban economist and to the economist specializing in intergovernmental fiscal relations. Again, the librarian will have an important role to play in facilitating interdisciplinary research.

VII

The pure theory of public goods, as distinguished from the empirical studies referred to in Section V above, may not increase in relative volume of output over the coming decade, at least in those respects that are of most direct interest to public finance. Many of the recent contributions have focused on jointness over consumers rather than on nonexcludability, and form a part of market microeconomics that is of particular significance for specialists in transportation and entertainment (theatres, television). The linkage of these studies with public finance is through the structuring of government subsidies that are necessary to supplement pricing for the attainment of economic efficiency. Here the research leads into the cash subsidy studies referred to in Section V above; indeed, even some of the tax subsidies can be explained in terms of jointness over consumers although excludability exists in sale of the product (e.g. accelerated depreciation for freight cars).

On the other hand, the theory of public goods delivered under conditions of non-excludability has by no means been exhausted, and some continuing contributions may be expected here.

Since environmental problems are increasingly the object of public concern, one might conclude that this sector of the public goods field, which deals chiefly with negative externalities generated in the production of marketable goods, will occupy a growing part of fiscal economics research. In practice, however, legislators have opted chiefly for direct regulation, despite all of the theoretical literature on taxation designed to limit these externalities to an optimal level. Unless fiscal economists achieve some break-throughs in formulating taxes of a kind that appeal to the legislator and the administrator, this area of fiscal economics seems likely to dwindle.

VIII

The theory of public choice, a subject that has developed rapidly over the past decade, is a stimulating mixture of economics and political science, with some sociology too. The tools employed are frequently mathematical, including game theory and advanced set theory familiar to several other fields of fiscal economics. In large part, the work has been the deducing of implications from appropriate axioms, but there has also been some attempt to distil generalizations from observed conduct, and this part of the field will probably become more important.

Some of the theoretical analysis can be placed under research on public goods (Section VII above), but much has only a tenuous connection, if any at all. Direct connection with tax policy seems even less; of the 92 titles of papers to be delivered at the April, 1975, meeting of the Public Choice Society, only two explicitly involve taxation. There is somewhat greater linkage with government budget techniques. The field supports a relatively new journal, *Public Choice*. In any event, the librarian must here cope with a highly interdisciplinary subject, more so than any of the other fields covered by the present paper.

IX

Economic stabilization, either as theory or as applied economics, obviously needs the expertise of the public finance scholar. In fact, however, this subject is coming more to be incorporated in macroeconomics and less in public finance, at least to judge by some of the recent public finance texts. Libraries that cover adequately the field of macroeconomics, which lies largely outside the scope of the present paper, will automatically be covering most of the fiscal economics contributions to economic stabilization.

There are, however, some crucial choices to be made among macroinstruments that require much more tax research. A notable example is that between an income tax and a consumer spendings tax as a counter-cycle instrument. Variations in the tax rate to combat inflation or unemployment would certainly be more effective under the spendings tax than under the income tax, owing to the former's substitution effect over time, but anticipation of the rate changes could induce destabilizing behaviour on the part of consumers. Both the tax economist and the macroeconomist are needed for research on this and allied issues.

A good many post-mortems will be submitted over the next few years on what went wrong with fiscal policy (or was it monetary policy?) in the first half of the 1970s, at least in the United States. Even more important for our profession, there will be attempts to explain why economists' forecasts had to be revised so frequently and so substantially. The latter question lies clearly in macroeconomics but has to be answered before stabilization policies can be improved. As the answers come in, they will probably be succeeded by a number of articles and even a few books on how to do better next time. Many of these articles will presumably appear in the general economic journals.

X

Country studies and area studies of entire public finance systems of developing countries may be somewhat less frequent than in the recent past, at least in book form, in view of the considerable amount of effort that has been expended in this field in the past decade, with relatively modest results in terms of subsequent policy action. On the other hand, articles, and intermediate length studies (see Section XII below) may increase relatively, as the finance ministries and planning or development departments continue to enlarge their research staffs with well trained fiscal economists who will be seeking recognition through publication.

The United Nations and the International Monetary Fund may also undertake, and publish, more studies of this type, in the form of 'staff papers' or 'technical papers'.

The creation of tax study commissions in the developed countries shows no sign of slackening (Australia supplies the latest example). A continued flow of reports from these sources can, therefore, be expected.

It would appear that each library will have to make some difficult choices as to how much of the world's output of these specialized country or area fiscal studies it is going to stock, in view of the shelf space taken up relative to the rather specialized demand. Perhaps here, more than in any other area of fiscal economics, some pooling and exchange system is needed.

XI

The structure and techniques of government budgeting will probably be studied more in the course of research in one or the other of the fields discussed above than in books devoted to this subject. Articles, however, may well become more frequent, especially in view of the recent attempts at budget reform, as in the United States, where the new Congressional Budget Office has started its promising, if perilous, journey. We may expect a number of descriptions and evaluations of this remarkable experiment.

The Brookings Institution's annual book-length analysis of each year's projected Federal budget may come to be duplicated in other countries.

Near the end of the coming decade there may be a good occasion for one or more book-length studies on 'modern' budgeting, including an evaluation of programme budgeting and allied techniques.

A matter of interest more to the political scientist than to the fiscal economist, at least as a research subject, is supplied by the recent controversy in the United States, at the Federal level, over the lengths to which the executive can go in impounding funds that have been appropriated by the Congress.

XII

Given these conjectures as to the various subject areas, what can be said with respect to modes of publication? Will there be more journals and fewer books, relatively? Or more public documents? More loose leaf tax services and the like?

My own guesses—and they are nothing more than that—are as follows.

Some new journals specializing in fiscal economics will be started in the next decade, but probably not more than over the past ten years, when there appeared the *Journal of Public Economics* in the United Kingdom, the *Public Finance Quarterly* and (somewhat earlier) *Public Choice* in the United States, and the *Japan Tax Law Review* in Japan. (This does not profess to be a complete listing.) More and more articles of interest to fiscal economists will be published in journals of accounting, political science, law, and other disciplines. New journals will doubtless appear in these fields. The total amount of journal literature of interest to fiscal economists may, therefore, grow rapidly.

The output of specialized books in one or another aspect of fiscal economics may not increase as much as in the recent past, owing to rising costs of publication. Research workers will be under economic pressure to condense their findings into article form, even when the studies have been carried out within research institutions. But compression to the length of the usual journal articles in, for example, the *National Tax Journal* or the *British Tax review*, or *Public Finance* is not feasible with respect to most of those shortened books. There may be a place for another journal like the *Finanzarchiv*, which publishes longer articles. Since English is now the nearest thing to a universal academic language in fiscal economics, virtually all of the articles in such a journal would be in English. (The *Finanzarchiv* itself publishes a considerable number of articles in that language.)

Meanwhile, this need can be met, in part, by 'Annals' or 'Staff Papers' published periodically by research institutions, as is now done by the National Bureau of Economic Research and the International Monetary Fund, or by book-length publications, at irregular intervals, that consist of several of these lengthier studies. Examples of this latter type are the recent United Nations' 'Technical Papers: Taxation', in its series of reports on multinational corporations, and the Compendia published in 1972–73 by the Joint Economic Committee (United States Congress) on *The Economics of Federal Subsidy Programs* and on each of a number of types of subsidy.

Elementary textbooks in public finance have multiplied recently in the United States, if not elsewhere, to a degree that is somewhat surprising, in view of the fact that many of them are not sharply differentiated products. In most university libraries, however, there will not be a call for all of these elementary texts. The intermediate-level texts, on the other hand (e.g. in English: Due and Friedlaender, Musgrave and Musgrave, and Prest) will need to be available in virtually every library.

As interest in international aspects of taxation quickens, libraries may want to carry more of the loose-leaf tax news services, tax information journals, and updated tax handbooks, notably those of the International Bureau of Fiscal Documentation, although only the larger libraries will be able to absorb the cost of subscribing to, say, the series on the value-added tax. Close co-operation between social science libraries and law libraries will be essential here.

Books of readings in public finance, or in some sub-field, will probably maintain their market share. This may be good news for libraries, since such books of readings, including volumes that bring together the contributions of some one author (e.g. the recently published volume of Head's papers, *Public Goods and Public Welfare*), tend to relieve the pressure to keep readily accessible, perhaps even on reserve, documents, proceedings, symposia, compendia, and remote issues of journals that are not widely used.

Unlike the usual book of readings, the *Festschrift* type of volume ordinarily covers a broad range of public finance topics, increasing the importance and the size of the task of cataloguing by subject. A number of

Festschriften in public finance have appeared in recent years, and more are on the way.

Reports of governmental and international commissions, committees, study groups and the like will probably continue to appear in increasing numbers. The larger libraries, at least, can hardly afford to be without them: for example, the (roughly) biennial reports of the United Nations Group of Experts on Tax Treaties between Developed and Developing Countries.

The need for libraries to purchase so large and so varied an output of specialized journals, reports, and similar publications in the field of fiscal economics is due, in part, to the fact, not readily explicable, that the general economic journals, for example the *American Economic Review*, the *Journal of Political Economy*, and the *Quarterly Journal of Economics* in the United States, and the *Economic Journal* and *Economica* in the United Kingdom, contain relatively few articles in the traditional public finance area, and not very many in other branches of fiscal economics. Accordingly, it seems likely that any one library's most difficult problem with respect to fiscal economics will be in deciding now many of these specialized journals, services, periodical and *ad hoc* reports they can afford to purchase and store.

Encyclopaedias are not common in most sub-disciplines of economics, but public finance has been a notable exception, thanks to the *Handbuch der Finanzwissenschaft*, which has appeared in two editions over the past several decades. A third edition, again under the editorship of Professor Neumark, will be available within a year or two. Like those in the earlier editions, the contributions will all be in the German language; this new edition will, nonetheless, be an appropriate acquisition for libraries in all universities, whatever the country, that offer graduate work in public finance.

XIII

The increasingly interdisciplinary nature of fiscal 'economics' suggests that any one university or research centre should physically centralize its journals in the various social sciences, in business, and in law. The public finance scholar who is studying, for example, some problem in public goods theory in an economics journal may find a reference to, say, the *Journal of Law and Economics*, which he realizes he should consult, but if that journal is in a separate law library some distance across the campus he may let the moment pass and perhaps lose something of consequence. A tax economist checking the contents of recent economic journals in the course of a study of tax subsidies may believe that he might benefit from glancing through the tables of contents of recent law reviews and sampling some of the articles, but unless those law reviews are right there in a section of a centralized current periodical collection, he may let the idea go. Or, in either of these cases, the researcher may delegate the task to someone who fails to carry it out properly.

If these remarks seem to indicate a deplorable lack of vigour on the part of the scholar, one need only recall the physical effort and, more important, the time expended, in trudging from one building to another in a modern campus of the extended type, to say nothing of trying to find what one is after, in an unfamiliar setting.

On the other hand, centralization decreases accessibility for the researcher whose interests are not interdisciplinary, and who would be saved time and effort if the economics journals were in a special economics library close to, or in, the building that contains his office, the computer terminal he uses, and so on. A similar remark applies to law, political science, business school, and other scholars, whether faculty or graduate research students.

Thus, the familiar problem of an optimal balance between promoting accessibility for any one discipline and facilitating interdisciplinary research is perhaps nowhere posed more acutely than in the kind of fiscal economics that promises to unfold in the coming decade.

REFERENCES

The following references are grouped by the section of the paper in which the reference is mentioned or which it serves to illustrate. The items are examples only; no attempt at comprehensiveness in listing is made, hence omission does not indicate less relative significance. The references are given chiefly for the convenience of those who wish to consult the particular books, documents, and articles. In general, the listing is restricted to publications that appeared during the past decade.

SECTION I SCOPE OF PUBLIC FINANCE

Prest, A. R., *Public Finance in Theory and Practice* (London: English Language Book Society and Weidenfeld and Nicolson, 1974), fifth ed., pp. 13–18.

Shoup, Carl S., *Public Finance* (Chicago: Aldine, 1969), pp. 3–6.

SECTION II INCOME TAX

Surrey, Stanley S., *Pathways to Tax Reform: The Concept of Tax Expenditures* (Cambridge, Mass.: Harvard University Press, 1973).

Shoup, Carl S., 'Tax Expenditures: A Review of Stanley Surrey's *Pathways to Tax Reforms*', *Journal of Finance* (forthcoming).

United Nations, Department of Economic and Social Affairs, *Tax Treaties between Developed and Developing Countries: Fifth Report of Group of Experts* (New York: United Nations, 1975).

United Nations, Department of Economic and Social Affairs, *The Impact of Multinational Corporations on Development and on International Relations. Technical Papers: Taxation* (New York: United Nations, 1974).

Bird, Richard M. and Sato, R., 'International Aspects of Taxation of Corporations and Shareholders', *International Monetary Fund* (forthcoming).

Prest, A. R., *Public Finance in Theory and Practice*, fifth edition (London: English Language Book Society and Weidenfeld and Nicolson, 1974), Chs. 13–18.

Brown, E. Cary, 'Recent Studies of the Incidence of the Corporate Income Tax', in

Warren L. Smith and John M. Culbertson, eds., *Public Finance and Stabilization Policy*, Essays in Honour of Richard A. Musgrave (Amsterdam: North-Holland Publishing Co., 1974), pp. 93–108.

United States Department of the Treasury, Internal Revenue Service, *Statistics of Income* (periodically) (Washington, DC: US Government Printing Office).

Kotowitz, Yehuda and Portes, Richard, 'The "Tax on Wage Increases"', *Journal of Public Economics*, Vol. 3, No. 2 (May, 1974), pp. 113–32.

Conrad, Ernst-Albrecht, 'Trends in the Level of Corporate Taxation', *Finanzarchiv*, Vol. 32, No. 3 (1974), pp. 361–405.

SECTION III SALES TAXATION

Due, John F., 'Alternative Forms of Sales Taxation for a Developing Country', *Journal of Development Studies* (January, 1972), pp. 263–75; reprinted in Richard M. Bird and Oliver Oldman, *Readings on Taxation in Developing Countries*, third edition (Baltimore: Johns Hopkins Press, 1975), pp. 309–24.

Guerard, Michèle, 'The Brazilian State Value-Added Tax', International Monetary Fund, *Staff Papers* (March, 1973), pp. 118–69.

SECTION IV PUBLIC DEBT

United States Department of the Treasury, *Treasury Bulletin* (monthly) (Washington, DC: US Government Printing Office).

SECTION V GOVERNMENT EXPENDITURES

Shoup, Carl S., *Public Finance* (Chicago: Aldine, 1969), Chs. 4–7.

Green, Christopher, *Negative Taxes and the Poverty Problem* (Washington, DC: Brookings Institution, 1967).

US Congress, Joint Economic Committee, *The Economics of Federal Subsidy Programs* (Washington, DC: US Government Printing Office, 1972–73); 'Staff Study', by Jerry J. Jasinowski and Carl S. Shoup, 1972; 'Hearings', 1972; 'Compendium of Papers', Parts 1–7, 1972–73.

Andel, Norbert, *Subventionen als Instrument des finanzwirtschaftlichen Interventionismus* (Tübingen: J. C. B. Mohr, 1970).

Berthold, Ursula, *Zur Theorie der Subventionen* (Berne: Paul Haupt, 1967).

Pryor, Frederic L., *Public Expenditures in Communist and Capitalist Nations* (Homewood, Ill.: Irwin, 1968).

Musgrave, Richard A. and Musgrave, Peggy B., *Public Finance in Theory and Practice* (New York: McGraw-Hill, 1973), Part Two, 'Expenditure Structure'.

Brennan, Geoffrey, '"Pareto-Optimal Redistribution": A Perspective', *Finanzarchiv*, Vol. 33, No. 2 (1975), pp. 237–71.

SECTION VI INTERGOVERNMENTAL RELATIONS; URBAN PROBLEMS

Advisory Commission on Intergovernmental Relations. Commission Reports; Information Bulletins; Information Interchange Service; News Releases (Washington, DC).

Break, George F., *Intergovernmental Fiscal Relations in the United States* (Washington: Brookings Institution, 1967).

Flatters, Frank, Henderson, Vernon, and Mieszkowski, Peter, 'Public Goods, Efficiency, and Regional Fiscal Equalization', *Journal of Public Economics*, Vol. 3, No. 2 (May, 1974), pp. 99–112.

Hogan, Timothy D. and Shelton, Robert B., 'Interstate Tax Exportation and States' Fiscal Structures', *National Tax Journal*, Vol. XXVI, No. 4 (December, 1973), pp. 553–64.

Vickrey, William S., 'The Economics of Congestion Control in Urban Transportation', in Frank C. Emerson, ed., *The Economics of Environmental Problems* (Ann Arbor, Mich.: Graduate School of Business Administration, 1973), pp. 55–70.

Crecine, John P., ed., *Financing the Metropolis: Public Policy in Urban Economics* (Beverly Hills, Calif.: Sage, 1970), Vol. 4 in Urban Affairs Annual Reviews.

SECTION VII PUBLIC GOODS; EXTERNALITIES

Head, John G., 'Public Goods; The Polar Case', in Richard M. Bird and John G. Head, eds., *Modern Fiscal Issues* (Toronto: U. of Toronto Press, 1972), pp. 3–17.

Shibata, Hirofumi, 'Joint Production, Externality, and Public Goods', in Bird and Head, *Op. cit.*, pp. 18–44.

Macaulay, Hugh, 'Environmental Quality, the Market, and Public Finance', in Bird and Head, *Op. cit.*, pp. 187–224.

Dorfman, Nancy S. and Snow, Arthur, 'Who Will Pay for Pollution Control?—The Distribution by Income of the Burden of the National Environmental Protection Program, 1972–1980', *National Tax Journal*, Vol XXVIII, No. 1 (March, 1975), pp. 101–16.

SECTION VIII PUBLIC CHOICE

Buchanan, James M., *Public Finance in Democratic Process* (Chapel Hill, NC: U. of North Carolina Press, 1967).

Buchanan, James M., *The Demand and Supply of Public Goods* (Chicago: Rand McNally, 1968).

Breton, Albert, *The Economic Theory of Representative Government* (Chicago: Aldine, 1974).

Olson, Jr., Mancur, *The Logic of Collective Action* (Cambridge, Mass.: Harvard University Press, 1965).

Buchanan, James M. and Tollison, Robert D., eds., *Theory of Public Choice: Political Applications of Economics* (Ann Arbor: U. of Michigan Press, 1972).

SECTION IX ECONOMIC STABILIZATION

Prest, A. R., *Public Finance in Theory and Practice*, Fifth ed. (London: English Language Book Society and Weidenfeld & Nicolson, 1974), pp. 96–117.

Musgrave, Richard A., *The Theory of Public Finance* (NewYork: McGraw-Hill, 1959), Parts One and Four.

Neumark, Fritz, *Wirtschafts- und Finanzprobleme des Interventionsstaates* (Tübingen: J. C. B. Mohr, 1961).

Examples of recent public finance texts that contain no chapters on stabilization are:

Buchanan, James M. and Flowers, Marilyn R., *The Public Finances* (Homewood, Ill.: Irwin, 1975), Fourth ed., revised.

Singer, Neil M., *Public Micro Economics* (Boston: Little, Brown, 1972).

Wagner, Richard E., *The Public Economy* (Chicago: Markham, 1973).

SECTION X COUNTRY STUDIES

Musgrave, Richard A., President of the Commission, and Gillis, Malcolm, ed., *Fiscal Reform for Colombia* (Cambridge, Mass.: The Law School of Harvard University, 1971). Final Report and Staff Papers of the Colombia Commission on Tax Reform. [In this case, substantial implementation occurred in 1975.]

Shoup, Carl S., Dosser, Douglas, Penner, Rudolph G. and Vickrey, William S., *The Tax System of Liberia* (New York: Columbia U. Press, 1970).

SECTION XI BUDGETING TECHNIQUES

Blechman, Barry M., Gramlich, Edward M. and Hartman, Robert W., *Setting National Priorities: The 1975 Budget* (Washington, DC: Brookings Institution, 1974).

SECTION XII MODES OF PUBLICATION

[References already given above are not repeated here.]

Head, John G., *Public Goods and Public Welfare* (Durham, NC: Duke U. Press, 1974).
Due, John F. and Friedlaender, Ann F., *Government Finance: Economics of the Public Sector* (Homewood, Ill.: Irwin, 1973), Fifth edition.
Gerloff, Wilhelm and Neumark, Fritz, eds., *Handbuch der Finanzwissenschaft* (Tübingen: J. C. B. Mohr (Paul Siebeck), 1952 to 1965), Zweite Auflage. Four volumes.
Schendstok, B., Frank, M., Peacock, A. T. and Senf, P., eds., *Essays in Honor of Fritz Neumark*, in *Public Finance*, Vol. XX, Nos. 1 and 2, 1965, pp. 1–250.
Haller, Heinz, Kullmer, Lore, Shoup, Carl S. and Timm, Herbert, eds., *Theorie und Praxis des finanzpolitischen Interventionismus*, Fritz Neumark zum 70, Geburtstag (Tübingen: J. C. B. Mohr, 1970).
Bird, Richard M. and Head, John G., *Modern Fiscal Issues*, Essays in Honour of Carl S. Shoup (Toronto: U. of Toronto Press, 1972).
Lascelles, David Wilfred, ed., *Public Finance, Planning, and Economic Development*, Essays in Honour of Ursula K. Hicks (London: Macmillan, 1973).
Cosciani, Cesare and Di Nardi, Giuseppe, eds., *Studii in Onore di Giuseppe Ugo Papi* (Padova: CEDAM, 1972), 2 vols.
d'Albergo, Ernesto, Pisanelli, G. Codacci, Cosciani, Cesare, del Prete, Pasquale and Amato, Angelo, eds. *Scritti 'in Memoria' di Antonio de Viti de Marco* (Bari: Cacucci, 1972), 2 vols.
Smith, Warren L. and Culbertson, John M., *Public Finance and Stabilization Policy*, Essays in Honour of Richard A. Musgrave (Amsterdam: North-Holland, 1974).

Comment by Alan Peacock (University of York)

As one might expect from such a distinguished public financier as Carl S. Shoup, his contribution offers as balanced and as perceptive a view of the future developments in his special fields of interest as one is every likely to find. A commentator brought up on the principle that 'if you have nothing to say, don't say it' faces an obvious difficulty. I believe that there is a *little* more to be said even if the net result is a meagre list of marginalia.

1. THE DEVELOPMENT OF FISCAL ECONOMICS

Though querying definitions is sometimes regarded as the last refuge of the intellectually bankrupt, I think that the term 'fiscal economics', which must imply a concentration on tax and revenue problems, is something of a misnomer, given the enumeration of topics in the paper which covers almost the whole range of subjects embraced by the term 'public economics', going even beyond the conventional boundaries of the AEA Classification Code item 320 'Domestic fiscal policy and public finance'.

Indeed, librarians still shackled by Dewey and Congress classifications of Economics subjects, though modifications are constantly being made, will have to run fast in order to take account of the re-grouping of sub-disciplines perpetrated by researchers.

In agreeing with Shoup that a broad view must be taken, an additional difficulty of 'linkage' becomes apparent. He stresses the links with law, political science and accounting. Important though these are, I would stress the growing links between public economic and other fields of *economics* concerned with public policy.[1] The kind of framework for policy decisions which is developing in many industrial countries stresses the need to compare different policy instruments in the achievement of a range of policy targets. This approach, which has developed out of the Theil-Tinbergen theory of economic policy, can be deployed at different levels of sophistication, but at all levels it calls not only for a comparison but, more difficult, for a ranking of alternative instruments. Thus, a public financier, particularly one concerned with giving advice to government, must be aware of both the relative merits of particular taxation and expenditure measures in achieving particular objectives and the 'opportunity costs' of using such measures requiring an awareness of 'non-budgetary' alternatives, e.g. monetary measures and direct controls.

2. THE COSTS OF SEARCH

My view about linkages reinforces the Shoup view about the polymathic character of public finance, but I do not think that it adds appreciably to the search costs of those engaged in its study and practice. There are already textbooks emphasizing this view of linkage, and the existing journals in public

[1] On this question, see Alan Williams' interesting view of the bibliographical needs of public financiers in Chapter 22, 'Public Finance' of J. Fletcher, ed., *The Use of Economics Literature, Information Sources for Research and Development* (London: Butterworths, 1971).

finance and public economics have terms of reference which easily embrace articles with linkage characteristics. If at all, I am inclined to think that Shoup may exaggerate the problems of search associated with his linkage example. Much depends on the nature of the consumer. The practised public financier who knows what he is looking for can turn over the retrieval problem to the library staff, which seems the logical thing to do, given the principle of division of labour, though hard-pressed librarians will emphasize that division of labour is limited by the extent of the market. At least, it is reasonable to assume that innovations in retrieval systems will, in time, take care of the locational problem presented by scattered sources. If he is lucky, the researcher can shift the costs of search back onto his research assistant (if he has one) if this seems an efficient use of his time! The problem of search is much greater for the untutored who do not know what they are looking for, and here Shoup's point is well taken.

3. THE FORMS OF DOCUMENTATION

Professor Shoup gives a very comprehensive picture of the forecasted reaction of supply of documentation to changes in demand. There is one important omission from his list, namely, the demand for knowledge of *work-in-progress*, which has its supply counterpart in the growing proliferation of circulated *working* or *discussion papers*, in public finance as much as in any other field. Even if one is plugged in to the specialist network, and given the linkage problems already referred to, it is difficult, if not impossible, for the practised hand to be fully informed by relying on the rising pile of these papers in his in-tray. There will be a continuing and growing need for a bibliographical and photo-copying service of the kind recently developed by the University of Warwick, England.

Will public financiers be expounding their subject by exploiting the latest gimmicks such as audio- and video-cassettes? Perhaps no more and no less than other teachers of economics, and with a close watch being kept, no doubt, on performing rights! It is perhaps not without significance that the commentator and Jack Wiseman were asked to tape two discussions—one on the general problems of public expenditure and the other on public enterprise—for a commercial enterprise who issued them in an Economics series.[2] It is an open question whether this innovation in the supply of knowledge will create its own demand, but it hardly borders on fantasy to suggest that it will not be long before audio-visual packs of seminar discussions will be available on sale or loan. One such discussion led by Professor Shoup himself would be something to treasure.

[2] When playing through our personal copy, Jack Wiseman was actually drowned out by the lowing of cattle and the stentorian tones of John Wayne shouting 'git along there', but this turned out to be a freak transmissional juxtaposition. Perhaps the tape would have sold better if this fault had remained on all the copies!

Summary of the Discussion

Dr Biehl simplified Professor Shoup's conclusions on the development of what he (Shoup) calls 'Fiscal Economics' for the next decade along the following lines: Interest would remain concentrated in public revenues, i.e. taxes, more especially income taxes and value added taxes. Apart from public borrowing, which Professor Shoup sees as a branch of Monetary Economics, research efforts and publications in the field of public expenditures will increase comparably only in the 'social security' lines as transfer payments, negative income taxation and old age assistance. Professor Shoup also expected some interest in inter-governmental fiscal relations, particularly as they involve regional, urban and environmental problems. Along more abstract lines, Professor Shoup anticipated continued interest in the theory of public goods, public choice, and public budgeting and programming. Publications are anticipated by Professor Shoup to become increasingly specialized in journal articles and working papers. Many of them will be inter-disciplinary, involving Law, Political Science, Sociology, and Psychology, along with Economics.

Dr Biehl agreed with many of Professor Shoup's conclusions, but thought that the revenue side of the budget had been given too large a weight in comparison with expenditures. He thought that European interest in problems particularly in connection with inter-governmental fiscal relations, revenue sharing, and regional development might remain more intense than in the United States, the main basis for Professor Shoup's surmises. Dr Biehl also commented on Professor Shoup's term, 'Fiscal Economics', since the conventional term has been 'Public Finance' and many writers use 'Public Economics'.

Professor M. Perlman digested a written comment by Professor Peacock. Besides preferring the term 'Public Economics', Professor Peacock thought that the paper should have laid more stress on bibliographical materials. To a list which Professor Peacock gave of such materials *Professor M. Perlman* added several UN publications. Professor Peacock was concerned about the rising cost of search, and mentioned the University of Warwick's attempt to centralize documentation for work in progress. Professor Peacock believed that audio and video cassettes might replace working papers in the relatively near future, and that audio-visual tracks of important seminars and interviews would also become available. (*Mr Evans* agreed, and added that these processes had already begun in some academic fields. *Professor M. Perlman* regretted the absence, thus far, of any feasible method for selectively condensing cassettes and eliminating the irrelevancies.)

Professor Kindleberger asserted that, however pleasant they might be as accompaniments for pleasure driving, cassettes were not well adapted to scientific research, not being reader paced.

Professor Bronfenbrenner inquired what might be expected of interest in income-averaging schemes, which he thought should increase in practicability with the onset of electronic computation.

Professor Wolfe feared that inter-disciplinary material might become difficult to come by. The Ohio plan, or something like it, would help in obtaining books, once they are ordered. But doesn't it, at the same time, reduce the probability of ordering a specific work, as each of several departments would expect its partners to order it?

Professor M. Perlman inquired what substantive issues, if any, were involved in the disagreements as to the proper nomenclature for this branch of economic science. *Professor Johnson* said that the main focus of the disagreement is in Great Britain, where the role of government has been expanding through public corporations, and where Professor Peacock's activities have been concentrated. In Great Britain, the public corporations have been more important than the Budget proper, as regards, say, income distribution. This is because of the importance of governmental and public corporation wages. This fact is less important in the United States, where local public bodies do not act in unison. Accordingly, one finds the term 'Public Economics' favoured in Britain, and 'Fiscal Economics' in the United States.

Dr Weise was not sure who were the principal addressees of Professor Shoup's list of topics—librarians, archivists, or economists? The paper appeared to be directed unduly at Professor Shoup's fellow economists, yet it pleaded for greater co-operation from others. In Germany, *Dr Weise* continued, the Central Statistical Office has special committees, including committees of users of particular statistical series. Such institutions could, perhaps, answer some of Professor Shoup's requirements.

Mr Fetterman claimed that the Center for Research Libraries (Chicago) can photo-copy any journal article in any language, and called it a resource which should be used more than it is. *Mr Evans* explained that the number of libraries which have access to its facilities is small, and *Mr Kilgour* noted that European libraries were superior to Americans with regard to duplicating equipment. *Mr Evans* also pointed out that copyright laws operated to restrict access for photocopying purposes.

Professor Johnson cautioned the group against forgetting the copyright laws, which were outside the range of conference discussions, but which might interfere with some of the proposals brought up. *Professor Wolfe* expressed pleasure that the issue had finally come up, and criticized certain other papers for not having mentioned it despite its relevance.

After requesting policy proposals from conference members, *Professor Giersch* wished that the Shoup paper had said more about regional and local taxation and expenditure problems.

Dr Biehl suggested a change in public-finance terminology. This should be designed in terms of *instruments*; specific taxes, expenditure items, price fixations, subsidies; then, movement should be from smaller to larger economies. *Professor Prest* complained that local and regional data are slow, hard to process, and often non-comparable between areas. In Australia, for example, local fiscal data is a year behind.

Professor Johnson criticized Professor Shoup's omission of the 'incentive' issue, which Dr Johnson believed was gaining in importance with the expansion of Social Security. People were making life-cycle decisions on the basis of such factors as these. Also, the definition of unemployment and its level hinged significantly on the availability of transfer income.

Professor Shoup answered his questioners on the initial issue of nomenclature. He might have preferred 'Public Economics' or 'Public Finance' because he thought that 'Fiscal Economics' was a misleading term. (In France, for example, *fiscale* is used exclusively with reference to revenues.)

On cash subsidies as possibly leading to shifts in willingness to work, *Professor Shoup* was aware of the recent availability of much experimental data from the United States, but doubted their quality and representativeness.

On income taxation, *Professor Shoup* commented on the numerous proposals, particularly during inflationary periods, to shift it to an expenditure tax, thereby encouraging saving, investment, and growth.

Even if public borrowing remains in 'Fiscal Economics', as it well might, *Professor Shoup* believed that taxation would continue to dominate the field, if only because more servicing is available on this front due to the natural interest of lawyers.

Whatever this conference paper may indicate, *Professor Shoup* has retained his interest in regional and local material. He has, in fact, suggested a Federal subsidy to States and localities keyed to the unemployment level. Up to 1975, he thought it applicable to the special situations of both New York City and many of its New Jersey suburbs.

Returning to the immediate subject of this conference, *Professor Shoup* complained of insufficient distribution of working-papers, they being restricted too much to the 'old-boy' network, with which he thought younger men would not intergrate quickly enough.

Professor Shoup then answered several individual questions. He attributed the lack of interest in more refined income averaging in the United States (responding to Professor Bronfenbrenner) to the self-assessment tradition of that country. Replying to Professor Wolfe on inter-disciplinary emphasis, *Professor Shoup* noted that essential works from other disciplines were not readily available in Departments of Economics. (For this situation, librarians were not to blame. Public finance scholars should tell colleagues what sorts of material would be welcome, and tell librarians to buy it when it appears.) Answering Professor Prest on obsolescent local-finance materials in Australia, *Professor Shoup* suggested that user pressure might induce acceleration. In response to Professor Johnson, *Professor Shoup* agreed that the incentive problem was a major inter-disciplinary one, and mentioned the tax-exemption of unemployment-insurance payments as increasing their value. He anticipated that increased interest might be generated by expanding Social Security systems of the 'welfare state' type.

15 Information Needs in Regional Economics

Edwin von Böventer
UNIVERSITY OF MUNICH

The paper discusses the information needs of policy oriented regional economic research. These needs have to be derived on the basis of policy goals, political decision processes, the policy instruments available, and a set of theories on the behaviour of the economic system. The lack of data has inhibited the development of operational theories. For the testing of theories as well as for the formulation of long-term regional policies, one needs additional information on: (1) the future demand for space by categories of economic units and the mobility of people and jobs; (2) the cost of changes in the spatial structure of the economy, particularly the social costs and benefits of (a) different degrees of the agglomeration of activities, (b) the utilization of infrastructure services (also as determined by distances) as well as (c) the input and output characteristics of production and the adaptations of firms to changes in their environments. More data on externalities are essential. A more flexible information system would make it easier to meet confidentiality requirements.

I. INTRODUCTION

It is often thought that the most extensive as well as the most flexible and, therefore, most desirable regional information system would be one that contains all relevant data on works and flows for spatial units that are as small as possible:

on their physical and financial resources,
on the kinds and levels of activities that take place at these points, as well as
on the interrelationships or the exchanges taking place between different points in space.

However, we shall argue in the following that this would be both much *more* information than one needs and much *less* than necessary for a comprehensive approach. It is *less* because, as in all social sciences, this reflects the results only of *past decisions* and is useful for future policy decisions only to the extent that decision processes and relevant behaviour functions and technical and ecological interrelationships, including significant external effects, have become known for the past *and* may be extrapolated into the future. Furthermore, one would have to know how, and how far, these processes may be influenced or controlled, and what (in the widest sense of the word), would be the *cost* of controlling them. All of this knowledge would go vastly beyond information about activities on, and between, different points in space. The main reason why so much information is wanted lies in the necessity to include *external effects* and their consequences for the individual decision units. On the other hand, it would be both impossible and unnecessary to collect and use all data on stocks and flows for all small spatial units, data which are anyway, only the results of past decisons.

As a starting point for our survey it should be stated that, through processing data, the amount of information is necessarily reduced by all kinds of aggregation (spatial or sectoral or other), as it is by the neglect of certain pieces of information that were originally available. Because of these simple facts, an information system can obviously be efficient only if its puposes have been clearly defined. For this, one needs *theory*, one needs to know what kinds of data are significant, which empirical relationships are important and what kinds of information losses through aggregation may be tolerated. Furthermore, one has to recognize that the term 'policy aims' involves sets of extremely complex matters, even if ultimate goals for the various spatial units are taken as given, because *policy aims* are multidimensional (and partly supporting each other, partly contradictory) and because there are also *many instruments* available about whose possiblilties and effects one knows too little.

In this situation, the tasks of the scientist may be summarized under these headings: he has to

analyse and systematize the policy aims that have been formulated by politicians,
obtain information about, and derive a comprehensive picture of, the developments of society in long-range terms, developments that seem *likely* on the basis of past events, and developments that are *possible*.

In particular, he has to

collect or derive information about the effects of policy measures that may be taken, particularly, in this case, with regard to the regional aspects.

All of this is done continually in theoretical and empirical research, and in all cases the use, as well as the improvement, of regional statistics is important both for the test of existing theories and for the formulation of new hypotheses and theories on the basis of empirical findings.

In this paper, we shall not present a survey of the problems of regional policy and planning—neither in general nor for a particular country, nor shall we present a complete catalogue of the regional data that are available or those are desired.[1]

The latest West German Government's Report on Regional Development (*Raumordnungsbericht*, 1974) points to the deficiencies of the information instruments and lists improvements on which work is in progress. Furthermore, there are the noteworthy investigations of the *Ministerkonferenz für Raumordnung* on the possible improvement of official statistics through a concentration of essential data and a more appropriate differentiation between censuses, current statistics and sampling. These publications show that governments have become increasingly aware of the information needs for regional economic policies and planning. There is no use in presenting a survey of all of these proposals, partly because some of them are not yet detailed or concrete enough.

The best approach to be taken in this paper seems to be a systematic presentation of the information needs of regional economics so that the interrelationship between (1) current problems, (2) information needs and (3) regional theory become evident and, hence, the usefulness of the data for forecasting purposes may be shown. The basis of our deliberations will be that

> *the primary orientation point for regional economics should be potential policy application.* From this basis, certain desirable lines of development for both theoretical and empirical research may be derived.

We shall focus both

> *on the lack of data and on the deficiencies of regional theory* and shall try to point out how a more efficient organization of empirical research may make regional economics a better instrument for giving advice in the fields of regional policy and planning.

[1]The problems of regional planning and of the available information systems in several industrialized, as well as in less industrialized, countries are discussed in A. Kuklinski (ed.), *Regional Information and Regional Planning* (Paris and the Hague, 1974).

A more detailed discussion of the problems of computer-based organization and processing of data is found in the following two publications of the West German *Bundesforschungsanstalt für Landeskunde und Raumordnung* (Bonn–Bad Godesberg): '*Informationssystem für Raumordnung und Landesplanung*', *Informationen zur Raumentwicklung*, 1974 (6): 213–250, and '*Dokumentation im ORL-Verbund. Ausweg aus der Literaturfülle*', *op. cit.*, 1975 (2/3): 33–116. In the latter publication, which came out after this paper was finished, ORL stands for *Orts-*, *Regional-* und *Landesplanung* (municipal and regional planning). This publication contains a discussion of computerized approaches to the literature of regional and urban economics.

II. REGIONAL ECONOMICS AS A GUIDE FOR POLICY DECISIONS

Before the regional scientist can help in shaping policy decisions, he has to know about the decision processes that are being taken in real life. He must know: who needs his aid? Who would be willing to accept his advice? Which actors are responsible for which kinds of decisions? What are their direct or ultimate goals? It is only then that he can pose the question: 'What kinds of information do they need for their decision processes?' So that he can start collecting the necessary basic information and start analysing it and deriving scientific conclusions.

Investigations in the decision-making processes of independent political authorities presuppose a minimum knowledge of political institutions and their realms of competence, as well as of the mechanisms and problems in the co-ordination of their decisions. The decision-making units act on the basis of certain goals, and these have to be studied with regard to their implications, their mutual compatibilities and their consequences. Recently, there have been published a number of investigations on the problem of *operationalizing* regional goals, because the formulations given by politicians are often rather vague. More important for practical work, however, is the analysis of *actual decisions* taken by politicians, with a view to deriving *implicit goals*, and to seeing whether these are compatible with each other and with explicitly formulated goals. In all of this, regional economists need the co-operation of other regional scientists, in particular of sociologists and political scientists.

The discussions between scientists and politicians should lead to the formulation of a coherent operational system of regional policy objectives. It is only on this basis that one may construct something which takes a few initial steps towards a social welfare function with *some* empirical content. The weights to be attached to particular goals have to be determined by political processes, but the scientist may indicate what conflicts and goal complementarities exist and may suggest appropriate measures for operationalizing both the goals and the indicators for the control and the evaluation of the effects.

It is due to the neglect of policy needs in regional economics that satisfactory indicators for the description of the qualities of spatial units have not yet been developed. The establishment of *social indicators* is particularly important for the evaluation of the spatial structure of an economy, because a highly differentiated spatial structure makes highly aggregated welfare indicators almost completely useless. Questions related to the aim of creating *equivalent* living conditions in all parts of a country may be answered only if supply levels of private and public commodities at different points in space and for various spatial units are measured in an appropriate way. Before this has been achieved, decisions with regard to establishing equivalent living conditions can certainly not in any way be called systematic or rational.

The measurement of living conditions in a space-economy and the development of regional goal systems presuppose the existence of methods for an adequate description and assessment of space itself. In spite of a long discussion about the right way of defining regions, the problem of how best to construct *planning regions* is far from being solved. This may be due to the facts

> that for this task one has to take into account not only (1) spatial goals; and (2) spatial interdependencies; but, also, (3) the complex regulations concerning the jurisdiction of various decision units at different levels and the kinds of decisions that they are allowed to take in the formulation and the execution of regional and national policies; and that one cannot neglect the various channels of co-ordination among all of these actors.

III. SPATIAL STRUCTURES: DEVELOPMENTS AND LONG-TERM PROJECTIONS

For most political decisions the underlying horizon is either short-term or medium-term. The regional scientist, however, has to take a different view. If more than *marginal* corrections of spatial developments are aimed at, regional policy has to be a long-term affair and, hence, needs the aid of scientists who are concerned with the spatial dimensions of the developments of the society. The long-term view of the interaction of economic, social and spatial structures implies the projection

of expected changes in the sectoral economic structure
of the development of household demand for space and, last but not least
of the willingness of people to migrate and commute.

All of these factors have a bearing on the spatial structure of an economy:

(*a*) Changes in the sectoral structure (which may be due to technical progress, resource limitations, and demand shifts or changes in the structure of international trade) have spatial consequences. They may significantly change the demand for space—either for the economy as a whole or for particular points in space. Changes in the tertiary sector certainly have had a great effect on the spatial structure of cities and concentrations within cities.

(*b*) The household demand for space, both for residential and recreational purposes, may be expected to change as new ways of family life and of spreading leisure time. These influence the growth of the whole system of cities, their relative sizes and locations and the intra-metropolitan degree of concentration.

(*c*) A third important factor for the development of regional economies is the spatial mobility of people and of commodities. Whether this mobility will rise or fall in the future depends on the development of new technologies—in particular, on the way that the telecommunications system will develop. It may increase the desire for more contacts and for taking advantage of the possibilities offered at far away places, but it may also reduce the need to go to these places in person.

Politicians very urgently need information about the implications of different spatial structures—in particular, the implications of different distributions of the population both within and between settlements of different sizes—if they think about the developments of society as a whole and about social policies for the future. Spatial development is one important dimension in a concept of overall development.

Apart from the influence of the three factors just mentioned, it is necessary to know about the implications and influences of *historical development* on the spatial structure and about the *cost of changing the spatial structure* if that is desired. Thus, one must know what kinds of spatial distributions of people and activities would best correspond to certain fundamental goals that one tries to accomplish for society as a whole.

In this context, one extremely important factor is information on the social costs and social benefits of different degrees of *agglomeration of activities*. The concept of an optimal development for a society has to be based, at least partly, on such cost and benefits; therefore, they have to be measured, as far as possible and *evaluated* for this purpose. Theoretical derivations on overall spatial structures exist in great number, but we know little about the cost and benefit implications of these structures for the agents who live in them. Different kinds of approaches have been used by architects and planners, but their models for physical planning have hardly been noticed by economists, much less been analysed in terms of economic criteria. The models of spatial economic structures of the Christaller-Lösch-Type have not been related systematically to systems of grids, directional grids, linear expansions in corridors of development, ribbon structures, star-shaped structures, broadcare cities and so forth, to name only a few important ones that are connected with the names of LeCorbusier, Miljutin, Buchanan, Hilberseimer, Hillebrecht and Frank Lloyd Wright. This is, indeed, a challenging field for systematic empirical studies. Economists cannot shy away from this task any longer. Who else should be asked to evaluate different spatial structures in terms of infrastructure costs, transportation costs, social costs, environmental degradation, as well as in terms of the relevant benefits as measured by the values added in different parts of the system? This cannot be done by economists *alone*, but economists have to determine what pieces of extra information they need and, in limited approaches, they may state *how* the outcome of certain evaluations depends on particular (relative) weights. All such evaluations are to be based in quantitative terms, on, admittedly, very difficult cost-benefit analyses.

In empirical investigations, the comparisons of different spatial structures in terms of costs are rendered very difficult by the fact that *sectoral* breakups are never the same in different structures. Now it seems to be almost impossible to derive any definite conclusions about the effects that different spatial structures in different countries have had in the past on levels and growth rates of incomes and other economic variables. Nevertheless, it remains important to study the *costs* of different spatial structures. In assessing some of the social costs, the economist will most certainly need the co-operation of ecologists and students of other disciplines.

Regional economics must supply the foundations for a theory of regional economic policy, as has been stressed above. For this purpose, regional economics must determine, in quantitative terms, the effects of regional economic and general economic policy measures on the spatial structure of the economy, because it is only in this way that spatially relevant decisions of economic agents may be influenced systematically and effectively in the direction that has been chosen on the basis of more fundamental policy goals for the space economy. This presupposes the existence of a body of regional economic theory which contains empirically testable hypotheses—i.e. is operationally defined and takes the data problems into account—and takes into account the available policy instruments for influencing locational decisions.

IV. SUGGESTIONS FOR FURTHER EMPIRICAL RESEARCH: LOCATIONAL DECISIONS

In the previous Section, we pointed out that we know too little about agglomerations and spatial structures and that much more research on this aspect of economic development is necessary. In the following one we shall make some suggestions for empirical research which we think are relevant from a regional policy point of view. This will be followed by remarks on additional statistics that are needed for this purpose. The context for these remarks will be the situation of West Germany with regard to its official statistics.

LOCATIONAL DECISIONS AS A MEANS OF SPATIAL ADAPTATION

Models of locational decisions do not put enough stress on the fact that entrepreneurial decisions on the location of new investment are only part of the total investment decision. An alternative to choosing a new location for a plant is the adaptation of existing plants at old locations to the changes in the 'economic environment' of the firm, in the locations of other economic activities and their interrelationships, and in other relevant data. A favourable environment is one of the most important advantages that large agglomerations offer, because in them the possibilities of effective adaptations are particularly great, due to the wide chances of securing other inputs for new lines of production, not least of which is labour input in a greatly differentiated labour market. For systematic studies of such possibilities, it is necessary to secure much more data for small spatial units—data in which plants are classified on the basis of a fine differentiation as between production programmes and/or production techniques.

For lack of statistical data, little is known so far about the way locational decisions depend on the size of the necessary capital stock or the magnitude of the capital stock that is available at a given location. This refers to sizes of both private capital and public infrastructure capital, as well as to the aspect of their limited divisibility. The important question in this context is, again, the degree to which the *historical* spatial distribution of the private and the public capital stock (including the parts that are invested in infrastructure) influences individual locational decisions and, hence, has a bearing on the *further development* of the whole spatial structure. Statistics on the capital stock should, therefore, contain information on the age structure and on the (embodied) production techniques, possibly in the form of productivity data. Indirect information concerning these questions might be obtained if more detailed information on the qualification of the employees were available. (Here the information needs are similar to those for foreign trade analyses—but much more difficult to obtain).

Locational decisions are also influenced by characteristics of the output side of the product. The degrees of standardization or non-standardization of a product or—as in the case of services—the degrees of differentiation and specialization of the commodities are important determinants of the extent to which agglomeration factors influence locational decisions. This is because the firms' communication and information needs are related to the product characteristics just mentioned.

More detailed information on both input and output characteristics would make it possible to give more empirical content to agglomeration and hierarchy models, regional growth models or growth pole models, and spatial diffusion models, among others. On the basis of such information, some models which so far have been formulated more in a static than in a dynamic context, might be reformulated. As dynamic models they would become much more useful for regional policy applications than they have been hitherto. Central Place theory might be a good example for this. In such models and applications, the influence of special social characteristics of a spatial unit should also be included. In trying to obtain the relevant data and in formulating operational theories, economists should seek a close co-operation with sociologists.

THE INFLUENCE OF 'ECONOMIC ENVIRONMENT'

The locations of other activities and the characteristics of other interaction points (including the natural surroundings for recreational purposes) are reference data for the locational decisions of firms and households; they are the relevant 'economic environment' that was mentioned above. While the influence of man's environment on his well-being—the emotional content of the environment—has, for a long time, been the subject of intensive investigations by social psychology and sociology, comparable studies are missing in economics. Indeed, the tendency of neoclassical models has been to neglect this aspect or even to explain why spatial adaptation processes beyond the market mechanism have been given only scanty attention in the past.

The questions which empirical research should try to answer may be characterized in this way. How does the economic environment influence economic locational decisions and the economic behaviour of economic agents at pvocation? How do the various *distances* from other space points influence these decisions? How do the relevant distance elasticities differ for different activities and different interaction points? How are selection processes within particular spatial units governed by adaptation processes versus adaptation processes ('adaptation' by the environment, if the old distinction by Alchian is used here)?

It is obvious that, for such analyses, much more detailed data are necessary than are available so far on the characteristics of different points in space. One should start with case studies.

SPATIAL INTERACTIONS

If the set of spatial *inter*actions between spatial units and the decisions taken there are considered, the following data are important

the traffic and communication streams that are created, and which may lead to bottlenecks,
the (secondary) adaptations on neighbouring lots, which may imply significant changes in the land-use patterns,
further adaptations in production at other points,
the needs for extending infrastructure services, as well as
effects on the whole ecological system.

The data should contain detailed characteristics of the past changes that have taken place at various points in space, and, therefore should be available in the form of time series.

In this context, the sum total of the external effects has to be studied much more systematically than has been done heretofore. Indeed, the deficiencies of present spatial economic theory are such that its application to empirical problems is difficult and its use in designing regional economic policy is extremely limited. Regional problems are the results of sectoral and spatial structural adaptations—with different durations or time-lags, and with processes that may be equilibrating as well as cumulative. It is to be lamented that it is not only the lack of data, but, also, the neoclassical orientation of many theoreticians which has led to a situation in which industrial geographers seems to be much more interested in analysing problems of adaptation processes under external effects than economists are.

INFRASTRUCTURE AND LOCATIONAL DECISIONS

The availability of infrastructure services certainly looms large in all locational decision processes. A certain degree of flexibility in the potential infrastructure services of a region is, therefore, important. A great degree of flexibility in the infrastructure and the absence of effective bottlenecks in the uses of infrastructure services makes it possible for private economic units to take investment decisions and other locational decisions only on the basis of the interrelationships with other *private* economic agents. This makes it easier for them to adapt to new conditions in their markets. The demand for infrastructure services offered at a given location is certainly dependent on the distances from potential users; hence, the great attractive power of large agglomerations with a good infrastructure. In quantitative terms, however, we have much too little information about the demand functions of infrastructures. From the point of view of regional policy, this is a serious handicap, because infrastructure investment is a primary instrument for attaining regional policy aims.

To what extent should infrastructure investment *follow* private relocations; when and where should it be used to *induce* private investment decisions and/or other relocations; and under what conditions may a co-ordination be achieved (or relied on) by which the two kinds of investment decisions are carried out simultaneously? Answers to such questions certainly have to be based (at least partly) on the degree of flexibility of the capacity restraints for various kinds of infrastructure and on the relevant distance elasticities. As yet, regional theory has little to offer—beyond certain generalities—if it comes to answering these questions. But the theoretical statements must, necessarily, remain general as long as it is impossible to test operational hypotheses on supply-demand-distance interrelationships and, thus, to determine (numerical) parameters, as long as there are not good data available on infrastructure services: kinds, capacities, use levels at various points in space during various periods in time.

REGIONAL INTERRELATIONSHIPS

In the macroeconomic part of regional economics, regions are considered as homogeneous spatial units without spatial dimensions and, hence, with zero intraregional transportation costs. It is only in some models that transportation costs arise *between* regions. The interregional interrelationships that are normally considered may be summarized as the exchanges of goods, factors and information. Commodity flows are often analysed within multiplier models, which are used in order to determine regional income levels, and regional growth rates, as well as in order to analyse cyclical changes. Theoretical instruments are available from macroeconomic theory, but empirical estimations on input-output relations, as on regional and interregional multipliers, are severely limited, due to the lack of statistical data on regional flows and on incomes for small spatial units. The availability of continual data on purchase and sales relationships and their changes would be of great help in determining the effects of public expenditures for various points in space.

V. SPECIAL DATA COLLECTION PROBLEMS

An improvement of the theory of regional policy necessitates the reduction of the deficiencies as listed above, with theoretical work being done along with empirical tests of operationally specified empirical hypotheses. It has been shown again and again that a most severe bottleneck is the lack of data with which to test meaningful operational hypotheses. But it is also to be stressed again that one should *not* want to obtain just all of 'the' data on persons, firms and lots, and make it available in a huge centralized databank. The order of doing things ought to be that *additional data* should not be collected before a *problem* has been specified for whose solution the data are necessary. One may then discuss whether the problem is really (i) an interesting and meaningful one and (ii) one whose solution is of such an interest to the community that additional data collection costs are justified. This may also reduce by *a bit* the danger that data are being misused.

In the following section, we shall try to summarize what we consider legitimate interests in obtaining additional information. (Some of the points have already been mentioned above in connection with deficiencies of the theory.) Here one starts with the observation that, from the point of view of regional policy, some significant improvements would be possible even on the basis of *existing* data if the registration, processing and retrieval were improved, to be done by the utilization of administrative processes in the updating and collection of data that are stored for various administrative purposes.

Various public and semipublic agencies (labour offices, social insurance offices, fire insurance agencies, revenue offices) are, indeed producing and using millions of individual data on persons, firms and lots—partly with computer based data collection and processing techniques. These primary elements—persons, firms and lots—could serve as the basis of the official regional data of the Bureau of Statistics, which would have to be supplemented by relatively few additional characteristics, though a unified system of classifying definitions and standard codes would have to be used.

With regard to the millions of data that are collected in West Germany, the following points are of interest.

(*a*) Only a small fraction of the data has been incorporated into the body of official statistics and, thus, been made generally accessible. The most important example is the data on incomes and sales for counties (*Kreise*), data which are taken from the statistics of the tax bureaus.

(*b*) These statistics may be taken as a good example of a general problem: data that originate from different sources are, in general, not comparable. In West Germany, this holds for statistics on incomes and sales as compiled from tax statistics, from industry statistics sources and from the census of manufactures. In statistics published by public authorities outside of the National Bureau of Statistics, different criteria are often used for the same series and, often, the classifications are not comparable—e.g. the standard industrial calssification for all economic activities of the National Bureau of Statistics and of the National Labour Office.

(*c*) What creates particular difficulties for regional statistics are the confidentiality regulations. These make it impossible to publish precise locational information—above all, about production and sales of enterprises. Due to these regulations, data are often aggregated over many spatial units or over groups of industries, and in this way become useless for detailed regional analyses.

(*d*) But, independently of all confidentiality considerations, the data often cover large geographical areas and are not disaggregated because either (1) financial limitations demand this or because (2), for large regions or for the whole economy only (relatively small) samples are taken which can not be evaluated on a spatially more disaggregated basis. Furthermore, often, areal units are used which can not be compared at all with basic *administrative* units. An example is transportation statistics: they use large spatial units which are not identical with the administrative units for which other data are available and, hence, these data are largely useless.

(*e*) Furthermore, it is again the financial limitations which affect the possible classifications of the statistics according to categories—with regard to the collection, the storing and the processing, as well as the publication, of the data.

(*f*) It is to be lamented that too few data are collected on an annual basis. This is true, in particular, of such basic statistics as population, total employment, sales and incomes. These should regularly be made available on an annual basis for the same small spatial units (*Kreise* in West Germany) every year and should be classified in some categories. Above all, it would be necessary to have annual sales and employment data for the tertiary sector. So far, these may be taken only from Census data which are collected once every ten years.

VI. EXPANSION OF THE INFORMATION SYSTEM

In the following section, we should like to discuss some suggestions for the expansion of the production of regional information, the basic criterion for all suggestions being the above-mentioned development of regional science.

The minimum requirement is a greater differentiation of the Census data on population and employment, so as to give more information on the characteristics of persons, employees and plants. For the census of employment this implies the modification of the standard industrial classification of all economic activities and an extension so as to build in more characteristics of the production process and/or of the product. This means, above all, a classification according to the technical standard of the equipment and/or in terms of the technical quality of the product.

With regard to *new surveys*, there would be no point in offering a catalogue of wishes for the expansion of the supply of regional statistics. We list only a few that we consider particularly important.

What is lacking, above all, is statistics (*a*) on regional and interregional flows, (*b*) on infrastructure and (*c*) on the uses of land.

(*a*) Statistics on *flows of goods* classified according to some categories, statistics on *truck traffic* and certain informations on shopping trips, as well as regional surveys of *expenditures* are among the most desidesirable flow statistics.

(*b*) Statistics on the *infrastructure* of regions should include all *kinds* of infrastructures. What is needed is, in particular, data on the use of infrastructure services. Data on infrastructure investment *outlays* by the Federal Government and the states (*Länder*) on a regional (county) basis are necessary to complete the statistics on community expenditures.

(*c*) What is also urgently needed for the planning processes of cities and metropolitan areas is *land use* statistics. Such data should be collected within a land use accounting system. This should also give information on the amount of dwelling space that is utilized for other purposes, in particular in ubanized areas.

Many pieces of information can certainly be obtained only by undertaking case studies. This refers above all to information on interfirm and interpersonal contacts, on the distance elasticities of such contacts and on the evaluation of the qualities of locations from the point of view of households and firms.

VII. IMPLICATION FOR THE ORGANIZATION OF ECONOMIC KNOWLEDGE

If regional economic theory is to be made more useful as a basis for regional policy decisions, some of its most serious deficiencies must be eliminated. A first step might consist of a systematic stock-taking of the existing body of theories with a view to determining which of them may be of value for regional policies and planning. Many theoretical models of regional economics have not been scrutinized from this point of view. But, at the same time, there exist many regional policy programmes and development programmes which make it hard to recognize any (explicit or implicit) theoretical foundations.

Future research must focus more strongly on the investigation of functional relationships or causal chains. In doing so, all those factors should be stressed which might be used as regional policy instruments. Since external effects and cumulative processes loom so large in all real word developments of regions and agglomerations, it is imperative that the neoclassical tradition be abandoned. In any case, the theory should focus more on adaptation processes. Dynamic processes, in particular cumulative disequilibrium processes, should be given much more attention.

Our suggestion would be to sift all regional economic analyses sytematically; all those that are not explicitly concerned with formal methods or are not trying to extend theoretical instruments, should be related to the *problems* to whose solutions they are supposed to contribute. In these policy-orientated investigations, the methods used should be evaluated in view of the possibilities of serving as *instruments* for regional policies or programmes. One should, thus, focus on usefulness in contributing to the solution of concrete problems of regional policy, rather than simply stress e.g. the possibility of just *testing* certain hypotheses.

Since many regional development plans have been formulated without explicit references to theories or hypotheses underlying them, it is necessary for regional scientists to be in much closer contact with planners and politicians. The scientist must convince the politicians and planners of the use of his theories and instruments, and he must, in return, get information on actual problems and political restrictions. In particular, the scientist needs information on the way decision processes run in reality; he must try to recognize what the implicit values are. It is not enough just to demand an 'operationalization of explicitly formulated value judgments', or the establishment of priorities.

The problems that regional policy makers and regional planners have to deal with are too complex to allow for *simple* solutions. In any case, regional scientists alone cannot solve them, but need the co-operation of other scientists—sociologists, social psychologists, political scientists, geographers. Furthermore, regional scientists cannot *take over* the results of these other disciplines and then work with them. Operational models and solutions must be worked out in continuous—partly tedious, partly fascinating—co-operation and discussion among scientist in all of these diciplines.

The role of statistical information is, in many fields, crucial for the advancement of regional economics. At the same time it remains true that even on the basis of *available* data a great deal of additional empirical research is possible. The *problems* whose solutions are made more difficult by the statistical data deficiencies are related in particular to

- the development of *lagging* regions,
- *cyclical* changes as they affect various parts of the country,
- the availability of *infrastructure* services on levels that may be described as *equivalent* in different geographical areas,
- the solution of problems of *urban and metropolitan* areas. Adaptation processes may be described and analysed in a satisfactory way only if more data are available on
- spatial distributions of natural and produced resources (including infrastructure)
- spatial interrelationships—commodity flows, financial flows, information and communication flows, migration and commuting, in particular on the spread or diffusion of technical progress and the adaptation of production techniques to changing technological and economic conditions,

And all of this necessitates research on

- functional relationships and causal chains, and
  the effects of potential, regional policy measures, which, again, presupposes that the analyst knows
- what kinds of instruments are available and
  how policy measures are co-ordinated and executed.

(*a*) There is no doubt that the information system suggested here costs money. But the costs of continued muddling through are also substantial. I hope that the present paper contains arguments that can be used in a cost-benefit analysis and I am convinced that the result is a justification for undertaking the efforts.

(*b*) It is also obvious that the statistics which regional economics urgently needs are only part of the sum total of all of the information that has to be collected and evaluated. Therefore, there would be no use in working out a *separate scheme* for the organization of *regional data*. This has to be part of an overall information system whose organization I am not in a position to discuss here further.

(*c*) Such a system must be flexible, and it is in connection with the confidentiality regulations that the demand for flexibility of such an information system attains additional importance. A flexible organization of the databanks—the core of the sytem—should make it possible to aggregate the original data on an ad hoc basis and, thus, to make available much more different-rated statistics, as far as spatial units and categories are concerned, than would be possible if confidentiality regulations were applied in an undifferentiated way.

Summary of the Discussion

Professor Chamley introduced Professor von Böventer's report. He first gave a summary of it, for which purpose he briefly reviewed the contents of all its parts. The following points emerged particularly.

Although Regional Economics is ancillary to policy, and although it must take into account historical legacies and institutional surroundings, there is an interdependance between policy, theory, and information.

In this nexus, theoretical work and provision of data appear to be weak links. On the last point, information on which to build long run forecasts leaves most to be desired. However, more generally speaking, the limitations set to research by the lack of statistical data are stressed again and again. As to the research lag, apart from the difficulties inherent in the matter itself, it is being blamed on interdisciplinary barriers, and on the obnoxious influence of neo-classical economics.

In his comment, Professor Chamley reported himself in substantial agreement with Professor von Böventer on many of these points, especially when Professor von Böventer underlines the importance of political constraints and the weight of historical factors. For his own part, judging from contrasting experiences provided by the British 'Town and Country Planning', and by the French case, he suggested that a distinction might be drawn between small scale regional imbalance and large scale disequilibria, which are deep-rooted in history and geography. While in the first case strong personalities may seemingly succeed in doing miracles, nothing of this kind is to be expected in the second one, where wider constellations of data are to be taken into account, and forecasts pertain to futurology. On the other hand, much of what Professor von Böventer said about the deficiencies of existing information is largely borne out also by the French experience.

However, Professor Chamley was not convinced that externalities and cumulative processes were sufficient reasons for discarding neoclassical economics altogether.

Dr Biehl doubted that neoclassicism had interfered with regional development or data collection. On the conventional demand side, if a region is lagging, one might consider increasing the demand for its outputs but this is only a short-term solution. Long-term regional development is a function of the relative endowment with especially immobile and indivisible resources (ranging e.g. from climate and location to agglomeration and social overhead capital), and the productivity and wage relationship which determines the relative competitivity of this regional resource endowment. Up to a certain point, infusion of social overhead capital into lagging regions may encourage national growth; beyond that, the process would be basically one of regional redistribution. The data we need for such a supply-oriented approach to regional policy, centre on matters of comparative resource endowment, among them human capital, for adequately defined regions (e.g. labour market regions if employment is a policy goal).

Professor Blaug agreed that conventional Economics had tended to neglect regional problems, but denied that the historical record implies uselessness, once one attempts to apply the analysis.

Professor Giersch inquired what body of theory, might replace the conventional one. Was it Keynesian macroeconomics that in Professor von Böventer's view, he had in mind? Marxism in some form? Location theory or *Raumwirtschaft*? *Professor Giersch* feared that Professor von Böventer was also being too abstract, and not considering realities. He added that growth theory had also been inadequate, and suggested that regional production functions might be developed to take account of limitations of space and the existence of externalities.

Professor Johnson felt that the criticism of conventional Economics was directed at obsolete or misunderstood versions. Nothing in neoclassical doctrine, as he understands it, requires the maintenance of any sort of regional balance, or sets it up as a goal. The problem of the lag is primarily political constraint—political resistance to out-migration in the lagging region, and/or to in-migration in other regions. Viewed as Economics, *Professor Johnson* thought Regional Economics to be largely a collection of non-problems and nonsense problems. A region is a geographical concept. Consider, for example, the Highlands of Scotland. This region is lacking in resources, industry, and people. Why waste time and resources trying to develop it? Why not just leave it alone?

Professor Morgan said that regions are infinite in number. One cannot collect and store data for all regions on all topics at all times. Specialists should agree on sufficient theory for data to be collected on a 'nested' sample basis, and the results stored. *Professor Morgan* feared that Professor von Böventer's suggestions were uneconomic.

Dr Biehl insisted that public decisions, not only market forces, have disadvantaged certain regions. For flexibility, one should estimate some sort of minimum-size regions, then agglomerate over such regions. (Labour market areas are the sort of minimum-size regions *Dr Biehl* had in mind.)

Professor Johnson returned to the attack. The Canadian maritime provinces have been depressed for a century. Their comparative advantage appears to lie in the production of emigrants. Why engage in public intervention to alter this situation? (*Professor Bronfenbrenner* mentioned the Tennessee Valley Authority in the American South as a counter-example, and *Professor Kindleberger* the Italian *Mezzogiorno.*) In *Professor Johnson's* view, what happens in successful regional development is that people emigrate and industry immigrates, possibly after the supply of quite specific resources, and all on good neoclassical grounds.

For some reason, intervened *Professor Blaug*, people prefer to live in the 'wrong' places. Is not the explanation of this phenomenon what Regional Economics should be about? Professor Johnson implies that this branch of Economics need not exist, but there *are* such people as regional economists, with needs for data. Should we not do something for them? *Professor Johnson* agreed only that they should be free to do something for themselves to justify their own existence, but he was opposed to spending national resources on purely regional problems. As another horrible example, *Professor Johnson* mentioned a Cambridge University research project to devise social accounts for the local county (Cambridgeshire). This project took eight years, then fell apart. It should have been recognized as wasteful from the start.

Professor M. Perlman took a doctrinal-historical approach. Regional Economics has developed from neoclassical economics, he believed, on the basis of location theory, two important names being Lösch in Germany and E. M. Hoover in the United States. It later developed social accounts, and sometimes even input-output analyses. Demographic Economics grew from the same root, in analysing job needs and skills. Regional Economics may, indeed, have concentrated on nonsense problems, since there is no need for all areas to grow and some should, indeed, be permitted to decline.[1] But, on the other hand, neither librarians nor economists have any right to insist on people's justifying whatever claims they may choose to make for particular areas.

Professor Chamley observed that in opposing Professor von Böventer on that point, he did not mean to suggest that neoclassical economics could be sufficient by themselves, since information was biased in favour of existing regional structures. *Professor Tyler* claimed that the same analysis applied also to some national states, but *Dr Biehl* pointed out that since a region is part of a nation, it lacks the capacity for self-help through taxation that the nation has. *Professor Diaz-Alejandro* wondered whether Regional Economics has met any kind of 'market test' to justify survival as a discipline, but *Professor M. Perlman* denied that a market existed in the usual sense. *Professor Kindleberger* said that the different regional boundaries for different activities (finance, manufacturing, agriculture) made 'regions', as such, difficult to study. *Dr Biehl* replied that administrative units collect data and make decisions. It is these which deserve separate study. Pragmatically speaking, he approved of Professor Morgan's 'nested sample' strategy.

Professor Kindleberger felt that the regional economists present proposed to start with data to generate problems, whereas he preferred the contrary procedure on methodological grounds. *Professor Johnson's* position was that most data are inevitably generated by operating civil servants, so that the question was how much of it should be used and how much confined to dead storage.

Professor Shoup asserted that the regional aspects of Public Finance (local finance, inter-governmental fiscal relations) are alive and well. Special problems arose in governments where 'equity' was constitutionally required, e.g. the American States, and where political questions were inevitably involved.

Professor von Böventer, in summary, admitted that some Regional Economics was being done out of 'idle curiosity', but would not rule out the possibility that even these results might be of great value. As for data, there is great 'practical' demand by business firms, and a great deal supplied. Furthermore, the fact is that planning, administrative, marketing, etc. regions do exist.

The conference participants, in *Professor von Böventer's* view, seem to have no clear idea of what regional analysts do. They do, in fact, use neoclassical analysis, *plus* Keynesianism, plus other supplements. In many cases the usual assumptions of neoclassical theory—in particular with regard to the properties of production functions—are not justified when one studies regional problems.

One should bear in mind that there is a great difference between the position that wrong applications of neoclassical models have caused harm (as when *externatives* or *total conditions* v. marginal conditions were ignored) and the position that neoclassical theory should be discarded.

The whole paper discusses problems which one finds in *reality*, and tries to derive the data needs from these problems, not the other way around, and the focus is much more on supply characteristics than on the demand side.

Normatively speaking, *Professor von Böfessor* asserted that people should

[1] He reported personal failure in trying to interest colleagues and students in studying 'the Economics of Senescence', a counterpart of Economic Growth.

be allowed to live where they wish, and not be forced out by economic considerations. He felt that, within certain limits, they should be guaranteed minimum incomes wherever they choose to live. Possibly a trade-off approach—greater income for greater mobility—might be suggested. In some cases, he agreed, particular areas should be allowed to decline. But which ones? To answer this question, more data are needed to render more concrete the existing melange of theories.

16 Information Needs and Data Requirements for International Economic Research

William G. Tyler
UNIVERSITY OF FLORIDA

This paper argues that, barring a spectacular theoretical breakthrough, the greatest gains in the field of international economic research will come in the form of empirical work. Comparable to other fields of economics, the data relevant to international economic research are relatively reliable, complete, and conducive to more intensive use in useful quantitative empirical work. The paper provides a discussion of the major data sources available through international organizations, focusing on their limitations and presenting some suggestions for their improvement. In addition, problems of information retrieval and accessibility are briefly discussed, with the argument made that libraries should become more responsive to the needs of researchers by expanding their handling of machine readable data.

I. INTRODUCTION

There has long been manifested a certain uneasiness, expressed both by economists and policy-makers, about the established theory of international economics. In recent years, partly as a reflection of the concern over the theory itself and partly owing to the improved data availability, there has been a growing interest on the part of many economists for empirical testing of existing international economic theory and its challengers.[1] Much of the empirical research suggests that there are gaps between theory and observed reality. Moreover, many of the most important policy issues in international economics are clouded with misunderstanding. We know little, for example, even of a descriptive nature, about such questions as the trade and employment impacts of foreign direct investment and the other international implications of the increasingly important multinational corporations. Uncertainty and ignorance are also apparent in such vital concerns as (1) the employment and distributional effects of trade policy changes, (2) the implications of

[1] A good survey of empirical attempts to test trade theory is contained in Robert M. Stern [8].

the growing financial interdependency of countries, and (3) the environmental dimensions of international economic transactions. In view of such limits in our understanding, and barring a spectacular theoretical breakthrough, I believe that the greatest scientific contributions in the field of international economics, over the next decade or so, will come in the form of empirically oriented, i.e. econometric, research. This is not to suggest that there should be, or will be, a reversion to indicative empiricism or research efforts with little theoretical base or content. I am merely suggesting that large gains in economic understanding can be attained by using empirical analysis to assess, improve, and expand existing theory and those analytical tools which are already available. In contrast to some other fields in economics, the data base for such empirical efforts in international economics is relatively good.

To be sure, the development of increasingly sophisticated econometric tools, the advent of the computer, and the existence and growing availability of large amounts of quantitative information facilitate empirical and econometric work in international economics. Yet, even disregarding analytical and information problems for the moment, there are other noteworthy impediments and barriers to empirical research. First, such research is generally more expensive than are theoretical efforts since it frequently involves tedious data manipulation, expensive computer time, and programming assistance. In addition to the financial costs, empirical work normally involves greater time costs. In fact, team efforts, on a full time basis, are frequently necessary. Secondly, on the reward or benefit side, we must also ponder the individual incentives for doing empirical work in a profession where the greatest kudos and scholarly recognition are awarded to those contributing to the advance of theory. Consequently, unless it is more adequately funded than at present, I believe there will continue to operate professional disincentives to undertaking empirically oriented research in international economics.

Compounding the professional bias impeding empirical work, the information needs for doing theoretical research in economics are less complex. Well organized and current conventional libraries can aptly fill the information needs of most economic theorists. What is important is ready and quick access to the theoretical literature as it appears in journal article, book, and, perhaps, working paper form. To satisfy such requirements, even modest library resources can suffice. With the mushrooming of the scholarly literature and the quickened pace of scientific advance, library resource requirements have grown, and speed in acquisition and cataloguing has become increasingly important. Long publication lags accentuate the desirability of institutionally acquiring working papers on a regular basis.

To undertake empirical research in international economics, additional information needs are immediately apparent. A distinction can be made between historical and institutional research, on the one hand, and mainly quantitative research, on the other. The information needs for the former, while far more extensive than those for theoretical research, can still be readily handled by most conventional libraries. However, for more quantitatively oriented research, the information needs become more complex and are less easy for conventionally organized and funded libraries to satisfy. Statistical materials are required, which may or may not be available in published form. If published, publication is normally carried out by government statistical offices or international organizations. The library acquisition of such materials, especially those from the developing countries, is rendered more difficult than is the simple purchasing of books and journals, which is frequently effected through agents and almost always done through the mails. Even discounting the natural predilection of many traditional libraries to focus on books and serials, there are some special problems in acquiring statistical publications. With such materials one must know exactly what to look for, where to look, and how to proceed in their acquisition—for which normal commercial channels may not suffice. And few conventional libraries possess the resources adequate for successfully undertaking such acquisitions.

With statistical materials that are not published, yet are available for dissemination, the problems are still greater. Few libraries are presently equipped, either professionally or psychologically, to handle machine readable data. Yet, in the future to service researchers adequately in the field of international economics, or in other fields, it is essential that libraries be willing to hold and able to process such data. The rapid growth of data banks, expressly established for this purpose, highlights the growing demand for their rather unique services.

So far I have argued that impressive gains can be made in the field of international economics with empirically oriented research. I have also indicated some of the special problems in undertaking such work and in attaining the necessary statistical information. Yet, as mentioned earlier, there is now a wealth of information available to the researcher. The rest of the paper will involve (1) a discussion of the important data sources and requirements and (2) some suggestions for improving upon the available data base and its usage, consistent with the needs of empirical research in international economics.

II. EXISTING DATA AVAILABILITY

While the type of information and data required for empirical research in international economics varies according to the specific topic examined, several important, but not all-inclusive, data categories are noteworthy. They are: national economic statistical series, trade flow data, price information, tariff and other information related to trade restrictions, data on capital movements, and multinational firm operations. In the following pages these data categories will be discussed separately.

A. NATIONAL ECONOMIC STATISTICAL SERIES

International economic analysis is most relevant if it is undertaken in the context of national economies. An examination of trade flows, for example, is more meaningful, if it is related to the national economic characteristics of the trading countries. With the advent of the computer and improved national income accounting techniques, national income accounts, however estimated, are available for practically all of the countries in the world. Other national economic series, such as sectoral data, employment figures, and financial accounts vary greatly over countries in their coverage and quality, with the best information being available for the more developed countries.

Individual country governmental agencies and statistical offices normally publish much of the data that is collected and made available. However, the acquisition of this material by libraries, as indicated above, is frequently difficult and time consuming. Even if such materials were universally available, there still would be problems in using them for comparative research. Difficulties in language and presentational format render data comparison tedious, at best. More important still is the problem of the lack of comparability emanating from differences in national statistical systems. Fortunately, for some types of comparative research it is not necessary to resort to the statistical publications of individual countries. Since World War II, international organizations have played a major role in collecting data from individual countries, simplifying formats, and publishing statistical materials. Moreover, these same organizations have exercised decisive influence towards the standardization of the economic data series compiled by individual countries. For the economist interested in undertaking comparative empirical research in international economics, the data published by the international agencies constitutes the point of departure.

One of the primary concerns of the United Nations in standardizing and collecting statistical information has dealt with national income accounts. In fact, during the early postwar period, the UN provided effective assistance to a large number of developing countries to establish their own national income accounting systems. Thus, it is not surprising to find a certain degree of standardization in the different national collection, estimation, and accounting procedures. This has, undoubtedly facilitated the dissemination of national income data for different countries, with the UN being the main and central source of publication. Table 16.1 lists some of the major published sources of national income account information, along with those for other types of data relevant for research in international economics. Making international comparisons

TABLE 16.1 REPRESENTATIVE STATISTICAL PUBLICATIONS OF INTERNATIONAL ORGANIZATIONS WITH INFORMATION OF RELEVANCE FOR INTERNATIONAL ECONOMIC RESEARCH

Type of Data (Principal Category)	*Publishing Agency*	*Name of Publication or Form of Dissemination*	*When Published*	*Data and Informational Features*
National Economic Statistical Series	UN	*Yearbook of National Income Account Statistics*	Annually	National income amount data
National Economic Statistical Series	UN	(a) *Statistical Yearbook* (b) *Monthly Bulletin of Statistics* (c) *World Economic Survey*	Annually Monthly	National income accounts, population, manpower, mining, manufacturing, construction, energy, agriculture, international trade, wages and prices, finance
National Economic Statistical Series	OECD	(a) *National Accounts of OECD Countries* (b) *National Accounts of Less Developed Countries*	Irregularly Irregularly	National income accounts National income accounts
National Economic Statistical Series	IBRD	(a) *World Tables* (b) *Trends in Developing Countries*	Irregularly Irregularly	National income accounts, population, employment, socio-economic indicators, trade, external indebtedness
National Economic Statistical Series	FAO	(a) *FAO Commodity Review and Outlook* (b) *Agricultural Commodity Projections* (c) *Production Yearbook* (d) *Food Balance Sheets*	Annually Irregularly Annually Irregularly	Agricultural output and consumption, some price information
National Economic Statistical Series	ILO	(a) *Yearbook of Labour Statistics* (b) *Bulletin of Labour Statistics*	Annually Quarterly	Employment, wage, and manpower data
National Economic Statistical Series	IMF	*International Financial Statistics*	Monthly, with periodic supplements	International reserves, aggregate trade, foreign exchange, money stock, credit, prices, government finances
National Economic Statistical Series	UN	*Demographic Yearbook*	Annually	Demographic information
National Economic Statistical Series	OAS	*America en Cifras*	Annually	Western hemisphere country information on population, agriculture, industry, trade, transportation, balance of payments, national income accounts, finance, wages, prices, consumption

International Trade Flows	UN	*Yearbook of International Trade Statistics*	Annually	Individual country, SITC disaggregated imports and exports in US dollars, world trade totals by regions and countries, total world exports by provenance and destination for regions and principal countries, price and quantum indexes of trade
International Trade Flows	IMF	*Direction of Trade*	Monthly	Individual country export and import totals by destination and provenance
International Trade Flows	UN	*Commodity Trade Statistics*, Series D	Annually	Individual country exports and imports disaggregated by commodities and listed by destination and provenance
International Trade Flows	GATT	*International Trade*	Annually	Trade flow aggregates
International Trade Flows	UNCTAD	*Handbook of International Trade and Development Statistics*	Irregularly	Developing country trade and balance of payments information, network of world exports, by selected commodity classes and by regions of origin and destination, developing country national income accounts and other economic indicators
International Economic Transaction Flows	IMF	*Balance of Payments Yearbook*	Annually	Individual country balance of payments data
International Economic Transaction Flows	BIS	*Annual Report of the Bank for International Settlements*	Annually	International financial and currency market data
Trade Restrictions	GATT	*Basic Documentation for Tariff Study*	1970	Tariff and trade summaries by BTN headings, tariff and trade profiles by product categories, tariff and trade profiles by stages of processing

Source: relevant publications as indicated.

with national income account estimates is subject to widely recognized limitations. While in one series the UN publishes country data denominated in a standard currency unit, i.e. US dollars, it also provides information as to what exchange rate was used for conversion purposes. In addition to UN publications, both the OECD and the World Bank publish national income accounts, making some adjustments to national data different from those made by the UN.

While not as comprehensive or complete as national income account data, sectoral information is also published by the UN agencies, with industry, commodity, and country disaggregation frequently apparent. Probably the best of this information is for manufacturing, where data collection problems seem to be less severe. Much effort has been devoted by the UN to standardizing manufacturing data, and the revised international standard industrial classification (ISIC) presents a system by which most countries now classify, or roughly classify, their manufacturing data. Agricultural data compilation and organization present other problems. While these are largely unsurmounted, the best data available are published by the FAO. The statistical information for other sectors in national economies is rather spotty and not amenable to aggregation. What is available on a comparable basis, again, is published by the UN.

Population, manpower, and employment data from individual countries are also collected and published by UN agencies. Especially active is the ILO, whose publications constitute the best single source of such materials. Financial information, frequently essential to international economic research, is available in a number of forms. The most convenient and comprehensive is the IMF's *International Financial Statistics*, which is also computerized and available in the form of machine readable tape.

Census information, both demographic and economic, constitutes another important data source in most countries. While summary tabulations are generally published in the individual countries concerned, library acquisition in other countries is frequently difficult, and at best comparative research employing census materials is a painstaking process. Other than some use of the broad aggregates in UN statistical publications, there is little systematic collection, centralization, and dissemination of census materials on an international basis. This type of information is best made available through dissemination by data banks and archives maintaining files of machine readable data. There are already in existence several such facilities, holding country census files or samples (e.g. the Centro Latinoamericano de Demografia (CELADE) and the Latin American Data Bank at the University of Florida).[2] It can

[2] For a discussion of data banking and a description of the data sets available for social science research on Latin America through the principal existing data facilities see William G. Tyler, ed. [10].

be expected that the future will witness a growing demand for such services in social science research.

B. INTERNATIONAL TRADE FLOWS

Of all the data utilized in empirical, international economic research, the most heavily used and relied upon is information on trade itself. These data are among the most extensive available in economics. In many countries, international trade time series, at least at the aggregated level, go back into the nineteenth century or before. The reason for the relative length of these time series is that trade statistics are relatively easy to compile, with foreign trade frequently being transacted through one, or a small number of ports. In addition, since, historically, taxes on trade have constituted the major source of public revenue for many countries, it is natural that reasonably good records were kept. Detailed disaggregation of trade figures, both by commodities and markets, normally comes at later stages, but, in general, even these more disaggregated time series are reasonably complete in many countries for extended periods of time.

Undertaking research comparing the trade flows and performance of two or more countries quickly becomes a complicated task if the nationally published statistics are used. Library collections are apt to be incomplete, and the data, at least on a disaggregated basis, may be incomparable. As in the case of national income accounting, the United Nations has played an important role, not only in collecting information from different countries, but, also, in trying to bring about the standardization of the trade statistics that are compiled.[3] On the whole these efforts have been rather successful.

Pre-dating the activities of the UN agencies, international co-operative efforts to standardize and compile international trade statistics date back at least one hundred years. With the blossoming of international commerce during the Industrial Revolution and the growth in the relative importance of trade in the economic life of individual countries, there was a clear need to know more about the nature and pattern of trade relations. Therefore, during the latter part of the nineteenth century, serious attention was devoted to problems of the uniformity of customs nomenclature, product classification, valuation, and market denomination. This attention and its concomitant deliberations culminated in the Brussels Convention of 1913, setting forth certain guidelines and providing for the compilation of international trade statistics. Publications of these data, according to a standard classification, was initiated and subsequently improved upon by the later statistical work of the League of Nations. Although publication ceased with the advent of World War II, in many

[3] For an early discussion of UN efforts to improve and standardize trade data see R. G. D. Allen and J. Edward Ely, eds. [1].

cases national statistical systems were improved during that war owing to the necessity for wartime economic planning.

The period since the end of World War II has witnessed an acceleration of international co-operative efforts to standardize, compile and disseminate international trade statistics. The League's trade classification system was scrapped by a UN special commission in favour of a new system that is far more detailed, yet thought to be more amenable to compilations on a quarterly basis. The new system—the Standard International Trade Classification (SITC)—was formally endorsed in 1950 and has been subjected to some minor changes since then. At the present time, nearly all of the world's countries either use the SITC system in their own compilations or have introduced cross-referencing to enable the UN to publish their trade data on a basis comparable to other countries.

The first issue of the *Yearbook of International Trade Statistics*, including trade data for over 90 individual countries, was published by the United Nation's Statistical Office in 1951. Since then, additional countries have been included and minor improvements have been made in the statistical presentation. Individual country exports and imports are published according to the SITC system. World totals are also published, not by commodity, but by regional and principal country totals. Other than for regions and a few industrialized countries, trade data published in the *Yearbook* are not directional, i.e. no attention is paid to the destination of exports or the origin of a country's imports. The International Monetary Fund, however, has compiled and published aggregate directional trade data since 1949 in its *Direction of Trade*. This series is now published monthly and is also available in a magnetic tape version.

For the researcher who is interested simultaneously in both the commodity composition and the direction of international trade, the data are less conveniently available and are, therefore, more difficult to work with. Fortunately, the UN publishes a commodity and directional breakdown of trade flows for individual countries in its *Commodity Trade Statistics*, Series D, with the commodity disaggregation listed first. Countries are listed individually and the published volumes appear as the national data become available. The UN has computerized the information published in the *Commodity Trade Statistics* up to the four digit SITC level. While the availability of these tapes to outside academic research institutions is uncertain, their use could greatly facilitate international economic research.[4]

One of the problems entailed in using Series D of the *Commodity Trade Statistics* is that data for some countries, mostly small ones, are

[4] To illustrate this point, reference can be made to the existing econometric research on international trade flows—most of which either concentrate on commodity composition or on total directional flows, but seldom on both. For example, one of the pioneering analyses in the field is that of Hans Linnemann [7]. Yet, Linnemann's study focuses almost entirely on the direction of total trade flows.

not included. These countries either do not report their trade statistics or do not report them in the SITC format. To overcome the latter problem, the UN Statistical Office has attempted to reorganize incomplete data along lines similar to the SITC system. These data, while not published, are stored on magnetic tape. Again, accessibility to this information by scholarly institutions would appear to be warranted on efficiency grounds.

Another problem in comparability is more serious. In order to make many types of international economic research meaningful it is necessary to relate trade performance to the domestic economies and the economic policies of individual countries. While the standardization of an industrial classification system (the ISIC) and of a trade classification system (the SITC) represent major statistical accomplishments of international organizations since World War II, these two systems are not readily comparable. Although the UN does publish a manual cross-indexing the ISIC and the SITC systems, the conversion of trade data to an ISIC basis is, at the very best, a laborious task. The cross-referencing could be easily computerized, and it would be a relatively simple matter for the UN Statistical Office to publish trade data according to an ISIC format. Such a service would constitute an important aid to research.

A further comparability complication is apparent when one tries to relate tariff schedules to trade and production data. For most countries, tariff information is not available either on an ISIC or a SITC basis. It is generally kept in a highly detailed and disaggregated form according to the Brussels Tariff Nomenclature (BTN). Again, the UN or, possibly, the GATT, could perform a major service to economic research by cross-referencing the BTN with the ISIC and SITC systems and periodically publishing tariff, production, and trade data on a comparable basis.

Another major contribution by international organization in bringing about the standardization and improvement of data relating to international economics transactions has occurred through the efforts of the International Monetary Fund dealing with balance of payments data. The extensive use of the Fund's *Balance of Payments Manual* and the frequent provision of technical assistance by the IMF to individual countries has led to considerable improvement in both the quality and comparability of balance of payments statistics. Using the *Manual* format, the Fund has, since 1949, published balance of payments data for its member countries in its *Balance of Payments Yearbook*. The Fund's balance of payments accounting system, as outlined in the *Manual*, not only determines what information is available on an internationally comparable basis, but, for a large part, it also determines what information is available on an individual country basis, as most countries now base their data collection systems on the IMF format.

While the Fund's balance of payments methodology and definitions have been subjected to periodic modifications and improvements, there are clearly some components in the balance of payments accounts for which the information collected and published is not completely satisfactory for research purposes. The data for movements of merchandise, i.e. commodity trade flows, are sufficient in terms of reliability and detail of coverage. Also, as indicated above, there are a number of other statistical sources which provide commodity trade data in varying detail. This is not the case, however, with most other types of information reflected in the balance of payments. Information shortcomings, which will be treated separately below, exist for capital flow data. Even in the current account of the balance of payments, statistical incompleteness exists, thereby precluding some types of international economic research. For example, there exists a relative paucity of statistical information on international trade in invisibles. Yet, such trade is of considerable importance. Aggregating figures published in the *Balance of Payments Yearbook* for 1958, Devons conservatively estimated that invisible items accounted for about 28 per cent of total world trade [4]. More complete information on foreign investment income and on payments for technology, to mention but two types of data, is essential for research on the changing international economic order. Tourism has also recently grown in economic importance in many countries, but extensive tourism and travel information is not readily available from balance of payments figures. It is suggested that the IMF (1) broaden its current account balance of payments coverage to reflect international service transactions more adequately and (2) that it encourages the upgrading and extended collection of such information on the part of member countries.

C. PRICE INFORMATION

One of the main concerns of international economic research has been the role of comparative cost and advantage in the determination of trade flows. Price information can also be of crucial importance in explaining developments in the balance of payments for different trading countries. Price information for these types of research, while always considered highly valuable, has not generally been sufficient to base comprehensive research efforts entirely upon it. Some information on international prices does exist on an aggregated level, but index number problems, aggregation difficulties, and other conceptual limitations abound. Most of the available price data is unit value information, constructed from value and weight measures of trade.

Many of the UN publications dealing with trade, e.g. the *Yearbook of International Trade Statistics*, publish aggregate export and import price indexes, based on unit value calculations, for the different regions of the world, along with accompanying series of the net barter terms of trade for these developed and developing regions. More detailed unit value information can frequently be computed from the disaggregated trade data itself as published in country tables. In the case of agricultural commodities, the resultant unit value estimates are much more meaningful than those made for non-standardized, manufactured goods, even at high levels of disaggregation, although one may find some research use of the unit value of manufactured products as providing something of an index to the embodied technology. In any case, direct price observations are vastly superior to unit value measures, but there is little such information collected and made available in the international statistical publications—other than some direct price data for agricultural commodities published in the FAO's *Production Yearbook*.

The difficulties in using unit value information in research are now widely recognized. Clearly, improved international price information would constitute an important contribution to research potentiality in international economics. The most promising approach to improve price information is that suggested in a recent study by Kravis and Lipsey [6]. They advocate the establishment of a clearinghouse system of trading export price information, that would, presumably, be best organized under the auspices of an international agency. With such information from trading firms and government organizations, price indexes based upon actual prices or price offers, not on unit values, could be constructed. Furthermore, the price indexes should reflect export prices, not domestic transaction prices, for exporting countries, and the indexes for different countries should pertain to the same basket of goods. The work by Kravis and Lipsey indicates that such international price indexes can be computed without excessive difficulties. It is to be hoped that international organization will interest itself in this important task.

D. INFORMATION ON TRADE RESTRICTIONS

One of the greatest empirical quagmires in international economic research is that of restrictions on international trade. Although, for the most part, the problems involved are not overly complex theoretically, the relative paucity of information makes empirical research time-consuming and difficult. Tariff information is sparse and relatively inaccessible, while precise information on nontariff trade restrictions is still harder to come by. In view of the successive reduction of tariffs by developed countries to relatively low levels, much recent attention by economists has been focused on nontariff barriers to trade.[5] Yet there is no systematic descriptive delineation of the various forms of such trade impediments and their quantitative magnitude for different countries. What information does exist is in the form of individual country studies.

The situation regarding tariff information is a little better. While frequently unwieldy, tariff schedules can usually be obtained for in-

[5] For an example, see Robert E. Baldwin [2].

dividual countries through domestic agencies or importer organizations. On an internationally comparable basis, GATT has made some efforts to centralize, collect, and disseminate tariff schedules, primarily in conjunction with multilateral trade negotiations. As a part of these efforts, the GATT secretariat has assembled highly disaggregated machine readable tariff and import files for the principal developed signatory countries.[6] From these detailed files, presumably unavailable to the scholarly community, GATT, in 1970, published some summary tables in three separate volumes, all bearing the title *Basic Documentation for Tariff Study*. In addition to this comparative information, the spate of interest in effective protection has resulted in a number of empirical studies quantifying the structure and level of protection for a number of different countries. Yet, much of this work is incomparable and, therefore, not conducive to undertaking comparative studies.[7] To be sure, a more systematic and comprehensive compilation of information on trade restrictions would be beneficial for international economic research.

E. CAPITAL FLOWS AND MULTINATIONAL FIRM OPERATIONS

As stated above, nonmerchandise movements in the balance of payments are less adequately recorded than are commodity transactions. Short term capital flows, for instance, are inherently more difficult to measure than are most other types of international economic transactions. Yet, in a world rendered increasingly small economically through improved communications, increased trade, and multinational firm operations, short term capital movements have become increasingly important as a cause of balance of payments instability. At the same time, however, many gaps exist in our understanding of international capital flows. Both theoretical and empirical research are needed to bridge some of the existing gaps. For the empirical study of short term and portfolio capital movements, individual country balance of payments and financial data are required. The available data base, with the exception of some disguising of credit and debit flows in the listing of only net flows is largely satisfactory for macroanalyses.

In all types of international economic research, data available at the firm level are extremely scarce. This is dramatically illustrated by the paucity of information on multinational firm operations. While there has been a rush of scholarly literature on multinational firms, there still exists remarkably little concrete understanding of the way in which such firms operate in the international economy and the overall impact of foreign direct investment on international trade. Gaps exist with respect to both

[6] For a description of these files and the GATT tariff study the reader is referred to GATT [5].

[7] A notable exception is Bela Balassa and Associates [3].

theoretical and empirical knowledge. Data on multinational firm output, exports, input structure, profitability, transfer prices, and factor usage are largely unavailable in any form.

A number of studies and information gathering efforts are currently under way to analyse the operations of multinational firms, including those organized by the United Nations under the auspices of the UNCTAD.

The most ambitious and comprehensive attempt, to my knowledge, to generate and analyse increased multinational firm information is that of the Harvard Multinational Enterprise Study, directed by Raymond Vernon. The Vernon group has painstakingly assembled a data bank covering some 187 United States-based multinational firms and about 200 large non-United States enterprises. A number of studies relying on this data base have already been published,[8] and it evidently is the intention to make the data bank available to outside scholars for analytical purposes.

In a period in which we have witnessed the dramatic growth of international organization and of international co-operative efforts in the economic sphere, it is somewhat surprising to find no international institution whose function it is to establish rules of conduct for international direct investment. The proliferation of multinational firms throughout the world in recent years underscores the need for such an institution, preferably based upon some sort of international consensus about foreign investment behaviour. Even in the absence of well defined agreement, an international organization might prove useful for establishing a livable standard of good behaviour. Should some sort of international institution, primarily concerned with international direct investment, eventually be established, as I believe it should, one of its tasks, important for economic research, should be the compilation and publication of information on multinational firm operations.

III. CONCLUDING REMARKS

In the past few pages I have sketched out the various statistical series, published by international organizations, which are important for international economic research. In doing so, I have made some suggestions specifically as to improving data coverage, collection, and comparability. In general, the data base—at least in comparison with other areas of economics—is relatively good. Even without further refinements, the available stock of statistical information can profitably be employed to bring about important contributions to our knowledge of the international economic order and the functioning of the international economy, both by testing and building upon existing theory.

[8] See, for example, Raymond Vernon [11], and John M. Stopford and Louis T. Wells, Jr. [9].

National data collecting agencies could contribute to research capabilities by further standardizing their own statistical systems in accordance with UN or accepted international practices. If such standardization, for one reason or another, is not considered desirable by individual countries, data cross-referencing, while not entailing great difficulties on the part of data collecting agencies, would considerably facilitate the task of making the data comparable at some later point. For developing countries, technical assistance from international agencies for improving statistical systems and increasing data standardization is highly desirable.

For their part, in the last thirty years, the international organizations have become the major repositories of national economic information of interest to researchers in international economics. The international institutions have responded sympathetically to the statistical responsibility thrust upon them, but there is still room for improvement in the dissemination of information for research purposes. International agencies collecting data but not publishing or otherwise making them available should be urged to do so. The World Bank, for example, has established a large socio-economic data bank containing a 20-year time series of about 165 variables for some 140 countries[9] and, while the Bank has had the intention of making this valuable data resource available to outside researchers, the status at present is unclear. One way to facilitate a wider dissemination of statistical information is through a wider reliance on machine readable data files. Those international institutions which possess computerized data holdings should be urged to make them available to academic data archives and libraries on a marginal cost basis.

Libraries should become more data conscious and computerized to respond properly to the needs of empirical research in economics. The capacity to handle machine readable data will become increasingly more important if libraries are to continue to provide adequate information services to economic researchers. While such innovations may be considered extremes by most conventionally minded and trained library managers, the changes are essential.

REFERENCES

[1] Allen, R. G. D. and Ely, J. Edward, eds., *International Trade Statistics* (New York: Wiley, 1953).

[2] Baldwin, Robert E., *Nontariff Distortions of International Trade* (Washington: Brookings Institution, 1970).

[3] Balassa, Bela and Associates, *The Structure of Protection in Developing Countries* (Baltimore, Md.: Johns Hopkins University Press, 1971).

[4] Devons, Ely. 'World Trade in Invisibles,' *Lloyds Bank Review*, New Series, No 6 (April, 1961), p. 39.

[9] For a description of IBRD data systems see William G. Tyler, ed. [10], pp. 119–21.

[5] GATT. Activities in 1969/70 and Activities in 1970/71 (New York: Unipub.).

[6] Kravis, Irving B. and Lipsey, Robert E., *Price Competitiveness in World Trade* (New York: Columbia University Press, 1971).

[7] Linnemann, Hans, *An Econometric Study of International Trade Flows* (Amsterdam: North-Holland, 1966).

[8] Stern, Robert M. 'Testing Trade Theories,' paper presented at the Conference on Research in International Trade and Finance, March 30–31, 1973, Princeton University.

[9] Stopford, John M. and Wells, Louis T., Jr., *Managing the Multinational Enterprises: Organizations of the Firms and Ownership of the Subsidiaries* (New York: Basic Books, 1972).

[10] Tyler, William G., ed., *Data Banks and Archives for Social Science Research on Latin America* (Gainesville, Florida: Consortium of Latin American Studies Programs, 1975).

[11] Vernon, Raymond, *Sovereignty at Bay: The Multinational Spread of U.S. Enterprises* (New York: Basic Books, 1971).

Summary of the Discussion

Professor Tyler's paper was presented by *Mr Hibbert*, who found its main motivation in Professor Tyler's dissatisfaction with the allegedly relevant theory. Contemporary international economic theory, said Professor Tyler, is not, in general, borne out. There is at present no clear understanding of the effects of the operations of multinational corporations on the domestic economy. As for the empirical work in International Economics, it is not well funded or recognized professionally. Yet, it is argued, very substantial gains in our knowledge can now be made through empirical work in international economics.

The main gaps in the data are quantitative. Libraries do not know where to look for it, especially in the absence of formal publication. The data, themselves, are, for the most part, derived from national accounts. They have been standardized by international agencies—a good starting point, but inconsistencies remain and detail is inadequate. On trade flows, there are good time series, with commodity classifications standardized according to the Brussels Convention. The International Monetary Fund (IMF) and various UN agencies have improved the data further after 1945, and they are of great value. They are, however, not well adapted for input-output work, and are not completely congruent as between countries. (Similar conclusions apply to tariff classifications and customs receipts data.) Balance of Payments (BP) data are weak as far as invisibles and short-term capital movements are concerned. Data on international prices remain poor; Professors Kravis and Lipsey have criticized indirect methods of finding proxies by trade volumes and trade 'quanta'. A clearing house may be established for international price data, including both prices paid and prices received. On tariff and non-tariff barriers to trade, data are poor. As for capital flows, the internal ones within (MNC's) are the weakest spot in a poor set of data. A Harvard Business School study under the direction of Professor Raymond Vernon is the best we have on the MNC's. It is unfortunate that no international agency has yet proposed a standard 'code of conduct' for these organizations, but compilations of specific decisions and rulings should be attempted. In general, national agency reports should be made congruent with international ones; this reform would be particularly useful to LDCs. And, finally, data should be available from more libraries in machine-readable form.

In the first comment from the floor, *Dr Schwartz* maintained that Professors Krause and Lipsey had done, at the Brookings Institution, much of what Professor Tyler had wanted, and that the work was proceeding on a continuing basis.

Dr Horn doubted that prices had much to do with BP under regimes of flexible exchange rates. He also doubted that progress in this field (or many others) must be predominantly empirical and computer-oriented. He saw some danger of neglecting new questions and problems for the sake of further refining existing data.

Mr Fetterman inquired whether libraries have failed to collect basic data in numerical form. He wondered also how much Professor Tyler might be willing to pay for how much additional speed in obtaining it.

Professor Bronfenbrenner criticized Professor Tyler's paper as reflecting 'immanent empiricism', the doctrine that if one examined enough facts hard enough, their meaning and significance would automatically become clear through some mystical process of instant enlightenment or *satori.*

Professor von Böventer inquired whether fixed production functions were not being generally assumed in international trade theory. He would himself prefer their replacement by input-output analysis. He also thought the 'product cycle' to be more important than either the paper or its discussant had made it.

Mr Evans referred to libraries as data suppliers, and inquired how they could convert to machine-readability. They did back away from supplying data in this form, because they are not technically equipped to provide it. They have inadequate budgetary support and, at many institutions, their relations with the corresponding computation centres are not of the best. *Mr Evans* doubted the possibility of turning any librarian into a computer scientist 'on the cheap'.

Professor Kindleberger turned the group's attention to Project LINK, which sought to construct a model of the world economy from country models of national economies. He hoped that it is not being anticipated that each library should duplicate Project LINK's ambitious activities.

Professor Blaug saw no reason for storing machine-readable data in libraries and doubted that this was a serious proposal. Storage should be at computer centres and specialized institutes, not at ordinary all-purpose libraries. *Mrs N. Perlman*, however, claimed that the University Pittsburgh and the Carnegie-Mellon University both do, in fact, store machine-readable data and avoid duplication. *Dr Schwartz* added that in many cases a terminal in a library is enough. *Professor M. Perlman* raised the issue of payment for the costs of transforming data into machine-readable form. *Professor Morgan* also objected to Professor Wolfe's suggestion that data be reserved for computer-centre storage. He said that such a proposal would be wasteful, because of the danger of *n* people on a single campus ordering the same data separately *n* times from a computer centre, with no user knowing of the others' existence. Professor Wolfe agreed that payment for data banking will be a real inter-departmental fight however it was done, and foresaw the economists competing with other academic departments for library purchases of machine-readable data.

Mrs N. Perlman shifted the subject. She wished to see more concern with both promptness and accuracy in international economic data and wished that UN agencies, in particular, were more speed- and accuracy-conscious.

On MNC, *Professor Kindleberger* feared that the UN Commission would not be helpful, because its staff is largely biased and seeks mainly to accumulate evidence for pre-established positions. He criticized Professor Vernon's Harvard Business School data as being more useful for Business Administration than for Economics. He also felt that data were of dubious comparability over time or space when collected under different exchange regimes: Fixed rates? Fluctuating rates? Special drawing rights (SDR's)? Pre-1914 gold standard rules? *Professor Diaz-Alejandro* replied that the IMF is keeping accounts in SDR's, but has not yet seriously considered going back in time and putting all of its data on this basis.

Professor Tyler began his reply by specifying the role of econometric analysis in International Economics as one tool among others; he did not think that the charge of 'immanent empiricism' was justified against either his paper or his general methodology. He did feel it better to use trade data even with errors—a problem no worse than in many other fields—in preference to theorizing with no data whatever. On library problems, he had found his main difficulty to be the obtaining of LDC data, since he thought that libraries prefer to use their funds for book purchases. If international organizations are slow in providing data, this is primarily because participating governments are slow. (*Mr Hibbert* suggested, on this point, that international agencies could adjust governments' regular statistical reports.) The reason that *Professor Tyler* wants libraries in the data-banking business is that no one else is doing it better. University data banks do even worse, mainly because of problems of funding, organizational structure and academic orientation. (*Dr Schwartz* suggested the use of commercial data banks in such cases, despite the added cost.)

17 Data Needs in Development Economics

Carlos F. Dias-Alejandro*
YALE UNIVERSITY

This paper first reviews the progress made since the Second World War in data availability for development research, mainly in the field of macroeconomic aggregates. It then focuses on data sources and data-gathering techniques deemed to be the most promising for large pay-offs in further development research. Greater understanding of the structure and workings of the modern sector of market-oriented developing countries could be obtained by analysing data on the 200 largest corporations in each country. But exclusive emphasis on large companies would neglect some very important research areas, such as income distribution, unemployment/underemployment and extreme poverty. The fresh data needed to get a firmer understanding of these matters are likely to come from the greater use of sample surveys.

I

There is much to be said for the argument that there are no facts without theory. But there is also some force in the line, that 'if you cannot measure it, it does not exist'. Theories of economic development and growth provide weak and uncertain guidance to empirical researchers in development economics, so that progress in this area is likely to arise from the interplay of hypotheses borrowed or adapted with laborious empirical work, from *all* branches of economics. In this process, standard economic theory itself should become richer by its greater exposure to Third World circumstances. Note how, nowadays, macroeconomists of industrialized countries try to catch up, after many years of neglect, with the inflationary experience of some Latin American countries, an experience which includes many instances of the 'stagflation' which fits so uneasily into standard models.

This paper, then, supposes that there is no shortage of hypotheses, hunches and insights which could be tested against Third World data, nor a lack of analytically oriented concepts, as phrased by Simon

* Comments on an earlier draft by Benjamin I. Cohen, Simon Kuznets and Hugh Patrick are gratefully acknowledged. The paper also benefited from discussions at the 1975 Kiel seminar of the International Economic Association.

Kuznets, to guide us (even if tentatively) in translating raw primary data into quantitative economic measures. The problem is choosing the more interesting hypotheses, establishing insightful categories, and finding or generating fresh data. Indeed, the latter aspect is so serious that one increasingly prefers to read papers which involve no elaborate hypotheses but present new solid data about an interesting issue without more than a coherent 'story' to bring the numbers together.

There has been a tendency, in the area of development economics, to manufacture pseudo-theories to explain pseudo-facts, often leading without much pause to persistent policy advocacy. The excuse that 'data are not there' has been used to justify much nonsense. Some of the most interesting work done in the development area, in recent years, involves this systematic examination of empirical evidence, which ends up giving a picture of reality significantly different from that commonly assumed in both the theorizing and policy-making of development. Examples include the Kindleberger work on terms of trade, that of MacBean on export instability and, more recently, the work of several authors on the nature and extent of the problem of marginality and unemployment. We will return to this type of empirical work below.

Rather than providing an exhaustive list of all data which it would be good to have, this paper will focus on data sources and techniques of obtaining data which, in my view, promise the largest pay-offs in development research. Such a view, of course, reflects my judgment as to which are the most interesting and important researchable topics in the area, as well as about how contemporary capitalistic developing economies work. Analysts with different interests in the pure research-policy spectrum, or located in other parts of the world, or with different preconceptions, could very well come out with different conclusions. Before getting into all that, one should start by reviewing the major progress made during the post-Second World War period in data availability for development research.

II

Much has been accomplished, during the last two-and-a-half decades, in expanding the data base available for researchers in economic development. The starting point was meagre, indeed: in 1950, the developing countries with national accounts, input-output tables and flow-of-funds tables were few. But, by 1975, just about every developing country appears in United Nations publications with *some* kind of national accounts, and an increasing number of countries boast of other components of comprehensive macroeconomic statistics, including those on international transactions and in the monetary field.

With all of their problems (and they have many), these masses of data have supported a narrowing of our ignorance regarding the process of growth and structural change which, by historical standards, must be rated as very impressive. The Kuznets–Chenery 'laws of development', of course, could not have been produced without such a data base. Those observed regularities and the discipline of available national accounts have limited fanciful and sterile debates (although perhaps less than they should have), channelling hypothesis-generation toward more fruitful areas. Furthermore, these data are, on the whole, easily available in the national and international publications that are found in most libraries all over the world.

Besides their usefulness for comparative work on growth and structural change, national accounts, in some developing countries, have been pushed back at least into the 1930s and 1920s, stimulating research on such topics as how well different types of developing countries fared during the Great Depression, and also providing longer time series for testing secular views on growth and structural change.

It is not a difficult task to point out that, in spite of the great deal accomplished in the area of national accounts, many gaps and imperfections remain. In many developing countries, the raw data on which the accounts are based leave much to be desired; furthermore, it is not clear that these matters are improving with time. In some countries, after an initial burst of enthusiasm in setting up the national accounts system, the collection and processing of raw data stagnate and are surpassed by the changing economic reality of the country. Increasingly, the frequent result is misleading national accounts. In some cases, the preparation of national accounts has drawn resources away from government statistical offices that generate raw primary data, leading to a decline in their output.

Most developing countries have not moved much beyond minimum national accounts. Input-output tables, flow-of-funds and, particularly, aggregate income distribution estimates remain relatively rare. Where they exist, it is even rarer to find systematic efforts for periodic actualizations of those tables. Even the core national accounts are seldom available at intervals more frequent than every year; quarterly series remain a rarity in developing countries. Indeed, prompt short-term economic indicators in developing countries are extremely scarce. Cyclical macroeconomic management in developing countries, an area neglected in the literature, typically evolves amidst great uncertainty as to what is really going on in the economy.

In the area of cross-country comparisons, the data base has not allowed an adequate separation of 'true' structural differences from those which show up in national accounts data simply because of differences in relative prices from country to country. One example which I have frequently used involves the substantial differences found in the relative prices of capital goods from country to country, differences which cast serious doubts about the meaningfulness of frequently seen comparisons of rates of capital formation among countries. Comparisons across input-output tables are also hampered by differences in relative price structures.

But it is not my intention to build up to an across-the-board plea for more and better national accounts in developing countries.[1] At zero opportunity cost, that, of course, would be splendid, and would stimulate some good research. But, given high opportunity costs and my preferences regarding research priorities, I will proceed to more specific pleading.

III

Aggregation into national macroeconomic magnitudes has been recognized for a long time as a less defensible procedure for developing than for developed countries, given the greater structural and regional heterogeneity of the former. If the national accounts were put together from regional and sectoral bits and pieces in such a way that disaggregation were only a matter of running the adding-up machinery backwards, much of the following discussion would be unnecessary. In fact, aggregate investment is not typically obtained from adding up estimates of all firms' investments, but from imports of machinery and equipment plus construction licences issued; national savings are derived as a residual from other magnitudes, and so on. In most countries, national accounts emerges as a precious package, and attempts to decompose it run the risk of leaving the researcher empty-handed.

Unless the national accounts of developing countries are substantially improved (an unlikely prospect), the juice which can be further extracted from them, either in time series or cross-section studies, appears limited. A more promising path toward greater understanding of the structure and workings of the *modern* sector of market-oriented developing countries would be to focus on, say, the characteristics of the 200 largest private corporations in each country. One can conjecture that such a group accounts for nearly all of the output generated by 'dynamic' industrial branches, public utilities and large-scale mining. Their share of private capital formation, outside of housing and consumer durables, is also likely to be very large. The same group will also account for a dominant share of foreign trade and of international capital flows. If, to that group, one adds the 30 or so largest public and banking enterprises, one would have the core of the modern sector of most developing countries.

Data on such a group of economic units are plentiful, but buried. Even

[1] Simon Kuznets has called for more comparative analysis of economic growth experience ([6], 1972, especially pp. 80–86). I share this view, but place that area of research more in the 'growth' than in the 'development' category, meaning by the latter the analysis of the early stages of growth acceleration and structural change in countries with an income per capita of, say, less than $1000.

developing countries with weak administrative machinery receive a steady flow of economic information from this group. There are income and sales taxes to pay or to seek exemptions from; labour legislation requiring the reporting of employment and social security taxes; import licensing demanding evidence of need; price control regulations demanding justification of price increases; banking regulations, and so on. These data sources, suitably processed, could, in most countries, provide a running census of the 'commanding heights' of the economy.

I became conscious of this rather obvious way of tackling data needs when studying the Colombian import control system. The officials in charge of that system kindly allowed me to examine a large number of import licence requests, which, I quickly discovered, were a golden data mine. Each company provided data for current and past years on such variables as employment, sales, taxes of various kinds paid, installed capacity, wages, inventories, etc. Once a decision had been made on the request, alas, these forms were destroyed. From the sample of requests that I was able to study, it was clear that a good deal of concentration existed. For example, just 80 industrial companies that were captured in the sample accounted for 30 per cent of all 1970 Colombian imports; these same companies accounted for 21 per cent of all income and sales taxes paid during 1970 in Colombia, and employed 19 per cent of all those engaged in manufacturing in the same year [3, 1976].

There are a large number of issues which could be fruitfully studied in the context of ample data for the core economic units. All of the standard development questions can be asked on such matters as efficiency of trade policy, choice of techniques, productivity changes, etc. Furthermore, the questions raised are likely to become more pointed when put in the context of the structural reality of the modern sector. Rather than imagining many atomistic firms behind some macro variable like total manufacturing output, one will have to face obvious departures from simplistic theories of the firm. Both empirical work and theorizing should benefit from the more realistic starting point; one is likely to understand the play better after having identified the major actors.

Let me again illustrate what I have in mind by reference to my work on Colombian foreign trade. From much of the debate on export promotion vs. import substitution, one could have imagined that the economic actors on both sides of that dichotomy were substantially different types: one type of unit seen as labour-intensive, competitive and small, while the other was pictured as capital-intensive, large and heavily dependent on government favours. Yet it turns out that in Colombia, for the period I examined, many of the firms engaged in new manufactured exports had been, or were still, engaged in much import substitution.[2]

While pure trade theory features individual industries having identical,

[2] In Asian countries, B. I. Cohen has found a greater degree of specialization [2, 1975].

linear homogeneous production functions within and across countries as units of analysis ('wine and cloth'), one often finds large firms producing jointly both 'wine and cloth'. Rather than attempt to separate the various activities of a given firm so that they can fit into standard industrial classifications, a process typically full of doubtful procedures, it may be better, in many instances, to focus on the large multi-product firm as the unit of analysis.

Focusing on the core economic units should advance research in a number of other lines. It obviously facilitates measurement of the degree of foreign ownership in developing economies, and provides a framework for comparing the behaviour and characteristics of domestic and foreign-owned firms in such things as exporting, research and development, and choice of technique. The history of a country's industrialization may best be written as the history of the rise and expansion of the core economic units, of conglomerates and economic groups embracing several of those units, and of their interaction with government policy which stimulated such industrialization. It may be much more difficult, however, to obtain data on the history of the core economic units and of economic groups than on their current operations.

The difficulty to which reference has been made is *not* the political, man-made variety. In addition, many may fear that focusing on core economic units for data gathering is but a first step toward their eventual socialization. Somewhat spurious pleas for protecting corporate 'privacy' will also be heard. Be that as it may, large companies and powerful economic groups are likely to feel more comfortable with their numbers diluted in macroeconomic aggregates than with schemes which highlight their largeness. Individual researchers may still obtain their co-operation for special projects; this is likely to remain the most realistic path toward obtaining a better understanding of the role and behaviour of core economic units and groups in a number of development topics. Individual researchers may find it difficult to cover all 200 top firms, and may have to remain satisfied with sample surveys. But that takes us to the next topic.

IV

Exclusive emphasis on large companies and groups would neglect some very important research areas, such as income distribution, unemployment/underemployment and extreme poverty, as well as sectors dominated by small firms and farms. The fresh data needed to get a firmer understanding and better measurement of these matters and sectors is unlikely to come from the further refinement of national accounts. Better and more frequent censuses may not be the answer either. The most efficient, although far from cheap, instrument here seems to be the greater use of sample surveys.

In a lively Presidential address to the Eastern Economic Association, Barbara R. Bergmann chided economists in the United States for not following the example of scientists in generating their own data base [1, 1974]. She also advocated a much greater use of sample surveys to find out 'first hand' about economic reality, rather than waiting for a government agency to produce numbers which are seldom exactly what is wanted. Her remarks, which make sense even in a country where government offices turn out massive amounts of high quality data, apply *a fortiori* to developing countries. Similar points have been made by G. H. Orcutt [8, 1970].

There is already evidence supporting enthusiasm for sample surveys in development research. During the late 1960s and early 1970s, the conjecture of large and growing unemployment in developing countries became so publicized that it soon was taken as fact. Dramatic policy proposals for how to deal with this problem followed. Only somewhat later came careful efforts to ascertain the extent and characteristics of open unemployment. Such efforts naturally involved increasingly sophisticated sample surveys.

The picture of open unemployment yielded by that research, such as that of J. Ramos [9, 1974], certainly has a richness and sophistication not present in earlier discussions of the topic. Heavy participation of non-heads of households and of young persons among the openly unemployed raises serious questions, for example, about the connection between open unemployment, poverty and income distribution. That research also probes toward better measures of underemployment in city and country. It is striking that only after two-and-a-half decades of theorizing and mostly casual empiricism about surplus labour in development, one now begins to see systematic empirical studies on the topic.

A related area where sample surveys show great promise is the mapping out of 'heterogeneous poverty' in the Third World. The logical data sources for researching this issue are, of course, national censuses, or stratified samples drawn from them. Impressive results have been obtained by Albert Fishlow via that route [4, 1972]. But the censuses are infrequent, and not all developing countries may have the administrative infrastructure to carry out as thorough a census as those recent ones for Brazil. Furthermore, if emphasis is placed on studying the characteristics of poverty, rather than income distribution, even partial surveys may provide more flexible and direct tools of research than do censuses. They certainly are a natural complement to infrequent censuses which remain necessary for guiding the structuring and design of samples.

Have the poorest 50 per cent of the population benefited from growth in developing countries? The conflicting answers that one hears to this question reflect the shabby state of empirical work in development economics. Answering it in a somewhat more scientific manner may involve not only greater reliance on tools such as sample surveys, but, also, the refinement of welfare indices and the taking into account of the poor's own perception as to whether they are better or worse off. A modest new rural water supply system may make villagers feel much better off, even though, in the national accounts, such projects would have a negligible impact on any sort of quantitative indicator. Much the same can be said about the provision of other public services in the areas of health, education, transportation, etc. How much of the welfare gains arising from the eradication of malaria and the decline in infant mortality have been captured in the national accounts of developing countries? Just about any junk-producing new import substituting industry has had a bigger impact on those national accounts!

United Nations efforts to develop indicators of social welfare could be very helpful. Simple data on numbers of bicycles, radios and shoes in a village, and on materials used for roofing may say more about welfare than 'guesstimates' on aggregate per capita consumption. My own favourite measure of welfare and its dispersion among social classes is life expectancy; there is no more brutal indicator of inequality than the higher life expectancy of the rich (and of their children) than of the poor.

One the whole, the sample survey may be the closest instrument we have to those in the experimental sciences, where the researcher typically generates his own hypotheses *and* his own data. Its greater use in development economics may limit the negative consequences of the impossibility of controlled experiments, as noted by Simon Kuznets: a great loss in data economy and the proliferation of competing hypotheses that survive for long periods of time [7, 1973, especially pp. 248–49].

Why have development economists been so slow in following the example of their sociology and political science colleagues in using sample surveys? Properly designed sample surveys require team-work, continuity of effort, and organization, not to mention faith in empirical research with long gestation periods. These are stiff requirements, particularly to a profession afflicted with extreme individualism, theoretical *hubris* and, in developing countries, the threat of institutional instability. But the sharply diminishing returns available in further squeezing public data sources is pushing us in the right direction. One hears that, in some developing countries, private consulting firms are emerging which offer to carry out sample surveys with a high degree of sophistication.

Autonomous research institutions in developing countries have a natural comparative advantage for this kind of empirical work *if* institutional stability can be maintained. Here is an area where economists in developing countries could take up an important research and pedagogical leadership role. Such a role would exclude both being simple gatherers of data to be processed in research centres of developed countries, and being gatherers of data which never get analysed in a systematic fashion. Neither danger should be dismissed lightly.

V

Trade and financial links between developed and developing countries have, historically, generated a disproportionate amount of data, contributing to the appeal of research in the area of trade and development. The international institutions which emerged from the Second World War have contributed much to stimulate and standardize the production of data on international trade and financial flows. Nevertheless, important gaps remain.

The biggest scandal in this field remains the lack of serious indices of international prices. After many years of arguments about trends in the terms of trade of developing countries, most international agencies still rely on unit value indices for imports and exports in computing terms of trade, in spite of widespread agreement that such unit value indices are rubbish, or close to it, as shown by Kravis and Lipsey [5, 1971]. As in the case of unemployment and underemployment, the amount of theorizing and policy debate on the terms of trade relative to the data base on the phenomenon itself makes the discipline of development economics appear singularly frivolous.

The rise of multinational corporations is a matter of hardly exclusive interest to development economists, but a greater flow of information on their activities would certainly facilitate objective research in the controversial area of their net contributions to development. The emphasis on obtaining data from core economic units, advocated earlier in this paper, should be helpful here. But, given the international nature of these units, international efforts at data gathering will also be necessary. The United Nations has started such an endeavour, but the field is a difficult one, as noted by Somavia [10, 1974]. Part of the difficulty lies in the conceptual weakness of economic ideas in areas such as that of technological transfer; measurement becomes particularly difficult when one is not sure about the nature of what one is trying to measure!

Pressures from the United Nations could be helpful in inducing the home countries of multinational corporations to co-operate in exchanges of information regarding their activities, a co-operation which has not been spontaneously forthcoming until now. These efforts may eventually lead to a commonly agreed-upon body of 'stylized facts' on which positive and normative theories about multinational corporations can be firmly based.

Finally, international agencies seem the logical bodies to improve data availability on the international migration of skilled and unskilled labour, a subject which is likely to become one of increasing interest to development analysts.

VI

From all that has been said above, it should be clear that I am sceptical about how successful the researcher in development economics will be in generating new insights just by relying on information already accumulated in libraries, whether they be located in developed or developing countries.

It is doubtful that libraries in developed countries should, or could, efficiently gather data on core economic units or on the small but growing body of sample surveys scattered throughout the Third World. International organizations may be able to provide an inventory of major bodies of such data and their location, particularly household sample surveys, a list which can then be disseminated through libraries. But the researcher will have to go, sooner or later, to the source of those data to check on gathering methods, robustness, and definitions.

Indeed, my bet is that, more often than not, already collected data 'lying around', unused and unanalysed, in the Third World, will prove of minor use to researchers. It is an old game in our profession to dream up hypotheses which can be tested against available data, a procedure frequently accompanied by many 'proxies' and 'dummies', and leading to murky results. But my conjecture is that the more interesting and focused a hypothesis in development economics, the less likely is it that data 'lying around' will be of help in testing it. Like the natural scientists, the pioneering development researcher may have to devise not only his or her own hypothesis, but, also, gather the fresh data needed for testing.

REFERENCES

[1] Bergmann, B. R., 'Have Economists Failed?' Presidential Address, Eastern Economic Association, Albany, New York, October 27, 1974 (mimeographed).

[2] Cohen, B. I., *Multinational Firms and Asian Exports* (New Haven: Yale University Press, 1975).

[3] Diaz-Alejandro, C. F., *Foreign Trade Regimes and Economic Development: Colombia* (New York: National Bureau of Economic Research, forthcoming, 1976).

[4] Fishlow, A., 'Brazilian Size Distributions of Income', *American Economic Review*, 62(2) (May 1972), pp. 391–402.

[5] Kravis, I. B. and Lipsey, R. E., *Price Competitiveness in World Trade* (New York: National Bureau of Economic Research, 1971).

[6] Kuznets, S., *Quantitative Economic Research: Trends and Problems* (New York: National Bureau of Economic Research, 1972).

[7] ——, *Population, Capital and Growth: Selected Essays* (New York: Norton and Company, 1973).

[8] Orcutt, G. H., 'Data, Research, and Government', *American Economic Review*, 60(2) (May 1970), pp. 132–37.

[9] Ramos, J., 'An Heterodoxical Interpretation of the Employment Problem in Latin America', *World Development*, 2(7) (July 1974), pp. 47–58.

[10] Somavia, J., 'Transnational Corporations: Information Gathering by The United Nations', *Development Dialogue*, 2 (1974), pp. 11–24.

Summary of the Discussion

Dr Hiemenz introduced Professor Diaz-Alejandro's paper, which he said, focused on sources and collection methods. The basic theory in the development field remains shaky, and data are necessary to identify relevant hypotheses. Considerable progress has been made in the last 25 years, chiefly with regard to macrodata related to the national accounts. Quality is also variable, even in the national income accounts, and the high level of aggregation frequently limits their usefulness for detailed analysis.

Professor Diaz-Alejandro's basic thesis in this report was that, outside of the national income accounts, the researcher should expect to gather his own data on a sample basis and on the principle of 'do it yourself', rather than waiting for usable published figures. In many areas, the largest 200 companies can be identified; tax and social insurance records can be investigated; and applications for business licences, import licences, etc., usually require much information that is useful to the investigator. A pool of all of these data can provide the answers to many questions. Difficulties remain, of course, but co-operation can usually be obtained. (*Dr Hiemenz* was himself less optimistic on this point.)

Evidence on such matters as small business, unemployment or poverty cannot, of course, be obtained from the sources just mentioned, but sample surveys can be undertaken. Teamwork is necessary, and there are usually research institutes in the LDCs themselves with whose staffs one can co-operate.

Some combination of sampling and the co-operation of key individuals can also secure data relating to such sensitive matters as international prices, MNC activities, and migration.

Dr Hiemenz doubted that a number of equally important data could be obtained by 'do-it-yourself' methods, and mentioned trade and payments as an example. He was, on the other hand, more optimistic than was Professor Díaz-Alejandro about census materials. Basic data were obtainable; and the LDCs were 'learning by doing', so that quality was improving. As for sample surveys, *Dr Hiemenz* maintained that these would have to be done by large organizations (not individual researchers) so that data could be standardized throughout the country or region under study. *Dr Hiemenz* also suggested that more use be made of UN documentation agencies and their domestic equivalents.

Dr Hiemenz also proposed two extensions of Professor Díaz-Alejandro's catalogue of data needs: (1) Given the growing regional dualism, detailed information on the workings of the agricultural sector is important for distributional and employment estimates and (2) small-scale industry data could improve our knowledge about linkages between the traditional and the modern branches of the economy. The generation of such data involves extensive field research concerning the mutual relations of growth poles and backward areas.

Professor Blaug criticized Professor Díaz-Alejandro's paper as failing to come to grips with the major problem of retrieval. He was convinced that all, or nearly all, LDCs had vast hoards of un-analysed data in their archives, and proposed that they be used. He wondered whether such data could not be taken out of the country or, at least, centralized in the capital.

Professor Blaug also criticized the UN agencies which had been mentioned, as collecting data too mechanically on the basis of questionnaires poorly adapted to LDC conditions. (Multiple-jobholding, for example, is overlooked.)

Professor Blaug's solution was to have special UN agencies, rather than the regular UN bureaucracy, do the surveying, but to inform outsiders of their projects, as was not done, he said, in the case of the 1968 survey of households in Sudan. *Miss Deane* and *Professor Tyler* agreed with Professor Blaug's point. *Miss Deane* added that UN documentation centres were slow and had large backlogs of high-quality but unavailable data, and *Professor Tyler* added that Latin American specialists at the University of Florida find it easier to use data banks in Los Angeles than statistical offices in the Latin American countries themselves.

Professor Giersch inquired why, if LDC data were so good, LDC economists did not use them to a greater extent. They did, in fact, Professor Giersch was told by *Professor Tyler*, but the results are seldom published in Western languages.

Dr Bartenbach claimed that DEVSIS, affiliated with ILO, was making special LDC studies under UN auspices. He also commented that the Economic Development journals were seldom cited by authorities outside of the development field, and that the LDC journals themselves seldom cite each other.

Professor Morgan was skeptical as to the quality of LDC data. He warned about collection errors resulting from obsolete collection methods, and sought evidence that the quality was actually as high as several previous speakers had maintained.

Dr Hiemenz issued two warnings: (1) The researcher with UN affiliations can often find out more than one coming from an MDC university, and (2) much available data cannot be released.

Professor Kindleberger raised the point that LDC librarians have trouble organizing retrieval in LDCs. (*Dr Heidemann* agreed, and mentioned inadequate funding to send people to LDCs to assist in the job.) *Professor Kindleberger* then suggested that US PL 480 counterpart funds might be used for financing purposes. He agreed that the quantity of good LDC data outran LDC cataloguing capacity, and added that spending time in the representative LDC may be a pleasant experience for an MDC economist.

Professor M. Perlman reminded the group that many interesting points in Economic History had been derived originally, from inferior data, and suspected that Economic Development was in the same position.

Professor Kindleberger wondered about the appropriate order of events. To him, it seemed that collection should be continuous and that analysis should begin early to expose difficulties in the collection process.

Professor Diaz-Alejandro insisted that Economic Development is a separate and 'different' branch of economic study. The funds of MDC libraries are better spent at home, and this is why development economists must develop their own data on a do-it-yourself basis.

Data should suggest hypotheses, continued *Professor Diaz-Alejandro*, although they do not always do so. It is not at all unusual for natural scientists to generate their own data experimentally, and Professor Kuznets might be cited as an example of an authority favouring extensive use of sample surveys.

Professor Diaz-Alejandro then formulated 'Diaz's Law' to the effect that 'the more interesting a hypothesis, the less the data relevant for its testing'. *Professor Diaz-Alejandro* accordingly doubted that an undifferentiated mass of data is of much value, and criticized UN agencies for centralizing data inadequately, although they catalogue well. He would prefer local Brookings Institutions to centralize LDC data. The political spin-off of such institutions, he was sure, would strengthen local institutions. Finally, *Professor Diaz-Alejandro* doubted that one really needs large, centralized, stored samples at all. (But, *Professor Morgan* objected, was there not potential bias in poorly-planned samples collected exclusively by LDC people?)

18 Information Needs for Agricultural Development, Policy and Planning

Montague Yudelman
INTERNATIONAL BANK FOR RECONSTRUCTION AND DEVELOPMENT, WASHINGTON

This paper identifies information and knowledge useful for agricultural policy analysis, with particular references to the world food situation and conditions in the less developed countries. Different kinds of data are described and means for obtaining and analysing them are discussed. Attention is given to micro and macrodata relevant to project level, national and international policy analysis.

I. INTRODUCTION

The main questions confronting economists working in the rural sector at this time are: can the world feed its growing population? What technological and institutional changes are necessary to enable it to do so? How can this be done while improving the wellbeing of the expanding rural population and without massive migration to the cities? These questions are currently being pursued within the context of a most critical outlook for food production in relation to population and income growth.

The growing sense of crisis about food has raised questions about our knowledge of the resource base, the appropriate technology and the means of organization to augment food production. This, in turn, has added emphasis to all of the issues that influence supply and demand: production levels, consumption patterns, prices, inventories, population structure, environmental factors and patterns of investment. All experience indicates that most economists concerned with these problems need more reliable and more recent information on the resource and technology base, as well as on trends in the supply of, and demand for, foodstuffs.

Within developed countries, the question of global food supplies has led to renewed emphasis on such things as: (i) early warning systems concerning cycles in farm production and in the production of farm inputs; (ii) building food reserves and buffer stocks, and their organization and management; (iii) research and development requirements for the technology needed to increase the productivity of available resources; and (iv) the provision of adequate service systems to ensure the supply of capital, technical and other inputs to agriculture. The information needs of these programmes far exceed the scope of traditional institutions and library systems. Consequently, a new family of information and knowledge storehouses has evolved under the rubric of 'extra-library programmes.' A feature of these is that they recognize the problems that the agricultural economist has in maintaining an awareness of the total pool of knowledge and information that he needs. There is still a major issue, though, as to how these programmes can be oriented to meet the urgent needs of agriculture and the formulation of food policy.

Economists concerned with developing countries are at a greater disadvantage than are those dealing with developed countries, as there is a paucity of both knowledge and appropriate knowledge and information programmes. For individual developing countries, more knowledge and better information needs include: (i) resource inventories of physical and human resources, and their rate of depletion or expansion; (ii) development trends in terms of GNP growth, population changes, and income distribution and productivity; (iii) studies of the dynamics of social organization, community structure and alternative institutions; (iv) surveys of settlement patterns and spatial factors; (v) analysis of alternative technology and its economics; (vi) motivation and incentive studies, price responses and the effects of other measures; and (vii) reviews of problems in organization, communication and participation in decision-making at all levels of rural society.

There are particular problems in obtaining and handling information about the agriculture of developing countries. First, there is the problem of how to estimate output, a problem inherent in an atomistic structure of millions of producers, very few of whom keep records, many of whom consume part of their output, and most of whom market their output through informal channels. Second, much of the information available is gathered by government departments, which are often inadequately staffed and under-financed. Third, because there are often competing demands for a limited number of capable professionals in statistical offices, information generation is literally put aside for shorter-run concerns. Fourth, rapid changes in the structure of industries and sectors, if not of the whole economy, very often have to be assessed without adequate base studies. Fifth, governments are frequently secretive, and individuals and groups are often reluctant to make available background material that is essential to sensible management and decision-making. Finally, due to the poor organization of institutions, inadequate training and other problems, the standards of measurement, data handling, and analysis are often inadequate.

Much of the limited information that is available is embodied in government reports, reports of international organizations, in planning bureaux, research centres and in libraries. Thus, traditional library services and infrastructures, even augmented by extra-library information programmes, are hard pressed to meet the needs of economists and policy analysts dealing with critical materials, shortages and the looming world food shortage. A shift in course is required to meet these pressing needs and to ease long-standing constraints. A first step in exploring the necessary new directions must be to: (i) differentiate between the knowledge and information requirements for policy analysis, along with requirements for operational management; (ii) specify these requirements in terms of detail and source; and (iii) separately specify the different needs at the global, national and project levels.

II. GLOBAL REQUIREMENTS

On a global basis, the knowledge and data requirements of economists surpass generic description. Only within the context of a single international programme—such as the World Food Program—which is aimed at increasing foodgrain production and averting a global food crisis, do the needs become more finite. As an example, the food programme illustrates the different data needs of long-term policy formulation for agricultural development and short-term needs for the aversion of acute food shortages in an area affected by natural disaster. A shortage of information hampers analysis in both of these areas. Though the data may have been generated, systematic mechanisms are often not created for its orderly storage and ultimate retrieval. This lack of conserved knowledge and information forces international development agencies to invest in extensive and costly fact-finding missions to the regions under study. Too often these missions uncover uncatalogued reports, undocumented knowledge and redundant studies. What causes such a dearth of readily usable data is that it lies within a proverbial sea of unuseful data. A lack of uniformity, or even co-ordination of objectives at a detailed working level by the many international organizations, contributes substantially to the information problem.

Clearly, international policy formulation must evolve from knowledge that is developed from the analysis of better data gathered at the national level and on a co-ordinated basis. A wider realization that data do not exist in adequate form, quantity, recency or detail for such global policy formulation is an essential prerequisite for future action. Action should be directed toward collecting more adequate data on a co-ordinated basis and examining in detail the policies to be formulated. In the case of inventories of buffer stocks, this would include identities, sources, quantities, qualities and locations of stores. Decisions on these can be made only after analysing, on a regional level, such interacting parameters as:

(1) *population size and growth data*—indicating demand profiles for foodgrain;

(2) *population income and nutrition data*—for the establishment of foodgrain needs;
(3) *arable land survey data*—covering current land conditions and then utilization, as well as estimations, of potentially usable land;
(4) *hydrological and cartographic data*—indicating the availability of surface and subsurface water resources for crop irrigation;
(5) *environmental and climatological data*—indicating rainfall, relative humidity and other sectoral conditions relevant to crop growth, as well as trends in climatic shifts;
(6) *agricultural and aquacultural production*—including data on yields for each food grain material for each regional sector and nation;
(7) *agricultural and aquacultural product prices*—nationally and worldwide;
(8) *agricultural input materials, inventory and flow data*—covering world production and its capacity to produce, inventory and balance of trade for fertilizer, seed material and pesticides;
(9) *infrastructural survey data*—covering land, sea and air facilities and equipment which can affect the transportation of agricultural input and output materials for LDCs; and
(10) *agricultural technology utilization data*—from site surveys and missions indicating present and potential uses of techniques and technology, with due consideration given to the limitations on the availability of infrastructure and labour that can inhibit the effective use of equipment.

It is clear that the information problem is atomistic in nature, with an enormous multiplicity of discrete but interactive components. There is little hope or need for ever maintaining complete current files of all data or knowledge concerning the effects of all such parameters within a global information system. (It is equally clear that the collection and management of such data falls well outside of the traditional function of libraries.)

However, within the implied matrix of parameters there are some data sets that should be maintained in a complete, current state; others can be maintained as sample data; still others can be maintained within a stochastic model. The analysis of goals and functions should determine which data sets need be complete. Obviously, environmental, production, consumption and other data associated with the operation of any system for assessing the world food situation must be organized in rather complete central files. Data associated with long-term rural development policy formulation might better rest in the specialized files of the regional sector agencies, but in such a manner that other potential users can be referred to their files. Such a referral mechanism could also lead the potential user to storehouses of knowledge available through economists working in each region.

An essential point here is that much of the unwritten knowledge possessed by economists, especially in the international arena, can be tapped only through direct communication with them. They produce, and can provide, much more intelligence or knowledge than can be obtained through the mere transfer of documents or data, since they have suffered through the analysis activity. These economists can also lead the researcher to the most productive libraries or repositories. Later in this paper, there is some description of the primary sources in existence today and those that are planned for the future.

III. NATIONAL NEEDS

Agricultural and other resource planning functions at the national level call for sets of information and knowledge at both ends of the spectrum. On the one hand, central government economists need information to satisfy requests for information from the international development community. On the other hand, these economists need decentralized information and co-ordination at the local level, because effective national programmes consist of composites of local projects.

Experience indicates that the planning and implementation of development activities call for a substantial measure of decentralization in functional programme management and the establishment of data collection at the local level. The adjustments needed vary significantly from country to country. Unless the functional aspects of development projects (including data collection) are completely delegated to some level of regional and/or local government, an unrealistic and probably undesirable situation will continue with regard to overlapping functions of central and local government departments. An institutional arrangement—perhaps through regional information centres and planning units, or through co-ordinating committees—must be found to resolve some of these issues. Where national investment priorities are concerned, provision has to be made to ensure that the central information gathering and planning authority is brought into the picture, and that the central units have the information needed to function effectively.

Decentralization of information gathering may also mean decentralization of authority: (i) to formulate projects; (ii) to administer projects, (iii) to allocate some expenditures, and (iv) to raise revenue. If three major levels of government are equally considered, the central (or federal), the state (or provincial), and the district will share the responsibility for planning, project monitoring via data collection, budgeting and executing development schemes. But, almost everywhere, central planning agencies and ministries have played a dominant role in directing and providing funds for development. In some countries, special ministerial or presidential agencies have been established to plan, co-ordinate and accelerate the development activities of central, as well as regional, agencies. This pattern must be changed. Local agencies will not be motivated to gather the accurate data needed for programme monitoring and management unless they have a hand in the management of the data.

Herein lies the only hope for the collection of information that will be needed for expanded agricultural development programmes in the future. The collection of raw data at the provincial level will provide the bases for knowledge building analysis at the national and, ultimately, at international levels. Any new problems arising from inconsistent and inadequate data resulting from essentially uncontrolled data collection at the provincial level are likely to be more than offset by general improvements in the quality of data in other respects.

Paramount among the current problems of evaluating the status of agricultural development programmes at the national level in developing countries is the lack of complete data on:

(1) the location and composition of populations comprising project target groups;
(2) the amount of arable land, water and other resources in use, or available, on a zonal basis;
(3) the agricultural yields and output available for subsistence and for the national market;
(4) the effects of environmental factors, technology, fertilizer and training on crop yields.

Data collection on the local level will make it possible to monitor development on the millions of small farms in the developing countries. With these new data, an international aggregation of small-farm yields will open new vistas for analysis at the global agricultural development level.

IV. PROJECT PARAMETERS

The principal information elements in agricultural project management can be defined within the conceptual framework of cost-benefit analysis. This method of analysis has been broadly applied to water resource development, agricultural credit programmes, new-crop tests, and multi-crop and agriculture-commerce development projects. The basic parameters deal with technical, managerial, organizational, financial, commercial and manpower development aspects of project performance. Development experts fostering and monitoring projects consider site visits to be the principal vehicle for their data gathering. The main information and knowledge-management issue appears to be the design of reporting modes so that project managers can adjust their own programmes in response to changing circumstances and events, thereby contributing to the overall knowledge base for the benefit of future resource development programmes.

But the appropriate structure can be built only after the framework has been conceptualized. Random collection and amassing of data will not build the required data base. Neither will proliferation or even systematic storage and indexing of project reports outside of the framework of a master knowledge development plan. Hence, a national viewpoint embodying knowledge of development goals and a series of milestones on the path to their achievement must come first. Within this framework, the project manager can then define his functional and information generating goals. It is hoped that this relatively new view of a project as a knowledge-generating activity will help alleviate current project management problems. If this approach works, projects will less frequently generate redundant data, and managers will be able to utilize knowledge gained in the past.

Out of this effort can grow new multi-project analysis techniques, since projects may be co-ordinated on a multi-province multi-region or even multi-nation basis. Opportunities for multi-parameter modelling, based on data that is better than the presently used shadow-data, may improve the usefulness of these approaches, and the coupling of research with national planning may be brought one step closer.

V. ON-GOING INFORMATION PROGRAMMES

Present world agricultural information programmes constitute a great deal less than a base for co-ordinated global agricultural knowledge, partly because the programmes have been developed without being co-ordinated by any kind of global strategy. However, presently existing programmes provide a useful stepping stone to the future. The principal components of today's programmes are exemplified by CRIS (the U.S. Current Research Information System), AGRIS (the FAO report index system), a multiplicity of environmental data programmes, and the potential for remote sensing by satellite for the collection of macro-phenomenological data. These are outlined more fully below.

CRIS

The information base for CRIS has been formed from the descriptions of research efforts sponsored by all six agencies of the USDA, 53 state agricultural experimental stations, and 25 other co-operating state institutions. The basic unit for documentation and reportage is the 'research work unit,' i.e. a research activity at a single location which focuses on a clearly definable problem, a sizeable phase of a very big problem, or a few closely related elements of interest which, together, form a logical and manageable package.

Approximately 24,000 project descriptions covering current projects are now held in CRIS. The total description for each current unit consists of a research resume, a classification report, a funds and manpower report, and a progress report. The two latter reports are submitted annually, while new resumes and classifications are submitted for revised projects. Each 'research work unit' is characterized by a set of keywords or terms describing the research objectives. Details of experimental programmes in which a worker is interested may be found by selecting keywords in the key-word authority list (this list contains some 11,000 terms) and sorting the 24,000-unit file for related projects. This system could be expanded, with minor modifications, to cover all worldwide agricultural research and development projects if data collection were designed and implemented.

AGRIS

The Food and Agriculture Organization (FAO) of the United Nations has an information collection and dissemination responsibility clearly defined in its constitution. This prescribes that 'The Organization shall collect, analyse, interpret, and disseminate information relating to nutrition, food and agriculture'. Hence, FAO has established an International Information System for the Agricultural Sciences and Technology, referred to by the acronym AGRIS. AGRIS encourages all nations contributing to the FAO to provide both input and output services, based on their own needs and facilities. AGRIS is basically a document and literature indexing system designed to meet research needs. AGRIS now performs several services, including the publication of AGRINDEX, and an index of the world agricultural literature. It does not pretend to perform any gathering, extraction, compilation or systematic dissemination of specific agricultural data for the purposes of global or national resource management. The importance of research data from the literature and their improved accessibility via the use of services such as AGRIS are not to be diminished.

If AGRIS indexing were co-ordinated with the CRIS key-word assignment, and if the coverage were expanded to cover the world literature (including World Bank, UNDP, FAO and other project reports), a single knowledge-searching capability could be established.

ENVIRONMENTAL DATA PROGRAMMES

Two worldwide meteorology and climatology data programmes are potential contributors to the co-ordinated agro-economic data and knowledge structure proposed in this paper. One is the Global Atmospheric Research Program (GARP) and the other is the World Weather Watch of the World Meteorological Organization. These provide an example of inter-agency co-ordination that might be studied further.

GARP presently is being planned to measure the motions of the entire lower atmosphere (below 30 kilometres) so that it can be studied as a single physical system leading to an improved physical and mathematical basis for medium and long-range weather predictions. The programme's sponsor is the International Council of Scientific Unions/International Union of Geodesy and Geophysics/Committee on Atmospheric Sciences, in association with the Committee on Space Research (COSPAR) and the World Meteorological Organization.

The operational programme that implements GARP policy is the WMO 'World Weather Watch.' WMO is encouraging its member nations to interact and co-operate in pursuing the following objectives: (i) to facilitate the building of a network of stations for making meteorological observations; (ii) to propose systems for exchanging meteorological information; (iii) to promote the standardization of weather observations and the uniform publication of observations and statistics; (iv) to further the application of meteorology to aviation, shipping, utilization of water resources, air pollution, etc.; and (v) to further research and training in meteorology and to help co-ordinate international activities in this respect.

Early in the planning of the World Weather Watch it was decided that there should be a number of world meteorological centres, forming an integral part of the global observing system. An integrated system of centres will eventually include world, regional and national meteorological centres. World centres have been set up in Melbourne, Moscow and Washington, D.C. This programme has developed substantial momentum. The linking of essential WMO models and data elements (joining forecasting rainfall and median temperatures with the agro-economic data monitoring systems) will contribute significantly to the ability to warn early about potential food shortages.

SATELLITE PROGRAMMES

A more accurate inventory of the world's food crops will be a major assignment for Landsat I and II (previously called ERTS A and B), the remote sensing imagery satellites launched by NASA. Images by the new Landsat's Multispectral Scanner (MSS) will enable agricultural scientists to make gross estimates of acreages and yields, and to correlate long-term relationships between yields and climatic patterns. At the recent World Food Conference in Rome, this new technique was characterized as being a 'promising and potentially vital contribution to rational planning of global production.'

Landsat II's continuous-strip photos will also be used to continue the mapping of surface water sources and forest-fire devastation, to locate underground water supplies, to update maps and navigation charts, to locate geologic formations indicating the presence of petroleum or minerals, to monitor spatial settlement and to evaluate fishery resources. The future roles of satellite images in agriculture will evolve with time. Tracing programmes will be required, so that the use of such images is not limited by a shortage of agro-scientists and economists capable of photo interpretation. In addition, active programmes to collect ground truth data will be necessary to ensure accurate image interpretation. Such programmes have already begun in several countries, including India.

Remote sensing ranks high as an option for data gathering. Furthermore, India's National Remote Sensing Agency appears to provide the appropriate medium for handling the data. A proposed National Resource Evaluation Agency Division of the Department of Science and Technology, which executes knowledge generation at the national level, and a separate planning group can effectively isolate, but integrate, the three key functions; data gathering, knowledge generation and knowledge application. The success of this programme does not imply universal applicability for all LDC's, particularly in view of India's capacity to apply this technique. Since there are few, if any, other practical options, the technique shows great promise.

AN ACTION PLAN

An action plan to meet the main information and knowledge needs of agricultural economists must satisfy two requirements: (i) provision of the data requirements for analysing discrete problems; and (ii) the measures involved should be complementary and self-reinforcing. The problems break down into two broad categories—those associated with knowledge management, and those associated with information and data management.

Knowledge, as mentioned earlier, usually rests in the minds of the generators. Researchers seldom find either the energy or the resources to communicate, or even document, more than a fraction of the knowledge that they generate, especially in the broad field of agro-economics. The best resource is the economist. This leads to the conclusion that more must be done to capture this knowledge by focusing more on recording the experience of economists. Such a system might comprise the organization of a computerized file of researchers, including a brief indexing or title listing of the key projects that each is now, or has been, engaged in. Organizing the file would pose some minor challenges, but its maintenance would become easy once the regular survey machinery had been set into motion.

The second problem of inaccessibility in the knowledge arena relates to project reports and studies, for they are seldom circulated, publicised, indexed, stored centrally or widely distributed. Yet they embody the cream of the work of most economists. A broadening of AGRIS' scope, so as to abstract and index reports from FAO, UNDP, the World Bank, the regional banks and from other development organizations, would be a major step forward. Such a file, however, would have to be maintained on an up-to-the-minute basis.

A major problem with reports, even when they are accessible, is that there is a time lag from the execution of research to its publication as a report. This lag extends from three months to several years. Thus, there is an inability to monitor the current generation of knowledge. However, if there were to be a CRIS or a CRIS-like information system to index and abstract *current* activities covering research beyond the USA, and extending into UNDP, FAO, the World Bank and the regional banks, a major improvement would result. If the expanded AGRIS and CRIS systems employed common or compatible indexing codes and vocabularies, a single search could uncover publications, reports and current research in a single topic area and on a global basis. Here, again, putting up the file would call for a sizeable effort in terms of manpower and financial resources, but its maintenance would be relatively easy once the input machinery had been established.

Agro-economic information and data management problems today have reached proportions that greatly exceed knowledge retrieval problems. As mentioned earlier in this paper, in the food area in particular, better information is needed on prices, production, consumption, inventories, population, environmental factors and on resource and technology utilization. A dual approach to the resolution of the issue is called for. First, and foremost, there must be experimental efforts to set up mechanisms for the collection of local data which is funnelled through to the national and to the international levels, with functional use all along the way. This step must be continuous so as to provide the detailed data for planning and to meet the need for observations to support satellite serving programmes. Data collection forms must be designed. Requirements for data collection must be set for all recipients of funds from all funding agencies. The enforcement of requirements and the checking of the data's accuracy by site visits and by other means must follow.

VI. CONCLUSIONS

The world is rapidly entering an era when there will be increasing pressure on existing resources, especially in relation to providing enough food for rapidly increasing populations. However, at present, economists working on problems related to food-population balances are severely handicapped by a lack of adequate information. This lack stems from two principal causes: first, there is a scarcity of reliable data and, second, when there are data they are usually not in a readily usable form, i.e. the information is not available as knowledge.

There is need for a much more systematic approach to generate both data and knowledge. This applies at national, regional and local levels. Libraries will be important, but many of the requirements of the agricultural sector will have to be satisfied by extra-library programmes.

Comments by Eric Thorbecke (Cornell University)

I find this paper somewhat incomplete on two grounds. First, the central issue, i.e. the data requirements for agricultural development planning are covered in a mechanistic and somewhat superficial way simply by listing a number of headings. I believe that it is essential to match the types of data required with the conceptual planning framework in use and the policy objectives which are sought. Thus, for example, if poverty alleviation and employment are important objectives, it would appear necessary to gather income and employment information by crop, by technology, and by socio-economic group to explain the determinants of income of these groups. Likewise, on the demand side, the consumption patterns of these socio-economic groups (e.g. landless farmers, small tenants, small farm owners, large farm owners) should be obtained. What I find missing in the paper is any analysis of the relationship between data requirements and the classification scheme of the planning framework. After all, information is a key input in the planning process and should, therefore, be closely linked to it.

Second, the inventory of on-going information programmes fails to list a number of relevant programmes such as: (*a*) FAO's data bank which, as I understand it, contains a large amount of international, cross-sectional and time series information, and (*b*) Michigan State University's computer library of agricultural sector analyses. Finally, I have great doubts about the present capacity of earth satellites to generate useful information. The statement made on pp. 374–5 appears greatly to overestimate that capacity.

Summary of the Discussion

Dr Palnicov introduced Dr Yudelman's report. Dr Yudelman has focused on two important problems: (1) inadequate knowledge of the world food situation vis-à-vis world population and population in specific areas, and (2) inadequate co-operation between international organizations. The paucity and low quality of data were important, particularly in connection with (1).

Dr Yudelman's problem is, accordingly, the improvement of agricultural data (prices, production, consumption, inventories, technology), especially in the LDC's. He has proposed improved mechanisms for collecting and processing local data and, then, concentrating them successively at regional, national, and international levels. The process should include the checking of accuracy; it should be set up on a permanent basis; it should include filing and storage facilities.

The unified efforts of international organizations, given these data, should then result in parameters for decision making and for world development policies. Demand profiles could be estimated, primarily involving population and its growth. Land surveys could be made, also including potentially fertile areas: these surveys should include water resources, climatic conditions, etc. Data should also include realized prices, outputs, and technology. Dr Yudelman believed that existing data were inadequate largely because of geographical non-comparability and the lack of international co-ordination.

The present programmes of certain countries, including Canada and the United States, are a promising basis for such an international programme as Dr Yudelman had in mind. Dr Yudelman noted particularly that they were well indexed and convenient to users. He felt that his proposed international system would be essentially this system expanded, and that the next step might be better dissemination of ecological materials and reports of individual-country experience.

Dr Palnicov thought the Yudelman proposals worth considering, perhaps in conjunction with Professor Diaz-Alejandro's proposals of the last session. *Dr Palnicov* felt, however, that Dr Yudelman might have gone further to consider retrieval of existing FAO data. The ambitious Yudelman proposals, then, actually included more duplication of existing work than Dr Yudelman may have realized.

Professor von Böventer, as chairman of the session, opened the discussion with a resume of a written comment submitted by Professor Thorbecke. Professor Thorbecke believed that Dr Yudelman's proposals were at once too mechanical and too aggregative. He felt that more should have been said about income and employment and that information must be more detailed by social classes. Agricultural data, in sum, should have been linked more closely with the problems and programmes of the remainder of the economies in question. Like Dr Palnicov, Professor Thorbecke criticized Dr Yudelman's failure to consider the availability of FAO data, and also mentioned data available at Michigan State University. Professor Thorbecke also characterized as 'science fiction' an ambitious suggestion by Dr Yudelman that earth satellites in outer space might prove useful in locating new areas of potentially fertile agricultural land on earth.

Professor M. Perlman then presented a resume of a second written comment, this one prepared by Professor Theodore Schultz (University of Chicago). Professor Schultz found Dr Yudelman's paper somewhat superficial, on the level of an administrative report. He was struck by the absence of either priorities or cost estimates. He believed that the LDC's themselves are imposing distortions of various kinds on their domestic agricultures, but doubted that either the International Bank of Reconstruction and Development (IBRD) or FAO was capable of analysing them objectively, because of fear of possible offence to the LDC's, *Professor Perlman* noted that Professor Schultz had not attempted such an analysis either.

The first oral comment was made by *Dr Scheper*, who claimed that Dr Yudelman had stressed food supplies in LDC's and the task of international agencies, but had inadequately stressed the problems of the MDC's and the data needs of agricultural policy makers in these countries. The lack of balance that *Dr Scheper* perceived, in the Yudelman paper led him to agree with much of Professor Schultz's written comment.

Dr Scheper continued in a more general vein. Agricultural policy, he pointed out, is a broad and heterogeneous field, with important relations to both income distribution and economic development. It requires a high degree of government involvement, where political problems are complex at both the national and international levels. While there is a large demand for information, there is also a large supply—more, perhaps, than can be used profitably. The problem is bringing supply and demand together—co-ordination, not assembly.

Why, *Dr Scheper* went on, are demand and supply so un-co-ordinated? Part of the problem is complex and specialized terminology and definitions. Another part is the difficulty of international communication. (The problem here is more than linguistic, but both IBRD and FAO are working on it.) Historical developments are by now well enough understood, but current information is slow, and forecasting ability needs improvement. (Dr Yudelman has stressed this last point, even to the extent of what some other commentators called 'science fiction'.) *Dr Scheper*, himself believed that information on farm structure, agricultural input-output, cost, and revenue data are better than Dr Yudelman has implied—but only in MDC's, and it is still too static. Data on investment and migration are poor, as are supply and demand data for individual crops, and income and welfare distributions of farm income. (Here we know little about income in kind, we have few forecasts, and are unprepared for possible transfers from wealthy to poor farmers.) Also, unwritten knowledge is especially important in agriculture. Although the farm bloc is important politically, the flow of information from farm to Agriculture Ministry is slow and uncertain.

Dr Scheper's final point was the heterogeneity of the demand for agricultural data. It ranged from the local area to the entire world, making impossible the single great leap to the global system apparently envisaged by the Yudelman paper. It might be better to concentrate, for the present, on individual problems, with results to be made understandable rather than sophisticated. Small institutes can do this on a collaborative basis, and have done so in West Germany. They may be able to do so on the international level also.

Professor Kindleberger commented that Dr Yudelman's title pre-judged issues of 'plan versus market' in favour of the latter. He suggested that private enterprise can not only work well but can generate information well. In West Africa, for example, private candy companies have better information about cocoa crop prospects than do the African governments themselves. He inquired how much information would be required to overcome the agricultural 'cobweb theorem', and suggested that published misinformation might make matters worse. As for Dr Yudelman's space surveys of potentially fertile land, *Professor Kindleberger* pointed out that ordinary aerial surveys of smaller areas were already 20 years old.

To *Professor Wolfe*, the question of what information could be useful was separate from the question about how existing information should be organized. For the present, he thought the second question to be the more important one. *Professor Wolfe* criticized Dr Yudelman's paper as too speculative, with its vision of a world agricultural plan. He might not go quite so far as Professor Kindleberger, but felt closer to him than to Dr Yudelman. Also, *Professor Wolfe* warned against losing sight of the relation between the availability of information and the desire to base plans upon it. *Professor Morgan* agreed, and was disturbed by what he interpreted as Dr Yudelman's implication that most, or all, existing data were worthless. He suggested a more positive focus: What parts of our present data are worth saving, and what parts are not?

Professor M. Perlman commented on agricultural economists. The planners among them seem to want us to accumulate a new set of data, while the anti-planners want to improve the data we have. (There is also a middle group, proposing both procedures at once!) But where does the scholar fit in here? Dr Yudelman has not made his own position clear and his paper needs more focus. Librarians, too, need to find out what the agricultural economists among their clientèle want, and act accordingly. Choice is necessary and unavoidable.

Dr Scheper stressed once more the heterogeneous demand for information, by level as well as by bias. (Also, the agricultural sector is somewhat isolated from the remainder of the economy.) In the MDC's, information needs income accounts (personal income distributions and rural welfare analyses, including comparison with urban dwellers). In some countries, he believed, data are kept confidential for security reasons. Also, land rent profiles by regions would be useful, especially in connection with taxation. For protection against agricultural instability, trade is most important, and it also increases the farmers' ability to bear what instability remains. Figures are available but do not seem useful. When it comes to the longer run, data are again available but their form is not good. Demanders should press suppliers to improve data and, particularly, to disaggregate it.

Professor Giersch argued that much data are supplied for policy reasons to 'Ministries *for* Agriculture' and, therefore, that their quality is suspect particularly as regards bias. *Dr Scheper* replied that *no* data are completely neutral and that, in the case of agriculture, consistency checks are relatively easy. *Professor Biehl* agreed with Professor Giersch, stating that many data are unusable because they cannot be made comparable with others.

Dr Palnicov responded in Dr Yudelman's absence. He began with the complaint that the discussion had ranged far from Dr Yudelman's original paper. He himself had found the paper more pragmatic, and focused on IBRD problems, but *Dr Palnicov* thought that the commentators seemed more interested in the scientific value of the Yudelman paper. *Dr Palnicov*, at the same time, agreed with Dr Scheper about the mechanical character of the paper, and about the degree of disaggregation required for usefulness. *Dr Palnicov* believed the separation between practical and speculative demands for information to be important, and had found the discussion helpful on this account. One moral derivable from it was that statistics should not be collected for their own sake.

19 Competition versus Planned Specialization in the Development of Resources for Research in Industrial Organization

Michael Gort
STATE UNIVERSITY OF NEW YORK, BUFFALO

There are two distinct problems: (a) the organization and retrieval of received knowledge; (b) the use of resources for the creation of new knowledge. Insofar as industrial organization is concerned, (a) presents no serious problems in the sense that the literature, which consists primarily of journal articles, is not so voluminous as to be beyond the storage and acquisition capacities of any good research library. On the other hand, (b) does present a serious problem, in that the sources of information are highly diverse and what information will prove useful is difficult to predict. The problem of diversity is accentuated by the expectation that industrial organization research will increasingly focus on data at the level of the firm or enterprise.

Unfortunately, librarians cannot contribute much to the stockpiling of information for future research of this type, since a decision as to what information is useful cannot precede research. It must either follow or, at best, be concurrent with new research. Consequently, the issue of where specialized research libraries should be located is subsidiary to the question of where research centres are to be located.

I shall begin with two fundamental issues that transcend the question of resource development for any single branch of economics. First, is specialization a desirable objective for research libraries? And second, to the extent it is, should the objective be achieved through an integrated long-term plan that allocates fields of specialization to particular libraries? This subject, though perhaps beyond the boundaries of my assignment, seems especially appropriate for a paper that focuses on research in industrial organization.

The central issue that must be faced at the outset is the measurement of the benefits and costs of regional specialization in *research*. To the extent that research centres for particular fields can be effectively designated in advance, the costs of regional specialization in library resources are minimal. Indeed, the elimination of duplication in library resources is only one component, and certainly not the most important one, of the reduction in aggregate costs through a reduction in duplication of research. It is for this reason that the issue of duplication versus co-ordination is a perennial one for governments and legislative committees concerned with the budgets of universities and other research organizations. Fundamentally, therefore, the issue we must consider is that of the benefits and costs of duplication in research.

Hard empirical evidence on the relation between advances in science and the number of competing research centres is difficult to find, but casual observation suggests a strong association. To some extent, casual evidence may be misleading, in that the number and geographical dispersion of scholars who devote their energies to particular problems is partly a consequence, rather than a cause, of intellectual breakthroughs. Nonetheless, there are compelling *a priori* reasons for expecting a positive association between the number of separate and competing research projects and the rate of scientific advance in a given field. First, competition is both a stimulant to effort and a control on continued investment in unproductive approaches. But, second, and even more decisive, the direction from which intellectual breakthroughs emerge is inherently unpredictable, with the result that limiting research on a given set of problems to a single centre is generally a prescription for sterility. The riskier the research—and almost all research with possibilities of high pay-off is characterized by high risk—the greater the adverse effects of regional specialization.

It follows, therefore, that regional specialization of library resources, to the extent that such resources are necessary for research, should be undertaken always reluctantly and only when the costs of duplication are high. But assuming that some specialization is unavoidable, how should the specialties be allocated? The view that the mere presence of rich resources automatically generates productive research is inconsistent with the overwhelming historical evidence of unexploited research opportunities and of resources remaining idle for successive decades. Clearly, an insight into how resources can be effectively used is necessary. This trivial statement has, however, important consequences. For it implies that the development of library specialties should at least accompany, and probably follow, the regional concentration of the relevant human resources. Thus, little purpose would be served in developing a library specialty in a given field unless scholars of distinction in that field were present in the region of the library.

Given the instability over time as to which research centres are distinguished in particular fields, it follows that plans for the specialization of library resources should generally be of limited duration, with periodic shifts in the assignment of preferential status to particular fields in a given library. Indeed, while there are serious obstacles arising from the parochial and bureaucratic interests of institutions, efficient co-ordination would entail periodic inter-library transfers of resources on a long-term basis to reflect the changing geographic distribution of superior scholars and research centres in particular fields.

Let us now consider the types of specialization possible and their implications. First, specialization may take the form of co-ordinated development of library resources within small geographical areas such as cities. Alternatively, it may involve broad regions within a country or, possibly, even co-ordination across national boundaries. Second, specialization may involve books and documents that are readily transferable through inter-library loans or, alternatively, may involve resources that are intrinsically difficult to transfer. The issues at stake clearly involve the balancing of alternative costs. On the one hand, there are the costs of duplication of resources, and on the other, there are the administrative costs of inter-library transfers and, much more important, a variety of costs to the scholar who uses resources not available in the library of greatest proximity.

It is customary in economics to translate all costs into monetary units. This can be effectively done with the costs to a scholar of using resources not present in the library of greatest proximity. On this basis, the social cost of even a trip across town is substantial in most developed economies if we assume that economists are paid at the opportunity cost of their time. Clearly, however, the problem becomes much more acute when library resources are located in distant cities.

What is at stake is not merely the potential travel cost, nor even the waiting time until publications can be transferred on inter-library loans, but something that is far more important. Normally, in the early stages of empirical research, one is not quite sure what types of information and data one will need. There is really no good substitute for browsing through potential sources of information for an intuitive assessment of the likelihood that a set of loosely formulated hypotheses can be tested. Under these circumstances, it is extremely difficult to provide a checklist of publications and data sources that one requires. Moreover, the riskiness of the research venture at this stage makes one disinclined to search for sources of information if the costs of research are high. The issue may be stated more generally. When the risks associated with research are modest, and when the models have been fully specified and the availability of necessary information ascertained, distance to a library is unlikely to be critical in the choice of research undertakings. But when the risks are high, the inclination not to venture into an area in which one is confronted with obstacles at the outset will surely be strong. Yet it is precisely the high-risk research ventures that often are associated with pioneering research efforts and the discovery of fundamentally new approaches to problems.

I shall now turn to a consideration of the types of library resources used in research in industrial organization. Next, I shall discuss the probable future trends in the types of information that research in this field will require, and the implications of these trends for specialization.

TYPES OF RESOURCES USED

Economics relies far less than do the humanities, and probably less than the other social sciences, on books. And industrial organization probably relies less heavily on this form of publication than do most branches of economics. With many notable exceptions, the main body of research in industrial organization is communicated through journal articles. While the number of journals that specialize in industrial organization has been rising slowly, most of the publications are general purpose journals, in the sense that they serve all of the applied fields and, in most cases, theory and methodology as well. Thus, any library which services economists in any field will have to subscribe to these journals. At a more specialized level in industrial organization there is only a handful of journals of sufficient quality as to be indispensable for research in this field. In short, neither the requisite books nor the indispensable journals are so numerous as to justify specialized libraries, or to create serious acquisition problems to any good research library.

A much more formidable problem is presented by government documents. The vast array of these publications, combined with the cryptic nature of the indexes (when they exist) and the sometimes inscrutable titles, raises not only a storage problem but a serious retrieval problem. For at least the larger economies, a good research library should find it possible to maintain the principal published statistical sources of relevance to research in industrial organization. For special government studies, as distinct from regularly published data, and for data for the smaller economies, some specialization seems inevitable.

In general, however, the central problem for maintaining resources for research in industrial organization arises neither from books nor from journals, nor even from special government studies, but from the data requirements in this field. Because the needs for microeconomic data are far greater in this than in other branches of economics, and because the sources of microeconomic data are extremely varied, a very serious obstacle to the diversity of research centres, all working on common problems, presents itself. As I shall presently argue, while multi-purpose data are usually sufficient for most applied problems in macroeconomics, hypotheses in applied microeconomics usually cannot be tested except with data developed for the special, narrow purpose at hand. As a result, the problem is not merely one of the capacity of a library to accumulate the necessary resources, but, rather, that stockpiling cannot take place before the problem has been effectively explored. This further reinforces my earlier argument that the development of specialized library resources should follow, or at least be concurrent with, the creation of a research centre in a specialized field.

DIRECTIONS OF RESEARCH AND TYPES OF DATA RESOURCES

From the universe of hypotheses about the history of science, the one which I believe is least vulnerable is that the *specific* problems and types of hypotheses which future generations of scholars will choose to examine are basically unpredictable. To be sure, the composition of the demand for knowledge, arising from social problems, tells us something about the general subjects that will be studied. And the record of past failures tells us something about what methods of analysis are likely to recede in importance. But when we come to specific types of hypotheses, these depend mainly on an exogenous variable, namely, where future intellectual breakthroughs will occur.

Data accumulated in advance of research must inevitably be of the general, or multi-purpose, type (e.g. data on production, number of producers, income flows, etc.). To the extent, therefore, that special purpose information is required for scientific progress, there is no effective way of accumulating it in advance of research—that is, in advance of the relevant intellectual breakthrough. Consider, for example, how futile the accumulation of data would have been if it were designed to answer the predicted future hypotheses of economists as of the year 1920.

All that can reasonably be hoped for, therefore, is the identification of broad categories of research. Even this is a hazardous venture. Who would have predicted, even a decade ago, the current interest in energy problems, or, two decades ago, the current preoccupation with environmental control? Nevertheless, one can draw some limited inferences from a combination of the current demand for knowledge and the record of past successes and failures. From these two elements in my predictive model, I conclude that the degree of disaggregation in industrial organization research will increase. Whereas the principal focus of attention in the past has been on behaviour at the industry level, I believe that it will now shift to the individual firm level. This projected shift involves data problems of a new dimension.

PRESENT AND FUTURE TRENDS IN RESEARCH

The dominant tradition of research in industrial organization in the last twenty-five years derives from ideas that emerged in the 1930's from Edward H. Chamberlin, Joan Robinson, and Edward S. Mason. Essentially, it focuses on the competitive structure of markets and proceeds to make behavioural predictions with respect to such variables as price,

price-cost ratios, output, product quality, advertising, etc. from some simple structural characteristics of the market. At the empirical level, this approach has been associated either with case studies of individual industries or, alternatively, with econometric cross-section studies at the industry level of disaggregation.

Though the type of research I briefly identify above continues to account for a large proportion of journal articles on industrial organization, I hazard the prediction that, for a number of reasons, its importance is likely to diminish in the future. First, at the level of theory, first principles in economics have not been sufficient to carry us very far in the analysis of oligopoly. Seemingly small modifications in the assumptions about the information available about each other to competing oligopolists, about the utility functions of managers, about the nature of the barriers to entry, etc., lead to drastic consequences for predicted behaviour. The number of *ad hoc* assumptions, in theoretical literature, on the consequences of market structure is embarrassingly large.

Second, at the empirical level, it has proved difficult to derive generalizations from the case studies, while the cross-section studies with industry data have tended to yield either weak or negative results. This has had the effect of casting doubt on some of the key postulates of the hypothesized link between market structure and behaviour. A striking illustration of this is the absence of strong affirmative results from the roughly forty econometric studies that have examined the relation between monopoly power and profit rates. Some have attributed the unimpressive record of cross-section studies at the industry level to a lack of correspondence between conventionally defined industries and markets. If this interpretation is valid, it appears that most multi-purpose data are unsuitable for studies of market organization.

A third and, probably, decisive reason for the anticipated shift in the focus of research is that the market structure-behaviour relation fails to address a range of questions that increasingly need to be answered. Among these are: (i) the internal organization, incentive structure, and system of rewards within firms—a subject on which, at present, there is little information that can be characterized as more than casual observation; (ii) the response of firms to increasingly pervasive regulatory constraints in all of the developed economies. Little is known about the systematic biases inadvertently introduced by regulation, and about the relative effectiveness of alternative regulatory techniques; (iii) the variables that influence innovative activity and the reaction time of firms to changes in technology; (iv) the incentive structures and patterns of behaviour of public and private non-profit enterprises—a sector that is rapidly expanding in all non-socialist economies.

The common attribute of all of the above problems is that they require information at a high level of disaggregation—that is, information at the level of firms or establishments. While there are some instances of detailed data of this type being published by government agencies—the Federal Power Commission's publications on the electric power industry in the United States is an example—generally, the information needed is not produced through governmental statistical agencies.

CATEGORIES OF DATA

The sources of information are highly diverse for the type of research that I have predicted will assume increasing importance. Data development in this field require considerable inventiveness, and the division of labour that has become standard in some branches of economics—the data producer, on the one hand, and the econometrician, on the other—is not likely to be productive. Indeed, among the reasons for the slow development of research in industrial organization in the last two decades has been the fact that scholars engaged in the testing of hypotheses have generally restricted themselves to the largely irrelevant, published, multipurpose data.

It follows from the above that the range of possible information which scholars will find useful is difficult to determine in advance. As an indication of the afore-mentioned diversity of sources, one can include the following: (i) Published microeconomic records for firms from corporate annual reports, plant directories, directories of product producers, proceedings before regulatory commissions, lists of patent recipients, etc.; (ii) Bodies of data on computer tape. In the United States, these would include the 'Compustat' financial records of public corporations, the Dun and Bradstreet plant employment and product tapes, similar tapes produced by Economic Information Systems, Inc. and still others. To the extent that this form of information—data on computer tape—assumes increasing importance, its acquisition by many libraries is facilitated; (iii) Business histories and document files pertaining to individual firms. Relatively little use has thus far been made of this class of information because of difficulties in quantifying it. However, it is a potentially rich source of relevant data; (iv) Data buried in a vast array of trade publications and publications serving selected industries, professions, and occupations (e.g. the hospital industry); (v) Industry data containing microeconomic information maintained, and sometimes published, by regulatory agencies, insurers (e.g. Blue Cross plans and processors of Medicare Claims in the United States), Boards of Education, etc.

To repeat, the above list is, at best, only partial. The development of new sources of information itself requires an intellectual breakthrough and, therefore, cannot proceed in advance of research. All that libraries can do is to accumulate information that has proved useful in the past. In industrial organization, this constitutes a rather limited subset of what scholars will need in the future. In effect, we are somewhere between the polar cases of the humanities, on the one hand, and most of the physical sciences, on the other. For the former, libraries constitute the principal stockpiles of as yet unused information; for the latter, they are mainly repositories of received knowledge. While, in industrial organization, libraries will be indispensable in maintaining the required resources, the process of stockpiling cannot be effectively carried out, independently, by the libraries themselves.

THE FEASIBILITY OF SPECIALIZATION PLANS

At the outset of this paper I discussed the beneficial effects of competition in research among scholars and research centres. Is there not a similar beneficial effect emanating from competition among libraries? In the humanities and in the various branches of history, the development of unique library resources is, itself, an important stimulus to the creation of distinguished research centres. A library that acquires the heretofore unpublished papers of James Joyce, or the documents of a former President, becomes a centre for scholarly studies in the relevant field.

It is obvious that opportunities for such stockpiling of information are vastly less in economics than in the humanities, and it is my contention that they are less in industrial organization than in most branches of economics. My views on the feasibility of planning specialization of library resources in industrial organization, whether by region or country, are, therefore, pessimistic. The standard sources of information such as books, journals, multi-purpose data at the industry level for the larger economies, are not so voluminous in this field as to be beyond the capacities of large research libraries.

To be sure, some specialization by country is necessary for government documents and other publications, and facilities need to be expanded for the effective exchange of such materials among libraries in various countries. Improved indexes, and improvements in other methods by which retrieval can be carried out at a distance, would help. Fundamentally, however, this will not solve the problem of accumulating resources for research in industrial organization. And it is my contention that such accumulation cannot proceed in advance, or independently, of research, or even at a physical distance from it. Specialization of library resources in this field is, therefore, subsidiary to a more fundamental question, namely, is it possible (or desirable) to plan regional specialization of research centres? While my prejudices on the latter issue are easy to discern, I propose to leave to some later conference a more definitive discussion of this question.

Comment by Michael Lynch (University of Sheffield)

Professor Gort raises questions as to whether economic knowledge ought to be *stored* on a geographically and topically specialized basis; and, if so, whether the allocation of this storage ought to be made through a long term integrated plan. If I read him correctly, he concludes that long term planning is not generally feasible and that such specialization as is desirable will, and must, accompany or follow specialized research. In my view, advances in the technology of reproducing and transmitting information have made these questions relatively uninteresting, at least for Industrial Organization research. Any reasonably sized library that serves economists can afford to store or borrow most of the books, journals, microfilms that will be of interest to industrial organization economists. Trade publications are more of a problem, but here I think that the problem is more one of *retrieving* relevant information than of storage. Indeed, I think that the significant problems in this area concern the *production* of relevant economic information, rather than its storage.

Gort suggests that future industrial organization research will rely more heavily on information at the firm level and even at the extra-firm level. All of my experience at the Federal Trade Commission confirms this. As a result of the high degree of diversification of major firms in the United States, we have very little information on the financial characteristics and performance of such important manufacturing industries turning out turbogenerators, refrigerators, washing machines, synthetic rubber, soaps and detergents, electric lamps, storage batteries, and a host of others. The lack of relevant information makes it difficult, if not impossible, to test adequately even the most basic structure-performance hypotheses. It is in the *production* and publication of such data that long term integrated planning is needed, for here 'laissez-faire' will not work. Intra-firm data is usable only if it can be compared across time and across firms. The 'invisible hand' will not guide firms to produce or publish such comparable data on their own.

I believe that the FTC 'line of business' programme is an important step in the direction of providing more relevant microdata for industrial organization economists. The programme seeks varied financial information, by the line of business, from major corporations in the United States. The latter will be built up from basic components such as establishments, product lines, profit centres, etc. The 1974 data will be classified into some 261 manufacturing industries corresponding to 3, 4, and, in some cases, 5 digit S.I.C. categories.

A complete description of the information collected by the line of business programme, how cost allocations are made, etc., is too complicated to go into here. Any interested reader can obtain additional information by writing to the FTC.

Comment by F. A. Graham (United Kingdom Atomic Energy Authority Reactor Group, Warrington)

Mr Gort's initial question on the desirability of specialization in research libraries is self-answering. Research libraries cannot be general, non-specialized libraries unless they are of the Library of Congress or British Museum Library scale. The question really is 'At what stage do special libraries become research libraries?'

The question of planned distribution of resources on specific subject fields is of major importance. It must be recognized, however, that the basis on which the allocation of subject specialization is determined is not in the hands of the librarian; this decision is pre-empted by the direction of research in the organization which the library serves. It is, however, within the area of the librarian's responsibilities to develop, or allow to decay, the collections on specific topics or lines of research.

The extent to which the total amount of research effort, in few or in many centres, affects the rate of intellectual progress in the field of research is doubtful. The evidence of the United States and of the United Kingdom war effort indicates that the expenditure of effort on development produces greater impact than does an equivalent expenditure on research. This appears to hold true in any branch of science. It may be that there will develop centres of excellence in a particular aspect of research, but it is highly unlikely that the centres will be competitive among themselves. The competition will stem from within each centre. It would follow, then, that the library serving such centres would, of necessity, develop along the lines of research of the parent body. This would not, of course, preclude the libraries from entering into competition with each other for the acquisition of certain research material. It would obviously not be economic for this state of affairs to extend very far.

One of the areas which Mr Gort could have examined, and which would have provided some valuable data, is the relationship between literature search costs, data generation costs and total research costs.

I would accept the trend of Mr Gort's argument away from the long-term planning of the location of specialist material. I am convinced that the incidence of successful research under planned circumstances and in pre-ordained locations is extremely low. There is a further point here which leaves room for discussion. The ordering of society, industry, mankind, books or anything else reaches a limit on the grounds of economics or social desirability. This could be applied to the planning of research-oriented, regionally organized libraries.

The co-ordination of library resources is, and has been for many years, a prime objective of librarians. The inter-availability of material and the co-operation among librarians has led to an improving situation. The co-operation can go only so far in an industrial world or the exchange of information would dissolve the business world. There must, therefore, be a limit on co-operation, the limit imposed by economic factors. The competition starts beyond that limit.

Each of Mr Gort's major points may be interpreted in a different way. There is a great difference between the development of resources for research and the development of resource libraries for research. There is a difference between the development of library resources for research and the development of resource libraries. It is because of the different interpretations available that some of the points in this paper may be self-evident to one group and anathema to another.

It is, perhaps, worth reminding ourselves that society is not moving in one direction all of the time. Organizations are in a constant state of flux and industrial patterns are highly susceptible to fashionable management ideas.

There can, therefore, be no one ideal solution. We must be aware of the options open to us and must be prepared to adapt to changing situations. Mr Gort has provided a view of the possible developments in one field, but, as he would agree, it is one view, not a global solution.

Summary of the Discussion

In introducing Professor Gort's paper, *Professor Coase* hoped that, since the paper was among the shorter ones presented to the conference, his own introduction might also be short. *Professor Coase* interpreted Professor Gort's paper as agreeing that libraries should specialize in particular sorts of material, but (more importantly) as denying that such specialization should be planned in advance. This is because the timing and location of intellectual breakthroughs are seldom predictable, whereas, under planning, one knows where he would have been if 'things hadn't turned up.' If there is specialization, it should vary with the demands of scholars and of shifts in public interest, and such 'planned variability' is seldom practical.

Other speakers have mentioned that Economics relies less upon books than the other social sciences appear to do. This is especially true in Industrial Organization. The specialist in this sub-field requires documents, reports, court cases, and articles in scholarly journals, both general and specialized. In addition, he is always finding usable materials in a wide range of miscellaneous sources—primarily business records—which are difficult to forecast in advance.

Within Industrial Organization, there seems to be a shift in attention from problems of industries to problems of firms. The great tradition is one of market models; great names include Chamberlin, Robinson, Mason. But empirical work along this line seems to be reaching a dead end; replication is difficult, and the volume of figures outruns their significance. No general theory of oligopoly has been developed, nor has there been one of the relation between concentration and profit. We have learned little about the internal behaviour of firms, or of their response to technological change; nor do we know much about similar problems in non-profit organizations. 'Firm' data comes from such miscellaneous sources as internal files, reports, interviews, and tape recordings; the specifics cannot be determined in advance.

Thus, Professor Gort. In *Professor Coase's* view, the 'dead end' to conventional research might have been predicted in advance. Markets have been treated by economists as abstract agencies of 'silent trade,' not as social institutions with real people buying and selling real commodities. We need, said *Professor Coase*, not so much additional data as new approaches. Data are fine in themselves, but data of what particular sorts? The wrong sorts might as well stay in company files as in library dead storage. Brains, not libraries, are the bottleneck in Industrial Organization.

Professor M. Perlman summarized written comments by Dr M. Lynch and Dr M. Graham, suggesting that Professor Coase had largely covered the points they had made. The Graham comment had called 'development' more important in this field than conventional 'research', and would have liked data on the cost of existing research. Dr Graham felt that it might have been more helpful to fund specific research projects directly than to fund research libraries quite so fully for unspecified future research. *Professor Perlman* then raised several issues on his own. He felt that too much of the 'regulation' data was in Schools of Law, and too much of the 'technology' data was in Schools of Engineering, and would have preferred that more of it be more available to economists. Furthermore, *Professor Perlman* criticized industrial economists for slowness in shifting their major emphases from manufacturing to service industries.

Professor Giersch wondered whether there were alternatives to conventional imperfect-competition theory and, if so, what they were. He found it conceivable that Sir Austin Robinson's descriptive-institutional work might be considered eventually as significant as Joan Robinson's theoretical contribution. *Professor Giersch* also criticized the industrial economists for having too little to say about MNCs, or about adjustment processes within LDCs. Among the problems to be studied are, why Volkswagen and 'Detroit' have been so laggard in adjustment to automobile market changes and to the rise of 'service' sectors within manufacturing firms. *Professor Coase* agreed. Theory is lacking, he said, not only for MNCs, but, also, for domestic conglomerates and for the relations between multiple activities within firms.

Professor Diaz-Alejandro wondered what the appropriate unit of observation might be—the industry, the firm, the plant, or, perhaps the 'activity'.

While agreeing with many of Professor Giersch's points, *Professor Wolfe* found much of the industrial-economics discussion too narrow. As for information, much of it is improperly organized and disappears before it can be used. Examples are: financial reports of firms, bank accounts, annual reports, business histories. *Professor Wolfe* thought it unfortunate that neither Professor Gort nor Professor Coase had considered the so-called 'behavioural theory of the firm' as developed by the Carnegie-Mellon group, or expanded the concept of the firm to include such non-profit agencies as churches, hospitals, and universities in their economic operations.

Mr Evans called attention, as he had done in several previous sessions, to the problems of the librarian. He once more asked the practical but unanswered question: which libraries should collect what data? It is costly to move materials from place to place, and it may be administratively 'illegal'. The aggregation of one 'minor addition' after another to the responsibilities of the library has cumulated to a real economic nightmare: *Mr Evans* wondered how the costs of accumulating and using research materials should be divided among individual scholars, libraries, and institutional 'general fund' budgets. Mr Kilgour added that mere stockpiling was costly, too, especially if the process included scientific sampling of stockpiled materials for the avoidance of inadvertent bias, as recommended by Professor Morgan.

Professor Shoup agreed with Professor Gort that the individual firm should be the focus of research, but warned that the size of the task is larger than is usually realized. For any sort of new breakthrough, *Professor Shoup* felt, the researcher must 'live' with the firm for years, not merely visit periodically (referring to Marshall's dictum on the relations between Economics and Biography).

Professor Kindleberger inquired when a collection should be allowed to decay. He felt that some collections were continued too long, and cited the Industrial Organization collection at MIT as a case in point.

Professor von Böventer called the group's attention to the study of types of decision processes. He thought that this typology might be more important than the classification of types of products. *Professor Bronfenbrenner* mentioned the wide range of processes involved here, from the Japanese *ringi-sho* to the frequent Western (and, perhaps, particularly American) authoritarian order by 'the terrible-tempered Mr Bangs'.

Professor Gort, in his reply, expressed the feeling that titles, labels, and nomenclature might be taken too seriously at the conference. He wondered whether there really was an existing stock of knowledge which needed 'retrieval'. Most of the papers dealt with the creation of new knowledge from the accumulation of new data rather than with the use of existing data. In Industrial Economics, the problem is to guess intelligently which data are (or will be) useful and which not. Of course, librarians cannot decide for themselves. Dun and Bradstreet has a great deal of material on computer tape, but no historical record. Why? Because the collection was made for non-research purposes, without the interests of scholars in view. In general, *Professor Gort* felt that the *exchange* of existing materials might, indeed, be more useful at the margin than the accumulation of more.

20 Some Information about Technological Progress and Economic Growth

Yu. A. Borko
INSTITUTE OF SCIENTIFIC INFORMATION ON SOCIAL SCIENCES, USSR

The main topic of the article is the state of, and the needs for, information about technological progress (the author uses the terms 'scientific and technological revolution' (STR) and 'economic growth' (EG). The key nature of the relationship between STR and EG is determined by the content, scope, and rate of development of science and technology. The strong necessity for a new approach to providing scientists with information about STR-EG stems from the multidimensional interdisciplinary character of this field of investigation. The problem of satisfying their requirements is viewed from two angles: (1) does the information exist? (2) is it available? The author supposes that there is a timely question of expanding, improving, and unifying the necessary empirical data. As concerns the availability, the author analyses the experience of the Institute of Scientific Information on Social Sciences (USSR); different types of information retrieval systems used in the Institute, the organization of bibliographical and abstract information, etc.

I. PRELIMINARY REMARKS

First of all, I would like to offer some explanation about the content of, and the concepts in the title. First, there is information related to the *relationship* between technological progress and economic growth (let us designate this relationship as: system 'technological progress—economic growth'). Second, it is useful to identify the meaning of both parts of this formula. As far as 'technological progress' is concerned, I prefer to use another term—'scientific-technological revolution' (STR) because it is more comprehensive and, even more important, it reflects more adequately the essence of the qualitative transformation that is taking place, both in our scientific understanding of nature and the productive forces of society. The second concept—'economic growth' (EG) is employed here in a broad sense, having in mind not only 'growth' as such, but the entire set of changes in the economy stemming from the scientific-technological revolution.

Hence, my task is to determine the extent to which economists require information about the STR-EG system, and the degree to which these requirements are satisfied by present-day information systems. I proceed with two convictions in mind: (1) information about the STR-EG problem ranks among the primary requirements of economists in view of the first priority of the problem; (2) this requirement is obviously not sufficiently satisfied at present; possibly, it is less well handled than the information requirements of economists investigating other, less important, problems.

II. THE CONTENT AND SIGNIFICANCE OF THE PRESENT-DAY STR

The key nature of the relationship between the STR and economic growth emerged after the Second World War. It is determined by the content, scope and rate of progress of science and technology. The unparalleled nature of this change has been reflected in a multitude of widely used metaphors: 'the Atomic Age', 'the Age of Cybernetics', 'the Age of Computers', 'the Age of Outer Space', 'the Age of Synthetics', and so on, emphasizing the various aspects of our contemporary scientific-technological revolution. This assessment has been expressed even more clearly in the use of such general terms as 'the new industrial revolution' and 'the scientific-technological revolution'.

It is my opinion that the preferred phrase is 'the scientific-technological revolution'. Although there are quite a number of aspects to this concept, and I have no intention of 'adding oil to the fire', nonetheless I want to quote one apt definition which interprets the STR as 'a radical qualitative transformation of the productive forces, resulting from the merging of the scientific and technological revolutions, and the transformation of science into a direct productive force'.[1]

The revolutionary nature of the scope and rate of development of discoveries in science and technology becomes clear from their impact on the economy, on society as a whole, and on man. It is an extremely deep-running impact, with many extremely complicated and quite often contradictory facets. In a number of aspects, the impact of STR is global. It does not necessarily depend upon the nature of social relations; on the contrary, any social system will leave its imprint on STR and its socio-economic, and even its ecological environmental consequences. The 'technological progress—economic growth' relationship has thus become an integral part of the universal 'Man–Nature' relationship.

Having thus mentioned the problem of the contemporary STR, I realize that I am extending the framework of my topic to a maximum, going far beyond the limits set down in the title. In order not to be ac-

[1] 'Chelovek—nauka—technika' (Moscow, 1973), p. 30.

cused of expansionism, it is necessary to emphasize here that it is precisely the broad interpretation of the problem which paves the way to the study of a narrower topic—the relationships in the STR-EG system. The 'comprehensiveness' in this case has two meanings: on the one hand, one studying the impact of STR on the *totality* of social production must go beyond the framework of economic science and draw upon the results of investigations obtained in other branches of scientific knowledge (natural sciences, engineering, sociology, law and so on); on the other hand, one's study of the *economic consequences* of the STR should be of help to representatives of other branches of science (philosophers, sociologists, specialists in the field of international relations, biologists and so on), who are investigating various aspects of the STR's impact on human society and the environment.

The need for this kind of comprehensive approach and inter-branch scientific co-operation should lay the groundword for a new approach to providing scientists with information about the STR and how it affects social production.

III. BASIC TRENDS AND METHODOLOGICAL PROBLEMS IN STUDYING THE STR-EG SYSTEM

As is evident from the intensive stream of literature devoted to the given problem, the Soviet study of the relationship between the STR and economic growth has been conducted on a broad scale in recent decades. The catalogue at the library of the Institute which I represent has, under several headings devoted to different aspects of the economic and social consequences of the STR, a list of almost 4000 books, reviews, reference-bibliographies and other publications, with the great majority coming off the press in the past 8–10 years. This number does not include periodicals, whose number is even greater.

An understanding of the broad scope of investigations in the given field can be seen in the following scheme. This scheme should not be viewed as some abstract model of an all-round study of the problem, but, rather, as a rough draft for classifying the factual stream of literature.

THE STR-EG SYSTEM

1. Scientific-Technological Revolution: general characteristics.
   Content of STR, principal features, dimensions and consequences; theories, concepts and methodological approaches.
2. STR and development of productive forces.
   Science as an accelerating factor of technical and technological progress;
   new sources and methods of energy production;
   nuclear energetics;

new methods of extraction and use of raw materials;
growing significance of artificial raw materials;
new technology;
automation of production;
development of synthetic chemistry;
new kinds of end-products.

3. The impact of STR on social production.
On the structure of the national economy (branches and territories);
on the proportion of social production (consumption-savings);
on the structure and dynamics of consumption;
on increment and utilization of savings.

4. The impact of STR on labour force.
On employment;
on the structure of labour force (branches and occupations);
on the quality and costs of labour force;
on the nature of labour and working conditions, problems of psychological adaptation by a worker to the new technology.

5. STR as a factor promoting economic growth.
'Contribution' to boosting labour productivity and GNP;
economic efficiency of 'R and D':
at the level of enterprises and firms;
at the level of branches and the national economy as a whole.

6. The impact of STR on trade, credit and monetary mechanism.
On the structure and rate of growth of trade;
on terms and forms of market competition;
on the monetary-credit mechanism.

7. The STR and economic organization and management.
New dimensions of production ('economy of scale');
new methods of management:
using computers in management;
industrial and scientific-technological policy:
at the level of enterprises and firms;
at the macro-economic level (national economy).

8. Science and education in conditions of the STR.
New forms of ties between science and production;
organization and economics of scientific research;
influence of the STR on education (general, vocational, special) and on the training of scientific personnel;
economic role, and the efficacy, of education.

9. The influence of the STR on the ecological environment.
The problem of natural resources;
problems of the environment;
an economic appraisal of the influence of scientific-technological progress on the environment;
the policy of protecting and restoring the environment disputable

triangle: 'the environment—the population-economic growth'.

10. Forecasting scientific-technological progress and its economic and social consequences.
11. Social consequences of the STR.
    Influence on the social structure of society;
    influence on living conditions and mode of life;
    problem of the 'quality of life';
    influence on socio-political relations;
    the problem of criteria for a general evaluation of the socio-economic consequences of the STR.
12. The influence of the social system on the course and nature of development of the STR, on its social-economic consequences.
    A comparative analysis of the relationships of the STR-EG in different countries, groups of countries and regions.
13. The impact of the STR on international economic and political relations.
    On the forms of international economic competition and international economic co-operation;
    on the international division of labour;
    on the relationships between the industrially developed and the emerging countries;
    the political and military-political aspects of the STR.

This list does not claim to be complete. Even so, it gives an indication of the scope of the problem and, what is more important, its novelty and complexity.

In addition, there are other circumstances intensifying these requirements. A successful study of the above-mentioned problems presumes as pre-requisites: (1) a general methodological (conceptual) base and specific methods of investigation; (2) a large volume of systematic and sufficiently trustworthy empirical data. These pre-requisites are inter-dependent. The information that is precisely needed by a scientist depends on the methodology and the methods chosen. In turn, the volume and the nature of the factual information determine, to a greater extent, the choice of concept and methods of investigation.

However, in the sphere of studying the STR-EG system, as well as in any comparatively new field of scientific knowledge, these prerequisites are only just now crystallizing. Several examples may illustrate the present state of methodology and methods of investigation. Some examples are related to attempts in determining the role of scientific-technological progress as a factor of economic growth. Economists studying this question agree thus far only that this factor plays a significant ever-increasing role. Yet, the quantitative evaluations of this role are astounding by their diversity. For instance, Prof. Charles Stuart (United States), in one of his articles, notes that, depending on the chosen methods, the 'contribution' of scientific-technological progress to economic growth varies from 30 per cent to 90 per cent.[2]

Such contrasts have been noted by the Soviet economist, Dr V. Zubchaninov, who quite justly concludes:

> When a difference in opinion is expressed in quantitative differences of such scope, one cannot but have doubts as to the correctness of choosing the parameters for the initial data, as well as the calculating methods employed.[3]

Another example of unsolved methodological problems is seen in the ways of making an economic evaluation of the harmful impact of the scientific-technological revolution on the environment, without which it is impossible to compile a well-founded estimate for protection expenditures. In an interesting article, R. Poujade (France) notes the difficulties in resolving the need for full collection of reliable data about the environment in this or that region, determining the cost of separate elements of the environment, making a quantitative evaluation of a number of harmful consequences of scientific-technological progress (noise, air and water pollution, degradation of the flora and fauna, and so on).[4] Here, the difficulty lies not only in the choice of method for analysis, but in the absence, or incompleteness, of data.

And, finally, the third example is the problem of a general evaluation of the effectiveness of scientific-technological progress. For quite some time, the majority of economists in the West regarded this problem from the standpoint of economic efficacy and economic growth. Proceeding from these criteria, the proponents of the proposed methods took purely economic data as their basic indices: volume of GNP (absolute and on a per capita basis) and the rate of its growth, level and rate of growth of labour productivity, indices of technical equipment and economic efficiency (electric power capacity, capital-output ratio, etc.), as well as certain other indices of this type. However, representatives of Marxist economic thought, as well as a number of economists of the radical-critical trend who do not share Marxist views, pointed to the one-sided nature of such an approach, and to the need for taking into account the social consequences of scientific-technical progress.

More and more, economists today are coming to the conclusion that it is impossible to give a general evaluation of so tremendous a process as STR without taking into account its social efficacy. I refer to two promi-

[2] C. Stuart, 'A Summary of the State of the Art on the Relationship between R & D and Economic Growth Productivity,' in *Research and Development of Economic Growth, Papers and Proceedings of a Colloquium* (Washington, 1972), p. 11–19.

[3] V. Zubchaninov, 'How to Evaluate Technological Progress?' *World Economics and International Relations* (Moscow, 1970), 2, p. 75.

[4] R. Poujade, '*Le Coût des nuisances*' in *Urbanisation et environment*, Paris (1973), N 844, pp. 13–18.

nent American specialists—S. Kuznets and K. Boulding. The former stressed that the economic calculations used at present relate to only one system of evaluation and selection, which does not take into account either many of the shortcomings or many of the benefits of economic and technical development.[5] Kuznets believes that the balance of these benefits and shortcomings should be evaluated with due consideration to the relationships between technical and social factors. Boulding's stand is even more categorical. He believes that it is time to stop regarding the GNP as the real yardstick of economic progress and effluency and, instead, to take an ecological approach as the basis for evaluation.[6] Finally, one must remember that, in recent years, a very active group of extreme supporters of the 'ecological-demographic' approach has appeared, a group that is developing the concept of 'zero growth' of the economy.

I do not intend to analyse these views. I would only like to stress the tremendous difference in elaborating the methodology for making a summary appraisal of the efficacy of scientific-technological progress, the difficulty of the task of making a quantitative appraisal and comparing all of the parameters—economic, social, ecological, demographic—of the impact of the STR on production and society. This example, like the others, indicates the great need for developing, to a maximum, an exchange of information in this field of the economic science.

A similar conclusion results from any review of the state of empirical data which a specialist needs as the initial material for analysing the relationship in the STR-EG system. Much new information which previously was of little interest to economists has now entered scientific circulation. This shift has given rise to the timely question of expanding, improving and unifying the necessary empirical data.

The ultimate conclusion to be drawn from a review of the information requirements of scientists studying the STR-EG system can be defined as follows: these requirements are, indeed, very great because of (1) the complex nature, scope, and novelty of the problem; (2) the rapidly expanding investigations and the swelling flow of literature; (3) the many questions of methodology and methods of investigation that have not been fully elaborated in the intensive search for solutions and lively discussions in this field; (4) the imperfect nature of the accessible empirical base for investigations and the need to improve it.

IV. THE STATE OF INFORMATION ABOUT THE STR-EG SYSTEM AND WAYS TO IMPROVE IT

The problem of satisfying the information requirements of scientists is

[5] S. Kuznets, 'Innovations and Adjustments in Economic Growth,' *Swedish Journal of Economics*, Vol. 74, (1972), N. 4, p. 443.

[6] K. Boulding, 'Fun and Games with the Gross National Product—the Role of Misleading Indicators in Social Policy,' in *The Environmental Crisis. Man's Struggle to Live with Himself* by H. W. Helrich, ed. (New Haven-London, 1970), pp. 157–70.

viewed from two angles: (1) does the information exist? (2) is it available?

The question of whether *information exists* may seem pointless if one recalls what I have written about the tremendous flow of scientific literature devoted to the STR and its economic consequences. However, matters look quite different as soon as we go over to evaluating the state of information about empirical data which represent the starting point for any investigation. Such information may become the object of scientific analysis if it complies with such criteria as being full, regular, dependable and comparable. It has already been mentioned that the empirical material already in the hands of scientists falls far short of these criteria.

Without going into a specific description of the state of empirical information, I feel it necessary to emphasize the main point—the pressing task of determining the range and content of the necessary initial data about the STR-EG system, their classification and unification.

There are at least four main groups of empirical data:

(1) natural-scientific and scientific-engineering information without which it is impossible to forecast scientific-technological progress and its influence on the economy and the environment;
(2) economic information reflecting the relationship between scientific-technological progress and the development of social production;
(3) sociological information and the humane aspects of the STR;
(4) information about the scientific-technological policy of governments, non-government institutions, international organizations and so on. Each of these groups consists of a great number of parameters characterizing the relationships in the STR-EG system from different angles.

Each of these groups includes various types of empirical data: statistical rows and separate quantitative indicators, factual data of a non-quantitative nature, documents, questionnaires, expert appraisals and so on. Proper organization of this whole world of empirical information is imperative for developing further research in this field. It goes without saying that the solution of this task calls for the co-ordinated efforts of economists in different countries. In particular, it would be desirable to hold a special symposium on this problem, possibly under the auspices of the International Economic Association.

The second aspect—*the availability of information*—will be dealt with in greater detail because, in the light of the current 'information explosion', the problem of tracking down, choosing and retrieving the information needed by specialists (not only empirical data, but the results of investigations, also) has acquired cardinal significance for the success of all investigations.

Out of the whole number of questions dealing with providing scientists with information about the STR-EG problem, this paper examines two aspects: (1) the extent of the given problem reflected in information retrieval systems (IRS); (2) the organization of bibliographical and abstract information. I shall refer to both international experience, as well as to the experience of our Institute of Scientific Information on Social Sciences (ISISS) and to a number of other Soviet information centres.

The organization of modern ISR's reflects two simultaneously existing but diametrically opposite tendencies in the development of science: (1) the differentiation and specialization of scientific investigations; (2) the integration of science, giving rise to new fields of investigation on the borderline of two or several branches of science, as well as the broadening inter-branch exchange of methods and results of research work. The first of these tendencies is of a traditional character, because it passes through the entire history of the development of science; the second is novel and has appeared now, in the postwar period. Each of these trends has found significant reflection in one of the two main types of modern IRS: the first tendency—in general, classification systems built along hierarchic lines and based on the classification of the branches of science; the second—in subject indices and catalogues where classification is based on the object under investigation in all of its aspects, irrespective of what branch of knowledge this or that aspect belongs to.

As for the IRS of the first type, the problem of STR-EG is reflected in new divisions within the already existing classification system. An example of such a system can be seen in the international Universal Decimal Classification (UDC), where the information on a given problem is divided among the branches 'Technology', 'Science', 'National Economy', 'Law' and so on. With the branch heading of 'National Economy' there are wholly new rows of sub-divisions of the 4th, 5th and 6th order, containing direct references about technological progress (330.341.1 Development of productive forces. Technological progress; 330.836 Technico-economic theories. Technocracy; 333.041 The impact of engineering; 331.6.063.2 Technological unemployment; etc.).

The UDC also employs another method of classifying new problems—double indexing which makes it possible to overcome the rigid framework of branch classification (330.111.4: 001 Science as factor of production; 330.341:63 Technical factors of economic development).

It is apparent that, in the future, both methods of supplementing classification systems like the UDC with new concepts that point to the ties between the STR and different aspects of economic life in society, will be used. For instance, the proposals for improving the economic section of UDC that were tabled in 1974 in FID by a group of experts, including T. Földi and B. Bobocki (HPR), S. E. Müller (FRG), I. Soukup (CzSSR)—contain more than ten new headings related to the given problems.

The classification systems of the hierarchic type employed in the

Soviet Union are being improved along the same lines: for example, the library-bibliographical classification (LBC) which is employed at the V. I. Lenin State Library. In the ISISS, the hierarchic principle of classification lies at the basis of branch indices which are used in the monthly bibliographical bulletins, published at the Institute. For instance, the index on economics which was substantially redone in 1974 contains about 50 sub-indexes of the 3rd–6th levels reflecting the STR-EG problem, including: 'The STR in conditions of present-day capitalism', 'The STR in conditions of socialism', 'International scientific-technological ties', 'Technical progress in the national economy' (as a whole and in each branch), 'Labour and technological progress,' 'The economics of science' and so on.

The problems of interest to us are also widely reflected in another branch index—science of sciences. It contains indexes at the 2nd level as 'Organization of scientific research.' 'Management of science' (10 sub-indexes of the 3rd level, 35 at the 4th level, and 5 at the 5th level), 'Scientific personnel' (correspondingly—7, 9 and 1 sub-indexes); and 'The economics of science' (5 sub-indexes at the 3rd level). Other sections of the index classify such sub-indexes of the 3rd–6th levels as 'Communist and Workers' parties and questions of science and technology', 'The contemporary scientific-technological revolution', 'Science as a direct productive force,' 'Science and ecological problems', and so on.

However, there is a limit to improving the IRS of the above-mentioned traditional type. This limit is determined by the rigid initial structure of the branch classification of sciences. The introduction of sub-headings and double indexes makes it possible to overcome this rigidity only partially.

All of this is especially true of those new, complex problems which include the subject of the STR-EG. Bearing in mind the trend in modern science toward investigating such inter-branch problems, the fundamental library on social sciences of the USSR AS (now part of the Institute), has, for many years, been oriented toward the second type of classification, the one based on a thesaurus or subject-approach. This principle was used in its library for building a master catalogue which numbers about 200,000 subject headings and above 2 million bibliographical cards.

This catalogue consists of subject indexes reflecting the basic categories and concepts used in social sciences, as well as the most important processes and subjects studied by these sciences. In order to give a description of the whole range of indexes reflecting the topic or the problem as a whole, the concept 'complex' should be introduced because it plays a vital role in improving the subject catalogue. It makes it possible periodically to analyse, to some extent, the given group of subject indexes reflecting the problem in all of its aspects and relationships, and to introduce changes and supplements reflecting progress in science. The alphabetical order of the indexes and the absence of a hard-fast indexation lend the necessary flexibility to this system of classification, and help it to create new sub-headings which fit in quite easily with the system and to establish new ties between headings.

The catalogue envisages different methods of such ties. They include the use of complicated headings such as 'main headings—thematic sub-headings', or 'main heading—geographical sub-heading—thematic sub-heading'. Another method is to list all of these ties between affiliated headings like 'heading—reference from other headings—references to other headings'. In cases when identical or very close concepts are used in science, they are included in a catalogue as separate headings; moreover, information on the given object is collected in one place, while the rest of the headings are accompanied by references.

The index catalogue contains a great many headings dedicated to the STR-EG problem. First of all, there is the heading 'Scientific-technological progress' (the catalogue reflects the concept 'scientific-technological revolution', from which a reference is given to the mentioned heading). The essence of this concept starts with the help of a complicated system of relationships, in which 54 headings and sub-headings are connected with the main heading (not counting the sub-headings such as 'branch of production—technological progress', and 'the country—scientific-technological progress').

The problems of the STR-EG are broadly covered in the comprehensive headings of 'Industry'. The 'solution' is attained, not only by creating more than 20 main headings, directly pointing to ties between industrial production and scientific-technological progress, but, also, by forming a great number of standard headings of the same nature related to branches and factors of production, to countries and regions (e.g. 'machine engineering—comprehensive mechanization—automation': 'France—national economy—technological progress'). Out of the 98 standard sub-headings, more than 20 directly point to ties with scientific-technological progress and about another 40 envisage such ties.

It is understandable that the work performed by the Institute in labelling the given problems should not be considered as complete. In all likelihood, new thematic headings and sub-headings will appear, and new ties among different objects will emerge. Apparently, a more general task has matured—to unite all of the headings related to the given topic into a single complex 'The scientific-technological revolution. Economic and social consequences'.

However, from the point of view of today's—and, what is more important—tomorrow's requirements of specialists in information, as well as from the point of view of our contemporary understanding of an optimal system of information, the above-mentioned ways of improving systematic and subject IRS's are of a partial nature. The problem now is to create a unified automated service of information using electronic computers and other modern technical means. Such a service would merge into one all the different stages of selecting, processing, collecting, storing, searching for, and handing out, information, and all types of information retrieval languages and information services. Within the framework of such a solution, it may become possible to improve information about the STR-EG problems.

The task of creating such an information service in the USSR also covers the 'All-Union Information Classification of the Branches of Science, Engineering and National Economy' (AIC). This job has been tackled by the leading scientific and information centres in the country, including the Academy of Sciences of the USSR, branch scientific institutes, the All-Union Institute of Scientific and Technical Information (AISTI), the ISISS, and so on. The problem of STR-EG is widely covered in all four sections of AIC—'Marxism-Leninism', 'Natural Sciences', 'Natural sciences', 'Engineering—National Economy', 'Social Sciences'—as headings on the 3rd level. But, on top of all this, the AIC designates a special subject field, 'Comprehensive problems of social sciences', which has a separate division for the topic 'STR Problems', including 9 groups of the 3rd level: 'General methodological problems of the STR', 'Social problems of the STR', 'The environment and the STR', 'The STR in conditions of various social systems', and others.

The elaboration of classification systems, combining systematic and subject approaches, is being conducted at the international level. The draft Subject-Retrieval Code, tabled in FID in 1973, is developing precisely in that direction. In my opinion, the complex topic, 'Scientific-technological revolution', should be included in the number of object fields.

The last question with which I would like to deal concerns *bibliographical and reference information.* Its role as a kind of signalling system has, without a doubt, grown. The ISISS is the main centre in the Soviet Union for creating systems of bibliographical and reference publications on social sciences. These publications reflect the problems under consideration.

Bibliographical information on problems of the STR-EG is printed mainly in the following bulletins: *New Soviet Economic Literature*, *New Foreign Economic Literature*, *New Soviet Literature on Science and Scientific Research in the USSR*, and *New Literature about Science and Scientific Research Literature Abroad.* These bulletins are formed on the basis of branch headings, which makes it possible to track down the necessary literature.

The organization of information on problems of the STR-EG can be seen from the example of the *New Soviet Economic Literature* bulletin. The contents of each issue are under 18 sub-headings of the 2nd and 3rd level: *Problems of the STR Under Socialism*, *Technological progress in the national economy*, *Automation*, *Effectiveness of measures of technological progress and new machinery*, *Technological progress in industry*, *Scientific research in the national economy*, and others. A random study of several issues has shown that out of 3611 titles of published works, 750 (21 per cent) were either totally or mainly devoted to different aspects of relationships between scientific-technological progress and social production. At the same time, the analysis has illustrated that in specialized headings there were only 237 titles, i.e. one-third of all the works on problems of the STR-EG. This is related to the fact that a number of general headings—'Personnel', 'Labour', 'Planning' and others do not have a corresponding sub-heading, but contain works examining the given problem from the point of view of the STR. In all likelihood, the classification into such headings is expedient in some cases, while in others it is not. Yet, there is another way of raising the informativeness of bibliographical bulletins—by synopsis. This is the path that has been taken by the Institute which plans to increase sharply the share of symopsized titles, and, in the future, to go over to such a system in general. Reference information on problems of the STR-EG is presented chiefly in the reference journal (RJ) *Social Sciences in the USSR* (from the series 'Economics' and 'Science of Sciences'). The share of reference material on the given problem is quite high. In the first series it is 48 per cent (1974), in the second series it is 33 per cent (1973–74), and in the third it is 60 per cent (1973–74). In all three series, this problem is dealt with in special sections: In the first, 'Combination of achievements of the STR with the advantage of socialism. Economic problems of creating the material and technical base of communism' and 'Questions of determining and raising the efficiency of social production, improving its structure and proportions, raising productivity of labour'; in the second, 'Technological progress. Social-economic consequences of the STR'; in the third, 'Science and society', 'Organization of science' and 'Scientific personnel'.

It is noteworthy, however, that there is no total correlation between the above-mentioned sections and the problems of the STR-EG. On the one hand, the topic framework of the sections is, as a rule, broader; on the other hand, the rest of the sections of the given series of RJ's also include reviews of books and articles which take up problems of the STR-EG (this concerns those cases when the given problems are not the main ones in scientific research or when one of its chapters analyses it). That is why one of the conditions for raising the level of informativeness of the RJ's is to create indexes which reflect the problems examined in the paper.

The RJ is not the only type of review-reference publication used by the Institute. A promising type of publication are collections of reviews (RC). Unlike the RJ, which are of a branch nature and are compiled on the basis of current scientific literature, the RC's are problem-subject publications and can include not only new, but previously published works, which have made a substantial contribution to the scientific development of the given problem. In particular, the Institute is preparing for print a whole series of RC's under the general title of 'Problems of the Scientific-Technological Revolution'.

And, finally, another type of reference-review publication which has been planned for use in obtaining information about problems of the STR-EG are the analytical reviews of Soviet and foreign scientific literature.

Summing up this brief review of the state of information on problems of the STR-EG, it is necessary to emphasize that both in the Soviet Union as well as in other countries, efforts are being undertaken to expand and improve such information. Today, some valuable experience in this field has been accumulated from the experiences of various countries. A mutual exchange of such experience is extremely useful, not only for the development of national information systems, but also for generally expanding the stock of international scientific information which is so badly needed.

Summary of the Discussion

Dr Schatz introduced Dr Borko's paper with an exposition of Dr Borko's concept of STR-EG. This is an acronym for 'Scientific-Technological-Revolution and Economic Growth'; much of Dr Borko's paper is organized around the notion of the STR-EG complex. This concept can be justified by the intimate relations between science, technology, and production; moreover, the relation of STR-EG to society as a whole is necessarily interdisciplinary.

Dr Borko's work has been organized around a number of sub-fields. Six of these are: (1) Changes in resource allocation, to increase average labour productivity; (2) Changes in investment and production decisions; (3) Changes in the quality of factors of production; (4) Changes in the environmental and ecological consequences of production; (5) Changes in international trade relations; and (6) Improvements in forecasting.

Our STR-EG information needs, Dr Borko has said, are not yet met. This insufficiency, Dr Borko believes, has added to supply shortages. We know little about either the precise influences of STR or of the social costs of EG. Dr Borko believes that a narrowly economic approach to these problems will not suffice. More general approaches, such as he has found to be provided by Marxism-Leninism, are much more promising.

In Dr Borko's view, information about the STR-EG system exists in large quantities in many countries. It is, however, not readily available, is frequently incomplete, and is often of low quality. Storage and retrieval facilities are lacking. Moreover, there is a tendency toward too much specialization, which Dr Borko refers to as 'branch hierarchy', over the study of STR-EG as a whole. Offsetting this, however, are new integrations of the various branches of knowledge, such as are being attempted in the USSR. International co-operation will assist in the integration process.

Dr Schatz's own comments focused on the definition of 'revolution'. He wondered whether, in the context of history, the STR-EG developments should not be looked upon as a process of continuous evolution. *Dr Schatz* also felt that the paper should have examined in more detail the relation of STR-EG to environment and ecology. The relationship, he thought, was explainable on the basis of economic history, and Dr Borko's treatment was not well adapted to the needs of contemporary LDCs.

The initial comment from the floor was made by *Professor Gort*, who wondered whether economic study should revolve about STR-EG to quite the extent suggested by Dr Borko. He also wondered whether mere bibliographical information would help anyone except the somewhat superficial generalist, and whether the cost of the Borko proposal of widespread and comprehensive bibliography had been taken into account. Much of the accumulation will inevitably be rubbish, unless the accumulation process is more selective than that suggested by the paper. *Professor Gort* had himself attempted to describe the innovation process on a much smaller scale, for some 35 specific products. His initial strategy, which had placed great reliance on library catalogues, unearthed mainly useless information. His second, and more successful strategy, had been direct consultation with specialists in particular products, who were primarily engineers and technologists. *Professor Gort* believed that his experience would be equally applicable to developmental history in the large.

Professor M. Perlman noted, as an aspect of the so-called 'convergence hypothesis', the increasing empiricism in Soviet research, including the improved organization and availability of Soviet data.

Professor Giersch then inquired how the contemporary STR aspect of Dr Borko's thesis compared with the Industrial Revolution of the past. His own suspicion is that it represents a 'Kondratieff' cycle of wartime and pre-war innovations which are being absorbed into the economy. This explanation is applicable at least in the West, according to *Professor Giersch*. Is the situation significantly different in the USSR?

Mr Kilgour inserted the viewpoint of the librarian. About 20 per cent of catalogue items refer to specific subjects; in his view, only 20 per cent of these are helpful to users. He believed the arrangement of materials on library shelves to be the main determinant of their usefulness, and not the accumulation of catalogue references. In addition, such volumes as *Chemical Abstracts* have been extraordinarily helpful in their respective fields.

Professor Chamley noted that Dr Borko's concept of STR-EG is not being used in the West, and wondered whether it might be in some sense ideological. *Professor Kindleberger* suggested an alternative organization of 20th century technological history. During the period of World War I, *Professor Kindleberger* believes, great advances were made in mass production. The corresponding improvement during the period of World War II was in what *Professor Kindleberger* called 'mass precision'. The contemporary improvements might perhaps be described as 'materials precision'.

Professor Blaug introduced into the discussion the distinction between 'product innovation' and 'process innovation', which he had not found in Dr Borko's paper. (*Mr Kilgour* did not believe that the two should be separated too sharply.) In the West, *Professor Blaug* went on, product innovation is considered the more important of the two. Do students in the East come to the same conclusion?

Replying to these comments, Dr Borko denied that his term STR-EG was either substantially original or distinctively Marxist. It described, he thought, a process recognized all over the world. Similar terms such as 'the technotronic age' and 'the post-industrial age' had been devised by Western scholars like Brzezinski and Bell.

Dr Borko believed that the pace of industrial progress has accelerated qualitatively in recent years, and cited the work done under the auspices of the Club of Rome. He suggested that, if Western scholars disliked the term 'revolution', they might substitute the term 'qualitative change' to cover the association of scientific progress, technological progress, and economic growth in both East and West. (While the present EDCs are not yet full participants, *Dr Borko* forecast that some of them would become so in the relatively near future.)

Finally, *Dr Borko* defended the bibliographical aspects of his proposal as being merely first steps. He admitted the danger of negative returns from the accumulation of useless and low-quality items, and also raised the problem of classification. Any classification system would, unfortunately, be too coarse for some purposes and too fine for others.

21 The Relevance of Recent Trends in Economic History to the Information Needs of Research Workers in the Field

Phyllis Deane
UNIVERSITY OF CAMBRIDGE

This paper focuses on the library needs of economists doing research in economic history. After a brief reference to the special characteristics of the information required by the economic historian, it discusses recent trends in the subject—particularly the persistent interest in economic growth and development since the early 1950s and the 'new' economic history with its heavy dependence on statistical-analytical techniques. Both trends have increased the volume of quantitative data and widened the range of the qualitative data required for research in economic history. The last section suggests an order of priorities for university libraries providing economic historians with research material.

My brief in this paper is to consider the information needs of economic historians with particular reference to their implications for university library acquisition and discard policies over the next decade—a period which is likely to be characterized by particularly severe constraints on the financial and spatial resources of university libraries. I propose to focus on the needs of the academic research worker on the grounds that, when resources are limited, priority should be given to those who are actively concerned with strengthening the foundations or extending the frontiers of knowledge in the subject; and, also, in the belief that a library policy which meets the needs of those actively researching in the subject cannot be bad for those who are teaching or studying it at an academic level.

I. WHAT IS ECONOMIC HISTORY?

The first problem which arises is that of defining the subject and, especially, of deciding to what parent discipline economic history belongs. Is it history or is it economics? The superficial answer is to say 'both', and to start from the premise that the study of economic history is an interdisciplinary study which draws on the methodology and techniques of both disciplines. In practice, it is not as easy as that.

It is well known that economic history has two faces—one looking towards the discipline of history and the other to that of economics, that research in economic history tends to put a different set of questions to the historical record, and to assume a different form, when undertaken by history graduates, from what it does when the questions are chosen and formulated within the analytical framework suggested by an Economics Faculty. Traditionally, the historians have tended to set their explanations of economic change in a narrative-descriptive framework which gives more weight to the qualitative complexity of the historical process, whereas the economists have tended to select their problems and variables in relation to a deliberately simplified analytical framework, and to give special weight to aspects which are, (in principle if not always in practice), measurable in quantitative terms.

True, the modern economic historian reared in a history stable also adopts an analytical approach to his material, makes explicit use of the logic of economic theory and applies appropriate statistical techniques to answer questions which have a quantitative dimension, just as the economics graduate specializing in economic history cannot afford to neglect the chronologically changing qualities of his economic parameters or of the social, political and institutional context in which they operate. In principle, the results of approaching economic history from these divergent directions should be complementary and our attempt to define the information needs of one group of research workers should be applicable to those of the other group. In practice, however, the two kinds of economic history vary so widely in scope and methodology that an economist is perhaps unlikely to rank information priorities in the same order as does his historian counterpart.

For the economist, then, the study of economic history is a branch of applied economics, distinguished essentially from other areas of applied economics in that its raw material is drawn more from past periods than from the contemporary economy. Where the contemporary present shades into the historical past is, of course, debatable, but at present the Second World War makes such a sharp break in the continuity of recent events that the period before, say, 1950 can be conveniently regarded as 'historical.' The object of an economist's excursions into economic history is generally to trace the recurrent regularities of human behaviour in the economic sphere and to illustrate or test the economic laws or theories which anticipate such regularities.

II. GENERAL CHARACTERISTICS OF INFORMATION REQUIRED FOR RESEARCH IN ECONOMIC HISTORY

The applied economist formulates his research problem in the context of the paradigm he has absorbed in the course of his professional training as an economist. This may approximate to one, or a mixture of, several possible alternatives (e.g. neoclassical, post-Keynesian, monetarist, Marxist, etc.)—the mix depending on his own natural prejudices and acquired preconceptions which determine both the problem he chooses to investigate and the disciplinary matrix in which he specifies it. One result, however, is that the subject matter of economic history is far from stable. Different generations of economists focus on different questions and adopt different views of what is an orthodox and what is a heretical framework of analysis. Another result is that the raw material of economic history is scattered over a very wide area of primary and secondary sources. The modern economic historian may draw his conceptual, methodological and theoretical ideas from, e.g. sociology, political science, and demography, as well as from different areas of economic theory. He may use factual, descriptive and quantitative information from the natural sciences (e.g., technological and medical sources) as well as from other social sciences. He may draw data and inspiration from a wide range of historical and geographical origins and from a variety of published and unpublished sources (books and pamphlets, journals and newspapers, official and institutional papers, private and public archives, dissertations, academic working papers, *ad hoc* oral surveys, photographic records, etc.).

In these respects the study of economic history differs from that of contemporary applied economics, or, indeed, from any of the other social sciences, only as a matter of degree.[1] However, its interdisciplinary character and its potentially extremely wide chronological and geographical range ensure that the scatter of its material and the characteristic search techniques developed by its scholars are significant in determining its information needs. In particular, for example, the research material assembled by past economic historians, the primary records relating to past events or institutions, are rarely outdated in the sense that they will no longer yield fruitful answers to new questions or that they have been fully exploited in relation even to old questions. As a result, the economic historian tends to resist obsessively any suggestions that librarians or archivists should be permitted to discard or destroy material—however apparently ephemeral or however thoroughly worked

[1] Kyle [22] (1958) notes that the literature relating to the social sciences differs from that of physical science or technology by virtue of: (1) its quantity, variety and scatter; (2) its imprecision and the great size of vocabularies (making effective indexing that much more difficult); and (3) the unstable character of its subject matter.

over—and to put great stress on the serendipity that might stem from free, direct and unstructured access to primary and secondary source materials.[2]

III. RECENT TRENDS IN ECONOMIC HISTORY

Theoretical economists have a long and respectable tradition of going back to economic history for the empirical material with which to justify their assumptions or test their theories of the way the economic system works. Adam Smith's *Inquiry into the Nature and Causes of the Wealth of Nations* contained a strong element of 'conjectural history' as, indeed, did Karl Marx's theory of the laws of evolution of the capitalist system. The first edition of Alfred Marshall's *Principles* . . . contained more than a hundred and twenty pages of historical introduction; and, although by the 5th edition, this material had been heavily cut, or relegated to appendices, the historical bias was always implicit in the Marshallian analysis.[3] Keynes' applied theory of money, (Vol. II of the *Treatise on Money*) [18], went back to Spanish experience in the 16th–17th century price revolution, *inter alia*, for its historical illustrations. Schumpeter's theory of business cycles was supported by a detailed historical, statistical study of 19th century business cycles in England, Germany and the United States. Modern monetarism stands on the foundation of such works as M. Friedman and A. J. Schwartz, *Monetary History of the United States 1867–1960* [11] (1963).

Since World War II, however, interest in the determinants of long-term economic growth, and particularly in the factors limiting the industrialization and development of today's low-income countries, has become a prime interest for applied economists generally and has encouraged many of them to embark on research in economic history. Journals such as *Economic Development and Cultural Change* have reflected the close connection between research in economic history and in development economics.

One consequence of the contemporary concern with the problems of economic development from a backward starting point has been to give economists an incentive to pursue their researches in economic history into periods of pre-modern history which used to be considered outside of the usual sphere of interest of economists *qua* economists. Even today, the study of economic history for the typical Economics Faculty tends to

[2] Serendipity, according to the Oxford English Dictionary, is the faculty of making happy and unexpected discoveries by accident. It is a term coined by Horace Walpole after *The Three Princes of Serendip*, a Ceylon fairy tale.

[3] For an indication of the importance which Marshall attached to economic history, see his letter to C. R. Fay, the Cambridge economic historian, reprinted in Pigou [33]. 'A thousand years hence, 1920–70 will I expect be *the* time for economic historians. It drives one wild to think of it. I believe it will make my poor *Principles* with a lot of poor comrades, into waste paper.'

start from the Industrial Revolution. An interest in economic development, however, takes one back to pre-industrial periods. For example, Colin Clark's *Conditions of Economic Progress* [4] (1940) contained an appendix on the economy of Imperial Rome. More recently, Sir John Hicks' *Theory of Economic History* [17] (1969) sketched a model of economic development focused on the transformation from a traditional to an exchange economy. More recently still, North and Thomas have 'developed a comprehensive analytical framework to examine and explain the rise of the Western World' from 700 to 1700 [31] (1973).

Another consequence of current interest in explaining the variety of contemporary patterns of economic development has been a tendency for research in economic history to take a comparative form and for Western economists to take a deeper research interest in the past growth experience, not only of countries other than their own, but, also, in countries further afield than, say, Europe or North America. Thus, a noticeable effect of economists' preoccupation with the theme of growth and development has been to extend the scope of their researches in economic history, both chronologically and geographically.

Since growth is a quantitative concept, a further effect has been to inject a strong bias towards large-scale statistical studies at a macroeconomic level. Thus, for example, Professor Simon Kuznets' comparative studies of the rate, pattern and structure of the growth of nations have directly and indirectly stimulated an international programme of research focused on long-term estimates of national income and capital formation and their principal components.[4] Whereas historians using quantitative data mainly for illustrative purposes were often content with anecdotal statistics relating to a particular firm or region or discrete time-period, economists concerned to examine the pattern and structure of national economic change set out to create continuous (preferably annual, at least benchmark) estimates of the main economic aggregates. This kind of research called for systematic compilation and cross-checking of data on prices, quantities, incomes, expenditures, assets, etc. in as much detail, and over as long a period, as the records would permit. It thus guaranteed an insatiable demand for more and more statistical information over a wider and more comprehensive framework of reference than ever before. Moreover, it has become an ongoing international programme of research in which new work at a

[4] This programme was launched in the early 1950s under the auspices of the International Association for Research in Income and Wealth and the early results were published in the conference proceedings series of IARIW—particularly [19] 1952 (which contained two substantial papers on the long-term growth of U.S. national income and wealth); [14] 1953 (papers on Japan and France); [20] 1955 (papers on U.K., France, Germany, Denmark, Hungary and Japan) and [7] 1958 (Canada). See Simon Kuznets, *Modern Economic Growth,* [21] (1966) for analysis and bibliography of subsequent work in this field.

deeper, more informed level of research is constantly making it possible to refine, revise and redefine the earlier crude estimates.

As the numbers of those doing basic quantitative research on long-term growth grew, the range of raw or processed statistics becoming available in secondary sources (e.g., in the historical statistical abstracts that were sometimes a by-product or extension of a growth study) expanded the scope for applied economic research reaching back into the nineteenth and late eighteenth centuries. This data explosion permitted the post-World War II econometric revolution in economics to spill over into economic history and gave rise to the 'new' economic history, otherwise known as cliometrics.

The distinctive characteristic of the 'new' economic history are: (1) the systematic application of statistical-analytical techniques (most commonly regression analysis); (2) the explicit formulation of testable hypotheses within the framework of established economic theory (and, also, sometimes, of accepted theory in other social sciences, e.g. sociology, psychology, demography); and (3) the attempt to test hypotheses in terms of what might have happened (the counter-factual proposition) as well as in terms of what did happen. A main difference between the 'old' and the 'new' economic history is that the 'new' version systematically spells out and seeks to test the counter-factual propositions that were always implicit in the 'old'.

The 'new' economic history has tended to focus on narrower, more precisely defined issues than did the economic growth studies inspired by Simon Kuznets and to yield correspondingly less general conclusions. Nevertheless, like the economic growth studies inspired by Kuznets, the cliometric studies opened up an inexhaustible mine of new research problems and set off a continuing programme of related projects, most of which depended heavily on being able to generate new quantitative estimates.

In effect, then, these two broad and often inter-related trends in research in economic history since the early 1950s have done three things for the discipline. They have (1) widened its theoretical and empirical horizons; (2) introduced into it more elaborate analytical techniques; and (3) given it a 'cutting edge'.

The widening of horizons shows itself in a tendency for economic historians to develop in systematic fashion the interdisciplinary and the comparative (inter-spatial and inter-temporal) aspects of their subject. It has never been a satisfactory procedure to keep studies of economic development penned within the narrow confines of 'pure' economics, and current interest in the problems of today's developing countries has encouraged the traditional propensity for economic historians to view society more in the round than most other applied economists find necessary. Old areas of research have been given a new lease of life in this broader context and there has been a fruitful revival or expansion of interest in such specialisms as historical demography, business history, labour history and urban history. Interestingly enough, cliometrics, which seemed, at first, to many traditionalists to constitute a narrowing of the historical vision, is beginning to lead the way in the process of broadening the horizons of research in economic history. The latest contribution to the long cliometric debate on slavery in the U.S. for example [10], Fogel and Engerman *Time on the Cross* (1974)—illustrates not only the widening range of social theory involved in the 'new' economic history, but, also, a tendency to revert to the use of the 'old' narrative history which, for a while, was wholly out of fashion among modern economic historians.

The use of statistical-analytical techniques has been the most distinctive feature so far, of the recent trends in economic history, and has created an increasing demand for new quantitative data. This has had two implications. On the one hand, it has generated a long shopping list of research topics feasible at the level of the individual research worker—i.e., a list of potential dissertation topics—which has helped to encourage an increasing number of applied economists to specialize in economic history. On the other hand, even more significantly, it has opened up an unprecedented scope for institutionalized or team research in economic history, for the long-term growth studies, and many of the exercises in testing counterfactual propositions or multi-disciplinary models, have data requirements which can be met only by setting teams of researchers to work on the primary sources. Even for those who remain wedded to an essentially 'old' variety of economic history, research based on anecdotal, or regional, or otherwise partial sources of evidence no longer suffices to support a serious piece of analysis. Today's economic historian needs to know how representative his information is (whether qualitative or quantitative), how it relates to the universe of which it is a part, and where it stands, chronologically, in the dynamic process.

Finally, the new trends in economic history have given the discipline an identifiable frontier of knowledge, a direction in which progress is expected to be possible, an area where new research can be systematically fitted into previous work, in short, a 'cutting edge'.[5] Traditionally, research in economic history has tended to be diffused over a very wide area, each project emerging from a particular mine of primary data and having little relationship with recent past research—except by analogy (e.g., by comparison with similar studies for other regions or periods or

[5] 'All scholarship has a corpus and an archive but science has a cutting-edge too. While they are at the research front, papers behave, as is known from citation network studies, as if they were pieces in a jigsaw puzzle. Each paper fits into two or three closely related previous papers and in turn becomes the point of departure for new research, so that old knowledge breeds new knowledge at a constant and rapid rate' [35].

industries, say) and except to the extent that discovery of a new and richer data-source made it possible authoritatively to revise an accepted interpretation based on more partial evidence. In these circumstances, research progress was ragged, heavily dependent on the brilliance of individual research workers and not easily envisaged in wider perspective. The newcomer seeking to make a 'contribution to knowledge' had only his (or his supervisor's) intuition to guide him on research priorities and had little scope for reaping external economies by choosing a topic which would enable him to build and improve upon past research in a systematic fashion. Indeed, if he wanted to establish a claim to originality he might be well advised to steer clear of past research. Today's research worker in the field of economic history, however, has endless scope for starting where his predecessors have left off. He can usefully revise or extend a national income or wealth series, for example, by taking the estimates into greater depth or over a longer period or into a different structure of disaggregation than did his predecessors. He can fruitfully examine the logic of a cliometric model or of a counter-factual proposition, or, by developing a new set of quantitative estimates, he can test the empirical validity of its assumptions or extend the range of its conclusions.

Looking forward, rather than backward, in assessing trends in economic history, then, it seems certain that the two basic post-war trends will continue to be important determinants of the choice of research topics by students, institutional research workers and university teaching staff over the coming decade. The problem of economic development shows no sign of diminishing in intensity as the primary interdisciplinary problem of the social sciences—though the focus of active interest may well shift from a study of growth rates and the performance of national economies to the exploration of patterns of structural change and of income or wealth distribution. However, there is still much to be done in trying to explain the determinants of long-term economic growth and change. Similarly, the intellectual attractions of applying rigorous techniques of analysis to the historical record are more likely to increase by expansion of the field over which they are applied than to diminish in strength because some themes have been relatively overworked. So, although the demands for fresh quantitative data are unlikely to fall away, the demands for more systematically compiled sets of *qualitative* data are highly likely to increase as the questions are reformulated in response to deeper insights into the complex process of social and economic change.

IV. RESEARCH NEEDS OF THE MODERN ECONOMIC HISTORIAN

Clearly then, the research needs of the individual economic historian operating in the 1970s are typically more various and more scattered than was normal even twenty years ago, and, also, more scattered by source and type of primary material as well as by range of theoretical and 'inspirational' material than is the case for most applied economists. It is less likely today that the bulk of this primary data will come from a single, main archival source or that his conceptual and methodological ideas will be exclusively based on an economist's paradigm. Partly because there has been a spate of new work on economic history over the past quarter of a century, but, also, partly because research priorities today are more often defined in terms of an identifiable, if rather long, frontier of knowledge, it is now important that the newcomer to a particular research area familiarizes himself with a substantial volume of current (and past) research in secondary sources, published and unpublished, in his own and other countries or languages, on the same and different periods, from the one in which he is to be concerned.

Nor, indeed, have most of the pre-war monographs and research articles become out-dated and, therefore, dispensable. To judge from the citations in articles on economic history in current journals, a researcher is as likely to use monograph material published before 1950 as after. This is not surprising, of course, for today's research worker has new questions to pose to the narrative-descriptive material compiled by yesterday's researchers and new uses for their factual conclusions. At the same time, he may have to go back to already exploited public and private records, papers and archives, official publications, books, pamphlets, newspapers and assorted ephemera to extract data at a greater level of detail and more systematically than his predecessors deemed necessary. A glance through the citations of recent issues of journals specializing in economic history indicates that the raw material of current research in economic history comes predominantly from such sources as unpublished Ph.D. dissertations; statistical abstracts; government reports and other official papers (central, local, national and international); company and estate reports and other private records; contemporary books, pamphlets, journals and newspapers; as well as from a wide range of modern books, journals, recent conference proceedings, and working papers privately circulated. To an increasing extent, moreover, the modern economic historian is coming to rely on direct personal contact with his colleagues in other universities and is participating in conferences focused on specific topics in economic history.

In short, the research needs of the modern economic historian are so extensive and various that even the longest-established, most affluent university library is unlikely to meet more than a fraction of them. So what can one say about relative priorities?

It is a daunting task to try to lay down priorities for research workers whose potential range of fruitful inquiry is so enormously wide, and it does not seem sensible to attempt to do more than suggest rather general guidelines. It seems reasonable to suppose that faculties and research institutes will tend to specialize in particular areas, as they have already begun to do, and that particular university libraries will develop certain areas of documentation in considerable depth. More generally, what is required is to give the research worker a series of leads to current and past research and to primary sources of data and ideas, bearing in mind, of course, that economic history is a sub-field of both economics and history.

(1) The first thing, then, that a university library should do for its economic historians is to provide them with direct or indirect access to as wide a range as possible of the learned journals currently specializing in economic history. As long a run as is available of the two leading specialist journals in English—*Journal of Economic History* and *Economic History Review* (and its predecessor, *Economic History* originally published as a supplement to the *Economic Journal*)—is the first requisite. The footnotes to the articles, the bibliographical essays, the reviews and the lists provide a lead-in to much of the primary and secondary material available in English and other accessible languages. Beyond these, it is convenient to have complete runs for the other leading journals in the field (most of them, as it happens, are fairly recent in origin) such as *Explorations in Economic History* (with its predecessor, *Explorations in Entrepreneurial History*), *Economic Development and Cultural Change*, *Annales*, *Economia e Storia*, and, also, some of the specialist journals, e.g. *Agricultural History Review*, *Labor History*, *Business History*, *Transport History*. In any case, it is important to have a complete listing of the periodicals currently available on inter-library loan (e.g., the current List of Serials kept up-to-date by the Cambridge University Library) including the numerous specialist newsletters (often in mimeographed form) which constitute checklists of information on recent research, published or unpublished, e.g. *Urban History Newsletter* (Leicester) now supplemented by an *Urban History Yearbook*; *Historical Methods Newsletter* (Pittsburgh); *Oral History Newsletter* (Essex); *The Family in Historical Perspective* (Clark University) to cite a very few examples.

(2) It is useful to have a full range of statistical abstracts[6] and basic source books (e.g. census reports) and of authoritative commentaries on certain kinds of statistical raw material.[7] Since most research workers will gravitate towards topics bearing on their own country, domestic primary sources (e.g. Censuses of Population and Manufactures and certain other official papers) have a claim to first priority.

(3) The economic historian needs access to a wide range of

[6] Examples include [40] 1960; B. R. Mitchell [28] (1971); N. Urquhart and K. Buckley [41] (1965); [39] (1971); E. B. Schumpeter [36] (1960).

[7] Examples include Colin Clark, *Guide to English Commercial Statistics 1697–1782*, and J. C. Stamp, *British Income and Property*.

bibliographies, ancient and modern. These would range from such sources as J. B. Williams, *Guide to Printed Materials for English Social and Economic History 1750–1850* [42] (1926) or the Catalogue of the Goldsmiths' Library [1] (1970–75) to J. Fletcher's listing of academic working papers on economics [8] (1974), plus such specialized listings as reflect the research interests of Faculty members.[8]

(4) The economic historian doing original research in economic history needs instant access to the wide variety of guides to archival sources, records, and official papers, so that he has advance knowledge of how to proceed before he begins to sample the primary data, as well as some reliable clues as to what kind of data is likely to be available to him.

(5) Since many of the seminal articles currently or recently published in economic history appear elsewhere than in the main specialist economic history journals, it is also useful to have a fairly wide collection of anthologies bearing on special topics in economic history. Examples include the readings collected in the volumes of *Debates on Economic History* edited by Peter Mathias, e.g. Hall [15] (1968) and Taylor [38] (1975), W. E. Minchinton [27] (1968), M. E. Falkus [6] (1968), and R. Fogel and S. Engerman [10] (1971), etc.

(6) It is convenient to have at hand complete sets, not only of the major series of volumes specifically focused on economic history (e.g. Postan and Habakkuk [34] (1963–66) or Cipolla [2] (1972–73), but, also, of other standard historical series such as the *Cambridge Modern History.*

(7) It is worth acquiring as many as the budget will permit of the major classic research monographs on economic history—some old, some new—e.g., Clapham [3] (1932–39), Matthews [26] (1954), Hecksher [16] (1965), Gayer, Rostow and Schwartz [12] (1953), Lockwood [25] (1954), and Friedman and Schwartz [11] (1963). Even a complete coverage of such classic monographs would not, in practice, entail a very large number of books.

(8) Finally, the researcher in economic history needs to have direct access to, and the possibility of browsing in, a fairly wide range of inspirational material, including such items as e.g., Gerschenkron [13] (1962); Hicks [17] (1969); Kuznets [21] (1966); Lewis [24] (1955); and Moore [29] (1967). It is less easy to see, perhaps, where this group begins and where it ends, and it could clearly become a rather large collection in the more affluent library.

In sum, these suggestions amount to putting a high priority on the leading journals, bibliographical books, statistical abstracts and search guides, and a moderate priority on authoritative series volumes, specialized anthologies, classic monographs and inspirational material, which, taken together, offer the research worker scope for fruitful brow-

[8] Examples are G. Ottley [32] (1965); H. M. Larson [23] (1948).

sing. Beyond this, however, given the vast potential range of economic history research and of the serious work already reaching publication stage, it seems likely that the pressure on particular institutions to specialize will help to predetermine library acquisition policy. There are obviously considerable advantages in selecting amongst the wide variety of recently published monographs with a view to developing certain subject areas in considerable depth; and in discarding monograph material where it has been largely outdated by more recent research or where it lies patently outside the area of faculty specialization. Given that the university research worker specializing in economic history will normally have a ready access to a wide range of secondary material on economics and history, a departmental library can afford to develop the kind of acquisition-to-discard policy which reflects the research interests of its current body of users.

REFERENCES

[1] Canney, Margaret, Knott, David and Gibbs, Joan M., *Catalogue of the Goldsmiths' Library of Economic Literature* (London: Cambridge U. Press, 1970 and 1975) 2 vols.

[2] Cipolla, Carlo M., *The Fontana Economic History of Europe*, Vols. I–VI (London: Wm. Collins and Sons, 1972–73).

[3] Clapham, J. H., *An Economic History of Modern Britain* (Cambridge: Cambridge U. Press, 1932–39), 3 vols.

[4] Clark, Colin, *Conditions of Economic Progress* (London: Macmillan and Co., 1940).

[5] — —, *Guide to English Commercial Statistics 1697–1792* (London: Office of the Royal Historical Society, 1938).

[6] Falkus, M. E., *Readings in the History of Economic Growth* (Oxford: Oxford U. Press, 1968).

[7] Firestone, O. J., 'Canada's Economic Development 1867–1953', *Income and Wealth Series* (Cambridge: Bowes & Bowes, 1958).

[8] Fletcher, J. ed., *Economics Working Papers, January–December 1973* (New York: Trans-Media Pub. Co.; Warwick: U. of Warwick Press, 1974). Available on subscription quarterly and annually.

[9] Fogel, R. W. and Engerman, S. L., eds., *The Reinterpretation of American Economic History* (Boston: Little, Brown & Co., 1974).

[10] — —, *Time on the Cross* (Boston: Little, Brown & Co., 1974), 2 vols.

[11] Friedman, M. and Schwartz, A. J., *A Monetary History of the United States* (Princeton: Princeton U. Press, 1963).

[12] Gayer, A. D., Rostow, W. W. and Schwartz, A. J., *The Growth and Fluctuation of the British Economy* (Oxford: Clarendon Press, 1953), 2 vols.

[13] Gerschenkron, A., *Economic Backwardness in Historical Perspective* (Cambridge, Mass.: Belknap Press of Harvard U. Press, 1962).

[14] Gilbert, Milton, ed., *Income and Wealth Series III* (Cambridge: Bowes & Bowes, 1953).

[15] Hall, A. R., *The Export of Capital from Great Britain 1870–1914* (London: Methuen, 1968).

[16] Hecksher, E. F., *Mercantilism*, 2nd edn., ed. E. F. Söderlan (London: Allen & Unwin; New York: Macmillan, 1965).

[17] Hicks, J. R., *A Theory of Economic History* (Oxford: Clarendon Press, 1969).

[18] Keynes, J. M., *A Treatise on Money*, reprinted in *Collected Work of J. M. Keynes*, ed. D. Moggridge (London: Macmillan, 1971).
[19] Kuznets, Simon, ed., 'Income and Wealth of the United States. Trends and Structures', *Income and Wealth Series II* (Cambridge: Bowes & Bowes, 1952).
[20] ——, *Income and Wealth Series V* (Cambridge: Bowes & Bowes, 1955).
[21] ——, *Modern Economic Growth* (New Haven: Yale U. Press, 1966).
[22] Kyle, B., 'Some Further Considerations on the Application to Social Science Materials of Up-to-date Methods of Bibliographical Control and Information Retrieval', *Journal of Documentation* (1958).
[23] Larson, H. M., *Guide to Business History* (Cambridge, Mass.: Harvard U. Press, 1948).
[24] Lewis, W. A., *The Theory of Economic Growth* (London: Allen & Unwin, 1955).
[25] Lockwood, W. W., *The Economic Development of Japan* (Princeton: Princeton U. Press, 1954).
[26] Matthews, R. C. O., *A Study in Trade-Cycle History* (Cambridge: Cambridge U. Press, 1954).
[27] Minchinton, W. E., ed., *Essays in Agrarian History* (Newton Abbot: David and Charles Ltd., 1968).
[28] Mitchell, B. R. and Deane, Phyllis, *Abstract of British Historical Statistics*, 2nd ed. (Cambridge: Cambridge U. Press, 1971).
[29] Moore, Jr., Barrington, *Social Origins of Dictatorship and Democracy* (Boston: Beacon Press, 1966).
[30] *New Cambridge Modern History*, 12 vols. (1957–68).
[31] North, D. C. and Thomas, R. P., *The Rise of the Western World* (Cambridge: Cambridge U. Press, 1973).
[32] Ottley, G., *Bibliography of British Railway History* (London: Allen & Unwin, 1965).
[33] Pigou, A. C., ed., *Memories of Alfred Marshall* (Oxford: Macmillan, 1925).
[34] Postan, M. M. and Habakkuk, H. J., eds., *The Cambridge Economic History of Europe*, Vols. I–VI (Cambridge: Cambridge U. Press, 1963–66).
[35] Price, D. J. de S., 'Networks of Scientific Papers,' *Science* (1965).
[36] Schumpeter, E. B., *English Overseas Trade Statistics 1697–1808* (Oxford, 1960).
[37] Stamp, J. C., *British Incomes and Property* (London: P. S. King & Son, Ltd., 1915).
[38] Taylor, A. J., ed., *The Standard of Living in Britain in the Industrial Revolution* (London: Methuen, 1975).
[39] U.K. Department of Employment, *British Labour Statistics Historical Abstract 1886–1968* (London, 1971).
[40] U.S. Bureau of the Census, *Historical Statistics of the United States, Colonial Times to 1957* (Washington, D.C.: U.S. Govt. Printing Office, 1960).
[41] Urquhart, M. C. and Buckley, K. A. H., *Historical Statistics of Canada* (Cambridge: Cambridge U. Press, 1965).
[42] Williams, J. B., *Guide to Printed Material for English Social and Economic History 1750–1850*, 2 vols. (New York: Columbia University Press, 1926).

Summary of the Discussion

Opening his presentation of Miss Deane's paper, *Professor Kindleberger* commented on Economic History as a discipline. Both he and Miss Deane, *Professor Kindleberger* thought, regarded the discipline as primarily applied economics and only secondarily as historical narrative. (Perhaps the term Historical Economics might be as useful as Economic History.)

The information required by the ideal economic historian is unfortunately, 'everything'. While there are new trends in the field, summarized under the heading of 'cliometrics', *Professor Kindleberger* did not consider it particularly critical to discuss these at this conference. (It seemed to him that cliometricians get out of their data only what they put in, and that their models have been static rather than dynamic, in that they do not explain why group or nation A overcomes some economic obstacle, whereas group or nation B waits for solutions from outside.)

Professor Kindleberger also felt that *comparative* economic history provides a generally more promising approach than does the cliometrician's characteristic analysis of counter-factual situations. He added that comparative methods can test the generality of one's models. An example was the fall in world wheat prices centring in the 1880s. Whereas Italian farmers reacted primarily by emigrating, other European farmers reacted by less 'parochial' means, such as technological improvements or tariff protection.

As a positive suggestion for fellow-economic historians in both the United States and Britain, *Professor Kindleberger* recommended the learning of more foreign languages. In the United States, at least, he felt, there was an erroneous hierarchy of languages; mathematics was not only recognized as a language, but as the only language that the scholars needed to know. (Of course, there would be advantages, for English-speaking scholars, in having everyone learn English, or in having more materials translated into English from other languages.)

Turning to current trends, *Professor Kindleberger* described as hopeful both the establishment of the new *Journal of European Economic History* and the preparation of collected essays in Economic History for teaching purposes. On the other hand, he found strange and unfortunate the suspension of the Irish University Press project for reprinting the British *Parliamentary Papers* because of inadequate demand, particularly in Europe.

Mrs Schwartz opened the oral discussion with a question: Why was there not more study of economic diffusion? *Professor Kindleberger* suggested, in reply, that the comparative study of diffusion processes would generally be more useful than would the narratives of individual historical cases that he believed Dr Schwartz had in mind.

Professor Morgan criticized economic historians generally for their failure to face issues of cost. Again, as in connection with many other disciplines, Professor Morgan felt that scientific sampling of data might provide a viable alternative to 'saving everything'. (His illustration involved hospital records in Ann Arbor, as an aid to research in Health Economics.) (*Mrs Schwartz* added that widespread micro-filming of larger samples, or even complete universes, of data might be an alternative.)

Professor M. Perlman sought to reopen the issue (from earlier discussions) of whether academic libraries should drop their subscriptions to journals once economic conditions force breaks in their series. He felt that this would often be a false economy.

Mr Kilgour felt it desirable to make a careful distinction between Economic History and the History of Economics, since materials relatively useless for one of these fields might be extremely helpful for the other. *Professor Kindleberger* commented that much Economic History was re-written when the dominant school of Economic Theory changed, citing as an example the capital movements from Britain to Canada at the turn of the century, which had been re-examined in 'verifying' each successive change in trade theory.

Miss Deane replied to these several comments. While she was herself no cliometrician or numerologist, she hoped that everyone now realized that both quantitative and non-quantitative methods were necessary. She agreed that her paper should have contained more comparative economic history or, at least, more discussion of this field. She also agreed with Professor Kindleberger on the 'linguistic hierarchy' and the need for more translations. Once one decides to discard original records, *Miss Deane* feared (and *Professor Blaug* agreed) that a separate research project might be required to decide what, and how, to sample, even if one accepts Professor Morgan's faith in scientific sampling as a semi-panacea. She also doubted the possibility of the desirability of one generation attempting to define or limit the next generation's methods, as might be implied by wholesale weeding out of allegedly 'useless' materials. (*Professor Giersch* suggested 'competitive' storage for new materials as a compromise here, with old materials limited to single copies 'in storage somewhere'.)

22 The Information Needs of Economic Researchers in the Field of Comparative Economic Systems*

Paul Chamley

FACULTÉ DES SCIENCES ECONOMIQUES, STRASBOURG

I. *A distinction is drawn throughout between four types of systems: market system (developed), plan system, self-management system, economic system of developing countries, subdivided in two groups: South and Central America, Africa and Asia. As to the approach, research is assumed to aim at analysing the systems and at explaining their emergence and their evolution.*

II. *The references relating (expressly or implicitly) to economic systems contained in the latest issue of the* International Bibliography of the Social Science (Economics) *were taken as a sample for the purpose of supplying a list of indicators and of characterizing the trend of research and the state of the documentation. Out of 6430 titles, 1053 were selected.*

III. *As to the tendencies of research, the following points (illustrated by a number of tables) emerge: Comparative studies proper are scarce; few studies are devoted to the comparative investigation of economic structures. However, market countries display more interest for such kind of studies than do plan countries; more precisely, the former appear to be more extroverted, the latter more introverted.*

IV. *From an essentially external point of view (location, languages, number of periodicals and newspapers . . .) the available information is much less concentrated than is research. On the other hand, the various fields of research are being covered very unequally, all the more since a great deal of duplication is to be expected among studies from Eastern countries. In order to illustrate the existing facilities of documentation, three agencies are briefly described* (International Bibliography of Social Sciences, Institut für Weltwirtschaft, Glasgow Institute of Soviet and East European Studies). *To conclude, some propositions are made for developing comprehensive means of information in this field. A final word is devoted to interdisciplinary research.*

* The annexes referred to are available from the author.

I. *DEFINITION AND APPROACH*

An Economic System will be *defined* hereafter as a certain principle of organization characterizing a concrete economic whole. It is fairly generally admitted that there are, in fact, only two systems so defined: the market system and the plan system. This conception—old as to its principle[1] of organization—seems presently to rest on the observation that the only concrete economies which carry weight are built upon either of these two principles. Furthermore, even the economies which give a significant place to some other principle belong, in the main, either to the market system or to the plan system and, therefore, constitute simple varieties of them.

This view seems to be well-grounded. However, there is no inconvenience in taking into account the contrary opinion, according to which the principle of organization characterizing a concrete economy is not necessarily that one which is dominant in it, but rather the principle to which it owes its origin and its significance. Again, the importance of an economic system should not be measured by its economic weight. Consequently, the system of Yugoslavia ought to be given a separate place, under the name of self-management. Having gone so far, we can take one more step in the same direction and include the Israeli kibbutz in the same category.

In order to take all opinions into account, and since it is easier to do away with a useless distinction rather than to introduce a necessary one belatedly, the second view will be adopted here, however disputable it may be in itself and in the application made of it.

As to the *method*, the researcher is assumed to elect the *integrated approach*: in opposition to the 'operation approach', systems are not considered as given. The investigation of them is supposed to aim simultaneously at analysing them and explaining their emergence and evolution.

Such an approach makes the task of researchers particularly difficult, because of the sheer extent of the field to be explored. First, the evolution of a system depends upon its day-to-day working. In this respect, studying a system includes analysing the mechanisms of the economy which it characterizes. Comparative research in economic systems, therefore, involves economic research at large. Furthermore, inquiries into the emergence and development of economic systems are not likely to be successful without an awareness of the contribution of the whole of social sciences: history, anthropology, social psychology. Finally, an overall interpretation of economic systems is scarcely conceivable without some resort to philosophy.

Little wonder then, that, so understood, research in economic systems has as yet made small progress. However, in addition to the difficulties

[1] Hegel, G. W. F., *Grundlinien der Philosophie des Rechts*, § 236.

attendant upon the scope and diversity of its field of investigation, it runs counter to considerable, perhaps insuperable, epistemological and practical obstacles, to which recent works[2] have drawn attention. How is the distinction to be drawn between 'systemic' factors and accidental factors belonging specifically to a real economy? In other words, how is a concrete system to be isolated from a concrete economy? How are the limits of a system to be drawn? From which degree of change onwards, from which date on is one system replaced by another? There also arises the problem of objective scientific research, here perhaps more acutely than anywhere else. How can research avoid putting into question the object of its investigation? How is it to be isolated from the ideological game? How is one to settle the conflict between the rights of research and the right—or the duty—of a system to defend? Finally, is it not self-contradicting to attempt to organize knowledge—and, consequently, to assign it a fixed analytical framework—in a field where everything is supposed to be moving, and nothing is to be 'given'?[3]

In the course of the present study, such difficulties were met with almost at every step. Of course, no general solutions were given to them. They were dealt with quite empirically, with the conviction that, in such a matter, scarcely anything is logically clear cut, and that, according to Aristotle's saying, 'in every science, one has to be content with the degree of precision which belongs to its object'.

II. *PROCEDURE OF INQUIRY LIST OF INDICATORS*

In order to assess the needs of researchers in this field, and with a view to reducing the risk of subjecting appreciations, the documentation contained in the *International Bibliography of the Social Sciences, International Bibliography of Economics*, XXI, 1972 (last volume published) was taken as a starting point. Since it constitutes the main source of integrated documentation covering the whole field of economic knowledge, and provided that some supplementary sources were taken into account, it was thought that this could serve as a sample for a threefold purpose:

1. to supply materials for a list of indicators that were to be used eventually in an integrated system of documentation;
2. to yield information about the nature and direction of research in the field of Comparative Economic Systems; and
3. to help determine the present state of available documentation. Conclusions reached under points 2 and 3 should make it possible to know the information needs of researchers better.

The whole of volume XXI of the *International Bibliography* was in-

[2] See, for instance, *Comparison of Economic Systems* (A. Eckstein, ed.), 1971.

[3] 'Das Wahre ist so der bacchantische Taumel, an dem kein Glied nicht trunken ist. . . , (G. W. F. Hegel, *Phänomenologie des Geistes*). (Vorrede) ed., 1952, 39.

spected. For lack of time, the inspection extended only up to Nr 6430. (All together, there are 6968 items.) The classification scheme preceding the *Bibliography* is joined to the present report (Annexe 1).

Most of what relates directly and mainly to economic systems (N, Public Economy) has been retained. The same was done with G 32 (Economic concentration), G 33 (Organization of the firm), H 112 (Forms of agricultural enterprise and land tenure), H 212 (Forms of industrial enterprise, legal status), H 412 (Forms of commercial enterprise, legal status), I 2124 (Price formation under planning), K 21 (Local studies), K 32 (Profits andreturns), M 2 (Standard of living), M 3 (Social and welfare policy, general and descriptive studies), M 4 (Social security, social assistance, work safety). Furthermore, in the whole of the Bibliography, all studies relating significantly to economic systems and likely to be useful for the comparative investigation of them, have also been selected. On the other hand, as a rule, references relating to matters dealt with in seperate reports (History of Economic Thought, Economic History, etc.), were left out. In these fields, only studies referring explicitly to economic systems were selected.

The selected references, 1053 in all, weres analysed in the light of a quadruple classification set up beforehand, but expanded in the course of the work, so as to make it possible to accommodate correctly all of the selected studies, and to take into account all aspects of them (Annexe 2).

The fourth part ('Subjects') of this classification is, in fact, a list of complex indicators, since each of them includes a scale of specifications. Once reduced to its components, it yields a list of *elementary indicators* (Annexe 3).

The frequencies of occurrence of complex indicators have been transcribed on both lists. They have, of course, only limited significance, as far as they concern complex indicators compounded from several elementary indicators, for example, (in Annexe 2, Nr 451111, 451112, 4511421, etc.) or elementary indicators taken from them (tabulated in Annexe 3 under 'mixed frequencies'). Although derived in both a deductive and experimental way, and tested in terms of frequencies, this list of indicators is evidently only a tentative one. As a consequence of the approach adopted here, it is likely to overlap the lists drawn up for other special fields. The list of indicators given under 'Economic System' in the *Macrothesaurus* edited by OCDE has been added for the sake of comparisons (Annexe 4).

III. *TENDENCIES OF RESEARCH*

The selected data have been processed with the help of a computer, using the facilities given by the PASTIS program at the university's 'Centre de Calcul de Strasbourg-Cronenbourg'.

The results of the analysis are summed up in Tables 22.1–7 (pp. 438–45). The following points may be particularly stressed:

1. On the whole, there is a marked disproportion between studies bearing on points of detail and general studies. Works of synthesis seldom occur. For types of publication 112, 113, 114, 116, 117 and 118, no publication was registered during the year under examination (Table 22.5). Expressly comparative studies are scarce, witness the small frequency of most of the corresponding indicators (Annexe 2, indicators 40361, 40362, 414734, 4231, 4232, 4331, 4332, 4432). Comparative studies proper ('inter-system comparisons') rank particularly low. This tendency is being confirmed by the scarcity of general interpretations of the origin and development of economic systems (Annexe 2, indicator 415).
2. Few studies are devoted to investigating the institutional structure of economic systems (indicators 43 . . .), an essential point for comparative studies.
3. However general these tendencies, scientific behaviour is far from being homogeneous. Differences appear from one system, or one group of countries, to another.

Contributions coming from the market system (developed) bear the character of synthetizing studies to a higher degree than to contributions coming from other systems or groups of countries. This conclusion is supported by consistent evidence from Tables 21.5, 6 and 7.

Table 21.5. Types of publication 111, 115 and 120 are being supplied almost exclusively by countries belonging to group 21 (Market, developed). The same countries are largely dominant for types of publication 21 and 22. By the way, it may be interesting to note the greater abundance of collective studies in the market countries.

Concerning articles, the plan countries prevail (in absolute numbers and, all the more, in percentages) as to *small contributions* (types 123 and 124), the market countries as to large ones (types 125 and 126). In percentages *in each group*, the distribution is as follows:

		Types of publication				
Groups of countries		123	124	125	126	Total
Market (developed)	(21)	17·9	31·3	34·5	16·3	100
Plan	(22)	36·8	38·5	19·0	5·7	100

Table 21.6 For all groups and all types of publications, *modal* indicators frequency is 2, except for group 23 (self-management), where it is 1.

However, from left to right of the table, there appears a clear tendency towards concentration on studies dealing with special points, since putting into operation small numbers of indicators. This tendency seems to reverse itself at the extreme right of the table, but the number of studies with high numbers of indicators is too small in that region (3 in all) for the deviation to be significant.

Table 21.7. Concerning articles alone, for all countries of origin and all types of articles, the *modal* number of indicators is 2 again, except for articles of type 24 (10 to 14 pages), where it is 1.

There is, however, a clear divergence between the market countries and the plan countries as to the distribution of articles according to the number of indicators. For all kinds of articles, the concentration on the two first lines (1 or 2 indicators) is stronger, with 41·3 per cent and 44·5 per cent, for studies coming from plan countries (group 22), than for studies coming from market countries (group 21), with 35·9 per cent and 36·64 per cent.

As evidenced by Table 21.4, the interest taken by each group in the system to which it belongs is not of the same magnitude for all groups. It increases from left to right of the table (squared percentages). In this sense, it may be said that group 21 (market, developed) is the least 'introverted' of all. On the other hand, the percentage of studies devoted to the market system in plan countries is larger than conversely. Again, studies devoted to 'unspecified areas' loom larger in market countries than they do in plan countries.

A difference of behaviour may also be noted between North America and the USSR as to the relative place given respectively to their own system (211/311, 221/321) and to the overall system to which they belong (211/31, 221/32). *Within the limits of its own system*, the leading country would appear less 'introverted' in the case of the plan system than in the case of the market system. This difference might be related to a higher degree of 'systemic' integration on the side of the plan countries. Whatever the explanation, from the present point of view, 'introversion' is, of course, of lesser consequence when it occurs within the same system than it is between different systems.

To conclude on points (1) and (2), contributions from plan countries have a more limited scope, simpler contents and are more self-centred. In short they bear the character of comparative studies to a lesser degree than do contributions from market countries. This conclusion is fully borne out by a closer scrutiny of the distribution of studies by countries of origin. In particular, for indicators 4521 and, more significantly, 4522—the only cases of *comparative studies with sizable frequency figures*—the distribution is as follows:

IV. *THE INFORMATION NEEDS*

Within the limits of the present sample, the information needs may be defined as follows:

(a) The available information is extremely plentiful and widely

Indicator	*Countries of origin*		*Frequencies* No.	%
4521	211		10	27·00
	212		5	14·00
	213		7	19·00
	214		3	8·00
	215		3	5·00
	216		2	3·00
	217		1	8·00
	221		3	8·00
	226		2	5·00
	24		1	3·00
		Total	37	100·00
4522	211		8	57·00
	213		4	29·00
	214		2	14·00
		Total	14	100·00

scattered. However strictly the preceding bibliography has been delimited—especially with respect to the history of economic thought and economic history—about 1/6 of the whole economic literature registered in the *International Bibliography of Economics* had to be selected as relevant for the comparative investigation of economic systems. This state of dispersion is still being aggravated by the relatively low linguistic concentration (see Table 21.2), at least among the five principal languages, and by the diversity of research directions, especially on the part of market countries.

(b) In spite of its over-abundance, documentation seems to be lacking on certain points essential for the comparison of economic systems, notably concerning the quantitative characteristics of institutional sectors. It is well known that research in market countries aims especially at closing the gaps of current documentation on that point.[4]

Moreover, the information supplied by documents is not necessarily in proportion to their number. Considering the introverted tendency and the narrow scope of documents coming from plan countries, duplications are likely on that side.

Finally, on certain aspects of the working of economic systems, signalled in the preceding analysis by zero frequencies, information is completely inadequate, at least within the limits of the sample.

(c) On the other hand, as to the areas in which they appear, information needs are much more concentrated. While English studies concerning economic systems amount to only 20 per cent of the total number, about half of the strictly comparative studies are in English. More generally, the bibliographical analysis has shown that market countries take a major part in the work of synthesis in this field.

[4] See F. Pryor's enquiries.

It remains to be seen how *access to information* is being organized. Quite a number of agencies are at work in order to facilitate it, and some of them can be examined. They will be briefly commented upon, beginning with the Bibliography from which the preceding sample has been borrowed.

International Bibliography of Economics. Valuable as it is for the extent of the field that it surveys, the *International Bibliography of Economics* unfortunately also presents certain conspicuous deficiencies:[5]

(1) It is edited with considerable delay—about two years after the data of publication of the registered studies.
(2) Each study is registered under one heading only, a practice particularly ill-suited for the needs of researchers in comparative economic systems. On that account, the International Bibliography is strewn with inconsistencies and arbitrary choices.
(3) However numerous, the sources used are too limited:

(*a*) On the whole, articles are taken from specialized publications. While this selection may be adequate for conventional research conducted in special fields with small ideological implications, it is not sufficient for researchers in comparative economic systems. A larger and more variegated survey would do away with some of the 'zero frequencies' noted before (e.g. black market, bureaucracy, economic delinquency, etc.).

(*b*) Even as to specialized periodicals, only part of those which are relevant for research in comparative economic systems are being tapped for the *International Bibliography*, as appears from the list of periodicals of the same kind received at the *Institut für Weltwirtschaft* (Annexe 5).

(*c*) Very scant attention is paid to the economic system of China. (See, again, Annexe 5.)

Institute of Soviet and East European Studies, University of Glasgow. The publications of this Institute enjoy a well-deserved renown. Among them, the ABSEES (*Soviet and East European Abstracts Series*) calls for some remarks. Going beyond the *International Bibliography*, and partly over the *Institut für Weltwirtschaft*, it has the advantage of supplying extensive summaries, and not restricting itself to specialized journals. In fact, it devotes plenty of space to newspapers, so as to provide almost immediate knowledge of the actual working conditions of the system and of the society in which it is embedded.

Apart from the necessary limitation of its field of enquiry, the main deficiency of this publication lies in the fact that each contribution is

[5] Apart from its constitutional weaknesses, it is impaired by frequent flaws, especially in the translations from the German.

registered under only one heading, which entails the same inconveniences as in the case of the *International Bibliography*.

To go into more detail, some practical improvements would be welcome, such as occasionally repeating the classification scheme and the list of surveyed publications, and printing on only one side of the page, as in the French *Documentation Economique*.

V. *CONCLUSION*

However incomplete, the foregoing review of information agencies shows that the information needs of researchers in the field of comparative economic systems are far from being completely satisfied. In spite of the high quality of some contributions, each agency gives these needs only a fragmentary response, sometimes an imperfect one even within the limits set to it beforehand. Moreover, there is apparently little co-ordination between the agencies co-operating in the same information task.

It seems that the search for thorough-going interpretations, at least for researchers from market countries, is hampered on one side by the number, the heterogeneous character and the uneven quality of raw materials and, on the other side, by the scarcity of precise and comparable data concerning certain aspects of economic systems. Just the number of periodicals to be reviewed runs to the hundreds. Those relating more particularly to economic systems or to certain aspects of them have been listed in Annexe 5.[6] Yet studies relating to economic systems are currently published in general economic reviews, and ABSEES shows that newspapers ought to be included, at least in the area surveyed by this paper.

In order to make research easier, it would seem proper to devise some co-ordinated information system operating at three levels:

elementary analysis and filing of documents,
developed analysis, in the form of abstracts,
translations.

It remains to be seen to what extent the information—work, at each level, should be selective, and to what extent it should be undertaken at the initiative of researchers.

Finally, one word ought to be said about the co-operation among the different scientific disciplines that are involved in the comparative investigation of economic systems. According to the integrated approach defined at the beginning, such co-operation is necessary. On the part of at least some of those disciplines, it is invited.[7] Yet it seems to be little practiced and poorly organized. The *International Bibliography of the Social*

[6] Even the combined list of 169 periodicals mentioned in Annexe 5 would not be altogether exhaustive. The *Russian Review*, for instance, is absent from it.

[7] See *Confluences*, Paris, I, 1960, p. 168.

Sciences is also editing an *International Bibliography of Social and Cultural Anthropology* and an *International Bibliography of Sociology*, both of which include sections relating to economic systems. However, these Bibliographies suffer from the same shortcomings as does the preceding one, at least on the two first accounts mentioned before. In addition, it seems that each of these three Bibliographies ignores what the others are doing.

TABLE 22.1 DISTRIBUTION OF STUDIES BY COUNTRIES (OR GROUPS OF COUNTRIES) OF ORIGIN

	Numbers	*Percentages*
North-America, English-speaking	184	17·5
Western-Europe, German-speaking	112	10·6
Western-Europe, French-speaking	94	8·9
Western-Europe, English-speaking	66	6·3
Scandinavia and the Netherlands	44	4·2
Italy, Spain, Portugal, Greece and Turkey	41	3·9
Australia, Taiwan, Japan, New-Zealand, South Africa, Singapore, Philippines, South Korea	13	1·2
	—554	—52·6
Russia	216	20·5
Poland	80	7·6
Rumania	34	3·2
GDR	29	2·8
Hungary	15	1·4
Czechoslovakia	14	1·3
Bulgaria	1	0·1
Albania	0	—
Continental China	0	—
	—389	—36·9
Yugoslavia	35	3·3
Israel	1	0·1
	— 36	— 3·4
South-America and Central America	54	5·1
Developing countries of Africa and Asia	20	1·9
	—74	—7·0
Total	1053	99·9

TABLE 22.2 DISTRIBUTION OF STUDIES BY LANGUAGE (PERCENTAGES)

Languages	*Percentages*
English (English-speaking countries of America and Europe + Group 217 + half of Group 25)	26
Russian	20·5
German (German-speaking Western Europe + GDR)	13·5
French (French-speaking Western Europe + half of Group 25)	10
Polish	7·5
Spanish	(approx.) 5
Yugoslavian languages	3
Rumanian	3
Other languages	less than 3

TABLE 22.3 DISTRIBUTION OF STUDIES BY COUNTRIES OR AREAS OF APPLICATION

	Numbers	*Percentages*
Group as a whole	161	15·3
North-America, English-speaking	72	6·8
Western-Europe, English-speaking	23	2·2
Western-Europe, French-speaking	27	2·6
Western-Europe, German-speaking	27	2·6
Scandinavia and the Netherlands	21	2·0
Italy, Spain, Portugal, Greece and Turkey	24	2·3
Australia, Taiwan, Japan, New Zealand, South Africa, Singapore, Philippines, South Korea	15	1·4
	—370	—35·2
Group as a whole	185	17·6
Russia	73	6·9
Albania	0	—
Bulgaria	3	0·3
GDR	14	1·3
Hungary	13	1·2
Poland	22	2·1
Czechoslovakia	3	0·3
Continental China	3	0·3
Rumania	21	2·0
	—337	—32·0
Group as a whole	7	0·7
Yugoslavia	26	2·5
Israel	10	0·9
	—43	—4·1
South-America and Central America	85	8·1
Developing countries of Africa and Asia	62	5·9
Unspecified area	86	8·2
Heterogeneous application area	70	6·6
	—303	—28·8
	1053	100·1

TABLE 22.4 DISTRIBUTION OF STUDIES BY COUNTRIES (OR GROUPS OF COUNTRIES) OF ORIGIN AND BY COUNTRIES OR GROUPS OF APPLICATION

Originating countries or groups	*Market System (developed)*				*Plan System*				*Self-management System*				*South and Central America*		*Developing countries Africa and Asia*	
Countries or groups of application	Group 21		North-America (211)		Group 22		USSR (221)		Group 23		Yugoslavia (231)					
	No.	%	No.	%	No.	%	No.	%	No.	%	No.	%	No.	%	No.	%
Market System (31)	297	53·61	96	52·17	67	17·22	47	21·76	5	13·89	5	14·29	1	1·85	0	—
of which North-America (311)	66	11·92	58	31·52	6	1·54	5	2·31	0	—	0	—	0	—	0	—
Plan System (32)	60	10·83	10	5·43	275	70·70	142	65·74	1	2·78	1	2·86	1	1·85	0	—
of which USSR (321)	12	2·17	5	2·72	60	15·42	58	26·85	1	2·78	1	2·86	0	—	0	—
Self-management (33)	12	2·17	4	2·17	1	0·26	1	0·46	29	80·50	28	80·00	1	1·85	0	—
of which Yugoslavia (331)	4	0·72	0	—	0	—	0	—	22	61·11	22	62·86	0	—	0	—
South and Central America (340)	38	6·86	19	10·33	3	0·77	3	1·39	0	—	0	—	44	81·48	0	—
Developing countries Africa and Asia (350)	38	6·86	12	6·52	5	1·29	3	1·39	1	2·78	1	2·86	2	3·70	16	80
Unspecified area (360)	72	13·00	32	17·39	9	2·31	4	1·85	0	—	0	—	3	5·56	2	10
Heterogeneous area (370)	37	6·68	11	5·98	29	7·46	16	7·41	0	—	0	—	2	3·70	2	10
TOTAL	554	100·01	184	99·99	389	100·01	216	100·00	36	100·01	35	100·01	54	99·99	20	100
(A + B + C + D + E = 1053)	A	%		%	B	%		%	C	%		%	D	%	E	%

TABLE 22.5 DISTRIBUTION OF STUDIES BY COUNTRIES OF ORIGIN (OR GROUPS OF COUNTRIES) AND TYPES OF PUBLICATION*

Originating country / *Type of Publication*	*211*	*212*	*213*	*214*	*215*	*216*	*217*	*Total*	*221*	*222*	*223*	*224*	*225*	*226*	*227*	*228*	*229*	*Total*	*231*	*232*	*240*	*250*	*Total*
111	1							1										—					1
115	3			2				5										—					5
120	1	2	1			1		5						1				1					6
121	46	9	12	16	4	5	1	93	28			1		6	1		1	37	3	1	1	3	138
122	57	18	25	30	6	10	4	150	76		1	3		21	1		1	103	8		13	6	280
123	12	5	4	16	9	4	2	52	36			7	1	19	6		22	91	3		4	2	152
124	25	13	16	22	9	5	1	91	49			13	9	17	3		4	95	6		7	3	202
125	21	14	22	18	11	10	4	100	22			4	4	10	3		4	47	14		16	4	181
126	9	5	14	7	5	6	1	47	5			1		6			2	14	1		13	2	77
127	8							8										—					8
128	1							1										—					1
129				1				1					1					1					2
	184	66	94	112	44	41	13	554	216	0	1	29	15	80	14	0	34	389	35	1	54	20	1053

* Types of publications with occurrence zero have not been mentioned.

TABLE 22.6 DISTRIBUTION OF STUDIES BY COUNTRIES (OR GROUPS OF COUNTRIES) OF ORIGIN AND NUMBERS OF INDICATORS

Originating countries or groups / *Number of Indicators*	*Market System Group 21*		*of which North-America 211*		*Plan System Group 22*		*of which USSR 221*		*Self-management System Group 23*		*of which Yugoslavia 231*		*South and Central America Group 240*		*Developing countries of Africa and Asia 250*		*Total*	
	No.	%	No.	%	No.	%	No.	%	No.	%	No.	%	No.	%	No.	%	No.	%
1	195	35·20	57	30·98	148	38·05	77	35·65	21	58·33	21	60	13	24·07	4	20	388	36·18
2	202	36·46 (71·66)	62	33·70 (64·68)	168	43·19 (81·24)	88	40·74 (76·39)	11	30·56 (88·89)	11	31·43 (91·43)	21	38·89 (62·96)	7	35 (55)	409	38·84 (75)
3	88	15·88 (87·54)	38	29·65 (85·33)	53	13·62 (94·86)	37	17·13 (93·52)	1	2·78 (91·67)	1	2·86 (94·29)	11	20·37 (83·33)	6	30 (85)	159	15·10 (90)
4	45	8·12 (95·66)	19	10·33 (95·66)	15	3·86 (98·72)	11	5·09 (98·61)	3	8·33	2	5·71	9	16·67	1	5	73	6·93 (97)
5	18	3·25 (98·91)	4	2·17 (97·83)	4	1·03 (99·75)	2	0·93 (99·54)							1	5	23	2·18
6	1	0·18 (99·09)	1	0·54 (98·37)	1	0·26	1	0·46							1	5	3	0·28
7	3	0·54	1	0·54													3	0·28
8																		
9	2	0·36	2	1·09													2	0·19
TOTAL	554		184		389		216		36		35		54		20		1053	100

TABLE 22.7 DISTRIBUTION OF ARTICLES BY SIZE AND NUMBER OF INDICATORS, FOR WORLD, MARKET SYSTEM (DEVELOPED), PLAN SYSTEM

Number of indicators	Articles of less than 10 pages (123)						Articles from 10 to 14 pages (124)					
	World		group 21		group 22		World		group 21		group 22	
	No.	%	No.	%	No.	%	No.	%	No.	%	No.	%
1	55	36·18	18	34·62	34	37·36	93	46·04	38	41·76	48	50·53
2	74	48·68	23	44·23	48	52·75	72	35·64	31	34·07	35	36·84
3	16	10·53	7	13·46	6	6·59	24	11·88	15	16·48	9	9·47
4	5	3·29	2	3·85	3	3·30	11	5·45	5	5·50	3	3·16
5	2	1·32	2	3·85	—	—	2	0·99	2	3·85	—	—
6	—	—	—	—	—	—	—	—	—	—	—	—
7	—	—	—	—	—	—	—	—	—	—	—	—
8	—	—	—	—	—	—	—	—	—	—	—	—
9	—	—	—	—	—	—	—	—	—	—	—	—
	152	100·00	52	100·01	91	99·97	202	100·0	91	101·66	95	100·00

Table 22.7 (*cont'd*)

Number of indicators	Articles from 15 to 25 pages (125)						Article more than 25 pages (126)						Total Articles					
	World		group 21		group 22		World		group 21		group 22		World		group 21		group 22	
	No.	%	No.	%	No.	%	No.	%	No.	%	No.	%	No.	%	No.	%	No.	%
1	64	35·36	33	id.	17	36·17	22	29·87	15	31·91	3	21·43	234	38·20	104	35·90	102	41·30
2	66	36·46	34	id.	21	44·68	31	40·26	18	38·30	6	42·86	243	39·70	106	36·30	110	44·50
3	30	16·57	20	id.	7	14·89	13	16·88	7	14·89	3	21·43	83	13·60	49	16·90	25	10·10
4	14	7·73	8	id.	1	2·13	5	6·49	3	6·38	—	—	35	5·70	18	6·20	7	2·80
5	4	2·21	4	id.	—	—	4	5·19	2	4·26	2	14·29	12	2·00	10	3·40	2	0·80
6	2	1·10	—	id.	1	2·13	—	—	—	—	—	—	2	0·30	—	—	1	0·40
7	1	0·55	—	id.	—	—	2	2·60	2	4·26	—	—	3	0·50	3	1·00	—	—
8	—	—	—	—	—	—	—	—	—	—	—	—	—	—	—	—	—	—
9	—	—	—	—	—	—	—	—	—	—	—	—	—	—	—	—	—	—
	181	99·98	100	100·00	47	100·00	77	101·29	47	100·00	612	100·00	290	100·00	247	100·00		

Summary of the Discussion

Dr Borko presented Professor Chamley's paper, pointing out its originality. Professor Chamley has defined an economic system as a principle of the organization of economic activity, and has distinguished five groups of systems on this basis: Market systems, Planning systems, Self-management systems, Latin American systems, and Asian-African systems, the last two characteristically less developed than the others. Using this framework, Professor Chamley has classified both existing documents and what he considers to be the demand for further information. The resulting set of tables and appendices constitute, in Dr Borko's opinion, the most interesting and valuable portion of Professor Chamley's paper. It is important, in *Dr Borko*'s view, for different systems to study each other impartially, and the material that Professor Chamley has assembled will help to fill a vacuum. His material is of interest in itself, both quantitatively and qualitatively; *Dr Borko* was appreciative of the breakdowns by language, by country under study, and by the country from which the various studies have been undertaken.

At the same time, *Dr Borko* found Professor Chamley's definition of an economic system too vague and general for his liking. Rather than by 'principle of organization', *Dr Borko* maintained that the basis for classification should be on some such basis as the system of property in the means of production, or the system's role in the world economy. (Why, for example, had Professor Chamley put Israel and Yugoslavia in the same category?) *Dr Borko* also noted that Professor Chamley had made only a partial selection of documents and tables from UN sources, and had omitted others which he *Dr Borko* would have considered equally relevant; *Dr Borko* inquired, therefore, to the basis of Professor Chamley's selection.

Turning to more detailed aspects of technique and method, *Dr Borko* noted that Professor Chamley had attempted breakdowns by general vs. detailed accounts of economic systems and, likewise, by intra-system vs. inter-system studies. He noted also that different aspects had been stressed—a broader range, he thought, than in most studies made in market-system countries, which had been the sources of the great bulk of Professor Chamley's material. On the other hand, Professor Chamley's quantitative data refer to a single year. The basis of classification is not always clear; perhaps because the title of an article a book may not adequately summarize its contents. Of 169 periodicals cited, only 41 per cent are listed in the *International Bibliography of Economics* (IBE), and there appears to be under-representation of Soviet and Eastern European journals. In short, the paper needs considerably more work, but *Dr Borko* believed that co-operation could be secured from Soviet economists and information specialists.

In his reply, *Professor Chamley* expressed gratitude for the expressions of support, particularly those from Soviet sources. He did not consider the criticisms of his method or of the detailed categorization of particular countries to be really justified. All studies quoted in the IBE in the classes relevant for the comparative investigation of economic systems were examined one by one. After inspection of their title, some were selected, some not. It finally happened that some classes were selected in their entirety, some not. It was never decided beforehand to select a complete class of studies. As to the inclusion of

Yugoslavia and Israel in a separate category, it is only tentative. The main justification for this procedure was that some people might prefer it, and that it was easier to undo it if it should appear unjustified rather than to introduce it once the study was completed.

Professor Giersch, from the floor, claimed that the paper needed to draw a clearer line between facilities to be supplied by libraries and facilities that researchers should supply for themselves. He inquired how much of his own job the researcher could reasonably expect a library to do for him, and felt that the *number* of researchers was important in this respect, because of the possible strain on library facilities. (*Professor Chamley* agreed, adding that the JEL classification suggested that the number of researchers in comparative systems was falling, perhaps because their work was becoming more difficult.)

Mr Weiss pointed to the mass of information which must be processed if some such scheme as Professor Chamley's were to be adopted. Who would do the processing, and might it not be more difficult than in most other branches of economic study? (Professor Chamley felt that it was too early to determine relative difficulty without further testing. Meanwhile, library networking might help and multiple indexing is necessary. As for IBE, by contrast Professor Chamley believed its indexing to be incomplete for his purposes.)

Professor M. Perlman claimed that the history of the comparative systems sub-discipline was 'catching up with itself'. It had previously concentrated on abstract studies of market vs. planning. (Here *Professor Johnson* commented that he had found the field highly descriptive and institutional in the 1930s and 1940s, with descriptive studies of Communism, Fascism, and Sweden's alleged 'middle way'.) Currently, *Professor Perlman* continued, countries were experimenting with mixed systems and there was much talk of 'convergence' between them. Also, mathematics and statistics have been slow to permeate this field. Although not himself a mathematical economist, *Professor Perlman* had heard of experiments to use multi-dimensional surfaces in a geometrical presentation of some comparative-systems problems. (*Professor Chamley* was dubious about the usefulness of exclusively mathematical methods in an essentially interdisciplinary field like Comparative Economic Systems.)

Professor Morgan reported that multi-dimensional classification causes problems unless one uses a computerized approach in classification. In particular, he thought that multi-dimensionality was not compatible with the 'key word' approach to bibliography, which many speakers were advocating at this conference. (*Professor Chamley* agreed.)

Dr Heinemann observed that the list of periodicals imparted to the Institut für Weltwirtschaft in Annexe 2 of the report was incomplete—*Professor Chamley* apologized for the errors and said it would be easy to correct them.

To close the discussion, *Dr Borko* requested the floor once more in clarification of his earlier statement. He did not want his earlier criticisms to be taken too literally. He wanted to make it clear that he supported Professor Chamley's efforts and, furthermore, that he did not feel it necessary to have all data summarized in advance before research is undertaken.

23 Data in the Planned Economy of the USSR

M. S. Palnicov
INSTITUTE OF SCIENTIFIC INFORMATION, USSR

At the present time, in the Soviet Union there is a rapid development of computerized economic information systems primarily in connection with the requirements of its economic planning and management. In some aspects this work is being carried out together with other CMEA member-countries and will result in the creation of an international network of information in economic statistics.

The proper organization and development of information services requires that the information needs of researchers be carefully studied in order to avoid duplication both in data and research or the collection of unnecessary or relatively insignificant data.

Among possible ways to study users' needs that are discussed in this article are: the systematic study of structure and tendencies in economic literature flows, the classification of actual requests according to identified categories of users, and some other practical steps.

The aim of this paper is to describe the general characteristics of the data used in economic research.

In a planned economy, the collection of statistical economic data, as well as of data in the form of ideas, is closely connected with economic planning. All forms of planning theory, as well as improvements coming from practice, inevitably result in improvement of data, too. In fact, the experience of the last few years convinces us of the importance of users' needs. In this case, the users are planners and planning researchers. What, then, are these planning needs, by which this influence is determined?

I. MAIN TRENDS OF RESEARCH IN PLANNING

During the last few years, particular attention has been paid in the Soviet Union to the creation of a general system of connected and well-balanced long, medium, and short-term plans for economic development.

Some substantial changes have taken place in the mode of primary statistics gathering. This gathering is now being reorganized in accordance with the requirements of computerized planning and management systems, and methods of working-out of all types of balances and of indicators.

On the whole, this programme of improvement in methods and statistical background of planning includes more than one hundred research issues and an unusually large number of statistical indicators. It is enough to say that the list of necessary additional research in working out the long-term plan for 1976–90 includes 126 problems about, and prognoses for, science and technical development. Its successful realization will essentially increase the amount of statistical data given to researchers in planning and all other branches of economic science.

II. ECONOMIC RESEARCH AND ECONOMIC INFORMATION SCALE

The above-mentioned improvements in planning goals, methods and procedures have produced a strong impact upon the whole complex, both basic and applied, of research activities. The volume of economics publications, including those dealing with planning, grows continually. According to the bibliographical bulletin, 'New Soviet Economic Literature' (published by the Institute for Information in Social Sciences, USSR Academy of Science), the number of books and papers with the term 'planning' in the title increased from about 724 to 960 instances per year during the period 1970–74. For the period, 1963–73, the number of books and booklets on planning, accounting and management increased from one-quarter to one-third of the total publications on economic topics. There has been a marked addition in the number of statistical publications. The regularly published statistical yearbooks, *National Economy of the USSR*, present a full-scale description of the development processes in the economy, and this description is now much more detailed than it used to be at the beginning of the post-war period, to say nothing of pre-war times. The introduction of new material is now more frequent. Current observations, as made by state statistical organizations, target figures and prospective plans for economic development are also now regularly published; on the other hand, it ensures a higher level of statistical data presentation.

Yet, in spite of this wide (and constantly growing) publication of data, our yearbooks are still far from reflecting the total amount of statistical information presently being collected and processed by the various state statistical offices. That is why, along with such yearbooks, other publications appear more and more. In a yearly periodical collection, *The USSR and Soviet Republics*, one can regularly find reports on the fulfilment of quarterly, semi-annual and annual plans. In fact, every issue of the magazine *Vestnik statistiki* (*Statistics Herald*) presents current developments of statistical data. The frequency of its publications has been doubled in the last few years.

Since the end of the 1960s and the beginning of the 1970s, important material has been collected for publication, once in a five-year period, in such special data collections as *Industry of the USSR, Technological Progress in National Economy, Rural Economy of the USSR, Soviet Trade, Finances of the USSR, Public Education, Science and Culture, Health Protection in the USSR, Apartment Construction in the USSR*, etc. Statistical periodicals of the individual Soviet Republics, as well, present valuable information. One should also bear in mind that the Central Statistical Office of the Soviet Union and agencies of the various republics supply research centres directly with necessary data on request.

At the same time, our economists and statisticians fully acknowledge the importance of the further qualitative improvement of statistical data, along with its quantitative growth, that can be secured through the publication of more new value indices, the extension of the groupings used, etc.

As for the quality characteristics of statistical data, one cannot help but mention the important work being done in the field of the unification of statistical methodology through the joint efforts of CMEA member-countries. At present, this work touches upon the accounting activities in all, or almost all, spheres of industry and the other structural units of the national economies of these countries. Because of these efforts, they have been able, for some years, to exchange comparable statistical data.

It is evident that this exchange between the USSR and the other member-countries, in connection with the co-ordination of economic plans and other mutual tasks, leads to an eventual expansion of data now in possession of Soviet scientists, as well as those of all other socialist countries.

It is impossible to imagine modern information services without computerized systems of collection, storage, retrieval and dissemination of economic information. In order to raise information servicing to the level of the tasks mentioned above, there has been undertaken in the Soviet Union, within the last few years, a strong effort to create automated systems of state statistics (ASGS). Being a sub-system of the all-Soviet system of automated collection (including the processing of information for accounting, planning and decision-making (OGAS), ASGS allows for further improvement of the methodological and technical bases of statistics. It will have a large bank of data connected with the banks of the other OGAS sub-systems. The manifold effects of the ASGS development will become apparent in the full unification of comparable accounting statistics, in the possibility of working out numerous new statistical aggregates, in reducing decisively the period necessary for information processing and retrieval, and in supplying a much wider circle of its consumers with economic information. Along with this process, there is being carried out the creation of another OGAS syb-system, one involving an automated system of planning calculations (ASPR). ASPR is considered to be a necessary tool for the optimal planning of the national economy. It includes all calculations and decisions (represented by the system of models, algorithms and computer programs), basic data, and the turnover of current documentation. ASPR will be put under partial operation during this year (1975). Its creation will not only increase the efficiency of planning decisions, their operativeness and variability, but will also facilitate the essential research activities of the scientific centres.

Great attention to the mechanization of statistics gathering and processing is being paid by the Permanent Commission of CMEA Countries on Statistics. It now prepares a mutually acceptable system of economic information, which provides for a single type of technical and economic data classifications and codes, a unified type of documentation, unified algorithms for data handling and the other necessary elements of the system. Works presently undertaken are an important step in creating the future international network of economic statistics for CMEA countries.

Alongside of these statistical data channel improvements in the Soviet Union, there has continued large-scale work on the development of a nation-wide network of information in basic and applied economics. The world-known VINITI (All-Union Institute of Scientific and Technical Information), one of the numerous functions of which is to collect and disseminate current information of a techno-economic nature, was supplemented recently with INION (The Institute for Information in Social Sciences). One of INION's functions is to retrieve and disseminate, in abstract or any other required form, information on fundamental works in political economy, whether issued at home or abroad. With the creation of this centre there has been formed—at least institutionally—the system of information which controls and organizes all existing flows of economic data. These flows can be roughly divided among basic economic data (handled by INION and subordinate information centres with the Academy of Science), applied techno-economic data (handled by VINITI and industrial information centres), and current business accounting and statistical information (handled by agencies belonging to the Central Statistical Office). The research process in economics now rests upon a solid information basis, subject, of course, to further necessary improvements.

III. POSSIBLE WAYS TO STUDY RESEARCHERS' NEEDS AND THEIR IMPLICATIONS FOR THE GENERAL IMPROVEMENT OF DATA AND ECONOMIC KNOWLEDGE

Of the many problems connected with further improvements in the national network of economic information (e.g. the necessity (1) to organize properly all information flows and their handling on sequential levels of this network, (2) to involve fully all modern sources of information, and (3) to create a universal information retrieval language), only one will be discussed in this paper. It is the problem of recording and analysing the researchers' needs.

It is evident that past retrieval of information, its completeness, and the optimal effectiveness of creative research labour (which manifests itself in the quality of economic research and planning decisions) are closely connected with the study of users' needs.

It will not be an overstatement to say that, in a situation of some overproduction of primary information, everywhere called the 'information explosion', thoughtful investigation of researchers' needs on the part of secondary information producers acquires special importance.

Let us consider some possible ways and means of demands analysis. It seems that such a procedure should rely on:

(1) the systematic study of structure and tendencies in flows of scientific documents—their quantitative parameters, regularities of distribution and ageing;
(2) a thought-out classification of scientific workers, i.e. users of information, according to their position, scientific training, specialization and character of scientific work (basic or applied research);
(3) a study of concrete demands according to fixed categories of users and to kinds of demands in direct connection with stages of their research work;
(4) a study of possible changes over time in the demand for various types of information services.

1. Although primary document flows analysis is not a direct study of demands, it is important in order to reveal possible requests, their *epicentrum*, and the directions of search for answers. All of this is made easier by the factor that, while handling documents, information specialists inevitably deal with primary sources, opening up new directions of research, and they can register increases or, *vice versa*, decreases in the flows of literature on certain themes, etc. Continued control over these changes gives them the possibility of orienting themselves with regard to the general structure and character of present and future requests. On the other hand, such control makes it possible to find out, and to fill, the gaps in information flows, e.g. giving to a wider circle of users information about sources that are otherwise non-available to them (shorthand records of conferences, unpublished scientific and technical reports, and the like).

2. The classification of information users could also serve as one of the fundamentals of rational information activities. At present, we have a rather clear notion about the mechanism shaping information requirements, as well as a set of objective and subjective factors that in-

fluence their content and structure. For example, it is well-known that the leading staffs of scientific institutions are interested in theoretical information. Within the total number of requests for data from all branches of knowledge, those from economists with doctor's or master's degrees exceed the number of requests from experts having other qualifications. Depending on the scientific specialization of scientists, their need for political economy data, econometrics or other economic discipline fluctuates widely. However, this information on users' requirements is still insufficiently generalized and classified. It seems that the possibilities for the quantitative and qualitative analysis of requests, inherent in scientific workers' classification, and the extent of their satisfaction can be more completely analysed. In particular, with the help of a thesaurus used by certain categories of specialists, it would be possible to establish subject attributes and then to analyse document flows, revealing their subject saturation and the degree of correspondence with the needs of these categories of users.

3. A clear understanding of types of requests and of their peculiarities permits us to have the most direct influence upon economic knowledge. This can be achieved by directly finding out what are researchers' needs; namely, whether they need information in the form of an analytical survey, whether they are interested in acquiring data on a specific narrow subject, or on the main aspects of the problem, or, on the contrary, whether they want to receive information of a somewhat broader character than just the scientific subject of their research, etc. All of this is quite possible. Practically, it is the question of a systematic combination of information services with Five Year plans or longer plans of scientific centres (including university economics departments), and, also, the publication schedules of central and regional publishing houses (the latter is necessary to take into account works not provided by the scientific centres' plans. In our view, such knowledge could give the possibility: (1) to determine in advance the probable breadth of researcher subjects, and the depth, variety or number of previously published materials, and the correlation between narrow and large-thematic literature; (2) to prepare in advance information materials for the beginning of research projects and, thus, to speed them up; (3) to promote a higher quality of research activities; (4) to signal a possible duplicating of investigations and promote more rational use of data; and (5) to insert effective corrections in the acquisition of information holdings in classification schemes.

In other words, such co-operation between scientific and information centres would be useful for those who prepare data and for those who use them. To put this co-operation into practice would mean making a valuable contribution to the general organization of economic knowledge and to its ordering on the basis of a preliminary study of potential requests.

No less essential for the adequacy of information to researchers' needs is the active participation of information services on different stages of research. Experiments have shown that an economist-researcher goes through three stages while working over his theme:

a search for the starting point of an investigation, the formulation of a problem, the definition of goals and tasks, and the means and methods of research realization;

a development and transformation of accumulated knowledge, the formulation of preliminary hypotheses, and the elaboration of a scientific theory;

a materialization of theoretical theses, the verification of conclusions, the final formulation, and the publication of the results of the research.

Most of the required information falls into the second of these stages. It is desirable to have it in summary form, thus giving the researcher a panoramic vision of his set task in the light of the whole problem. Put in perspective, this stage may become a field for the most fruitful co-operation between researchers and information workers. As for the information services, the analytical survey seems to be a comfortable form of presenting highly concentrated information, combining conceptual, methodological and factographic data.

Other forms of recording and answering requests are also possible; for instance, the preparation of materials in the form of econometric or statistical data selections or files, in response to a specially formulated demand. With the development of computing centres and automated databanks this way of preparation by information services of ready-to-use materials will evidently be widespread, thus saving researchers' time for direct analytical studies. Even now, such work is carried out by many information services in academic and other scientific institutions.

Of course, needs for information are not reduced only to the level of initial research topics, as formulated in the working plans of scientific centres. Most demands appear in the course of subsequent investigations. Recording the contents and trends of such demands seems particularly useful for the rational acquisition of information holdings because it leads to a wider professional realization of what is necessary for research.

Apparently, the recording and analysis of the total volume of requests is not likely to be realized in full until construction is completed of the above-mentioned networks of economic data centres. At present, the main forms of recording demands are still questionnaire distribution and interviewing. In our view, these are useful in some respects, especially in showing up new requirements for information servicing, for changes in information users' structure, etc. But, on the whole, their future seems to be somewhat dubious. beyond these new opportunities, which will be opened by automatic recording of demands, there has appeared, in recent years, another serious competitor to these traditional methods, namely, discussions of magazine or journals specializing in abstracts. The users' wishes to see certain new materials in these abstracts are, as a matter of fact, not much different from demands revealed by questionnaires and interviews. They are, perhaps, simply more skilled and systematized demands, for they are based on studies of subject flows of secondary information. The results of such discussions are widely used for the betterment of secondary information flow.

4. A few remarks must be made about changes in demand for different kinds of information services. Their review permits us, of course, to judge, with some limitations, certain general tendencies in users' needs. So far, the statistics that could provide a detailed study of the structure of needs satisfaction according to different kinds of information service is not available. It is clear, however, that abstract services remain one of the main forms of information, retrieval or dissemination. At the same time, one finds, in the Soviet Union, a growing interest in analytical surveys. Also growing is the demand for the selective dissemination of information and delivery of factographic data. All of these positive changes are signs of the growing importance of the most effective and operative forms of information service—a process serving to guarantee further rises in the level of information service and in the scientific value of information for researchers.

IV. CONCLUSIONS

The analysis of the current state of data and the channels along which it goes to users, according to the structure and character of their needs, shows that, during the last few years, there were serious efforts undertaken in the information field, in the Soviet Union, to increase the general level of economic research. There now exists a ramified system of economic information embracing all the flows of economic literature and statistical data. It is to be based on the principle of the informational compatibility of all of its component parts.

One of the important aims of the system, along with the optimization of its scientific, technological and economic parameters, is the provision for maximum adequacy of information for researchers' needs. Practically, it means the necessity for securing maximum correspondence of data with the aims of scientific research; the avoidance of duplication of data and scientific activities; and thematic completeness of information supplies involving the filing of the most relevant and valuable ideas and statistical data, while excluding obsolete concepts and data. For this purpose, a constant and comprehensive study of information demands, their structure and peculiarities, is being carried on, along with direct cooperation between information workers and economic research scholars.

At the same time, the Soviet Union and other CMEA countries are undertaking efforts to create a broad international network of statistical information with a high level of methodological and technological compatibility. All of these efforts have already led to an essential expansion and improvement of the information bases of scientific research.

Nevertheless, there are still many problems, the solution of which requires not only Soviet efforts, but broad international co-operation as well.

Comment by T. Földi (Hungary)

In my comment I restrict myself to verbal information and would like to raise three questions.

Question 1. Are there any fundamental differences between the economic information needs in planned and market economies? The answer to this question is relevant from various points of view. Specifically, if there were too many differences they would limit somewhat the possibilities of international co-operation in the satisfaction of such needs, as well as in the development of tools that may serve this aim. As for me, fundamental differences do not exist, even if there are many important differences in the distribution of the needs of decision-makers and researchers according to the differences in the process of decision-making and of organizational structures both in management and research. Information needs are determined by three major factors:

(*a*) a striving for an economic and social policy, better founded scientifically to face the growing responsibilities of the leadership of society in securing the fundamental interests of human beings,
(*b*) the efficient utilization of the results of the scientific, technical revolution and, especially, of those in information and communication techniques for management and research,
(*c*) the recognized need for the further development of international economic co-operation, the task of its realization and, consequently, the need to become better informed about foreign economic facts and ideas.

If this argument can be accepted, one can also agree on the lack of fundamental differences, since the influence of the above-mentioned factors in *both* socio-economic systems can hardly be denied. While stating this, it is necessary to emphasize the really existing differences and to promote their study in order to find the focal points where effective co-operation can be developed. I stress this because I am convinced that the planning of information systems or co-operation cannot start from any other point than users' needs.

Question 2. Where do we stand now and in which direction should we go in the satisfaction of users' needs? The historical process of the satisfaction of the users' needs can be divided roughly into two phases:

1. In the first phase, the function of the storage of information prevailed. This lasted until about the end of the last century. Then the users themselves collected sources of information or had to go to different institutions (in historical research the latter is still the main access to information) and look for the information required. The 'information organizations', mainly libraries, had a conservation and stand-by function, and the volume of paper-work was not burdensome.

2. In the second phase, information organizations switched over, step by step, to an active position. Information dissemination had, by then, become prevalent and the system of values in information activity changed fundamentally. Competition started between information organizations: which could serve more extensive or specialized disseminated informations? Thus we run into an overproduction of secondary information. In Hungary, the number of periodicals which give secondary information on economic literature has grown fivefold during the last two decades and is now about 80. These serve about 2000 research workers. It is

a pity that the satisfaction of users' needs did not intensify at the same rate. The indicators of the efficiency of disseminated secondary information sharply decline as soon as they arrive at a critical point. I am afraid that we are not far from this point. I have to add that I do not believe that the use of computers, alone, will lead us out of this situation.

To answer the second part of the question, I cannot see the solution elsewhere than in the critical re-evaluation and revision of the information systems based on massive dissemination of secondary information. We cannot overcome the difficulties arising from this overproduction, unless we find a new philosophy. This philosophy should be based on (*a*) restoring the stand-by function of large scientific information bases which are to be shaped in order to face the present-day needs of inter- and multi-disciplinary research; (*b*) restricting the local information units to the service of the specific needs arising from the activities of their 'mother-organization' by acquiring specified information from the large bases and adapting them to the particular needs of their users; (*c*) establishing a standing interactive process between users and information units so that the teams of researchers or decision-makers should include information officers well qualified both in the respective field of knowledge and in information techniques. The transition to such a system needs a new aproach to the functions of large information organizations and preference to be given to their manifold development also in the social sciences; a new system of education, both of information officers and of users; and, last but not least, extensive international co-operation. This would be a long-range programme whose preparation may take more than a decade. Much human and technical investment will be needed, but it could hardly be more expensive than the present parallelism, overproduction and consequent waste of users' time.

Question 3. How to satisfy individual needs? I suggested above three major factors influencing information needs. Let me baptize them macrofactors, since, they create an environment in which *individual needs* arise. I do not believe that there exist two users with identical needs. At this point I would restrict the question—just as Mr Palnikov does— to the needs of researchers. An observation of the needs of some 60 research-workers of the Institute of Economics, Hungarian Academy of Sciences, over a period of more than a decade has led me to the following conclusions: (1) Researchers tend to be only slightly interested in scientific information other than that belonging strictly to their research field. Although they suffer from a lack of information on general developments in their science, they cannot afford the luxury of taking time regularly to consult them. (2) They complain more of too much information than of its absence, as they rarely get enough selected references on sources. One cause of this is that they cannot always formulate their needs precisely; the other is that even if they do, information organizations are not always capable of serving them with adequate information on the basis of the existing retrieval processes. Therefore, many of them reject the intervention of information devices into their instinctively shaped search for information, relying often on personal contacts with other researchers and, also, with practitioners. What conclusions are to be drawn from these experiences?

First—in accordance with Mr Palnikov's statement—there is a growing need for 'state of art' reports which should be satisfied in wide fields of knowledge in order to overcome the lack of information on general trends, due to growing specialization. This work is to be done in co-operation with researchers, mainly by information evaluation and repackaging centres. *Second*, to follow, as far as possible, the specialization and/or integration tendencies of research also by information activities aimed at satisfying direct research needs and, thus, to raise the selectivity of the information offered. The latter can be done only in very close collaboration with those who are served with information. Here direct human contact, a constant dialogue, cannot be fully replaced by written information.

Summary of the Discussion

Mr Weiss, introducing Dr Palnicov's paper, found it a highly useful means to estimate the present and future demand for data in the USSR. He noted the steady improvement in the technical aspects of Soviet planning processes: data, methods (statistics, accounting, materials balancing) and co-ordination between Gosplan and other ministries. The implications of these improvements, Dr Weiss believed, were an increasing quantity of published output and, also, more rapid publication. The quality also was rising, particularly as regards comparability with similar materials from other member countries of the Committee for Mutual Economic Assistance (Comecon, CMEA).

It would be difficult, and perhaps impossible, to estimate in advance how useful all of this might be to the individual researcher outside of the CMEA area, because researchers are so numerous and their desires so variegated.

Mr Weiss did not consider it impossible for some of Dr Palnicov's ideas to receive attention in the West, even though Western countries had no 'official' or 'imperative' plans. At the same time, demand for the Soviet materials comes largely from agencies whose needs form part of the central planning system, and one could expect demand and supply to develop together. In general, *Mr Weiss* thought, demand for data calls forth a corresponding supply if it is sufficiently specific, and if disclosure would not affect any important pressure group unfavourably.

Professor Bronfenbrenner made the first comment from the floor. He felt that researchers and technicians generally wanted data made public, while politicians and bureaucrats tended to favour secrecy to protect their exercise of 'discretion' and 'qualitative judgments' from effective criticism. This was true in both East and West, and had nothing to do with the issue of 'market vs. planning'. *Mrs Siefkes* added that when data are disclosed, there are important conflicts as to level and as to breakdowns, as between groups of users, so that the question should be rephrased: *what* materials were to become available for *which groups* of users? (With special reference to Soviet data, *Mrs Siefkes* also inquired what bibliographical materials were available in Western Languages.)

Professor M. Perlman then inquired what information was available to universities both in the USSR and abroad, and to special groups like that headed by Federenko, that are interested in cultural co-operation. As to the other CMEA countries, *Professor Perlman* understood that the situation differed widely from one to another, and he hoped that Dr Palnicov might indicate what materials might become available from which countries. Finally, *Professor Perlman* wondered whether Soviet databanks would ever become available on line to researchers outside of the CMEA.

After this introduction, *Professor Perlman* summarized a written comment by Dr Földi. Dr Földi felt that the differences between the information needs of different classes of users were not very important, and that the similarity of these needs would assist co-operation. Information is needed for domestic policy, for efficient use of the 'information revolution', and for international co-operation. But he went on to raise other and more fundamental issues.

For example, Dr Földi had inquired where we stand, and what was the useful next step toward the satisfaction of the users of economic data. Before World War I, users generally developed their own materials. Later, information organizations became more active and powerful. They also came to compete with each other, and sometimes supplied surpluses of low-quality, over-aggregated data at the secondary level. This has now reached the point of negative, and not merely diminishing, returns, and the whole information system needs a new philosophy. This should include 'standby' access to big data banks, interaction processes between sources and users, and accessibility to small and to local agencies.

But the expression of individual demands should change as well. In Dr Földi's country (Hungary), researchers seem to him to be too narrow in their interests, and too willing to complain of the surplus of irrelevant information which they receive. They do not ask questions well, and sometimes even actively avoid information offices in their work, preferring private contacts of various kinds. What is needed is closer collaboration and dialogue between researchers and suppliers of information.

Professor Tyler wondered whether Western data are available to Soviet researchers on the same basis as to Western ones. *Professor Perlman* saw no reason to doubt this. *Mr Kilgour* reported that exchange methods were being worked out to make more records machine-readable across more national boundaries, so that the key factor may soon be the bibliography of what is available.

Dr Palnicov chose to answer discussants individually. He had read Dr Földi's interesting comment, but felt that it had little to do with his own report. He agreed that there were few fundamental differences in information needs among users, but did not see why this point needed conference discussion. He was grateful for Dr Weiss' understanding introduction, but felt that Dr Weiss had drawn distinctions which had not been intended between the technical and the philosophical portions of his paper. In particular, Dr Palnicov's main concentration had been on specifically Soviet materials, and he did not know a great deal about the situations of other CMEA countries. Commenting on Professor Bronfenbrenner's observation, *Dr Palnicov* noted a new Soviet book entitled *Economic Information* (edited by Yassin) which gives a description of a more 'closed' system of terminals and databanks than his own. This volume proposed a 'closed system' of terminals and databanks for planners only. Dr Palnicov had no ready answers to questions raised by Mrs Siefkes as he had not studied the range of issues involved in the different demands of user groups, and his report had not been concerned with bibliographies. In general, *Dr Palnicov* stressed that the Soviet information system on economics was developing in step with the information systems of other countries. Special abstract and bibliography periodicals were regularly published and abstracts were being exchanged with foreign scholars in a continuing process. The Soviet Union was participating fully in UN organizations, such as UNESCO.

Following the close of formal discussion, *Professor Kindleberger* inquired whether Soviet planning procedures included estimates of consumer response to price changes. *Dr Palnicov* replied that up to the last few years such information was not collected, since the Soviets made a policy of charging only the lowest prices possible rather than experimenting with alternative prices. *Professor Diaz-Alejandro* added that in some 'model' planning systems, including a General Electric system used at Yale University, consumer demand functions can be, and have been, included. *Dr Weiss* wondered, with regard to data banking, whether this, too, might be subject to diminishing returns, since quantity was produced at the expense of quality. *Professor M. Perlman* admitted the GIGO problem of 'garbage in—garbage out', but said that the potentiality for improvement is always there. The computerized library, quite generally, has advantages and costs. *Professor Perlman* had been impressed with Mr Kilgour's accomplishments in this direction, and wondered why Mr Kilgour did not propagandize more actively for his system. (*Mr Kilgour* replied that propagandizing for the OCLC system was, in fact, one of his major activities.)

24 The History of Economic Thought and Analysis; Organization and Retrieval of its Content

Joseph J. Spengler
DUKE UNIVERSITY, DURHAM, NORTH CAROLINA

It is necessary to distinguish between information and knowledge since the latter is less easily communicated than the former. It is also necessary to attend to the input cost of communication, together with the willingness of potential users to meet that cost, particularly given the limited market provided by those with a relevant interest in the history of economic thought.

A number of limits exist to the utilizability of computerization and other or complementary apparatus available for organizing and retrieving information and knowledge in the history of economic thought. Among these limits are: (1) the degree to which an organized body of knowledge can be decomposed in utilizable parts; (2) the degree of specialization; and (3) the purposes to be served by the history of economic science.

Careful attention needs to be given to costs, particularly since these costs may be overhead in character and, hence, run high per unit if the warrantable rate of use of the aggregate apparatus and organization is low. If costs are variable, the risk of low use is less and high cost per unit is less. In short, the cost structure needs careful examination of unit cost is to be minimized.

The organization and facilitation of retrieval of information on the history of economic thought are of growing importance. At issue, therefore, is the selection and adaptation of the best means or sets of means. Among these means a major role can be filled by computerization, albeit in conformity with research purposes.

Interest in the organization and retrieval of knowledge in the field of the history of economic thought, as well as in other fields of social thought, has increased greatly as a result of (*a*) the rapid growth of economic literature actually or potentially of historical interest, and (*b*) the development of methods of organization and instruments (e.g. the computer and its ancillaries) that permit quick search and recovery in many scientific fields. In an inquiry such as the present one, our concern must be not with organization and retrieval in general, but with conditions limiting its use in areas of inquiry or imposing significant costs upon its use. In this paper, attention will be focused upon two relevant aspects of organization and retrieval: (i) limits and costs, and (ii) practical alternatives.

I. INFORMATION vs. *KNOWLEDGE*

Before turning to limits, costs, and alternative modes of knowledge organization and retrieval, it is to be observed that while the title of this report and the introductory paragraph refer to retrieval of knowledge, it may be more accurate to refer to retrieval of information. The term 'information' has a more utilitarian connotation (if not denotation) than has the term 'knowledge'. It is concern with knowledge in the sense of potentially, if not actually, utilizable information that is the source of interest in the retrieval of knowledge or information and, hence, in modes of organizing information so as to make locating it, together with communicating it, as costless as possible in temporal and pecuniary terms. Moreover, the content of information may range widely, as in the present case, from mere reference to sources to portions of what is covered in these sources.

Since attention to the organization and retrieval of information may be said to have originated and flourished in the field of organic and inorganic science, it may be questioned whether the concerns in these areas of science correspond closely to those in economics or social science generally. In the field of natural science, far more than in economics, the demand for information is problem-oriented and, hence, specifically oriented to the solution of the problem in need of solution. Moreover, the content of natural science is more subdivisible, as a rule, into utilizable parts than is that of social sciences. The cost in time of satisfying this demand turns on the specificity with which information can be requested and the adaptability of the information transferred to the solution of a given unsolved problem, as well as upon the capacity of the information-requester to grasp and apply the information supplied to him.

The instruments whereon the transfer of information currently depends include, in the main, computers, computer-based files of abstracts and indexes for specific subjects, the volume of useful—as distinct from redundant—information fed into these files, information networks, and the access of information-users to the contents of these abstracts and indexes.[1] Access is conditioned of course, by the state of computer hardware, and the structure of information networks and their

[1] Knox, William T., 'Systems for Technological Information Transfer', *Science* 181 (Aug. 3, 1973), pp. 415–19; Martin Greenberger, 'Computer and Information Networks', *Science* 182 (Oct. 5, 1973), pp. 29–35.

institutional or market organization, as well as by the size of data banks and the degree to which they are specialized.

What has been said in the preceding paragraph points to a problem peculiar to the history of economic thought, together with the humanities and at least some branches of social science. Everything connected with the gathering, storing, and dissemination of information involves human and capital inputs and, hence, is expensive in varying measure, particularly if the flow of inputs into information-related activities is restricted by artificial constraints or by the high alternative use value of these human and capital inputs. Accordingly, since the demand in the market for information relating to the history of thought is limited and not likely to be greatly supplemented by public funds, scholars and others interested in the history of economic thought are not likely to be able to compete effectively with others investing in the retrieval or organized information. For this reason alone the potential contribution of the current information-gathering-and-assembling apparatus to the progress of the history of economic thought may prove limited, at least in comparison with most branches of science. Only if, somehow, the current shortage of finance can be overcome is it likely that the history of economic thought will find comparable support. Even then there exists a danger, namely, an excess of concentration upon aspects of the history of economic thought, exploration of which is relatively inexpensive. There remain other obstacles to be discussed below.

II. LIMITS

The utilizability of apparatuses for the organization and retrieval of knowledge in any field of science or branch thereof is conditioned by a number of circumstances which vary with both science and branch thereof. Circumstances of especial concern to students of the history of economic thought will be identified and briefly examined in this section.

DECOMPOSABILITY

The content of any organized body of knowledge is decomposable into parts, the number of which is conditioned by the degree to which that knowledge can be divided into self-sufficient or self-subsisting conceptual components comparatively free of dependence upon other such components. Given such a component, one may further characterize it according to authorship, point in time, and other relevant assignable attributes. In general, the more decomposable a body of knowledge is into essentially self-subsisting components, the better suited it is to computerized specification and retrieval.

The history of economic thought is much less decomposable than are most bodies of knowledge. It is decomposable, of course, into somewhat arbitrary categories, but the components so identified cannot be subdivided beyond a point except at excessive cost. Two limits to decomposability are operative: (*a*) loss of meaning and relevance as a conceptualized component is abstracted out of its context and reduced in substantive content; (*b*) loss of that continuity in historical time which is of fundamental concern to the student of the history of economic thought.

Despite ideological and similar barriers, progress in areas of inorganic and organic science is continuous, though at rates that vary widely in time, accelerating as new paradigms—Kuhnian or otherwise—come into being, find confirmation, and are absorbed. Progress in some realms of science may thus trace a series of logistic curves, with a new curve taking off as its predecessor begins to flatten out. Economic science, on the contrary, has not been characterized by recurring Kuhnian paradigms and crucial experiments and, hence, has not been subject to a high degree of variation in rate of progress. Moreover, the absorption of new models (e.g. the Keynesian) tends to be slow, both because models must be sharpened and, having been sharpened, need to be tested empirically, usually with insufficiently satisfactory results, and then gradually absorbed into the corpus of economics even though remaining subject to further qualification and quantification. As a result of these differences between the progress of economic science and that of organic and inorganic sciences, the history of the former is much less punctuated by landmarks than is that of the latter. One may, indeed, say that hillocks mark the path of progress of economic science, whereas mountains may sometimes mark that of the natural sciences, the functioning of whose analytical apparatuses are quite free of the constraints of institutional matrices to which social sciences may be subject.

SPECIALIZATION

That economics consists of an analytical apparatus designed for the study of the functioning of economies developed slowly in the nineteenth century, is in part because of the structure of dominant economic theory before 1850. Only in the present century has the potential of this apparatus become fully appreciated, with the result that many branches of economics have come into existence and the emergence of new or newly recognized problem areas has tended to be succeeded by an adaptation of the economic apparatus to the analysis and search for ways out of these problem areas. An accompanying outcome has been a great increase in the empirical orientation of economic theory, a great increase in the quantification and the 'testing' of theoretical formulations, and much more focus on the interaction between theory formation and the development of problems that give rise to theory testing. Out of all of these developments has come a great increase in the number of cells required to accommodate today's self-subsisting components as compared with yesterday's. Continuation of this trend may present a greater problem in the future. While the large number of cells required to represent today's economics can easily be made to accommodate the simpler economics of the nineteenth century, the cell structure will need also to be flexible and expansible if it is to accommodate the still more complex economics of tomorrow. In sum, the requirements of organization and retrieval become more complicated as a science becomes more sophisticated, specialized, and complicated. This is evident in the multiplication of subfields in economics as in other sciences.

FUNCTIONS OF THE HISTORY OF ECONOMIC SCIENCE

The history of economics serves five sets of needs: (*a*) cultural, (*b*) those bearing upon the development of the organon of science as such, (*c*) those dealing with the contributions of particular economists, (*d*) those connected with the ideational evolution of the theories composing economics, together with their application, and (*e*) those illuminating the development of other sciences (e.g. sociology) concerned with phenomena of scarcity.

(*a*) Economic thought of sorts is part of the cultural heritage of diverse societies, e.g. the Chinese, the Indian, the Japanese, the Western, or one of its subdivisions. It is, therefore, a subject of concern to the cultural historian and the humanist, whose emphasis is only secondarily upon economics as an analytical apparatus. Accordingly, he will prefer a subdivision of economic thought suitable to his concerns, among which probably fall concerns lying within the area of the sociology of knowledge such as interaction between economics and comparable subdivisions of a society's culture and knowledge, or interaction between economic views and societal or national policies (e.g. emphasis upon autarkistic rather than upon cosmopolitan objectives). Schemes for the organization and retrieval of economic ideas within a cultural and humanistic context, therefore, need to be prepared by scholars with humanistic and cultural concerns in view.

It is to be noted that consideration of economic ideas under a humanistic rubric tends to play down the role of economics as an analytical apparatus, especially in respect to the past, since this apparatus did not require really definite, though changing, form until the nineteenth century. With the development and application of this apparatus, however, precise determination of its humanistic impact may become more elusive, for the instrumental orientation of the apparatus becomes dominant and the object to which it is applied becomes secondary, at least temporarily. Illustrative has been the application of this apparatus to the study of slavery in the United States, with the result that the functioning of the slave system has been largely reinterpreted, though not yet with widespread effect. In the end, however, if the new interpretation becomes ascendant, the improvement in the analytical apparatus may be seen as an important 'causal' element. In general, as the economic analytical apparatus is sharpened and focused upon the functioning of institutions in the past, historical reinterpretations will result, though acceptance of new interpretations will become widespread only after a temporal lag during which the significance of the new views is finally understood.

(*b*) The development of the ideational structure of economics may contribute to our understanding of the development of ideational structure in general, particularly if the evolution of the ideational structure of economics is contrasted with those of (say) physics, chemistry, biology, and sociology.

(*c*) Even though stress is put upon organization and retrieval from a theory-formation point of view, interest will always remain in a personal approach, especially today when the multiplication of economists is greatly reducing the significance and visibility of any one, though not yet to the complete removal of interest in the contributions of individuals *qua* individuals, an interest of importance to those who make a sociology-of-knowledge approach to the study of economic science.

A personal approach may best be viewed as a by-product of the theory-formation appoach, since completion of the latter entails identification of the distinguishable contributions and areas of interests of specific individuals.

(*d*) It is the development of economics as a science, together with its subdivision into branches and theoretical categories, that is of major interest to students of the history of economic thought. Here, development includes the formation and testing of theories and their assimilation and integration into the corpus of economics as such.

(*e*) Inasmuch as economics focuses mainly upon man's response to scarcity phenomena, knowledge of economics has, or may have, contributed to the understanding of parallels or analogues to scarcity encountered outside of the boundaries of economic science as such.

III. COSTS

The costs here under consideration are those associated with the abstraction and isolation of that which is transformed into communicable data for the apparatus of retrieval. Abstraction is costly in that it entails selective elimination of content of that which is being subjected to abstraction. Cost, in the form of loss of information, tends to increase with the process of abstraction, since more and more information has to be eliminated. Up to a point, of course, that which is eliminated is probably redundant for most purposes. But the individual performing the abstraction moves out of the area of redundancy into an area of what may be called 'importance'. Importance is not, however, an absolute or impersonal attribute of information; its value depends, as does that of exchangeable goods and services, upon the particular concerns or demands of those utilizing or wishing to use abstracted information. Users differ in the value which they attach to the abstractable components of that which is subjected to abstraction, not only at a given time, but over time.

Abstracts of given bodies of information (e.g. articles) are not isomeaningful as between individuals performing abstractions or between a given individual's abstraction of a given body at time t_1 and again at time t_2. If we conceive of abstractions as subsets we may say that the area of overlap of intersecting subsets done by a number of individuals abstracting a given body of information diminishes as abstraction is intensified and more information is discarded. Moreover, the area of overlap between sets containing the information required by diverse users of an abstract diminishes as its information content is diminished.

The significance of increasing cost in the form of shrinkage in the amount of information provided turns on the purposes of users. If the object of the user is merely to locate sources of information (i.e. in articles, books, etc.) with the object of consulting these sources, he needs much less information than if he counts upon the abstract to provide him with enough information to save his consulting the source directly. Even in the former case, the user may be misled concerning whether it is worth while to consult the original source, for an abstract is unlikely to suggest the whole content of a source.

Whereas loss of important information due to excessive abstraction probably is the principal possible cost of the way in which information is assembled or communicated, a second type of cost may be associated with abstraction. Abstraction may narrow an inquirer's range of interest and choice and, thus, tend to generate a psychological outlook unfavourable to imaginative inquiry and the search for implications and suggestions in the study abstracted—implications sometimes unapparent even to the authors of the study. Such narrowing is likely if the organization and retrieval of information, together with its use, are problem-oriented. There often is much more in studies than what immediately meets the eye, and its loss through a user's reliance on abstracts may slow the development of the lines of inquiry to which the study in question relates.

IV. PRACTICAL ALTERNATIVES

The principal sources of information relating to the history of economic thought are periodicals, books, encyclopedias and similar repositories of this information, along with many other kinds not relevant to the development of economic thought and analysis. There is, however, no growing collection of material analogous to the Cross Cultural Survey of geographical, social, and cultural information, 'extracted in full from the sources and classified by subject, on some 150 human societies, historical and contemporary as well as primitive'. This Survey was initiated in 1937 by the Institute of Human Relations at Yale University (New Haven, Conn., USA) and was designed 'to secure practically all the existing information on particular topics in any of the societies covered in an insignificant fraction of the time required for comparable library research'.[2] What is relevant here is that the information thus gathered, though accurate in itself, was found wanting by some scholars utilizing it, on the ground that making full use of this information required knowledge of the social context to which it related.

What constitutes information relevant to the history of economic thought is of two sorts. In one category fall the articles—which appear mainly in general-purpose economic journals—and books which deal in full, or only in part, with the growth of economics; within this category may be grouped encyclopedias, etc., and specialized journals (e.g. the French demographic periodical, *Population*, which contains many pieces and notes on authors who dealt with economic aspects of demography in the past). In a second category fall many of the articles and book-chapters which constitute the steady and growing stream of economic literature in most countries. The articles and book-chapters here referred to are of two types. *First*, many an author, when putting forward a more or less new theory, incorporates in his presentation a review of those developments in economic analysis which anticipated or paved the way for the formulation of his new theory; by so doing he facilitates the integration of his new theory into the corpus of received economics. *Second*, many an article or book-chapter published today may, in time, be considered important enough in its impact to warrant its inclusion in general or specialized studies of the history of economics. Potential candidates are papers which catalyse new lines of inquiry or include new theories or important modifications of already existing theories. As noted earlier, the content of these articles invariably falls short of being paradigmatic in the sense popularized by Thomas Kuhn or of supplying the results of *crucial* experiments. Progress in economic analysis is incremental, as a rule; even a work such as Keynes' *General Theory* may be described as a chapter in the 'natural history' of his major theme—of a natural history that made his theme, when it appeared, more acceptable and that thus accounted in part for acceleration in the development of this theme in the 1930s and thereafter.

What may be called the bank of knowledge, or information regarding

[2] On these files and their use, see George P. Murdoch, *Social Structure* (New York: Macmillan Co., 1949); preface.

the history of economic thought, is not one bank but two. Within the one bank fall the direct contributions made in the past, or being made today, to the stream of the history of economic thought, together with those papers which, because of their eventual impact, became a part of the stream of change or development in economic analysis. Within the other bank fall potential candidates for inclusion in the stream of the history of economic thought. The potential of articles and books to command entry is not, of course, always apparent. Whether they are admitted into the second bank depends appreciably upon the less than infallible judgment of authors who deal with economic analysis historically—a judgment difficult to make both because the significance of a contribution may be recognized only slowly and because what should have been so recognized escaped recognition when it appeared and, hence, did not affect the course of economic analysis ('the time was not ripe', it is sometimes said). It is possible, given this second bank, that those with an interest in the history of economic analysis will become more alert to studies that are potential candidates for inclusion despite the multiplication of articles, books, and so-called 'working papers' put into limited circulation though still in process of completion.

Any reasonably good method of organizing economic knowledge for purposes of easy retrieval becomes quite workable; one needs only some experience with the system of categories employed to know approximately in what category a particular topic is located. Economic journals have experimented, in the past, with categorizing very short abstracts of articles published in other journals and these have provided good checks on what was being written. In the early 1930s a comparable service was supplied to social scientists by *Social Science Abstracts*. Selective bibliographies such as those brought out under United Nations auspices afford an overview of what is being published in the areas covered.

Perhaps the most useful set of categories for organizing economic articles and books and facilitating their retrieval is that utilized by the American Economic Association in its *Index of Economic Articles* and its *Journal of Economic Literature* which succeeded its earlier journal of abstracts. One can form a fairly accurate impression of the content of articles from the way in which they have been entitled and distributed among the 23 categories, together with the sub-categories into which each of the 23 is divided. Moreover, this index is applicable to books and collective volumes as well. Unfortunately, this index includes only materials in journals in English and a few that allow considerable space to articles in English. Were similar indexes prepared of journals in other languages (e.g. French, German, Italian, Dutch, Russian, Japanese, etc.) it would be quite easy to construct a universal index running from the latter part of the nineteenth century to the present. One might then code the journals, the articles according to the article classification system utilized, year of publication, name of author, and other attributes, and, ultimately, computerize these coded materials accordingly. A similar system might also be devised for books as well. We should then have a fairly complete bank of titles of what economists have published since the 1870s, if not earlier. Of course, papers published before 1870, or in general-purpose quarterlies (e.g. *Edinburgh Review*), would not be included under this arrangement, but a separate index could be made of them.

Unfortunately, writings on the history of economic thought, as such, have not been adequately subdivided. For example, in the American Economic Association Index, articles on the history of economic thought and biography are assembled under eight sub-heads: general, ancient and medieval, pre-classical, classical, socialist, historical, institutionalist, and other. From the consultation of such a listing one cannot infer what the article is about specifically unless the title itself is quite indicative. What is required, therefore, is the addition of a number of attributes suited to specify, with sufficient approximation, whether the article is likely to contain what a potential user is looking for. Similar specification is required for books in the field. It is possible, however, to make use of the other 22 categories, together with their subcategories, to subdivide each of the eight subcategories into which the history-of-thought field is currently organized. While this arrangement would include many empty cells, it could accommodate the need for particularity in specification and fit in nicely with the system utilized in handling current economic literature.

The approach outlined in the preceding paragraph does not greatly facilitate easy identification of articles lying outside of the field of the history of economic thought, as such, but yet containing important contributions bearing upon economic thought. An additional attribute might be utilized, however, to identify such articles. A classification of articles and books along these lines would help the historian of economic thought quickly to identify articles likely to deal with economic topics of particular concern to him.

Two detailed indexes such as we have described would make it easy for the scholar to locate articles pertaining to his research interests, but only a quite subdivided or many-celled arrangement can meet most of his needs. A few-celled arrangement resting upon general abstraction could not meet the specific needs of researchers in the history of economic thought; an index, as such, can do little more than facilitate location of sources expeditiously. Abstraction of the content of these sources by other than the researcher or his equivalent cannot match, in value, the detailed examination of sources by the researcher himself, but it can narrow the researcher's area of inquiry. In general, that which a researcher in the history of thought seeks is seldom if ever very comparable to the request of a medical or physical researcher who is in need of a concrete solution to a quite specific problem.

V. CONCLUSION

The thrust of this report is to the effect that modern methods of retrieval can be marshalled to locate relevant sources quickly, given initial organization and preparation of these materials. A preliminary to the development of these modern methods is improvement in the organization and cataloguing of relevant materials in the world's leading libraries and the assembly of these materials in data banks.

Modern methods cannot, as a rule, free the scholar from the need to abstract or screen the materials in question unless quite complete abstracts are prepared and made readily transmissable from banks of abstracts to researchers in the history of economic thought. This latter condition can be met only in part, at best, because of financial limitations, difficulties attendant upon locating and organizing all relevant sources, and great variations in what historians of economic thought find relevant.

Summary of the Discussion

Professor Blaug introduced Professor Spengler's report as not a 'typical Spengler paper', because of its paucity of detailed footnote references. *Professor Blaug* went on to treat Professor Spengler's remarks under three main heads. (1) In dealing with doctrinal history, the scholar is more concerned with knowledge in a broad and organized sense than with specific bits of numerical or factual information. There are no funds for the retrieval of 'knowledge' in this sense, and it would hardly be worth while to appropriate them. (2) Further, there are definite limits to the use of information (in the usual information-theory sense) in doctrinal history. Knowledge seems less 'decomposable' than in other branches of Economics, leaving less scope for computerized or otherwise-mechanized retrieval. In Professor Spengler's view, non-decomposable research is more 'agreeable' to most researchers than is the mechanical variety. (3) Professor Spengler thought it more important and practical to improve the availability of standard sources. He would like to see indexes and bibliographies extended to cover a broader range of foreign-language materials. As a postscript, Professor Spengler took a dim view of computerized research and retrieval, not only in the History of Economic Thought but in Economics quite generally, and would like to see an 'anti-information-science' counter-revolution to reduce the influence of such mechanical methods.

The initial interpellation from the floor was *Professor Kindleberger*'s. He insisted that more information, regardless of its type, was needed and available for doctrinal-historical research. For example, the archivists of the old League of Nations at Geneva had collected a substantial stock of League correspondence with the major economists of the inter-war period; this was only one example of similar collections which have not been explored systematically. *Professor M. Perlman* mentioned several other collections which are lying relatively fallow, in both Europe and America. His examples included the Goldsmiths' holdings in London, the collections in the Baker Library at the Harvard Business School, the Hollander papers at the University of Illinois, and the Einaudi collection at Turin. (*Professor Kindleberger* expressed doubt as to the value of the last-named item.)

As for the value of computerized retrieval, *Professor Perlman* was more optimistic than was Professor Spengler. He pointed out that Professor Spengler has a tremendous memory which few other scholars can match, and suggested that this may have biased his judgment. *Professor Chamley* agreed, and recalled that he had himself used computerized retrieval to good advantage as early as 1948 in locating material on Hume from the files of the *London Advertiser* in the Library of Congress (Washington).

Professor Bronfenbrenner ascribed his Duke University colleagues' (Professor Spengler's) bias (which he himself shared) against computerized-retrieval less to the uselessness of the method than to the subjective desire to reserve at least one branch of economic research for intelligent human beings, as distinguished from the 'desiccated robots' and 'disappointed mathematicians' currently being processed out by most departments of Economics.

Mr Kilgour, however, insisted that computer techniques are as applicable to doctrinal-historical research as to other types of historical work, and insisted that historians were using them to great advantage. One key technique, Mr Kilgour mentioned, was the putting of indexes in machine-readable form; one example that he recalled was the index to the seven-volume collection of Tukey's statistical papers. He added that author and subject indexes could be processed separately. *Dr Bartenbach* added that foreign-language economic bibliographies exist in Germany, Holland, France, and, likewise, New York. *Professor Blaug* did not consider any of these as useful as the *JEL* index in English, and *Professor M. Perlman* characterized them as particularly weak in doctrinal history.

Professor Wolfe reminded the conference of the small market for information-retrieval materials in doctrinal history. It was particularly unlikely, *Professor Wolfe* thought, that anything could be done on an un-subsidized basis. His own suggestion was that more materials should be made available on microfilm, where a good-sized book could be produced at low cost. *Professor Wolfe* wondered, however, whether microfilmed books would be at all saleable, and whether they would be noticed by reviewers. *Mr Evans* replied that, while libraries buy microfilms, users have not yet shown much willingness to read them. *Mrs Schwartz* suggested that users might learn to use microfilm materials after more time had elapsed. Both *Professor and Mrs Perlman*, and likewise *Miss Deane*, added that economists tended to refuse to review microfilmed materials for journals.

Mr Evans called the conference's attention to the SUNY Press, which publishes *exclusively* in microfilm. He also asserted (in response to a question from Professor Kindleberger) that microfilm publication counted as publication in connection with personnel decisions within the SUNY system. (Second-class publication, suggested *Professor Kindleberger*.) *Professor Wolfe* said that a 300-page book, which might have to be priced as high as $40 to pay for itself because of limited demand, could be produced for $0.50 by microfilm technique, once the typescript had been prepared. *Professor Kindleberger* said that, at MIT, practice was to prepare microfiche plus print-out materials, so that print-outs were read. In MIT terminology, manuscripts were often described as 'camera-ready'.

Professor Biehl mentioned what he called the 'intermediate technology' of computer-typesetting, such as was in use at IBM. *Professor M. Perlman* replied that, while this was common, it was not cheap. When publication costs are broken down by processes, composition is not the basic reason why publication costs are so high. (*Mr Evans* added that if such methods increased in popularity, authors and libraries would soon have to face problems of microfilm and microfiche pirating.)

Since Professor Spengler was unable to attend the conference, *Professor Blaug* attempted to respond to these comments in the role of Professor Spengler rather than by expressing his own views. He then expressed the hope that the old-fashioned, non-computer types of information retrieval might be satisfactory for an indefinite period in the history of economic thought. At any rate, such methods should be exhausted first. For example, translations should be made more available. *Professor Blaug* mentioned Walras' writings on applied economics, which may have taken up more of Walras' time and energy than did the more abstract general-equilibrium theorizing for which he is almost exclusively remembered. As for publication of the results, *Professor Blaug* (in the role of Professor Spengler) reminded the conference that books were often published as loss leaders by houses interested in up-grading the reputability of their lists. Libraries need not specialize in doctrinal history, *Professor Blaug* continued, but every economic library should have a good collection of perhaps 500 books plus 1000 secondary sources and specialized journals. And of course, there would remain many more specialized collections centred about particular individuals or schools of thought.

Comment by the author on the Discussion*

I am not opposed to computerization in the organization and retrieval of knowledge, but to use of the tool(s) in conformity with the objects of research and in such ways that selection of these objects becomes determined largely by the tools. Accordingly, as Professor Kindleberger and others suggest, banking the physical universe of sources and thus facilitating their retrieval is of very great importance. Unfortunately, some of the discussants failed to distinguish sharply between banking *sources* and banking *supposedly representative segments* of sources, or, what seems more useful, appropriately prepared terse abstracts of books and articles. I am grateful to Professor Blaug for his statement of my position and to Professor Bronfenbrenner for his summary and for his calling attention to the increase in danger lest the environment of research be tilted by diverse apparatus against scholars gifted with imagination, creativity, perception, and insight and in favour of robots and choosers of the path of the short-run and least resistance.

* This comment was written after the conference by Professor Spengler, who was prevented from attending because of illness in the family.

Part Four

The Nature of Economics and Its Implications for the Organization of Economic Knowledge

25 Economics and Contiguous Disciplines

Ronald H. Coase
UNIVERSITY OF CHICAGO, LAW SCHOOL

Economists are working more in the other social sciences. To discover whether this trend is likely to continue, we need to know the reasons why it is happening. It has come about largely because of the use of such techniques as quantitative methods or cost-benefit analysis with which economists are familiar and, more recently, by economists using economic theory as a basis for studying political science, sociology, law and the like. To the extent that such work by economists depends on the possession of superior techniques or approaches, it is not likely to continue, since other social scientists should be able to master such techniques or approaches where they are valuable and will be more familiar with the subject matter. But economists also study other social systems because their working is so intermeshed with the economic system as to make it impossible to discuss usefully the economic system without simultaneously considering these other social systems. This is particularly true of parts of the legal system. This being so, we may expect the scope of economics to be permantly enlarged to include studies in the other social sciences.

I wish to start with two general observations. First, what I have to say is largely based on my knowledge of developments within the United States and Britain. But I have sufficient confidence in the international character of science to believe that what can be observed in these countries is paralleled by similar developments elsewhere. My second observation is that a paper which deals with what is happening within a series of disciplines and which ranges so widely within economics itself, must inevitably mean, at any rate in my case, that it deals with many subjects about which the writer's knowledge is extremely vague. What I have to say will often have the character of assertion rather than of a conclusion based on a careful study of the literature in the many fields covered by my subject. I believe that such a careful study would confirm what I assert. But it is equally true that it may refute my views. Papers presented at international conferences are not usually high-risk ventures, but this one is. However, I do not think what is called for at this stage is a paper guarded by qualifications and difficult to attack because it says so little except what is generally accepted.

What is the subject with which I am dealing? What I am concerned with is what determines the boundaries between disciplines, in particular with what determines the boundaries between economics and the other social sciences, sociology, political science, pyschology and the like (without excluding the possibility that there may be overlaps). What the boundaries are at any particular time can, of course, be discovered by examining the range of activities engaged in by members of any given professional association, by the subjects treated in the journals devoted to particular disciplines, by the courses given in University departments, by the topics covered in textbooks and by the books collected in libraries concerned with the various areas of knowledge. A forecast of the boundaries of a discipline is, thus, a forecast of what topics will be covered by professional associations, journals, libraries and the like. I have long considered the definition of economics which Boulding attributed to Viner, and has since often been repeated, 'Economics is what economists do',[1] as essentially sound but only if it were accompanied, which it never is, by a description of the activities in which economists actually engage.

If the question is asked, how do these boundaries between disciplines come to be what they are, the broad answer I give is that it is determined by competition. The process is essentially the same as that which determines the activities undertaken by firms or, to take another example, the extent of empires. Gibbon describes how Augustus came to accept the boundaries of the Roman Empire. Gibbon says that it was easy for Augustus to discover that

> Rome, in her present exalted situation, had much less to hope than to fear from the chance of arms; and that, in the prosecution of remote wars, the undertaking became every day more difficult, the event more doubtful, and the possession more precarious, and less beneficial.[2]

The same kind of calculation ultimately led, and this is Gibbon's grand theme, to an abandonment of much of what had been contained within the Roman Empire and, finally, to its division within quite another set of boundaries. It is much the same with disciplines. The practitioners in a given discipline extend or narrow the range of the questions that they attempt to answer according to whether they find it profitable to do so, and this is determined, in part by the success or failure of the practitioners in other disciplines in answering the same questions. Since different people are satisfied with different answers, victory is not necessarily clear-cut, and different answers and different ways of tackling the same question may exist side by side, each satisfying its own market. One group of practitioners need not drive another group from the field,

[1] Kenneth E. Boulding, *Economic Analysis* (New York: Harper, 1955), p. 3.
[2] Edward Gibbon, *The Decline and Fall of the Roman Empire*, chap. 1.

but may merely, to use an economist's terminology, increase their market share. Of course, when the number of those who are satisfied with the answers given by any group of practitioners becomes so small and/or the questions for which this is true are few or trivial, the field may be abandoned altogether except by those whose competence is so low elsewhere that they cannot compete in a wider, more active and more profitable market.

If we look at the work that economists are doing at the present time, there can be little doubt that economics is expanding its boundaries or, at any rate, that economists are moving more and more into other disciplines. They have been conspicuously active in political science, where they have developed an economic theory of politics and have done a great deal of empirical work analysing voting behaviour.[3] Economists have also moved into sociology and we now have an economic theory of marriage.[4] Nor should we be surprised that there is also an economic theory of suicide.[5] Other subjects on which economists have worked are linguistics,[6] education,[7] and national defence.[8] I am sure that it is only my lack of familiarity with what is going on in the other social sciences which restricts my list. One striking example, with which I am familiar, is the use of economics in the study of law.[9] The general movement is clear. Economists are extending the range of their studies to include all of the social sciences, which I take to be what we mean when we speak of economics' contiguous disciplines.

What is the reason why this is happening? One completely satisfying explanation (in more than one sense) would be that economists have by now solved all of the major problems posed by the economic system,

[3] Among the works on the economic theory of politics are: Duncan Black, *The Theory of Committees and Elections* (Cambridge: Cambridge U. Press, 1958); Anthony Downs, *An Economic Theory of Democracy* (New York: Harper, 1957); James Buchanan and Gordon Tullock, *The Calculus of Consent* (Ann Arbor, Mich.: U. of Michigan Press 1962); Mancur Olson, *The Logic of Collective Action* (Cambridge, Mass.: Harvard U. Press, 1965); W. A. Niskanen, *Bureaucracy and Representative Government* (Chicago: Aldine, Atherton, 1971). For a study of voting behaviour, see George J. Stigler, 'General Economic Conditions and National Elections', *American Economic Review* (May 1973).

[4] Gary S. Becker, 'A Theory of Marriage: Part I', *Journal of Political Economy* (July-August 1973) and '*A Theory of Marriage*: Part II', *Journal of Political Economy* (March-April 1974).

[5] Daniel S. Hamermesh and Neal M. Soos, 'An Economic Theory of Suicide', *Journal of Political Economy* (January-February 1974).

[6] J. Marschak, 'Economics of Language', *Behavioral Science* (April 1965).

[7] John Vaizey, *The Economics of Education* (New York: Free Press of Glencoe, 1962); Theodore W. Schultz, *The Economic Value of Education* (New York: Columbia U. Press, 1963); Theodore W. Schultz, *Investment in Human Capital* (New York: Free Press of Glencoe, 1970).

[8] Charles J. Hitch and Roland N. McKean, *The Economics of Defence in the Nuclear Age* (Cambridge, Mass.: Harvard U. Press, 1960).

[9] See Richard A. Posner, *Economic Analysis of the Law* (Boston: Little, Brown and Co., 1972).

and, therefore, rather than become unemployed or be forced to deal with the trivial problems which remain to be solved, have decided to employ their obviously considerable talents in achieving a similar success in the other social sciences. However, it is not possible to examine any area of economics with which I have familiarity without finding major puzzles for which we have no agreed solutions or, indeed, questions to which we have no answers at all. The reason for this movement of economists into neighbouring fields is certainly not that we have solved the problems of the economic system; it would perhaps be more plausible to argue that economists are looking for fields in which they can have some success.

Another explanation for this interest in neighbouring fields might be that modern economists have had a more broadly based education than those who preceded them and that, in consequence, their interests are wider, with the result that they are naturally dissatisfied with being restricted to so narrow a range of problems as that presented by the economic system. Such an explanation seems to me largely without merit. If we think of Adam Smith or John Stuart Mill or Alfred Marshall, the range of questions with which they deal is greater than is commonly found in a modern work on economics. This impression is reinforced if we have regard to the articles which appear in most of the economics journals, which, to an increasingly great extent, tend to deal with highly formal technical questions of economic analysis, usually treated mathematically. The general impression one derives, particularly from the journals, is of a subject narrowing, rather than extending, the range of its interest. This seems inconsistent with the concurrent movement of economists into the other social sciences, but I believe that there is a connection between these two apparently contradictory developments.

If we are to attempt to forecast what the scope of economists' work is likely to be in the future—which is surely what is needed if we are to be helpful to the librarians and others for whose benefit this conference was planned—we have to understand the reason why economists have been moving into the other social sciences and what the situation is likely to be in future. To do this, we have to consider what it is that binds together a group of scholars so that they form a separate profession and enables us to say that someone is an economist, someone else a sociologist, another a political scientist and so on. It seems to me that what binds such a group together is one or more of the following: common techniques of analysis, a common theory or approach to the subject or a common subject matter. I need not conceal from you at this stage my belief that in the long run it is the subject matter, the kind of question which the practitioners are trying to answer, which tends to be the dominant factor producing the cohesive force that makes a group of scholars a recognizable profession with its own University departments, journals and libraries. I say this, in part, because the techniques of analysis and the theory or approach used are themselves, to a considerable extent, determined by what it is that the group of scholars is studying, although scholars in a particular discipline may use different techniques or approaches in answering the same questions. However, in the short run, the ability of a particular group in handling certain techniques of analysis, or an approach, may give them such advantages that they are able to move successfully into another field or even to dominate it. In making these distinctions, I do not wish to deny that techniques, approaches and subject matter will all exert some influence at any given time. Nor would I argue that it is inevitable that techniques and approach should exert their influence only in the short run. They could be dominant in the long run as well. But I believe that there are reasons for thinking that this will not usually be the case. If my description of the binding forces of a scholarly discipline is correct and if my assessment of their long and short run influences is also valid, then we will have to decide whether the current movement by economists into the other social sciences is the triumph of a technique or of an approach, or whether such an extension of their work illuminates, and is interrelated with, the solution of the central questions which economists attempt to answer that is, is necessitated by the nature of the subject matter which they study. To the extent that this movement is based on technique or approach, we can expect a gradual displacement of economists from their newly-won ground. To the extent that it is necessitated by their subject matter, we may expect the range of studies undertaken by economists to be permanently enlarged.

My first example of a technique, linear programming, is one which I am particularly unqualified to discuss, but, fortunately, extensive discussion is not called for.[10] It is, if I understand correctly, a mathematical method for discovering the proportions in which inputs should be combined in order to achieve a certain result at minimum cost. Such a technique has, potentially, applications in many fields. It is, however, difficult to believe that such a highly mathematical technique could not be as easily acquired or as well handled by suitably endowed scholars in other disciplines. Indeed, some of these might find such a technique easier to acquire or handle than would most economists. To the extent that economists have moved into other fields using linear programming, I would expect the forces of competition to be such that they would be largely displaced, although individual economists might still do useful work using linear programming. In any case, it seems improbable that knowledge of a technique such as linear programming would become such an essential part of any discipline as to outweigh command of the theory or knowledge of the subject matter. One would not expect economists to dominate such fields as nutrition or oil refinery engineering even if (which seems improbable) economists as a class were particularly adept in linear programming.

[10] On this subject, see J. R. Hicks, 'Linear Theory', *The Economic Journal* (December 1960).

The employment of quantitative methods, now so commonly part of the equipment of the modern economist, has also enabled a number of economists to move into neighbouring disciplines. To the extent that economists find it easier to acquire these techniques and/or can handle them with greater dexterity than can their colleagues in the other social sciences (in part because they use them so frequently), it is possible that this may offset their unfamiliarity with the subject matter of these other disciplines and the analytical framework within which these other social scientists work. But it seems a rather fragile basis for predicting a long-run movement by economists into the other social sciences.

My next example, cost-benefit analysis, is more difficult to discuss.[11] My guess would be that the great bulk of the incursions made by economists into contiguous and not-so-contiguous disciplines in recent years have been in connection with the undertaking of cost-benefit studies. Cost-benefit analysis seems to me best described as a technique. But since it is essentially applied price theory, having as its aim the giving of a monetary value to what is gained and what is lost by following a particular course of action, it is certainly an activity in which economists have some obvious advantages. However, since these studies are usually carried out with a view to facilitating decision-making, particularly by public bodies, with the problem to be investigated selected by such bodies, rather than with a view to understanding the system of which these public bodies are a part, and since economists working in unfamiliar fields will tend to rely on the work of others for their data, economists engaged in these studies will tend to play a useful but subordinate role, except to the extent that the particular decisions being investigated are closely related to their main concerns.

More important and more persuasive is the view, which I associate with the name of Gary Becker, that economic theory or the economic approach can form the means by which economists can work in, if not take over, the other social sciences.[12] But before examining this point of view, I will consider what I believe to be the normal binding force of a scholarly profession, its subject matter.

What do economists study? What do they do? They study the economic system. Marshall, in the first edition of the *Principles of Economics* defined economics thus: 'Political Economy, or Economics, is a study of man's actions in the ordinary business of life; it inquires how he gets his income and how he uses it.'[13] A modern economist, Stigler,

[11] On cost-benefit analysis, see A. R. Prest and R. Turvey, 'Cost-Benefit Analysis: A Survey', *The Economic Journal* (December 1965); E. J. Mishan, *Cost-Benefit Analysis* (London: Allen and Unwin; New York: Praeger, 1971); G. H. Peters, *Cost-Benefit Analysis and Public Expenditures* (London: Institute of Economic Affairs, 1966).

[12] See Gary S. Becker, 'The Economic Approach to Human Behaviour', in *Essays in the Economic Approach to Human Behavior* (forthcoming).

[13] Alfred Marshall, *Principles of Economics*, 9th variorum edition (London and New York: Macmillan, for The Royal Economic Society, 1961), II, p. 131.

has phrased it differently: 'Economics is the study of the operation of economic organizations, and economic organizations are social (and rarely individual) arrangements to deal with the production and distribution of economic goods and services.'[14] Both of these definitions of economics emphasize that economists study certain kinds of activity. And this accords well with the actual topics dealt with in a book on economics. What economists study is the working of the social institutions which bind together the economic system: firms, markets for goods and services, labour markets, capital markets, the banking system, international trade and so on. It is the common interest in these social institutions which distinguishes the economics profession.

A very different kind of definition is that of Robbins: 'Economics if the science which studies human behaviour as a relationship between ends and scarce means which have alternative uses.'[15] Such a definition makes economics a study of human choice. It is clearly too wide if regarded as a description of what economists do. Economists do not study all human choices, or, at any rate, they have not done so as yet. However, the view that economics is a study of all human choice, although it does not tell us the nature of the economic theory or approach which is to be employed in all of the social sciences, certainly calls for the development of such a theory.

I said earlier that there are, at present, two tendencies in operation in economics which seem to be inconsistent but which, in fact, are not. The first consists of an enlargement of the scope of economists' interests so far as subject matter is concerned. The second is a narrowing of professional interest to more formal, technical, commonly mathematical, analysis. This more formal analysis tends to have a greater generality. It may say less, or leave much unsaid, about the economic system, but, because of its generality, the analysis becomes applicable to all social systems. It is this generality of their analytical systems which, I believe, has facilitated the movement of economists into the other social sciences, where they will presumably repeat the successes (and the failures) which they have had within economics itself.

The nature of this general approach has been described by Posner in his *Economic Analysis of the Law*:

> Economics is the science of human choice in a world in which resources are limited in relation to human wants. It explores and tests the implications of the assumption that man is a rational maximizer of his ends in life, his satisfactions—what we shall call his 'self-interest'.[16]

By defining economics as the 'science of human choice', economics

[14] George J. Stigler, *The Theory of Price* (New York: Macmillan, 1952). p. 1.

[15] L. C. Robbins, *The Nature and Significance of Economic Science* (London: Macmillan and Co., 1932), p. 15.

[16] Richard A. Posner, *op. cit.*, p. 1.

becomes the study of all purposeful human behaviour and its scope is, therefore, coterminous with all of the social sciences. It is one thing to make such a claim, it is quite another to translate it into reality. At a time when the King of England claimed to be also King of France, he was not always welcome in Paris. The claim that economics is the science of human choice will not be enough to cause sociologists, political scientists and lawyers to abandon their field or, painfully, to become economists. The dominance of the other social sciences by economists, if it happens, will not come about simply by redefining economics, but because of something which economists possess and which enables them to handle sociological, political, legal and similar problems better than the practitioners in these other social sciences. I take it to be the view of Becker and Posner that the decisive advantage which economists possess in handling social problems is their theory of, or approach to, human behaviour, the treatment of man as a rational, utility-maximizer.

Since the people who operate in the economic system are the same people who are found in the legal or political system, it is to be expected that their behaviour will be, in a broad sense, similar. But it by no means follows that an approach developed to explain behaviour in the economic system will be equally successful in the other social sciences. In these different fields, the purposes which men seek to achieve will not be the same, the degree of consistency in behaviour need not be the same and, in particular, the institutional framework within which the choices are made are quite different. It seems to me probable that an ability to discern and understand these purposes and the character of the institutional framework (how, for example, the political and legal systems actually operate) will require specialized knowledge not likely to be acquired by those who work in some other discipline. Furthermore, a theory appropriate for the analysis of these other social systems will presumably need to embody features which deal with the important specific interrelationships of that system.

I am strengthened in this view by a consideration of the part played by utility theory in economic analysis. Up to the present it has been largely sterile. To say that people maximize utility tells us nothing about the purposes for which they engage in economic activity and leaves us without any insight into why people do what they do. As Stigler has told us, the chief implication of utility theory is that, 'if consumers do not buy less of a commodity when their incomes rise, they will surely buy less when the price of the commodity rises'.[17] But that consumers demand more at a lower price is known to everyone, whether an economist or not, who is at all familiar with the operation of a market. Utility theory seems more likely to handicap than to aid economists in their work in contiguous dis-

[17] George J. Stigler, 'The Development of Utility Theory', in *Essays in the History of Economics* (Chicago: U. of Chicago Press, 1965), p. 155.

ciplines. Recently, the work of Lancaster on 'characteristics analysis'[18] and of Becker on 'commodities',[19] which relate the satisfactions derived from goods and services to certain, specified, more fundamental needs, shows promise of being more fruitful. But it seems improbable that the list of the important 'commodities,' to use Becker's term, will be the same in the various social sciences or that they will be uncovered, except by specialists in those disciplines.

Economics, it must be admitted, does appear to be more developed than the other social sciences. But the great advantage which economics has possessed is that economists are able to use the 'measuring rod of money'. This has given a precision to the analysis, and since what is measured by money are important determinants of human behaviour in the economic system, the analysis has considerable explanatory power. Furthermore, the data (on prices and incomes) is generally available, so that hypotheses can be examined and checked. Marshall said that

> the steadiest motive to ordinary business work is the desire for the pay which is the material reward of work. The pay may be on its way to be spent selfishly or unselfishly, for noble or base ends . . .. But the motive is supplied by a definite amount of money: and it is this definite and exact money measurement of the steadiest motives in business life, which has enabled economics to outrun every other branch of the study of man.[20]

If it is true that the more developed state of economics, as compared to the other social sciences, has been due to the happy chance (for economics) that the important factors determining economic behaviour can be measured in money, it suggests that the problems faced by practitioners in these other fields are not likely to be dissipated simply by an infusion of economists, since in moving into these fields, they will commonly have to leave their strength behind them. The analysis developed in economics is not likely to be successfully applied in other subjects without major modifications.

If I am right about the relative unimportance of technique as a basis for the choice of professional groupings, if subject matter is really the dominant factor, with the theory or approach in large part determined by the subject matter, what is the outlook for the work of economists in the other social sciences? I would not expect them to continue indefinitely their triumphal advance and it may be that they will be forced to withdraw from some of the fields which they are now so busily cultivating. But such a forecast depends on the practitioners in the other disciplines making a competitive response. The success of economists in

[18] Kelvin Lancaster, 'A New Approach to Consumer Theory', *Journal of Political Economy* (April 1966); *Consumer Demand* (New York: Columbia U. Press, 1971).

[19] Gary S. Becker and Robert T. Michael, 'On the New Theory of Consumer Behaviour', *The Swedish Journal of Economics* Vol. 75 (1973).

[20] Alfred Marshall, *op. cit., I, p. 14*.

moving into the other social sciences is a sign that they possess certain advantages in handling the problems of those disciplines. One is, I believe, that they study the economic system as a unified interdependent system and, therefore, are more likely to uncover the basic interrelationships within a social system than is someone less accustomed to looking at the working of a system as a whole. Another is that a study of economics makes it difficult to ignore factors which are clearly important and which play a part in all social systems. Such a factor would be that, to a large extent, people choose their occupations on the basis of money incomes. Another would be that a higher price lowers the demand. Such factors may appear in various guises, but an economist is likely to see through them. Punishment, for example, can be regarded as the price of crime. An economist will not debate whether increased punishment will reduce crime; he will merely try to answer the question, by how much? The economist's analysis may fail to touch some of the problems found in the other social systems, but often the analysis can be brought to bear. And the economist will take full advantage of those opportunities which occur when the 'measuring rod of money' can be used.

But if the main advantage which an economist brings to the other social sciences is simply a way of looking at the world, it is hard to believe, once the value of such economic wisdom is recognized, that it will not be acquired by some practitioners in these other fields. This is already happening in law and political science. Once some of these practitioners have acquired the simple, but valuable, truths which economics has to offer, and this is the natural competitive response, economists who try to work in the other social sciences will have lost their main advantage and will face competitors who know more about the subject matter than they do. In such a situation, only the exceptionally endowed economist is likely to be able to make a significant contribution to our knowledge of the other social sciences.

Economists may, however, study other social systems, such as the legal and political ones, not with the aim of contributing to law or political science, but because it is necessary if they are to understand the working of the economic system itself. It has come to be realized by many economists in recent times that parts of these other social systems are so intermeshed with the economic system as to be as much a part of that system as they are of a sociological, political or legal system. Thus, it is hardly possible to discuss the functioning of a market without considering the nature of the property right system, which determines what can be bought and sold and which, by influencing the cost of carrying out various kinds of market transaction, determines what is, in fact, bought and sold, and by whom.[21] Similarly, the family or household and the

[21] On property rights, see Erik Furubotn and Svetozar Pejovich, 'Property Rights and Economic Theory: A Survey of Recent Literature', *Journal of Economic Literature* (December 1972).

educational system are of concern to the sociologist, but their operations affect the supply of labour to different occupations and the patterns of consumption and production and are, therefore, also of concern to the economist. In the same way, the administration of the regulatory agencies and antitrust policy, while part of the legal system and, as such, studied by lawyers, also provides the framework within which firms and individuals decide on their actions in the economic sphere.

The need to take into account the influence of other social systems, above all the legal system, in analysing the working of the economic system, is now widely accepted by economists. It has resulted in numerous studies of the effect of the legal system on the performance of the economic system.[22] Such work, because of its focus on the economic system, is likely, in general, to be best done by economists. Unlike the movement by economists into the other social sciences which has as its aim, the improvement of these other social sciences, a movement which, for reasons I have already given, seems to me likely to be temporary, the study by economists of the effects of the other social systems on the economic system will, I believe, become a permanent part of the work of economists. It cannot be done effectively by social scientists unfamiliar with the economic system. Such work may be carried out in collaboration with other social scientists, but it is unlikely to be well done without economists. For this reason, I think we may expect the scope of economics to be permanently enlarged to include studies in other social sciences. But the purpose will be to enable us to understand better the working of the economic system.

[22] It is necessary here only to refer to the kind of articles which appear in the *Journal of Law and Economics.*

Summary of the Discussion

Professor Johnson introduced Professor Coase's report as ' a theorist's paper applying a general principle', namely competition, to the determination of the boundaries of economics. As the paper pointed out, the discussion had been motivated by the recent spread of economic analysis in the hands of professional economists to consider aspects of other social studies, particularly Politics, Law, and Sociology, and, likewise, by the resentment of this intrusion in some quarters as 'intellectual imperialism'.

This extension of the boundaries of Economics is hardly prompted by any remarkable successes achieved by economists in their own fields, nor yet for securing broader cultural bases. Professor Coase proposed, rather, that the boundaries of a discipline were set by its technique, its approach, and its subject matter. In cases of inter-disciplinary competition and disputed boundaries, Professor Coase suggested, technique tended to dominate in the short run and subject matter in the longer term. Accordingly, excursions by economists applying such techniques as linear-programming and cost-benefit analysis to problems of Law, Politics, and Sociology will not permanently extend the boundaries of Economics. Once political scientists, lawyers, and sociologists have mastered the applicable aspects of these techniques, their superior knowledge of their own subject matters will repel incursions. (In the same way, applied mathematicians have not taken over Economics by reason of the application of programming techniques, despite some anticipations to the contrary in the 1950s, as witness the MIT–Harvard study by Dorfman, Samuelson, and Solow.)

But what *is* the subject-matter of Economics? *Professor Johnson* preferred the Marshallian definition involving 'the ordinary business of life' to the later Robbins one involving 'the allocation of scarce means among competing uses'. The former is, indeed, a 'subject-matter' definition; the latter, a 'technique' definition without content. They do, however, explain the ability of economists to expand their frontiers.

As for 'the economic approach', neither Professor Coase nor *Professor Johnson* believed it had much to offer elsewhere in the long run. The notion of rational utility maximization, for example, has no content. It can be quantified where some 'measuring rod' applies, as does money in economic arguments, but hardly elsewhere. And the notion that a social system is, indeed, a system (rather than anarchy, chaos, or 'jungle law') does not seem to be gaining ground in other disciplines; it has difficulty holding its own within Economics, itself.

So subject-matter is the deciding factor; the incursions of economists into other disciplines will produce competitive responses; economists will not hold much new ground. Economists such as Professors Becker, Buchanan, Tullock, and their followers will continue working in other fields, but, primarily, to understand Economics better. This conclusion is not a mere rationalization for 'empire-building', in that nobody expects political scientists, lawyers, or sociologists to suffer displacement or technological unemployment. Rather, to understand economic policy, one should understand why and how governments act irrationally and alternate among 'sub-optimal' policies. Professor Johnson's only criticism of Professor Coase's paper was that it offered little by way of guidance for librarians and information specialists.

Professor Giersch maintained that the relations between Economics and other disciplines were less exclusively competitive than Professors Coase and Johnson seemed to maintain. He felt that complementary relations were of equal importance, and spoke of building bridges to Law, Geography, History, etc. He felt, in addition, that bridges with Technology had been neglected, but that the Kiel group was attempting to build them, in connection with the industrial development of Europe and the adjustment problems of the LDCs. In fact, he thought that there was little conflict, and also, that while Technology is dominated by Engineering and the natural sciences, Library Science can be included.

Mr Vaubel inquired further as to the relevance of the Coase paper to the 'library industry'. He agreed that the paper would be highly relevant for the specialized economic library, but saw no reason for such libraries. Rather, the 'fuzzy', and shifting nature of the boundaries between disciplines could be translated into a case for the *general* library. The efficiency of a library is largely a matter of economies of large scale. Specialization is important in purchasing and cataloguing, but there is no need to dispute about which discipline particular titles 'belong to'. Specialized libraries are second-best solutions; while separate fields exist in general libraries, the boundaries are arbitrary. Perhaps 'Economics' is what economic libraries collect and general libraries classify under this head.

Professor Morgan presented a different view. Economics consists, he said, of the analysis of a social system plus a less-systematic analysis of actual behaviour. To improve economists' results, they must enter disputed areas, but the division of labour remains important; the relation is not all-or-none. What *Professor Morgan* feels to be needed is a team approach in these disputed areas. This approach may be either multi- or inter-disciplinary in character. As to the classification of the results, librarians should use the nature of the problem rather than the dominant discipline as the basis of their decisions.

How university libraries, at least, function depends on how university teaching is organized, said *Professor Wolfe*. Sometimes one finds strict separation; sometimes jointness and co-operation. There is danger that 'interstitial' materials will not be purchased, and that interstitial areas will be neglected in research. Professor Morgan's solution is important for funded research on special problems (the regulation of cable TV is an example), but libraries can hardly anticipate the needs of such special research groups. *Professor Wolfe* has doubts about the arguments for general or universal libraries on cost-saving grounds, because of the high labour and administrative costs. Rather, since no library can specialize in everything, libraries should adjust to their institutions' research strengths, even to the extent of weeding out volumes which become surplus merely because these strengths change. And, in particular, libraries should not resist changes in the boundaries of specific disciplines, but should recognize that these boundaries will shift continuously.

Professor Giersch proposed a revision of the Viner definition of Economics, to read, 'Economics is what economists *believe they can* do'. Accordingly, the boundaries depend on the supply of economists rather than on the demand for their services. *Professor Giersch* regretted that the academic-tenure competition had forced the concentration of economists in 'safe' fields, such as on 'MIT Economics', 'Chicago Economics', etc., rather than in Economics as such. Had the boundary depended on the demand for economists—including the demand by librarians—the results might have been different.

Professor M. Perlman replied to Mr Vaubel and Professor Morgan. It seemed to him that Mr Vaubel was answering his own criticism in admitting that choices had to be made in libraries along fairly conventional disciplinary lines. As for Professor Morgan's comment, it seemed to *Professor Perlman* that every discipline involved elements of systems analysis. The question was, what sort of system, and the Marshallian definition of Economics seemed to *Professor Perlman* too broad for usefulness. It was unfortunate, he concluded, that boundaries are both so necessary and so difficult.

Normative research, said *Professor Kindleberger*, is where one finds conflicts between practitioners of 'rival' disciplines. Money and MNC are cases in point in his own field. The meeting of minds is very difficult, and is made more so by the prevalence of such value-loaded terms as 'exploitation'. Moreover, it seemed to *Professor Kindleberger* that the implicit model of most economists is Adam Smith, while that of most political scientists is Bismarck or, perhaps, De Gaulle.

Professor Blaug felt that the discussion had wandered into a blind alley. Professor Coase had, he thought, minimized the differences of *approach* between the disciplines, relative to those of technique and subject matter. *Professor Blaug* wondered why other disciplines had not adopted the economic approach long ago, and suspected that this approach did not apply well there. For example, economists were biased toward individualism as against group consensus, and toward maximizing rather than satisfying. When two or more social-science disciplines attack the same problems, it is interesting to see whether their approaches are the same or not. (*Professor Bronfenbrenner* suggested that inter-approach conflict might also be settled by competition. One approach might yield more useful or workable answers than another.)

Mr Evans again inserted the viewpoint of the librarian. It appeared to him that academic departments were self-centred in carrying on their teaching functions, particularly in adding new courses and requirements. As a result, total expansions were too high, and duplications resulted. The same problem affected libraries, which were unable to meet all demands at once. As has been said many times already but still needs repetition, a general library cannot be a cluster of specialized ones.

In his own summary, *Professor Coase* turned first to Professor Johnson's charge that he had not assisted in solving librarians' problems. Librarianship, however, was a subject others understood far better than he did. His main conclusion was that economists must interact with other social scientists. Though his paper had stressed competitive effects, complementary ones were obvious. Economists will, therefore, continue to expand their interests, but will not take over those of others. As against Professor Morgan, *Professor Coase* doubted that formal 'team research' was usually necessary or even helpful. As for Professor Kindleberger's point about 'normative issues', *Professor Coase* thought that these could be discussed and even resolved most easily within a single institution (which includes a library). On the basis of his own Law School experience, *Professor Coase* felt that separate Law Libraries should be retained, but that their services might be improved by inter-disciplinary staffing.

Once again, discussion continued 'after the bell'. *Professor Kindleberger* referred to the MIT situation, where Statistics is taught in 11 departments, Mathematics in 7 or 8. (Economics will soon experience the same difficulty, although it is resisting.) The problem is that nobody wants to be a 'service department', and that it is difficult to avoid 'master-servant' relationships in teams involving contiguous disciplines. *Professor Coase* replied that these views support a position of his own, namely, that crossing of departmental lines should involve some knowledge of 'the other fellow's' subject matter. (Joint appointments tend not to work out well. Individuals must either fish or cut bait, i.e. they must concentrate their attention in one department or the other.) *Professor Coase* then turned his attention to Professor Blaug's attempt to distinguish between 'approaches' and 'techniques' or 'methods'. *Professor Coase* was not sure whether such distinctions are valid. Differences of 'approach', he thought, might be results of differences in subject matter and technique. (*Professor Blaug* himself suggested that his problem might not be as significant in connection with the Economics–Law relationship as with certain of the other continguous disciplines.)

Mrs Schwartz pointed out that Economics is not infrequently taught in Law Schools, but never, so far as she knows, in Department of Sociology. *Professor Morgan* explained the difference on the ground that sociologists saw no way in which they could use economic analysis in their field, despite the occasional intrusions of economists.

26 Methodologies of Economics

Harry G. Johnson
UNIVERSITY OF CHICAGO; UNIVERSITY OF GENEVA

The central question is whether there will be a reaction from the dominance of mathematics and econometrics. Affluence has meant problems of space and cost for libraries, while demands for more amenities, permissiveness about theft and vandalism, as well as graduate work and empirical research impose new demands. Reaction towards conventional library scholarship may follow from 'radicalism', diminishing returns from mathematical and quantitative techniques, declining enrolments and junior staff ratios, and the need for new ideas. One likely line is ethics and welfare economics. Rising publishing costs may reduce library storage problems.

The last two sections of this paper were added in the light of the discussion, in particular on the basis of comments by Phyllis Deane, John Fetterman and James Morgan.

I. INTRODUCTION

My assigned purpose in the paper is to discuss the evolving characteristics of economics teaching and research, with special reference to the implications for the storage and retrieval of economic knowledge in libraries. The word 'methodology' is, of course, an unlovely American neologism, inferior to the older concept of 'method', and I shall use it in the broader sense of methods of economics as a university-based teaching and research discipline. I shall also define my terms broadly to include some remarks on what I conceive of as broad social forces affecting, particularly, the teaching of economics, and a few remarks on some problems of publication in economics.

Any sort of projection of the shape of economics as institutionalized learning is bound to be a hazardous undertaking at the present time (at least for the 'western' countries to which my argument primarily refers), since the present is a period of reversal of the trend in public opinion on, and support for, universities. Economics rode on the band-wagon of the high promise of basic scientific research in the period after the Sputnik went up. This esteem promoted both an emphasis in research on empirical study, especially econometric study, which depended on constantly-improving computer technology and relied very little on library sources of data and ideas; as well as an emphasis, in teaching, on mathematical general equilibrium theory and on econometrics. Neither of these had a lengthy history embodied in library holdings and, in any case, neither one emphasized the accumulation of knowledge through the work of successive generations of scholars. Subsequently, economics, though less so than 'hard science', has paid the price of having generated hopes of painless human betterment that were unfulfilled because of relative deprivation of funds for research support and teaching posts and a change of popular attitude that was expressed in criticisms of 'lack of relevance'. This change has coincided with the 'accelerator' effects of demographic change on universities as producers of human capital and, also, of the human capital required to produce human capital. (Universities produce graduates to participate in the productive process of society, a certain proportion of whom go to replace the university teaching staff themselves. A sharp deceleration or reversal of growth of demand for undergraduate training has a catastrophic effect on the employment opportunities open to new PhDs, especially those from the less eminent institutions.) The effect, for present purposes, is to raise, in severe form, the question whether the changes in the nature of professional economics teaching and research that have occurred, most notably since the late 1950s, will persist, or whether economics will revert to its previous position as a largely undergraduate-teaching, largely individual, literate-scholarship, profession. One aspect of this question is how far the demands for 'radical' or 'relevant' economics will go in dictating the structure of teaching and research, since Marxist scholarship, in contrast to 'positive' economics, places great weight on the reading of, and references to, published authorities, especially those of vintages mostly available in libraries. But this aspect is probably far less important than the fact that the mass of economists, like the mass of scholars in most fields, is not by (human) nature oriented towards new discovery, but, rather to the organization and marginal improvement of existing knowledge, and that the university as an institution is, by very long tradition, oriented towards the maintenance of cultural capital intact rather than towards the creation of the obsolescence of capital by planned technical innovation.

These issues are extremely vague and highly debatable, too much so to justify producing a paper promised on the validity of the hypothesis that the past twenty years have been 'rather abnormal'. This paper will, instead, proceed on the assumption that future directions of evolution in economics can be extrapolated from past trends. Discussion of this main theme will be sandwiched, however, between some general observations on the university and university-library environment within which economics teaching and a considerable amount (not by any means all) of university staff research effort is conducted, and some observations on the publication of textbooks and monographs.

II. THE CHANGING UNIVERSITY AND LIBRARY ENVIRONMENT

It is a commonplace, requiring more detailed specification to save it from banality, that ours is an increasingly affluent society, that the main economic characteristic of such a society is a rising explicit, or implicit, price of time relative to commodities, and that this rise imposes on individuals and organizations the need to adjust their methods and practices to the relative costs of implicit time prices and explicit money prices. Such adjustment includes, among other things, being prepared to introduce prices for services that in less affluent times were free and to fix these prices at appropriate economic levels, to abandon pricing for goods which have become cheap enough to make the transaction costs of charging prices not worth while, and to differentiate products that differ substantially in their costs of production.

It is also commonplace to observe that university libraries, and libraries in general, are extremely slow to make the adjustment indicated. One major factor is the tradition of the university as a store of knowledge, in the form of scarce and irreplaceable books, which leads libraries to value their collections in terms of numbers of titles and the scarcity value of individual items, substantially independently of the needs of the typical borrower, and to be particularly reluctant to 'stream' readers into a mass of readers of standard works that should be quickly available, and occasional readers of recondite source material who are interested enough in particular books to be willing to pro-rate the time cost of waiting until the book or books they want can be fetched from some out-of-the-way storage space. Another example is the wildly uneconomic nature of library fines and related charges. One might argue reasonably, I think, that a really irreplaceable book—which would include books published by long-dead firms, except for the standard commercial editions reprinted by others—should never be allowed out of the library, and that the library should provide and charge the customer for the cost of verifying his credentials, providing a place to sit and read (together with a Xerox machine), and, if necessary, policing readers against clipping pages, etc. Conversely, if hard-to-replace books are allowed out into circulation, there is no reason why the borrower should not make a deposit equal to, or in excess of, the cost of replacement, providing again that the reader can opt to stay in the library to read (again, at a charge or on a subscription basis).

Finally—as the Regenstein Library at Chicago has found to its embarrassment—there is never a limit to the demand for carrels from the staff—especially if the library is air-conditioned while department offices are not—so long as carrels are not let out on a cash-rent basis. It is worth repeating that such difficulties arise because convention persists in regarding as an immutable right the free use of scarce and expensive resources, which, in earlier, less affluent (and populous) times were either free, or not worth the effort of charging for separately.

The problem of space in the modern university and the modern university library is, in fact, a consequence of the general upward trend of the value of labour relative to 'capital' or material goods, and of technical change economizing on labour by substituting capital for it. Perhaps it would be more accurate, in the specific context of universities and their libraries, to say that it is a consequence of the upward trend of the cost of unskilled labour relative to skilled (specifically 'educated') labour. Cheap unskilled labour and expensive educated labour make the construction and administration of spacious libraries possible, while keeping relatively small the number of books to be housed and readers to be accommodated. Technological progress in paper-making and printing, and advancing literacy, have vastly increased the numbers of readers and of books to be stored, while rising wages of unskilled and semi-skilled workers have made the cost of construction of buildings, and of the administration of library services, increasingly expensive.

The solution has to be found in continuous pruning of the library's book holdings, and the development of cheap offsite storage and retrieval systems for rarely used books.

Two other features of affluence, as it particularly affects libraries, are worth mentioning, both of which are suggested by the experience of the Regenstein Library. The first is that affluence tends to be accompanied by a blurring of the line between the work and the play-cum-social activities of the student body. One relevant aspect is the tendency towards more or less continuous 'snacking', and the expectation that the library will provide drinks and candy and, in some cases, sandwich and soup machines and appropriate space for consumption of the produce on site. Another is the tendency for the library to be turned, at least in part, into a social centre. Both aspects, and more subtle aspects involving noise generation and comfortable sitting arrangements, demand the allocation of library space to not-directly-functional activities. In some cases they increase the problem of policing the library against theft and vandalism.

The problems of theft and vandalism reflect the third feature of affluence worth noting, and that is the general increase in permissiveness towards illegal actions promoted by the ambiguity and shifting illegal actions promoted by the ambiguity and shifting nature of the line between 'free' and 'scarce' goods and between public and private property created by the progress of affluence. With the free provision of certain kinds of goods, and the consequent encouragement to waste them, goes the effect of the reduction of the typical family to the nuclear unit, and an associated attenuation of property rights, and of respect for them, in respect of certain kinds of goods. Given the large role of the opulently-illustrated perishable magazine (often 'given away' to customers) and of the paper-back book in modern literate life, there is an understandable transference of ideas to include the tearing of pages and pictures out of the library books and journals if they are particularly important to the individual's interests, and the purloining of the whole books from libraries on the rationalization that if they need a copy badly enough they can easily buy another one. This problem of contemporary libraries fits easily into the more general sociology of white collar crime.

The foregoing remarks clearly are not about economic methodology, but about its application to the economics of libraries and the improvement of their usefulness. Two main conclusions stand out, each of which is applicable to a number of other contexts. The first is the need to give careful consideration to the pricing system used for libraries. Here there are two aspects: securing greater efficiency by using money prices as substitutes for the unpriced use of increasingly valuable human time, and transferring a larger part of the cost of providing library facilities from the state, the university, and the private donor to the user of library services—a process which, it seems, is becoming crucial to universities in the coming decade. The second conclusion is that the standards of spartan living and non-spartan personal honesty and respect for cultural mausoleums that universities conventionally expect of their reading clientele cannot be taken for granted, but, instead, as in many other aspects of life in modern conditions of populous affluence, standards of proper behaviour towards 'public goods' must be inculcated by an appropriate system of rewards and punishments.

In conclusion of this section there is one further point to be made, which is made here instead of in the list above because it concerns the composition of the prospective clientele of the university. Up until the Second World War, or shortly thereafter, the bulk of the university library's readers consisted, on the one hand, of undergraduates, largely preparing for a degree as a symbol of cultural attainment and a general preparation for a career of a not necessarily closely specified nature in adult life, and, on the other hand, of university teachers whose research was both of a rather leisurely kind and based primarily on the reading of historical sources and great books. One of the effects of affluence, in combination with the more recent scientific approach to managerial, governmental, and other education-oriented carriers, has been the insertion between these two groups of a quantitatively significant third group of graduate students. Depending on the wealth of the country in question, the extent and degree of state support of graduate students, and the nature of the demand for the educated product, this group may be aiming at the one or two years' MA (as in Britain), the PhD (as in the United States), or the PhD examination qualifications without actual completion of the PhD (as in Canada). Whatever their degree objective, they constitute a different group of readers from the highly seasonal undergraduate-readers and contra-seasonal staff-readers, in that they tend to be steady attendees and careful and serious readers, readers, moreover, who concentrate much more than either of the other groups on the reading of fairly recent issues of the journals, and of selections from a variety of supra-textbook-level monographs and collections of papers. They place a much heavier strain on the resources of the library than is usually realized; on the other hand, that strain could frequently be considerably reduced by liberal provision of xeroxing facilities.

III. METHODOLOGICAL AND RELATED TRENDS IN ECONOMICS

As suggested earlier, there has been a revolution, or perhaps a series of revolutions, in economic method in the period since the war, and especially since approximately the late 1950s. In one real but limited sense this change has represented the victory of Milton Friedman's 'positive economics' over the negative economics of theory of the 1920s and early 1930s, with its emphasis on questioning the assumptions of theoretical analysis and disputing value judgments asserted to be implicit in the pure competition model of the economic system. But that sense is very limited, and contradicted by the evidence of strong and idiosyncratic value judgments underlying the use that is made of positive economics by its proponent himself. More important casual factors have been, on the one hand, the unattractiveness both of pushing scholarship into the meaning of the classical economists to points of diminishingly small marginal scholarly returns, and of continuing the name-calling over assumptions and hidden value judgments that was essentially a reaction to the evident inconsistency between a very general and timeless theory and a number of very particular and very short-run observations of the apparent real world. On the other hand, the increasingly easy availability both of the mathematical methods of analysis and of the methods and, especially, the means of computation of statistical and econometric analysis, to those who are young enough and recently enough educated to be 'numerate', as compared with the time-intensive methods of acquiring knowledge by traditional literate scholarship, have made the use of such methods an attractive means for the neophyte to overlap his elders and establish his professional reputation quickly and securely.

The results are evident in a number of indicators of the quality and thrust of scholarly work in economics. Examples are the level of intellectual difficulty and mathematical and econometric technique typical of articles in the leading journals, the rapid turnover of names of contributors as each generation of graduates shoots its technical bolts and retires to more obscure publication (often in textbook form), the proliferation of new journals based on the further development of a particular mathematical or empirical technique, and the generally low status of textbook writers (with one or two notable exceptions) and of writers of economics in readable and literate plain English.

This style of work in economics and, more generally, the standards of professional accomplishment and reward that encourage it, have some important observable consequences for the library services required by contemporary economics.

In the first place, each major graduate training institution, regardless of what it tells its students to read and how it pads its reading lists, is likely, in reality, to concentrate its training on the intensive study of a few 'classic' books, which may differ from institution to institution, and a rather larger, but still restricted collection of articles. The collection, in total, will consist partly of some generally-recognized seminal articles—which may or may not be available in collections of readings, including those sponsored by the American Economic Association—and authoritative commissioned survey articles, and partly of articles by current or past teachers of the course in question. The result is a relatively small range of materials being called for, but calling for intensive use. This, in turn, implies relatively large numbers of copies of particular books and of particular journal issues, and/or generous facilities for xeroxing. It also suggests the possibility, which has been tried in various ways but with mixed results, of putting together *ad hoc* books compiled from reproductions of essential articles, to be sold as a relatively cheap alternative to providing library copies of issues of the relevant journals and seating space for reading them.

As a side issue, a number of graduate departments are now processing a fairly regular flow of Spanish-speaking students. In this case, and comparable cases involving other language groups, it would be extremely useful for the library to carry a collection of translations of standard English articles into the other language concerned. Such collections, I have found by experience, seem very difficult for a library to handle. A great deal of material, often prepared at some cost, and useful to foreign students trying to catch nuances of meaning in a language foreign to them, seems to wind up in the waste-basket because the libraries do not understand the point of it.

In the second place a graduate school, like a rocket in a vacuum in the old unscientific age was presumed to do, keeps going by pushing against what is pushed out previously. In other words, one of the intellectually safe and relatively riskless ways of producing a successful PhD thesis, or a post-PhD article, is to do more elegantly and with greater generality a piece of work previously done by someone else in the same institution—because if B does better than A something that A got a PhD for, it is very difficult for the staff who approved A's thesis to turn down B's. This is one important reason why so many promising young PhD-stage economists are never heard of again. Without someone else's shoulders to stand on, they get lost in the crowd of intellectual midgets. Be that as it may, the counterpart of this characteristic of graduate training in economics—which, incidentally is associated with the fact that, unlike university teachers in the natural sciences, teachers in economics are very reluctant to tell a student what to do and how to do it for his PhD, out of subservience to a vague idea that the PhD ought, in some sense, to be 'original work' by the candidate—is an intense interest on the part of thesis-subject-seeking candidates in the theses accepted previously by their departments. This, in turn, requires the library to keep an adequate back-file of successfully completed dissertations and to houseclean the shelves from time to time, an operation that should not be conducted mechanically because the best theses have a habit of becoming alive again at intervals of time.

This is, of course, a rather narrow and minimal standard of what should be available to the aspiring PhD candidate. A broader and more ambitious objective, as well as one more oriented towards the ideal of a community of scholars, would be to maintain a collection of PhD dissertations from all of the leading graduate departments, the foreign as well as the domestic. This would merge into maintaining a central collection of working papers and discussion papers, a medium of publication very important to advanced work in a number of fields but one that proves difficult, indeed, for the typical library to handle.

In the third place, a great deal of research work at present and in the prospective future—as has been, indeed, a main theme of this conference—has come to be empirical in character. This emphasis is generally accompanied by a merely perfunctory acknowledgement that generations of past economists have worked on the problem, at least in literary and philosophical form, and have shaped the concepts applied in the contemporary empirical formulation of it, except to the extent that those concepts can be identified with important and recent work by economists still active in research, especially senior members of one's own or some other distinguished department. Its corollary is intense concern about raw economic data and the proper processing of them. The centre of such interest lies outside the library, in the econometric seminars, the workshops and the computer centre. On the other hand, there is a definite need for the establishment and maintenance of a data bank, or data banks corresponding to graduates' areas of research interest (such as the economics of human capital, consumer economics, income distribution, labour economics, development economics, the international monetary system) especially where published data need to be subjected to a number of more or less standard purification processes before they match the numbers that correspond to the concepts of theoretical analysis. As an illustration, in the field of international monetary theory there is a crying, but unsatisfied, need for reasonable series for world reserves, world money supply, and world prices and activity, which has only partially been substituted for by partial series constructed from OECD official statistics. Obviously, an officially-constructed and published IMF series would be a near-ideal solution;

but, failing that, researchers should not be in the position of constructing whatever *ad hoc* series they have the time and money to construct.

The foregoing observations rest on the usual assumptions of extrapolation from what has gone on already, namely, that already, evident trends will continue. However, there are various reasons for expecting that, in the next decade or so, economics may become very different from what it has been in the past fifteen or so years, in ways which have certain implications for the provision of library resources. Prediction of change in this sort of context is, of course, extremely difficult, because when we speak of 'economics' we refer, even within the United States, and certainly in other countries where it is difficult even to envisage a 'national' economics profession, to an extremely diversified and fragmented profession or intellectual discipline, the parts of which tend to lead lives of their own. Even in the United States, the officers and activities of the American Economic Association have become decreasingly representative of the profession as a whole, as the profession has grown in size, and leadership has been diffused from the North-Eastern seaboard—the New England private universities with Chicago as a lonely outpost only one third of the way west—towards the west as population and economic activity have shifted westward. Four major factors working for a change in professional approach and 'method' are worth singling out for comment; these vary in their political and scientific content.

First, there is the so-called 'radical challenge' and demand for 'relevant economics', spawned, fundamentally, by the loss of American political self-confidence associated with the War in Vietnam. As so frequently happens, 'radicals' in other countries have taken their cue from American radicals under the impression that they are being anti-American-imperialist and anti-capitalist. The important point about the 'radical challenge', apart from the fact that its original *raison-d'être* has disappeared with the former regime in Vietnam, is that it met, and profited by, weakness in a significant number of the great universities and has been proceeding to capitalize on exploiting this weakness. Thus, the demands have moved on, with the ageing of the successful radical generation, from 'relevance' and the elimination of examination discipline at the undergraduate level, to the same thing, including acceptance of 'radical' dissertation topics, at the graduate level, to employment of a quota of 'radical' staff members, to the creation of radical journals commanding publication credit, to the creation of parallel tracks of promotion to tenure and full professorship for radicals. The movement could be—and, in the past, has been, on similar occasions—eventually stalled by the ambiguity of academic promotion standards and their dependence on assessment, by senior colleagues, of the originality and quantity of work performed, and of the prospects for continued performance. But, assuming that it makes some mark at least temporarily, it will involve library services in the form of demanding provision of a different set of old books, a different set of newly-published books, and a different set of current journals. It will also, to the extent that it has serious scholarly pretensions, probably involve a much greater relative emphasis on library reading and research as contrasted with quantitative work, model-building, and the use of computer technology.

The second factor is the sharp decline in national government support of research. One alternative, described in Prof. Eckstein's paper and discussed also by the heads of some of the newer universities in the United Kingdom, is the development of research support through the commercial market—which probably implies a shift from dependence on the university library and computer centre to dependence on new, non-university, data banks and computer facilities. A commercial enterprise must necessarily pay attention to the cost of storing the knowledge that it decides to keep; the associated danger is a loss of old information that falls between the stools of collection by private non-university sources and storage for cultural heritage purposes by the university libraries. Another alternative, already in evidence, is for research interest to follow political concerns from the national to the local state or city government level; this would imply pressure on libraries to convert from the collection of general cultural items, related to western civilization as a totality, to the collection of local cultural data, history, and contribution to knowledge.

The third factor, so far most evident in the United States, but likely to be characteristic of western civilization generally (as distinct from less developed countries) is the decline in the rate of growth—in the United States it is an actual reversal of the numbers attending universities as students. This factor is a result of both demographic trends, and the élitist and authoritarian tradition of the university, neither of which is as congenial to a larger and more democratically-generated cohort of adolescents as the alternatives in the form of local and small community colleges. The demand for graduate training to the PhD level, and the economic opportunities open to those with such qualifications, are extremely highly geared to the rate of growth of undergraduate university teaching. With a slowing down or a reversal of the rate of growth of the market, coupled with a decline in the level of outside research support and a strong evident tendency for such support to be concentrated on 'applied' and 'policy-relevant' problems rather than on 'pure' research, there is a strong likelihood that the practice of economics will shift back to the pre-explosion-period pattern of departments containing a much lower ratio of young freshly-trained, technology-oriented (i.e. either pure mathematical, economic theory, or computer-aided econometrics) economists, and a dominant group of established university academics heavily involved in teaching and university administration and conducting research as a side-line and largely on the basis of reading books from the university library's resources. (By my observation, the avid collectors of old and classic books in the profession now consist almost exclusively of people near retirement, and trained in the pre-war scholarly tradition.) This factor implies that the traditional role of the university library as a store of rare books for reading by leisured people in the fullness of time, and as a provider of a limited range of undergraduate reading material will, to some extent, reinstate itself—presumably to the comfort and consolation of librarians.

The final factor I present with some hesitation, since it represents a personal view of the history of the profession in this century. Briefly, the view is that by the first decade of the century, the subject had reached a state of apparent completeness, symbolized by the necessity for a qualified economist to have a deep knowledge of the preceding literature, both as a source of ideas for personal scientific contribution and as a guarantee of receiving a respectful hearing for any new ideas that he advanced for serious consideration. That state of homeostasis was broken as a result of developments only partly attributable to the profession itself—notably the rapid growth of mathematical competence, the drastic cheapening of statistical computation by the substitution of machines for men, and the pressure exerted by the nation-state for quantitative answers to policy problems, within the framework of a general 1930s-inspired faith in the superiority of economic planning over *laissez-faire*. But the possibilities of progress through mathematization and empirical quantification have been rapidly reaching into the region of diminishing, and, more important, of low, marginal returns precisely because the techniques involved can be learned relatively easily and quickly by young recruits to the profession. The reasons are different in the two cases. Mathematics has the limitation of setting its own problems, which are dictated by its logical structure and standards of economy and elegance; and these problems—for example, the associated questions of stability and multiplicity of general equilibrium—are of very little, and sometimes of no, economic interest. (Moreover, insofar as they are of interest, it should be possible to condense the possible solutions and the parameter values on which they depend into a standard map, rather than to have the individual mathematical theorists publish the same tedious manipulations over and over again, with slightly different symbols.)

As regards empirical work, there are, in my view, at least three problems: the quality of the data, improvement of which used to be the sphere of 'economic statisticians', but is now the vested interest of an almost immovable bureaucracy; the improvement of the microcomponents of the models, which further requires that the economist concerned accept the role of a technician rather than of a scientist, and is unattractive to university economists except when PhD candidates can be dragooned and bribed into doing it, at the longer-run risk of their own career prospects; and the improvement of the basic theory that suggests the causal interdependences involved in the models and also determines the appropriation, or otherwise, of the available statistical series and the manipulations performed on them prior to use. In this connection, economics has certainly come a long way towards clearing up the conceptual mess created by Keynesian theory and national income account ing, progress symbolized by the development and clarification of such concepts as stock and flow equilibrium, human capital, life-time income and consumption profiles, and the difference between purchase and consumption of consumer durables. But, in my judgment, a great deal of this apparent progress has represented the working out, by sustained application of many trained intelligences, of ideas explicit or obviously implicit in the thinking of the past great economists, thinking transmitted to the post-war-II generation of economists as a consequence of the scholarly knowledge of the literature of the pre-war-I and 1920s and early 1930s generations. With the prolonged studied neglect of the history of the subject that has come to characterize the PhD preparation stage and the immediately ensuing publication stage of a professional career, the subject is very likely to deteriorate sharply intellectually, unless revivified by fresh and deep draughts of literary scholarship on the works of the great economists of the past. This, however, is likely to occur more or less automatically, as the sterility of purely technologically-based work becomes increasingly obvious. And this, in turn, will (if it occurs) imply a re-invigoration of the university library as a store-house of inherited wisdom and knowledge, to the extent, that is, that libraries use their limited storage facilities with discrimination.

In concluding this section, it may be interesting to speculate on the new directions in which economics may go. Some guidance may be provided by the state of economics in the immediate prewar I period. The marginal revolution had seemed to clear up the remaining problems of production theory, and for society, at least in Britain, which then dominated economics, material prosperity and affluence were apparently ensured. The consequence was, in a sense, a switch of interest from production to consumption theory, in the particular form of concern about equity in the distribution of income as expressed in Pigou's *Economics of Welfare*. The simple utilitarianism of the Pigovian construction was blasted by Robbins' *The Nature and Significance of Economic Science*, and remained so despite the efforts of 'the new welfare economics' to salvage something of scientific value from the wreckage. In the meantime, first the great depression and the Keynesian Revolution and, subsequently, the related problem of competition with Russia and the Eastern bloc countries in the generation of economic growth, and the efforts to promote economic growth in the less developed countries, switched attention back to production theory and away from consumption and welfare theory. This phase, in turn, has been undermined by changes in public concern away from growth towards equity and 'the quality of life'. Economics has so far responded largely by adaptation of the standard tools of production theory, for example, introducing 'pollution' as a 'bad' or as undesired product in the familiar Leontief input-output matrix. But the more fundamental philosophical problems of finding a satisfactory ethical foundation for welfare analyses and prescription obviously await analysis with better logical and philosophical tools: and one might interpret the recent flurry of interest in Rawl's theory of justice as a harbinger of a more determined and sustained intellectual endeavour.

IV. SOME OBSERVATIONS ON ECONOMICS PUBLISHING AND ITS ECONOMICS

The justification for including this final section is that published books and journals are the raw material of both libraries and much of economic scholarship, and the production of such material has certain economic characteristics obviously relevant to the purposes of this conference.

To be brief, publishing involves the same sort of compromise between the public good and the private profitability necessary in a private enterprise system as is involved in patents and copyrights. It is subject to a high, fixed investment cost and a low, marginal unit cost in two senses. From the standpoint of the author, the effort of writing is largely independent of the *ex-post* number of readers, in the sense that it costs the author nothing for an additional reader to read his work. From the standpoint of the publisher, there is a high cost of type-setting and correction, advertising, etc., but a low cost of printing and distributing the marginal copy. An ideal system of production would involve marginal cost pricing (nothing for the author, pure replication cost for the publisher), with overheads being covered somehow by society, on the basis of some means of judging whether the social benefit of having the book or article produced justifies the expense. In academic publishing, the author is rewarded indirectly by career advancement, but the publisher adds on to prime cost a margin out of which he expects to recoup overhead costs. The hope is that sales will cover the overhead and normal profit, and, with luck, yield a windfall in addition. The economic expectation is that competition will lead to average sales just recouping overhead costs with normal profits.

This system has some economic consequences that make it extremely vulnerable to changes in demand. These include, most noticeably, a tendency for rising demand to lead to proliferation of firms and expansion of titles published, followed by 'shake-outs' and financial difficulties even if rapid demand expansion is not followed by rapid demand contraction (as has, in fact, occurred). The difficulties are reinforced by the fact that the pay-off is long-delayed after the investment, requiring the use of short-term capital, which is difficult to handle and makes the firms vulnerable to rising interest rates and credit squeezes, and also by the fact, that, for reasons not altogether accountable for, firms tend to keep on adding staff in good times, transferring expected future profits into commitments to sustain overhead labour, and thereby increasing their vulnerability to interruptions or a slowing down of demand growth. Something of the same kind applies to academic journals, though these tend to be cushioned against financial risks by university or learned society support and reader loyalty and willingness to pay higher subscriptions.

The point of these remarks is to suggest that the so-called 'information explosion', which has increasingly been worrying libraries through its effects on acquisition, storage, and cataloguing costs, may well become considerably less severe in the next decade. If publishers become less willing to publish books, libraries will have less to store. Authors will be forced to settle for journal publication of the guts of their work, without so much literary fat, and journal editors will have to become more discriminating in their acceptance standards, the former tendency saving library storage space and the latter easing the librarians task of selection of books by transferring the task to journal editors as selectors of articles. The fly in the ointment, unfortunately, is the possibility of the authors' finding their own way out, through cheap mechanical reproduction of limited quantities of non-book, poorly-evaluated typescripts and machine print-outs, and of discussion and working papers. An obvious, but not very specifically helpful, suggestion for dealing with this problem would be central storage of master copies of papers at the authors' cost, possibly including the cost of publishing an evaluated catalogue of material.

Summary of the Discussion

Professor M. Perlman introduced Professor Johnson's paper under four heads:

1. Economics as taught in universities had been an 'unstable' discipline, both as to content and teaching methods.

2. The university and library environment of economic instruction was likewise variable. Under these circumstances, the administration of a library involved more than the passive retailing of traditional library services, and librarians had not thought adequately about adjustment to the changes. Under the 'Carnegie' concept of libraries as free public institutions, some libraries were becoming social centres, cafeterias, even 'rip-off centres' for thieves and vandals, thereby increasing costs of operation at a time when labour costs were rising, particularly the wages of professional librarians. A simultaneous change had been the increasing numbers, and importance, of graduate students, with their special demands for relatively recondite materials and for private spaces in the library stacks.

3. If we define methodology not as method but as the *choice* between methods, the methodology of Economics had been changing rapidly, with new demands on libraries. Professor Johnson described the economist's basic methodological choice as being between and among deductive logic, quantitative and historical empirical, and moral suasion. Deductive theory had played an essentially negative role, in rendering useless its more mundane and obvious illustrations, while the 'positive economics' of Professor Friedman had increased the importance of empirical verification. In addition, or in consequence, the role of mathematical and statistical research had been rising, partially at the expense of the 'bibliographic tradition' of Great Books and doctrinal history. A wider range of sources was demanded by students and teachers, in connection with the increasingly large number of small classes and the increasing volume of dissertation research. Some of this demand was for quantitative numerical data which could be, and often was, banked elsewhere than in libraries.

Moreover, the end is not yet. Future pressures will make the future different and difficult for economists and librarians alike. These pressures include the rise of Radical Economics', declining enrolments and financial support, and changes in the relative pay-offs of different sorts of research. (Mathematical Economics, for example, may have reached its peak.)

4. There is a changing role and rate of publishing. Professor Johnson characterized the 'information explosion' as a disease which might produce its own cure, as publication prices rose and the demand for additional publications fell off.

Professor Perlman commented that the materials assembled above under (3) were the heart of Professor Johnson's paper, and that Professor Johnson had regarded the paper as a welcome opportunity to let the spleen out of his system. *Professor Perlman* himself saw signs that the role of traditional classroom teaching (textbooks, lectures, and all) might be restored by the budgetary crunch and by student demand. Also, libraries might be centralized in the interest of reducing both vandalism and the diversion of space for eating and social activities. *Professor Perlman* also felt that the traditional 'Economics shelves' of libraries might increase in importance as the 'Political Economy' aspect of economists' functions revived in importance and economists were called upon for immediate decisions, rather than left free to run to the capital for research funds. On the other hand, Professor Johnson may have exaggerated the extent of retreat from such recent fads as quantitative empiricism, and warned that the empirical economist cannot increasingly rely on 'someone else' to collect more and more of the data that he needs. Finally, *Professor Perlman* anticipated some revival of normative economics and, likewise, a retreat from the excesses of the 'Carnegie principle' as applied to university libraries.

Professor Kindleberger took the floor in favour of the Carnegie tradition for university libraries, particularly after students have paid tuition. He felt that libraries should try to encourage the use of their facilities, rather than restricting them. *Professor Kindleberger* also doubted that 'weeding' of library collections would be worth its own cost, and cited a study by Raffel and Shisko[1] to this effect.

Professor Giersch suggested that some recent changes in libraries replace what might otherwise have been costly changes in university departments, so that libraries might be looked upon as subsidizing departmental budgets. *Professor Bronfenbrenner* also mentioned a recent American trend of separating an undergraduate library (with social facilities and a limited collection) from the more traditional graduate library facility. *Professor Prest* added that an attempt to charge admission to the undergraduate library at the Australian National University had led to a student protest.

Professor Blaug saw no reason for libraries to be more 'collectivized' than, say, universities or hospitals, where public institutions raise part of their expenses by charging fees. *Professor Blaug* also noted that university libraries are generally more congested than public libraries. This suggested to *Professor Blaug* that marginal-cost pricing might be particularly useful in a university setting, not so much to relieve congestion of space as to reduce the amount of labour demanded. *Professor Blaug* agreed that the marginal cost of certain library facilities might well be zero or even negative, in which case fees should not be charged.

Mr Kilgour discussed the history of library charges in the United States. Approximately 100 years ago, institutions such as Harvard and Yale charged college library fees of $5 per year. Students then founded competitive undergraduate libraries; it was these which first developed cataloguing systems. *Mr Kilgour* noted also that academicians, when they do not patronize their own institution's library, are more apt to use public libraries than the facilities of other schools. As for public library admission fees, *Mr Kilgour* recalled that they had been suggested for the main New York Public Library, but that the public had objected. Turning to the problem of weeding out collections, finally, Mr Kilgour suggested to Professor Kindleberger that computerization might reduce costs sufficiently to make weeding worth while.

Mrs N. Perlman claimed that the under-utilization of library materials extends only to the basic collection (books). Other university library resources, and public library resources in general, were used widely.

Professor Blaug mentioned a new British law, by which British authors would

[1] Raffel, Jeffrey A. and Shisko, Robert, *Systematic Analysis of University Libraries: Application of Cost-Benefit Analysis to the M.I.T. Libraries.* (Cambridge, M.I.T. Press, 1960.)

be paid rental fees for their books when these were withdrawn from British libraries. When this system is combined with free libraries, it will add to library deficits. *Professor Blaug* added that this system had an obvious appeal, and might go round the world, providing state subsidies for authors. *Mr Kilgour* added that Denmark already has such a system in operation.

Dr Bartenbach reminded the conference that 'information on demand' business had been established in the United States. Most such firms are located near major libraries.

Professor Wolfe foresaw a return to the 'undergraduate orientation' in teaching and research, and *Professor Blaug* expressed the view that Professor Johnson's paper did not justify its title by its distribution of emphasis.

In his final summary, *Professor Johnson* said that 'methodology' means all things to all men. He had tried to forecast a near-future trend. He feared that the 'community of scholars' might be breaking down, but foresaw a corrective shift to graduate teaching and the use of libraries. The recent expansion of the profession had changed the age distribution of economists, who were now a relatively young group, but he anticipated a reversal of this trend in consequence of the relative decline of funding.

Index

Entries in the index in **bold** type under the names of participants in the conference indicate their papers or discussions of their papers. Entries in *italic* type indicate contributions by participants to the discussions.

For Product Safety Concerns and Information please contact our EU representative GPSR@taylorandfrancis.com Taylor & Francis Verlag GmbH, Kaufingerstraße 24, 80331 München, Germany

Batch number: 10726013

Printed by Printforce, the Netherlands